# Engaging in the Language Arts

## Exploring the Power of Language

# Engaging in the Language Arts

## Exploring the Power of Language

**Donna Ogle**
National-Louis University

**James Beers**
College of William and Mary

PEARSON

Boston New York San Francisco
Mexico City Montreal Toronto London Madrid Munich Paris
Hong Kong Singapore Tokyo Cape Town Sydney

Executive Editor: Aurora Martínez Ramos
Senior Development Editor: Shannon Steed
Associate Editor: Barbara Strickland
Series Editorial Assistant: Kara Kikel
Executive Marketing Manager: Krista Clark
Production Editor: Annette Joseph
Editorial Production Service: Becky Dodson/Black Dot Group
Composition Buyer: Linda Cox
Manufacturing Buyer: Megan Cochran
Electronic Composition: NK Graphics
Interior Design: Deborah Schneck
Photo Researcher: Annie Pickert
Cover Administrator: Linda Knowles

For related titles and support materials, visit our online catalog at www.pearsonhighered.com



ISBN-10: 0-205-43093-7
ISBN-13: 978-0-205-43093-2

**Library of Congress Cataloging-in-Publication Data**
Ogle, Donna.
Engaging in the language arts : exploring the power of language / Donna Ogle, James W. Beers.—1st ed.
p. cm.
Includes index.
ISBN 0-205-43093-7 (alk. paper)
1. Language arts (Elementary) I. Beers, James W. II. Title.
LB1576.O363 2008
372.6—dc22

2008017740

Printed in the United States of America
10 9 8 7 6 5 4 3 2 1 RRD-MO 13 12 11 10 09 08

Credits appear on page 579, which constitutes an extension of the copyright page.

**Allyn & Bacon**
**is an imprint of**

PEARSON

www.pearsonhighered.com

# About the Authors

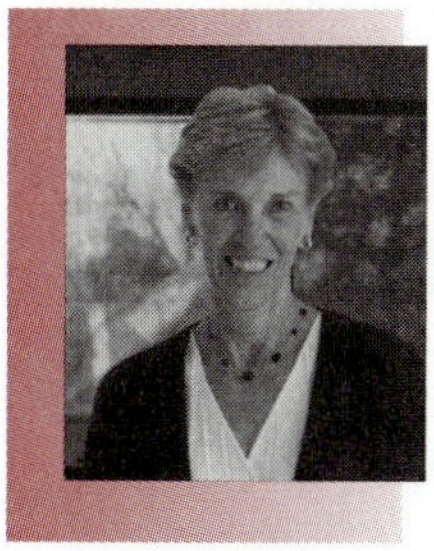

DONNA OGLE is Professor of Education at National-Louis University in Chicago, Illinois, and is actively involved directing staff development projects in the Chicago Public Schools, the Reading Leadership Institute, and in other U.S. districts. She also serves as a literacy consultant internationally and as a part of the editorial review boards of *Lectura y Vida* and the *Thinking Classroom.* Together with her husband, she participated in the Reading Writing for Critical Thinking Project in Russia. She is a past-president of the International Reading Association (IRA) and is a member of the Reading Hall of Fame. Donna also conducts research on visual literacy and content comprehension, having developed both the K-W-L (know, want to know, learned) and PRC2 (partner reading in content, too) strategies. She is the author of many books, book chapters, and professional articles, including *Reading Comprehension: Strategies for Independent Learners, Building Literacy in Social Studies* and *Coming Together as Readers.* She is a consultant for Holt-McDougal's literature program.

JAMES BEERS is Professor of Reading, Language, and Literacy in the School of Education at the College of William and Mary, Williamsburg, Virginia. He is also the Director of the Eastern Virginia Writing Project of the National Writing Project, which teaches educators how to help their students become better writers. He has a B.A. in English from Johns Hopkins University, an M.A. in English, and a Ph.D. in Reading from the University of Virginia.

Jim Beers has taught reading, writing, and spelling to students at all grade levels and has published books, chapters, and articles on reading, writing, and spelling. Among these publications are *Developmental and Cognitive Aspects of Learning to Spell* and *Writing for Competency.* He is also an author of the Scott Foresman Reading and Spelling Programs. He has given numerous in-service workshops throughout the United States and Canada for teachers and administrators on the teaching of reading, writing, and spelling. He has assisted a number of school systems in developing K–12 reading and writing curricula and the three- to four-year plans for implementing the curricula.

Along with his wife, Carol Beers, James has participated in the Reading and Writing for Critical Thinking Project through the International Reading Association's International Volunteer Program. This project has helped teachers in Eastern European countries promote critical thinking and independent learning through reading and writing in their students. James and Carol are currently co-authoring a book that addresses what every principal should know about reading.

# Brief Contents

# Contents

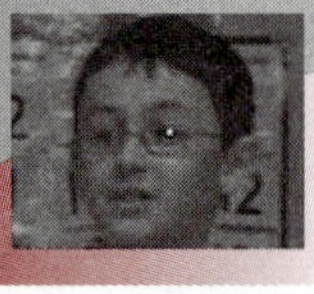

chapter 3
## Developing Speaking and Listening 70

chapter 4
## Supporting Diverse Learners 104

chapter 5

## Assessing Language Arts 138



chapter 6

## Reading in the Primary Grades 178

## chapter 7 Writing Development 216

## chapter 8 Writing Conventions 260

## chapter 9 Spelling Development 282

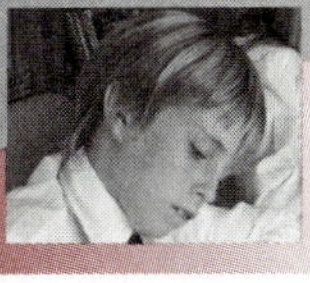



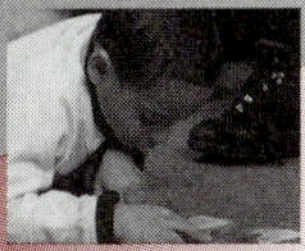

## chapter 14

## Creating Classrooms for All Learners 488



## chapter 15

## Incorporating Technology 516

**Denise Johnson,** College of William and Mary

# Special Features

## engaging in Visual Literacy

## engaging in Oral language

## exploring diversity

## engaging in Assessment

## exploring technology

## exploring Children's Literature

# Preface

Language is best learned when it is used well. This book provides a guide for ensuring that language is alive in classrooms and that children regularly explore varied ways to engage in language. That's why the title of this book has two parts: ***Engaging in the Language Arts*** and ***Exploring the Power of Language***. Students need to have experiences that engage them in listening, reading, speaking, viewing, and writing. It is through the meaningful engagement in language arts activities that students will explore, analyze, and discover the power of their own language.

We have written this book because we know you can make a difference in the lives of students you will teach. We are eager to share with you, the future teachers of our children, what we know about the foundations of language arts instruction and what we have learned from outstanding teachers across this country and around the world.

To show how you can actively engage students in language arts, we have included pictures, examples of student work, and video clips of teachers demonstrating what they do in their classrooms. We do this because we know how important seeing and hearing are in communicating and learning. We also know that students need to learn to view, construct, and think critically about visual media, pictures, and film. As visual literacy has joined the other language arts, we are delighted that our book publisher, Allyn & Bacon, has moved into the use of visual media, too. The photographs and the video clips that accompany this book are from classrooms of teachers we respect. We share the photos and clips as another way to help you create your own visual images of what you want to accomplish in your future classrooms. During our years preparing teachers, many students ask, "Do you have a video that shows this?" or "Where can we see teachers using these approaches?" Now, the resources that accompany this book do just that. Both on the website for MyEducationLab and with the web links that we have included in the book, you have a rich set of resources to support the reading you will do.

Refining classroom instruction is a life's work. New teachers have much to orchestrate: learning to relate to individual students and create productive classroom groups; knowing the expectations of society reflected in standards and curriculum guidelines; understanding the social and cultural expectations of the families represented by the students in each class; and knowing the foundations of language arts and how students can develop over time with expert guidance from teachers. The content in this book is designed to provide a road map for the start of your journey. We welcome you to the exciting future—explore your language and learn how to guide students in becoming more proficient language users.

## Organization of the Book

We begin this book with an overview of the field of language arts in Chapter 1 so readers can develop a framework for their thinking and study. The next two chapters focus on oral language, the foundation for speaking, listening, reading, and writing. Chapter 2 addresses language development during the preschool and school years; Chapter 3 focuses on the ways classrooms can foster speaking and listening in social, exploratory, and informational contexts. This examination of oral language is extended in Chapter 4 where the focus is on diversity and ways teachers can weave together the language strengths of all their students and build their competence and respect for each other. Chapter 5 addresses the important topic of language arts assessment, provides a framework for thinking about the purposes of assessment, and presents assessment techniques that teachers can use to identify their students' language arts abilities and plan appropriate instruction. Chapter 6 provides an introduction to reading development in the primary grades and includes instructional strategies that promote phonemic awareness, phonics, reading fluency, vocabulary development, and reading comprehension.

The next four chapters focus on writing. Chapter 7 provides a foundation by examining the development of writing and explaining the nature of the writing process. Chapter 8 focuses on the conventions of written language and ways to address grammar and usage. Chapter 9 examines the development of students' understanding of spelling and strategies for teaching spelling as well as handwriting. Chapter 10 provides a framework for exploring key writing genres and helping students develop as writers using them.

The role of literature in children's literacy is explored in Chapter 11. Suggestions for ways teachers can build on the power of literature and help all children find themselves in stories and informational texts are included. Chapter 12 addresses the continued development of reading beyond the primary grades with frameworks for developing integrated units and inquiry projects with oral and visual media presentations. Chapter 13 addresses ways teachers can stimulate the development of academic and general vocabulary through their own modeling, explicit instruction, and by providing a metacognitive orientation with students. The final two chapters take a broad perspective on two important elements for successful and supportive learning in the language arts. Chapter 14 provides suggestions for how classrooms can be organized to provide optimal experiences for all students and helps new teachers think about the use of resources, space, and time; Chapter 15 brings technology into the central spotlight and introduces readers to the rapidly increasing instructional technology resources available for language arts teachers.

## Special Features

Throughout the book, special features focus on issues of recurring importance to language arts teachers and extend understanding of key concepts in language arts instruction.

**Classroom Challenge.** Chapters open with a narrative vignette that shares a language arts teacher's experience in an active classroom. Each vignette models key concepts and demonstrates the challenges of today's classrooms and considerations for addressing the needs of diverse students.

**classroom challenge**

To get ready for his new class of third-graders, Mr. Bergen spends one day before school looking over assessment information he has gathered on his incoming students. Sitting at a large round table, he has several sources of information before him, including a stack of cumulative folders that contains the past academic performance of each student and comments from past teachers. He also has each student's test results of the previous year's language arts standards of learning assessment. His school began portfolio assessment in the language arts last year, so he has all of his students' portfolios.

These portfolios contain samples of writing and responses to reading done by the students. Each portfolio also includes student and teacher comments about each student's progress and challenges in reading and writing last year. As he looks through all of this information, Mr. Bergen begins to develop a picture of each student. He sees those who passed the Virginia Standards of Learning (SOL) test and those who did not. He identifies students who enjoy writing and those who are more reluctant writers. He notices the instructional strategies that teachers used last year in conjunction with the students' portfolios. As he looks more closely at the portfolios, he realizes that many of them contain only finished writing products,

**Questions for Reflection**

1. What additional language arts assessment information should Mr. Bergen obtain early in the school year?
2. How can he monitor his students' progress during the year to ensure that his instruction will advance his students in the language arts?
3. What language arts assessment should be carried out at the end of the school year to see how his students have progressed?

**Questions for Reflection.** Students are asked to reflect on their knowledge of the subject matter before reading and to connect their experiences to those within the chapter-opening *Classroom Challenge.*

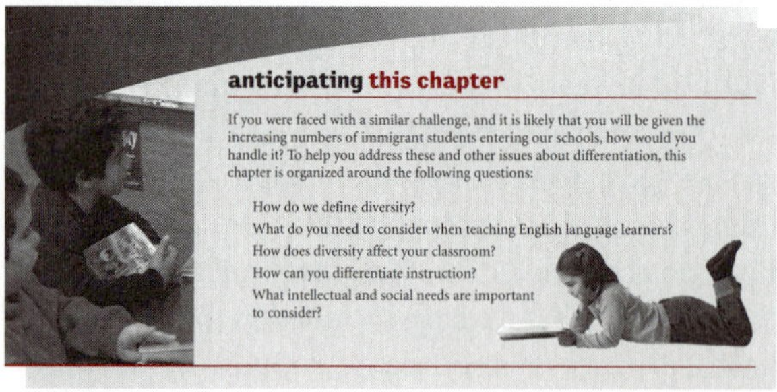


**Focus Questions.** Each chapter begins with a series of key questions that guide students' reading of the chapter and outline important topics.

**Engaging in Visual Literacy** shows how to incorporate viewing with lessons in reading and writing. This feature provides examples and ideas for reading visual images, developing strategies for interpreting visual information, drawing and visualizing, and connecting visual and narrative information.

## engaging in Visual Literacy

### Sketch to Stretch

Most students love to draw. In the **Sketch to Stretch** strategy (Short, Harste & Burke, 1996), students learn to listen to or read a text and create a single visual image that captures the essence of the story and that illustrates what the story means. Students work in small groups (usually four to five students) and, after creating a visual response to the reading, they gather to share their sketches. Each person takes a turn by showing his or her sketch to the others. The students study the sketch and take turns explaining to the group what they see in the drawing and what they believe the illustrator wants to express about the story. This sharing lets the illustrator hear what other students see in the visual image and provides a good way for all children to engage in exploratory talk. After everyone else has shared, the illustrator then explains what he or she was trying to illustrate. Sharing continues in this way until all group members have been able to share their sketches and get the group's responses. One way of bringing the small group activity to the whole class is to have each group select one sketch they want shared with the class. Either the same day or in a subsequent class period, these sketches can be shared on a visualizer or transparency so the whole class can view them and participate in interpreting the drawings. Sharing visual images provides a nonthreatening way for children to share ideas, participate in discussion, and learn how to express ideas in a new sign system (visual illustration) that may be easier than using words and language.

## engaging in Oral language

### Sharing Folk Tales across Cultures

Comparing similar folk tales and legends as they are interpreted by different cultures can lead to interesting discussions of social values and cultural lessons. For example, the story of the Frog Prince has a very harsh ending in the Japanese version of the story compared to the English one; the German version is somewhat in between. If no versions are available in the different languages, a display of books containing variations of Cinderella can make a good discussion. From Mufaro's *Beautiful Daughters* to *Cinder Ellie* to *The Rough-Faced Girl* and the *Egyptian Princess,* there are great cultural lessons that can be compared to the French and modern American versions. Reading these folk tales and legends orally can highlight the different ways stories are told in particular languages. This can lead to rich discussions of the themes and the ways language is used.

**Engaging in Oral Language** gives ideas for in-class activities, assessments, and lessons that connect students' use of oral language with the other language arts.

## exploring Children's Literature

### Bilingual Picture Books

#### Grades K to 3

*A Magic Pocket: Selected Poems*—Written by Michio Mado, illustrated by Mitsumasa Anno, translated by the Empress Michiko of Japan, and published by Margaret McElderry (1998).
Japanese and English versions of each of the fourteen poems about simple childhood experiences are available.

*Gathering the Sun: An Alphabet in Spanish and English*—Written by Alma Flor Ada, illustrated by Simon Silva, and published by Rayo (1997).
This is a book of poems about working in the fields and nature's bounty, one for each letter of the Spanish alphabet.

*Hairs/Pelitos*—Written by Sandra Cisneros and published by Knopf (1994).
A girl describes how each person in the family has hair that looks and acts different. For example, Papa's is like a broom, Kiki's is like fur, and Mama's has the sweet smell of bread before it has been baked.

*I Love Saturdays y domingos*—Written by Alma Flor Ada, illustrated by Elivia Savadier, and published by Atheneum (2002).
A young girl enjoys the similarities and differences between her English-speaking grandparents and her Spanish-speaking ones.

*Jambo Means Hello: Swahili Alphabet Book*—Written by Muriel Feelings, illustrated by Tom Feelings, and published by Dial (1974).
This book presents a word, with English translation, for each of the twenty-four letters in the Swahili alphabet. A brief explanation of each word introduces an East African custo

*Kobo, the Li'L Rascal*—Written by Masashi Ueda a published by Kodansha International (2001).
The story centers on five-year-old Kobo and his mischievous antics centering on the small in dents of daily life in Japan. English and Japanes versions are available (Manga format).

*Owl Babies*—Written by Martin Waddell, illustrat by Patrick Benson, translated by East Word, and published by Magi (1995).
Three owl babies whose mother has gone out int the night try to stay calm while she is gone. The Vietnamese text is placed into the illustrations.

*Table, Chair, Bear: A Book in Many Languages*—Written by Jane Fedor and published by Ticknor and Fields (1995).
This book presents illustrations of objects found a child's room, labeled in thirteen different languages: English, Korean, French, Arabic, Vietnamese, Japanese, Portuguese, Lao, Spanish Chinese, Tagalog, Cambodian, and Navaho.

**Exploring Children's Literature** features are a resource for teachers, providing an annotated list of materials to use in the classroom, organized by theme and also by grade level. These features include books, journals, newsletters, magazines, manga, dictionaries, and web-based resources for classroom teachers.

## exploring diversity

### Working with Students Who Are English Language Learners

Second language learners often feel uncomfortable speaking in large group settings while they are still gaining control over English. This is particularly true when the class is engaged in content-area discussions. These students deserve support in learning how to participate in talk about content material they are learning. One approach we have found useful in developing the PRC2 framework is to make explicit to students several ways they can respond and extend talk with their partner. The key responses students can make are listed on a bookmark for them to use during their partner reading sessions. It is good to model a partner discussion using these starters. Let students hear other partners discuss; it may be useful to have a second teacher join you to model exchanges. If there are some student partners who easily discuss their texts, ask them to model for the rest of the class. It is also possible to audiotape a discussion between two partners and listen to their talk; sometimes, following a good demonstration, let students hear one not well executed and ask them how it could be improved.

Giving students a transcript of a segment of partner talk is yet one more way to help children develop an internal expectation of what they can sound like talking together around content ideas.

If there are some students from other cultures in the classroom, it may be possible to get them to compare and contrast the expectations for partner reading that the class has established with ways of engaging in other cultures. For example, K. Au has identified a shared-group construction pattern in Hawaiian society; no one person answers a question but answers emerge as children add to one another's contributions. In some other contexts, older children have precedence over younger and each knows their time to contribute to exchanges. Yet, in other cultures students are never expected or given time to talk in class; the idea of listening to other students is foreign and their ideas would never have been solicited. For students from these cultures, building a sense of how talking and listening can enhance learning may take time to develop.

**Exploring Diversity** gives readers examples of how to consider factors of diversity, differentiate classroom activities, and help students access their language strengths as they relate to academic instruction and management.

**Engaging in Assessment** illustrates practical applications or brief "case studies" that build on and enhance each chapter's coverage of assessment.

*engaging in*
**Assessment**

**Modifications for Students with Special Needs**

One of the greatest challenges when working with diverse students is assessing their current knowledge and progress in the classroom. Documenting the progress made by students with language or learning needs, such as ELL populations, including Sonya who was introduced in our classroom challenge at the beginning of the chapter, can be difficult when the students are not able to read or understand the questions on a test or other assessment tool. Assessment information can be extremely useful to teachers for planning future lessons and activities, but only when the information collected through the assessment tool is an accurate reflection of their students' learning. To help ensure that the assessment information you collect from your students is accurate, you may need to make some slight modifications. For example, students who are easily distracted may benefit from working in a quiet location or away from visual distractions. Students with slower processing speeds may require extra time to complete their work and

**exploring**
**technology**

**Sites for Developing Oral Language**

**Storytelling Tips for Oral Language Development (www.literacyconnections.com/Storytelling.html)**
Shirley Raines and Rebecca Isbell, authors of the book *Tell It Again!: Easy-to-Tell Stories with Activities for Young Children*, share information and resources on selecting stories and using storytelling tips.

invaluable resource with directions on how to conduct reader's theater, tips, scripts, and links to online resources.

**Scaffolding Oral Language Development through Poetry (www. readwritethink.org/lessons/lesson_view.asp?id = 69)**
In this lesson from ReadWriteThink, students work in small groups to develop a choral reading of two poems about an assigned insect. The poems serve as an introduction to a research

**Exploring Technology** provides readers with information about assistive and instructional technologies that can be employed with all students.

**IRA/NCTE Icons.** Each chapter contains marginal icons that correlate chapter content to the twelve English Language Arts standards developed by the International Reading Association (IRA) and National Council of the Teachers of English (NCTE).

**ɪorting Students Who Are ELLs**

ɪry in how they support students who come with limited English. In some ɪmigrant children are immediately placed in English only classrooms in which s the only language spoken. In other states and districts, students begin their g in bilingual or dual language programs in which their first language is used ı of the content area instruction and they learn English as a new language.

IRA/NCTE 10

ɪudents' First Language in the Classroom Research indicates that students ɪst effectively when they can use their first language in developing both literacy ɪsh language. This can happen in bilingual programs in which students begin to read and write in their first language and then transition into English as they ɪre of the English language. These are called *one-way immersion* programs the goal is that the students will function in a totally English environment

**revisit the classroom challenge**

More and more, teachers are being asked to welcome students who are still learning English in their general education programs. Therefore, it is important that teachers such as Mrs. Jones learn more about the needs of these students and adapt instruction to meet their needs. By looking more deeply at students such as Sonya, it is possible to determine if her reluctance to speak in the book discussion group is due to shyness or to deeper issues in her production of English. By giving students more time to prepare their responses before speaking and letting them practice voicing their thoughts with a partner first in settings where there is little risk of failure, teachers can support students who are ELLs journey to English competence. Teachers schools receiving more English learners can join together to study about second language acq sition and ways to scaffold instruction for these students.

**Revisit the Classroom Challenge.** Each chapter concludes with a return to the chapter opening *Classroom Challenge* section that encourages students to monitor their learning of key concepts in relation to the development of the teacher and student scenarios.

**Chapter Review.** Each chapter closes with a review section that is presented in a question and answer format so that students can revisit chapter materials and assess their understanding of key topics.

**chapter review**

Our classrooms are filled with unique students. It is our privilege as teachers to get to know each of them and create both nurturing and challenging opportunities for them to continue to learn and grc It is important that, as teachers, we think deeply about the individuality of each child we welcome in our classroom. What are their life experiences, what interests capture their attention, how to do they learn most productively, and what kinds of interpersonal contexts bring out their best efforts?

**How Do We Define Diversity?**

This chapter looks at diversity from a variety of perspectives. One of the most obvious areas of diversity at this time of large-scale immigration is language and cultural diversity. Differences in language are clear immediately when we receive students who are English learners in the classroo However, there are many layers of diversity beneath the surface, too. Cultural expectations for ho schools run, what teachers and students should do, and the roles of parents in education also var by culture. Schools need to invite parents to share their experiences and expectations and also create contexts so parents can develop an understanding of the school's instructional practices and expectations. Many families who have not had positive school experiences often hesitate to take an active role in their own children's education. It is important to be sensitive to their emo-

## Supplements and Learning Aids

The following supplements provide an outstanding array of resources that facilitate learning about language arts. For more information, ask your local Allyn & Bacon Merrill Education representative or contact the Allyn & Bacon Merrill Faculty Field Support Department at 1-800-526-0485. For technology support, please contact technical support directly at 1-800-677–6337 or http://247.pearsoned.com. Many of the supplements are available for download from the Instructor Resource Center at www.pearsonhighered.com/irc.

## Resources for Instructors

**Instructor's Manual.** The Instructor's Manual includes a wealth of interesting ideas and activities designed to help instructors teach the course. Each chapter includes a chapter-at-a-glance grid, chapter overview, learning objectives, lecture outline, key terms and people, discussion topics, activities, web links, and additional readings. (Available for download from the Instructor Resource Center at www.pearsonhighered/irc.)

**Test Bank.** The Test Bank includes multiple choice, true/false, and essay questions. Page references to the main text, suggested answers, and skill types have been added to each question to help instructors create and evaluate student tests. (Available for download from the Instructor Resource Center at www.pearsonhighered/irc.)

**Computerized Test Bank.** The printed Test Bank is also available electronically through the Allyn & Bacon computerized testing system, TestGen. Instructors can use TestGen to create exams in just minutes by selecting from the existing database of questions, editing questions, and/or writing original questions. (Available for download from the Instructor Resource Center at www.pearsonhighered/irc.)

**PowerPoint™ Presentation.** Ideal for lecture presentations or student handouts, the PowerPoint™ Presentation created for this text provides dozens of ready-to-use graphic and text images. (Available for download from the Instructor Resource Center at www.pearsonhighered/irc.)

**VideoWorkshop for Language Arts Methods.** An easy way to bring video into your course for maximized learning! This total teaching and learning system includes quality video footage on an easy-to-use CD-ROM plus a Student Learning Guide and an Instructor's Teaching Guide—both with questions and activity suggestions. The result? A program that brings textbook concepts to life with ease and that helps students understand, analyze, and apply the objectives of the course. VideoWorkshop is available for students as a value-pack option with this textbook.

**Professionals in Action: Literacy Video** (© 2000, 90 minutes in length). This Professionals in Action video consists of 10- to 20-minute segments on Developing Phonemic Awareness, Teaching Phonics, Helping Students Become Strategic Readers, Organizing for Teaching with Literature, and Reading Intervention, plus discussions with experts on literacy and brain research. The first four sections of each segment provide narrative along with actual classroom teaching footage. The final section presents, in a question-and-answer format, discussions by leading experts in the field of literacy.

## Resources for Students

**VideoWorkshop for Language Arts Methods.** An easy way to bring video into your course for maximized learning! This total teaching and learning system includes quality video footage on an easy-to-use CD-ROM plus a Student Learning Guide and an Instructor's Teaching Guide—both with questions and activity suggestions. The result? A program that brings textbook concepts to life with ease and that helps students understand, analyze, and apply the objectives of the course. VideoWorkshop is available for students as a value-pack option with this textbook.

**Themes of the Times for Literacy.** Available as a value-package, this collection of 46 *New York Times* articles provides students with real-world information about literacy.

PEARSON
**myeducationlab**
**Where the Classroom Comes to Life**

MyEducationLab is a research-based learning tool that brings teaching to life. Through authentic in-class video footage, interactive simulations, rich case studies, examples of authentic teacher and student work, and more, MyEducationLab prepares you for your teaching career by showing what quality instruction looks like.

MyEducationLab is easy to use! In the textbook, look for the MyEducationLab logo in the margins and follow the simple link instructions to access the multimedia "**Homework & Exercises**" and "**Building Teaching Skills**" assignments in MyEducationLab that correspond with the chapter content. Homework & Exercises offer opportunities to understand content more deeply and to practice applying content. Building Teaching Skills assignments help you practice and strengthen skills essential to quality teaching through your analysis and response to student and teacher instructional encounters and artifacts.

The rich, thoughtful, and interactive elements you will encounter throughout MyEducationLab include:

**Individualized Study Plan.** The study plan is designed to help students perform well on exams and to promote deep understanding of chapter content. Readers have the opportunity to take tests before and after reading each chapter of the text. Test results automatically generate a personalized study plan that identifies areas of the chapter that students must reread to fully understand chapter concepts, as well as interactive multimedia exercises to help ensure learning.

**Video.** The authentic classroom videos in MyEducationLab show how real teachers handle actual classroom situations.

**Case Studies.** A diverse set of robust cases illustrates the realities of teaching and offers valuable perspectives on common issues and challenges in education.

**Simulations.** Created by the IRIS Center at Vanderbilt University, these interactive simulations give you hands-on practice at adapting instruction for a full spectrum of learners.

**Student and Teacher Artifacts.** Authentic preK–12 student and teacher classroom artifacts are tied to course topics and offer you practice in working with the actual types of materials you will encounter daily as teachers.

**Lesson and Portfolio Builders.** With this effective and easy-to-use tool, you can create, update, and share standards-based lesson plans and portfolios.

**MyEducationLab is easy to assign, which is essential for providing the greatest benefit to your students.** Visit www.myeducationlab.com for a demonstration of this exciting new online teaching resource.

# Acknowledgments

We want to thank the following reviewers for their valuable suggestions, comments, and feedback:

Deborah Farrer
California University of Pennsylvania

Rose Heilman-Houser
Slippery Rock University

Linda Kleeman
Harris-Stowe State University

Lonnie McDonald
Henderson State University

Barbara Rahal
Edinboro University of Pennsylvania

Sara Runge-Pulte
Northern Kentucky University

Elke Schneider
Winthrop University

This book represents collaboration among several colleagues. We are enormously grateful to all who have contributed to the development of this book. In particular, we thank Carol Beers, Executive Professor of Curriculum and Instruction at William and Mary, for writing the language development chapter. As a teacher, principal, assistant superintendent, superintendent, and professor, Carol has a unique perspective and valuable insight into students' language. We also thank Denise Johnson, Associate Professor of Reading at William and Mary, who wrote the chapters on children's literature and technology. This book is much stronger because of their willingness to share their areas of special expertise.

Donna would not have taken on this project without Susan Pierce's help. Special thanks go to Susan's mother, Lillian Stevens, who was Donna's mentor when she began teaching language arts methods to undergraduates at NLU and who also introduced Donna to the exemplary Glenview Schools. Lillian's daughter, Susan Pierce, reading specialist and assistant principal of Winkelman School in West Northfield, Illinois, continues Lil's wonderful leadership and has worked closely with Donna providing advice, contributing vignettes and examples from her school, and taking many of the photographs found throughout the book.

The TREE team at Pleasant Ridge School in Glenview has opened their classrooms to us and invited us to videotape them in action. They are an amazing team and meeting with them is always a pleasure: their dedication to their students and their carefully crafted research process show what teachers and students can accomplish together. Our deepest appreciation and respect go to Jan Hinton, Deanna Santini, and Kathy Pattengale, the teachers, and the students of the TREE team.

Donna's thinking about visual literacy has been developed and shaped through work with colleagues at NLU. Ideas coming from her collaboration with Mark Newman and Xiuwin Wu on two visual literacy projects, the Adventures of the American Mind and Picturing Chicago, are important parts of this book. She is grateful for their insights and energy in helping students interpret and respond to visual images. The needs of English learners have been central to Project ALL, a grant funded by the Chicago Community Trust and the Chicago Public Schools. Donna wants to acknowledge the important contributions of the Project ALL team and especially the insights of Amy Correa that continue to inform her ideas about the language needs of English learners. The PRC2 framework and the guidelines for discussion included in this book have been developed as part of that project.

Jim would like to thank Mark Gulesian, retired William and Mary English Education professor, who invited him to become part of the Eastern Virginia Writing Project (EVWP) over twenty years ago. Jim's association with this site of the National Writing Project afforded him the privilege of working with countless numbers of outstanding teachers and principals to develop K–12 writing curriculum for a number of local school districts. Special thanks go to EVWP Co-Directors Deb Farina, Liz Ackert, Susan Pongratz, and Ron Wheeler for their support and feedback. Our thanks also go to Kathy Kryscio, fourth-grade teacher at Sanford Elementary School in Newport News and Amy LeBrec, fourth-grade teacher at Matoaka Elementary School in Williamsburg for sharing their students' writing with us.

Our chapter on reading in the primary grades and spelling could not have been possible without the mentoring that we both received from the late Ed Henderson at the McGuffey Reading Center at the University of Virginia. Not only did we learn the role of spelling for writing but also for reading under his tutelage. Jim also acknowledges the support of two lifelong friends who helped shape his understanding of language and literacy instruction: Ron Cramer and Dorsey Hammond.

Many thanks go to our graduate students who have been enormously helpful in this project. Meagan Boyle, special education teacher and doctoral student at NLU, edited the chapters for consistency and contributed suggestions for working with students with special needs. Lauri Leeper, experienced teacher, media specialist, and doctoral student at William and Mary, developed the Index and also reviewed the manuscript.

The classroom examples, photographs, and video clips are from classrooms and schools where we know and respect the teachers and administrators. Our thanks go to all these talented educators.

Writing a book like this requires uninterrupted time and support from some very special people. Special thanks go to Donna's husband Bud for his incredible support and encouragement at every phase of this work and Carol Beers, Jim's wife, for her insights, encouragement, and support.

Finally, our editors, Aurora Martinez and Shannon Steed, have become like "family." In fact, we celebrated the birth of Shannon's baby before we could celebrate the birth of this book. We are deeply grateful to both of them for their subtle yet persistent encouragement and support.

DONNA OGLE
JIM BEERS

# Engaging in the Language Arts

## Exploring the Power of Language

chapter 1

# Introducing the Language Arts

Language is best learned when it is used well. A major responsibility of you, the language arts teacher, is developing students' abilities to use language well. The choices you make in organizing your instructional programs and the quality of the language environments you create have a measurable impact on students' language growth. Research has demonstrated that the instructional focus, the types of activities, and the feedback students receive all influence their continued development of their oral and written language abilities (Myhill, 2006; Paratore and McCormick, 1998). In addition, teachers will often have children who are English Language Learners (ELLs) in their classrooms. How teachers accept the English learners' levels of English proficiency is important in students' ability to take risks and learn a new language. Teachers' responses to the language of different social classes and to gendered uses of language also have noticeable impacts on students (Jones and Myhill, 2004; Tatum, 1997).

## What Is Important about Classroom Language Use?

Research on the oral context of classrooms makes it clear that taking some time to focus on how you will understand, respect, and use language can make a difference to your students (Johnston, 2004). As Allen (1991, p. 361) explained, "Teachers can, (despite not feeling competent to integrate the acquisition of English with the learning of curricular content) however, create a classroom environment that will allow linguistically and culturally different children both to acquire English and to move ahead cognitively. In order for this to happen, teachers will need to examine the amount and types of linguistic input that children receive and the ways language is used in the classroom." Students need to have clear input from the teacher and also have regular opportunities to talk with their classmates.

## Teacher Talk

An important study by Mehan (1979) found that much of the talk in classrooms is "teacher talk" and follows a predictable routine of the teacher initiating a question, a student responding, and the teacher giving an evaluative closing like "Good," "Yes, that's correct," or "Does someone else have another answer?" He labeled this routine the IRE (Initiation, Response, and Evaluation). This traditional, teacher-centered form of classroom talk, not really discussion, gives students little opportunity to use oral language for thinking or exploring ideas. In fact, in traditional classrooms teacher talk dominates, with over 70 percent of the talk being done by the teacher (Pinnell and Jagger, 1991, p. 702).

## Engaged Students

More recently, literacy instruction has moved away from reliance on whole-group, teacher-led routines so students have more time to engage with other students and explore their own ideas. Structuring classrooms so students can engage actively, using both oral and written language to explore, share, and inquire, promotes language growth. So, too, students need guidance in becoming more proficient in oral, written, and visual language forms. Teachers who have a good understanding of the English language can guide students at the points of their learning potential. Each chapter of this text provides the foundation for understanding the different aspects of English and ways teachers can maximize language learning and growth by varying the classroom routines with teacher-to-students and student-to-student language activities.

These collaborative and varied classroom routines come close to John Dewey's (2001/1900) vision for schools. A seminal educational psychologist, Dewey argued that schools should provide ways for children to be active, engaged participants in the intellectual and social life of the classroom and school. He explained that school should be focused on drawing out of students rather than a pouring in, and that teaching reading, writing, and oral language should be done in a related way, as an outgrowth of a child's social desire and experiences.

## Personal Reflection

We begin our introduction to this language arts methods text with an invitation to explore your own language and the various ways you use language. As a teacher, much of your impact on students will be through your oral language; you will be a model for students of how to use language, you will provide much of your instruction verbally, and you will help students refine what they know and do through the feedback you give students. Your oral language will be a major instructional tool and a way you will establish your personal connections with your students. Your written language is also important. You will model how to construct pieces of written text; you will demonstrate ways students can improve their writing; you will give students written feedback on their assignments. Your use of visual images and texts in your teaching and the ways you will guide students to represent ideas in visual formats can help them become thoughtfully engaged with visual literacy. How you use language will be a significant component of language in the classroom.

Think for a few moments about yourself as a language user and the variety of ways language enhances your life. What do you most enjoy about language—savoring lyrics to songs and poems, reading favorite authors, keeping a diary, or debating and arguing opinions with friends? Think about experiences that helped you expand your confidence in language uses. As you reflect on your own language, your interests and uses, you may identify some of your teachers who helped you gain skill and confidence in oral, written, and visual forms of expression. Consider these questions while you reflect on your own experiences with oral and written language:

- How does language enhance your life?
- How did you develop your abilities in writing and how did you learn to share your thoughts in more formal, structured pieces of writing?
- What do you recall about learning to read and participate in discussions in school? Can you visualize some positive experiences?
- Have you learned to speak another language, or communicated with people who do not speak English?

## What Is the Authors' Perspective?

As a teacher, you will want to ensure that your students continue to develop their own language skills and will have many opportunities to talk, read, and represent their ideas. Students at all grade levels need regular opportunities to use language—oral, written, and visual—for meaningful purposes and also to examine how language functions in different contexts, from intimate home settings to small group projects in clubs and religious settings, to school learning, and to formal presentations in writing and before audiences. Throughout this book the focus is on helping students gain understanding of their language and expanding their competence in using language meaningfully. The ability to use language well is a foundation for success in life; it enables the language user to present himself or herself, to express ideas, to engage in exploration of varied perspectives, and to reflect and rehearse ideas. For example, bullying presents a challenging issue in schools. There is an increased importance in helping students learn to use language to express their feelings and to problem-solve in group experiences to make schools more humane and accepting for all students.

IRA/NCTE 11

Language gives us the ability to remove ourselves from a situation, to think about it, discuss it internally, diagram the context, and explore varied resolutions before taking action. As one frustrated mother explained, "If I hadn't decided to write a note to my daughter explaining just how angry I was with her antics, I think I might have taken my frustration out on her physically. The act of writing out my frustration lowered my emotional level amazingly!" Language allows us to argue with words, not our bodies, and make reasoned decisions. It also opens up to us the record of what others have done—in books, articles, and visual formats. With all the potential uses of language, students deserve learning to use it well. The more students can engage in situations in which they can explore ways to express their own ideas and feelings, in which they can talk and listen, read and write with their peers, and use language meaningfully, the more successful they will become. In this spirit we approach writing this text, sharing a basic commitment to the primacy of language use for learning and living well.

## Language at the Center of Learning

Language, and guidance in using language well, need to be at the heart of all instruction—not just during times designated for language arts. Students need to be given opportunities to use oral and written language to participate in the social life of the classroom and school. Teachers model and explain how a focus on language makes learning in science, mathematics, literature, and the social sciences more productive. Opportunities for students to learn to use language to engage in inquiry—asking questions, discussing with others, considering alternatives, and communicating what they learn and the results of their investigations—are also essential to their development.

From the first experiences in school—when teachers gather children to discuss the calendar in kindergarten or when first-graders guided by their teacher together compose a Morning Message, an updated summary of activities and information contributed by the class—children can learn about language by using it meaningfully. Regular opportunities to collaborate in peer groups, share responses to reading and writing activities, and explore new ideas expand students' abilities. In later years, students can engage in student-led literature discussions, take part in teams solving mathematical problems, and participate in inquiry-focused integrated units. Throughout the grades, children and teachers can use language in a variety of ways for specific, meaningful purposes.

## The Many Uses of Language

As you begin this study of the language arts, know that the authors of this text share an understanding that the key to language arts is *language* being used throughout the day and across the curriculum for a wide variety of purposes. In the more formal vocabulary of the field of language study, this attention to the varied uses of language is called **pragmatics.** Throughout the book, a recurring theme is that students will grow in their understanding and command of language when they are given regular opportunities to exercise and expand their competence as active language users. And, as we hope to make very clear, they also need the guidance of caring and knowledgeable teachers such as yourself to become adept and skillful language users!

# What Are Important Aspects of Language Study?

We humans are social beings; we want to connect and communicate with others. We want to make sense of our experiences, store them in our memories, and share them with others. The over 6,000 languages currently spoken in the world attest to human creativity and our ability to construct languages, our basic means of communication and thinking (www.yourdictionary.com, 2006). Yet, the variety of these languages also makes it important to understand some fundamental concepts about language and be alert for situations in which communication needs careful attention. All languages are not structured the same, nor are the physical signals listeners and speakers use to emphasize meaning the same. For example, when Turkish speakers want to emphasize disagreement, they shake their head up and down—just as English speakers do when indicating agreement. So, even the nonverbal signs need to be attended to carefully. These linguistic differences can be very confusing, but they make the study of language fascinating and important.

## Oral Language Acquisition

Human ability to create languages is evidenced in every society as babies learn to communicate in their parents' language. It is also evident when young people develop "secret" or special languages, such as Pig Latin, as workers and professionals create languages specifically for their groups (truck drivers, teachers, publishers, and other professionals), and as the use of new technologies creates contexts for variants of language and writing, such as those used in instant messaging.

Language acquisition is impressive; it is certainly a cause for respect and wonder. Most children acquire their mother tongue without special effort usually in the first three to four years of their lives. Young children begin this process almost from birth and, by the time they are around one year old, can use language to communicate thoughts and wishes. As they develop an ear for what sounds count and learn how to construct meaningful utterances, they also acquire new words at an astonishing rate of approximately nine words per day as toddlers until they reach first grade (Carey, 1978).

By the time we meet kindergartners in public schools, they have already developed impressive communication abilities. As teachers, we need to respect these accomplishments and encourage their further development. Those with language delays and special issues need our support so they can participate confidently in the classroom contexts, too. Students continue to differentiate aspects of syntax during elementary grades and need to learn to participate in a variety of oral and listening settings. They also need guidance in understanding the conventions of written language, including spelling. Reading doesn't come naturally to children, either. Most need continued guidance to build their skills and strategies in decoding and making sense of the texts they read.

Children who expand their language competence in school carry their new abilities back into their homes and community settings where families and friends reinforce and build on the emerging capabilities. Home and school experiences can reinforce each other during the elementary years if children are encouraged to explore language and use it in increasingly varied contexts. A key to continued language growth is teachers who understand, are sensitive to, and supportive of, children's language development. This continued growth in language skill and communication competence characterizes children in healthy environments. See Figure 1.1 for an example of the cycle of language development.

## Second Language Acquisition

The ability of children to acquire their first language without any instruction makes language learning seem simple. Yet, when adults try to learn a new language, they often experience frustration and must expend concerted energy to develop new linguistic competence. What was easy as a young child becomes more of a challenge in adulthood. During the first years of life, children seem to be very receptive orally to their language environment and learn to discriminate key sounds as they try to communicate.

**Figure 1.1** Cycle of Language Development

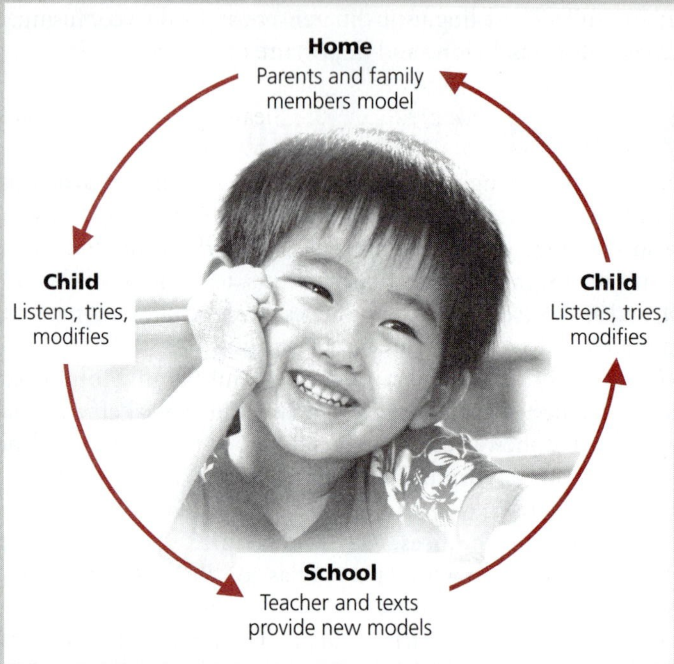


One of the factors contributing to the difficulty of learning new languages as adults is that languages don't use the same **phonemes,** or significant speech sounds, to indicate differences in meaning, as in *rap* and *lap.* The /r/ is distinguished from the /l/in English, but not in some other languages, such as Chinese, for example. The /r/ and /l/, therefore, are phonemes in English but not in Chinese. The flexibility of our voice mechanism has led to significant differences in the ways we humans use our vocal abilities to convey meaning and feelings. If you have traveled abroad or listened to people from other cultures speak, you probably noticed that some languages require sounds that we don't make (like the rolled /r/ in Spanish or the tonal variations in Chinese). At birth, children can distinguish a full range of sounds. However, within a few months of life they have selectively narrowed their attention to those sounds that are important in their language community. By adulthood, most people don't even hear differences in sounds that are unimportant to meaning. This makes learning tonal languages especially difficult for English speakers. **Phonological awareness,** the ability to recognize and produce the sounds that are used in a language, has a positive impact on the ability of children to acquire reading skill according to several recent research studies (Stanovich and Siegel, 1994). The implications for teaching students to read are discussed in Chapter 6.

## Communicating Ideas

The tremendous variations in world languages also mean that understanding others is not simple. The labels created by each cultural group to express ideas and describe the world are often specific to that group. Inuit people in Alaska, for instance, have over twenty words for what we label as *snow.* Russians have only one word to describe *assessment* or *testing.* In English, we have several and seem to keep expanding our lexicon of terms—formative assessment, summative evaluation, progress monitoring, etc. Translation from one language to another poses real challenges, given the variations in terms and ways of expressing the nature of the relationships among the ideas themselves both within words and across them.

Being aware of English **morphology,** the meaning-bearing units of language, and **semantics,** how ideas are communicated, helps teachers make decisions about how to teach vocabulary and word usage. With the increasing numbers of immigrant children from around the globe in our schools now, an understanding of the way languages function and the great variations they represent will help you meet your students' language struggles with understanding and will help you support their language learning. The process of language development and what research has confirmed about this fascinating human facility are explored in Chapter 2. Chapter 11 focuses on the important area of vocabulary development and provides many insights into how teachers can facilitate this important area of ongoing learning in general vocabulary and give special attention to content-specific vocabularies.

IRA/NCTE 10

## Written Language

Humans have developed ingenious ways of sharing experiences and ideas throughout history. Some of the earliest records of human written communication are drawings on caves that show animals and human figures. The early humans created these images to record important events so they could be shared and remembered later. The early systems of communication evolved from these drawings and stylized representations. Later, the Chinese invented paper and were able to share the records of their ideas more easily. They also developed a very complex writing system using pictographs, designs, and lines. In Mesopotamia papyrus, which has lasted until today, contains cuneiform records that reflect a shift to an alphabetic approach to written communication but one that also includes visual images.

Written records provide an important window into human history. In the *New York Review of Books* (October 20, 2005), Anne Carson explained that she was able to create a translation of a poem by Sappho, a Greek poet who lived about 600 BCE, because of the recent identification of a new text of fragment 58. She quotes Martin West, who explained that it was found through the identification of a papyrus in the University of Cologne, as part of a roll containing poems by Sappho. This text, recovered from Egyptian mummy cartonnage, is the earliest known manuscript of the female poet's work. It was copied early in the third century BCE, not much more than 300 years after she wrote it (p. 47). It is from careful records kept by many early civilizations that we have glimpses into our past not otherwise possible.

Written language systems have provided a major form of communication across time. Early records that have survived reveal important information about our various ancestors and various cultures. Archaeologists are still unlocking some written languages and opening windows to other times and places. The varieties of ways humans have created to represent ideas in written form is an interesting study in itself.

## Writing Development

One area of current research on written language has focused attention on the processes by which young children learn to differentiate how a particular language is represented in written form. Even before children know the individual letters, their scribble writing shows their awareness of the physical features of writing. Harste, Woodward, and Burke (1984) described examples of preschoolers' scribbling to make this point: the Chinese child made marks like the characters in Chinese calligraphy; an Arab child's scribbling resembled Arabic flowing script; and an English-speaking child's scribbling showed his awareness of English **orthography**—the way words are represented in written language. All this occurred before the children received any formal instruction in writing or reading. Children who are in a literate environment notice how language is communicated and will try to adopt more adult forms. Children may pretend to write grocery lists when they have seen their parents write and use these for shopping. Many parents encourage young children to draw pictures for their grandparents and absent family members and include these with birthday cards. Children also learn to compose messages on computers as they watch their parents work at home. The connection between children's drawing and early writing has also been established; drawing precedes writing as a way of communicating (Dyson, 1993).

Studies of early writing and reading development show how important the role of preschool literacy experiences in the home are for subsequent learning. When children have been read to in the home and are encouraged to draw and play with writing instruments, they develop a personal identification with literacy. They also build an understanding of how stories are structured and learn a vocabulary that is often more expansive than what they hear in their oral experiences. Chapters 6 and 7 in this book focus on children's early literacy development. Chapters 8 through 10 examine ways students can be helped in developing competence in using our written language conventions, spelling, handwriting and typing, and structures and formats for particular writing genres.

## Visual Literacy

A major component of written communication in books and magazines for young children is the pictures that complement the stories. It is often the pictures and images that students are attracted to first and that they use to confirm their interpretation of the narrative they read in the text. The power of visual images to attract, communicate ideas, and shape opinions is being rediscovered again in this twenty-first century. We are very fortunate to live at a time when publishers of materials for children contract with outstanding artists to illustrate children's books and also attend carefully to the photographs and visual content in informational books. See the Exploring Technology feature for resources to use in creating visual representations.

Our students live in a highly visual world. According to recent surveys (Scholastic, 2005), children spend on the average four hours a day with media—watching TV, playing video games, and communicating via the Internet. Many of the images they attend to are *moving* images—movies, computer games, videos, and advertisements, etc. Most of those they will encounter in the elementary grades in school materials are *still* images, in books, magazines, workbooks, and instructional materials teachers use on transparencies and other visual aids. It is important that students learn to "read" both types of images and know how to interpret, use, and evaluate their impact. Rather than taking what they see at face value, students need to be aware that there are often subtle messages and biases included in visuals. This is one of the reasons the national language arts standards, developed by the International Reading Association (IRA) and the National Council of Teachers of English (NCTE) include viewing as one of the basic standards.

As you think about the types of visual images students will be reading, make a list of what you yourself encounter regularly. On this list are probably the following:

## exploring technology

### Visual Representation

**PowerPoint: Creating Classroom Presentations (www.educationworld.com/a_tech/tech/tech013.shtml)**
This article from the online magazine *Education World* provides information and resources for using Microsoft PowerPoint to create interactive presentations for teachers and students containing text, art, animation, and audio and video elements. Resources include a link to an online tutorial, project ideas, and a student evaluation rubric for using PowerPoint.

**Digital Storytelling (www.coe.uh.edu/digital-storytelling)**
Digital storytelling combines the traditional art of storytelling with multimedia tools such as graphics, audio, video animation, and web publishing to create stories that can be shared electronically all over the world. This site outlines a step-by-step process for creating digital stories, information on technology applications, examples of projects, links to other resources, and more.

**Visual Learning (www.inspiration.com/vlearning/index.cfm)**
This website, sponsored by Inspiration and Kidspiration—software products that support visual learning in the classroom—provides information and project ideas for combining visual learning and technology to clarify thoughts, organize and analyze information, integrate new knowledge, and think critically.

- Pictures
- Photographs
- Maps
- Cartoons
- Comic strips
- Diagrams
- Charts
- Tables
- Movies, videos, and documentaries
- Sketches and drawings
- Posters and advertisements

Helping students develop a thoughtful approach to this visual environment, to become visually literate, is a big task, and luckily, it is one that is shared across the content areas. We teach students to read graphs and charts, primarily in connection with their mathematics curriculum; we teach interpretation of maps, historical primary source documents, and political cartoons as we teach history; and in science we teach students to read charts and diagrams. If there is an arts program then the interpretation of artifacts (such as sculpture, carving, and folk arts) as well as paintings is introduced in those programs.

**Interpret and Create Visual Images** In the language arts, however, we have a major responsibility to help students develop their abilities to use all of these forms of visual representations well. We need to help them both *interpret* visual images and *create* their own. Sometimes, depending on the grade and the class, it may be easier to focus on one of the visual formats by having students create their own. At other times, a more directed approach to introducing the visual format and its key attributes is preferred.

**Combining Information** The combination of visual and verbal messages and images creates new forms of communication, and the new technologies make it very easy to include photographs and images along with texts. The advances in film, photography, and computers have created a powerful set of tools that facilitate the use of visual images. Film, computer-generated graphics, and all sorts of written texts that combine pictures, graphs, charts, and maps with narratives are characteristic of the kinds of messages we receive and create.

**Electronic Tools** As visual communication increases in our times, so does the use of the computer, and specifically, the Internet, as tools for communication. In the 1980s, an argument was made that young people wouldn't need to learn to read in the future because the technological revolution would make this form of language unnecessary. In contrast, with more technological resources we are reading more than ever. And new forms of literacy are required to fully participate in this society as Karchmer, Mallette, Kara-Soteriou, and Leu (2005, p. 1) explain in their book, *Innovative Approaches to Literacy Education,*

> If students are prepared only for the foundational literacies of book, paper, and pencil technologies, they will be unprepared for a future in which the new literacies are required by new information and communication technologies (ICTs). . . . New literacies emerge almost every day as new ICTs emerge. As a result, it becomes important to understand the new skills in reading, writing, viewing and communication that these technologies demand.

Rather than losing value, the importance of language and communication skills is gaining importance in the twenty-first century. The demands on both students and teachers alike are ever-expanding. Therefore, this book includes support for you, as a new teacher, in guiding your students to be thoughtful and knowledgeable with the technologies. We give particular attention to visual literacy in Chapter 12 and new technologies in Chapter 15. The wide variety of tools that are available for teachers' use means that a new teacher needs to check with the school district to see what forms are available and what technological supports are in place. The possibilities for sharing ideas are greatly enhanced when computers, video cameras, and digital cameras are available to teachers and students.

## How Do We Organize and Structure Ideas?

In order to communicate complex ideas, language needs to be organized to show relationships among words and phrases and to indicate time and location.

### Grammar and Syntax

The varieties in how human communities express ideas through **grammar,** the rules that define how language is organized, and **syntax,** the accepted ordering or arrangement of words in sentences, is striking. Grammar includes parts of speech, types of sentences, and punctuation. Children learn the basic rules of grammar and syntax

The possibilities for sharing ideas are greatly enhanced when computers, video cameras, and digital cameras are available to teachers and students.



before they begin school. They develop knowledge of the written grammatical rules usually in elementary school.

There are great variations in both grammar and syntax across languages. Some languages, however, don't separate words or indicate boundaries of sentences and the reader has to determine how ideas are connected. Ancient Hebrew, for example, didn't include vowels or separate words, so readers have to infer a great deal in making sense of these texts. Modern languages also vary in how they organize ideas and indicate relationships. German, for instance, generally places the main verbs or indicators of action at the end of sentences. English has developed a special form to express momentary, ongoing progression of action; for example, "She *was taking* a nap when the phone rang." As humans have developed systems of language, both vocabulary and the structuring of language with what we call grammar and syntax have varied widely. Knowing something about the basic structure of language can help students to use language more effectively. Students who speak more than one language can then compare and contrast the linguistic systems and identify points that may cause confusion. They may also note points of commonality.

## Levels of Formality

Young language users also need to learn how to use different levels of formality appropriate to their purposes and the audiences with whom they are communicating. Each language has its own way of differentiating intimate from formal language. Each has markers for the various language functions, such as giving commands and asking questions, too. The chapters on Understanding Oral Language Development (Chapter 2) and Writing Conventions (Chapter 8) investigate this information.

## Longer Texts

Beyond these basic levels of language structuring, the majority of the energy spent in elementary classrooms is helping students learn to use the structures and conventions common in English to communicate ideas in longer texts. Students learn by reading and writing stories, informational texts, poetry, and procedural guides. Most students begin schooling with a good idea of what the structure of "stories" is; as they develop the ability to read, they are introduced to an increasingly wide array of stories and are transported to different times, places, and contexts. The literature now available for children is a rich treasure that teachers read to and with children. Chapters 6 and 9 outline the early literacy development process and are full of suggestions for how to expand students' literacy with literature. Chapter 11 also focuses exclusively on engaging with literature.

**Informational Texts** Children are much less familiar with the organization of informational texts such as content textbooks, news articles, essays, editorials, persuasive pieces, and procedural "how-to" guides. Yet, by sixth grade, the majority of the material students read is informational, no longer in story form. In fact, Moss and Newman (2002) claim that 75 percent of all reading materials by that time are informational. It is important for intermediate grade teachers to provide guidance into the ways these texts are structured and how students can use the organization to identify important ideas and see relationships among them. Chapter 12 includes ideas on how to help students attend to the organization and structures used in informational texts.

**Structure in Writing** The knowledge of text structures is also foundational for writing. With a growing emphasis on testing writing, students' ability to organize pieces of writing is important for academic success. This knowledge comes from both reading and writing pieces with a variety of text structures. Chapter 10 on writing genres and forms explores this connection fully.

**Reading and Writing** A majority of the time in early elementary classrooms is spent in developing reading and writing and communication competencies. In the intermediate grades, children put these skills to use as they continue to explore in more depth the content of all the curriculum areas and engage in inquiry projects that cut across the traditional disciplines. Learning to use a range of resources, including both print and electronic, is a major focus of the intermediate and upper grades. While all the language arts develop and reinforce each other, the literacy processes receive focused attention in Chapters 12 and 13. These chapters also explore the important relationships between reading and writing.

## How Do Our Communities Influence Language Development?

Learning and using languages well is challenging and a lifelong venture. Yet, when children are young, it is a natural process. Researchers explain (Brown, 1973; Vygotsky, 1962) that there is a seemingly innate ability of humans to acquire language. Yet, the ability requires speakers of the language to surround the child/children with language and to give them supportive feedback. Our natural proclivities need modeling and reinforcement from others who care for us. There have been a few instances of children separated from other humans who have been raised by animals or basically in isolation; these children don't develop normal language skills. Families and nurturing contexts are basic to language development in children.

## Social-Cultural Context

A long-term research study by Hart and Risley (1995) revealed the profound differences in the oral language environments in which children develop in the United States. By taping home conversations/talk at random times over four to five years, Hart and Risley's team was able to derive a picture of the oral language environment of families of different economic levels. (In the study, six families were headed by welfare mothers, thirteen were lower-class working families, ten were middle class, and thirteen were families of upper socioeconomic means.) For over two years, the researchers collected monthly transcripts of the oral language used in the homes as children between one and three years of age were developing. After analyzing the transcripts, the team was able to derive a picture of the oral language environments of these families. They noted that all the families engaged in the full range of communication types and all had quality interactions with their young children.

However, in analyzing their data they also found major variations. They found a tenfold difference in the amount of language directed to the children from the professional homes compared to the welfare homes. The quality of the oral language heard by children of welfare mothers and those children of professional families from working class families was also markedly different. They reported that in the welfare homes, most of the communication directed to the children was in short commands and reprimands. In professional homes, children were given encouragement and modeling of more adult ways of expressing their ideas. For example, a parent might receive a child's query, "Daddy go?" with the feedback, "Yes, Daddy is going to work now." Both the richness of the language used and the purposes for which adults use language in the home have striking impacts on children's linguistic development.

**BUILDING TEACHING SKILLS: Case Study Exercise**

*On the Frontlines*

Go to the Building Teaching Skills section in Chapter 1 of MyEducationLab and read the case study, "On the Frontlines: Connecting with Families," about a veteran teacher who conducts interviews with the families of his students. Complete the activities that follow, and save your work or transmit it to your professor as assigned.

Hart and Risley (1995, p. 149) also identified five factors of parenting that accounted for over 60 percent of the differences in communication related to socioeconomic status. These were (1) the variety of words used, (2) a positive feedback tone, (3) elaboration on topics, (4) giving children choices as they engaged in verbal interactions, and (5) listening to and responding to the children. As Hart and Risley (p. 164) report:

> For the children in welfare and professional families in the longitudinal study, we compared the number of new words added to the recorded vocabulary between the ages of 30–36 months, when all the children were regularly using sentences and clauses appropriately. The welfare children added an average of 169 words in the 6 months from age 30–36 months; the children in professional families added an average of 350 or twice as many. The welfare children were adding fewer numbers of words to vocabularies already smaller. At 30 months the welfare children had an average recorded vocabulary of 357 words, less than half as many as the 766 words in the average vocabulary of the children in professional homes.

**Vocabulary** The implications of these differential rates of vocabulary acquisition were clear in a follow-up study done when the children were in third grade. High correlations were found between language development at three years of age and their language skills and vocabulary at nine years on tests of vocabulary and language. However, there was no association found between students' vocabulary growth and their academic performance in reading, writing, and arithmetic (p. 161).

**Implications** These findings are interesting at many levels. For teachers, it means that children enter classrooms with considerably different depths of language familiarity, vocabulary, and linguistic experiences. However, it is curious that these differences didn't have any impact on their school success. This finding is one that deserves further reflection. What levels of language are being elicited by teachers? Are levels of required language ability low enough that children are not challenged or stretched enough that any differences would be noted?

## Home Language Environment

This study adds important data to our understanding of the importance of the home language environment for children's oral language acquisition. Children seem to use the older speakers of language around them to guide their search for the words and patterns that allow them to communicate with one another. Their attention to vocabulary is directly related to the richness of adults' vocabulary in their home. Earlier research in child language development by Roger Brown (1973) provided insight into ways children search for the structure and regularity of language. Children don't mimic adults as much as they use adult language to help them look for patterns in language. By using cross-national studies, Brown was able to identify similar patterns of children's search for structure. Young speakers tend to label and use one-word utterances. They combine ideas and then create language such as "Daddygo?" an utterance they have never heard, but have constructed from their own sense-making instinct. It is the feedback from older language speakers that helps children revise their "grammatical" utterances and begin to appropriate more adult patterns.

As children develop, they continue to learn more about how to use language effectively. Carol Chomsky (1969) showed how the development of our understanding of the structure of language continues into elementary years. Children at this stage are still sorting out the language and using adult feedback and models to use it effectively. But language learning doesn't stop in childhood; the refinement of our capabilities to express ideas in unique and powerful ways continues in our adult years. And, as we all know, the expansion of our vocabularies and communicative abilities continues throughout our adult lives. The creativity of the human language user is impressive. The study of our shared efforts and the human products should be exciting and stimulating, too!

## Vygotsky and Social Impact

According to language researchers, the modeling and feedback from those around them is essential for children to become more mature language users. As Vygotsky said, "What the child can do in cooperation today he can do alone tomorrow" (1962, p. 104). The power of the external social community to provide the examples, stimulus, and support for language and cognitive development is clear. We learn what those around us make possible (Vygotsky, 1978). We do this because of a relationship between the individual and the social processes according to Vygotsky. He labels this the **zone of proximal development**. The zone of proximal development describes the space between a child's present actual level of functioning and what he/she can do with support, or his/her potential level of functioning. An example may help to clarify this relationship. If you can recall learning to ride a bicycle, for most of us, it was not easy. We needed help if we were to move from our current level of competence to being able to ride independently. One form of support many parents provide is to have smaller, training wheels put on the bicycle to steady it. Another is for a parent to hold onto the bicycle and stabilize it while the child explores how to balance and move forward. Both of these scaffolds make it possible for the child to gain control over a higher level of functioning. Parents running alongside their children generally call out some guiding verbal instructions, "Keep pushing on the pedals" or "Keep your balance in the center of the bike." The combination of physical and verbal mediation soon permits the child to master the art of riding independently. We use this metaphor to illustrate the way children continually move into higher levels of competence in all sorts of physical, cognitive, and social activities.

Children use the older speakers of language around them to guide their search for words and patterns that allow them to communicate with each other. Their attention to vocabulary is directly related to the richness of adults' vocabulary in their home.



## Second Language Learners

Teachers have particular responsibility to know enough about language development and second language acquisition that they can create supportive language environments for all students. This is not an easy task, but one that teachers working together are taking on. Programs such as the Sheltered Instruction Observation Protocol (SIOP), explained in Chapter 4, include very concrete and specific guidance for teachers in meeting language learners' needs. At a very basic level, teachers need to be aware that if they speak clearly and slowly and don't overwhelm children with complex words, students are more likely to be able to differentiate the words. Krashen (1992) has called this "**comprehensible input**" and suggests teachers take some time to monitor their language use for students learning English. Adding physical gestures and actions is also helpful. Ways to be supportive of the needs of children as they learn English are described in Chapters 3 and 4.

IRA/NCTE 10

We started our discussion of language by describing the nature of language and the human experience. We introduced several aspects of language related to both oral and written language. Figure 1.2 provides an overview of these aspects.

Figure 1.2

### Aspects of Oral and Written Language

| Oral Language | Written Language |
|---|---|
| Pragmatics<br>Phonemic Awareness<br>Syntax/Grammar<br>Semantics<br>Vocabulary | Pragmatics<br>Orthography<br>Syntax/Grammar<br>Semantics<br>Text Structure/Genre |

# What Is Your Role?

Teaching about language and helping students become more adept language users are both exciting and essential components of what you will do as a teacher. Students need to be encouraged to use language in all their learning; this means they need regular opportunities to *talk*, to *think aloud*, and to *listen* to many voices—both yours as their teacher and those of their classmates and other adults in the community. They need to learn how to participate as members of a language community, how to give signs they are listening actively and respecting others who speak, and how to share their ideas clearly and appropriately within the varied contexts of school and home. You can help them explore the varied ways we communicate and develop understanding of the differences in styles and expectations among ethnic and cultural groups.

## Examine Language

Making *talk about language* a part of your classroom will help all students gain confidence as language users. The United States is a multicultural and multilingual society. Your interest in language will set the stage for your students' attitudes toward their and other students' languages. Rather than shying away from children and their parents who come from other cultures and speak other languages, your openness as a teacher to learning *from* and *with* them can create a positive context for language arts and all you do. By opening language as an area for exploration, everyone will learn and expand their knowledge and understanding. Explain why it is important to be able to use the formal and polite form of English such as, "My brother and I went to the game," not "I and my brother went," or the dialect form, "Me and my brother," when in situations that demand formal English usage. Explore the alternative forms that are used informally in some communities. Explain why English tradition calls for the other person to be indicated before yourself. When you talk about language with students both the rationale for particular constructions and interest in the evolving nature of the language can be explored. Read aloud to students from books that provide good models of English structures that might not be well practiced. Poetry can provide a powerful tool because it can be memorized and serve as a model for the language learners.

Your interest in language will set the stage for your students' attitudes toward their and other students' languages.

## Model Good Language Use

As a teacher you can think carefully about how you construct classroom activities so students have the opportunity to hear from adults like you who are more competent language users. They need to hear you read aloud from well-written texts, both informational and narrative literature. They need to hear you think aloud about how you respond to what you read, how you compose messages, and how you revise your understandings of what you hear, see, and read. They also need to experience other adults and older students who come into the classroom and engage with them around literacy.

Many primary teachers have developed strong "buddy" programs in which older students read or write with young K–3rd grade students, thus providing social modeling and support for the young learners. Such "buddies" become scaffolds for the younger children and let them experience developmentally more mature language users. Remember that many elementary schools are filled with women and conscious attention to bringing some men into the school and classroom is important so boys will develop clear role models of what they can become. Special days when community members come into the school to read to students can be the ideal opportunity to let children enjoy hearing the mayor, a police officer, and the maintenance personnel share some of their favorite readings. Some schools also have authors and actors visit the school, so students can hear firsthand about their work and interests.

## Encourage Collaborative Learning

You also want to structure the classroom so students can work with each other regularly in partner and small group settings. This permits students to try out their ideas using language and to get feedback from supportive others. Both cognitive and affective engagement can be stimulated when students work with their peers. One of the best ways for students to grow in language is to have regular opportunities to engage in language use. As teachers consciously create classroom opportunities that involve students in expressing their own questions, ideas, and feelings, students become more interested in expanding their language capabilities. When they write to other pen pals or Internet buddies they become more interested in communicating well. When they discuss the themes in the literature they read with others, they gain more insight into the text. Students working on a collaborative team can explore questions and issues more deeply than they can alone.

IRA/NCTE 11

## Fill Your Classroom with Print and Electronic Resources

One of the best resources we have available to us is the wealth of excellent books, magazines, and electronic resources for children and adolescents. These materials provide great models of good language, writing, thinking, and ways of representing ideas. Good books are often the entry point for students to want to read. Think of the impact of the Harry Potter series; thousands of children have become avid readers thanks to this one engaging series. For some more reluctant readers, comics and manga, the Japanese visual cartoon-type books, are the entry point to reading. Yet other children enter literacy online. See the Exploring Children's Literature feature for more ideas on books and resources to use with your students.

A starting place for any new teacher is to identify some key books and articles that can be read orally to students. Then, after finding out students' interests, help them select the kinds of materials they want to read. There are many memorable books that can also stimulate students' deeper thinking and examination of how humans survive in a variety of challenging settings. Books can take students around the world and across time. Create a good classroom library for your students. Also, connect with the school and public librarians to help you locate the "just right" materials to deepen what you are teaching and to provide memorable independent reading materials. Chapters 11 and 15 are filled with resources and ideas to use in your classroom. Each chapter of this book also contains many books and technological supports that will build connections to students. See the Exploring Children's Literature and Exploring Technology features in each chapter for practical ideas and applications.

Throughout this book, we will share ideas for how students can work together with partners and in collaborative small groups. As a teacher, you need to think through the ways student-to-student engagement can be maximized so students will be as active in extending their own learning as possible. Think about classrooms you know of where students have worked together. Literature study groups and book clubs, writing workshops and peer conferencing, students engaged in science and social studies inquiry groups, reader's theater and choral reading are all examples of how teachers enhance language learning and engagement in classrooms from kindergarten through eighth grade. When we discuss assessment, we will explore ways that you can use the opportunities when students are working in partner and small group arrangements to listen to and observe the children and assess their thinking and learning. Information about how to plan and organize your classroom is highlighted in Chapter 14.

## exploring Children's Literature

### Bilingual Picture Books

#### Grades K to 3

*A Magic Pocket: Selected Poems*—Written by Michio Mado, illustrated by Mitsumasa Anno, translated by the Empress Michiko of Japan, and published by Margaret McElderry (1998).

Japanese and English versions of each of the fourteen poems about simple childhood experiences are available.

*Gathering the Sun: An Alphabet in Spanish and English*—Written by Alma Flor Ada, illustrated by Simon Silva, and published by Rayo (1997).

This is a book of poems about working in the fields and nature's bounty, one for each letter of the Spanish alphabet.

*Hairs/Pelitos*—Written by Sandra Cisneros and published by Knopf (1994).

A girl describes how each person in the family has hair that looks and acts different. For example, Papa's is like a broom, Kiki's is like fur, and Mama's has the sweet smell of bread before it has been baked.

*I Love Saturdays y domingos*—Written by Alma Flor Ada, illustrated by Elivia Savadier, and published by Atheneum (2002).

A young girl enjoys the similarities and differences between her English-speaking grandparents and her Spanish-speaking ones.

*Jambo Means Hello: Swahili Alphabet Book*—Written by Muriel Feelings, illustrated by Tom Feelings, and published by Dial (1974).

This book presents a word, with English translation, for each of the twenty-four letters in the Swahili alphabet. A brief explanation of each word introduces an East African custom.

*Kobo, the Li'l Rascal*—Written by Masashi Ueda and published by Kodansha International (2001).

The story centers on five-year-old Kobo and his mischievous antics centering on the small incidents of daily life in Japan. English and Japanese versions are available (Manga format).

*Owl Babies*—Written by Martin Waddell, illustrated by Patrick Benson, translated by East Word, and published by Magi (1995).

Three owl babies whose mother has gone out into the night try to stay calm while she is gone. The Vietnamese text is placed into the illustrations.

*Table, Chair, Bear: A Book in Many Languages*—Written by Jane Fedor and published by Ticknor and Fields (1995).

This book presents illustrations of objects found in a child's room, labeled in thirteen different languages: English, Korean, French, Arabic, Vietnamese, Japanese, Portuguese, Lao, Spanish, Chinese, Tagalog, Cambodian, and Navaho.

## Grades 4 to 8

*ABC x 3: English, Español, Français*—Written by Marthe Jocelyn, illustrated by Tom Slughter, and published by Tundra (2005).

Each of the 26 letters shared by the English, Spanish, and French alphabets is represented with a striking cutout illustration paired with a corresponding word in the three languages.

*Arctic Memories*—Written and illustrated by Normee Ekoomiak and published by Holt (1990).

This text, in Inuktitut and English, describes a now-vanished Inuit way of life.

*Can You Greet the Whole Wide World?: 12 Common Phrases in 12 Different Languages*—Written by Lezlie Evans, illustrated by Denis Roche, and published by Houghton Mifflin (2006).

This book introduces young readers to common phrases such as "good morning," "thank you," and "please" in German, Hebrew, Spanish, Arabic, Russian, Hindi, Chinese, Zulu, Japanese, Italian, French, and Portuguese.

*Diego*—Written by Jonah Winter, illustrated by Jeanette Winter, and published by Random House (1991).

Through Spanish and English captions and paintings, this book discusses the childhood of Diego Rivera and how it influenced his art.

*In My Family/En mi familia*—Written and illustrated by Carmen Lomas Garza and published by Children's Book Press (1997).

Through bilingual text and illustrations, the author describes her experiences growing up in a Hispanic community in Texas.

*Liu and the Bird: A Journey in Chinese Calligraphy*—Written and illustrated by Catherine Louis and published by North-South (2006).

A young Chinese girl has a dream that leads her on a long journey to her grandfather on the other side of the mountains (includes activities intended to teach Chinese characters).

*Tigers, Frogs, and Rice Cakes: A Book of Korean Proverbs*—Edited by Daniel Holt, illustrated by Lu Han Stickler, and published by Shen's Books (1998).

This collection contains traditional Korean proverbs followed by brief explanations of their meanings and comparisons made with English equivalents.

*We All Went on Safari: A Counting Journey through Tanzania*—Written by Laurie Krebs, illustrated by Julia Cairns, and published by Barefoot (2003).

Three children learn to count in English and Swahili as they cross the Tanzanian plains.

# What Does Good Instruction Look Like?

Children learn that which is important to them. Therefore, the foundation of good teaching is providing students with interesting and meaningful contexts for language use. When children have purposes for developing new abilities they are most likely to focus their attention and engage fully in taking the risks to learn something new. Therefore, we begin with the focus on **immersion in language-rich opportunities.** This means that the classroom provides regular opportunities for students to hear good language, to be engaged with other students in meaningful oral and written activities, and to have a variety of choices in their activities. Classrooms that provide immersion have a variety of places in the room where students can go to engage in meaningful work. There may be a table with headsets so students can listen to oral readings of interesting books and text materials, an area with computers so students can connect and explore ideas, a writing corner with resources to encourage elaboration and revision, and a classroom library and reading nook for personal quiet reading. The walls and bulletin boards will show examples of strategies students are using and guidelines to refresh their memories. Student work will be visible and clearly honored. Chapter 14 provides a fuller exploration of ways to create such classrooms. See the Engaging in Visual Literacy feature for an activity that will help you to envision and design your own language arts classroom.

engaging in

# Visual Literacy

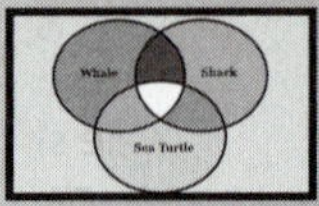

## Classroom Drawing

Imagine what an inviting classroom looks like. Now, take out a piece of paper and draw the room. Make it like a planning sheet for an architect's drawing of the classroom. Place on it the arrangement of the student desks, the teacher's desk, and the other work areas. Where are books stored and where are places for students to keep their work? Is there a reading corner with comfortable pillows or rugs on which students can stretch out and read? Where does the teacher keep necessary supplies? What makes this room special? After creating your illustration, skim the textbook and see whether you notice any classrooms or photographs that might give you ideas for adding or subtracting things from your own room. You may want to share this drawing with others, but keep it as you build your own plan for how you can create an inviting space where students will learn with you.

## Explicit Instruction

Then teachers need to focus *explicit attention* on the selected aspects of language for development. There are two basic avenues for instruction open to you as you build students' understanding of language arts. The first is to provide **explicit instruction** about language, especially about how the English language functions. All students need to have a clear understanding of the variety of ways we use language, the ways we represent ideas in different forms of discourse and engage in inquiry with language, and how to use language appropriately in speaking, writing, and creating visual representations. When aspects of language are highlighted by teachers, all students have the opportunity to develop a vocabulary to describe the particular aspect, think about why it is important, and practice thinking about and using it appropriately. Take for example the ability to produce cursive handwriting. Some teachers don't want to spend time on such basic-level skills. However, when students are shown how to hold their pencils, how to form letters, and see models of good writing, the quality and ease of their writing improves. This is also true of most of the aspects of oral, written, and visual language; attention to and identification of what makes quality production help students learn. At all grade levels you, the teacher, have an obligation to help students develop their skills in using oral, written, and visual language.

## State and National Standards

The state and national standards for English Language Arts provide an important framework for your planning. Examine Figure 1.3 and look at the 12 basic areas outlined by the IRA/NCTE standards. Note that these are general areas and that a more clear delineation of what needs to be learned at each grade level is missing. That is where the state and pro-

Figure 1.3

## IRA/NCTE Standards for the English Language Arts

The vision guiding these standards is that all students must have the opportunities and resources to develop the language skills they need to pursue life's goals and to participate fully as informed, productive members of society. These standards assume that literacy growth begins before children enter school as they experience and experiment with literacy activities—reading and writing, and associating spoken words with their graphic representations. Recognizing this fact, these standards encourage the development of curriculum and instruction that make productive use of the emerging literacy abilities that children bring to school. Furthermore, the standards provide ample room for the innovation and creativity essential to teaching and learning. They are not prescriptions for particular curriculum or instruction. Although we present these standards as a list, we want to emphasize that they are not distinct and separable; they are, in fact, interrelated and should be considered as a whole.

1. Students read a wide range of print and non-print texts to build an understanding of texts, of themselves, and of the cultures of the United States and the world; to acquire new information; to respond to the needs and demands of society and the workplace; and for personal fulfillment. Among these texts are fiction and nonfiction, classic and contemporary works.
2. Students read a wide range of literature from many periods in many genres to build an understanding of the many dimensions (e.g., philosophical, ethical, aesthetic) of human experience.
3. Students apply a wide range of strategies to comprehend, interpret, evaluate, and appreciate texts. They draw on their prior experience, their interactions with other readers and writers, their knowledge of word meaning and of other texts, their word identification strategies, and their understanding of textual features (e.g., sound-letter correspondence, sentence structure, context, graphics).
4. Students adjust their use of spoken, written, and visual language (e.g., conventions, style, vocabulary) to communicate effectively with a variety of audiences and for different purposes.
5. Students employ a wide range of strategies as they write and use different writing process elements appropriately to communicate with different audiences for a variety of purposes.
6. Students apply knowledge of language structure, language conventions (e.g., spelling and punctuation), media techniques, figurative language, and genre to create, critique, and discuss print and non-print texts.
7. Students conduct research on issues and interests by generating ideas and questions, and by posing problems. They gather, evaluate, and synthesize data from a variety of sources (e.g., print and non-print texts, artifacts, people) to communicate their discoveries in ways that suit their purpose and audience.
8. Students use a variety of technological and information resources (e.g., libraries, databases, computer networks, video) to gather and synthesize information and to create and communicate knowledge.
9. Students develop an understanding of and respect for diversity in language use, patterns, and dialects across cultures, ethnic groups, geographic regions, and social roles.
10. Students whose first language is not English make use of their first language to develop competency in the English language arts and to develop understanding of content across the curriculum.
11. Students participate as knowledgeable, reflective, creative, and critical members of a variety of literacy communities.
12. Students use spoken, written, and visual language to accomplish their own purposes (e.g., for learning, enjoyment, persuasion, and the exchange of information).

*Source:* Excerpt from International Reading Association (IRA) & National Council of Teachers of English (NCTE). Standards for the English Language Arts (p. 3). 

fessional standards documents are very helpful. Chapter 5 on assessment examines a developmental set of guidelines. These are important in planning instruction so there is a continued development of students' command of the language arts skills and processes. There is so much that students need to learn to do that each grade level needs to build on the preceding one. Standards documents can be a starting place for a good schoolwide discussion on how students can be assessed and then instruction planned so all can learn.

## Contextualized and Incidental Teaching

A second important form of instruction is through **contextual and incidental teaching.** Teachers learn that students are most responsive to instructional coaching when they have an immediate context for using the guidance. Helping students phrase a request and thank administrators when they want special permission to take a field trip is much more effective than teaching an isolated lesson in how to use polite language to make requests. Using students' own writing to illustrate the need for agreement between subjects and verbs is much more effective than a lesson on agreement taught outside any particular writing context. Many teachers find their leads from what their students are struggling to do and create focused lessons as the opportunities arise. Both these forms of teaching are important and need to be utilized. Examples of direct and contextualized teaching are provided throughout this book.

## Gradual Release of Responsibility

The next steps in teaching are equally important. Students learn from their teachers' modeling and attention to aspects of language, then they need guided opportunities to use the strategy or process with feedback and support from the teacher and other students. Finally they can move to more independent use of the new competency. This gradual release of responsibility model was first developed by Pearson and Gallagher (1983) and is shown in Figure 1.4. The goal is that students can demonstrate their newly developed abilities in meaningful activities where they can demonstrate for themselves and others all they have learned. Finally, students also need to evaluate their own learning and success in using the targeted competence, whether it is in their writing, oral participation in discussions, oral report, or an artifact for their portfolio. This is where attention to rubrics, matrices with descriptors of levels of performance on particular tasks, and other descriptions of what good performance is like are important. For example, a new teacher, Elizabeth, wanted her students to learn to give an oral report to the class as part of their social studies research. She developed a rubric with her students and then asked all students to use it in preparing their reports. By doing so, the students and she could more easily determine the focus of their efforts and also evaluate the success of the project presentations. You will find examples of rubrics and read more about using them for student assessment in Chapter 5. The Engaging in Assessment feature on page 24 also discusses how both students and teachers can benefit from using rubrics.

The language to describe attainment of competence is helpful to all—teachers and students. It helps us talk with each other about growth and helps us mark achievements. It also makes learning a shared endeavor, not a guessing game, for students trying to find the answers their teachers want.

Figure 1.4

## Gradual Release of Responsibility Model

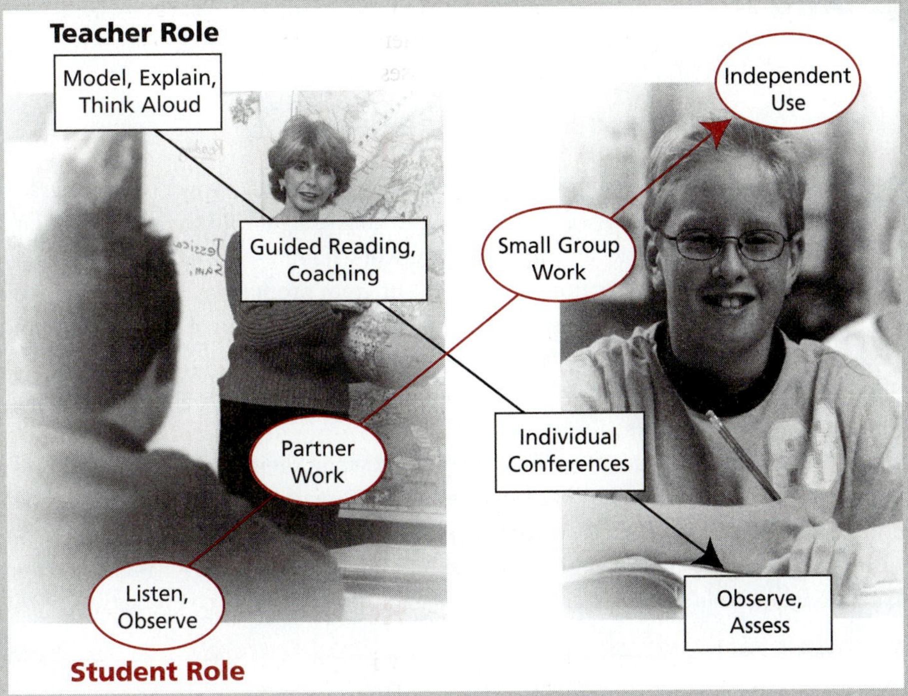


*Source:* Based on Pearson and Gallagher, 1983.

## Students' Metacognitive Control of Learning

Our goal is that the teacher does not need to be with students for them to employ their knowledge of and competence with language. Students deserve experiences so they can evaluate situations, select from a range of options, and take their own actions as communicators. This ability to monitor one's own learning and engagement and evaluate oneself is called **metacognition**—meaning looking at one's own thinking and making decisions about it. Students need to gain control of their own "tool kit" of strategies as independent learners. It is helpful to think of metacognition as involving several levels of knowledge (Paris and Ayers, 1994):

IRA/NCTE 6

- **Declarative knowledge**—being able to describe tasks and processes (what is a research paper as distinguished from a personal learning journal; what is a grammatically correct command; what do the letters stand for in the KWL strategy?) Know that each of these activities is explained later in the book. In fact, you will be gaining a great deal of declarative knowledge about teaching routines you may use.
- **Procedural knowledge**—knowing how to engage productively in an activity (how to write a clear research paper; how to construct directions or create a KWL—Know, Want to Know, Learn—chart while learning). The procedural level is more difficult because it involves actually using the strategies or routines. It will take

**engaging in**

## Assessment

### Using Samples and Rubrics

Students and new teachers can develop more accurate expectations of quality work at their grade level when they see samples of other students' work. Teachers can gain insight into their own standards for their students by making comparisons to state and national work samples. For example, states often provide sample papers of what students have done to score at different proficiency levels on state writing examinations. Check your state's website to see whether it contains examples of student work in writing, reading, and oral communications. As a new teacher, you may need to study these and compare them to the state rubrics or scoring guides so you can build your own internal representation of what you can expect at various developmental stages.

It is helpful for students to see examples of the work of others in their grade level when they go online. The students themselves can reflect on the papers or projects they find and build their skills in establishing criteria for what makes excellent work. They can also study less-than-excellent papers or projects and decide how these examples could be improved. Developing a plan for revising a document and providing a rationale for the choices made can be a useful metacognitive task.

several attempts to use a new strategy before you will feel secure in implementing it. Procedural knowledge builds more slowly and requires trials and feedback.

- **Conditional knowledge**—knowing when to use a particular set of processes or strategies (does the paper need to be edited and prepared for publication or is a draft for class discussion sufficient; when should one express the way to complete a task, when does one use the KWL framework in learning?) Knowing what one can do is important; knowing when to do it comes with more experience and reflective practice.

The more teachers talk about learning and describe the processes and outcomes inherent in the classroom activities, the more likely it is that students will be able to function successfully. How many times have students complained, "If only the teacher had told us what she expected!" Do teachers know how to make their expectations clear and do students know to ask for clear explanations and models of work? When students can use rubrics and see sample papers, they can form images of what they should be doing. When you help students keep learning logs to describe what they are doing and how they are doing it, students grow in their own ownership of their activities in school. See Chapter 10 on genres of writing for explanations of how learning journals and learning logs can be used.

## Consider Student Diversity

IRA/NCTE 9

Classrooms and schools are increasingly diverse, with inclusion of students with special needs, English language learners, and children from a variety of social and cultural backgrounds. This makes it important to listen carefully to students and find out as much as possible about each student early in the school year. Teachers who take time to meet with families to learn more about each student can plan for more personalized instruction and bring in the knowledge and experience of the students more effectively. Often, par-

## exploring diversity

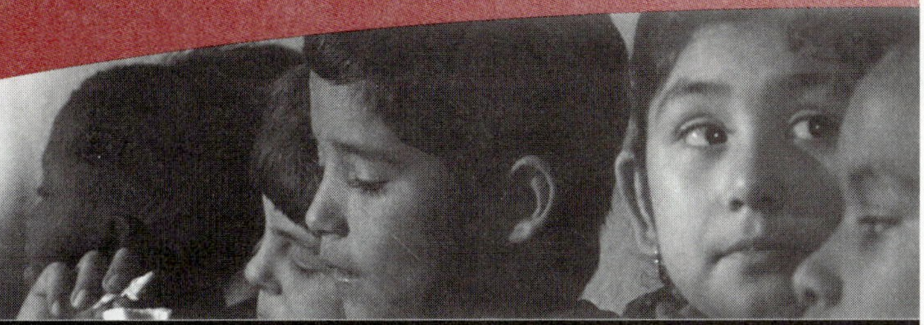

### Get to Know Your Students

There are many ways to become acquainted with your students at the start of the school year. When parents bring their children to school, take special time to get to know them and ask them about their child.

Feel free to ask, Is there something special about ____________? What has ____________ done this summer that ____________ might like to share? What activities does ____________ enjoy? Then, make notes on a card of what you learn. The more information you have about your students, the better. When there are parents who do not come to school, send a letter home asking for information that might help you involve the child and adjust to her or his needs and interests.

Dear ____________,
I am delighted that ____________ will be in my class this year. To help ____________ feel comfortable and confident this year, I would like to know some special things about ______. I would greatly appreciate your responses to the following:

1. Something special about ____________ is ____________________________.
2. A favorite activity of ____________ is ____________________________.
3. In the family, ____________________________.
4. This summer, ____________________________.
5. A favorite book (magazine, comic, movie, video game) of ____________ is ____________________________.
6. We hope this school year includes ______.

ents can be great resources and help in the classroom, too. Making early efforts to know students and their families is an important first step in being able to create a classroom that will be differentiated for the particular group of students. In many schools, differentiating instruction also means that there will be aides and special teachers in the classroom during some parts of the day and week. Careful thinking can ensure that these support personnel are available when they are most needed and when they can work with individuals or small groups of students. Chapter 4 and the Exploring Diversity features of this book examine the importance of differentiating instruction.

In summary, good instruction begins when teachers create rich, engaging contexts for language use, where there is:

- Immersion in language
- Explicit attention to specific aspects of language arts
- Modeling and guided release of responsibility for use
- Demonstrating real performance
- Reflection on use by the students themselves
- Differentiation of instruction to meet the needs of students

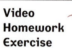

# How Can the Standards Help Your Teaching?

One of the general responses from preservice teachers is that they feel overwhelmed. "How can I possibly teach all that is expected of me?" "How can I be accountable for all this content!" One of the best ways to keep focused is to let the state and national standards guide you. The process of helping students become competent language users is one that is shared by teachers at all grade levels. The standards and benchmarks try to provide a developmental profile of what students should be learning to do. They also provide a common vocabulary that we can use with other teachers, parents, and our students. It is good to take a look at the English language arts standards now and return to them often.

We, the authors of this book, and practicing teachers, have also used these standards regularly as we have written these chapters. We will refer to them as we explore each aspect of the language arts and make suggestions for teaching. They also are a basis for the assessment chapter so you can learn to look to your students for indications of their stages of development as language users.

**Video Homework Exercise**

*Content Standards*

Go to the Homework and Exercises section in Chapter 1 of MyEducationLab and view the video, "Content Standards" about a first year teacher and her questions regarding the standards. Complete the activities that follow, and save your work or transmit it to your professor as assigned.

## Use for Self-Assessment

Take a few minutes to read through the IRA/NCTE standards in Figure 1.3 and mark with a plus (+) those you feel most comfortable teaching and with an asterisk (*) those you will want to spend more time developing. Then, go online and look up your state's own standards for language arts and compare them. We suggest putting the state standards in your notebook for this course. It will help you become very comfortable with the language and expectations of those in your area-wide professional community. Most school districts have spent considerable time aligning their own curriculum and assessments to the expectations of the state and national groups.

As you will regularly have to make decisions about how to spend the limited time you have with students, the standards can be very useful. Ask yourself, "How will this develop my students' knowledge and abilities of what is expected of them? How does it reflect the grade level or developmental standards? What research base is there for what I want to do?" You may also need to refer to the standards periodically to ensure that you are not overlooking some important area of the standards. We have found that we gravitate to those areas we feel most comfortable teaching and avoid those with which we are less confident. Checking against the standards can help nudge us into trying those areas.

## Establish Teaching Priorities

Another way the standards can be useful is in setting priorities. The school day is too short for you to accomplish all that you want. Therefore, it is important to set priorities. Standards are a great way for you to balance some of the engaging activities you may want to do with the curriculum expectations for the children. Ask yourself, "What's most important?" Then, talk with other teachers to see if you are all moving in a common direction and giving students the learning experiences they most need. You might even make a list of the standards and benchmarks for your grade and decide which of them you will assess and teach each month or quarter of the year.

At each grade level, there is much that teachers do to help students move forward in their command of language. Teachers need to identify their students' zones of proximal development and structure appropriate activities for language exploration and use. With an understanding of what students should be able to do by the end of your grade you can look for evidence of their level of accomplishment in informal instructional assessments and in regular, assigned class work. These give you an indication of how much attention needs to be devoted to each area of the curriculum. For students who show command of grade-level work, differentiating for their level of achievement is important. For those needing additional work with some standards in the curriculum, there are many ways you can set up meaningful learning activities to help them move forward, too.

You will want to provide a rich context in which students regularly use language in meaningful contexts. Research studies continue to conclude that teaching the forms and structures of language does little good if students are not actively engaged in purposeful use of language (Langer, 2002; Applebee, 1994). Grammar and spelling taught as a series of skills has little impact. When students want to communicate clearly to others, they are much more interested in making sure that they use language well. Therefore, the more opportunities students have to work on projects and activities of interest to them and where they have an audience for their work, the more likely it is that they will attend to the important features of language. With our increasing numbers of English language learners and students with special needs in the classroom, the advantages of providing multiple extended contexts where children can learn together are clear. Student-centered exploratory study units can integrate content with language arts with exciting results. See Chapters 4 and 12 for ways to develop rich, integrated instruction.

## How Can You Get Started in This Study of Language Arts?

As you begin this study of language arts, you probably are thinking of how you have been taught aspects of language arts. Many new teachers draw heavily on their early experiences as they begin their own teaching. It is very useful to think critically about those experiences: Which were most helpful to your development? What is your internal image of a good teacher of language arts? Is it current? Can you visualize the situations in the Classroom Challenges that you will find introduced in each chapter? If you can't, you may want to watch some videos of good teachers in action or visit some classrooms. The MyEducationLab activities found in the margins of each chapter are also designed to enrich your reading and enhance your experiences in this course and in your classroom.

As you read this book, use the chapter structure with the Classroom Challenge and key questions to guide your thinking. At the end of each chapter we return to the Classroom Challenge; use this as a time to reflect on how you would now handle the challenge that was posed. Take time to return to the key questions, too: they are reviewed at the conclusion of the chapter. It is our hope that you will be able to elaborate on each of them, using ideas you have gained from reading, viewing, and discussing.

Use this book as a guide to test your past experiences as a learner against some of the examples provided in the vignettes of contemporary teachers and teaching methods. Keep a journal comparing and contrasting your experiences with these different options. Make notes of ideas you want to try as you begin teaching. If there are some ideas that seem unclear, ask your instructors for suggestions of schools to visit where you can see this kind of teaching in action. Use the web resources presented in the Exploring Technology feature. These websites are all examples of teachers in action. Use this study to expand your vision of how you can be an outstanding language arts teacher; think of all you as a teacher will be able to do to support students' developing language capabilities.

## What Are Your Interests and Questions?

As you think about your previous experiences, it is also good to identify your major interests and the questions and concerns that you have now. Make notes of what you want to gain from this study and write down the questions you most want answered. Then check the text Table of Contents and Index to see if there is direct reference to these concerns. You may want to start your use of the textbook by checking for help with these immediately and then build your understanding of these issues as you continue through the course. Refer to them periodically and keep adding to what you learn. There is no substitute for writing to help you build your understanding and retain good ideas. When you find ideas or websites, write them down so they will be yours when you find yourself alone in the classroom as the teacher in charge. Remember that your classmates and instructor are important resources, too. Make a list of questions that may help elicit their experiences and knowledge and can help you deepen and expand your own thinking. Listen actively so each experience helps build your strength and confidence. Use this course as an opportunity to reflect on your own learning strategies and expand your understanding.

## chapter review

### What Is Important about Classroom Language Use?

Children continue to expand their abilities to use language during their elementary years. Teachers can do a great deal to facilitate this growth. First, teachers serve as models of more proficient language users for young students. Second, teachers can set up classroom routines so students can engage actively together in using language for a variety of purposes; when students use language, they can expand their abilities to use language and can also deepen their understanding of language.

### What Is the Authors' Perspective?

We believe strongly that students need regular activities to use language in meaningful settings for real purposes. It is by using language and learning new ways to express ideas and feelings that students will grow in their abilities to use language for learning and living well.

It is our intent to provide you with tested and practical ways to organize your classroom, to focus your instruction, to develop your students' language and learning potential, and to meet the demands of the national and state standards.

### What Are Important Aspects of Language Study?

As a teacher, you will want to know about how children acquire language, both their mother or first language as well as second languages. The development of written language is also important to understand. Finally, visual literacy is a central form of communication that needs to be understood and included in the language arts curriculum.

### How Do We Organize and Structure Ideas?

Languages are more than words; they are structured and organized with shared rules or conventions called *grammar* and *syntax*. There are conventions, also, for how to express longer chunks of meaning. Narratives follow a story structure, and informational texts are organized by some common "frames." There are many commonalities between reading and writing, yet each develops independently.

## How Do Our Communities Influence Language Development?

Children learn the language that is spoken in their homes and by those who they love. Recent studies of language development in diverse homes also indicate that there are distinctly different patterns of home language interaction that influence the extent of language children acquire: in fact, there can be a threefold difference in the entering vocabularies of kindergarten children related to the socio-economic conditions of the families.



## What Is Your Role?

Teachers need to help children explore language, use language in a variety of ways, and then reflect on their language options and uses. Teachers serve as models of more mature language users and can develop enthusiasm for language and word use. As children grow, providing more explicit explanations of what mature language use is like through rubrics and written descriptions and models can help students develop metacognitive control.

## What Does Good Instruction Look Like?

Teachers who immerse students in language-rich activities and then provide explicit instruction as needed create the context for learning. Building on contextual and incidental opportunities brings life into the classroom and can help students make connections. Good instruction doesn't look the same all year; teachers who model and guide then provide settings for students to take more control over those same strategies or behaviors and support students until they are in control themselves. Teachers know how to differentiate instruction and practice according to individual student needs. They also want students to have metacognitive awareness of their learning so they can determine what to do personally. The gradual release of responsibility model means that teachers have clear goals, know how to model and instruct students, establish safe ways for students to practice new routines and language as they engage together, and then turn over the learning to the students, individually and corporately.

## How Can the Standards Help Your Teaching?

One of the first things new teachers learn is that there is too much to teach for the amount of time available. Therefore, teaching *is* decision making. Standards provide a good starting place for prioritizing what gets included in the school week. They also help in initial assessment of where students are functioning by providing a template for performance based on national and state expectations. With this information, it is easier to select materials and activities to include in the instructional program.

Welcome to this study of language arts!



Now go to www.myeducationlab.com to take a Pretest to assess your initial comprehension of chapter content, study chapter content with your individualized Study Plan, take a Posttest to assess your understanding of chapter content, practice your teaching skills with Building Teaching Skills exercises, and build a deeper, more applied understanding of chapter content with Homework and Exercises.

chapter 2

# Understanding Oral Language Development

**Carol Beers,** College of William and Mary

## classroom challenge

**Ms. Paredo** is a third-grade teacher who has twenty-five students in her classroom. She has been concerned about some of her children's use of the past tense, noting that they often drop the endings to their verbs when they talk with her. She decides that a lesson is needed to introduce and reinforce past tense markers to her students. After talking with her colleagues, she decides to try a lesson the other teachers have used in their classes.

During the lesson, she reads a story to her students, placing particular emphasis on the past tense verbs. She has planned several activities for when the story is over. She reviews present tense verbs and past tense verbs with her students. As she reviews these verbs, she asks the students about the verbs within the story. After identifying these verbs together, she asks them to talk about some things they did yesterday. As students respond to her questions, she lists the past tense verbs on the board.

After this brief discussion, Ms. Paredo writes five sentences on the board, omitting the verb. Possible verb choices are posted on the board near the sentences. The sentences include the following: Yesterday, I __________ with my dog. Last week, she __________ to the store. My mother __________ hard for her family.

Ms. Paredo asks students to come to the board, read the sentence, and fill in the blank space with a verb. She follows this with a worksheet that her students do

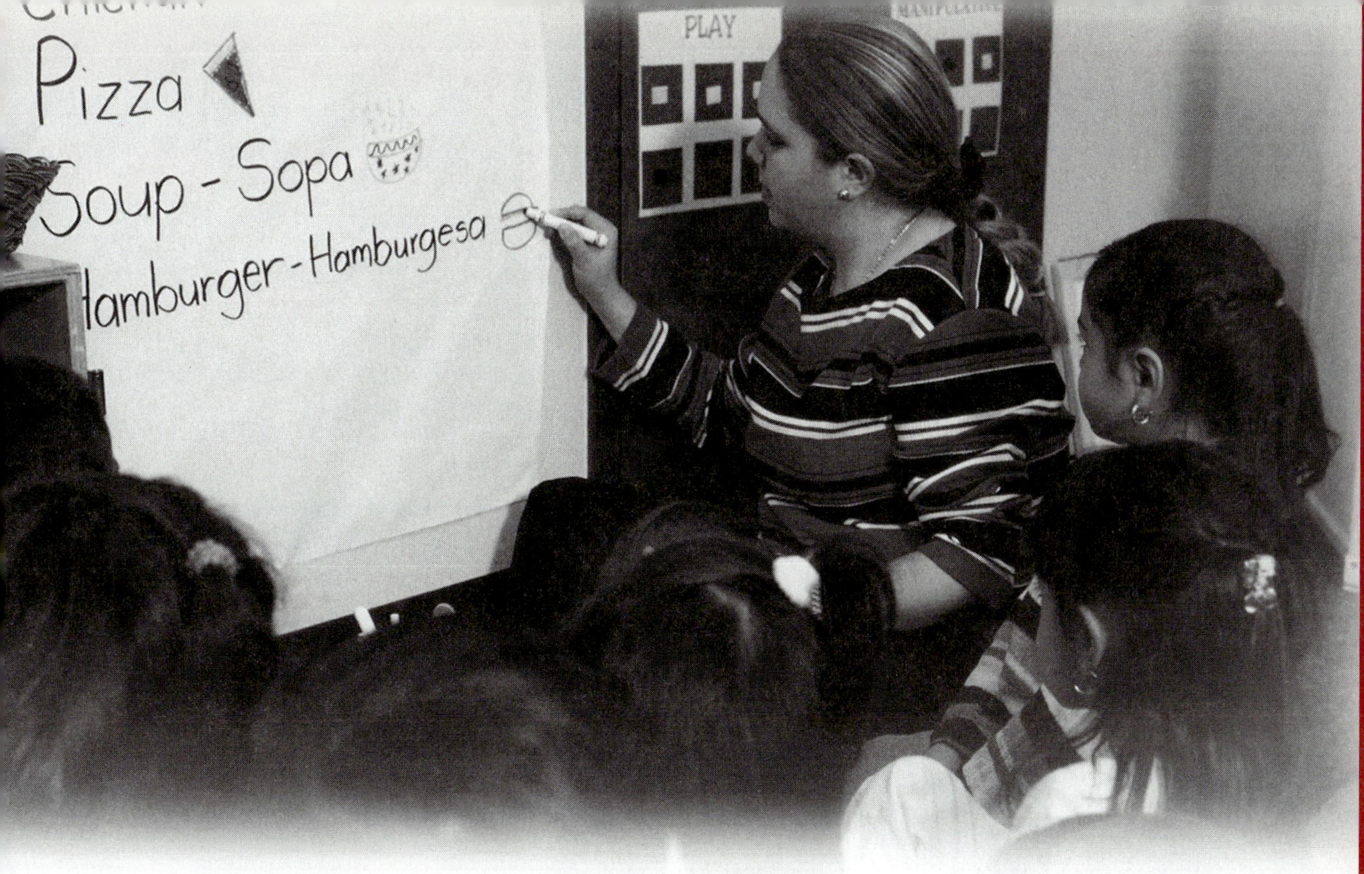


individually. She is pleased when they seem to fill in the blanks correctly.

After the lesson, the students have a break before moving into their social studies lesson. During this time, she moves around the room, chatting informally with her students. While talking to several students, she notices that they are still leaving the past tense off their verbs. Miguel, for example, says, "Yesterday, I walk to school." Brian chimes in and says, "I walk too. My mother, she carry my books for me." At this point, Ms. Paredo is not sure what she should do. Should she correct them? Should she ignore them? Should she do the lesson again? Feeling somewhat frustrated, Ms. Paredo returns to her desk.

## Questions for Reflection

1. Why do you think the students were not using past tense markers in their conversations?
2. How could Ms. Paredo have done her lesson differently?
3. What should Ms. Paredo do now to address what she sees as a continuing problem?

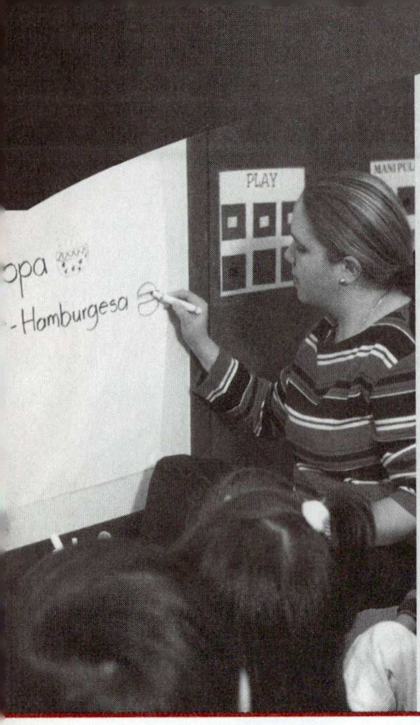


## anticipating this chapter

These questions help focus attention on the importance of oral language in classrooms.

What is language?
Why is oral language important?
What do we know about oral language development?
How does language grow?
How does language change during the preschool years?
Is language development "finished" when children enter school?
What do we know about dialects?
How do students use language?
How can we promote language growth?

# What Is Language?

Language is an essential part of our humanity. It is what allows us to relate with other people, learn of a past we never experienced, and imagine the future yet to come. Most of us take our language system for granted, even though it is quite complex. Many different definitions of language exist, but they all tend to include three key elements: Language is a system; language includes arbitrary symbols; and language allows us to classify everything in our experience, such as thoughts, processes, and events.

- **Language is a system.** Several rules govern how language systems operate. In the English language system, for example, adjectives are placed before nouns. In the French language system, however, adjectives appear after nouns. We are referring to these and other rules when we classify language as a structured system.
- **Language includes arbitrary symbols.** Our language system uses the word *house* to designate a building in which families reside. The Spanish use the word *casa.* These are examples of the arbitrary symbols used in a language system and agreed to by the users of that language.
- **Language allows us to classify everything.** Has anything ever happened to you that you could not describe in your mind? Is there anything in your range of experiences that you cannot name or find the name to? This aspect of language is limitless.

There are four modes of language: talking, listening, reading, and writing. Talking and writing are *expressive* modes of language. Listening and reading are *receptive* modes. Most attention in elementary schools is focused on teaching children how to improve their reading and writing skills. Very little attention is focused on teaching children how to improve their talking and listening skills. The integral nature of these four components is essential to language arts.

## Why Is Oral Language Important?

Recognizing the role of talk and listening in today's classrooms is crucial, perhaps now more than ever. Our society is becoming increasingly divided over very important issues, but often, adults do not engage in conversations in which true differences of opinion are fully expressed. The ability to engage in a conversation in which both parties are willing and able to listen to each other's points of view is an essential skill. These conversations enrich participants and often motivate deeper thinking about their own worldview.

The importance of oral language in the classroom cannot be overstated, and understanding its role is crucial for students who will be entering a workforce very different from the workforce seen today. Students today will live and work in an increasingly diverse society that will require the ability to communicate well. The minority portion of the U.S. workforce is expected to double by 2020, while the majority portion is expected to decline by 25 percent (The National Center for Public Policy and Higher Education, 2005). Being able to communicate well with a variety of people is an increasingly important skill.

### Talking Improves Students' Ability to Communicate

Oral language in the classroom, however, has other more immediate purposes. For example, we know a great deal about how children learn their oral language system and the stages through which they progress. We also know that language growth does not stop once a child reaches school age. In fact, much of a child's oral language learning occurs between the ages of 5 and 10. Teachers must recognize this and find opportunities to be effective with students during these years.

Planning such opportunities for students to talk and listen to other students and teachers will improve their ability to communicate (Eeds and Wells, 1989). This is especially important for children who come from homes in which "school language" is not the norm, such as homes in which English is spoken as a second language or environments in which the home language reflects a cultural variation not acceptable in the world of school. Where else will children have the opportunity to get better at this "school language" than in school?

> Talking and listening in classrooms helps students to think more critically about what they are reading and to engage in higher level discussions.

## Talking and Listening Promote a Deeper Understanding of Text

The education philosopher R. S. Peters (1967) states: "There is a sense in which we do not really know what we think about anything until we have had to state it explicitly." Palinscar (1987) and Palinscar and Brown (1984) have conducted research that supports this contention. Palinscar's work on reciprocal teaching, during which students are involved in structured conversations about text, revealed that these students had better reading comprehension than those who did not engage in these conversations. Long and Gove (2003) found that these "engagement" strategies are crucial for students to promote a personal connection with the text.

## Talking Promotes Critical Thinking and Problem Solving

Talking and listening in classrooms help students to think more critically about what they are reading and to engage in higher-level discussions. Almasi (1995) found that when teachers use discussion in classrooms, there is more focused student talking and higher-level thinking about the text. Hudgins and Edelman (1986) found similar results. Other studies have found that students may more readily solve problems with math manipulatives, for example, when asked to explain what they are doing at the same time (Gagne and Smith, 1962). In fact, Britton (1970) argues that the ability to solve problems and cope with the world is largely dependent on the quality of oral language in the early years.

## The Interdependence of Oral and Written Language

Oral language is the basis for reading and writing. Students who have great facility with their oral language systems can easily tap into these systems when they come upon words they do not know. Studies with older children and adolescents have demonstrated that competence in oral language is essential for satisfactory performance in reading, writing, and spelling (Gray, Saski, McEntire, and Larsen, 1980). The relationship with younger children does not seem to be as clear. Researchers suspect this may be because of the nature of children's language development. Young children's language abilities are far more advanced than their reading abilities. As a result, the texts they use in early reading do not readily match their language abilities (Corson, 1984).

Goodman and Goodman (1982) note that the methods children use in literacy learning are first established as they develop oral competence. Students' competence with the oral system, particularly the representation function, has a direct impact on how well they progress with the written system (Corson, 1984).

## The Pressing Issue of Talking

In many classrooms today, teachers feel pressure to be accountable, and this pressure seems to be exerted more profoundly now than in any previous generation of teachers. Coming from inside and outside the education system, this pressure has created environments in which teachers have become intensely concerned with tests and test scores. In such an environment, it is easy to forget about the way students learn best.

Although schools may see a rise in test scores in the short term, this does not necessarily mean that students are stronger.

The classroom is often the first place students receive exposure to a wide range of students and backgrounds. Talking and listening facilitate an honest exchange of ideas, promote better understandings, and develop deeper appreciations for other points of view. Students do not come by this naturally. The responsibility lies with the language arts teacher to plan for these experiences and to ensure that students develop the necessary skills to be prepared for the world that awaits them outside the school environment.

## What Do We Know about Oral Language Development?

Have you ever thought about language and wondered why we can communicate as much as we do? Have you ever wondered whether other species have a language system and can communicate as humans do? Have you ever watched a child who has not developed language in a normal pattern and marveled at how complex language truly is? To truly understand its complexity, teachers must have some knowledge of language basics.

### The Properties of Language

Several features of language are essential to our understanding of what language entails. These features, or properties, seem to be unique to human languages and are universal features of language cultures across the world. Hockett (1958) first set out to describe these properties as a way to distinguish human language from animal communication. Four important properties are: (1) the generativity of language, (2) its rule-governed nature, (3) its arbitrariness, and (4) its duality.

- Language is **generative.** Theoretically, no limit exists regarding the number or length of sentences humans can produce. Users of a language system can create perfectly understandable sentences that relate to things about which they have never known.
- Language is **rule-governed.** The rules describe the relationships between sounds, words, and meanings. Rules in the English language, for example, tell us that adjectives come before nouns. Rules also dictate which sounds may combine to express meaning.
- Language is **arbitrary.** Words are assigned meanings by the language system in which they occur. For example, English-speakers might say "house" to describe a residence, while a Spanish-speaker might say "casa" or "maison."
- Language has a **dual** quality. This duality allows us to experience both the sound and the concept that represents the meaning. The sound /wan/ could be "one" or "won." A simple sentence such as "John loves Mary more than Jamie" can be heard two ways: "John loves Mary more than he loves Jamie" or "John loves Mary more than Jamie loves Mary." The meaning cannot be determined until it is heard in context.

## The Components of Language

Linguists also have studied several components of language and learned a tremendous amount about how children acquire these aspects. The areas of study they have focused on include phonology, morphology, syntax, semantics, and pragmatics.

**Phonology** The study of speech sounds (*phonemes*) and how they are produced and combined is referred to as **phonology.**

- In the phonetic alphabet, there are forty-four phonemes in the English language. The sound of "o" in the words *love, prove,* and *cot* is represented by three different symbols.
- Phonemes can be classified in several different ways, including by whether they are voiced or unvoiced; by their position in a word (initial, medial, or final); by the place of articulation; and by the manner in which the breath stream is blocked as it flows through the mouth.
- When phonemes are *voiced,* the vocal cords vibrate. When they are *unvoiced,* the vocal cords do not vibrate. Many pairs of sounds in English differ only in this quality. When an individual says the /p/ sound, for example, the mouth is in the position to say both the /p/ and /b/ sound. The only distinction the speaker will make is whether their vocal cords vibrate as they attempt to say the sound. If the cords vibrate, the individual will say the voiced /b/ sound. If they do not vibrate, the individual will say the unvoiced /p/ sound. Pairs of consonant sounds that differ only on this quality include /p/ and /b/, /t/ and /d/, /k/ and /g/, /f/ and /v/, and /s/ and /z/. Vowels may also be distinguished with this voiced or unvoiced quality. The short /i/ sound is the unvoiced counterpart of the long /e/ sound. The short /e/ sound is the unvoiced counterpart of the long /a/ sound. Many children experience confusion when they begin to read and write because of these very fine distinctions.
- Some rules tell us how many consonants we can cluster together; other rules tell us which sounds can be combined with other sounds. In English, for example, we can cluster together a maximum of three consonants in either the initial or final position. We also must make the plural sound by putting the unvoiced /s/ sound after words that end with other unvoiced sounds and the voiced /z/ sound after words that end with other voiced sounds. Thus the /s/ on the end of *cats* has a soft s sound. The /s/ on the end of *legs* has a /z/ sound. The study of phonology helps us understand these rules, although most of them are understood implicitly, not explicitly.

**Morphology** Morphology is the study of morphemes—the smallest unit of meaning in our language. Morphemes are not, however, synonymous with words.

- There are two types of morphemes: *free* morphemes that stand alone and *bound* morphemes that are always attached to other morphemes. The word *cat,* for example, is one morpheme. When we make it plural by adding /s/, we have added a morpheme. The word *cats* contains two morphemes. The /s/ in *cats* is a bound morpheme; *cat* is a free morpheme.
- Some bound morphemes change the meaning of the word or change the part of speech, such as in *un + happy, walk+er.* Other morphemes only refine and give extra information about already existing meanings, such as in b*ook+s.*

- Morphemes can have more than one sound. When adding an *s* to make a plural word, that *s* can be pronounced as /s/ or /z/, depending on the final consonant in the original word. Thus *cats* makes a /s/ sound at the end of the word; *bugs* makes a /z/ sound.

**Syntax** Syntax is concerned with the arrangement of words into acceptable sequences.

- Several possible rules can be applied to change sentences without changing the meaning. These rules help us to know how to transform a sentence to make it into a question or a negation.
- Syntactic rules help us to know that we can say "John will not ride" but not say "John not will ride."
- Syntactic rules help us produce and understand an infinite variety of sentences.

**Semantics** Semantics deals with meaning and how it is communicated in our language system.

- Semantics refers to the concept that is understood when the word is read or spoken. These concepts grow in young children through their exposure to various experiences.

These four areas of study examine the structure of language as isolated areas, but children learn all the components when they are learning language. More importantly, each of the four areas can influence the other. When children talk about something that happened yesterday, they are simultaneously using all four systems.

**Pragmatics** More recent study of language has focused on how children develop communication skills such as turn-taking, conversational repair, and topic introduction and maintenance. **Pragmatics** refers to the rules that help us navigate our conversations.

Children's language learning does not occur in isolation. It develops in the context of conversation, usually with the primary caregiver. Over time, children learn to communicate with peers and other adults. Pragmatics concerns itself with how children learn how to do this so that they become conversationalists.

## The Importance of Talking and Listening

Listening is defined by the International Listening Association as the process of receiving, constructing meaning from, and responding to verbal (spoken) and nonverbal (unspoken) messages. Most of us listen far more than we talk. It has been estimated that 45 percent of the time we spend engaged in communication is devoted to listening. In school, children spend far

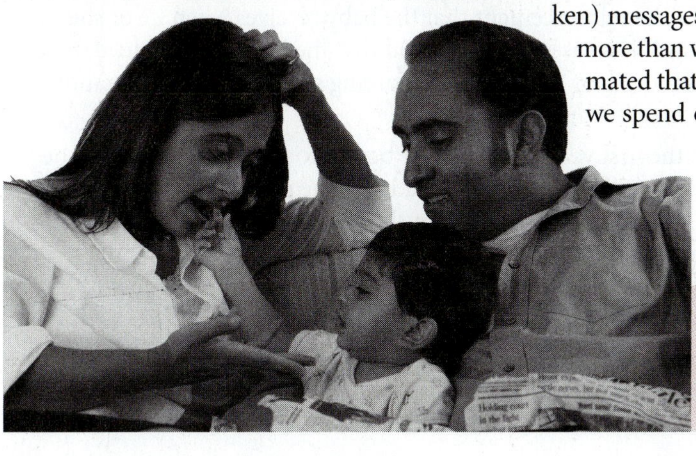

Children's language does not develop in isolation. It develops in the context of conversation, usually with the primary caregiver.

more time listening than they do talking. They listen to teachers, to peers, to dramatic productions, to videos, and the like. The list is endless, and that is only during the school day.

As children develop language, they do so by listening. Generally, children's comprehension is far greater than their **production.** Infants begin to listen to the sounds of language earlier than they begin to produce the sounds of language. Because listening occurs before speaking, we often refer to listening as the primary form of language. That is not to say, however, that children must learn to listen before they can learn to talk. The development of talking and listening occurs together.

It is difficult to separate the steps in learning to listen from the steps in learning to talk. As children learn to use different forms of their oral language system, they do so in an integrated manner. It is for this reason that talking and listening are discussed as integrally related modes of language.

## How Does Language Grow?

Over the past fifty years, several different perspectives have been proposed about how language develops. These perspectives have contributed some significant ideas and concepts about language learning and have provided keener insights into the development of language in children.

### Skinnerian Theory

B. F. Skinner (1957) set out his theory of language in the book *Verbal Behavior.* Skinner viewed language as a verbal behavior that was learned just as other behaviors were learned. Key components of Skinner's theory include:

- Language takes place through a process of shaping, which controls how speech sounds are acquired.
- Later children learn how to acquire abilities such as naming objects through a process called *discriminate learning.* During the first year of life, Skinner believed that children learn to produce the sounds in their language system through selective reinforcement. The reinforcement that the baby receives when he or she produces these sounds increases the likelihood that the baby will produce these sounds again. This process of selectively reinforcing successive approximations to a desired response is called *shaping.*
- Toward the end of the first year, the caregiver begins to reinforce sounds in the presence of objects. Thus if the baby says "dada" in the presence of a father, the baby is reinforced. If the baby says "baba" in the presence of a father, the baby is less likely to be reinforced. Through this process of reinforcing for some responses and not all responses, the baby learns to discriminate. Skinner referred to this process as discriminate learning.
- Imitation also plays a role. The example in the above paragraph illustrates how imitation may occur. The father may say "yes, I'm daddy" to the baby who has

just said "dada." That baby then says "daddy" in imitation, thus setting up a cycle of imitation and reinforcement.

## Psycholinguistic Theory

**Psycholinguistic theory,** developed in the late 1950s and early 1960s, offered an alternate (and opposing) approach to the behaviorist view that had dominated the first half of the century. Noam Chomsky (1965; 1975) was a leading proponent of this theory, which focused on the syntactic system and the rules that govern this system. Some key components of psycholinguistic theory include:

- Humans have innate capabilities that predispose them to learning language. Language acquisition is similar to other genetically determined skills that humans are programmed to learn, such as learning to walk on two legs (Lennenberg, 1981).
- According to Chomsky, the LAD (language acquisition device) explains how children acquire and process language (1965; 1975). The environment triggers the LAD into operation and determines the specific language and cultural variation of the language.
- Two types of syntactic structures in grammar exist: the *deep* structure and the *surface* structure. These two structures recognize that we cannot always interpret what we hear or see easily. The sentence "They are visiting relatives," for example, could mean that someone is visiting relatives. It could also mean that the relatives are visiting. This discrepancy in meaning requires that there be two sets of syntactic structures: deep structures to help us understand the meaning; surface structures to help us phonetically represent this meaning.
- A set of transformational rules helps us move from the deep to surface structure and back again. Some rules can help us convert active voice to passive voice; other rules can help us convert statements to questions. For example, a basic kernel sentence such as "The boy hit the ball" can be transformed several ways, including: Did the boy hit the ball? The boy did not hit the ball. The ball was hit by the boy. The boy hit the small ball.

More recent expansions of these ideas have been offered by Chomsky (1986; 1995).

## Semantic-Cognitivist Theory

The **semantic-cognitivist** perspective is based on the works of Jean Piaget, although Lois Bloom (1970) was the one most noted for her work in expanding this theoretical perspective. Bloom attempted to examine the language of children in relation to its intended meanings. In doing so, she determined that syntactic rules were inadequate to account for the different meanings that children were communicating. Her studies signaled a move from syntactic analysis to semantic analysis. Simultaneously, other linguists had reached conclusions similar to Bloom (Brown, 1973; and Slobin, 1978). This shift in study has been called the *semantic revolution.*

- The semantic-cognitive approach assumes that language development is deeply rooted in early cognitive development and that *thought* precedes *language.*
- The role of the adult is crucial in this model because the adult models language and provides experiences that expand children's concepts.
- One critical concept that theorists believe is necessary for language is the development of *object permanence.* When children develop this concept, they realize

that objects still exist even when they are not in sight. This concept signals that the child has a general concept of the object and is thus ready to learn its label.

- Early utterances are the result of semantic, not syntactic, relationships. These semantic relationships are developed as the child develops cognitively, through the interactions with the people in the environment and the experiences within the environment.

## Sociolinguistic Theory

The **sociolinguistic theory** was developed in response to the focus on the structural elements of language in the previously discussed theories. Sociolinguists argue that language develops from the need to communicate in context, such as families and schools. Thus, the primary motivation for language acquisition is effective communication.

- The speech act is the central focus of analysis, rather than the syntactic or semantic element. As such, the speech act is seen as a larger unit of language.
- There are three speech-act principles: **illocutionary force,** which refers to the speaker's intention as interpreted by the listeners; **conversational principles,** which refer to the listener's expectations of the speaker; and **presuppositions,** referring to assumptions that both the speaker and listener may have (Heatherington, 1980).
- The speaker's intention may be *implicit* or *explicit.* Examples of implicit intentions include imperatives, questions, and assertions. Sometimes, the speaker's implicit intention is not clear. For example, a woman might make the statement "I am cold." If her spouse is with her, however, she may be asking him to turn up the heat. So, on the surface, the statement may seem to be a simple assertion, but the true intention may be an imperative ("Turn up the heat"). Explicit illocutionary forces in speech are statements that contain an action. "I promise I'll turn up the heat" is an example of an explicit illocutionary force as it constitutes the act of promising.
- Conversational principles refer to the listener's expectations. When listening to someone, individuals assume that the speaker is sincere and truthful. They also assume that the speaker will provide the amount of information needed (neither too much nor too little) and will say something relevant to the topic at hand. If an individual asks, "What time is the party," that individual expects the responder to state the exact time and does not expect to receive an elaborate discourse on the appropriateness of partying at this time of year.
- Presuppositions refer to what both speakers and listeners expect of the information provided in an utterance. Suppose, for example, a friend is greeted with "You are not going to believe what happened to Jean yesterday at the dress shop!" The speaker is assuming that both individuals know Jean and that both know that Jean is a woman. Presuppositions underlie a good deal of our communications. Effective communication requires that speakers continually adjust their presuppositions to ensure that their communications are effective.

## The Value of Language Theory

Each of the theories just discussed helps develop a fuller picture of language. The Skinnerian behaviorist theory, for example, focuses on the important role of adult modeling. The psycholinguists emphasize an apparently innate potential for processing language. They also stress that children learn far more than what they hear. The semantic-cognitivists bring the role of thought into the process, emphasizing that much of language growth reflects children's thought processes and cognitive stages. The sociolinguists look beyond the structure of language and examine the way children use language with others. Each theory has an important role in helping teachers fully appreciate how complex language is.

# How Does Language Change during the Preschool Years?

Language develops and changes early in a child's life. It progresses from the prelinguistic period in infancy to the beginning of speech and into the beginnings of sentences. Between eighteen and twenty-four months, children's vocabulary increases significantly. Children at this stage understand much more language than they can produce. By the time they are ready for school, these young students have become very adept at understanding and using their oral language.

## The Prelinguistic Period

Before children begin talking, they develop many language abilities that are believed to be crucial to subsequent language development. This period before the first word is spoken is known as the **prelinguistic phase.** During it, the infant goes through the following stages:

- ***Crying*** Vocal communication begins with crying, the earliest of which is the birth cry. The birth cry is important because it is the first indication that the vocal apparatus is intact. Crying at later stages helps children become accustomed to using vocal folds and modified breathing. These are all critical for subsequent oral language.

- ***Cooing*** As early as the third week after birth, babies begin to coo. Cooing is largely reflexive. All babies, even deaf babies, coo. Cooing is a period of learning to use the sound production mechanisms. The first cooing sounds are vowels. Often, an infant in this stage can produce sounds that an adult has difficulty imitating. Gradually, the infant develops enough control to produce sounds that more closely approximate the sounds in their environment.

- ***Babbling*** When infants reproduce the same sound repeatedly, usually in a state of contentment or relaxation, they have started to babble. This occurs anywhere between six weeks and six months. The first babbles are usually long strings, such as *ba, ba, ba* or *ma, ma, ma.* The emergence of babbling does not appear to depend on auditory input. Deaf babies babble; hearing babies of deaf parents also babble. Owens (2005) notes, however, that deaf babies have a smaller repertoire of sounds. Babbling is usually done for one's own sake as a kind of play. See Figure 2.1 for some reasons why babbling is important. This may be the time when babies practice the phonemes found in their family. Babies produce the greatest number of phonemes between eight and twelve months.

The communication cycle is established by the end of the first year. By the time a child begins using words to express himself or herself, a well-developed interaction cycle is present. The next step is to put words into these communication cycles.

**Figure 2.1**

### Why Is Babbling Important?

1. Babies are developing more precise control over their articulators.
2. Adults in the environment generally respond favorably to babbling, thus encouraging babies to produce more sounds.
3. Babies are developing the inflectional pattern of their language. These features (force, quality, and pitch characteristics) are referred to as the melody of language.
4. The mother-child interaction pattern is emerging. The mother (or primary caregiver) often treats the communication as if it had meaning. The baby sometimes confirms the interpretations, sometimes not.
5. The baby also develops ways to engage in joint activities through mutual gazing, peek-a-boo, and pushing objects back and forth. This process helps the baby learn that communication is a social tool.



## The Emergence of Speech

Somewhere between twelve and eighteen months, babies intentionally utter their first word to indicate someone or something in their environment. Piaget (1954) suggests that the first word is acquired through vocal contagion and mutual imitation. Vocal contagion is a process during which we talk as though it were contagious. During mutual imitation, not only does the baby imitate the adult, but the adult imitates the baby. For example, a mother may hear her baby say "mama" spontaneously and may then respond by saying "mama." The baby repeats "mama," and the parent says it again.

Nelson (1973) found that first words were more likely to include food, toys, and articles of clothing, whereas words for immovable objects were rare. Words such as *shoe, hat, sock, clock,* and *key* were found in the first fifty words. Owens (2005) notes that the first ten words were likely to be the names of animals, foods, and toys. He also states that nouns account for 60 to 65 percent of the first fifty words; action words account for less than 20 percent of the total.

Those who have studied this stage of language development explain the first words in relationship to cognitive development. During the sensorimotor period, toddlers build an understanding of their world by physical action—what they are able to do to the *things* in their environment. Toddlers bite, bang, drop, or shake hats, shoes, socks, keys, and (toy) clocks. They do not have that same repertoire of action available to them with tables, even though they may sit at a table every day.

Somewhere between twelve and eighteen months, the holophrase emerges. A *holophrase* is a single word used to communicate a variety of messages. A child who says "milk," for example, may mean "That's a glass of milk," "I want a glass of milk," or "Oops" (I spilled it). The adult generally needs to be with the toddler in order to determine the meaning of the holophrase.

## The Beginnings of Sentences

Somewhere between eighteen and twenty-four months, toddlers begin to combine words in a way that is often referred to as *telegraphic* speech. This is because the communication is limited to content words and the short bursts of word pairs are reminiscent of the ways telegraphs used to work. The toddler may say, for example, "Baby go" or "Milk fall." Brown (1973) described this period intensively, identifying several meanings expressed during this early word combination period (see Table 2.1).

As mentioned earlier, context is important when trying to determine the meaning being conveyed. A toddler who says "Mommy sock" could be trying to say that the sock belongs to Mommy or could be trying to say that Mommy is trying to put on the sock. We only know the intended meaning when we are actually present and observing the scene.

In later stages, toddlers begin to add endings to words and to combine several words so that sentences become longer. "Put doll" and "doll here" becomes "put doll here" or "I draw" and "draw puppy" becomes "I draw puppy." After this point, language explodes in terms of sentence structure. As children approach their third birthday, they begin to acquire more varied sentence structures, including negatives, questions, passive, and imperatives. Table 2.2 presents the developmental sequence of these sentence structures.

Overgeneralization is common during this period. Children often form the simplest and most general rule they can; they then use that rule whenever they can. It is not uncommon for a preschooler to use words such as *bringed, doed, singed, foots,* and *mouses.* These "mistakes" are seen in all children and do not reflect poor grammar. Children may learn, for example, the rule for forming past tense and may actually say the right past tense form with a word (such as *brought* for *bring*). They often learn the

**Table 2.1**

**Basic Semantic Relations**

| Category | Characteristics | Example |
|---|---|---|
| Nomination | labeling and naming | *this baby* |
| Recurrence | commenting on or requesting more | *more cookie* |
| Non Existence | the absence of something | *allgone boy* |
| Agent + Action | the agent performing an action | *mommy push* |
| Action + Object | someone or something receiving an action | *push truck* |
| Agent + Object | noting relationship between agent and object | *Kate truck* |
| Action + Locative | place of an action | *sit chair* |
| Entity + Locative | relationship between person or thing and its location | *sock chair* |
| Possessor and Possession | relationships between an object and its possessor | *baby food* |
| Entity + Attribute | noting an attribute of someone or something | *big boy* |

**Table 2.2**

**Development of Sentence Structure**

| Sentence Type | Early Stage | Later Stage |
|---|---|---|
| ***Declarative*** | | |
| Big truck. | That big truck. | That's a big truck. |
| ***Negative*** | | |
| No play. | I no want to play. | I don't want to play. |
| ***Interrogative*** | | |
| See kitty? | You see kitty? | Did you see the kitty? |
| ***Imperative*** | | |
| No run! | You no run! | Don't run! |



correct form before they learn the incorrect. As children learn that *ed* is used for the past tense, they may start to say *bringed* rather than *brought.*

## The Development of Vocabularies

By eighteen months of age, toddlers will have a vocabulary of approximately fifty words. As mentioned earlier, nouns are produced most frequently. Most words are people, animals, or objects that children can manipulate. Between eighteen and twenty-four months, there is usually a tremendous jump in vocabulary, with estimates of up to 300 words at twenty-four months. As their vocabulary grows during this period, the child will exhibit more verb usage. It has been estimated that preschool children add two to four words to their vocabularies each day. Their vocabularies seem to grow with only a few exposures and without a lot of specific feedback. This process, known as *fast-mapping,* has been well documented (Bloom, 2000; Crais, 1992; Markson and Bloom, 1997).

Vocabulary continues to increase rapidly during the preschool years. A three-year-old may have a vocabulary between 800 and 1,200 words. By the time children are four years old, that number will have risen to between 1,500 and 1,900 words. Their words also become more complex as they add more inflectional (plural and past tense markers) and derivational morphemes (prefixes and suffixes). Three major theories attempt to explain how this development occurs.

■ ***Semantic Features Hypothesis*** Children seize on some particular perceptual feature of the object and use that term for all objects that possess that particular feature (Clark, 1974).

- Upon receiving feedback, children will add additional features that will help them be more discrete. As they learn the word *moon,* for example, they might focus on the shape. Thus, they name all round things "moon."
- Shape, size, and movement seem to be the most salient features they notice. As they develop more words, they begin to focus on more than one feature at a time, thereby refining their vocabularies.

■ ***Functional-Core Hypothesis*** Children focus on motion features rather than static perceptual features as they develop their vocabularies (Nelson, 1974). Children's early vocabularies include words that have a high degree of motion or something they can manipulate.

- Children understand words in relation to the actions (or motion) that they require. An apple, for example, is something to eat. A dog is something that runs and barks.
- Concepts begin to develop with the formation of these understandings. Only later do children begin to add perceptual features.

■ ***Prototypic-Complex Hypothesis*** Children have a model, or prototype, that they use when they learn new words. The closer the new concept is to the stored prototype, the more likely that concept will be labeled by the word for that concept. A robin, for example, is a good example of a bird. It is seen frequently and has many of the probable characteristics of a bird (it flies, has a beak, and chirps).

- Children identify those birds that most closely resemble their prototype more readily. Only later do they recognize that some birds do not fly and thus, they begin to recognize members that are farther from their prototype.
- These prototypes are critical to vocabulary development and may vary widely across children, depending upon their experiences.

Each of these theories can help us understand how children develop their speaking vocabularies and how their vocabularies become more elaborate. The semantic feature hypothesis explains the frequent overgeneralizations we see when children call all tiny specks they see a "fly." The functional-code hypothesis can explain why children often define words in terms of an action. What is a horse? "It eats carrots," replies the young child happily. The prototype-complex hypothesis helps us understand the valuable experiences that help children develop more elaborate and inclusive prototypes.

## Comprehension versus Production

There is a tremendous difference between children's ability to produce language and their ability to understand language. Productive vocabularies typically lag behind receptive vocabularies. Benedict (1979), for example, found that toddlers comprehended their first fifty words by thirteen months yet did not produce them until nineteen months. Griffiths (1986) found that toddlers between the ages of eighteen and twenty-four months have receptive vocabularies that may be four times larger than their expressive vocabularies. By the age of five, that difference may be six times larger.

There may be a difference between these two areas, but it does not necessarily mean that comprehension always precedes production (Owens, 2005). The relationship between comprehension and production is very complex. Even though, for example, toddlers may have larger receptive vocabularies, we know that they do not fully comprehend words before they can produce them. At the early stages, comprehension depends greatly on context. As children approach two years of age, the differences between comprehension and production decrease.

The growth in language between one and five years of age is tremendous. See Table 2.3 for an illustration of the gap that exists in oral language between a typical five-year-old as compared to a one-year-old. The five-year-old has developed a receptive vocabulary of 13,500 words, a speaking vocabulary of 2,200 words, has learned

**Table 2.3**

**Oral Language Development: The One-Year-Old and the Five-Year-Old**

| One-Year-Old | Five-Year-Old |
|---|---|
| Understands less than 10 words | Understands up to 13,500 words |
| Uses up to 3 words other than mama and dada | Uses up to 2,200 words |
| Uses up to 18 phonemes | Uses all phonemes but r, s, z, ch, j, zh, and blends |
| Has one-word sentences | Average sentence length is 6 words; uses questions and negations |
| Has no endings on words | Uses plural, past tense, and possessive markers |

nearly all his phonemes, has an average sentence length of six words, can form a variety of sentences, and can use plural and past tense markers with ease. That development is in stark contrast to what he or she could do at one year of age.

It is no wonder, then, that linguist K. Chukovsky (1963) states: "It seems to me that, beginning with age of 2, every child becomes for a short period of time a linguistic genius. Later, beginning with age 5 or 6, talent begins to fade."

## Is Language Development "Finished" When Children Enter School?

By the time children reach school, they are adept with language. They understand the functions and use of language. The have acquired most of the individual sounds, but they will still continue their development in this area. Their receptive and expressive vocabularies will expand dramatically. They will have mastered most of the syntactic structures but continue refining more complex structures. They will begin to understand irony and figurative language and other kinds of subtle meaning changes signaled by intonation.

The school-age period is crucial for ensuring that language continues to grow. Until recently, most people assumed that language growth was "finished" by school age and that the main thrust was primarily in syntax, but a lot more has been learned. During the school-age years, a tremendous amount of growth occurs in all aspects of language, including syntax, vocabulary, phonology, and pragmatics.

### Syntax Continues to Grow

During the school years, children's language becomes more elaborate and more specific. Their syntactic knowledge increases as they expand forms they learned as preschoolers and acquire new forms. Their language becomes more complex as their noun and verb phrases become more elaborate. During this period, children learn how to differentiate between subject pronouns (such as *he* and *we*) and object pronouns (such as *him* and *us*). They learn to use reflexive pronouns such as *myself* and *herself*. They begin to use and understand the use of pronouns in sentences and can order adjectives correctly. (For example, they learn to say "a large blue dump truck" rather than "a dump blue large truck.") They can use *many* with count nouns appropriately, so they learn to say *many bikes* but not *many water*.

In addition, children's sentence structures at school age become more elaborate. Between first and third grade, young students learn to use sentences with a comparative relationship. By age nine, they begin to understand promise/tell sentences (such as "John promises Mary he'll leave"). By age ten, they understand ask/tell sentences (such as "Ask Mary what she wants").

Embedding and conjoining within sentences also increases, leading to more complex sentences. **Conjoining** (or joining two clauses together) begins around age seven. Children, however, do not understand or use conjoining with any consistency until age ten, and even then, there are some forms not fully understood until thirteen to fifteen years of age. Clauses joined with *because* are the easiest, followed by clauses joined with *if* (age eleven), *although* (age thirteen), and *unless* or *until*. Conjoining is not easy for younger children because often the clauses that are joined are not in the order they appear. The sentence "I went because I was asked" is an example of this. Which came first?

**Embedding** is also complicated. Embedding consists of a dependent phrase or clause within a sentence. There are generally two types of embedding: *parallel* embedding in which the sentence shares the same subject or object and *nonparallel* embedding in which the sentence does not. Examples of parallel embedding are seen in the following two sentences:

He hit the boy that I did not like. (shares same object)

The girl, who lives next door, called me. (shares same subject)

Examples of nonparallel embedding are seen in these sentences:

He hit the girl who lives next door. (different subject/object)

The girl that was chased by the boy is scared. (different subject/object)

Generally, parallel embedding is understood and acquired earlier than nonparallel embedding. By seventh grade (age thirteen to fifteen years), children can understand and use both types of embedding.

**Passive sentences** are understood in a limited way in the early school years and understanding grows throughout the school-aged period. There are three types of passive sentences. *Reversible* ones are those in which either noun in the sentence could be the subject or object, as we see in the sentence: "The girl was chased by the boy." *Nonreversible* ones are those in which the nouns cannot be switched, as we see in the sentence: "The ball was thrown by the machine." Nonreversible passives can be instrumental, when an instrument is the subject, as seen in the earlier sentence. They can also be *agentive*, when an agent is the subject, as seen in the sentence: "The ball was thrown by the girl."

Before age four, children can produce reversible passives, although only 50 percent of five-year-olds can interpret them correctly. Just before age eight, there is a marked increase in children's ability to produce nonreversible passives with people as the subject. It is not until children are between the ages of eleven and thirteen, however, that they are able to produce and understand nonreversible passages with instruments as the subject.

## Vocabulary Continues to Grow

During the school years, vocabulary generally increases in both size and specificity. There are two types of increase in word meaning that occur: *horizontal* and *vertical.* When horizontal increases occur, children add features to the definition that are common to adults. So, the word *bird* will include birds that fly and those that do not. Their understanding of the word *bird* will increase as a concept because of the added features.

When vertical growth occurs, children add more definitions to a single word. Thus, they begin to understand that the word *run* can mean to move fast or it can mean to blur or it can mean to operate. The recognition of all these definitions leads to a more specific vocabulary.

Children's understanding of words does not resemble adults' understandings during the early school years. A specific type of shift in a child's understanding has to occur before this level of understanding arises. Before age seven, children often define words based on their syntactic relations. If, for example, a young child is asked to define what a girl is, the child might say "She combs her long hair" or "She runs." Later, children begin to define words based on their semantic attributes. In response to the question about a girl, the older child might say "She's like a woman." This change in how children associate and define words is called the **syntagmatic-paradigmatic shift.** The period of most rapid change generally occurs between seven and nine years of age. Once children make this shift, their definitions and understandings of words become more elaborate, and they begin to include larger concepts. No longer does the child define *dog* as something that barks. Rather, the child defines a dog as an animal that has four legs, a tail, and a bark.

## Phoneme Awareness Continues to Grow

Children's understanding and use of phonological rules develops quite early. Although children master most of the phonological system before entering school, there is still some growth as children refine their understandings and begin to apply them to words they write.

***Voiced and Unvoiced Sounds*** Evidence suggests that children can distinguish between voiced and unvoiced sounds relatively early. As soon as they can distinguish between /p/ /b/, they also start to distinguish between /t/ /d/, /s/ /z/, and other voiced and unvoiced sounds. Berko (1958) found that children as young as five years of age knew which plural sound (/s/ or /z/) to add with words ending in various sounds, as well as which past tense sound (/d/ or /t/). Five-year-olds knew implicitly that unvoiced sounds were added (such as /s/ and /t/) when words end with an unvoiced sound. They also knew that voiced sounds were added (such as /z/ and /d/) when words end with a voiced sound. It appears that they have a fairly well developed understanding of acceptable sound combinations in their language system. During the early school years, they refine these understandings to include more combinations.

***Phoneme Segmentation*** Another aspect of the phonological system involves **phoneme segmentation.** Six-year-olds can identify phoneme segments in syllables, but they have more difficulty when asked to do this in words. Although preschoolers can rhyme simple words such as *bat* and *cat,* it is not until later that they understand that the only difference in these words is the beginning sounds. Children grow in this understanding between kindergarten and third grade. By age seven, children can determine new words when the initial sounds are removed. Thus, they can say *ink* when the *s* is removed from *sink.* They can also say *oap* when the *s* is removed from *soap.* Younger children have more difficulty repeating meaningless strings.

■ ***Sound Associations*** School-aged children do not appear to associate sounds, however, the same way adults do. Read (1975) conducted a series of experiments to determine how children see relationships between sounds. In one study, he asked children to identify pictures of words that began like *truck* or *dragon.* He found that most kindergarten children saw words that begin with /t/ or /ch/ beginning the same as *truck.* He also found that most kindergarten children regarded words beginning with /d/ or /j/ beginning the same as *dragon.* He also found that first-graders do the same. These same associations occur in children's early spelling development (see Chapter 9).

Further studies demonstrated that children do not associate vowels the same way either. When asked, for example, whether *Ed* would like *aid* or *add* better, children clearly preferred *aid* while adults preferred *add.* Children clearly preferred short *e*-long *a* relationships as well as short *i*-long *e* relationships. Read explains that these relationships are phonetically appropriate. These same preferences also appear in children's early writings (see Chapter 9).

## Conversational Abilities Continue to Grow

Conversation is not something that comes easily to young children (or for that matter, many adults). In order to carry on a conversation, we must be able to participate in a give and take, with each participant asking and answering questions, replying with statements, and recognizing the contributions made by the other individual. More specifically, participants in a conversation need to be able to introduce and maintain a topic, use conjuncts (that connect ideas) and disjuncts (that contrast ideas) effectively, and engage in conversational repair. As mentioned earlier in this chapter, when we listen to someone, we assume that the speaker will say something relevant, be sincere and truthful, and provide us with the amount of information we need. Conversations also assume that we have enough information about the other person to ensure that when we do communicate, it is effective.

IRA/NCTE 4

■ ***Topic Maintenance*** The ability to introduce and maintain a topic develops gradually during elementary school. Preschoolers may be able to sustain a topic only 20 percent of the time. By the time children are in elementary school, this ability has increased dramatically, although most of the conversation may be very concrete in the early years of school.

■ ***Conversational Repair*** Conversational repair is crucial to the ability to participate in lengthy conversations. Young children seem to respond with silence or repetition when confronted with a listener who says "I don't understand." Repetition seems to be the major repair strategy that children use until age nine. After this point, children understand that they need to provide additional information, by providing more background, being more specific, or both.

■ ***Comparison between a Five-Year-Old and a Ten-Year-Old*** The change between five and ten years of age is not as dramatic as the change that occurs between one and five years of age, though the change is still remarkable. The five-year-old enters school not fully understanding the syntactic system, with limited abilities to understand and use passive voice, to embed and conjoin, and to elaborate on noun and verb phrases. The ten-year-old has a much richer understanding of the syntactic system and is able to use a variety of passive sentence structures, to understand and produce sentences with a variety of embedding and conjoining, and to use elaborate noun and verb phrases. The vocabulary of the five-year-old, though large, is limited. The five-year-old often uses syntactic relationships to define words. The ten-year-old has a much deeper understanding of concepts and is able to define words using the class of words. The five-year-old will have good understanding of the phonetic system; the ten-year-old will know it well.

It is important to recognize all the growth that occurs during these school years. Our responsibility as teachers is to help students grow in their oral language as much as possible, so that they become efficient and effective communicators. See the Exploring Children's Literature feature for recommendations of books to use for choral reading and reader's theater.

## exploring Children's Literature

### Books for Choral Reading and Reader's Theater

#### Grades K to 3

*I Am the Dog, I Am the Cat*—Written by Donald Hall, illustrated by Barry Moser, and published by Dial (1994).

A dog and a cat take turns explaining what is wonderful about being who they are. This story can be easily adapted for choral reading or reader's theater.

*Brown Bear, Brown Bear, What Do You See?*—Written by Bill Martin Jr., illustrated by Eric Carle, and published by Holt (1996).

This book is a pictorial representation of a question-and-answer game played by a teacher and her group. This story can be easily adapted for choral reading or reader's theater.

*Bringing the Rain to Kapiti Plain*—Written and illustrated by Verna Aardema and published by Dial (1975).

This tale is a cumulative rhyme relating how Ki-pat brought rain to the drought-stricken Kapiti Plain. This story can be easily adapted for choral reading or reader's theater.

*Dirty Laundry Pile: Poems in Different Voices*—Written by Paul B. Janeczko, illustrated by Melissa Sweet, and published by HarperTrophy (2007).

A scarecrow, washing machine, cow, and other objects and animals express themselves in this collection of poems.

*Farmer's Garden: Rhymes for Two Voices*—Written by David L. Harrison, illustrated by Arden Johnson-Petrov, and published by Boyds Mills (2000).

A farmer's dog asks various animals and plants what they like about the farmer's garden and what they do in it.

*You Read to Me, I'll Read to You: Very Short Stories to Read Together*—Written by Mary Ann Hoberman, illustrated by Michael Emberley, and published by Little, Brown (2006).

Seventeen familiar nursery rhymes are set in three columns with color-coded type as a script for two voices to read separately and together.

*Why Mosquitoes Buzz in People's Ears: A West African Tale*—Written and illustrated by Verna Aardema and published by Dial (1975).

This retelling of a traditional West African tale reveals how the mosquito developed its annoying habit. This folk tale can be easily adapted for reader's theater.

*Yo! Yes?*—Written and illustrated by Chris Raschka and published by Scholastic (1993).

Two lonely characters, one black and one white, meet on the street and become friends. This story can be easily adapted for choral reading or reader's theater.

## Grades 4 to 8

*Anansi and the Moss-Covered Rock*—Retold by Eric A. Kimmel, illustrated by Janet Stevens, and published by Holiday House (1988).

Anansi the Spider uses a strange moss-covered rock in the forest to trick all the other animals, until Little Bush Deer decides he needs to learn a lesson. This story can be easily adapted for reader's theater.

*Big Talk: Poems for Four Voices*—Written by Paul Fleischman, illustrated by Beppe Giacobbe, and published by Candlewick (2000).

This collection of poems is to be read aloud by four people, with color-coded text to indicate which lines are read by which readers.

*The Great Kapok Tree*—Written and illustrated by Lynne Cherry and published by Harcourt (1990).

The many different animals that live in a great kapok tree in the Brazilian rainforest try to convince a man with an ax of the importance of not cutting down their home. This story can be easily adapted for choral reading or reader's theater.

*I Am Phoenix: Poems for Two Voices*—Written by Paul Fleischman, illustrated by Ken Nutt, and published by HarperTrophy (1989).

This collection of poems about birds is to be read aloud by two voices.

*Joyful Noise: Poems for Two Voices*—Written by Paul Fleischman, illustrated by Eric Beddows, and published by Laura Geringer (1988).

This collection of poems describing the characteristics and activities of a variety of insects is to be read by two voices.

*Math Talk: Mathematical Ideas in Poems for Two Voices*—Written by Theoni Pappas and published by Wide World (1993).

This book presents mathematical ideas through poetic dialogues intended to be read by two people.

*Sleeping Ugly*—Written by Jane Yolen, pictures by Diane Stanley, and published by Coward, McCann & Geoghegan (1981).

When beautiful Princess Miserella, Plain Jane, and a fairy fall under a sleeping spell, a prince undoes the spell in a surprising way. This fractured fairy tale can be easily adapted for reader's theater.

*Wham! It's a Poetry Jam: Discovering Performance Poetry*—Written by Sara Holbrook and published by Boyds Mills (2002).

More than thirty poems along with tips on how to perform them.

# What Do We Know about Dialects?

A **dialect** is a language rule system used by an identifiable group of people that varies in some way from the ideal (Owens, 2005). All of us are, in fact, dialect speakers because the ideal standard is rarely used in oral communications. There is nothing inherently good or bad about a dialect, but evidence suggests that the differences in our dialects are becoming more pronounced (Schwarz, 2005).

It is not by accident that part of the definition of a dialect states that there is a "rule system." All dialects have rules that govern how phonemes are used, which word endings are used, how word order functions, which vocabulary is used, and how language is used in conversations. In other words, they are language systems in their own right. It may appear strange to hear words pronounced or combined in a different way when one does not know the system. These variations are perfectly natural to those who do know the system.

IRA/NCTE 9

Our society places different values on different dialects, although the value of the dialect is not intrinsic. The value placed on dialects is both extrinsic and biased. One person may value, for example, a dialect associated with higher income levels, while another person may see this same dialect as pretentious.

Differences in dialects appear to be related to several factors, including geography, socioeconomic levels, race and ethnicity, context, peer group, and primary language. In the United States, there are ten regional dialects and two major racial/ethnic dialects. The regional dialects include those of New England, New York City, the mid-Atlantic, western Pennsylvania, the North Central region, the Midlands, the Northwest, Southwest, Southern, and the Appalachian region. The largest racial group with a dialect is African American. The largest ethnic group is Hispanic or, more specifically, Latino. The following sections focus on these two dialects, although many more could be discussed.

## Characteristics of African American English

Any discussion about **African American English** (AAE) or African American Vernacular English (AAVE) needs to begin with three important points: (1) The linguistic differences between AAVE and Standard English (SE) are minimal and rule-governed; (2) the linguistic differences that AAVE exhibits have considerable overlap with southern dialects and other dialects. For example, British Cockney often omits the final consonant in a word, so that a listener might hear the word *ak* for *act.* Scottish frequently uses subject stress, so that one might hear sentences such as "My father he be taking me out;" and (3) not all African Americans use a dialect. Those who do use the AAE dialect do not use its features at all times.

Some of the major differences in the rules that govern AAVE may be seen in the areas of phonology and syntax, although there are other differences as well (Dandy, 1991). In phonology, consonants show the most distinctive differences. The initial *th* can become *d,* so we might hear the word *then* pronounced *den.* The final *th* may become *f,* as we hear with *bath* becoming *baf.* Final consonant clusters are reduced so that not all are pronounced. The sound of *r* may be deleted after a vowel. A list of some of these differences is seen in Table 2.4.

Morphological and syntactic differences are also well known. Some of these differ-

### Table 2.4
### Some Features of African American English

| Phonetic Features | Example |
|---|---|
| Elimination of l or r sounds | hep for *help* |
| Deletion of final consonants | fine for *find* |
| Use of /f/ sound for th at end of word | wif for *with* |
| **Syntactic Features** | **Example** |
| Use of the verb *be* to indicate continuing action | *He be working.* |
| Elimination of verb *be* when contractible | *He bad.* |
| Deletion of plural marker when number indicated | *I know five boy.* |
| Deletion of past tense marker when other words indicate past | *Yesterday I walk.* |
| Use of subject stress | *My father, he tall.* |
| Nonuse of possessive /s/ | *My friend truck.* |

ences include the omission of a past tense marker. This occurs when the past tense is obvious in context, as seen in "Yesterday I walk." Plural markers are omitted when words have a numerical quantifier is in front of them, as in "two cat." In both examples, the markers are viewed as redundant and not necessary in order to be understood. It is obvious that when a speaker uses the word *two* in front of *cat,* she is talking about more than one. There is little redundancy in AAVE.

Perhaps one difference that teachers frequently notice is the use of the verb *be.* The presence of *be* in many sentences indicates habitual action or something ongoing. "We be playing after school" means that we do play after school on a regular basis, not just today. "He be tired" means that he is always tired. When *be* is omitted, it means that the condition is temporary. "*He cold*" means that he is cold today, but he may not be cold tomorrow (see Table 2.4 for other differences).

Some African American children use different types of verbal interaction that are often misunderstood in the classroom. Teachers who learn more about these cultural differences will know how to respond to them in the school setting. The Exploring Diversity feature displays examples of the types of verbal interactions used by students who are African American.

## Characteristics of Latino English

As mentioned earlier, the largest ethic population in the United States is Hispanic. Within this Hispanic population, two major groups exist: Puerto Rican-Caribbean and Central American. The dialect that many of the members of this group speak is Latino English (LE). The same three points made about AAVE are valid for LE as well. The linguistic differences between LE and Standard English (SAE) are minimal and rule-governed. The linguistic differences evident in LE have considerable overlap with other dialects. Not all Latinos use a dialect.

Just as in other dialects, there are differences in the phonological and syntactical rules that govern LE. Many speech sounds in English do not exist in Spanish. English vowels, for example, are more varied and more irregular. In some instances, sounds associated with English vowels are in direct contrast to the Spanish. The English sound of long *e,* for example, is represented by the Spanish vowel *i.* Many of the consonant sounds in LE also vary from English. Sounds such as /m/, /w/, and /f/ are often omitted. Sounds such as /b/, /g/, and /k/ may be distorted or replaced by their voiced/unvoiced counterpart. Spanish does not distinguish between the /b/ and /v/ sounds and uses them interchangeably. These are only a few of the phonetic differences evident in the language of children speaking Latino English.

Other differences relate to the syntactic/morphological system. In LE, the plural /s/ and the past tense /ed/ are not obligatory, and thus are often omitted. Articles are often omitted. Negation is placed before the verb, such as "She no like." There is no noun-verb inversion to ask questions. Some of the differences between LE and SAE may be seen in Table 2.5.

There are nonlanguage differences between LE and SAE. In Latino cultures, for example, it is acceptable to maintain a closer speaking distance with more touching between speakers. Avoiding eye contact is viewed as a sign of respect.

## Guidelines for Working with Diverse Language Learners

As you prepare to teach students, it is important to consider your own assumptions about language variations so that you are better prepared to accept your students' language and

## exploring diversity

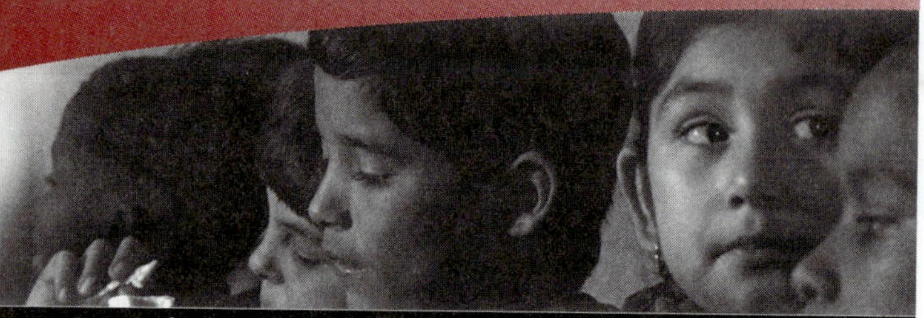

### African American English

Many teachers misunderstand the behaviors of some of their students, primarily because they do not understand the cultural values of that student. The African American culture, for example, places great value on verbal abilities. As Toni Morrison so aptly put in an interview in 1981:

> [Language] is the thing that black people love so much—the saying of words, holding them on the tongue, experimenting with them, playing with them. It's a love, a passion. Its function is like a preacher's: to make you stand up out of your seat, make you lose yourself and hear yourself. The worst of all possible things that could happen would be to lose that language.

Some verbal strategies African American students value include "woofin" and "playing the dozens". *Woofers* use strong language primarily to intimidate others. One of the major intents of "woofin" is to keep the anger, hostility, or both at the verbal level and to "best" someone at a verbal level. Ali, the boxer, was adept at using this strategy to intimidate potential opponents. Students use this strategy in school with one another and sometimes with adults. Students who stand in the hall and block the way or who yell in a menacing way about a grade may be woofin. It is important for teachers to avoid showing fear of these students. One effective strategy for handling a student who is woofin is to ask a question that diverts attention away from the situation.

Another verbal strategy valued in the African American culture is "playing the dozens". When *playing the dozens,* opponents verbally spar with each other, usually trading insults about each other's family member (often the mother, specifically). During the game, participants avoid speaking about a deceased family member or playing with strangers. The participants exchange insults that escalate in intensity, while they try to maintain their composure. This game was played frequently on plantations in the eighteenth and nineteenth centuries where young black males were taught to ignore insults from their masters. An effective way to handle this game in the classroom is to acknowledge that it is being played and to remind students that it is a game to be played at home, not in school.

at the same time to help guide them in their expanding linguistic competence. As a teacher of students who speak a variety of dialects, you have the dual responsibility of seeing their language as something very much a part of them and, at the same time, of helping them expand their use of standard English.

It is essential to recognize that dialectal differences are common. There is enough information to suggest that negative attitudes toward low-prestige dialects directly affect how well students learn. Teachers are role models for students and should take advantage of opportunities to demonstrate the interesting qualities of language differences. Some recommended steps to take are:

- Learn more about the culture and dialect of students, whether through reading, attending workshops, or talking to others.

## Table 2.5
### Some Features of Latino English

| Phonetic Features | Example |
|---|---|
| /b/ and /v/ indistinguishable | *It is balentine's day.* |
| Only five vocalic phonemes, not short or long depending | *I heat (hit) him.* *These (this) is good.* |
| Many English sounds, such as /z/, /l/, /th/, and /j/, do not exist | *Can you unsip (unzip) it?* |
| **Structural Features** | **Example** |
| Deletion of plural marker | *I know five boy.* |
| Nonuse of possessive /s/ | *The truck of my friend.* |
| Deletion of past tense marker when other words indicate past | *Yesterday I walk.* |
| Use of *no* before verb to negate | *I no want this.* |
| Omission of subject pronouns when subject identified in prior sentence | *Mother is working. Works hard.* |

- Help students develop an understanding and respect of others' dialect differences. One way to introduce students to other dialects is by including literature from the cultures and dialects represented in your class.
- Model a curiosity and interest in other cultures and dialects by inviting into your class different speakers from other cultures. When teaching geography, for example, introduce the major dialect areas associated with various regions so that students learn that different dialects are common.

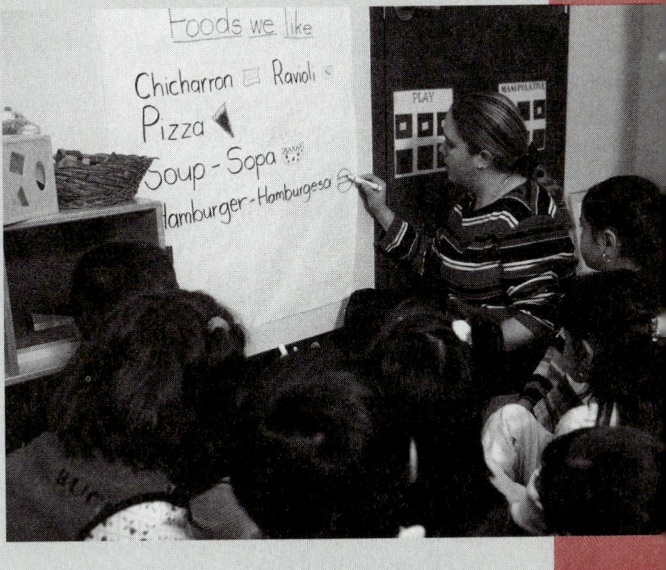

It is important to model standard English rather than correct it. There is evidence that correction is one of the least effective ways to change language. Modeling language is the most powerful way to change language.

## Teaching Standard English

Within a sensitive and appreciative atmosphere, teachers must teach Standard English—the language of schools and textbooks and, in most cases, the language of the business and professional community. In the school environment, Standard English helps students access resources and opportunities that will help them succeed from grade to grade. Beyond the school and neighborhood, Standard English is the predominant language of many other important communities, and the degree to which students use SAE (or do not use it) can affect the outcomes of job interviews, scholarship applications, public presentations, and job promotions. Some recommended steps to take in teaching SAE are:

- Introduce language differences by discussing examples of and differences between *home language* and *school language.*
- Examine children's writing samples to determine which linguistic features should be taught first, starting with the features that are common to most students.
- Teach components of school language in a direct, explicit way.
- Expect older students to use school language in the classroom, especially when that school language has been modeled and taught in the classroom.
- Model language rather than correct it. Evidence suggests that correction is one of the least effective ways to change language, but modeling it is the single most powerful way to elicit change (Lindfors, 1991).

# How Do Students Use Language?

How children use language in the classroom provides insight that can help classroom teachers. Classroom teachers who understand the tremendous language growth that occurs during the elementary school years will want to provide a full range of activities to ensure that language continues to grow. Similarly, understanding the importance of teaching Standard English to students means you will want to provide many speaking and listening activities for students. Sociolinguists provide some insight into how teachers can design a variety of language experiences that expand, rather than narrow, the type of language used in classrooms.

## Halliday's Model for Language Use

The British linguist **Michael Halliday** (1973; 1982) focused attention on how individuals use language by identifying seven functions. The functions identified were instrumental, regulatory, interactional, personal, heuristic, imaginative, and representational (see Table 2.6 for definitions of each function).

While Halliday's work was seminal by bringing focus on the use of language rather than the structure, he acknowledged that his list of functions was not meant to be all-inclusive. Tough (1982) expressed concern that these functions did not adequately allow teachers to analyze children's use of language in normal discourse within classrooms.

## Tough's Model for Language Use

**Joan Tough's** (1981; 1982) work was built upon several theoretical bases that helped answer two major questions: What does a child achieve by using language? What meaning does the child attach to language? Tough's functions included self-maintaining, directing, reporting, reasoning, predicting, projecting, and imagining. These functions, she believed, more adequately allow teachers to analyze children's discourse as well as plan assessment and teaching activities. For each function, Tough identified several specific strategies that further provide support to the teacher:

## Table 2.6
## Halliday's Model of Language

| Category | Definition | Example |
|---|---|---|
| Instrumental | Used to get things done | *I want milk.* |
| Regulatory | Used to regulate others | *You can't do that!* |
| Interactional | Used to interact with others | *Nice to meet you.* |
| Personal | Used to express individuality | *That was a good book.* |
| Heuristic | Used to learn about things | *What is that?* |
| Imaginative | Used to create own environment | *I'm the mommy and you're the daddy.* |
| Representational | Used to convey specific messages | *A tree fell on my house!* |

- **Self-maintaining language,** expressed frequently by younger children, is used to satisfy children's physical and psychological needs. Criticisms and threats, such as "That's messy!" are examples of self-maintaining language. Another example is any statement referring to their physical or psychological state, such as "I'm sad." When children use this language, they are generally concerned with supporting or asserting themselves in relation to other children or adults.
- **Directing language** is used to control themselves or others. Children using it are generally concerned about monitoring their own actions, directing other people's actions, or guiding their own actions. Statements such as "Don't do that!" or "I'm almost done. I'll be ready in a minute!" are examples of directing language.
- **Reporting language** may entail labeling, referring to details or sequences, making comparisons, and reflecting on central meaning. "This is the house, and here is the truck" is an example of a statement with labels. "The house is big and green" refers to details. "It is bigger than my house" demonstrates the ability to make comparisons. "Houses are important because they keep us warm and safe" provides an example of central meaning.
- **Reasoning language** is used to express relationships within experiences or to express a reason or reasons for some course of action. A typical reasoning statement will make cause-effect relationships clear. The child will not just say, "There's been a fire," but rather "There's been a fire because I can see the fire trucks." Reasoning statements may explain a process, such as "First, you coil the clay by pushing your hand back and forth over it. Then, you take your coil and make a circle. Then, you make more circles with more clay. Then, you put your coils on top of one another." Reasoning statements may also recognize problems and solutions, draw conclusions, and justify actions.
- **Predicting language** helps children use their past experiences to make predictions about the future. They may anticipate and forecast events, anticipate details or sequences of events, anticipate problems and solutions, recognize alternative courses of action, and predict the consequences of events. Children may say, "We're going to get a new guinea pig today," indicating that they can anticipate events. "We'll need to buy some food" demonstrates their anticipation of details.

A statement such as "We better have the food pretty soon or the guinea pig might not be happy" illustrates how children might anticipate problems and solutions.

- **Projecting language** includes the ability to project a point of view into experiences or situations the child may never have experienced. It also includes the ability to project a point of view into the feelings and reactions of others. The statement "The bus driver must have a hard job" is an example of projection, as is "He is going to be real mad if we fight on the bus."
- **Imagining language** is used when the whole content of language is the product of imagination. Developing an imaginary situation based on real life or fantasy are examples of imaginative language. When we hear a child say, "Let's pretend you're the prince and I'll be the princess," we know that that child uses imaginative language.

Tough (1981) found that, by the age of three or four, children are able to use language that appears to contain elements of all seven categories. She also noted that, among all children, directing, reporting, and self-maintaining language seems to be used most frequently, with reasoning, predicting, and imagining language beginning to emerge during the preschool years. Projecting language emerged later.

When comparing children whose parents held unskilled and semiskilled jobs to children whose parents held professional positions, Tough (1981) found that children from families whose parents held unskilled and semiskilled jobs used speech three times as often to secure attention for their own needs and to maintain their own status as well as monitor their own actions. Children from families whose parents held professional positions used speech five times as often to predict, to collaborate actions with others, and to imagine.

## Using Tough's Framework to Guide Questions

Students come to classrooms with a range of experiences. Your job as their teacher is to build upon these experiences and help children's language continue to grow. Knowing that there are differences in how students use language provides more compelling reasons for teachers to "level" this language playing field. Asking questions that elicit more elaborate and varied responses from children is a first step.

IRA/NCTE 11

When planning questions to use in the classroom, focus on the higher levels of language use. Questions that encourage children to report, reason, predict, and project are easily designed for many classroom topics. It is useful to make notes of students' responses to your questions, too. This can provide a window on their levels of language development. Some sample questions for each of these areas are listed in Table 2.7.

To assist children in becoming more adept with language functions, teachers should consciously plan the types of questions they ask. As teachers begin to promote more varied usage in their modeling, students' ability to use language will improve.

# How Can We Promote Language Growth?

As we discussed in the earlier part of this chapter, it is essential for classrooms to be places where children have ample opportunity to talk and listen to one another. Not only does such conversation improve students' abilities to communicate, it also helps students

**Table 2.7**
**Sample Questions Using Tough's Framework**

| Function | Sample Teacher Question |
|---|---|
| Self/Group Maintaining | Are you hungry? |
| Directing | Is your group finished? |
| Reporting | What did you find out? |
| Reasoning | Why were there so many hurricanes last year? |
| Predicting | What can be done to help people understand? |
| Projecting | How would you feel if you had no water or electricity? |
| Imagining | Can you think of a different ending to this story? |

understand text on a much deeper level and promotes critical thinking. Student conversation needs to be valued in our classrooms, so how do we start?

## Examine Assumptions about Language

Teachers' assumptions about language will affect how verbal their classrooms become. Meaningful talk does not just happen because a teacher says "Let's talk." The teacher must consciously and strategically plan for the classroom environment to become a place where children are meaningfully engaged in conversations throughout the school day. Lindfors (1991) suggests that there are several assumptions that should guide our efforts. Some of these assumptions are:

■ ***Language Growth Continues*** Language continues to grow in structure, in vocabulary, and in usage. As discussed earlier, the language of a five-year-old is dramatically different from that of a one-year-old. Likewise, the language of the ten-year-old is also markedly different than that of the three-year-old. The ten-year-old, for example, can easily understand passives as well as sentences with embedding and conjoining. These are not simple structures for the five-year-old. Vocabulary continues to grow as well. Many people did not understand the role that levee systems were supposed to play before a hurricane occurred along our coastal region. Many graduate students do not know what a phoneme is until they read about it and start to use it in context. Similarly, the ten-year-old has a far more developed vocabulary than that of the five-year-old.

The use of language also continues to change. Children learn to use language in different settings (home versus school) and with different people (adults versus peers). They also learn how to use language differently with the adults outside the home versus those inside the home.

If language growth continues throughout the school years, then teachers have a critical role in determining the direction and quality of that growth. Teachers must provide ample time and opportunity for children to speak to one another as well as to the teacher.

***Language and Cognitive Growth Intertwine*** Earlier in this chapter, there was a discussion of the first words a toddler says. Among them were *clock, shoe,* and *sock*—all words that had meaning to the toddler and represented things that they could manipulate. The teacher's role is to provide ample experiences for children, so that their cognitive and language abilities continue to grow. Children need ample time to develop a concept so that their vocabulary becomes more enriched. Simply looking at pictures of an elephant and talking about an elephant may not be enough. When children have the opportunity to see, hear, and smell an elephant, they begin to fully understand what an elephant is.

***Language Growth Occurs with Active Involvement*** Children do not learn language just by listening to it. Unfortunately, this is what happens in many classrooms today. Staab (1992) found that 78 percent of class time was devoted to the teacher talking or to quiet time, with 49 percent of teacher time being lecturing. The remaining 29 percent was spent asking students to listen quietly. Oral language does not grow in these environments.

Fortunately, many children live in environments in which there is ample opportunity to talk with others about what they learn. Unfortunately, other children do not live in such environments. School is the one place where teachers can ensure ample time for talk. The teacher's task is to provide experiences in which children become involved, so that they have ample experiences about which to talk.

***Language Growth Occurs in a Student-Oriented Environment*** Not all children are alike. Some children prefer to work and learn alone; others prefer working and learning in small groups. Some children like to talk a lot; others like to listen and observe. Teachers should provide a variety of language activities to meet the needs of all students, particularly those students who are reluctant to participate in class discussions.

Initially, **low-risk activities** can be provided to accommodate differences. Speaking always involves a risk of some sort, more so than writing. (Writing can be erased; not so with speaking.) Providing low-risk activities alleviates this risk, and here are some steps to consider:

- Reduce the size of the group for listening. Begin with partner exchanges. Keep the size of larger groups small enough that students feel comfortable. Talking to a group of three or four is much easier than talking to a group of twenty-four.
- Reduce the need for correct responses. Ask open-ended questions that allow more than one response. Encourage students to let each one complete their turn before others respond.
- Allow children to speak as part of a group, so that the opinion of the group, rather than the individual, is being expressed.

**Shared-risk activities** are another vehicle for reducing stress and encouraging talk. Several ways to have students share the risk include the following:

- Establish opinion trios in which every child is in a group of three. Ask an opinion question and allow each student up to one minute to respond in their trio. After three minutes, move to another question. The questions can be personal, such as "What is your favorite place to visit and why?" Or they can be content-related, such as "Do you think the Native Americans were treated fairly? Why or why not?"
- Set up think-pair-share time, in which each student is paired with a partner. After asking a question, give students time to think individually about their response before they share it with their partner.

## exploring technology

### Sites for Developing Oral Language

**Storytelling Tips for Oral Language Development (www.literacyconnections.com/Storytelling.html)**
Shirley Raines and Rebecca Isbell, authors of the book *Tell It Again!: Easy-to-Tell Stories with Activities for Young Children,* share information and resources on selecting stories and using storytelling tips.

**Aaron Shepard's Reader's Theater Resources (www.aaronshep.com/rt/index.html)**
Created by reader's theater expert Aaron Shepard, this comprehensive website is an invaluable resource with directions on how to conduct reader's theater, tips, scripts, and links to online resources.

**Scaffolding Oral Language Development through Poetry (www. readwritethink.org/lessons/lesson_view.asp?id = 69)**
In this lesson from ReadWriteThink, students work in small groups to develop a choral reading of two poems about an assigned insect. The poems serve as an introduction to a research investigation about the insect. Students compile factual information about the insect and present the information, along with their choral poetry readings to the class.

In these examples, it is not necessary for the teacher to hear all the responses. What is crucial is that all children have an opportunity to talk in a meaningful way.

Technology can also stimulate and support language growth in students. The Exploring Technology feature contains ideas for using technology to develop oral language in your classroom.

**Video Homework Exercise**
*Language: Classroom*
Go to the Homework and Exercises section in Chapter 2 of MyEducationLab and watch the video, "Language: Classroom," about how one teacher encourages communication using sign language for both hearing impaired students and typical students. Complete the activities that follow, and save your work or transmit it to your professor as assigned.

***Language Growth Occurs in Responsive Environments*** Responding to what children are trying to do is difficult, but it is essential in the teaching of reading/language arts. Research shows that beginning teachers focus primarily on themselves. Only after a few years of teaching do teachers start to ask questions such as "What does Miguel care about? How can I help him?" (Conway and Clark, 2003). Several ways to be responsive include:

- Show acceptance of what children say. Children need an environment in which it is safe to speak.
- When trying to build confidence in speaking, do not correct students' language. Research suggests that positive support builds confidence and language skills better than correction.
- Listen. Many studies indicate that a lot of classes are weighted toward large group lessons that are teacher dominated. Lindfors (1991) noted that teachers in fourth- and sixth-grade classrooms asked an average of forty-seven questions every twenty minutes; children as a whole group asked 6.9 questions every twenty minutes with only 1.67 percent of all questions in a classroom being asked by children. Teachers waited for children to respond to all these questions an average time of . . . one second.
- Avoid repeating (parroting) what the child has just said (see Dialogue 2.1).

Dialogue 2.1

## Parroting

| | |
|---|---|
| Teacher: | Boys and girls, yesterday we read the story "Little Red Riding Hood." Can anyone tell me what this story was about? |
| Child 1: | It was about a little girl visiting her grandma's house. |
| Child 2: | And she met a wolf. |
| Teacher: | Yes, she met a wolf. What else happened in the story? |
| Child 3: | Well, the wolf went to the grandma's house and pretended to be the grandma. |
| Teacher: | Yes, the wolf went to the grandma's house and pretended to be the grandma. |
| Child 4: | And then, Little Red Riding Hood went to the house and talked to the wolf. |
| Child 5: | And a hunter came in and saved her from being eaten by the wolf. |
| Teacher: | The hunter saved her from being eaten. Why did he do that? |
| Children: | [No response.] |



Teacher parroting encourages children to listen to the teacher, not to one another. In fact, children learn early that they do not need to listen to one another because the teacher will always repeat what is said. Parroting also communicates a strong nonverbal message to children. Parroting says to children: You are not a competent language user by yourself; therefore, I must repeat after you. And, finally, parroting closes discussion. A key strategy for teachers who are truly concerned about developing listening skills in children is to reduce the amount of parroting.

**BUILDING TEACHING SKILLS: Video Exercise**

*Discussion of The Scarlet Letter*

Go to the Building Teaching Skills section in Chapter 2 of MyEducation Lab and watch the video, "Discussion of the Scarlet Letter," that demonstrates a teacher carrying on a discussion with older students. Complete the activities that follow, and save your work or transmit it to your professor as assigned.

## Increase Time for Discussion

What is discussion? Discussion can be referred to as an earnest conversation in which people exchange ideas and feelings. It is not recitation, in which the teacher asks a lot of questions and students take turns answering those questions. In discussion, there is a real interaction among the students. In order to have a true discussion, those participating are generally interested in exploring more than one point of view, are willing to put forward and respond to different points of view, and have a true interest in understanding the matter under discussion.

Discussion is important for several reasons, including that it promotes a deeper understanding of text (Gambrell, 1996). Morrow and Smith (1990) found that kindergartners who engaged in small group discussion about stories that had been read aloud showed excellent story recall. Discussion has also been found to increase higher-level thinking. Hudgins and Edelman (1986) found that students in small group discussion were better at providing more evidence for conclusions. Reznitskaya et al. (2001) found that fourth- and fifth-grade students who read a story and discussed controversial issues before writing essay responses produced significantly better essays than did students in the traditional classrooms. As mentioned earlier, discussion also improves communication skills. Prioritizing time for students to talk together about content is time well spent. Unfortunately, discussion is used very little in classrooms. Goodlad's classic study (1984) estimated that there was a 4 to 8 percent probability of finding discussion across all levels of schooling in all subject areas.

The quality of discussion is affected by the type of text being discussed, the size of the group, and the quality of the leader. Gambrell (1996) notes, for example, that informational storybooks (such as the *Magic School Bus* series) enhance discussion more than narrative or expository texts. In fact, she notes that students actually prefer informational texts over narrative when there is discussion. Gambrell also notes that children demonstrate better comprehension when there is ample discussion.

Group size also affects the quality of discussion (Gambrell, 1996). Small group discussion appears to provide more time for all students to talk. Generally, there is agreement that the group should be large enough for diverse opinions, yet small enough to allow everyone a chance to talk. Research confirms that students recall information and have better comprehension in small groups (Morrow and Smith, 1990; Palinscar and Brown, 1984).

Leadership also appears to be an important factor affecting discussion. Although a growing amount of research on student-led discussion groups is being conducted, research seems to support the role of teachers in discussions. Teachers have an important role in helping students develop their discussion capabilities (McGee, 1992). Because real discussions are rare, teachers can help students learn to listen to one another, to present their own ideas, and to provide positive feedback that moves conversations forward.

## How to Begin

■ ***Discussing in Class*** Here are several steps you can take to incorporate more discussion in the classroom:

- Determine the social skills that students need in order to participate in a discussion (Vogt, 1996). Very young children may need modeling and role-playing. Older children can benefit from brainstorming to learn how to make a discussion work. Vogt suggests having students complete a *looks like/sounds like/feels like* chart.
- Determine the size group that you want for the discussion. There are times when you will want a whole class discussion. At other times, you will want to have smaller groups of four to six students. During this group time, students should be assigned member responsibilities, such as recorder, timekeeper, facilitator, and summarizer.
- Decide how to present questions for discussion, including writing on a wall chart, sharing in a discussion web, or presenting verbally at the whiteboard.
- Make sure the students have developed the discussion rules and that they understand them.

■ ***Supporting the Discussion*** Here are several general strategies teachers can use to help students become more involved in discussions:

- Assist students who repeat others or who use non-sequiturs, by seeking agreement or paraphrasing.
- "So you agree with Miguel then?" is a helpful comment for students who repeat.
- With comments unrelated to the topic, paraphrase the student and draw him or her back to the topic at hand by saying something similar to: "You just visited your granddaddy's house. Maybe when Jack went home, he wanted to visit his granddaddy, too. But why did Jack leave home to go visit the Giant?"
- Increase the wait time—the amount of time between the questions and the response— to three seconds. There is ample evidence to suggest that the amount and quality of discussion increases when wait time increases. Suggest that students make notes on what they want to say so they will not forget their own ideas. With added wait time, students talk more, more students talk, and the talk is more relevant.
- Seek clarification from students when the meaning is unclear. Say something similar to: "I'm not sure I understand. Could you say this another way?"

- Ask students for evidence: "Can you point us to the paragraph where it says that?"
- Help students see common points of agreement: "Oh, so you agree with Manuel and Miguel?"

## Promote Language Growth Using Other Activities

Tough's model of language use provides a helpful framework for developing varied language activities in the classroom. This framework helps ensure that a range of language opportunities is provided.

***Directing Activities*** Teachers may give directions to simple art projects and activities. Students may even be given the opportunity to give the directions themselves, with other students following their directions. Some directing activities to consider are:

- A simple activity such as sharpening a pencil or making a sandwich can challenge students to give directions that are specific and sequential.
- The use of origami (paper folding) provides many opportunities for students learning to give and follow directions.
- Having simple shapes stacked (see the Engaging in Visual Literacy feature) and having students give the class directions to make these shapes can be fun and rewarding. Such activities help the other students to focus as they listen.

***Self-Maintaining Activities*** These activities allow students to express their opinions in a variety of situations. Some self-maintaining activities to consider are:

- Students could read a simple story and share their opinion about the story in the opinion trios. They could also change a key opinion in the story. What would have happened, for example, if Goldilocks had liked the first chair she sat in?
- **Think-pair-share** is an effective tool for helping children learn to express their opinions in safe environments. During this process, a pair of students first think about a topic and share their opinion with each other. Then, they join with another pair of students to share their opinions.

***Reporting Activities*** Summarizing favorite books and television shows to present to other students is always useful. Some reporting activities to consider are:

- Students place objects or photographs in a bag, then a student selects one object and describes it without naming it. The listeners must write down what they think it is and share their answers with their group.
- Show and tell for younger children also promotes reporting, especially when it is in small groups.
- Paired reading is a good opportunity for students' use of reporting in the classroom and is advantageous because all students are actively involved (Dansereau, 1986). Students work in pairs with two distinct roles: that of a reporter who summarizes and that of a responder who questions. The teacher takes a reading assignment (which has been read by the entire class ahead of time) and subdivides it twice. The first time, it is divided into four sections. The second time, each of the four sections is divided into two parts: A and B (see Figure 2.2 for directions on paired reading).
- Another technique which involves all students uses expert groups. Elliot Aronson developed expert groups in 1971 as a means to facilitate student interaction (Gilbert, 2001). This is a cooperative learning strategy that helps students develop deeper understanding of text. In this process, students are reassigned

## engaging in Visual Literacy

### Communicating Directions

Having students learn how to discriminate and interpret the objects or symbols is important. This exercise helps students learn how to communicate this information effectively. Choose a student volunteer and ask him or her to provide directions on how to recreate this visual to the rest of the class. In no time at all, the students will learn that their directions must be clear and concise. The listeners learn that they must listen carefully or their reproduction will not resemble the original at all. Variations of these drawings are easily made for subsequent lessons.

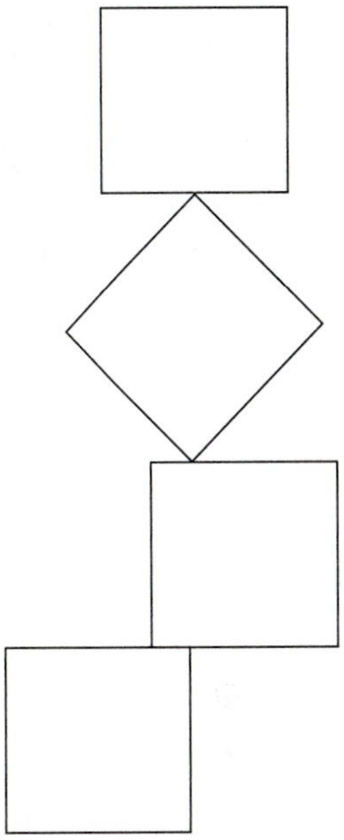

---

from their home group to an expert group. In the expert group, students discuss only one or two aspects of an assigned reading or topic, with the goal of reaching a common understanding. After students reach an understanding, they return to their home group and present the information they learned.

- The **three-step interview,** which is similar to think-pair-share, is more structured. In pairs, students interview each other about an announced topic. Times are assigned for each interview, and when the time is up, the partners switch their roles, with one being the interviewer and the other the interviewee. Pairs join each other to form groups of four. Students then take turns introducing their partners and sharing what the pair partner had to say about the topic. The three-step interview can be used for various activities.

***Reasoning and Predicting Activities*** These activities encourage students to think and make connections as they learn. Some reasoning and predicting activities to consider are:

- Playing **Twenty Questions** helps students listen carefully. During this game, a student selects an object, concept, or category. The classmates have twenty questions to determine what the student has selected. The twenty questions, however, must be yes/no (closed) questions. The purpose of the game is to identify the item in the fewest number of questions. Students must listen and reason carefully as they choose their questions to ask.
- **Story mapping**, another good example of reasoning and predicting activities, is explained in Chapter 5, as are DRTAs (Directed Reading Thinking Activity). This is a specific strategy developed by Russell Stouffer.

**Figure 2.2**

## Paired-Reading Strategy

- Students are responsible for reading the entire chapter or article.
- Divide the selection into four sections.
- Divide each section into two sections, called A and B.
- Have students placed in pairs for a second reading.
- Each member of the pair has a distinct role for each section.
- The reporter: reads the section carefully and summarizes the section for their partner. The summary must be in his or her own words.
- The responder: reads the section carefully and asks the reporter questions that clarify (e.g., "What does that mean?" "What about . . . ?").
- The partners then choose whether they are the A or the B person.
- When the partners read the A section, the A person is the reporter. The B person is the responder.
- When the partners read the B section, the B person is the reporter. The A person is the responder.
- Pairs then develop a graphic organizer and use this organizer to report out to the group.
- There will be multiple pairs reporting out on the same section. They may emphasize different items as they report out. This is a way of reinforcing the material with students.

***Projecting*** Projecting activities help children learn to see different points of view.

- The **Intra-act Procedure** (Hoffman, 1979) requires students to silently read a selection and then discuss the selection in small groups. Chairs of the groups summarize the selection's content. Teachers provide four value statements pertinent to the selection. Students agree or disagree with these statements individually, noting their position in writing. Students then write predictions about what position the other members of the team will take on each of these statements. Discussion then occurs, as students share their predictions about the other members and students reveal their actual responses to the statements. An example of this may be seen in Figure 2.3.
- **Discussion webs** (Alvermann, 1991) are also an effective tool to develop the projecting function. To start this process, the teacher writes a thought-provoking question that can be answered positively or negatively. Students then work in pairs to discuss the question and list four or five reasons why the question could be answered yes and four or five reasons why the question could be answered no. The pairs then combine with another pair to discuss their reasons, modifying their lists for both responses. The group of four then considers all their reasons and tries to reach consensus on their answer to the central question. Groups report to the whole class or write their own response.

***Imagining Activities*** Creative drama and role-playing are very important in the classroom. Asking students to change different elements of the story (the characters, the setting, or the problem resolution) can help them use language imaginatively. The Engaging in Assessment feature presents two informal ways to monitor the oral language development of your students.

## Figure 2.3 Example of an Intra-act Procedure

Do you agree or disagree with the following?

How will members of your group respond?

- I think Ivan's parents are unimportant in this story.
- I think Ivan is a mean person for taking her coat.
- I think the seal would have been better off if she had never met Ivan.
- I think Ivan was punished for keeping the seal skin.



## *engaging in* Assessment

### Oral Language Samples and Activities

A classroom teacher can use several informal ways to assess language. Language samples are one important way. Here is an example of a language sample from first-grade students. What can you tell about Jeremiah's language from this brief conversation?

Jeremiah: Look at dis. You don' cut dat. You don't s'pose to cut dis paper. You s'pose to color. Dis how Jeffrey color. Dis how Lauren color . . . color everywhere. Joshua used to color like date, didn't he? When he come, he color nice.

Carlos: Where's Joshua?

Jeremiah: Dis is how James draws.

Carlos: No it isn't.

Jeremiah: James did.

Carlos: Did not.

Jeremiah: Did too. [making clucking sounds like a chicken while playing with his feathers] I'm done. Now I gotta use yellow . . . blue. Den yellow. Yellow.

Carlos: That's ugly. [looking at Jeremiah's headband]

Jeremiah: What's ugly?

Carlos: That picture . . .

Other ways to assess language include specially designed activities designed to elicit language. A teacher, such as Ms. Paredo, may want to design a task similar to one that Berko used in her study. In this task, a series of figures with nonsense words is presented to the students. The teacher might say: This is a *wug;* now there are two of them. There are two ________. In this example, of course, the teacher is listening for the plural marker. Past tense could also be used by changing the verbal prompt: This is a *wug*. He likes to *wop*. Yesterday, he ________. In this example, the teacher listens for the past tense marker. Remember that Berko found that five- and six-year-old children could complete these tasks. Ms. Paredo's third-graders also should be capable of completing such tasks.

## revisit the classroom challenge

Why were the children in Ms. Paredo's class not using past tense markers in their conversations? Could Ms. Paredo have done her lesson differently? What should she do now to address what she sees as a continuing problem? Check the statements below that provide guidance to Ms. Paredo.

1. _______ Some dialects do not have an overwhelming need for past tense markers.
2. _______ Ms. Paredo did not allow enough time for the children to apply their new learning about past tense markers.
3. _______ Ms. Paredo should correct the children every time she hears them leaving off the past tense in their speech.
4. _______ Ms. Paredo should spend more time on this topic and provide more time for talk in small group settings.

## chapter review

This chapter provides an overview of language development and its integral role in the language arts. Our students come to school with a tremendous amount of language abilities, including phonology, morphology, syntax, semantics, and conversational skill. In the elementary school years, students continue this remarkable journey toward full language use. Our role as teachers is to ensure that all our students have as many opportunities with language as possible. Ensuring that our classrooms are alive with conversation will bring our students a long way in that journey.

This chapter answered the following questions about oral development in today's classroom:

### What Is Language?

Language is a system of arbitrary symbols that allows us to classify everything in our experience, such as thoughts, processes, and events. There are four modes of language: talking, listening, reading, and writing.

### Why Is Oral Language Important?

Oral language improves students' ability to communicate and promotes a deeper understanding of text, critical thinking, and problem solving. It is also important because oral language is the basis of reading and writing.

### What Do We Know about Oral Language Development?

Oral language has a generative, rule-governed, arbitrary, and dual (linking sound and meaning) quality. There are five components of language: phonology, morphology, syntax, semantics, and pragmatics. Children vary in the rate and order in which these components develop, so it is important to respond to children and young students individually. Preschool children already manifest amazing control over most of these features.

### How Does Language Grow?

Several different theories about how language develops include: the Skinnerian, psycholinguistic, semantic-cognitivist, and sociolinguistic. Each theory contributes to a more complete picture of how language grows and helps us appreciate the complexities of language and its development.

### How Does Language Change during the Preschool Years?

Language develops and changes early in a child's life. It progresses from the prelinguistic period in infancy to the beginning of speech and into the beginnings of sentences. Between eighteen and twenty-four months, children's vocabulary increases significantly. Children at this stage understand much more language than they can produce. By the time they are ready for school, these young students have become very adept at understanding and using their oral language.

### Is Language Development "Finished" When Children Enter School?

No. Syntax continues to grow as students develop and use more complex sentence structures. Vocabulary continues to grow and is crucial to students' comprehension of the world. Children continue to expand their awareness of how their sound system works with respect to phoneme segmentation and sound associations. An important, ongoing development is in students' conversational abilities. They become more able to listen to others, to respond verbally and nonverbally, to engage in dialogic exchanges, and to learn from these shared engagements and discussions.



### What Do We Know about Dialects?

Language dialects are common, and there are many types. Each dialect is a complete rule-governed language system suited to the language users in the dialect community. Guidelines for working with diverse language learners include recognizing that dialectical differences are common, teaching Standard English (SE), and monitoring our own behaviors to ensure that we do not communicate low expectations to our students but that we do create an environment of high expectations.

### How Do Students Use Language?

Halliday identified seven functions for how students use language: instrumental, regulatory, informative, interactional, personal, heuristic, and imaginative. Tough's language functions address the question of what is achieved by using language. Specific kinds of questions raised by teachers can stimulate students' ability to use these language functions. The ways in which teachers respond also influence students' willingness to participate orally in the classroom. Giving children good models of oral language, providing wait time for them to frame their ideas and decide what to say, and creating a variety of contexts of language use are all important.

### How Can We Promote Language Growth?

As teachers, we need to recognize that language continues to develop during the elementary years and that language and cognitive growth are intertwined. Language growth is supported and encouraged when students are actively engaged in a student-oriented classroom environment. Within this context, it is important to actively respond to students and support frequent opportunities for students to talk—with partners, in small groups, and in larger group discussions. Teachers also need to create opportunities that promote students' use of all language functions.

PEARSON
**myeducationlab**™
Where the Classroom Comes to Life

Now go to www.myeducationlab.com to take a Pretest to assess your initial comprehension of chapter content, study chapter content with your individualized Study Plan, take a Posttest to assess your understanding of chapter content, practice your teaching skills with Building Teaching Skills exercises, and build a deeper, more applied understanding of chapter content with Homework and Exercises.

chapter 3

# Developing Speaking and Listening

## classroom challenge

**Ms. Fotopoulos** likes to have her fourth-grade students work in partner and small group activities. However, this fall she is having trouble keeping her students on task and engaged in the designated activities. As she goes around the room, she notices that there is little talk back-and-forth in the small groups but a single student or two seems to be dominating and taking control of the group time and not involving others. She is noticing that even when she asks students to work with partners using her favorite "Think-Pair-Share" activity, some students seem not to listen to each other; when she asks the pairs to share their ideas, she often feels uneasy that there is no consensus of ideas. She is concerned that the students do not seem to respect each others' ideas and have yet to understand the value of looking at ideas from multiple points of view. Before she begins her book clubs, she knows the class will need to have a more respectful way of interacting and have a better appreciation of what can be learned in partner and small group discussion.

She sits at her desk after school and begins to think of ways to get students

engaged productively. She knows students need to both value shared thinking and talking *and* develop good communication skills. Perhaps she should use an assessment tool to become more specific about what skills students do possess in speaking and listening and the range of abilities and skills of her students. She thinks about the value of modeling some specific behaviors she would like to see students use. This may be a time to slow down and focus on oral communication.

## Questions for Reflection

1. What can Ms. Fotopoulos do to assess her students' oral language and social skills?
2. What skills in communicating with other students can Ms. Fotopoulos expect her students to possess?
3. What can this teacher do to improve students' social communication?
4. How important is it to focus on developing common speaking and listening patterns and behaviors?

## anticipating this chapter

In exploring ways to develop speaking and listening, the following questions provide the structure for the chapter and can help guide your reading and thinking:

How do state and national standards inform oral language instruction?

How can social interaction and communication be developed?

How can you develop exploratory uses of language?

How can you help students gain confidence in speaking?

How can students learn to use language to inform others?

In what ways can you develop students' ability to listen?

The preceding chapter provided an in-depth foundation for understanding oral language development and how language varies across ethnic groups. It also gave ideas for how to develop school language directly. This chapter builds on these ideas, linking them to specific instructional settings and activities. Instead of revisiting Tough's functions of language, the functions are clustered in three basic categories: social interaction, exploratory, and informational. This clustering permits us to focus on the many classroom venues for speaking and listening. Specific activities and assessments are provided that can be used when grouping students in partner, small group, and large group settings. This attention to group settings reflects the National Communications Association guidelines that elementary children need to develop oral communications in varied small group and cultural settings (NCA, 2000).

Both children and adults spend most of our time communicating orally. Our home life is characterized by personal communication. Our time in school is also grounded in speaking and listening. According to research cited in the National Communication Association curriculum guidelines, researchers have found that people spend 75 percent of their day engaged in communication (www.natcom.org, Guidelines for Developing Oral Communication Curricula in Kindergarten through Twelfth Grade, pdf p. 8). Of that 75 percent, students spend 53 percent listening, 17 percent reading, 16 percent speaking, and 14 percent writing. In the current climate of electronic communication, the percentage of time students spend in informal writing is probably increasing. As norms for communication change, it is important that teachers think carefully about how they can guide students in becoming effective communicators across informal social settings, in more structured school and classroom learning, and in the larger mix of cultural and formal settings. In this chapter, we focus on what teachers can do within the school context to build students' oral communication skills. We focus attention on three major contexts for speaking and listening in the classroom: (1) in individual or partner communications, (2) in small group contexts, and (3) in large group settings. Both social and academic discourse are addressed.

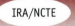

# How Do State and National Standards Inform Oral Language Instruction?

Oral competency is an essential part of state and national standards in language arts. The general framework developed by the International Reading Association (IRA) and the National Council of Teachers of English (NCTE) includes four that are particularly focused on oral language.* These are:

IRA/NCTE

- **Standard 4.** Students adjust their use of spoken, written, and visual language (e.g., conventions, style, vocabulary) to communicate effectively with a variety of audiences and for different purposes.
- **Standard 9.** Students develop an understanding of and respect for diversity in language use, patterns, and dialects across cultures, ethnic groups, geographic regions, and social roles.
- **Standard 11.** Students participate as knowledgeable, reflective, creative, and critical members of a variety of literacy communities.
- **Standard 12.** Students use spoken, written, and visual language to accomplish their own purposes (e.g., for learning, enjoyment, persuasion, and the exchange of information).

## National Communications Association (NCA) Standards

A good resource for more specific grade level standards has been developed by the National Communications Association's (NCA) National Project on Speech Communication Competencies. Separate standards have been developed for Fundamentals of Effective Communication, Speaking, Listening, and Media Literacy.

Figure 3.1 includes the NCA standards for Speaking and Listening. More information about particular grade levels and what teachers should focus on to develop students' competencies can be obtained from the NCA website.

## State Standards for Speaking and Listening

Most states also specify areas of oral language proficiency expected of students. Recently, the need for communication skills has become a concern of high schools, too, since when students leave school for the workforce many employers have found their new employees lacking in these basic skills. The more teachers can do in the elementary grades to develop social communication abilities, the better prepared children will be for their lives. Take some time to look up the speaking and listening standards and benchmarks for your area. Look at the Engaging in Oral Language feature on state standards for an example of what one state has included for fourth grade. Ask your district personnel about available support materials and projects to help you develop your students' oral language.

*Source: International Reading Association

**Figure 3.1**

### NCA Standards for Speaking and Listening

**Speaking**

9. knowledge and understanding of the speaking process
10. the ability to adapt communication strategies appropriately and effectively according to the needs of the situation and setting
11. the ability to use language that clarifies, persuades, and/or inspires while respecting differences in listeners' backgrounds
12. the ability to manage or overcome communication anxiety

**Listening**

13. knowledge and understanding of the listening process
14. the ability to use appropriate and effective listening skills for a given communication situation and setting
15. the ability to identify and manage barriers to listening

*Source:* International Reading Association

## Sheltered Instruction Observation Protocol (SIOP)

Another good source for attention to oral language is the **Sheltered Instruction Observation Protocol (SIOP)** and the teaching suggestions contained in the program (Echevarria, Vogt, and Short, 2007). Designed for teachers who have English language

### engaging in Oral language

#### Focus on Standards

Many states have developed specific standards and benchmarks that focus on particular types of oral language use. For example, the state of Virginia has grade-level standards and benchmarks for oral language. This is a good time to check the state standards for oral language in your areas. Look at the state standards first. Then look at what the school districts are doing to support teachers in implementing and monitoring students' development of these skills. Which of the standards and benchmarks do you feel most comfortable teaching? Which will take more thoughtful preparation? As you read the rest of this chapter, collect ideas that you can use when you are teaching.

learners in their classrooms, it lays out a powerful model with eight specific features that support language learners. One of these is to have both clear content and language objectives. As teachers plan lessons, they think specifically about the language students will need to understand and use. They establish specific objectives for each lesson, so they don't overlook guiding students in language development. An example of a language objective related to helping students learn to engage in discussions could be to clarify the differences among these terms: *discuss, brainstorm,* and *share.* At the intermediate level, the additional terms *explain, argue, debate,* and *support* might be added since we often use them without being sure students know their precise meanings and how and when to engage in each.

With so many school districts around the country now having increasing numbers of students for whom English is not the home language, it is valuable to take time learning more about what regular education teachers can do to support students' language development. The SIOP framework is certainly a valuable tool to support language growth. In addition to attending to the language students need to use, it also has teachers focus on their own language of instruction. This is described as "comprehensible input" and is an important aspect of the language used in the classroom; what words teachers use, how they find the appropriate level of explanation and elaboration; and how they link oral and visual forms of language can all make a tremendous difference for students. Your attention to language use can also raise all students' awareness of the importance of thinking of the listener when speaking orally.

### Assessment of Oral Language Development of English Language Learners

Another important support for teachers in developing students' oral language comes from the **World-Class Instructional Design and Assessment (WIDA) Consortium. WIDA standards** and their framework for large-scale assessment (State of Wisconsin, 2004) identified communication in English for social and instructional purposes within the school setting. It also includes specific proficiencies for academic success in each of the academic areas: mathematics, science, social studies, and language arts. See Chapter 4 for more elaboration on these useful guidelines for students developing their oral English proficiency. See Figure 3.2 for an example of the WIDA standards.

## How Can Social Interaction and Communication Be Developed?

The more teachers understand the development of children's language during the elementary years, the more we can be constructive in planning activities and experiences in the classroom. Most importantly, teachers set the tone and expectations for how students will be expected to use language. Since informal exchanges and talk among peers is the most frequent language use, it is where we start in this chapter.

Figure 3.2

**WIDA English Language Proficiency Standards: Grades Three through Five**

WIDA English Language Proficiency Standard 2: English language learners communicate information, ideas, and concepts necessary for academic success in the content area of **Language Arts**

| Language Domain of | Level 1 Entering | Level 2 Beginning | Level 3 Developing | Level 4 Expanding | Level 5 Bridging |
|---|---|---|---|---|---|
| **Speaking** | name story elements depicted visually | describe explicit story elements supported by illustrations | summarize issues or conflicts in various genres | discuss relationships among ideas and offer opinions | make connections and propose options or solutions |

*Source:* WIDA ELP Standards © 2004, 2007 Board of Regents of the University of Wisconsin System. Used by permission.

The most powerful models for students are the adults in the school. Right from the first day, you can establish a positive way to greet and interact with your students. The whole school may also have some clearly established routines you will want to learn about. For example, some principals await children at the front door of the school and welcome them individually as they enter. "Good morning, Josh. I'm glad to see you. How's that little sister of yours? Is she joining us this year?" Each student gets a personal welcome over the course of a week or so, and all are greeted with a smile and short word or two—"Hi, Shenee," and "Welcome, Darius!," etc. When adults take time to acknowledge each child and find out about their lives, it sets a personal and important tone.

## Classroom Routines

You will want to develop this same type of communication as you meet your class at your classroom door or establish other morning rituals. At the end of the day, it is also good to think of a closing routine that communicates personally with each student. You may close the day with a song, a class poem, or a class journal entry reflecting on the day and the key events. At that time, you may thank students for some creative work they accomplished, some hard tasks they attempted, or some problem-solving they entertained. Acknowledging two to three students for individual recognition each day also establishes a personal connection that most students crave from their teachers. For example, "Darnel, thanks for getting all those books in order today so we could begin our literature discussion groups," or "Samanda, I am going to keep thinking about your wonderful analogy about the rap lyrics."

When teachers and administrators establish positive connections with each student, they send strong messages about the importance of each person and the value of social greetings within the school community. This practice provides a great starting place to encourage student-to-student communication, too. At the beginning of the year, listen to students as they greet each other and get settled into their desks or pods. Find out if they engage each other positively, notice those who seem shy and may be left out of the informal social exchanges. You may want to initiate a routine through which

The most powerful models for students are the adults in their school. Right from the first day you can establish a positive way to greet and interact with your students.



you guide students as they gather together to create a daily schedule or write a "Morning Message," a brief news update about the status of the class. As part of the routine, you can incorporate a short thirty-second student-to-student exchange. Ask students to turn to someone near them and greet that person, "Good morning, _______. Glad you are here today!" or something appropriate to your group. Given the increasing diversity of our classrooms, it can be an important modeling of the kinds of social greetings common in our mainstream culture. Later, you can explore with students other ways their communities may extend and share greetings.

## Other Contexts for Developing Social Interaction

Students can quickly develop routines for meeting and greeting classmates and key adults in the school environment. Don't overlook attending to such basic greetings as saying "Good morning" and "Hello!" The next step is helping them become comfortable greeting and talking with newcomers to the classroom: visitors, new students, and parents. At each grade level, children need to learn how to receive visitors. In some schools, students learn to greet them orally in unison, "Good morning. Welcome to our class." At the primary level, this is a good way to get students more comfortable with social exchanges. Students may learn to stand up to greet adults, too. Norms vary by school, so it is good to think through the practices in the school where you will teach. Ask other teachers what is done and then think through how you can guide your students in developing appropriate behaviors.

Some intermediate grade teachers assign "Daily Greeters" or class hosts/hostesses who have responsibility for greeting newcomers and introducing them to the class. This gives students a real personal way to develop their skills; and for shy students or those not accustomed to meeting unfamiliar adults, this practice can be important in their development. Before making these assignments the whole class needs to practice ways of meeting adults and welcoming them. Students can work with a partner and follow a script provided by the teacher or developed by the class. Figure 3.3 shows one script developed for this use.

Figure 3.3

## A Model for Meeting and Greeting Guests

Student: Hello, I'm Jeremy Bransford. I'm part of Mr. Hanson's class and am the Class Greeter this week. We are glad you are visiting us. Have you ever been in our classroom before? [*Introduce yourself and welcome the guest. Ask a question to start some conversation about the visit.*]

Guest: Thank you, Jeremy, for being my greeter. It is nice to have someone meet me and take me to the classroom. I don't think I have been in your classroom before. I was in the school last year, however, when there was an all-school assembly. Where is your room? [*Most adults will respond to what you say and extend the conversation with a question or connection. If the guest doesn't then go ahead with your introduction to the principal.*]

Jeremy: Before we go there we would like you to meet the principal. I know Ms. Stolz would like to welcome you herself. We have a few minutes before the class expects us. [*Explain to the guest what you would like him to do.*]

Guest: That's a good idea.

Jeremy: Ms. Stolz, this is our guest, Mr. Kuhlman, who is going to speak to us about being an aeronautical engineer. He's helped design the new Boeing planes and we are excited to have him here. [*This helps the principal have some information so she can make a connection to the guest.*]

*After this brief conversation, Jeremy takes Mr. Kuhlman to the classroom and introduces him to the class.*

Jeremy: Class, we are lucky today to have Mr. Kuhlman visit us. He is an aeronautical engineer who is working on the development of new passenger planes for Boeing Aircraft. I know from the letter he sent us that he always wanted to be either a pilot or an engineer; even in high school he was designing models and took glider lessons. In college he studied engineering so he could get a job in this area.

Mr. Kuhlman, we are ready to learn more about your work. We have prepared questions, too, that we would like to ask you.

Reading through and practicing scripts like this one can help intermediate and middle grade students gain more confidence in how they can be a class greeter and meet and introduce adults to other students. Students often are very uncomfortable initially with the idea of meeting new adults and giving some attention to these skills can be very useful. Even the practice of shaking hands and making eye contact with adults may need some practice before it feels comfortable. If your students are not accustomed to these kinds of interactions, set up a schedule with other adults in your building and ask them to be visitors to your classroom over the course of the year so students gain confidence with these social practices. Think of the many ways teachers help develop students' engagement with adults; as you read this book, you will find examples that may help give you ideas for your own teaching. For instance, in Chapter 12, the Authors' Tea is one way children can host a special event for parents during which they share their own writing.

Social interactions are also important as students meet other children, perhaps as new children join the class or are visitors in the room. Discuss with the class how they would greet unfamiliar or new students. Students can develop dialogues similar to the one in Figure 3.3 for Jeremy and Mr. Kuhlman, but with modifications for greeting a new student. Finding good questions to ask or ways to elicit the students' experiences and interests can be included in this kind of dialogue. Then have students practice meeting and greeting each other. If appropriate you might invite older students from another class to practice these routines.

The suggestions and examples presented in this section underscore the goals of all teachers: we want students who are confident and competent in a variety of oral communication settings. We know students will grow when there is good modeling and support from the adults in the school. We also know that students need direct guidance in developing some of these social and cultural practices. Helping students develop sensitivity to the different contexts, purposes, and audiences is an important part of language development.

In this chapter two additional purposes for oral language are highlighted: talk that is exploratory in nature and talk that is to share information. Both purposes involve both speaking and listening. However, there are specific skills associated with each of the expressive and receptive aspects of communication. Therefore, ideas for developing speaking and listening are presented separately. Because classroom language arts and other content area activities are the major contexts for teachers to help students, three different groupings in which oral language can be developed are also discussed: partner, small group, and whole class.

## How Can You Develop Exploratory Uses of Language?

Using oral language to explore ideas and to consider different interpretations and variations of perspective is an important part of school life and thinking. If you go online and look at the Virginia standards and benchmarks, you will find that by fourth grade students are expected to contribute their ideas in group discussions and to use evidence to support their opinions. They are also expected to develop the ability to seek the ideas of others as part of the exploration of ideas and development of understanding. This means that students need to know how to ask good questions and make connections between their ideas and those of their classmates.

There are many instructional settings in which teachers can help students use language to explore, predict, imagine, solve problems, and reason together. Because this use of language is so central to learning, it is useful to identify particular ways students can be nurtured over time in using language for exploration. The section following provides a framework for thinking about how teachers can develop these aspects of communication during regular classroom activities. As you look at the areas listed, think of where you have seen students in the schools you have visited or have worked in engaging in similar activities. Think about the following questions:

- How can students be most productively engaged together?
- What skills do they need to develop to work in these settings productively?
- What kinds of guidelines are important to provide?

**Video Homework Exercise**

*During Reading*

Go to the Homework and Exercises section in Chapter 3 of MyEducationLab and view the video, "During Reading" where a teacher uses whole class discussion while students read informational text. Complete the activities that follow, and save your work or transmit it to your professor as assigned.

## Creating Safe Contexts

**CASE STUDY HOMEWORK EXERCISE**

*Coping with Problems Effectively—Elementary School*

Go to the Homework and Exercises section in Chapter 3 of MyEducationLab and read the case study "Coping with Problems Effectively - Elementary School," which is about fifth grade class discussion among a group of students that is not working. Complete the activities that follow, and save your work or transmit it to your professor as assigned.

For many students, and particularly those from other language backgrounds, it is important to give them time to talk and think in nonthreatening contexts before expecting them to feel comfortable in whole class or large group discussions and learning activities. Providing regular opportunities for students to first work out their ideas orally with a partner is a content and language essential. Once they have tried out ideas in that safe setting, they can move into a more risky, small group context. It may take real scaffolding before students feel comfortable sharing ideas in a large group.

As a teacher, advance planning is important so you can maintain a safe environment for students' language exploration and growth. One good way to begin is to select one or two partner, small group, and large group oral frameworks and become comfortable using them. Then you can adjust them to your style of teaching and to your students and, eventually, you can add more teaching frameworks to your repertoire. Students will feel more comfortable and able to participate if you use a small repertoire of oral frameworks, too. By introducing them to the expected types of talk (polite routines, turn taking, ways to ask questions, etc.) students will grow in their discussion skills and learn to explore their own ideas and those of classmates.

As you think of the many contexts in which students can engage with each other in thinking about ideas in an exploratory way, this list can continue to expand. Not all of the suggested activities are explained in this chapter; you will learn about many of them later in this book. However, they are listed as a sample of how you can elaborate your own repertoire of activities. See Table 3.1 to begin exploring oral language activities. As you develop your own routines for classroom instruction, this framework may be helpful so you can be sure that students have opportunities to engage in partner, small group, and large group contexts. Remember, choose only a few activities or routines initially so you and your students can become comfortable in using them. Include all three levels of grouping. Beginning with partner activities, then moving to small

**Table 3.1**
**Oral Language Activities**

| Partner Activities | Small Group Activities | Large Group Activities |
|---|---|---|
| Say Something/ Turn and Talk | Think-Pair-Share-Square | DL-TA; DR-TA |
| Think-Pair-Share | Sketch to Stretch (Feature) | K-W-L Brainstorming |
| PRC2 (Partner Reading & Content, Too) | Book Club/Literature Discussion | Great Books Discussion |
| Peer Writing Conference | Writing Workshop: Generating writing ideas and sharing drafts | Discussion using The Discussion Web |
| | Science Team Inquiry | Teacher-led discussion of content-area problem |
| | | Teacher guiding revision of student writing pieces |

group, and finally to large group contexts also provides more support for risk-taking and exploration of new ways of engaging.

## Planning for Partner and Group Discussions

We suggest careful planning before asking students to use language for exploration together. Before deciding which of these activities to introduce, take time to assess students' readiness and ability to articulate expectations. For example, before initiating a book club format, ask students to think about what makes a good book discussion group. Begin by discussing with the class how they think they should participate; what is expected of each, and what a good participation is like. One way to begin is to ask students to think about the activity and create a chart (Vogt, 1996) that includes the three categories: looks like, sounds like, and feels like.

IRA/NCTE 4

As students contribute their ideas they can be put on the chart. This is a good introduction to shared thinking and helps you gain a better idea of students' experiences and preparedness for working together. This also provides a starting point for you to determine how much modeling, practice, and support is needed for students to work collaboratively.

**Say Something/Turn and Talk** An easy way to get started with student-initiated talk in the classroom is to teach students a simple routine called **"Say Something,"** or **Turn and Talk**. Even in kindergarten and first grade, children can learn to share ideas in this easy format. Initially, the teacher needs to help students develop the concept of speaking in a "twelve-inch" voice, a "secrets" voice or a "knee to knee" voice; just loud enough for the partner to hear, but no one else. The teacher also helps organize the group so everyone has a partner. Children can hold up their hands together to show that they know their partner. The partners should sit next to each other on the carpet or in their chairs. Then the teacher can model the process with one student, sitting in front of the large group. The teacher explains that he or she is going to ask a question and wants each student to turn to another child and "talk about that question." Begin with something easy that isn't necessarily text-based such as, "What special location in the school would you like to visit (e.g., library, cafeteria, nurses' station, etc.) and why?" Later, this routine is good to use when reading aloud to students. Stop at an interesting point and ask the children to turn to their partner and predict what will happen next or how they might solve the problem.

**Think-Pair-Share** This activity was mentioned in Chapter 2 as a good way to help students use their oral language to discuss questions posed by the teacher. The teacher asks a question that requires some exploration and gives the students time to think about it (the length of time depends on the age of the students and the nature of the question) and make some notes or sketches about their response. Students then turn to their partner who is seated next to them and each shares what they thought. After one to two minutes of talk between the partners, the teacher can call the whole class back for some sharing with the whole group. Often, it is one partner who will share the other student's ideas. "I really liked what my partner thought about this. . . ." The teacher can then draw the connections among the different partners' ideas and probe further into cases where some aspects have not been discussed.

The variant on this activity, **Think-Pair-Share-Square,** provides the added step of having two partnerships join together after the first discussion to share ideas among the two sets or four students. This shifts the dynamic of both talking and listening and requires all students to be respectful and interactive.

**Book Club and Literature Circles** These small group interactions provide a good context for students to learn to explore ideas together around a single book they all are reading. For the group meetings to be productive, students need to be taught how to both share their ideas and listen to others. Some teachers have students write out questions they want to have shared in their groups; others may have students keep journals in which they respond to the stories and then raise issues for discussion when they come to the groups. Sometimes one student is designated as discussion leader and develops questions for the group to answer. No matter which structure is used, students still need to develop an understanding of what makes good discussion behavior. See the Engaging in Visual Literacy feature for another activity that promotes communication skills in a small group setting.

IRA/NCTE 12

## Establish Student Norms for Oral Engagement

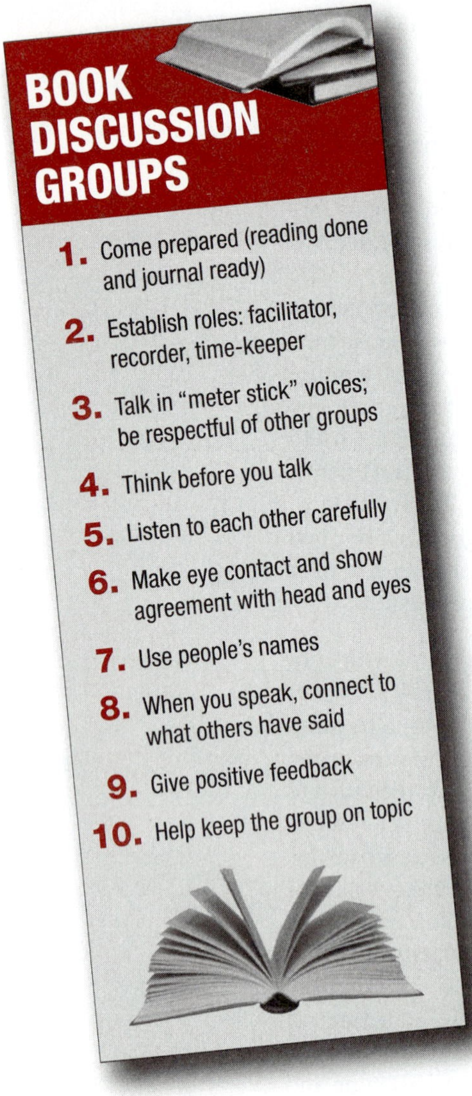


As teachers introduce students to particular oral discussion routines, students become more able to understand when their talk is productive. They can add to the chart on what good talk "Looks like, Sounds like, and Feels like" periodically during the year. With the foundation in asking students what they think makes for good partner and group work, next steps can be determined. One way to make these expectations clear to all students is to keep them written on large chart paper and visible in the classroom. When the group has established norms and expectations for participation they can also be put on a bookmark and inserted in students' notebooks or texts as constant reminders. That list of behaviors can also become the students' individual and group assessments. The bookmark shows an example of what one class developed as a guide for their book discussion groups.

With this kind of a guide developed for each group activity, students will all have a clearer idea of how they should behave and how they can improve their own and group members' talk and listening. Teachers can easily turn this guide into a checklist that the groups fill out. It can also become a framework to be used at the end of a class session when teachers want students to do a quick self-assessment. For example, the teacher may ask students as they complete their book discussion time to respond to questions such as:

- How was my participation today?
- What did my group do well?
- How could we do better when we meet again?

Primary teachers can also build children's discussion abilities in a variety of ways. A discussion of what group work is like is just as important for them as it is for older students. Then teachers can write the rules or guidelines on a piece of chart paper, using visual icons to indicate terms students may

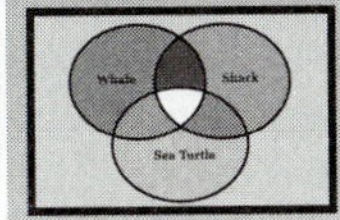

## Sketch to Stretch

Most students love to draw. In the **Sketch to Stretch** strategy (Short, Harste & Burke, 1996), students learn to listen to or read a text and create a single visual image that captures the essence of the story and that illustrates what the story means. Students work in small groups (usually four to five students) and, after creating a visual response to the reading, they gather to share their sketches. Each person takes a turn by showing his or her sketch to the others. The students study the sketch and take turns explaining to the group what they see in the drawing and what they believe the illustrator wants to express about the story. This sharing lets the illustrator hear what other students see in the visual image and provides a good way for all children to engage in exploratory talk. After everyone else has shared, the illustrator then explains what he or she was trying to illustrate. Sharing continues in this way until all group members have been able to share their sketches and get the group's responses. One way of bringing the small group activity to the whole class is to have each group select one sketch they want shared with the class. Either the same day or in a subsequent class period, these sketches can be shared on a visualizer or transparency so the whole class can view them and participate in interpreting the drawings. Sharing visual images provides a nonthreatening way for children to share ideas, participate in discussion, and learn how to express ideas in a new sign system (visual illustration) that may be easier than using words and language.

not know how to write. For example, a picture of an ear can signal that students should listen; a pair of eyes can indicate that looking at the speaker is important, etc.

## Exploring Ideas in Writing Workshop

As teachers build a writing workshop in their classrooms, it is also important to take stock of how well-prepared children are to discuss their and others' pieces of writing while in process. Children can be very cruel if they don't know how to preface suggestions by first "receiving" the piece that another child has worked on. Teachers may need to model a clear routine: begin by identifying something you like about the draft that is shared. Then think of one area that we have been working on (colorful words, elaboration, direct quotation, etc.) where you can highlight an example from the text. Finally, make one suggestion related to this area that might help the writer.

There are several ways teachers can help students structure their group time in writers' workshop. Just as in the other settings for exploratory talk, having clear guidelines and careful development of routines will make the time valuable. There are no more important words than, "I really like how you wrote . . ." and "That was interesting, can you tell me more?"

# Preparing Ideas to Share in Group Discussions

A key to good discussions is some thoughtful reflection before talking or sharing ideas. Students can develop the habit of thinking personally before they speak in several ways. Primary students can prepare for group discussions by drawing or writing ideas before a discussion begins. They don't have to be elaborate, but having a written visual note helps them hold onto their thoughts and be able to contribute when it comes to their turn.

In the intermediate grades, students can learn to keep a journal of their responses to the chapters they are reading that may include graphic organizers, plot lines, character grids, and drawings of ideas. These give them "texts" to contribute when a small group convenes. Some teachers ask students to respond to their reading by composing questions for the group discussion in preparation for meetings. In large group discussions, like the Great Books framework suggests, students take a few minutes to write their answers to the interpretive questions the leader poses before the oral discussion begins. This helps students frame their thinking and keep track of their ideas even when others may be sharing theirs first.

IRA/NCTE 6

At the upper grades, students can be asked to prepare a **Discussion Guide Think Sheet** (Alvermann, 1991). On the guide, students are given the discussion focus question and then have to find reasons to both support and disagree with the question. For example, a teacher might want to focus a large group discussion on the importance of the 19th Amendment to the U.S. Constitution that gives women the right to vote. The teacher frames the question: Do women in the United States consider the right to vote an essential right? The student think sheet then has two columns and students must include arguments and facts that support both sides of the question. To take part in the oral discussion, students must come to class with their Discussion Guide (see Figure 3.4) completed. The teacher can easily check the sheets to ensure that students have been thoughtful in their preparation. Then, at the end of the class discussion, students can add to and revise their original ideas and points of view.

**Keep Written Notes** Children often have a hard time holding onto their ideas during discussions. They want to blurt out ideas immediately as they think of them. A good habit to develop when they are engaged in a large group discussion is to write down any particular ideas that come to them during the discussion that they want to share rather than waving their hands frantically while others are speaking.

A good place to introduce this note-making strategy is during the **Directed Reading-Thinking Activity (DR-TA)** discussions (see Chapter 6 for a full description of this teaching strategy). Teachers ask students to predict what they think will happen in a story from the initial title, picture, genre, and author information. Then, as students read more of the text, the teacher again stops them to ask for confirmation of their original predictions and for evidence that supports those predictions or that causes them to modify or change the predictions. Often, as students get engaged in the story they have much they want to share. Giving them a few sticky notes or blank pieces of note paper can help them keep track of evidence they noted in the text or connections they can make to other ideas suggested by the text. This can help the Directed Reading-Thinking Activity process because students become more conscious of their ideas and can also listen to be connected with other students or to be sure that other students have not made similar contributions.

Figure 3.4

## Sample Discussion Guide

***Question: Do women in the U.S. consider the right to vote an essential right?***

| **Disagree** | **Agree** |
|---|---|
| 1. Fewer than 50% voted in the last election. | 1. They vote and they serve our country in many roles, civilian and military. |
| 2. There are almost no women in Congress. | 2. Some women on the political right think it is more important that they raise families than engage in politics. |
| 3. Most political leaders are men. | 3. Neither men nor women vote in as large numbers as should! |

Final point of view: ____________________

____________________

____________________

____________________

Name ____________________

# Learning to Ask Questions for Discussion

When using language to explore ideas, an essential beginning point is asking good questions. Many less secure students seem almost afraid to ask questions of ideas they are encountering in school. And, many teachers seem in such a rush to explain and tell students what they should learn that they forget that inquisitiveness is the foundation of learning. Teachers need to slow down, ask good questions themselves, and encourage students to frame questions of their own.

**Know, Want to Know, Learned** A good way to develop students' willingness to ask real questions is with the **KWL (Know; Want to Know; Learned)** framework (Ogle, 1986, 2008). See Figure 3.5 for an example of the graphic guide for KWL. A unit of study can be initiated by asking students what they already know about the topic. In the primary grades, this might be as a class starts to study about animals—penguins, dinosaurs, or pond critters. In upper grades, teachers may begin any number of units for which teachers think the students have a moderate, but not extensive, background. The discussion time is particularly important if there are some students for whom the topic is not well known; they can gain from hearing other children share what they know and can learn to use terms that may not be familiar. The teacher initiates the process by explaining that the first step in this large group activity is for the students to **brainstorm** what they think they know. In brainstorming, everyone is to just share what comes to the top of their heads—being right isn't the point, but the purpose is to

**Figure 3-5**

## K-W-L Guide

| 1. K–What We Know | W–What We Want to Learn | L–What We Learned and Still Need to Know |
|---|---|---|
| | | |

| 2. Categories of Information We Expect to Use: | | 3. Where We Will Find Information: |
|---|---|---|
| A. | E. | 1. |
| B. | F. | 2. |
| C. | G. | 3. |
| D. | H. | 4. |

*Source:* Ogle, Donna M. "K-W-L: A Teaching Model That Develops Active Reading of Expository Text," *The Reading Teacher* (© 1986), 39(6), pp. 564–570. Reprinted by permission of the International Reading Association.

share associations and quick thoughts. No ideas are considered wrong or unworthy—what is wanted is immediate associations.

After the initial brainstorming and shared talk, students are then guided to think about the major categories of information they might expect to be included in what they will study. For example, if the class is going to study the desert region of the United States, then they might expect to learn about the physical features of a desert, what animals live there, what plants grow in the desert, and how people live in that environment.

The teacher writes all the ideas the students generate on the board or on large sheets of paper so they can be saved and referenced later. By writing them down for the students, no one has to worry about whether they can spell the words before sharing ideas. It also speeds up the process because students are often quite slow in their writing. (They can create their own KWL records in their notebooks later.)

When the teacher has elicited a good range of ideas and some categories, the students and teacher can organize the ideas into categories. This process helps the group assess where they have the most knowledge; it also leads into their asking questions. For example, if there have been several different animals included in the brainstormed list but no information about how people live on the desert, this becomes a good point for the teacher to suggest that the class frame a few questions about people: students may suggest, "How long have people lived on the deserts in the United States? Where do they get their water? What cities or towns are in desert areas? Do the desert animals hurt people?"

The group process permits the teacher to model the construction of questions that come out of a prior thoughtful process of accessing what is known. The teacher can use this as a time to explain that good questions arise after we reflect on what we know and what is likely to be important in a unit of study. If students have trouble generating questions at first, showing some photographs or reading a text about a desert can stimulate their deeper response to the unit ideas.

**Sorting Pre-Generated Questions** Sorting questions is also a good initial activity. The teacher may prepare 8–10 questions and ask students in small groups to decide which of the questions they most want to study about. This could be a time to introduce the idea of "**thick and thin questions**"—those that don't take one very far (thin) and those that are really meaty and for which lots of ideas can be generated (thick). See the example of this activity of identifying questions in Figure 3.6.

Some teachers have also used question sets to help students think about stories they are reading. When children need help asking questions, cards can be a good support. Some general questions that can be put on cards for student use include:

- What is the main problem the characters have to solve?
- What do you think the characters can do to solve the problem?
- What has the author told about the characters to give an idea of their personal strengths and ways of solving problems?
- How does the setting affect this story?
- What is the author trying to do—entertain us, teach us a lesson, or recall some experience?

**Figure 3.6**

### Sorting Activity: Thick or Thin Questions

Sort these questions into two piles: Thin, or easily answered, questions and Thick, or meaty, questions that will lead to broader learning.

1. What is the average temperature on the Sonora desert?
2. What happens to animals when there is no rain or river water?
3. How often do desert animals have to drink?
4. Where do desert animals get their food?
5. Were there ever camels on American deserts?
6. Who named the Sonora desert? Why that name?
7. How can desert areas be useful?
8. Why do people move to desert cities?
9. Why do scorpions sting?
10. What cities are built on desert land?

Figure 3.7

**PRC2 Question Starters**

| | |
|---|---|
| What was most important? | What was most interesting? |
| What connection can you make to these ideas? | How could the author have made this section clearer? |

**PRC2 Partner Reading Process** Students can learn to ask good questions while reading and discussing texts with partners. Teachers who use the PRC2 process with their students have noted that some children have trouble writing their own questions and may require an extended amount of time to construct questions. Therefore, teachers have developed a scaffold for students using the PRC2 partner reading process. They have a guide sheet with four basic questions on it (see Figure 3.7). Students can use one of these questions or make a modification to fit their own text. This support has helped students think of general types of questions and feel more confident in their probes of their partners. Not all students need this support, but having it as a bridge for students who need some modeling and support can be useful. See the Exploring Diversity feature for additional information on providing modeling and support for students who are English language learners.

## How Can You Help Students Gain Confidence in Speaking?

Many of us remember being afraid to speak before a group of people, and many of us still may not enjoy having to address groups. There is a great deal teachers can do to help students gain confidence in making oral presentations, from the most informal to formal talks.

### Poetry

A great way to involve children in speaking is by having them memorize and recite poetry. From nursery rhymes, Dr. Seuss, and Shel Silverstein and all the way to Shakespeare, learning and performing poetry can be enjoyable—and valuable at the same time. A very easy and natural starting place is for children to learn to recite poetry together. When the poetry is combined with movements, children take great pleasure in participating orally and kinesthetically; it gets them up in front of others in the class and helps them relax. Teachers can develop hand signals to indicate different aspects of a poem so students can perform both orally and kinesthetically.

There are great collections of poems by J. Prelutsky (1977), Shel Silverstein, May Arbuthnot, and many others. Autobiographical poetry such as Gary Soto's *A Fire in My*

## exploring diversity

### Working with Students Who Are English Language Learners

Second language learners often feel uncomfortable speaking in large group settings while they are still gaining control over English. This is particularly true when the class is engaged in content-area discussions. These students deserve support in learning how to participate in talk about content material they are learning. One approach we have found useful in developing the PRC2 framework is to make explicit to students several ways they can respond and extend talk with their partner. The key responses students can make are listed on a bookmark for them to use during their partner reading sessions. It is good to model a partner discussion using these starters. Let students hear other partners discuss; it may be useful to have a second teacher join you to model exchanges. If there are some student partners who easily discuss their texts, ask them to model for the rest of the class. It is also possible to audiotape a discussion between two partners and listen to their talk; sometimes, following a good demonstration, let students hear one not well executed and ask them how it could be improved.

Giving students a transcript of a segment of partner talk is yet one more way to help children develop an internal expectation of what they can sound like talking together around content ideas.

If there are some students from other cultures in the classroom, it may be possible to get them to compare and contrast the expectations for partner reading that the class has established with ways of engaging in other cultures. For example, K. Au has identified a shared-group construction pattern in Hawaiian society; no one person answers a question but answers emerge as children add to one another's contributions. In some other contexts, older children have precedence over younger and each knows their time to contribute to exchanges. Yet, in other cultures students are never expected or given time to talk in class; the idea of listening to other students is foreign and their ideas would never have been solicited. For students from these cultures, building a sense of how talking and listening can enhance learning may take time to develop.

*Hands* (1990), seasonal poetry, and even content-related poetry can enliven some of the content units of study.

Poetry memorization and sharing poetry has the added benefit of giving language learners an opportunity to hear and learn some standard English patterns of subject-verb agreement and to use a more elaborated vocabulary than they would in general conversation. Teachers may target particular poems that can achieve more than one objective. For example, in the poem "There was an old woman who swallowed a fly," students repeat over and over the standard past tense ("There *was* an old woman") and the future verb "I think she'll die." Memorizing these forms can then help students use them more easily in their speaking and writing.

## Choral Reading

This is another nonthreatening way to help children gain confidence speaking. In **choral reading,** much like reader's theater, students read together from a poem or song

Students' oral communication skills are enhanced through reader's theater because students need to speak clearly, enunciate so listeners can understand, and provide the subtleties of oral language that enhance communication.

or story. They may memorize the lines or use a printed sheet to read from. The key is that the text is rehearsed and performed in an engaging way. Students may have parts so the reading is broken up with different voices; some text is read by individuals and other parts are delivered by the whole group.

## Reader's Theater

**Reader's theater** is the oral performance of a script done with the "actors" reading directly from the text while seated or standing before the audience (Black & Stave, 2007). This fairly simple structure permits students to develop an interpretation of a script together without having to act out the parts. The performers create an interpretation through their voices, pacing, and some minimal props, such as wearing a hat, scarf, or piece of clothing that might suggest the context or setting. Because the script is followed carefully, students can be more confident in participating in the joint construction of a meaningful production.

Recently reader's theater has become more popular and there are many scripts available in children's magazines, online, and in printed collections. Teachers can also create their own scripts from children's literature and poetry. This takes more time, but can be a very personalized way to engage students in pursuing more deeply some particular class theme or project. Students' oral communication skills are enhanced through reader's theater because students need to speak clearly, enunciate so listeners can understand, and provide the subtleties of oral language that enhance communication. See the Exploring Technology feature for resources to support the use of reader's theater, poetry, and drama.

## Drama

More physically involving, teachers also can develop students' oral communication through **drama.** An easy starting place for drama is mime and the creation of tableaus. In these forms students don't have to speak but use their bodies to communicate. You can begin by helping students develop a visual representation of some scene in a story they have just read. Tell them you are going to create a scene from the book. Begin:

> Who should be in the scene?
>
> Where did the story take place or this scene occur and how can that location be shown?
>
> What were they doing?
>
> How can the feeling be communicated?

Then, members of the class plan together how to construct a scene that illustrates what the author created with words.

## exploring technology

### Supporting Reader's Theater, Poetry, and Drama

**Aaron Shepard's Reader's Theater Resources (www.aaronshep.com/rt/index.html)**
This comprehensive site created by reader's theater expert Aaron Shepard is an invaluable resource with directions on how to conduct reader's theater, tips, scripts, and links to online resources.

**Scaffolding Oral Language Development through Poetry (www.readwritethink.org/lessons/lesson_view.asp?id=69)**
In this lesson from ReadWriteThink, students work in small groups to develop a choral reading of two poems about an assigned insect. The poems serve as an introduction to a research investigation about the insect. Students compile factual information about the insect and present it, along with their choral poetry readings, to the class.

**Reading In Motion (www.readinginmotion.org/)**
Reading In Motion lesson plans allow children to get out from behind their desks and use their entire bodies and minds to master reading skills. These engaging activities are carefully tailored to the grade and developmental level of the students.

In some schools, teachers use mime to help students monitor their comprehension and imaging. After a certain portion of a text is read, the teacher asks the students to stand and take the posture of the main character or the antagonist. If there are more characters, students might work in groups to show the ways the characters are aligned in the text portion just read. Getting students involved kinesthetically helps develop both good listening and interpretation and increases the likelihood that they will deepen their mental engagement over time. See the Exploring Technology feature for the Reading in Motion website, which contains many valuable ideas on kinesthetic learning.

## How Can Students Learn to Use Language to Inform Others?

One of the important oral language activities in academic settings is communicating what one knows. It begins when students answer teacher questions and continues in the upper grades where students prepare and share formal oral reports. Again, it may be useful to think of one or two routines that you want to ensure all students know so they can gain confidence in sharing information. Some frequently used activities are listed in Table 3.2.

**Table 3.2**
**Activities to Practice Sharing Information**

| Partner | Small Group | Large Group |
|---|---|---|
| ReQuest | Book Club/Literature Discussion | Morning Message/carpet time |
| PRC2 | Question the Author | Sharing Amazing Facts |
| | Reciprocal Teaching | Presentations of inquiry and research KWL |

## Sharing Information in the Primary Grades

The ability to share information in an interesting way for an audience can be developed in comfortable classroom activities like "Carpet Time" or by composing a "Morning Message." Most children love to share what they know and are doing. Creating ways to make this productive for everyone is the key. Students who are shy or don't feel confident in their English can be encouraged to share in other ways, by bringing in artifacts or photographs or by creating pictures of events and special news. Many kindergarten and first-grade teachers use the morning gathering of students as a time to develop both speaking and listening. They ask, "What did we do yesterday? What is on our schedule for today? What makes today special?" Then the teacher honors what students contribute by writing their ideas on the large chart paper or the white board. For example, a first-grade class composed this message:

> *Yesterday we began the book Amazing Grace. We love it and know the teacher will finish it today. We are also going to see a video of Peter Pan. Michelle is missing today because she has to be at the dentist office. She will get a new tooth.*

With several questions, teachers help children think about the current events of the classroom and school and make connections to other special events. It is also a good practice to bring the class together at the end of the school day to write a class journal summarizing the events of the day and recalling interesting things that have been learned. One teacher who has developed this practice notes that parents are always pleased that when they ask their children what they did in school that day, they have answers. This is because the teacher has helped them reflect on the day and put the class activities into language that children can then share with their families. This is the beginning of helping children use more school-based language to communicate information.

**Reporting and Sharing Orally** As students continue through elementary school, they can be asked to share more extensively. Primary teachers who organize units of study can develop short **Amazing Fact Sheets** (McKee and Ogle, 2006) students can

**Figure 3.8**

**Amazing Fact Sheet**

Name ______________________________

Book ______________________________ pp. __________

Author ______________________________

An amazing fact I found is that ______________________________

use to fill out information they gain from their reading (see Figure 3.8 for an example). These are placed in a bin, and, periodically, the teacher calls the group together and asks students to share what they have learned using their Amazing Fact sheets. This activity helps children develop confidence in sharing with others.

## Sharing Information in the Intermediate and Upper Grades

In the intermediate and upper grades, students need to have time to talk about content they are learning. Yet, they are seldom given many opportunities to try out their own use of academic concepts and vocabulary.

**Partner Reading and Content, Too (PRC2)** For second language learners and students who need more time to internalize new concepts, PRC2 can provide a needed support. As teachers initiate a new science or social studies unit, they collect small trade books (publishers like National Geographic, Rosen, Benchmark, etc.) on a variety of reading levels on the topic being studied. Then the teacher matches students so two partners who are reading at about the same level and are compatible can share a book. Students learn to read orally to each other and then talk about the text ideas together in this structured routine. The sheet that is given to students to help them learn the steps in PRC2 is shown in Figure 3.9. The steps for reading and responding help students learn to speak orally as they explore both graphic, visual information and then respond to their partner's questions after reading. Specifically, students learn to:

1. Sit side by side so they can use the same book. They begin by previewing the book together, talking with each other about text features (titles, italics, headings) and talking about the graphic displays (pictures, charts, maps, cartoons, etc.).
2. Students read and talk about each *two-page spread* in a regular cycle. First, both read the two pages silently, then each rereads and practices the one page on their side of the book and selects a question from four stems given them (What is most important; what is most interesting; what connections can we make to this; what could the author have done to make this clearer for us to understand?). They each select a question and write it on the PRC2 question sheet (see Figure 3.7).

Figure 3.9

## PRC2 Guide Sheet

### Getting Ready to Read Together

Choose a book together.

Find a place where you can sit next to each other.

Come prepared with your Vocabulary Notebooks, *PRC2 Questions* sheet, and pencils.

### Previewing

Look at the cover and title, and ask each other, **"What do we think this book is about?"**

Look for a table of contents, and ask, **"How is this organized?"**

Look through the book together, and ask, **"Does the book have...?"**

- **Chapters**
- **Headings**
- **Pictures**
- **Special marked vocabulary**
- **Diagrams**
- **Maps**
- **Charts**
- **Index and glossary**

Talk about these features.

### Reading the Text Together

- Take turns reading the pages of this book by first deciding who will read page one, and who will read page two aloud.
- Both read the first two pages silently thinking about what they mean. If there are some words you don't know how to say, ask your partner. If your partner doesn't know, raise your hand and ask the teacher or use the glossary.
- Silently reread the page that you will read aloud thinking of good expression and pace.
- Choose one of the four questions on the *PRC2 Questions* you want to ask your partner.
- The first person reads his/her page aloud, while the other partner listens and thinks about the ideas.
- The reader asks the listener the question he/she chose for that page. The listener explains what he/she thinks. The partners talk about ideas and any questions they have.
- Then partner 2 takes a turn, reads page two aloud to the partner. The listener thinks about the ideas.
- The reader asks the listener the question he/she chose for that page. The listener explains what he/she thinks. The partners talk about ideas and any questions they have.
- Continue taking turns until finished.
- Fill out our *WOW! Informational Log.*

### Thinking and Talking About the Text

After reading the pages, share what you liked and learned about the text.

Attend to the vocabulary you wrote down on the *PRC2 Questions* sheet.

Together fill out *PRC2: Read and Recommend* sheet.

**Ask yourselves...**

Are there words we want to remember?

*If so, write them in the Vocabulary Notebooks.*

Do we have more questions? Do we want to read another book on this same topic?

Do we want to share any interesting information or thoughts with the class?

3. Students take turns reading their page orally to their partner and then asking the partner the question they selected. The two partners then talk about their responses to the question before starting the next page.
4. Students can use the discussion guide stems on the question guide sheet to help them engage productively and learn an academic discourse routine. This guide gives students specific suggestions for their talk together. See the Exploring Diversity feature for more elaboration on this support.
5. This routine continues for twenty minutes. At the end of the time, students reflect on what they have learned and each identifies two or three key academic terms they want to add to their vocabulary notebook section.
6. When they finish the entire book, they each write their reflection on what they liked about the book and learned from it.

**Inquiry Projects and Presentations** The practice of sharing what is learned from books and investigations also leads into more extended oral reports that students in fourth, fifth, or sixth grade can be expected to present. The TREE (Technology-Rich Educational Environment) team at Pleasant Ridge School in Glenview, Illinois, develops fourth- and fifth-grade students' oral communication skills as part of their extended inquiry/research projects which are done three times each year. Part of the culmination of their project work is making a formal presentation of what they have learned to their classmates, the younger third-grade classes, parents, and community members. Students know their topics well because they do the research, develop a PowerPoint presentation, and create a trifold, stand up visual display on their topic. In preparing for the final, oral presentations the teachers help develop students' oral skills by having them think of three major parts of their talks: (1) the talk begins with a good "hook" to invite listeners to attend; then, (2) the content portion is developed, which is accompanied with PowerPoint slides; and finally (3) it concludes with a strong closing.

IRA/NCTE 11

Elementary school students such as those at Pleasant Ridge School enjoy creating PowerPoint presentations to complement their oral reporting. At first, children may want to include every new technique they learn in their presentations. It is good to provide enough time to learn about using the PowerPoint options well before the students actually transfer their own learning onto this visual tool.

Preparing students to make these more formal presentations is important. They need to feel comfortable speaking to an audience, so their depth of knowledge and their practice in making presentations are both important. So, too, the teachers have found it very helpful to include the third grade children as part of the audience watching the older students give reports. The teachers at Pleasant Ridge School know that when children in the third grade listen to and see the visual results of the research projects done by the fourth- and fifth-graders, they are much more prepared to engage in doing oral presentations about their projects the next two years.

The TREE team at Pleasant Ridge School in Glenview, IL, develops fourth- and fifth-grade students' oral communication skills as part of their extended inquiry projects. Part of the culmination of their project work is making a formal presentation of what they have learned to their classmates, the younger third-grade classes, parents, and community members.

The more students can be part of classrooms and schools in which attention is paid to oral presentation skills, the better they will become. They can then evaluate what makes some of the speakers more effective and make a list for their own presentations. Teachers who keep videotapes of other class presentations can share some snips with the class to stimulate the same kind of reflection on what makes a talk worth listening to. Children can articulate a good list of guidelines that includes:

- Speak loud enough for everyone to hear.
- Make good eye contact.
- Give listeners an overview of your talk. (Create a "hook" to interest listeners and explain what you have done and what you will share.)
- Pronounce words clearly and correctly.
- Change speed and volume so you aren't boring.
- Use visual supports.
- Use gestures—your hands can help make points.
- Develop a conclusion.
- Thank the audience for participating.

## In What Ways Can You Develop Students' Ability to Listen?

Equally important with speaking is listening because oral discourse depends on the ability of communicators to be aware of and respond to each other. Teachers, as well as students, need to be active listeners. Pause for a moment and think of your ability to listen. How can you describe your own listening? What strategies or techniques do you use when you need to listen carefully, when the stakes are high for your listening?

Some people can describe particular strategies they use: look the speaker right in the eye if it is a personal situation; take notes and create a visual map of what the speaker is saying if it is in a large group meeting; make a formal outline of ideas if there is a formal speaking situation. A starting place is to repeat the gist of what a speaker has just communicated before moving on to share your own ideas. For example, "I just heard Camille say that she only liked the first part of the movie because it really confirmed the images she had in her own head when she was reading; after that the movie didn't seem to capture the book. Is that right?" There are many other ways to develop good listening skills, and it is worth making a list of those you may suggest to your students.

There are many ways to develop students' listening abilities in the normal instructional program. Table 3.3 can be used to help plan for maximizing learning opportunities. As you read this text and take part in classroom activities, add to the list and think of which students may need more time in each setting—partner, small group, or large group. It may be that the students who most need to learn to listen need more modeling and guidance from the teacher and so the large group settings may be more of a starting place than partner work.

## Table 3.3
## Activities to Develop Listening Skills

| Partner Activities | Small Group Activities | Large Group Activities |
|---|---|---|
| Think-Pair-Share<br>Retelling a story<br>Listening for partner to answer the question (PRC2)<br>Reading aloud sharing the text with a partner | Writing workshop: Listen to student in the Writer's Chair<br>Sketch to Stretch response<br>Book Club/Literature Circle discussion<br>Discussion Web sharing<br>Listening center | Directed Listening-Thinking Activity (DL-TA)<br>All group responses, i.e., "Thumbs up/thumbs down"<br>Teacher read-aloud<br>Student reports<br>Audience for Reader's Theater and other dramatic productions |

## Teacher Read-Alouds

Students need regular opportunities to develop good listening behaviors. A natural context to share ideas with your students is when you engage them by **reading aloud;** at every grade level, students can gain by having interesting and well-written texts read orally to them. We suggest you build a list of materials you can read to your students and then find good times during the day when students can be actively engaged as listeners.

Read aloud two to three different times a day at least! Read from different types of texts—fiction, nonfiction informational pieces from newspapers, magazines, and good trade books, literary nonfiction like biography and autobiography, poetry and word play, cartoons, jokes, etc. Establish ways students can respond to these oral listening opportunities and discuss not only the content of what you read, but also the strategies students should use to be good listeners. Then check their listening by having them respond when you stop periodically (in some texts) or make predictions or make connections. At times, ask students to draw their understanding or write a quick-write response after you are finished. Some teachers build in student responses during their pauses while reading aloud. They may ask students to use the "Thumbs Up; Thumbs Down" to indicate if they think a character is going to continue with some behavior. There are any number of ways the teacher can ask students for their responses to aspects of the story or article they are reading. Teachers can also use colored cards with "*Agree*" or "*Disagree*" on them or "*Yes*" and "*No*" to give students ways to all respond as they listen to the teacher doing a read aloud. By encouraging all students' responses, teachers can establish the importance of active, engaged listening. The same activity can be used when students read orally to each other. The expectation is that others listen and respond appropriately when asked.

## Ideas for Reading Aloud

You can read predictable pattern books to younger students; it stimulates them to listen carefully and predict subsequent events in stories. Books with familiar sequences of numbers, days, months, events help students engage and anticipate what they are hearing as you read. A long-time favorite pattern poem is "I knew an old woman who swallowed a fly" with its refrain, "Oh, my, I think she'll die!"(Hawkins and Hawkins, 1987). Another good book to read aloud is *Is Your Mama a Llama?* (Guarino, 1989).

As you read predictable poetry and books, you can omit words and repeated phrases so students participate in the oral reading. This helps ensure that they listen carefully to the exact words and sequence.

With older students, continue reading aloud. Two good ways to increase their active listening are to ask them to draw and illustrate as you read orally. At the end of a few minutes of reading, pause and ask students to share their visual images coming from what they heard. A Pair–Share is a good way to help students make their own listening and imagining public; it is also a good way to help them understand how differently individuals respond to the same text experiences.

Another activity to increase students' listening during reading aloud is to pause periodically and ask one or two students to predict where they think the story or article is heading. If students are not good at listening actively, then you could use the occasion to suggest they make notes on a scratch paper as you are reading orally to see if they could identify some key words or images that would summarize the ideas they were hearing. This is a good way to begin the practice of listening that students will need for note taking in the later elementary and middle grades. The sooner students develop the habit of listening and summarizing ideas at the same time the better they will be throughout life; both in school and in adult life good listening is critical. See the Engaging in Assessment feature for information on how to analyze students' listening.

## Directed Listening-Thinking Activity (DL-TA)

Russell Stauffer (1969) developed the basic Directed Reading-Thinking Activity as a way to model for young readers the active problem-solving nature of reading. This activity can also be introduced as a group listening Directed Listening-Thinking Activity (DL-TA) when the teacher reads the text to the students rather than having them do the reading individually. It is well suited to helping students develop good listening skills and provides the teacher a way to monitor how well students attend to important information in stories.

Teachers prepare for a DL-TA by reading the story and determining some key stopping points just after the author has introduced new information or raised issues that active readers need to consider as they build a meaning for the text. At each point, the teacher encourages students to predict what they think will happen in the rest of the story and why. When one is new to using this activity, it is good to mark stopping points and also make a note of the information the author provided in the preceding section—information that students should use in responding when the teacher asks students to predict or confirm earlier predictions. If students overlook important information, the teacher makes note of it and can return later to have students think again about the story. The teacher may also want to reread the section explaining to students that they need to be better detectives, better listeners.

## *engaging in* Assessment

### Analyzing Students' Listening

There are many informal ways a teacher can monitor how students are listening. We suggest monitoring listening in both small and large group activities. By making a chart with all students' names and listing the activities in which you are observing them, you have a matrix that you can use periodically to focus on listening.

For students who seem to miss a great deal orally, more individual assessments can be done. One simple individual assessment involves reading a short selection to a student and having the student summarize the text. Begin by explaining the task, so the student understands you want to check to see how well they listen to stories or materials read to them. Also, explain that after you read the selection to them, you want them to remember as much as they can of the text and retell it to you. The easiest way for the teacher to keep a record of students' responses is to copy the selection and check off or underline ideas the student contributes. If the student omits major portions, you can ask probing questions to find out whether they recall but just did not mention the portion.

The teacher also establishes the participation rules and writes them on a chart, so all students can see what is expected. These include:

- Listen carefully to the text as it is read.
- Listen to each other as you make predictions.
- Don't repeat the same prediction someone else has made; you can say, "I agree with _______'s prediction.
- Raise your hand to speak.
- Connect your ideas with those of others in the group.
- If you want to share something and aren't called on, write down your ideas or make a picture of what you want to share.

The teacher shows the cover, the title, and any picture and asks students to predict what they think the story may be about. This is brief because there is little information provided yet. Then after reading the first short section of the story, the teacher can elicit a better idea of the students' listening and thinking by asking students: What do you predict, or think is going to happen, in this story? Why do you think that? Three to four different ideas should be elicited. Then the teacher asks students to think for a moment and then vote on which idea they think is most likely. "Everyone who thinks _______ will happen raise your hands. Those who think _______ will happen raise your hands. Those who agree with the prediction that _______ will happen raise your hands." After all the students have made commitments to one or another of the predictions, the teacher says, "Good thinking, now let's hear more of the story," and continues reading.

This cycle of predicting, confirming, and revising predictions is continued three to four times in the story. The teacher constantly attends to how well students use the information provided by the author in confirming, revising, and making new predictions.

The DL-TA is a powerful way for teachers to monitor students' active listening and thinking. It works best when there are only eight to twelve students in the group so the teacher can monitor students' engagement and use of textual evidence. Keeping a chart with all children's names and spaces to write their contributions permits the teacher to return to assess the activity more fully later. With some practice, teachers can also chart the flow of talk and how students listen to each other and build on the group contributions.

## Large Group Discussions

IRA/NCTE 4

One of the most challenging settings for students and teachers is the whole class discussion. Too often, teachers use most of this time doing the talking (over 75 percent of class talk is teacher talk). When teachers do ask students questions, the majority fall into the category of literal questions with single right answers rather than the kinds of questions that encourage the sharing of perspectives and exploration of ideas. To move away from that standard initiation–response–evaluation (IRE) cycle of interrogating children to find out if they understand the basic information, careful attention to selecting good questions for discussion is necessary.

The first step is thinking ahead to select some good discussable questions. Then it is also important to develop some structure so all students can participate and focus on improving their listening. One important way to develop better discussions is to ask a question and then give students time to think-pair-share before responding. Some teachers keep a jar with tongue depressors with each student's name on one. When it is time to call on students to share ideas, the teacher can randomly select names and then not put the name back in the jar until all other students have had a turn. As a way to create more active listening, periodically the teacher stops the discussion and asks students to write:

- What ideas have you heard that you think are important?
- Whose ideas do you agree with and why?
- Who gave good evidence or support for their ideas?
- Who else would you like to hear from on this topic?

It is also good periodically to have students draw or illustrate what they think are the important points in what they have just heard. Some teachers ask students to fold blank sheets of paper in fourths. Then, when they stop during either reading to students or during a talk or discussion, students are asked to draw or list key ideas they have just heard. By having four stopping points, students keep a more active stance in large group settings. A regular reminder that listening leads to some production can be very motivating and instill a good habit in your students.

## revisit the classroom challenge

In the opening Classroom Challenge, we met Ms. Fotopoulos who was aware that her students weren't exhibiting good oral communication skills. The following questions were posed:

1. What do you know about evaluating students' oral language and social skills?
2. What skills in communicating with other students do you expect your students to possess?
3. What can you do to improve students' social communication?
4. How important is it to focus on developing common speaking and listening patterns and behaviors?

Ms. Fotopoulos considered several options. She began with an informal assessment of her students' behaviors and contrasted them with the kinds of oral communication skills she knew are needed to participate in book discussion groups. This led her to more conscious attention to students who seemed able to listen actively, respond to others' ideas, and also make useful contributions extending ideas or raising good questions. She then engaged the students in a discussion and listing of what good participants do. She found that with her guidance, the class could list some of the skills needed. She had to model with another teacher some of the basic behaviors, such as making eye contact, giving nonverbal feedback, and repeating and connecting to other members' ideas. With the list before them and some examples from the modeling to guide them, her students began to exhibit better listening and speaking behaviors. However, Ms. Fotopoulos also decided to develop a rubric for the groups that included the key behaviors they worked on: listening politely and actively, making eye contact, connecting to others' ideas, and giving everyone in the group a turn. This helped all her students to be more self-aware of what was expected in their groups, and raised their awareness level of their own behavior when the group discussed scoring their sessions with the rubric. Over the weeks as she watched the groups in action, Ms. Fotopoulos was pleased, yet she knew she would have to keep students focused on these important skills. She wanted her students to be both confident and competent in participating in group oral activities.

## chapter review

This chapter has provided a framework for teachers such as Ms. Fotopoulos to use in assessing her students' range of oral language skills and helping her students become more productive when they engage in oral language activities in the classroom. Talking and listening are essential language activities that deserve teacher attention because young students don't come with them well developed. Teachers need to focus attention on several areas of speaking and listening because students need to use language in social settings; in exploratory talk as they ask questions, make predictions, engage in inquiry, and solve problems; and in reporting on ideas and the results of inquiry and research.

### How Do State and National Standards Inform Oral Language Instruction?

State and national standards include the development of a range of oral competencies and expect students to be able to be aware of how language needs to be adjusted to the context and purpose. Respect for diverse ways of using language and expressing ideas is also a goal for elementary students, particularly as our students may come from a variety of different cultures. Knowing that oral communication conventions vary by culture is basic to developing sensitivity to how to communicate and realizing that options exist for adjusting communication to respect others. Teachers and students can learn to be sensitive to the difficulty of learning to communicate by prioritizing the study of oral language. National and state standards all can be useful in thinking about and planning for oral language activities. For English language learners both the WIDA proficiency standards and the SIOP model are helpful in guiding teachers to develop both content and language objectives for all lessons. This allows you to reflect as you plan each lesson to take into account the levels of language needed for students to be successful and also to plan activities to support and scaffold students' language development.

## How Can Social Interaction and Communication Be Developed?

Teachers are students' most available model of adult language users and can do a great deal to provide both examples of and develop ways to talk and think about good oral communication. An important starting point for developing students' oral communication is for teachers to be self-conscious in how we model communication with students and other adults in school. There are so many opportunities to help students learn the social skills they need, if only we slow down and realize that many students need to have these modeled and also explained directly. Teachers can create roles for students to take as greeters, guides to new class members, and hosts for visitors. They can also create contexts in which students can learn to communicate in standard ways for a variety of different purposes.

The use of the SIOP framework, especially identifying language objectives for all lessons, will help teachers to seriously address the language needs of students and be more conscious of building support for language into the life of the classroom. Teachers who use a set of benchmarks for their grade level can target areas of greatest need and provide settings for students to build their oral skills while learning content. Each teacher can make a list of activities that can stimulate speaking and listening as students work with partners, in small groups, and in large group settings.

Because it takes some self-reflection to improve speaking and listening, it is helpful to develop some common routines and patterns of interaction. Students then can know what is expected in each setting and can become more comfortable participating without fear.

## How Can You Develop Exploratory Uses of Language?

There are many ways teachers can develop students' use of language to explore ideas. Making a chart of the different ways partner, small group, and large group activities can build language facility helps teachers maximize the opportunities classroom content activities provide. Rather than just assume that students will know how to participate in book discussions or writing workshop small group activities, you can model, provide written guidelines, and help students reflect on their own participation in each context. Several specific group strategies work well in helping students use their own language to explore ideas: these include Say Something, Sketch to Stretch, PRC2, Book Discussions, Discussion Guides, and DR-TA. Asking good questions can be stimulated through KWL activities and developing students' awareness of the differences in questions as discussion starters.

## How Can You Help Students Gain Confidence in Speaking?

Many students are hesitant to speak up in groups. Teachers can do a lot to help them gain confidence by engaging them in group activities such as poetry reading, choral reading, reader's theater, and informal drama. When children feel comfortable expressing ideas in front of others, it is easier for them to move to the level of sharing their own ideas and questions. Partner and small group activities are often an easy starting place so students can test out their ideas before sharing them with the whole class.

## How Can Students Learn to Use Language to Inform Others?

Primary grade teachers begin developing students' ability to use oral language to inform others when they gather children together on the carpet to plan the day's activities or create a Morning Message—sharing news and setting the agenda for the day. As children engage in class explorations in social studies and science, they can learn to record ideas on Amazing Fact sheets to be shared when the class convenes to share their learning. Many teachers use a Current Events Time to involve children in sharing what is happening in the school, community, and world. When older children learn to engage in extended inquiry projects or research, it is important that they also learn the skills of presenting their findings orally. Teachers can give good guidelines on what is important in presenting informational reports, model for students, and provide examples of what other students have been able to do—either by doing cross-class sharing or by keeping videotaped samples students can watch later.

## In What Ways Can You Develop Students' Ability to Listen?

Students can become much more active and attentive listeners with guidelines and support from teachers. One of the easiest ways to check students' listening is to engage in some oral reading and then ask for students' responses—either by repeating patterned phrases or predicting coming events in the text they are hearing. When teachers can incorporate all student responses, such as "Thumbs Up; Thumbs Down" or by holding up Agree or Disagree cards, student attentiveness is enhanced. The Directed Listening–Thinking Activity is another powerful way to help students focus on active listening. These all lead students to more productive participation in group activities and discussions.



PEARSON
**myeducationlab**™
Where the Classroom Comes to Life

Now go to www.myeducationlab.com to take a Pretest to assess your initial comprehension of chapter content, study chapter content with your individualized Study Plan, take a Posttest to assess your understanding of chapter content, practice your teaching skills with Building Teaching Skills exercises, and build a deeper, more applied understanding of chapter content with Homework and Exercises.

chapter 4

# Supporting Diverse Learners

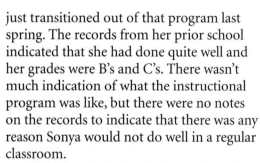

## classroom challenge

**Mrs. Jones,** a sixth-grade teacher, sat at her desk after her students had gone. She was troubled that she still hadn't been able to get Sonya to participate in the class literature discussion. What else could she do? She had tried so many ways to encourage Sonya to talk and take part in discussions. She knew that oral language was important and that for Sonya to develop her English she would have to start using language.

Mrs. Jones thought back about all she knew of Sonya—who had entered the class in October after the routines had already been established and students had formed good working relationships. She knew that might affect Sonya's confidence in jumping into classroom activities. She also knew that Sonya had begun school in another district in a bilingual classroom and had just transitioned out of that program last spring. The records from her prior school indicated that she had done quite well and her grades were B's and C's. There wasn't much indication of what the instructional program was like, but there were no notes on the records to indicate that there was any reason Sonya would not do well in a regular classroom.

Mrs. Jones had checked Sonya's reading ability with a silent reading test the district reading program provided. On that measure her reading comprehension put her just below the grade level and so Mrs. Jones had been careful to place her in a guided reading group that had fifth-grade level material. In the guided reading group, she didn't respond unless called on but would often answer with brief, but generally appropriate

responses. It seemed that Sonya did comprehend the materials the group read. However, Mrs. Jones thought that at times some of the vocabulary seemed to be an issue in limiting Sonya's responses. She also had made note that when they read informational selections, Sonya didn't seem as secure. Probably the vocabulary in those texts was part of the issue for her.

Mrs. Jones was concerned because she had few students who came from backgrounds with languages other than English. This was a new situation for her, and she wanted to do well by Sonya and the other students she knew she would be finding in her classroom in the future. Already other teachers had mentioned the changing population in other schools in the area. She pondered, what steps can she take to help Sonya succeed?

## Questions for Reflection

1. How can Mrs. Jones determine Sonya's knowledge of English?
2. What can Mrs. Jones do to help Sonya gain confidence in using English and participating in class discussions?
3. Mrs. Jones wonders if there are specific issues students face in learning academic English.

## anticipating this chapter

If you were faced with a similar challenge, and it is likely that you will be given the increasing numbers of immigrant students entering our schools, how would you handle it? To help you address these and other issues about differentiation, this chapter is organized around the following questions:

How do we define diversity?

What do you need to consider when teaching English language learners?

How does diversity affect your classroom?

How can you differentiate instruction?

What intellectual and social needs are important to consider?

# How Do We Define Diversity?

The Classroom Challenge you have just thought about focuses on students coming to our classrooms with different linguistic and cultural experiences. This is certainly an important type of diversity. However, we want to help you think about diversity as a much broader concept as you read and entertain the ideas in this chapter.

When you hear the expressions, "America is a land of diversity" or "We are a diverse people," think for a moment about who you see in your mind's eye. Are you including racial, socioeconomic, sexual, religious, gender, educational, and regional diversity in your conception? What about diversity in learning styles and intelligence? Think of your own community; how many types of diversity can you list? How many of those are represented in the schools? What do you know about the values each of these different characteristics represents and how they influence the expectations parents hold for the education of their children?

## Language and Cultural Diversity

In contrast to so many countries, our nation has been known for its respect for individual and social values and experiences, and also for learning from what each variety brings to our total cultural mix. Our culture and language continue to be enriched with the gifts from a variety of peoples, both local and international. With such diversity in America, it is important that teachers are sensitive to differences that students and other teachers may bring, that we listen carefully to each other, that we are sensitive to the possibility of differing values and what makes us feel comfortable and respected.

## Diversity in Intellectual and Personal Learning Preferences

Language and culture represent two aspects of an individual's diversity. Howard Gardner and others have also made us aware of intellectual diversity. There are people who are extraordinarily gifted in music, the arts, sciences, and abstract theoretical formulations who may not be as gifted in interpersonal or intrapersonal intelligence. The opposite holds true, too. In some cases, it seems that those who are most talented in a particular area are less developed in some of the social skills we assume. With the recognition of large differences in people's intellectual gifts, teachers have learned to provide a variety of learning activities that reflect different preferences: addressing physical, visual/spatial, emotional, kinesthetic, and linguistic ways of knowing can help more students have access to the content to be learned. The recognition of differences also helps teachers provide for students with more challenging learning needs, especially those with language-based learning disabilities.

The Myers-Briggs Personality Inventory, a forerunner in describing personal style preferences, has identified sixteen different traits that characterize us, from introversion to extroversion to thinking and feeling. Therefore, as we think of diversity, there are some obvious dimensions that are easily noted and others that are realized only as we know and work with others over extended periods of time. A point we want to make in this chapter is that to be an effective teacher, we need to know our students well and know their families. We need to listen to them and ask questions to clarify our observations and assumptions.

One easy way to continue to expand our cultural sensitivity is to talk with people from other cultural and social groups. Ask about their educational experiences and expectations. Another good starting point is to read books and articles about people whose experiences and values are different from our own. Teacher book clubs and study groups are a natural place to explore variations. See the list in Figure 4.1 for a sample of the kinds of books that you might read with a group of teachers.

## Students with Language and Learning Difficulties

Many students in your classroom may have special learning needs that require some extra attention. In many cases, you will notice some students who are below grade level

**Figure 4.1**

### Professional Resources: Books about Diversity

Alvarez, J. (1994). *In the Time of the Butterflies.* New York: Penguin.

Benard, C. (2002). *Veiled Courage: Inside the Afghan Women's Resistance.* New York: Random House.

Lahiri, J. (1999). *Interpreter of Maladies.* New York: Houghton Mifflin.

Obama, B. (2004). *Dreams from My Father.* New York: Random House.

Tatum, B. D. (2003). *Why Are All the Black Kids Sitting Together in the Cafeteria?* New York: Basic Books.

in reading or are struggling to learn to read. Some of these students may have diagnosed learning disabilities or other learning difficulties, while others may not. It is important to note that, in many districts, reading disabilities and many other learning disabilities are not diagnosed until third grade or later, leaving these students ineligible for Special Education services. Because in some cases, students are less likely to be diagnosed in the early grades, or may have "slipped through the cracks" until the older grades, it is important that you as a teacher get to know your students well, and watch for students who may need extra help with their reading, writing, spelling, attention, language skills, or organization. Studies have shown that early intervention for struggling students is essential—the sooner they get extra help, the better.

Today's classrooms include students with a wide range of learning differences. There are many ways you can support these students' learning. Struggling students may benefit from more explicit instruction in basic skills and strategy instruction, more practice with new concepts, and more guidance and one-on-one attention in their independent reading and writing. They may also require frequent review of previously learned material and additional opportunities for previewing or pre-learning ideas and concepts. Smaller instructional group sizes often are successful when working with struggling students. In addition to extra time, attention, and review, these learners may need additional strategy instruction and learning aids that the rest of the class does not need. Finding time to work with small groups or individuals can be challenging, but even ten or fifteen minutes a day carved out of transition times or other activities can make a huge difference for students who need extra help. Some students can even come in early or stay after school, depending on their schedules. Other ideas include finding time during centers, before the school day starts, or during reading or writing workshop time.

Finding the right support is essential. Get to know the specialists in your school, as they are an invaluable resource for working with students who are struggling. In addition to special education teachers, reading specialists, social workers, and speech therapists, you may be able to use the help of parent or community volunteers, other students, or "learning buddies" from older grades. Often, teachers bring in these types of helpers to work with struggling students; however, since you, as the child's teacher, are the expert who knows this child best, it is usually better to bring in outside help to work with the class while you provide extra instruction to those who need you the most.

Finally, all students, especially those with special learning and language needs, benefit from quality instruction with teacher scaffolding. Frequent informal assessments are key because teachers who know their students well know the best ways to support their learning!

## Socioeconomic Diversity

Diversity comes in many forms in our schools. Socioeconomic status is a factor that influences families' involvement in their children's education. As mentioned in Chapter 1, the longitudinal study of early language development by Hart and Risley (1995) revealed enormous differences among social groups in the amount of language children are exposed to and the impact that has on the extent of vocabulary they learn each year. Economic status can also influence how comfortable family members feel in coming to school. Terry Rodgers (2000) explored parent participation in elementary schools and found that working-class mothers were intimidated by the "tennis moms" who seemed to have a great deal of energy and involvement in the school. Unintentionally, many mothers felt left out and unwelcome in the school parent culture.

**Fear of School** From personal experience of working with low socioeconomic communities, we know well how reluctant many families are to enter the schools their children attend. Their own experiences of schooling were not positive; many have bad memories and still feel emotional pain when they think of school learning experiences. Some recount what seem, from their perspective, to indicate cruel and unfeeling treatment by teachers and administrators. One man in his sixties very emotionally explained that when he came to the town high school from a country elementary school, he wasn't allowed to take mathematics because his scores in algebra were too low. He begged to be allowed to retake that course or be given some help so he could continue with high school math; unfortunately, in his memory, the school was uncompromising and unhelpful and he never learned more mathematics; nor did he ever forgive the school. He, like many others, dropped out early and didn't finish high school. This experience is illustrative of the stories of negative school experiences that parents hold within themselves and that make collaboration with schools difficult.

**Gender Sensitivity** Another group often left out of elementary and middle schools is fathers. Most teachers communicate with mothers, and it is generally mothers who support special events, serve as guides on field trips, and volunteer in the school. Yet, half of our students are male and need to know that education is not a female-gender activity or priority. Therefore, finding ways to make your classroom and school father-friendly is also important. You can do this quite easily. As a starter, invite males to read to students periodically. You may focus on special occupations or simply have "Special Readers" days. Some schools have open conversations with fathers and call them "Donuts for Dads" events. See a sample of an invitation to send to fathers in Figure 4.2. If you are not sure when the fathers or male caretakers are available, send out an inquiry or talk with some of them via phone or e-mail and then establish an accessible time and event. Use the checklist developed by Gwendolyn Cooke (2002) as a starting point for considering ways to involve fathers in your classroom and school. A copy of it is shown in Figure 4.3. It may make a real difference to some of your students; we know that boys are not staying in school as long as girls and not achieving as well (NAEP, 2004).

**Figure 4.2**

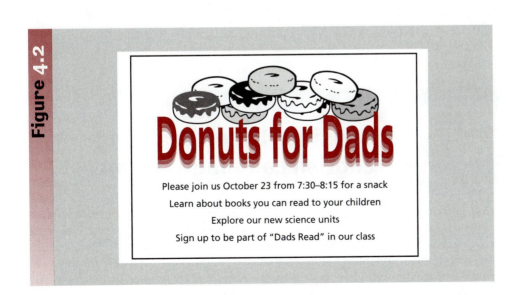

**Donuts for Dads**

Please join us October 23 from 7:30–8:15 for a snack

Learn about books you can read to your children

Explore our new science units

Sign up to be part of "Dads Read" in our class

**Figure 4-3**

**Is Your School Father-Friendly?**

Use this checklist to help you assess just how friendly your school is to fathers. If your school is not doing these things, or is not doing them well, now is a good time to start planning improvements. At your school do you:

____ 1. Actively and continuously encourage all men to participate—regardless of their backgrounds, attitudes, limitations, or age?

____ 2. Send a copy of notices to fathers not living in the home?

____ 3. Tell them directly (not through mothers) that the school needs their involvement?

____ 4. Display photos or drawings and publish stories of men involved with children at school?

____ 5. Show a genuine interest in fathers by greeting them at the door and asking them casual questions like, "So what have you been up to lately?"

____ 6. Give both dads and moms special activities to do with their children at home, and ask them to do specific "jobs" at school?

____ 7. Find out what men are interested in, what they would like to do, and what information/help/skills they need?

____ 8. Provide programs and activities geared to meet the specific needs of fathers and other significant male adults in students' lives?

____ 9. Schedule home visits, conferences, and other events at a time when fathers can attend?

____ 10. Offer something that is unique for men only, like a "Fathers' Club" or weekly "Donuts for Dads" coffees?

____ 11. Include in the parent room *Sports Illustrated*, special books and notices for dads, and other items of interest to men?

____ 12. Speak to mothers and fathers equally when they are both present at meetings, conferences, and home visits?

____ 13. Call or visit men when they don't attend a planned event and ask them why?

____ 14. Use men to recruit fathers and other male volunteers in the community?

*Source:* Gwendolyn Cooke, *Keys to Success for Urban School Principals,* Skylight Training and Publishing. Thousand Oaks, CA: Corwin Press, 2002. Used by permission.

## What Do You Need to Consider When Teaching English Language Learners?

One particular group teachers need to be sensitive to is students who are English Language Learners (ELLs), children like Sonya in the Classroom Challenge. This term refers to students who come to our schools with insufficient English to participate in our classrooms successfully. By the year 2020, it is estimated that 1 in 7 students will speak English as a second or third language. According to Genesee, Lindholm-Leary, Saunders, and Christian (2005), the number of English language learners has increased dramatically in the last decade. More than five million school-age children have been identified as ELLs. That is equivalent to more than 10 percent of the total K–12 public school population. Students who come as immigrants have traditionally been clustered in a few states and concentrated in urban school districts in California, New York, Florida, Texas, New Jersey, and Illinois. However, this pattern is changing. In fact, a report in 2006 indicated that six states with the highest increases in ELLs included Indiana, Nevada, North Carolina, and Connecticut. This changing pattern of immigration provides evidence of the dramatic changes taking place as immigrant families are now entering schools across the nation. Therefore, no matter where you may teach, it is likely that you will have students who are ELLs. It is important that well prepared teachers have an awareness of the language needs of students who are ELLs and know ways to make classrooms productive learning environments for all students.

## Supporting Students Who Are ELLs

States vary in how they support students who come with limited English. In some states, immigrant children are immediately placed in English only classrooms in which English is the only language spoken. In other states and districts, students begin their schooling in bilingual or dual language programs in which their first language is used for much of the content area instruction and they learn English as a new language.

IRA/NCTE 10

**Using Students' First Language in the Classroom** Research indicates that students learn most effectively when they can use their first language in developing both literacy and English language. This can happen in bilingual programs in which students begin learning to read and write in their first language and then transition into English as they learn more of the English language. These are called *one-way immersion* programs because the goal is that the students will function in a totally English environment. Other programs are designed to maintain the first language throughout elementary schooling while the students also learn English. These dual language or two-way programs are often open to both ELLs and to English speakers who want to learn a second language, too. A large-scale study of second language learners conducted by Thomas and Collier (2002) concluded that dual language bilingual enrichment programs were the only ones that successfully prepared students so they reached at least the 50th percentile in both languages, and from which there were the fewest dropouts.

The synthesis research on early literacy done by Snow, Burns, and Griffin (*Preventing Reading Difficulties in Young Children,* 1998) also concluded that children should learn to read in their home language if at all possible before beginning English reading instruction. The national panel that reviewed the research on literacy programs for ELL students also concluded that, wherever possible, students should learn to read in their first language before being taught in English (August and Shanahan, 2006).

Given the variety of programs in our schools and the resistance found in some areas toward instruction in languages other than English, there is no one single pattern of instruction that is dominant. Adding to the challenge is the reality that many schools will have students from a variety of languages and can't find teachers qualified to teach in the first language. In the best situations, students who come to your school speaking languages other than English will be placed in special programs in which they receive either dual language instruction or at least English instruction. Many students who come also have already achieved some level of English proficiency from instruction they received in schools in their home countries or from family members. However, it is good to know as much as possible about second language development and the roles that regular education teachers can play in fostering students' language development. Many districts offer courses in supporting language learners. Universities and other educational agencies also are good resources to help you continue your education.

**Social and Academic Language** While many teachers may initially feel uncomfortable with their familiarity with language issues and different cultures, our new classroom composition also provides new opportunities for us to learn. One of the gifts of our new students is that they make clear that we need to think consciously about how we use language and how we make English comprehensible. English language instruction is crucial for these students. And, it is critical throughout most of their schooling. Cummins and Corson (1998) make clear that while second language learners can develop a command of social or conversational English in two to three years, it takes four to seven years to develop command of academic English. That means that for most teachers, sensitivity to the level of language development of students who are English learners is important. Students may speak and converse easily in English and still not have the full understanding of the academic terms and language of instruction that is needed for success in our schools. In districts where students have bilingual education for two to four years, students may sound very confident in English and be very fluent with conversational language. However, those same students may flounder in the upper grades because they may lack the vocabulary and experiences needed to do well in social studies and science, for example. Research studies have confirmed that it is in the areas of academic language and procedural directions and commands that students who are ELLs are likely to need continued adapted and scaffolded instruction, what many call sheltered language instruction, the kind of instruction provided by the Sheltered Instruction Observation Protocol (SIOP) program (Echevarria, Vogt, and Short, 2007).

**Nonverbal Communication** In addition to the need to deal with the actual acquisition of English, there are also nonverbal communications—the gestures and body movements we use to enhance our verbal communication—that need to be understood across linguistic and cultural groups. Sharing these ways of communicating and making a chart of what nonverbal communication signals mean can be interesting and add to understanding. For example, a tacher might ask students, "How do we show that we are listening carefully to someone as they speak? How do we show our respect if we are being corrected?" A child from Mexico will respond that they show respect by keeping their eyes down and not connecting with an adult's eyes. An Asian child will most likely respond in a similar fashion. However, an American student will explain that we are to make eye contact with someone speaking to us and that even while being corrected it is polite to keep one's eyes on the speaker. Asking students how they indicate agreement nonverbally is also important. For Greeks shaking the head up and down and clicking the tongue indicates "no" or "I disagree." Moving the head from right to left signals "yes."

Another area of cultural difference that affects how teachers interact with students and their families is the physical distance between persons engaged in conversation. Hispanic families are physically warm and often hug to show greetings and leave-taking. Hispanic children also often keep close physical contact with their friends and enjoy a hug from their teacher. Many Northern European and Asian families find close touch uncomfortable and prefer handshakes to other forms of social connection. Asian students, too, are prone to wanting more private space around their physical bodies.

Arab and Muslim cultures often separate girls from boys after age twelve, and some newly arrived families may find our mixing of male and female students and teachers uncomfortable. An example of how important it is to make these differences explicit comes from a school experience of one of our teacher friends in Virginia. Shortly after a family arrived in the school from Saudi Arabia, the father came to the school office asking that his son be moved to a different classroom. He didn't want the boy taught by a woman. It was very difficult for him to understand how, in American schools, boys and girls were mixed in the same classrooms and that they would be taught by teachers of both genders. Something that most American teachers would never consider offensive was very difficult for this father to accept for his family.

If you have students in your classroom who come from a variety of cultural groups, being curious about their nonverbal communication signals and preferences is important. It can be an entry into an ongoing study of communication for your whole class. Most elementary students need to learn how to participate fully in a multicultural world; they also need to learn how to be productive members of their classroom community. Establishing a classroom protocol for talking and listening is useful to all involved. Small group discussions work well when children know to look at the speaker, give nonverbal feedback that is encouraging, and then respond in ways that acknowledge the ideas that the speaker shared.

## Support for Teachers of English Language Learners

Support from a variety of sources is available to teachers who have ELLs in their classrooms. Most states have guidelines for students who are ELLs and also provide some forms of assessment to help in placing students in appropriate programs. More and more resources are also available to help teachers in adjusting instruction so all students can be successful. The SIOP framework for instruction is an important response that has been developed for general education teachers who are experiencing more ELLs in their classrooms. In addition, the national consortium for ELLs, World-Class Instructional Design and Assessments (WIDA), has elaborated specific proficiencies for ELLs at five levels of English language development.

**WIDA Standards for ELLs** A set of national proficiency standards for English language learners has been developed by a consortium of state education agencies. These standards include the four domains of listening, speaking, reading, and writing, and delineate benchmarks for five levels of language from entering (level 1), beginning (level 2), and developing (level 3), to expanding (level 4), and bridging (level 5).

Several states have used these standards and benchmarks in developing their own versions and are also using the WIDA assessments that measure students' levels of proficiency with English. See Figure 4.4 for one part of the standards for Grades 3 to 5 focused on social and instructional language. These WIDA standards can be very useful for teachers because they highlight a variety of areas of English language development critical to students' success in school and beyond. For example, the standards for social and instructional language for the third through fifth grades focus on students' ability to engage in oral communication (speaking) by making personal introductions, exchanging personal information, and asking and responding to questions. In the area of listening, the standards focus on following directions and responding to questions by identifying main ideas and implied details of oral discourse. In each area, speaking, listening, reading, and writing, there are usually just one or two benchmarks so teachers can attend to these specific language elements. By keeping notes on the progress of

Figure 4.4

## WIDA ELP Standard 1: Social and Instructional Language Framework for Classroom Instruction and Assessment

| Level 1 Entering | Level 2 Beginning | Level 3 Developing | Level 4 Expanding | Level 5 Bridging |
|---|---|---|---|---|
| **Speaking** | | | | |
| Ask for assistance with a task or needed supplies | Ask or provide the meaning of words, phrases, or uses of relevant resources | Ask questions to seek information or provide opinions, preferences, or wishes | Ask for or provide clarification of information by restating ideas | Ask for or provide specific information that confirms or denies beliefs |
| **Listening** | | | | |
| Identify materials needed to complete tasks from realia and oral statements | Match materials or resources needed to complete tasks with their uses based on realia and oral directions | Select materials or resources needed to complete tasks based on realia and oral descriptions | Sequence use of materials or resources needed to complete tasks based on oral directions | Evaluate use of materials or resources needed to complete tasks based on oral discourse |

*Source:* WIDA ELP Standards © 2004, 2007 Board of Regents of the University of Wisconsin System. Used by permission.

English language learners in the classroom, it is a manageable task and can also highlight instructional opportunities you can provide for all students.

## Instructing English Language Learners

The WIDA standards and student assessment focus on what students need to be able to do as they develop English proficiency. There are also supports for teachers in adapting instruction so we can be more sensitive to students' needs. There are two terms that are generally used to describe instruction that is adapted to take into account the needs of ELLs. These are sheltered instruction and Specially Designed Academic Instruction in English (SDAIE). The latter term is used most extensively in California.

**Sheltered Instruction** *Sheltered Instruction* is a term that has been in use for many years and refers to ways teachers adapt their content instruction to recognize the demands academic instruction places on students still learning English. Sheltered English immersion (SEI) programs are provided in some districts in which there are enough students who have basically mastered conversational English but still need support in content learning. SEI programs provide support in several ways. Some include classrooms led by a native language teacher who teaches groups of students from the same home language or classrooms with students of mixed language backgrounds needing more carefully orchestrated English support. The teacher provides all instruction in English but helps clarify concepts in the home language of the students.

Other schools support the academic language development of ELLs by including an extra teacher on a grade-level team to help support teachers in modifying instruction and to help students needing additional bridging between languages.

**The SIOP** In most districts, there are not enough resources to provide additional teachers so the responsibility for assisting ELLs falls on the classroom teacher. Knowing what the needs of ELLs are and how to create instructional environments in which they can grow as learners is important. One good resource for all teachers is the Sheltered Instruction Observation Protocol (SIOP). This framework for classroom instruction was developed through an extensive research program focused on identifying those instructional elements essential for the development of English language learners (Echevarria, Vogt, and Short, 2007). As the authors explain, "The SIOP operationalizes sheltered instruction by offering teachers a model for lesson planning and implementation that provides English learners with access to grade-level content standards" (2007, p. xi). The protocol identifies eight elements that are essential in classrooms that are supportive of ELLs (see Figure 4.5 for a list of these elements).

All of these lesson elements need to be developed if students are going to reap the benefit from good instruction. It takes your concerted attention to the elements and reflective practice to become proficient with all these components. As a new teacher, you may want to ask if your district has a professional development strand where you could work with other teachers in developing your own skills in focusing your instruction so all

**Figure 4.5**

## SIOP Essential Elements

1. Careful lesson preparation that includes objectives for both content and language development
2. Building background for the lesson—both activating what students know and providing essential foundations when needed, with special attention to content vocabulary and the procedural and functional terms students need to know
3. Providing comprehensible input by slowing down speech and using visual, body, and artifactual enhancements
4. Using teaching routines that build students' learning strategies so they become more independent as learners
5. Provide multiple opportunities for students to use language orally and in written form as they are learning; working with partners, small groups, and cooperative teams provides engagement and practice
6. Opportunities to rehearse and practice content and language objectives and integrate their learning
7. Carefully prepared and delivered lessons that build from what students know and can do
8. Providing time for review and assessment as an ongoing part of developing, teaching, and adjusting instruction to improve students' learning and insure the achievement of the objectives

students will be able to learn effectively. Some groups of teachers and some schools start by focusing on one element at a time and build understanding and implementation of all eight elements over a one- to three-year period of time. We present this framework here because we think it is important for new teachers to include in your own initial teaching experiences as comprehensive and inclusive an approach to teaching and learning as possible. Each experience you have working with students will help you reflect on and analyze your own planning, pacing, and development of instructional activities.

## Determining Language Development Needs

New teachers can begin supporting their students who are learning English and those who are language-delayed by listening to them and engaging them in personal communication. Take some time to talk with them about the content that is going to be developed and attend to their vocabulary and language use. This informal pre-assessment of your students' knowledge and language takes very little time but can reap big benefits. From this information, you can work on establishing language objectives that will help your students grow. As a language arts teacher, you have a special opportunity to put into practice your knowledge of English and good language arts instruction.

Always consider both the academic content needs *and* the instructional language that will need to be understood by students. In this book, you will find many ways to

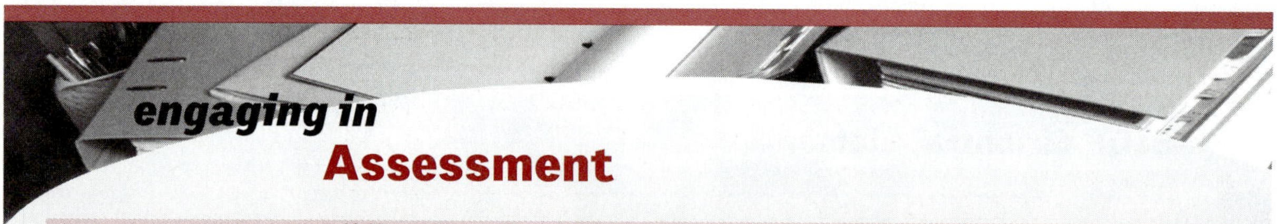

### *engaging in* Assessment

#### Modifications for Students with Special Needs

One of the greatest challenges when working with diverse students is assessing their current knowledge and progress in the classroom. Documenting the progress made by students with language or learning needs—such as ELL populations, including Sonya who was introduced in our classroom challenge at the beginning of the chapter—can be difficult when the students are not able to read or understand the questions on a test or other assessment tool. Assessment information can be extremely useful to teachers for planning future lessons and activities, but only when the information collected through the assessment tool is an accurate reflection of their students' learning. To help ensure that the assessment information you collect from your students is accurate, you may need to make some slight modifications. For example, students who are easily distracted may benefit from working in a quiet location or away from visual distractions. Students with slower processing speeds may require extra time to complete their work and would benefit from tests that are not timed. Other students may need test questions read to them or may need words or phrases translated into their primary language to ensure they understand what the question is asking. When a great deal of writing is involved, sometimes students may need to dictate their answers or use a computer to type their responses. Many of these modifications will be included in the individualized education program, or IEP, for students who are receiving special education services. However, to develop an accurate measure of their current abilities and progress in your classroom, it is important to be aware of all of your students' learning needs, even though they may not be currently receiving special education or ELL support.

assess students' knowledge of important content vocabulary, especially in Chapter 11. The One-Minute Fluency Snapshot (explained in Chapter 12) provides a quick check on the basic accessibility of a text for the student. A short writing piece can also give you an initial idea of the skills the student has in expressing thoughts related to your topic of study. See Chapter 12 for more ideas on Assessments and see the Engaging in Assessment feature for more on assessing students with special needs.



## Providing Opportunities for Language Development

IRA/NCTE 10

Learning a new language is not easy. Many of you may have struggled to gain a basic fluency in some languages other than English. Others of you may have learned English as a second language yourselves. As you were learning, you probably did a lot of translating using your first language to help you as you tried to find ways to express yourself in a new language. This is true of most speakers, even when they are very proficient in a second language. A good starting point is to remember that ELLs have a first language that they can use and should use as they need it to clarify and extend what they know. Let students use all their language resources. Remember, though, that it takes more time to think in two languages. ELLs will need additional time to think through the content and find ways to express their ideas in English. You will help students by giving time to process ideas and information. You can encourage students to turn to another student who speaks their same language and talk together to see if they do understand. Establishing a supportive environment in which students can work together on class activities is important.

Students in your classroom may be at varied levels of command of English. At the earliest stage, students may understand what you say and what they read but lack confidence to articulate their ideas in English. This is termed the *comprehension or preproduction stage* (Terrell, 1981). The next stage is called the *early production stage* and is characterized by students' responses that are very short, usually one- or two-word utterances. The third stage, the *emergence* of speech, is typified by children's construction of longer and more varied oral language utterances. Being aware of the levels of your students can help you scaffold the tasks you ask of them and the activities in which they are engaged.

Let students use all their language resources. Establishing a supportive environment where students can work together on class activities is important.

**Pacing and Wait Time** No matter their level of English proficiency, it is important to monitor the pacing of instructional activities and provide enough wait time after asking questions so all students can respond. Remember, some ELLs may have to translate from English to their home language and then back to English before they can respond. Giving them ample time to think and formulate a response is important. Students need to feel relaxed and have time to think, and make the associations in English that are appropriate for the activity. Establish regular routines so students can anticipate that you will stop your lessons and activities and give students time to turn to a partner and share what they are thinking and ask questions if they are unclear about the lesson. This kind of student involvement establishes a clear respect for their language processing needs. Students need to frame what they are doing in English and be sure they understand. All students benefit from times to **"Think-Pair-Share"** (McTighe and Fyman, 1988) or turn to a partner and **"Say Something"** (Short, Harste, and Burke, 1996) about the lesson. Students benefit when you have routines that put them with partners or in small groups to read, write, and talk together. In addition to the explanations provided below, see Chapters 2 and 3 for more on group routines.



IRA/NCTE 9

**Encourage Student-to-Student Engagement** Students develop their language by using it. Therefore, one of the most important components of your classroom activities is structured talk routines. Teachers who assume students should know how to participate in small group discussions, or even whole class discussion, without having appropriate routines modeled and behaviors defined quickly get frustrated. It is in these unguided classrooms that teachers often stop using discussion and revert to teacher-dominated activities. It takes time and effort to build social routines that fit within the classroom parameters. Yet, they are essential to students' language growth and development. In Chapter 2, we introduced several ways to develop students' awareness of the conventions of group talk. With second language learners and students from other cultural settings, building routines for safe talk is also important. Several classroom routines that help students share their ideas are explained in the following examples.

**Partner Students Who Speak the Same Language** Many teachers get frustrated when immigrant students enter their classrooms mid-year and are not fluent in English. Finding a partner for the new student who speaks the same home language and letting them sit beside each other can help the newcomer feel at home quickly. Students should be told that the English-speaking partner will periodically be explaining things to the new student orally while the class is working. The partner will use a soft voice so others won't be disturbed. This talk is important and the whole class needs to acknowledge the value of these translations. Periodically, the teacher can ask the English-speaking partner to share some of the other language, especially when new content topics are being introduced, so the whole class can learn more about both languages and how they are alike and different. Writing words and phrases in the new language can be a special learning experience for English-only students. Visually seeing how words are written, how accent marks and punctuation are used, and identifying similar cognates adds interest to the language classroom.

**Think-Pair-Share** In the Think-Pair-Share activity, the teacher stops periodically during a discussion or mini-lecture so students can process and respond to some aspect of the content being studied. The first step in this routine is to ask a question for reflection. Students respond in writing to this teacher-initiated question about the ongoing lesson. After each student writes—or in the case of ELLs or students with language and learning difficulties, they might draw or diagram their ideas—then the students turn to a partner and share their ideas. Finally, the teacher brings the class back together as a group and asks for some students to share their discussion. In a reading lesson, the teacher might ask students to pause and make a prediction as she reads aloud. Each should write their own prediction on paper. Then they turn to their partners, share their ideas, and come to a common decision on one or two possible next steps in the story. Finally, the groups reconvene and the teacher writes on the board some of the groups' predictions. This activity helps students—ELLs and other students with language delays—gain confidence in speaking because they have a chance to rehearse their ideas orally with just one other person.

At the beginning of the year, the single language partner may be the one who shares with the whole group. A student might say, "My partner had a great idea about why Frederich wouldn't move. She thought . . ." When the English speaker contributes ideas from the ELL partner, the student feels included and honored. Without a partner, ELLs may be too intimidated to speak or share their ideas with the whole class. The partner can be the voice and also the model for how to contribute. Later in the school year, as the students who are ELLs see that their ideas are acceptable, they enter the discussions much more confidently.

**Say Something** A variant of this activity is to have students "Say Something" to a partner at points in the lesson where you stop and instruct them to turn to their partner and say something about what they are learning. It may be something you are telling them, something you are reading to them, or something they are experiencing as a science activity. By periodically stopping the flow of classroom activity so students think about what is occurring and share their thoughts with someone else, you establish how important using language to process ideas is in thinking and learning.

Many teachers ask students to use knee-to-knee voices or eighteen-inch voices to help moderate the noise level in the room when children are conversing with their partners. Teach this moderation of voice levels at the beginning of the year. Primary children often lack an understanding of how their voices carry unless there is some attention to this aspect of classroom talk. Periodically, you can ask a partner team to model again for the class how they engage in their conversation; remember, praise for appropriate conversations is important. Having a few students model the appropriate voice level can pay off in rich dividends later.

**Reading and Writing Buddies** English language learners and students who struggle with reading often don't know how to read fluently and pronounce the words in the materials the class is reading. Many teachers have success by partnering a more able and less able reader for oral reading. When the able reader goes first, the less able reader hears the text read accurately and can copy the pronunciation of words and follow the intonation patterns of the partner. It may be useful to have the partners engage in repeated reading. The able reader reads one paragraph or page and the partner repeats the same section. Reading proceeds in this way for the designated five- to ten-minute period. If there are wide variations in the reading abilities in a class, some teachers establish partners across grade levels. For example, a first-grade teacher may establish a partnership with third-grade classrooms. Once a week, the classes come together and engage in partner reading or writing. The older and more able partners can either read to their partners, do repeated readings, assist their younger partners in reading a text orally, or help them prepare for a reader's theater or other oral production the class will do. The buddies can also be great support for writing and composing ideas. Some classrooms involve buddies on computers. Others ask buddies to assist with writing by taking dictation from the younger students. Some teachers have the buddies send notes to each other periodically, thus establishing a great motivation for writing in both classes.

**Partner Reading** The partner reading routines generally involve two students of comparable reading ability working together. The partners each take responsibility for one side of a page of text or one paragraph. Each is responsible for reading that section silently and preparing to read it orally. As each is ready, they share their parts with their partner. After reading the section, the listener responds with what they learned or liked. (See Chapter 3 for a more elaborate description of this activity.) A variant is that the reader asks a question of the listener. Then, the other partner shares his/her oral reading and the listener responds. The reading continues in this manner for the duration of the activity which shouldn't be more than fifteen to twenty minutes. Engaging older students in writing responses can help both students and teacher ensure that the content is being accurately recalled.

While these activities that encourage talk and sharing between students are essential for students who are ELLs and students with learning and language needs, they are also very important for *all* students. As we wrote in the first chapter, students need more opportunities to talk in the classroom than many teachers provide. If you establish a few regular routines, such as the Think-Pair-Share and Say Something activities, students will begin to expect that they can and will use their language to respond to content and also construct their own ideas.

Move at a pace that helps students process the content they are learning and share their ideas with each other. This will help students develop oral language skills as they think about content.

## How Does Diversity Affect Your Classroom?

As we think about the language needs of students, we also need to think about the cultural expectations and values they bring that may be quite different from what we expect. For example, one newly arrived immigrant family was quite critical of the education their children were receiving. The parents explained that, in their European schools, the students received homework every night and the parents were able to help them with the academic assignments. The mathematics their children did in Europe was at least a year beyond that which they were receiving here. In addition, the parents complained that there was little writing required. They wanted their children to become expert writers in English, yet the teachers hardly ever assigned written papers. The children spoke English quite well, but needed help expanding their command of this language. As the family's frustrations were shared, it became clear to the teachers that the forms of schooling and the uses of homework represented a difference, or at least perceived difference, in the expectations of the schools. Luckily, the teachers communicated regularly to the parents, and before much time had passed, the teachers and parents set up meetings where they discussed the curriculum and the kinds of expectations the school had for the children.

**Video Homework Exercise**

*Teacher Rigidity*

Go to the Homework and Exercises section in Chapter 4 of MyEducationLab to watch the video, "Teacher Rigidity," about a Native American expert who discusses the misrepresentation of cultures. Complete the activities that follow, and save your work or transmit it to your professor as assigned.

Many families come to our schools with more formal experiences in education. In many eastern European countries, students are never to question what teachers say and engaging in discussion of literature is not permitted. Students memorize the interpretations that the "authoritative theorists" have determined to be correct. When students from these contexts enter our schools, they are understandably confused. Why would teachers want to hear their opinions? Why would teachers waste time in discussion of what students think about literature? We had interesting experiences working with Russian teachers who argued strongly that students should *NOT* engage in exploratory discussions of literature; making personal connections to texts or even reading across texts just wasn't appropriate. They were convinced that students should learn the "expert" interpretations of pieces of literature. Even primary students read only respected authors and learned what texts meant from their teachers. For students from educational systems such as Russia that honor the expert interpretations, we need to be very explicit about our approaches and the theoretical positions informing our pedagogy.

**BUILDING TEACHING SKILLS: Video Exercise**

*One Teacher's Influence*

Go to the Building Teaching Skills section in Chapter 4 of MyEducationLab to watch the video, "One Teacher's Influence," about how one school addresses cultural diversity. Complete the activities that follow, and save your work or transmit it to your professor as assigned.

## Mexican Immigrants

Because so many of our newly arriving immigrant students are coming from Mexico, it is important to note that there are significant differences in the approach to education between our two countries. In many Mexican elementary schools, there is little emphasis placed on reading. In contrast, students spend a significant portion of their time learning to write, that is, learning to use correct handwriting and spelling. The formation of the letters and words is important; copying models from the board is often a task for students. Jiminez (2005) provides a clear explanation of these basic differences in the ways elementary schools prioritize their goals. Think of how confusing it must be for parents who expect to have their children practicing handwriting and instead learn that their children will be listening to teachers read aloud and be asked to discuss their own connections to the text ideas. In schools where handwriting and spelling are not a high priority, these parents can easily develop negative impressions of the education we provide.

Our work in Chicago with Mexican immigrant families has taught us a great deal. Perhaps most important is that the families value education and want their students to do well in school. In fact, they honor teachers so much that many are hesitant to interfere with the work their children are doing in school. They don't see themselves as their children's first teachers; they reserve that honor to the school teachers. In many cases, the families are coming to get employment that is sufficient to support their families; they are from poor, rural areas of Mexico. Their own educations have been very little; many have attended only a few years of school and don't have confidence in themselves as "teachers" of their children. The idea that they, as parents, should be involved in helping their children develop literacy is often a new and intimidating idea. Therefore, sensitivity is needed in building a good relationship with families. At the first level, we need to understand the life circumstances of the families. Many may be holding down two jobs and find little time to be engaged with either the school or their children. Most want to do what they can for their children and are part of a larger family constellation. Building bridges to the extended families can be helpful. So, too, is meeting with parents when translators are present. We find there are significant differences in the command of English even within one family. Having a translator can put parents at ease. It is also good to consider having groups of parents attend parent conferences together rather than talking with each family separately. As an outgrowth of their Bridging Cultures Project (Quiroz, Greenfield, and Altchech, 1999, p. 69) where teachers studied cultural values, one teacher decided to hold group conferences. She concluded that:

> The group conferencing was relaxing for the parents . . . . It was a less threatening environment than the individual conferencing style; parents supplied support and were company for one another. This format provided a group voice from the parents rather than an individual voice. The conferencing time was also structured so that after one hour, parents could sign up for a private conference or ask a few questions without others present.

For additional ideas on supporting students from diverse backgrounds, see the Exploring Technology feature on websites to support diverse classrooms.

exploring technology

## Websites to Support Diverse Classrooms

**Supporting ELL Students (http://english-zone.com/index.php)**
English-Zone.com is a website for students who are learning English as a second language, or studying English in general. The site is divided into "zones" in which students can find information and play games about grammar usage, verbs, idioms, spelling, conversation, pronunciation, vocabulary, reading, writing, language skills, and much more.

**Supporting the English Language Learner (www.learner.org/channel/workshops/readingk2/session2/index.html)**
The Annenberg Channel provides several programs for teacher professional development. In the video for this session, Dr. Mileidis Gort presents research-based principles that support English Language Learners' literacy and language development. She describes the characteristics of beginning and intermediate second-language learners, then presents instructional practices that best meet their needs.

**Supporting Students with Special Language and Learning Needs (www.ldaamerica.org/aboutld/teachers/index.asp)**
The official website of the Learning Disabilities Association of America (LDA) provides resources, strategies, accommodations and modifications, research, and information for parents and teachers of students with learning disabilities, including Attention Deficit Hyperactivity Disorder (ADHD). They also hold local and national conferences and workshops for teachers.

**Council for Exceptional Children (www.cec.sped.org)**
The Council for Exceptional Children's website provides information about a wide range of disabilities and special education topics you may experience in your classroom, including ADHD, learning disabilities, autism, and gifted and talented students. Teachers can also find information about current special education topics, evidence-based practices, and assessment.

**ASHA (www.asha.org/public/speech/development/schoolsFAQ.htm)**
On ASHA's website teachers can find information about language-based learning disabilities, hearing impairments, and speech and language disorders. The website includes useful definitions, information on how language disorders can affect learning, tips for working with students in your classroom, information on collaborating with speech-language pathologists and other specialists, as well as links to other online resources.

**Recording for the Blind and Dyslexic (www.learningthroughlistening.org)**
The Learning Through Listening organization provides audio recordings of books and textbooks on CDs for students with visual impairments or reading disabilities, such as dyslexia. Teachers and educators can also find lesson plans, teaching tools, and strategies on this website.

**E-Buddies (www.ebuddies.org)**
E-Buddies is dedicated to enhancing the lives of people with intellectual disabilities by providing opportunities for one-to-one friendships via e-mail. Its website provides information about membership and how to start a chapter in your community.

## New Formats for Communication

The example of Mexican immigrant families illustrates how important it is that teachers learn about the values and sensitivities of the families of our students. Creative thinking can also help us develop new formats for communication. Some schools have special programs for parents in which they model the practice of reading aloud to children. They bring in books that are in both the home language of the parents and in English. A nice way to engage parents in reading to and with their children is to provide copies of the same story in English and the other language (in many cases, Spanish). That way, the parents can read or tell the story using the Spanish book and the child can read or tell the English version if their English skills are that developed. In some schools, there are special reading events for parents in which they can experience responding to stories in the same way their children are. One middle school in Chicago has a book club for parents in which they read and discuss the same books their children are reading. It opens up great opportunities for parents to engage their children in talk about literature. It has also helped the school communicate the reason they want students to discuss books they are reading rather than always listening to teacher lectures.

Some schools have programs in which they celebrate authors and stories from other cultures. Displays of books from different parts of the world in different languages can be very interesting and informative. Identifying the most important authors, both for children and adults, from different countries adds interest. When parents can write or illustrate their own favorites, these intercultural sharing opportunities can take on a personal and rich tone. See the Engaging in Oral Language feature for more ideas on integrating stories from other cultures into your classroom.

IRA/NCTE 1

## Understanding the Cultures Represented in Our Classrooms

There are many ways teachers can expand understanding of the different cultures represented in the school and community. Even if you don't have a student from a cultural group one year, it is likely that you will be introduced to children from a variety of cultures eventually. The more teachers can learn about the special characteristics of different cultures, the more sensitively they can meet and support the children. One of the easiest ways to learn more about different cultures is to invite speakers into the school to share during teacher meetings and professional development sessions. Local community representatives are often very eager to be recognized by the schools and serve as liaisons as new families settle in the area. Churches, synagogues, and mosques are also places where community leaders can be found and invited as speakers. Parents of children in the school are also great resources to the faculty and individual teachers. Inviting speakers to teacher meetings is important; it is also good to invite guests to speak to students. When this is done, teachers have a great opportunity to introduce the rules for polite etiquette in meeting and welcoming adults. Students can learn to be greeters, to introduce speakers, and to be escorts to show them the classroom and school. Learning to shake hands, introduce oneself, and thank guests are important skills that can easily be developed with these events.

**Seek Information about Your Students** In the fall, it is very useful to send a note home to parents (translated for those needing languages other than English) asking for information about their children, their interests, what they have done recently, any special concerns the teacher should know about, etc. One teacher explained recently that he would have had no idea that his seventh-grade student had just lost his father

## engaging in Oral language

### Sharing Folk Tales across Cultures

Comparing similar folk tales and legends as they are interpreted by different cultures can lead to interesting discussions of social values and cultural lessons. For example, the story of the Frog Prince has a very harsh ending in the Japanese version of the story compared to the English one; the German version is somewhat in between. If no versions are available in the different languages, a display of books containing variations of Cinderella can make a good discussion. From Mufaro's *Beautiful Daughters* to *Cinder Ellie* to *The Rough-Faced Girl* and the *Egyptian Princess,* there are great cultural lessons that can be compared to the French and modern American versions. Reading these folk tales and legends orally can highlight the different ways stories are told in particular languages. This can lead to rich discussions of the themes and the ways language is used.

over the summer if the parent hadn't included this in the note sent back to him. What a difference it made in his understanding of the child's reluctance to engage in some activities! Another way to get to know students better is to read books and engage in faculty book club discussions on those readings. There are many good adult and children's books that provide rich insights into other cultures.

Teachers who have students respond to personal interest surveys and questionnaires can also learn about students quickly. It is also important to know these interests because they can be a powerful connection to students for language arts instruction. Special needs students of all types do best when they can use their own interests as a starting point for literacy learning (see suggestions in Fink, 2006). Figure 4.6 gives ideas on what to include in an inventory that can help you get acquainted with your students.

Later in the year, as you continue to get acquainted with your students you can add notes about them to these initial inventories. As you teach each of your units and introduce new topics, you will want to find out what students know and where their interests lie, too. One of the easiest ways to do this when you start new topics in reading and inquiry units is to follow the steps of the KWL (Ogle, 1986) and ask students what they know and want to learn about the topic. These quick brainstorming activities give teachers great insights into students' knowledge, vocabulary, and interests. For ideas on books to bring into your multicultural classroom, see the Exploring Children's Literature feature.

## Communicating the Curriculum and Pedagogy to Families

One important way teachers can translate the school curriculum and pedagogy to all families is through continuing communication. Don't assume that the fall parents' night and a spring open house are adequate. Rather, think of creating weekly

Figure 4.6

## Sample Student Inventory

Good questions to include on teacher-designed inventories:

- What do you most like to do on the weekends?
- What stories or books do you like to read?
- Who are your best friends and what do you do together?
- What do you do with your family?
- Draw or describe your family.
- What words describe you best?
- What's the happiest time you can remember?
- What is your favorite TV program?
- What is your favorite sport?
- What is your favorite music?
- What is something you would like to have others know about you?

communication with parents and then introduce them to key curriculum frameworks during the year.

***Curriculum Night*** Some schools invite the parents to come to school to experience the same instruction their children receive. Parents sit in the students' desks and teachers present lessons they are using with the children. Teachers also explain the purpose for the instructional routines and take parent questions. By having parents experience instruction, they can understand it more fully. They also use the materials the children have in the classroom and can see how the standards and curriculum objectives are implemented in the instruction students receive.

***Home Links*** Teachers can send home weekly summaries of what the instruction will be about during the week and include activities for families to engage with their students. Some teachers go into quite a bit of detail explaining the nature of instruction so families will understand the rationale behind activities. With the major changes that have occurred in instruction, even for parents from this country, interpreting the curriculum is important. The focus on standards-based testing and accountability makes informing families an important part of your responsibility.

## Becoming Part of a School Planning Team for Students with Special Needs

With the changes implemented in special education legislation (IDEA 2004), it is important that you think of your classroom as a community for all students.

# exploring Children's Literature

## Multicultural Books

### Grades K to 3

*Bringing Asha Home*—Written by Uma Krishnaswami, illustrated by Jamel Akib, and published by Lee & Low (2006).
Eight-year-old Arun waits impatiently while international adoption paperwork is completed so that he can meet his new baby sister from India.

*Brothers in Hope: The Story of the Lost Boys of Sudan*—Written by Mary Williams, illustrated by R. Gregory Christie, and published by Lee & Low (2005).
Eight-year-old Garang, orphaned by a civil war in Sudan, finds the inner strength to help lead other boys as they trek hundreds of miles seeking safety in Ethiopia, in Kenya, and finally, in the United States.

*Calavera Abecedario: A Day of the Dead Alphabet Book*—Written and illustrated by Jeanette Winter and published by Harcourt (2004).
Every year, Don Pedro and his family make papier-mache skeletons, or *calaveras,* for Mexico's Day of the Dead fiesta. From Angel and Doctor to Mariachi and Unicornio, each letter of the alphabet has its own special *calavera.*

*Celebrate! Connections among Cultures*—Written by Jan Reynolds and published by Lee & Low (2006).
Through photographs, the book explores the similarities among celebration rituals in several indigenous cultures around the world and compares them with celebrations in the United States.

*I Lost My Tooth in Africa*—Written by Penda Diakité, illustrated by Baba Diakité, and published by Scholastic (2006).
While visiting her father's family in Mali, a young girl loses a tooth, places it under a calabash, and receives a hen and a rooster from the African Tooth Fairy.

*How People Live*—Written by Penelope Arlon and published by DK Publishing (2003).
This book describes different parts of the world and how people live in each, from the Eskimos and Inuit of the Arctic to the Amish and Maya of North America and the Asante and Zulu of Africa.

*Jingle Dancer*—Written by Cynthia Smith, illustrated by Cornelius Van Wright and Ying-Hwa Hu, and published by Morrow (2000).
Jenna, a member of the Muscogee, or Creek Nation, tribe borrows jingles from the dresses of several friends and relatives so that she can perform the jingle dance at the powwow (includes a note about the jingle dance tradition and its regalia).

*One Year in Beijing*—Written by Xiaohong Wang, illustrated by Grace Lin, and published by Chinasprout (2006).
Ling Ling is eight years old and lives in Beijing, China. Through her journal, a month-by-month account tells about Chinese culture and destinations, holidays and festivals, school and family life, and more.

### Grades 4 to 8

*First Day in Grapes*—Written by L. King Pérez, illustrated by Robert Casilla, and published by Lee & Low.
When Chico starts the third grade after his migrant worker family moves to begin harvesting California grapes, he finds that self-confidence and math skills help him cope with the first day of school.

*How We Are Smart*—Written by W. Nikola-Lisa, illustrated by Sean Qualls, and published by Lee & Low (2006).
Through direct quotations, verse, and prose, this book presents the achievements of a diverse group of people who illustrate Dr. Howard Gardner's theory of multiple intelligences (includes information about the eight basic ways people can be "smart" and suggested activities).

*In the Year of the Dog: A Novel*—Written by Grace Lin and published by Little, Brown (2006).
Frustrated at her seeming lack of talent for anything, a young Taiwanese American girl sets out to apply the lessons of the Chinese Year of the Dog, those of making best friends and finding oneself, to her own life.

*If the World Were a Village: A Book about the World's People*—Written by David Smith, illustrated by Shelagh Armstrong, and published by Kids Can Press (2002).

The idea of a world of 6.2 billion people becomes more understandable by exploring the lives of the one hundred villagers to gain a better understanding of the world's peoples and their ways of life. Facts about such topics as nationalities, food, language, and religion are brought to light.

*Quiet Hero: The Ira Hayes Story*—Written and illustrated by S. D. Nelson and published by Lee & Low (2006).

This is a biography of Native American Ira Hayes, a shy, humble Pima Indian who fought in World War II as a Marine and was one of six soldiers to raise the U.S. flag on Iwo Jima, an event immortalized in Joe Rosenthal's famous photograph.

*Paths to Peace: People Who Changed the World*—Written and illustrated by Jane Zalben and published by Dutton (2006).

This book profiles the lives of sixteen peacemakers, including Mahatma Gandhi, Eleanor Roosevelt, Cesar Chavez, Aung San Suu Kyi, and the most recent Nobel Prize winner, Dr. Wangari Maathai.

*Rickshaw Girl*—Written by Mitali Perkins, illustrated by Jamie Hogan, and published by Charlesbridge (2007).

In her Bangladesh village, ten-year-old Naimi excels at painting designs called alpanas, but to help her impoverished family financially she would have to be a boy—or disguise herself as one.

*Kampung Boy*—Written by Lat and published by First Second (2006).

This book (in graphic novel format) relates the life experiences, from birth to beginning boarding school, of a boy growing up on a rubber plantation in rural Malaysia.

Guidelines ask that students being considered for special education be considered in three tiers. The first tier is for classroom instruction to be modified with more explicit directions and often with the instructional sequences broken into small chunks. The second tier is for students to be provided with small group instruction that meets their specific skill and processing needs. Only at the third tier do students receive individual instruction from specialists rather than classroom teachers. With all the variety of activities and strategies language arts and reading teachers have available to them, you are important contributors to planning for students with special needs.

The habit you have developed of keeping notes on students' participation and the ongoing assessments you use means that you have data that is important in this planning process. You also know that it is not just the skills students lack. Many need to have adjustments made to the content so they bring their background knowledge to their language learning. Breaking apart the tasks they are asked to complete is important for many of these students. Deshler and Schumaker (2006) provide good guidelines to help analyze school tasks and the language used to explain what students are expected to accomplish. See Figure 4.7 for an example of one Unit Planning Frame developed by Keith Lenz (2008) of the University of Kansas team. Students with special needs may also require more extended periods of time to complete tasks.

## How Can You Differentiate Instruction?

Think of your classroom as a community of special students, each with their own gifts, special interests, and ways of learning. You will probably have students from several cultural backgrounds and ways of interacting. As you get to know your students, you

Figure 4.7

**Unit Planning Frame**

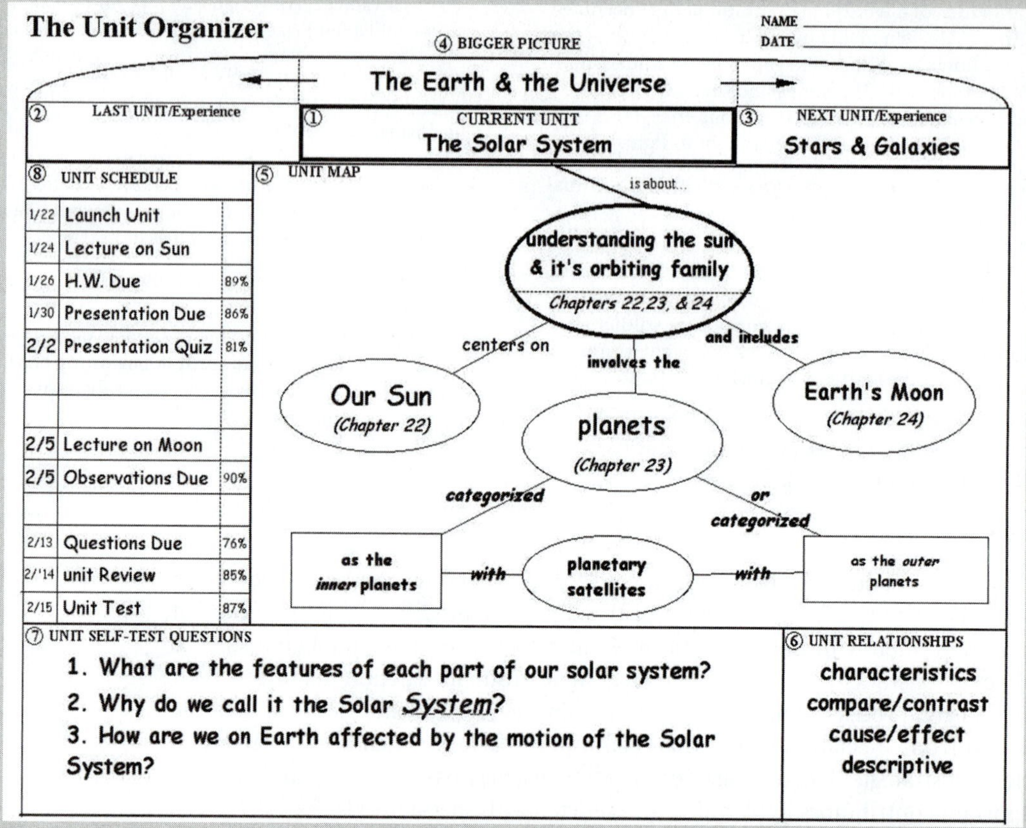


*Source:* Adapted from *The Unit Organizer Routine*. Copyrights for the template are held by the authors of *The Unit Organizer Routine*. Received through personal communication from Dr. Keith Lenz, University of Kansas, Feb. 15, 2008.

will identify varied ways of learning and different strengths and weaknesses. Some students are very gifted and deserve having stimulating opportunities to continue to grow and expand their competence. Other students may have special areas of strength and need to be encouraged to use those areas to grow. Some will be coming with Individual Educational Plans (IEPs) and you will be coordinating with special education support personnel for their participation. It is unlikely that as a new teacher you will be able to adapt your instruction to meet as many of the individual profiles as you would like. However, if you think of your role as one to learn as much as you can about each of your students and then to differentiate in ways that consider the most important aspects of your curriculum and your students' needs, you will be on your way.

## Defining Differentiation

C. Tomlinson (2000) describes differentiated instruction by focusing on three elements of differentiation that teachers can vary to respond to their particular students: content, process, and product. *Content* refers to the priorities you have for students in your grade level. These are generally determined by district objectives and are based on state and national standards. Most teachers use these as a starting point for planning for the year and for weekly lessons. They are very useful as you plan and work with teachers in the grades preceding and following yours; you want to see a continuation of the progress students make over years. Content also refers to the materials you use for teaching; students need appropriately leveled materials in order to be successful. They also need to learn with a variety of genres, so the materials need to be representative of the key genre and topics in the curriculum. *Process* refers to all the instructional routines and groupings used to help students understand, practice, and apply new learning. *Products* are the work students complete that ensure they have grasped the concepts and strategies you are teaching and have ways of sharing them with others.

**Classroom Artifact Homework Exercise**

*Attention Deficit Disorder*

Go to the Homework and Exercises section in Chapter 4 of MyEducation Lab to view the artifact of a sample of writing that exemplifies a student with an "Attention Deficit Disorder." Complete the activities that follow, and save your work or transmit it to your professor as assigned.

## Planning for Differentiation

Think of the content that you need to teach. The standards and objectives of your district are helpful as a starting place. Let's consider one example, the objective in this case is that: "All students need to learn to summarize what they have read." That is a content objective that you decide to focus on in the fall. You have listened to your students tell the class about their summer activities, and you know some can use an approach that highlights key aspects of their activities and also includes some main idea statements. You want to see if they can transfer that knowledge as they also summarize what they read and the classroom activities in science and other inquiries. As you consider ways to help focus on summarizing, you decide to start with the task of summarizing short stories and informational articles. You know, however, that many of your students are not able to read long texts and a few are not able to read grade-level materials. Therefore, you will help students develop this skill using different materials, appropriate to their reading levels. You also want to consider students' interests. You know some are very interested in informational articles they read in their news magazine. For others, you will begin with selections in the basal readers that are connected with the thematic unit. Finding the materials that meet students' reading levels and interests is also part of the *content* you consider in your planning.

A second aspect of differentiation relates to the *product* or outcome of this instruction. You decide to differentiate how the students share their summaries. The products will vary by students' development levels. The product for some will be a group composed summary. For others, it will be an individually drawn summary with four-to-six frames that will represent different aspects of the summary. (Each section of a divided paper is used for a different part of the story summary: beginning, setting, development of the conflict, and then the resolution. With informational texts, the frames may indicate main idea, examples and supporting facts, and conclusion.) For other students, the product will be individually written summaries and for yet others, you may ask that they summarize orally for the class and share their responses.

The *process* you use will be similar for the whole class initially but then reflect their varied needs. You will provide instruction in what makes a good summary to the whole class. Then you will involve the whole class with a guided practice activity. You decide to use a short article you know the class will find interesting which you read aloud to the group. Then you can help them together think aloud and write a summary. You put their ideas on the board and edit and revise as the class contributes. You know you will need to help the students chunk similar ideas and find the most succinct ways of capturing the main points. From this overview and guided practice, you are prepared to give students much more work with summarizing. You know some who will need to be helped by more group process, while others seem to know what to do and can work on their own. You decide to develop two activities that can be done in small groups.

Students will be asked to read a short text and then compose summaries together. One student in each group who writes well will take on the role of transcribing what the group decides. All students will participate in rehearsed oral reading of portions of the text. You also plan for other students to read articles on the social studies topic you are studying and then write summaries individually. You let them know they will share what they learn orally with the class. You have two students who need much differentiated arts-focused activities to grasp the larger concepts. You decide to see if they can work together to create a collage showing the major ideas in a videotape that parallels the social studies material. By comparing various forms of summaries, you hope to stimulate students' awareness of the varieties of ways we communicate.

**Differentiation Requires Planning** This example using the basic aspects of instructional differentiation illustrates how teachers can engage in careful planning that respects the individual students in their classes. The more teachers provide varied experiences, the more they learn about what their specific students need and respond well to. In language arts, we know how valuable a variety of learning contexts is and how each serves particular purposes. As you prepare to teach, think about your readiness to involve students in:

- Whole class instruction
- Guided small group instruction
- Book clubs and discussion groups (student led)
- Listening and viewing stations
- Partner work for fluency and reading engagement
- Centers and work stations
- Inquiry and project-based teams
- Individual inquiry
- Reader's theater and drama

The most basic form of differentiation in language arts instruction comes as we insure that students read regularly in materials at their instructional levels. Matching students with appropriate reading texts is essential if students are going to make the gains as readers that they are capable of making. As explained in the chapter on Assessment, there are very quick ways of getting a basic idea of the appropriate reading level for students. Most materials now are leveled by one of the major systems (e.g., Lexile, Fountas and Pinnell; Rigby; etc.), so once you know the students' reading level you can find appropriate materials. At the upper grades, a quick fluency check can provide good data about the appropriateness of class textbooks or main sources being used. If some students fall below or above the level, then it is important to supplement the content with different texts.

IRA/NCTE 7

**Student Interests** It is important, also, to remember that students' *interests* are as important as their precise reading levels. Often, what students know and are interested in means that they have a larger vocabulary and more ability to infer the unfamiliar words in texts on these topics. Therefore, it is always important to listen to students as they read particular texts. Reading level and interest need to be considered together.

You can honor students' interests by giving them choices in writing; students should be given much encouragement to write on topics of personal interest and knowledge. There is no reason to give out Topics for the Week when students have so much to say.

It is important to create environments in which students feel safe to express their ideas and experiences and also safe to experiment with spelling and written conventions. Too much "red pencil" can shut down personal expression very quickly. Students should be encouraged to keep personal writing folders with ideas and snippets of experiences that can be elaborated on later.

One way upper-level teachers have been very successful in responding to students' interests is through a joint language arts and social studies project. The students study the twentieth century through their own personally chosen topics. There are clear guidelines for the kinds of explorations they need to include—written documents, personal interviews, and media. What is important for this discussion is that the range of topics is enormous—students have chosen to study the century from the perspective of music (jazz, blues, and the guitar), famous film stars (Lucille Ball), developments in science (aviation, polio, and computers), women's styles, immigration (by a recent immigrant from Romania), and so many more. What is interesting is that each of these topics provides a window on the century and the combination of the reports gives the class a much deeper understanding of the period than would be possible if students just read from a common text or set of articles. Students take great pride in their research efforts and in the presentations they create.

You can honor students' interests by giving them choices in research and writing; students should be given encouragement to write on topics of personal interest and knowledge.

**The Importance of Choice** Throughout this discussion of ways to differentiate for students, there is an underlying reality. Students do better when they have choices in what they will do and how they will represent or share their learning. Recent studies have concluded that choice is one of the most important factors that leads to positive responses to school tasks. Therefore, with the varieties of instructional contexts and activities possible, the more teachers can provide choices the more likely it is that students will put more effort into their own learning. This is critical!

## What Intellectual and Social Needs Are Important to Consider?

It is possible to understand students on a personal level when we consider their individual characteristics and ways of learning. You may have taken coursework in psychology that introduces the theory of multiple intelligences. You may also be familiar with different personality typologies that provide words to describe variations in learners' preferred styles of functioning. In the language arts classroom, attention to students' intrapersonal and social intelligence is important because much of the learning activities involve working together in collaborative projects and in small reading groups. The Engaging in Visual Literacy feature contains ideas for creating visual reminders for both elementary and intermediate students.

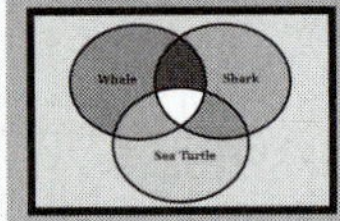

## Creating Visual Displays

We have found it very helpful with elementary students to be sure that directions and instructions are given both orally and in written and visual forms. Some students have great difficulty internalizing what teachers present orally. They need to hear and see the ideas and concepts. Teachers who develop hand signals find them very useful in keeping students' attention and reminding them of how they should be participating. For example, a class might develop a signal to show that it is time for listening by cupping one's hands behind one's ears.

In addition to physical signals, every classroom needs to include charts and lists of how to be successful as writers, speakers, and readers. When these charts include icons that represent each activity or strategy, students have additional keys to help them remember what they need to do.

In addition to displaying wall charts, give students bookmarks as a personal reminder of what they should do as they read and write or engage in oral conversations. Samples of bookmarks from primary and intermediate-grade classrooms are shown on the next page. Teachers can involve students in creating their own bookmarks and icons to represent steps that need to be taken in learning at all grade levels. The more students own the visual displays, the more they will use them. At the primary level, even having students color the graphics and putting their names on their bookmarks (before laminating them) gives students a greater sense of ownership. At the upper levels, students can also design their bookmarks and guides in their own personal ways.

> Every classroom needs to include charts and lists of what it means to be a successful writer, speaker, and reader.

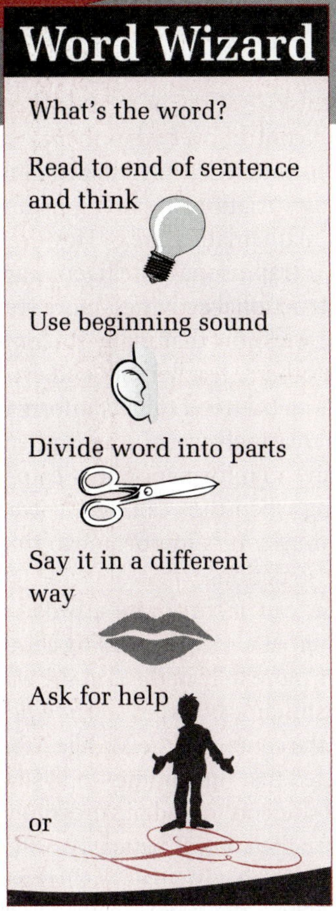


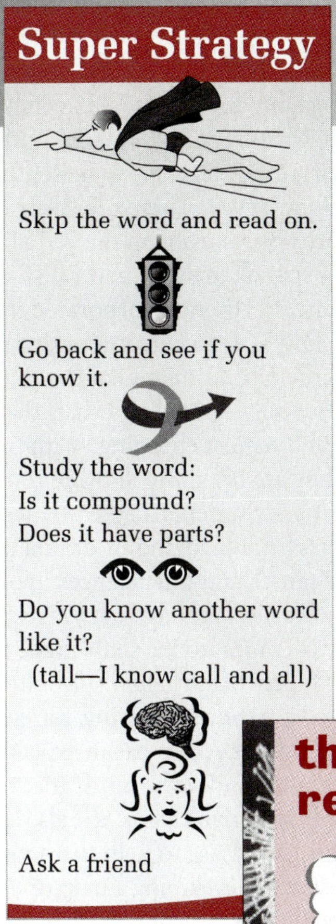


**Primary Grade Bookmarks**

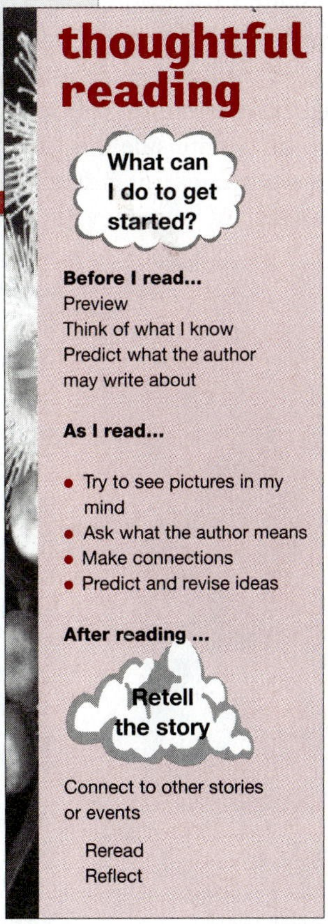


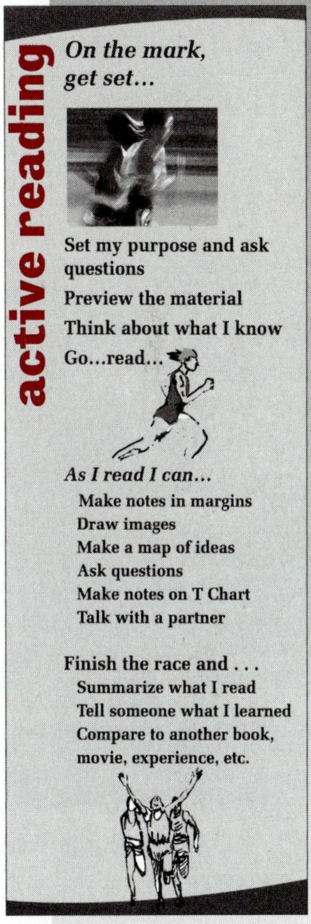


**Intermediate Grade Bookmarks**

## Accommodating Multiple Intelligences and Modes of Expression

IRA/NCTE 12

Classrooms are more engaging for all students when you use a variety of modalities in helping students learn new content and practice and gain control over what they need to master. It is also important for teachers to be sensitive to variations in students' multiple intelligences (Gardner, 1992). There are some strong variations in strengths our students possess; some are not as strong in the verbal and mathematical areas. However, when other strengths in spatial, artistic, naturalist, and intrapersonal intelligence are considered and ways to include them incorporated in instructional activities, more students can be successful. This is especially important since we know that many students are much stronger as learners in some modalities than in others. Teacher talk and even student oral discussion are only one way (verbal) that students attend to new information; in fact, it is often not the most engaging. With the increasingly visual environment in which students live, they are often much more responsive to information that comes in visual and media formats. Students also enjoy learning when they can be involved actively using their bodies and engaging in drama and music. It is important to find ways to involve all of the senses and intelligences in our instruction.

An example of how easily language arts instruction can incorporate a broader engagement of intelligences comes from a sixth-grade teacher. As a result of reading about multiple intelligences, Beth decided to help involve students more fully in the unit she was teaching on the Middle Ages. She was using Karen Cushman's book, *The Midwife's Apprentice,* as a core literature text. As she began explaining the context of the Middle Ages, she asked volunteer students to find some music that reflected that time frame—and suggested the church music of Gregorian chants. She also asked students to find pictures of the European countryside they could use to help them visualize the context better. Two students who seemed interested in developing a map of the countryside (spatial intelligence) drew a map of what they thought was the physical area in which the story was set. Some students also looked for examples of the clothing being worn and styles for both the common people and the wealthy. A few boys had learned something of the defense systems used in castles and wealthy estates and added their interests and knowledge. As they began studying the novel, the students were surrounded by music, visual images, and deeper appreciation of the context than was the case before this expanded frame. The combination of having an integrated unit with social studies and language arts that provided more time for the class activities, and thinking of multiple ways of knowing, allowed Beth to reach and engage all of her students.

Classrooms are more engaging for all students when you use a variety of modalities in helping students learn new content and practice and gain control over what they need to master.

## Teaching to Multiple Intelligences

A research study by Fink (2006) involved interviewing and studying sixty-six successful adults whom she characterizes as striving readers, people who struggled to read as children, some even as adults, and who had not responded to instructional interventions. These striving readers were compared to another group of successful adults who had not experienced problems learning to read. One chapter in her report is entitled "Learning to Read Through Multiple Intelligences." In it she describes an internationally known scientist, Roy Daniels, who is the youngest member ever elected to the National Academy of Sciences. As a child, he struggled in trying to read, and even now as an adult, he still struggles as a reader; however, his scientific intelligence is outstanding. Because of his intense interest in science, he has been an "avid" reader (p. 71) since he was young. Even though he couldn't read all the words and confused some letters, he kept reading. Daniels used visualization and retelling as strategies that helped him compensate when he struggled with materials that weren't in his interest areas. His high scientific intelligence kept him going during his school years, despite teachers' and counselors' warnings that he wouldn't succeed. Daniels's interest and his breadth of knowledge of the concepts he reads about help him overcome his decoding problems. Daniels is a clear example of someone with very different intelligences, and someone illustrative of those needing and deserving accommodations so their potential can be realized. We don't often have such extreme disparities in intelligence in our students, but recognizing the variations that exist and being alert for students' particular strengths is something we must do.

Another surprising finding from Fink's study was the powerful role of students' interest in their becoming expert readers. She reports, "individual interest emerged from the data as a powerful and unexpected result that could not be ignored" (p. 145). In each of the cases of striving readers, it was some compelling interest and support from some mentor that helped these readers achieve. Again, the importance of knowing students individually and finding their strengths and interests comes through as an important theme.

## Teaching Students Who Are Gifted

With much attention directed to struggling students through No Child Left Behind legislation, students who are gifted and talented are sometimes overlooked in planning instruction. These students deserve our attention, too. Rather than sending them off to read more difficult material or to do independent projects, students who are gifted need and deserve instruction appropriate to their learning needs. We need to be careful that students who are gifted are not given books and materials beyond their developmental and conceptual levels. Much of the fiction older readers can interpret is beyond the experiential and developmental level of younger, gifted readers. It is better to create tasks through which students become critical readers and thinkers. These challenges can be created by having students read several books on the same theme or topic and learn to compare and contrast them. Looking for differences in authors' purposes, styles of writing, use of examples, and other important features can help these able students stretch their minds by going more deeply into the content. Students can become discriminate readers and, in the process, begin to write more, too.

Students who are gifted need to be stimulated in their self-expression through a variety of writing activities. With the Internet available, these students can be linked with others in different parts of the country or the world. They can extend the class learning by linking it beyond the classroom. Some international exchanges have been very productive in helping students see themselves as citizens of a world community.

There are many ways students who are gifted can be stimulated through the language arts/reading program by deepening and extending what they do with the same basic units or themes the class is studying. It is differentiating their content through materials and thinking objectives, differentiating the processes they are asked to employ through teacher guidance (i.e., using thinking maps and graphic organizers to compare and contrast, Question the Author, or create another parallel text), and differentiating the products they create (producing a play or musical variation; creating a collage of the themes and characters; writing a critical review, etc.). Students who have special gifts and talents are not all alike. By working with families and coordinators, you will find the best ways to stimulate these students and help them maintain their role as part of the whole class.



## revisit the classroom challenge

More and more, teachers are being asked to welcome students who are still learning English into their general education programs. Therefore, it is important that teachers such as Mrs. Jones learn more about the needs of these students and adapt instruction to meet their needs. By looking more deeply at students such as Sonya, it is possible to determine if her reluctance to speak in the book discussion group is due to shyness or to deeper issues with her production of English. By giving students more time to prepare their responses before speaking and letting them practice voicing their thoughts with a partner first in settings where there is little risk of failure, teachers can support students who are ELLs journey to English competence. Teachers in schools receiving more English learners can join together to study about second language acquisition and ways to scaffold instruction for these students.

## chapter review

Our classrooms are filled with unique students. It is our privilege as teachers to get to know each of them and create both nurturing and challenging opportunities for them to continue to learn and grow. It is important that, as teachers, we think deeply about the individuality of each child we welcome into our classroom. What are their life experiences, what interests capture their attention, how do they learn most productively, and what kinds of interpersonal contexts bring out their best efforts?

### How Do We Define Diversity?

This chapter looks at diversity from a variety of perspectives. One of the most obvious areas of diversity at this time of large-scale immigration is language and cultural diversity. Differences in language are clear immediately when we receive students who are English learners in the classroom. However, there are many layers of diversity beneath the surface, too. Cultural expectations for how schools run, what teachers and students should do, and the roles of parents in education also vary by culture. Schools need to invite parents to share their experiences and expectations and also create contexts so parents can develop an understanding of the school's instructional practices and expectations. Many families who have not had positive school experiences often hesitate to take an active role in their own children's education. It is important to be sensitive to their emotional fears of schooling and find ways to reach them. It is also important to find ways to reach males—fathers and caregivers—who may not feel welcomed in the school. Diversity characterizes our school community at many layers. Successful teachers and schools listen, learn about their families, and build bridges across differences.

### What Do You Need to Consider When Teaching English Language Learners?

English learners develop oral language quite quickly when they have opportunities to hear English spoken and then to experience using English in a supportive environment. ELLs go from a stage of receptive language when they don't feel comfortable speaking to a stage of fluent conversational English before they are able to participate fully in academic language and learning. Both language and nonlinguistic elements of communication are important to consider; miscommunication can occur on the nonverbal level as well as the verbal. One of the best ways to help students experiment with English in the classroom is to permit them to work with partners and small groups. In these settings, students have less fear of making errors than in large group situations. There are several activities teachers can use that support ELLs. These include Think-Pair-Share, Say Something, Reading and Writing Buddies, and Partner Reading.



## How Does Diversity Affect Your Classroom?

The longer you teach, the more you will be aware of the diversity within even what seems a fairly "homogeneous" community. At the first level, it is important to learn about the families and their experiences with schooling. Be sure you take time to explain the curriculum and your instructional practices and expectations to the families of your students. Involve parents in school events and curriculum-focused events. Then learn as much as you can about each of the students in your classroom.

## How Can You Differentiate Instruction?

Students deserve classrooms that provide opportunities for them to succeed. That requires teachers to create varied approaches to learning. Using Tomlinson's framework, three dimensions of differentiation need to be considered: the content, the processes, and the products. The importance of creating varied ways for students to learn is highlighted by Fink's study of gifted adults. Some had severe learning problems with traditional literacy. Yet, with accommodations they all find ways to bypass their areas of weakness. This is a clear example to teachers to be problem-solvers in working with students with special needs.

## What Intellectual and Social Needs Are Important to Consider?

Students are quite different in their preferred ways of learning and in their psychological preferences. Some are verbal and thrive in traditional language arts activities; others think more visually or kinesthetically and will respond to visual arts and project work. Some enjoy working in groups; others prefer solitary or partner activity. The more you can provide multiple ways of learning to your students, the more students you will reach. Students who are gifted, students with learning challenges, and students learning English (in particular) need our attention. Yet, all students have specific learning preferences and ways of functioning most comfortably. It is the challenge of teachers to provide options for all to be successful learners.



Now go to www.myeducationlab.com to take a Pretest to assess your initial comprehension of chapter content, study chapter content with your individualized Study Plan, take a Posttest to assess your understanding of chapter content, practice your teaching skills with Building Teaching Skills exercises, and build a deeper, more applied understanding of chapter content with Homework and Exercises.

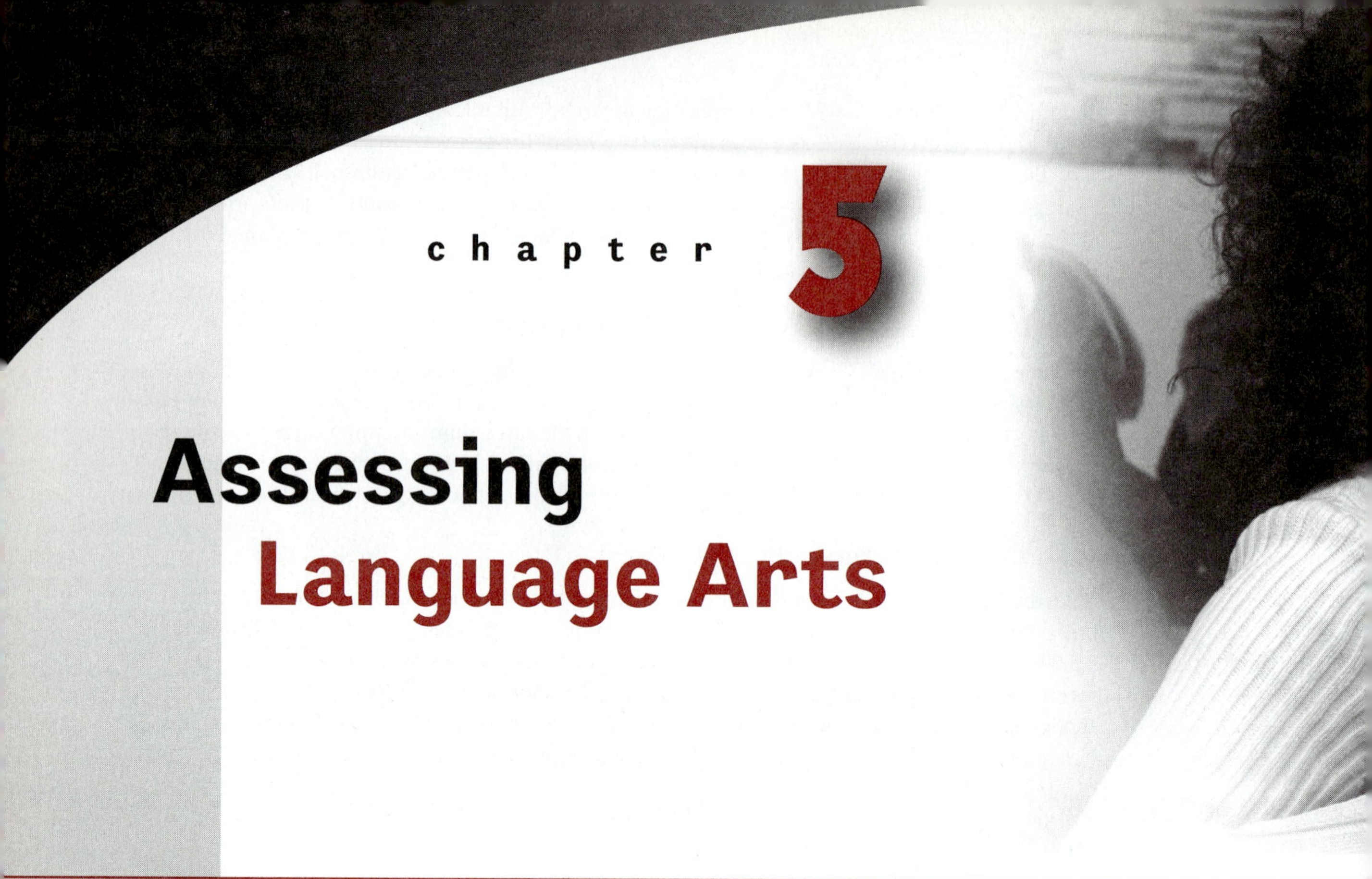

chapter 5

# Assessing Language Arts

## classroom challenge

**To get ready** for his new class of third-graders, Mr. Bergen spends one day before school looking over assessment information he has gathered on his incoming students. Sitting at a large round table, he has several sources of information before him, including a stack of cumulative folders that contains the past academic performance of each student and comments from past teachers. He also has each student's test results of the previous year's language arts standards of learning assessment. His school began portfolio assessment in the language arts last year, so he has all of his students' portfolios.

These portfolios contain samples of writing and responses to reading done by the students. Each portfolio also includes student and teacher comments about each student's progress and challenges in reading and writing last year. As he looks through all of this information, Mr. Bergen begins to develop a picture of each student. He sees those who passed the Virginia Standards of Learning (SOL) test and those who did not. He identifies students who enjoy writing and those who are more reluctant writers. He notices the instructional strategies that teachers used last year in conjunction with the students' portfolios. As he looks more closely at the portfolios, he realizes that many of them contain only finished writing products,

making it difficult to see what kind of writing process the students used. The writing checklists included in the portfolios reinforce this observation as they reflect more summative than formative assessment.

He needs to find out how his students write. Other than teacher comments and the results of the state language arts test, Mr. Bergen does not know how his students read. He needs a more complete picture. He has some useful assessment information but knows that he needs to gather more information about his students. This will enable him to develop the language arts instruction that will support his students in becoming better readers and writers.

## Questions for Reflection

1. What additional language arts assessment information should Mr. Bergen obtain early in the school year?
2. How can he monitor his students' progress during the year to ensure that his instruction will advance his students in the language arts?
3. What language arts assessment should be carried out at the end of the school year to see how his students have progressed?

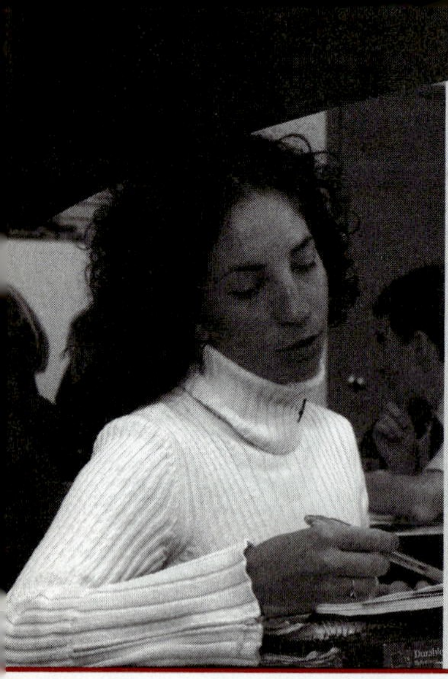

## anticipating this chapter

To help you answer these and other questions about language arts assessment, this chapter addresses these questions:

- Why is language arts assessment important?
- What are different perspectives on language arts assessment?
- What are principles to follow in language arts assessment?
- How can you assess language arts?
- When do you assess language arts?

# Why Is Language Arts Assessment Important?

With the advent of No Child Left Behind (NCLB) legislation (2001) and Reading First initiatives (2001) at the federal level, coupled with high-stakes testing and school accreditation at the school district level, language arts assessment has taken on greater importance than ever before. States feel the impact of NCLB as they put in place state-mandated assessments to measure student performance on statewide language arts standards of learning (SOLs). School districts feel the impact as they develop curriculum and instructional objectives that ensure their students succeed on the state-mandated SOL assessments. Student performance in individual schools in the district reveals whether all students are making adequate yearly progress (AYP), which ones are not, and whether a school becomes at risk for losing its accreditation. With this kind of accountability at the school level, teachers, curriculum, and instructional practices come under close scrutiny.

Because tax dollars fund public schools, various constituencies want to know how we are doing with our students. The U.S. Congress and Department of Education want to know how students perform in the language arts areas within and across all the states. State legislatures and departments of education want to know how students are doing within and across schools throughout the state. City, town, and county jurisdictions and local school boards want to know how students are doing within and across grades in each school of their respective school districts. Parents want to know how their students are doing compared to students in other classrooms, grades, and schools. Teachers want to know how their own students are doing and how their students' performance compares with that of other teachers at the same grade level. With so much emphasis on assessment coming from so many quarters, how can you ensure that your students will be successful on national, state, and local assessments and, at the same time, that they become successful readers and writers? In the final analysis, it is you, the classroom

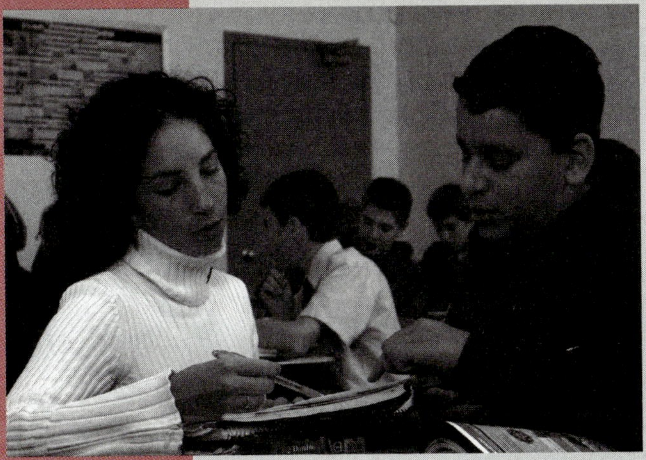

Through your own assessment and instruction, you will know more about the language, reading, and writing abilities of your students than any single national, state, or school district assessment can measure.



teacher, who best assesses student literacy performance and best instructs students based on your assessment (Johnston, 1987; Gunning, 1998). Through your own assessment and instruction, you will know more about the language, reading, and writing abilities of your students than any single national, state, or school district assessment can measure. The results of your assessment will guide you in instructional decisions and the results of your instruction will guide you in your assessment decisions. "Assessment informs instruction, instruction informs assessment."

# What Are Different Perspectives on Language Arts Assessment?

Fortunately, national, state, and school language arts assessment standards are quite similar although they approach assessment from slightly different perspectives.

## National Language Arts Standards and Assessment

At the national level, professional organizations such as the International Reading Association (IRA), National Council of Teachers of English (NCTE), and the National Association for the Education of Young Children (NAEYC) have worked together to create national standards for reading and writing instruction. A joint statement by the IRA and NAEYC (1998) has a strong developmental framework because the focus was reading and writing instruction for preschool through third grade. Even within this developmental framework, the joint statement does recognize that "development and learning occur in and are influenced by social and cultural contexts. Language, reading, and writing are shaped by culture" (p. 16). The statement goes on to recognize the cultural and linguistic diversity of our student population and that "Teachers should never use a child's dialect, language, or culture as a basis for making judgments about (children's) intellect or capabilities" (p. 16). A portion of the early reading and writing standards found in this joint statement contains this phase:

### Phase 3: Early Reading and Writing

First-graders can:

- Read and retell familiar stories
- Orally read with reasonable fluency
- Use letter-sound associations, word parts, and context to identify words
- Identify an increasing number of words by sight
- Write about topics that are personally meaningful

IRA/NCTE

The IRA and NCTE (1996) also developed a joint statement and set of standards to guide language arts instruction. As the preface to the twelve standards states: "The vision guiding these standards is that all students must have the opportunities and resources to develop the language skills they need to pursue life's goals and to participate fully as informed productive members of society" (p. 9). With this opening statement, both professional organizations created a larger context for the application of their standards that go beyond the classroom. Here are several standards that illustrate their real-world application:

***Standard 1*** Students read a wide range of print and nonprint texts to build an understanding of texts, of themselves, and of the cultures of the United States and the world; to acquire new information; to respond to the needs and demands of society and the workplace; and for personal fulfillment. Among these texts are fiction and nonfiction, classic and contemporary works (IRA/NCTE, 1996, p. 19).

***Standard 2*** Students read a wide range of literature from many periods in many genres to build an understanding of the many dimensions (e.g., philosophical, ethical, aesthetic) of human experience (IRA/NCTE, 1996, p. 21).

***Standard 3*** Students apply a wide range of strategies to comprehend, interpret, evaluate, and appreciate texts. They draw on their prior experience, their interactions with other readers and writers, their knowledge of word meaning and of other texts, their word identification strategies, and their understanding of textual features (e.g., sound-letter correspondence, sentence structure, context, graphics) (IRA/NCTE, 1996, p. 22).

Another feature of these language arts standards is that they are not assigned any grade level or developmental phase as are the IRA/NAEYC literacy standards. If you look at the Standard 3 of the IRA/NCTE standards, you will find some overlap with the IRA/NAEYC Phase 3: Early Reading and Writing standard. In Standard 3, you can see reference to understanding text structures such as "sound-letter correspondence, sentence structure, context, graphics" that is similar to students "can use letter-sound associations, word parts, and context to identify words" in the phase 3 standards. Standard 3 is a more general standard for all students while the Phase 3 standard is more specific to first-grade students. For the full joint IRA/NAEYC statement and standards, see the NAEYC website (www.naeyc.org). The IRA/NCTE joint statement and standards can be found on the NCTE website (www.ncte.org). For your reference, the full text of the IRA/NCTE Standards are also found inside the front cover of this text. National testing agencies have also become involved in national language arts standards and their assessment. The major national assessment that must be given in all the states in fourth, eighth, and twelfth grades is the National Assessment of Educational Progress (NAEP). In 2009, a new framework will be used for the first time, replacing the earlier 1992 framework. This new NAEP Reading Framework includes two types of texts: literary and informational. Poetry will be included at all three levels of testing. An important shift in the assessments is the inclusion of more informational texts, recognizing the shifting nature of reading in our society. By the twelfth grade, the majority of the reading will be in informational material. The fourth-grade test will have equal passages of literary and informational texts; the eighth-grade test will have 45 percent literary and 55 percent informational; by twelfth grade, the distribution will be 30 percent literary and 70 percent informational. The assessments will also include items that measure vocabulary knowledge as an aid to comprehension:

1. Reading literary texts

   Literary passages will come from three categories of literary texts: fiction, literary nonfiction (e.g., essays, speeches, biographies, and autobiographies), and poetry.
2. Reading informational texts

   Informational texts will come from three categories: exposition, argumentation and persuasion, and procedural texts and documents. The documents may include graphic representations that ask readers to draw on information presented in varied formats. Embedded documents will be used in grades 4 and 8 and in free-standing documents.
3. Reading multiple texts

   Reading and integrating information from more than one text is a common task for students at all grade levels. Therefore, the test includes intertextual passage sets to approximate the normal type of reading that schools require.

Four cognitive tasks will be assessed:

1. Forming a general understanding of text
2. Developing an interpretation of text
3. Making reader/text connections
4. Examining content and structure of text

A close examination of this framework reveals similarities between the NAEP reading framework and IRA/NCTE standards that pertain to reading. Look at the IRA/NCTE Standard 1 and the NAEP description of the materials to read. Both refer to being able to gain knowledge about the world through reading a variety of different texts. For the complete *Nation's Report Card: 2005 Reading* along with more discussion of the reading standards that are part of the 2009 framework and assessment go to http://nces.ed.gov/nationsreportcard/reading/. Other national organizations, forums, and study groups have published national language arts standards that also overlap with the language arts standards just cited (Educational Testing Service, 2003; National Reading Panel, 2000). This is important to remember as we turn to state language arts standards and the assessments based on state standards.

## State Language Arts Standards and Assessment

Although national standards and their assessment focus on general language arts performance by students across the country, the assessment of state standards compares the language arts performance of students across school districts. State standards generally adhere to national standards, though there is more specificity to state standards and their assessment. The state standards also have more impact on a school district's language arts curriculum, instruction, and assessment than the national standards because of their more detailed approach. Virginia and California, for example, have a language arts standard that requires third graders to read and demonstrate their understanding of stories in various ways. If you go to the Virginia Department of Education website (www.doe.virginia.gov/VDOE/Superintendent/Sols/2002) and the California Department of Education website (www.cde.ca.gov/be/st/ss/enggrade3.asp), you can see how similar Virginia's 3.5 and 3.6 reading standards are to California's 2.0 and 3.0.

Both states require nearly identical behavior from their respective third-grade students in reading comprehension of fiction and nonfiction. Notice also that these standards are more specific in identifying the standard and the indicators required to meet the standards than the national standards spelled out in the IRA/NCTE or IRA/NAEYC standards. They still echo these national standards but speak more specifically about how teachers should instruct students regarding reading and writing in the third grade. This becomes more evident when you look at the third-grade English assessments conducted in Virginia and California.

## School District Language Arts Standards and Assessment

Language arts standards used by school districts to develop appropriate curriculum and instructional strategies are derived from language arts standards adopted by the state. Because students will be assessed on these standards, school districts want to be included in the language arts standards and ensure that they are included in the guides that shape the language arts curriculum. School districts also have to consider the impact of NCLB and other national and state mandates as they develop their own language arts curricula and assessment plans. The careful alignment of national, state, and local school district standards of learning for language arts ensures that what you teach in your classroom prepares your students for the mandated assessments conducted each year in your school district.

As you cover the language arts standards identified by your school district and ensure that they reflect state and national standards, consider how you know they reflect how children learn and develop competency with all the language arts. How do you know whether or not you are teaching them in a developmentally appropriate manner? A look at developmental language arts benchmarks can help ensure that you do.

Development in the language arts occurs in stages that overlap one another, and students add onto what they have developed at one stage as they go to the next. This view makes language arts development continuous while recognizing that differences among individual students are a normal part of language arts development. When you place language arts standards within the context of this developmental perspective, students in the classroom can perform differently on these assessments. Table 5.1 presents benchmarks for language arts development.

We have modified the literacy development benchmarks so that they fit within the context of language arts assessment. We have structured the benchmarks in stages of language arts development and have added spelling as a separate area of development at each stage, creating four areas of development: oral language, reading, writing, and spelling; we call them stages of language arts development. The names of the stages, rather than grades 1–5, convey the idea that students are moving from one stage to another and take what they learn in one stage and bring it to the next. The names also reinforce the notion that students can be in two stages at once for different areas of language arts development. If you compare these expanded benchmarks with the national or state standards, you can see considerable overlap. The use of benchmarks allows you to follow your state and school district language arts assessment standards while keeping a developmental perspective in mind as you assess and instruct your own students.

## Table 5.1
## Language Arts Development Benchmarks

**Early Emergent Literacy** (Preschool)

- Oral Language
  1. Begins to use different language functions
  2. Listens to and enjoys stories
  3. Enjoys rhyming and other word play
  4. Knowledge of grammar and language conventions grows
- Reading
  1. Acquiring print concepts
  2. Knows purpose of print
  3. Knows familiar writing genres
  4. Predicts and constructs meaning
  5. Retells familiar story
  6. Enjoys listening to literature read aloud
  7. Beginning of phonemic awareness
- Writing
  1. Knows what writing is for
  2. Tries to write or pretends to write
  3. Learning left to right progression
  4. Uses variety of writing implements
  5. Asks what something says
- Spelling
  1. Knows some letters
  2. Knows sounds of some letters
  3. Beginning awareness of letter-sound links
  4. Writes letters and letter-like forms

---

**Emergent Literacy** (Grades K–1)
(adds to Early Emergent Literacy competencies)

- Oral Language
  1. Uses standard sentence construction
  2. Participates in discussions
  3. Facility with oral language
- Reading
  1. Knows most print concepts
  2. Can track written words spoken aloud in text
  3. Learning common phonic elements in words
  4. Matches upper and lower case letters
  5. Growing phonemic awareness
  6. Able to use story elements in retelling

*(Continued)*

## Table 5.1
## (Continued)

- Writing
  1. Uses letters in writing and other writing conventions
  2. Knows all letters of the alphabet
  3. Uses invented spelling in writing
  4. Writes on journals and shares writing
  5. Beginning to add story and informational writing to personal writing
  6. Starting to use the writing process
- Spelling
  1. Represents beginning and ending sounds in words
  2. Spells some words correctly
  3. Moving toward complete phonetic spelling of words

---

**Beginning Reading and Writing** (Grades 1–2 or 3)
(adds to Emergent Literacy competencies)

- Oral Language
  1. Use of standard English grows
  2. Ability to use language in variety of settings
  3. Interest in words grows
- Reading
  1. Sight vocabulary continues to grow
  2. Reading fluency grows
  3. Phonics and structural analysis for word recognition
  4. Uses context to learn words and their meaning
  5. Uses variety of comprehension strategies
  6. Has positive attitude about reading
  7. Begins to use text resources in all subjects
- Writing
  1. Widespread writing
  2. Shares writing
  3. Writes in different genres for different purposes
  4. Uses the writing process
  5. Gains control over writing conventions
- Spelling
  1. Spells more words correctly
  2. Recognizes common spelling patterns
  3. Becomes aware of features to spell words besides letter-sounds

---

**Almost Fluent Reading and Writing** (Grades 2–4 or 5)
(adds to Beginning Reading and Writing competencies)

- Oral Language
  1. Use of standard English continues to grow
  2. Learning to differentiate between standard and nonstandard English
  3. Use of all language functions grows
  4. Speaking and listening vocabulary growing
  5. Aware of language techniques used by speakers
- Reading
  1. All word recognition strategies being used
  2. Has instructional reading level at least at grade level
  3. Comprehension strategies continue to grow
  4. Enjoys reading independently in different genres for different purposes
  5. Silent reading grows
  6. Developing research skills through variety of media and texts
- Writing
  1. Writes for different purposes and audiences

2. Uses different writing forms and genres
3. Self-evaluates own writing
4. Shares writing
5. Uses feedback in revision
6. Grows in knowledge and use of writing conventions
7. Makes links between reading and writing

- Spelling
  1. Knowledge of spelling patterns grows
  2. Makes link between spelling, pronunciation, and structural elements in words
  3. Edits for spelling effectively
  4. Increases percentage of words spelled correctly in writing

**Fluent Reading and Writing** (Grades 5–12)
(adds to Almost Fluent Reading and Writing Literacy competencies)

- Oral Language
  1. Uses language in a variety of functions
  2. Uses language with a variety of audiences
  3. Able to move between formal and informal modes of talking
  4. Vocabulary continues to grow
- Reading
  1. Adjusts reading to meet purpose for reading
  2. Understands and reads different genres
  3. Uses variety of comprehension strategies
  4. Enjoys reading
  5. Expands research skills
- Writing
  1. Continues to expand purposes for writing
  2. Uses writing rubrics and self-evaluation to assess writing
  3. Uses writing process
  4. Uses different techniques for prewriting and revising
  5. Voice and style evident in writing
  6. Continues to make connection between reading and writing different genres
- Spelling
  1. Conventional spelling widely used
  2. Edits for spelling correctly
  3. Makes spelling connection among alternate forms of words
  4. Adds meaning to pronunciation and structural elements as guide to spelling

*Source:* Adapted from Cooper, J. and Kiger, N. (2005). *Literacy assessment: Helping teachers plan instruction.* Boston: Houghton Mifflin. Used by permission.

## What Are Principles to Follow in Language Arts Assessment?

Cooper (2003) identifies eight principles to help guide teachers in carrying out literacy assessment in the classroom. They can also be applied to all language arts, not just reading and writing, which is why we call them principles for language arts assessment.

### Principles for Effective Language Arts Assessment

1. Assessment is an ongoing process that occurs whenever a child speaks, listens, reads, writes, or views something and informs you.
2. Assessment is part of instruction. Whenever students engage in instructional activities, what they do and how they do it, informs you. When a student discusses a story with other students, you assess their language and their knowledge of the story.
3. Assessment is authentic. If you want to know how well a student writes sentences in an essay, have him or her write an essay instead of giving them a grammar test.
4. Assessment is a collaborative, reflective process. Self-assessment is important for students so they can learn on their own beyond the realm of the classroom. By making assessment collaborative, freedom, responsibility, and respect become hallmarks of the relationship between teachers and students.
5. Assessment is multidimensional. One test is not enough. Multiple measures yield more reliable measures. Writing portfolios with drafts, self-assessments, revisions, and final products in different writing assignments provides a more broad and complete picture of a student's writing performance at the end of a semester of work than does a single writing assignment.
6. Assessment considers cultural, developmental, and learners factors. This means there is not one assessment for all students. Accommodations need to be made in all these areas when considering assessment measures.
7. Assessment identifies students' strengths as well as needs. This provides a place to start and build upon as students move toward new learning. A student can extend a strong imaginative oral language through poetry writing.
8. Assessment reflects an understanding of how students learn to read, write, and use language. Because learning to spell has a developmental aspect to it, spelling assessment that focuses only on memorizing word lists is not in keeping with what we know about learning to spell.

It is important to keep these assessment principles in mind as you consider language arts assessment in the classroom. You can meet national, state, and school language arts standards within the context of these principles of language arts assessment by using the developmental language arts benchmarks as part of your formative and ongoing assessment. This keeps the student as your primary guide for instruction and not just a list of standards. See the Exploring Technology feature for a list of online tools and resources to support classroom assessment.

## How Can You Assess Language Arts?

We have discussed the relationship between national, state, and local school district language arts standards and their assessment, and we have addressed guiding principles for language arts assessment in the classroom. Now we turn to techniques and strategies that you can use to assess the language arts performance of the students in your classroom.

**exploring technology**

## Online Assessment Tools

**Reading Assessment Calculator (pt.liverpool.k12.ny.us/reading/rcalculator/assessmentcalc.htm)**
The reading assessment calculator is an online tool for scoring running records. After taking a running record of a student's oral reading, simply enter the number of running words in the text, the number of errors made by the student, and the number of self-corrections. With a click of a button, the error rate, accuracy rate, and self-correction rate are instantly calculated.

**Level Estimator (pt.liverpool.k12.ny.us/reading/levelestimator/estimator.htm)**
The level estimator is an online tool for determining a student's reading level. The assessor selects the student's grade level from a pull-down menu, which results in a display of a short passage with a picture for the student to read. When the student has finished reading, the assessor enters the number of errors, after which an accuracy percentage is calculated, along with information about the meaning of the rate. Based on the accuracy percentage, the level estimator determines whether the child's comprehension of the particular passage is above level, on level, or below level.

**Reading Assessment Database (www.sedl.org/reading/rad)**
This searchable database, developed by the Southwest Educational Development Laboratory (SEDL), provides information about eighty reading assessment tools for students in pre-K to grade 3.

Language arts assessment can best inform your language arts instruction when used in a five-part language arts assessment cycle. The steps in the assessment cycle include:

- Step 1: Identify the language arts standard or learning objective from the language arts curriculum
- Step 2: Develop and implement instruction to meet the language arts standard or objective
- Step 3: Assess student learning based on the instruction
- Step 4: Evaluate student performance and the language arts instruction
- Step 5: Identify new learning objective(s) based on teacher evaluation

Once the assessment cycle is complete, the cycle begins again. The assessment cycle is valuable because it informs you on your students' progress in the language arts curriculum. It also provides useful information that can be shared with students, parents, principals, and other school administrators to document student performance, the impact of the language arts curriculum, and instructional practices. Look at Figure 5.1 for a visual representation of the assessment cycle.

For assessment to be effective and informative, it must be authentic assessment (Valencia, Hiebert, and Afflerbach, 1994). Authentic assessment looks at what students

Figure 5.1 The Language Arts Assessment Cycle

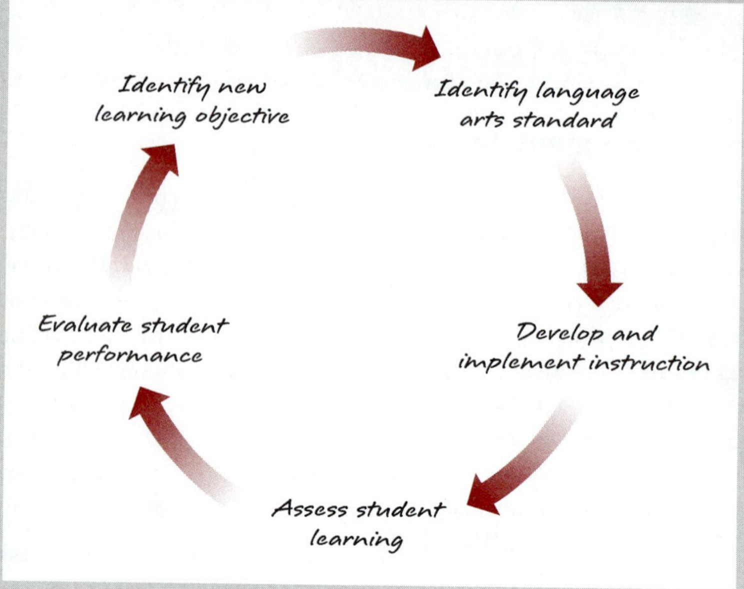


**BUILDING TEACHING SKILLS: Classroom Artifact Exercise**

*Goals and Self-Evaluation*

Go to the Building Teaching Skills section of Chapter 5 of MyEducationLab and examine the artifact, "Goals and Self-Evaluation," which is a sample of a student's self-reflection regarding a portfolio. Complete the activities that follow, and save your work or transmit it to your professor as assigned.

actually do in real reading, writing, and language experiences and falls into two broad assessment categories: formative and summative assessment. *Formative* assessment can occur at any step during students' learning experiences and can provide helpful feedback to students as they go through the learning experience (O'Connor, 2002). For example, it can address various steps in the writing process used by students as they work on a writing assignment. Monitoring students' predictions as they proceed through a story is another example of formative assessment. *Summative* assessment looks more at the end product or final result of a learning experience. The final draft of a writing assignment or an oral argument in a debate can be the object of summative assessment. Summative assessment can take the form of unit tests given upon the completion of an English unit or segment of the language arts curriculum. The assessment of student learning and teacher instruction should be important goals of each type of assessment. What follows are specific ways of doing both kinds of assessments.

## General Language Arts Assessment Techniques

There are formal and informal assessment techniques that can be used with any of the language arts. Others are particularly suited for a specific area such as writing or spelling. They can provide an assessment of an entire grade level in a school district or a single student in that grade. Here are examples of formative and summative general language arts assessment techniques.

**Standardized Norm-Referenced Tests** Tests that compare the performance of students to the sample of students used to create the scoring norms of the test are called *standardized norm-referenced tests* (SNRTs). The tests are *standardized* because they follow identical or standardized directions for administering and scoring the results. They are *norm-referenced* because a student's test score can be compared with the scores of students in the sample used to create norms for the test. When arrayed, the sample scores resemble a normal distribution, or bell-shaped curve. Figure 5.2 shows what this bell-shaped curve looks like. The numbers at the base of the curve represent the percentage of scores distributed along the curve. Once students' raw test scores have been compared to the sample norm scores, they can be converted to standard scores, percentiles, or stanines. Standard scores use the standard deviation to determine how far above or below the mean score an individual score is. For example, if a standard deviation is 10 and the mean is 50, a standard score of 60 represents a score that is one standard deviation above the mean score.

A percentile score expresses in percentage form how well a student did with respect to other students. For example, an 85th percentile score indicates that the student did as well or better than 85 percent of all students in the test sample. Stanine scores also use standard deviations to express test scores by dividing the normal distribution into nine equal parts. The fifth stanine represents the middle of the distribution,

Figure 5.2

## Standardized Test Scores

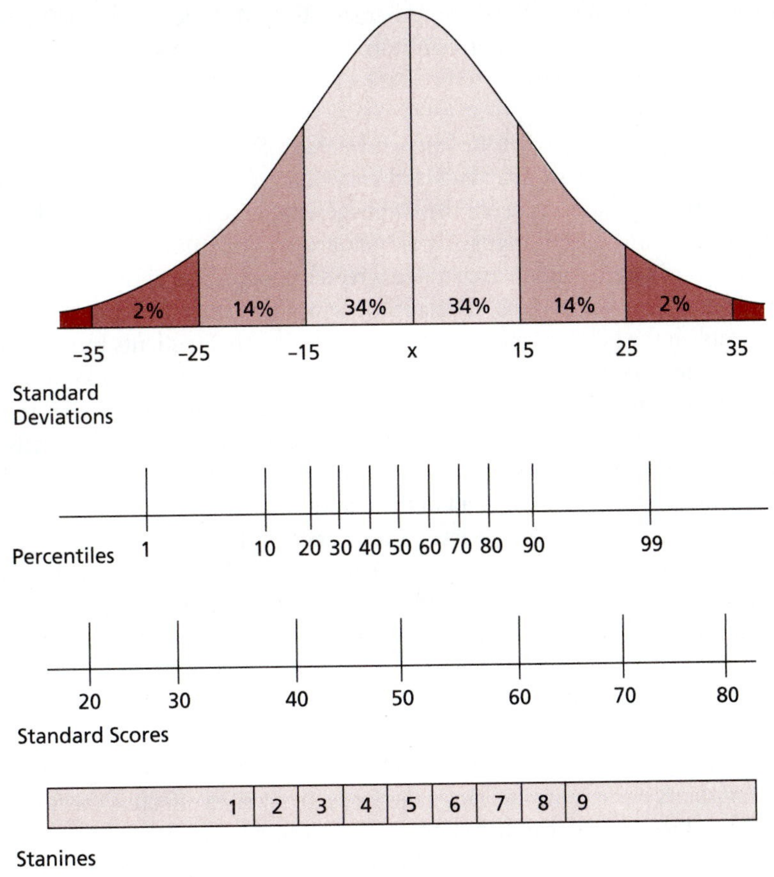

with four stanines falling below the middle and four falling above the middle of the distribution of scores. If a student has an eighth stanine score, the score would be more than 1 standard deviation above the mean of the scores.

If you look closely at Figure 5.2, you can see how all the scores are related to one another on a normal distribution of scores (the bell-shaped curve). The numbers at the base of the curve represent the percentage of scores distributed along the curve. For example, 68 percent of the scores on a normal distribution of scores fall within (±) one standard deviation of the mean of all the scores. This statistical conversion technique allows you to compare students across your class, school, district, state, and nation after all the students have taken the norm-referenced test.

School districts often use SNRTs at the end of the school year to measure student progress on general language arts measures. They also use them to compare groups of students within grades, across grades, and across schools. As such, they generally do not yield helpful information about individual students on specific language arts strengths or weaknesses. This can account for those occasions when students' performance on such a test does not compare well with other language arts measures such as running records or read-and-retells. The results of SNRTs are limited and only provide a gross measure of student performance. Their ease of administration and scoring, however, coupled with their general comparison value make them popular assessments around the country. The No Child Left Behind (2001) legislation also requires the use of standardized tests for assessing the academic progress of students. The more widely used ones include the Comprehensive Tests of Basic Skills (2000), the Iowa Tests of Basic Skills (2001), the Metropolitan Achievement Tests (2000), and the Stanford Achievement Tests (2000).

**Standards-Based Criterion Referenced Tests** State-mandated language arts assessment often relies on standards-based *criterion referenced tests* (CRTs) to determine whether students have mastered the language arts standards established by the state. For example, if a third-grade language arts standard is "The student will identify the author's purpose," a test item might have students read a passage and choose the answer that best completes a sentence such as "The author wrote this story in order to _______." CRTs also establish the performance standard or criterion that students must achieve in order to "pass" the tests. Standards-based CRTs are important for you to know about because they have an impact on the language arts curriculum and instruction in local school districts. The results of this type of assessment are used for school accreditation, to determine whether students are making AYP (adequate yearly progress), and whether an instructional program can be used in the school. This assessment yields general information about the overall language arts performance of the students in your classroom that can be useful for grouping and instructional purposes. If the standards-based assessment is closely linked to the curriculum used in your school, it will yield more specific information for instructional purposes. Most states provide online access to practice tests or previously administered standards-based CRTs. Explore your state's department of education website to review them.

**Observations and Anecdotal Records** Watching and noting student behavior while students participate in a language arts activity is an effective way to assess student behavior. Observations can help answer questions such as: What phases of the writing process do students use or ignore? How do students engage one another in discussion groups? How accurate are students' predictions about their reading? To address these and other questions about what students do in actual language arts activities, make and record observations. The objectives and instruction for your language arts curriculum serve as the guide for what you want to observe and record. Other more generic classroom behaviors can also be the basis for your observations (Acheson, 1997). These include students' classroom behavior and interaction with other students as well as completion of assigned tasks. You can use your observations to assess student learning, as well as the effectiveness of your instruction and subsequent plans for instruction. Figure 5.3 contains anecdotal records of a third-grade teacher based on observations of students working on their writing and helping group members with revising their writing.

**Checklists** One way to reduce the amount of time it takes to jot down notes during your observations is to create a checklist of the behaviors you expect to see in your students. These can be arranged from frequently observed to not seen at all. The checklist can also reflect a continuum of behaviors that you might expect to encounter with students engaged in the learning experience. As with anecdotal records, checklists can



**Figure 5-3**

### Anecdotal Records of a Third Grade Teacher

Lucia - asks the group for help with her beginning paragraph

Henry - offers suggestions for putting her sentences in a different order

Sue - needs ending for her report on frogs + toads

Marcus - helps by asking her to go back to intro. paragraph and use those ideas to form ending paragraph. Like bookends.

Latetia - needs help with sentence combining. Good topic for mini-lesson for her and Samuel.

**Figure 5.4**

## Checklist Used for Monitoring Story Retellings

| Story Elements | Student Responses | Points |
|---|---|---|
| Story Setting: (10) | | |
| Introduction | | |
| Place | | |
| Story Characters: (10) | | |
| Main Characters | | |
| Other Characters | | |
| Story Problem: (5) | | |
| Identifies Problem | | |
| Story Action: (10) | | |
| Identifies Story Events | | |
| Retells Events in Order | | |
| Story Outcome: (5) | | |
| Identifies Problem Solution | | |
| Describes Story Ending | | |
| Total Points out of 40 | | |
| Additional Comments | | |

provide information about student performance as well as your instruction. For example, if your instruction focused on helping students learn about noun-verb agreement and it persists as a challenge in their writing, having noun-verb agreement in your checklist would alert you to the need for follow-up instruction in this area. Your learning objectives and language arts curriculum can give you guidance on what to include on your checklists. Figure 5.4 gives an example of a checklist used for monitoring story retellings.

**Attitudes, Interests, and Motivation** Important areas to assess include how students feel about their learning, what interests them, and what motivates them. This helps ensure that students are positively engaged in their learning. Obtaining a measure on a student's self-concept as a reader or writer can identify the kind of support the student needs. Self-concept questionnaires can help identify the factors that inhibit students' participation when they are reluctant to talk or participate in class discussions. Interest inventories can reveal what students like to read or write about. By tapping into their interests, you will help in motivating students to want to read and write.

A variety of assessment formats can be used to obtain information about students' attitudes, interests, and motivations. Have younger students answer questions you ask or have them complete sentences orally. Encourage them to draw or cut out pictures that depict their interests. Have older students write their responses according to the format used or draw as a means for expressing their interests and likes or dislikes about their learning experiences. Students are more likely to provide valid responses about their self-concept or interests when they feel trust for and from you as their teacher. Be sure to explain that the purpose of gathering this personal information is to help you help your students learn in ways that are interesting and responsive to their concerns and needs. Figure 5.5 shows examples of attitude and interest assessments completed by students for their teachers.

**Conferences** Assessment conferences with individual students are ideal settings for talking about any aspect of language arts. The conversation could focus on comprehension challenges and how to solve them. It might focus on steps that the student can take to better revise his or her writing. The student can provide feedback about the instruction he or she has found helpful or what additional clarification or elaboration is needed. Here are five points to keep in mind when preparing for an assessment conference:

1. Have a specific purpose for the conference.
2. Have the student bring to the conference all necessary materials or work.
3. Makes notes of what you and the student say.
4. Agree on the follow-up to the conference.
5. Keep the meeting brief—no longer than ten minutes.

Keys to a successful assessment conference include mutual respect and a desire to improve, both of which must be shared by you and your student. In the conference, you are assessing yourself as well as your student. Figure 5.6 contains notes taken at an assessment conference with Alberto, a fifth-grader.

**Portfolios** One of the best sources of information about student performance and progress in all of the language arts is the student portfolio. Your school may have portfolios as part of its assessment plan for students. Portfolios can contain finished work as well as

**Figure 5.5**

## Excerpts from Attitude and Interest Assessments

My favorite subject is ______________________.

My favorite author is ______________________.

After school I like to ______________________.

My favorite TV show is ______________________.

My hardest subject in school is ______________________.

I like to write about ______________________.

The hardest thing about writing is ______________________.

I like to talk about ______________________.

What I like best about school is ______________________.

What I like least about school is ______________________.

**Figure 5.6**

## Assessment Conference Notes

Assessment Conference

Name: Alberto

Date: April 25

Purpose: Writing

Comments: Alberto is having trouble getting started on his next writing assignment.

topic – sharks – where to start?

I want to see if he can brainstorm ideas about sharks.

– he brainstormed questions to ask about sharks which helped him get started.

-- What do they eat?
-- How do they swim?
-- Do they lay eggs?
-- Do they have enemies?
-- How long do they live?
-- How many different kinds are there?
-- Are they endangered?

This helped. We'll meet again to see how he used these to guide his writing.

work in progress. They can also contain assessment checklists or rubrics used with assignments. Self-reflections, along with teacher notes and comments, also may find their way into student portfolios. Portfolios encourage students to reflect regularly on their learning. There is more emphasis on formative and ongoing assessment. Portfolios put greater importance on student-created language arts products and the process used to create them. They can also promote greater interaction across all the language arts: language, reading, writing, and visual literacy. See the Engaging in Assessment feature for an example of integrating electronic portfolios. Organizing and managing portfolios present challenges for students and teachers. Here are guidelines for helping you and your students with both:

1. Organize the portfolio with student and teacher input.
2. Decide on the language arts material to be included.
3. Have a place for works in progress (items still under construction).
4. Have a different place for completed work.

5. Include checklist, rubrics, and other assessment tools used with the student.
6. Include student and teacher comments.
7. Decide how the portfolio is to be used in teacher-student conferences.
8. Establish rules for reviewing, adding, or removing material from the portfolio.
9. Use the portfolio for formative and summative assessments.
10. Create a schedule for using the portfolio with the student.

Portfolios need to be dynamic and used frequently so that they do not become just a repository for student work. They should be a source of pride for the process of



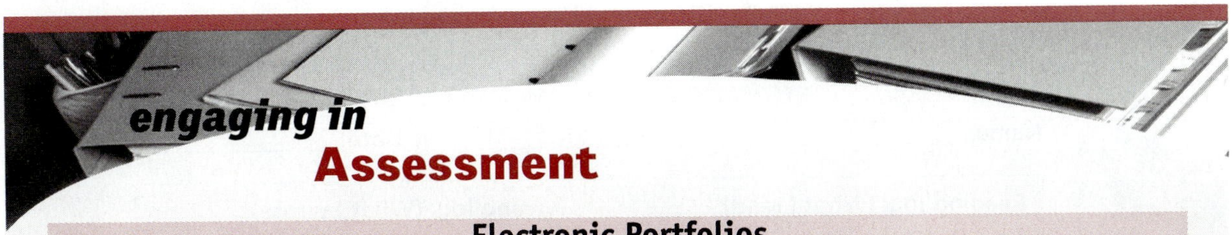

## *engaging in* Assessment

### Electronic Portfolios

To help in assessing the progress her fifth-grade students have made in writing, Ms. Gerelli has her students construct their own electronic portfolios. When students have completed writing assignments, the work goes into their portfolio along with a self-assessment of the assignment based on rubrics designed by Ms. Gerelli and her students. Each portfolio has three major sections, or *hyperlinks.* One section contains topics, assignment requirements, and works in progress. Another section contains conferencing notes, self-assessments, teacher assessments, and writing used for assessment. The third section is for completed writing. By using electronic portfolios, she can access information quickly, make her assessments, and get the information back to her students quickly. Students can do the same with her written assessments or the writing of others. She has even developed an easy way to include comments in a student's writing without having the note become part of the writing itself. Such notes can be written in any color and never have to appear on the students' papers themselves; this gets away from writing red pencil marks directly on a student's paper.

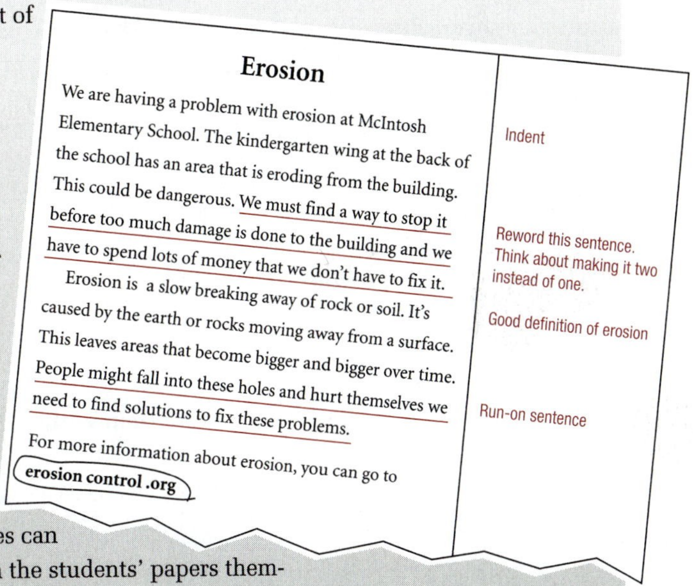

**Erosion**

We are having a problem with erosion at McIntosh Elementary School. The kindergarten wing at the back of the school has an area that is eroding from the building. This could be dangerous. We must find a way to stop it before too much damage is done to the building and we have to spend lots of money that we don't have to fix it.

Erosion is a slow breaking away of rock or soil. It's caused by the earth or rocks moving away from a surface. This leaves areas that become bigger and bigger over time. People might fall into these holes and hurt themselves we need to find solutions to fix these problems.

For more information about erosion, you can go to erosion control .org

Indent

Reword this sentence. Think about making it two instead of one.

Good definition of erosion

Run-on sentence

A page from the electronic portfolio of one of her students appears above. You can see marginal comments alongside a page from a first draft of a paper as well as a hyperlink on erosion.

Mrs. Gerelli was able to determine that this student had completed every writing assignment given. The student's self-assessment presented a picture of a student who saw one of his challenges to be in the area of making smoother transitions in his informational writing. His poetry is a great source of enjoyment and pride and shows how carefully he selects the words in his poems. For Ms. Gerelli, the student's electronic portfolio proves that technology is a valuable resource that enhances her ability to assess students.

learning as well as the products derived from that learning. See Figure 5.7 for a portfolio summary sheet used by students to monitor their portfolios.

**Rubrics** The use of rubrics is a popular means of assessment. Rubrics are guides or criteria used to assess student learning. They lend themselves well to writing assignments, reading responses, and oral language tasks. A good rubric contains the elements to be assessed and a rating scale to determine how well the element has been addressed. For example, a rubric used with a writing assignment identifies content, organization, sentence structure, vocabulary, and mechanics as the elements. Each element has a set



**Figure 5.7**

## Portfolio Summary Sheet

Name: ____________________ Date: ____________

| | |
|---|---|
| **Reading log: (What I read)**<br>1.<br>2.<br>3. | **Writing log: (What I wrote)**<br>1.<br>2.<br>3. |
| **Reading responses: (What I thought)**<br>1.<br>2.<br>3. | **Drafts of my writing (First steps)**<br>1.<br>2.<br>3. |
| **My favorite reading:**<br>1.<br>2.<br>3. | **Finished writing**<br>1.<br>2.<br>3. |
| **In reading, I am getting better at:**<br>1.<br>2.<br>3. | **My favorite writing:**<br>1.<br>2.<br>3. |
| **In reading, I need more help with:**<br>1.<br>2.<br>3. | **In writing, I am getting better at:**<br>1.<br>2.<br>3. |
| **Reading topics: What I want to read**<br>1.<br>2.<br>3. | **In writing, I need more help in:**<br>1.<br>2.<br>3. |
| | **Writing ideas: What I want to write**<br>1.<br>2.<br>3. |

of indicators that describe what should be found in the writing. The rating scale indicates how well the writer has included the indicators in each element.

Many assessment rubrics for reading and writing assignments can be found on the Internet, including formulas for generating your own rubric. Your language arts objectives and curriculum guides can help you get started. To create your own assessment rubrics, identify the objectives to be accomplished in the language arts task, the indicators of the objectives, and the scale that demonstrates how successfully the task is completed. For an example of an assessment rubric used with a persuasive writing assignment, please see Figure 5.8.

Figure 5.8

## Persuasive Writing Assignment Rubric

| | RATINGS | | | | |
|---|---|---|---|---|---|
| **Criteria** | **4** | **3** | **2** | **1** | **Points** |
| Ideas and content | Position is clearly stated and maintained | Position is stated but not maintained | Position is not clearly presented or maintained | Cannot determine the position or issue | |
| Voice | Voice is persuasive and consistently maintained | Voice is persuasive but not consistently maintained | Voice is not consistently persuasive or maintained | Voice is absent or ineffective | |
| Organization | Writing is clearly organized and clearly developed | Writing is organized but less clearly developed | Writing is less organized and clearly underdeveloped | Writing clearly lacks organization or clarity | |
| Sentence structure | Sentence structure is correct and varied | Some incorrect sentences with less variety | More sentence errors and little sentence variety | Poor sentence structure and no sentence variety | |
| Writing conventions | All conventions are correct | Two errors in spelling, punctuation, and/or capitalization | More than two errors in writing conventions | Many errors in writing conventions | |
| Word choice | Varies vocabulary to suit the position | Some variety in vocabulary | Little variety in vocabulary | Repetitive vocabulary and no variety | |
| Total points | | | | | |

**Self-Reflections (Formative or Summative)** One of the best ways to have students partner with you in assessing their learning is to help them learn to reflect on their own learning. You can model self-reflection by thinking out loud about your own learning experiences or by sharing your own written self-reflections. General questions that lead to self-reflection can include:

- How am I doing in school?
- How am I doing as a reader and as a writer?
- What do I like about my reading and writing?
- What is hard for me in reading or writing?

Questions that stimulate self-reflection can be specific to assignments or other language arts experiences:

- What was hard or easy about my last writing assignment?
- What words are hard for me to spell?

Students can use complete sentences, rather than questions, to respond about their reading, writing, or language activity:

- When I write, I need help with ______________________________.
- Two things that I liked about this book are ______________________________.
- Giving oral presentations makes me nervous because ______________________.

Regardless of the format you use to encourage self-reflection by your students, keep in mind that self-reflections can give you insight into your students' feelings about their learning and their work. These insights, in turn, can direct future instruction. See the Exploring Children's Literature feature for books that focus on school and student self-discovery.

## Oral Language Assessment

The purpose of oral language assessment is to determine whether language follows a normal developmental pattern and whether intervention is needed. Although language therapists have an important role in this assessment, the classroom teacher generally is the first to notice whether a student is having difficulties. Classroom teachers need to know enough about language assessment to use the information that a therapist may provide. To assess students, then, it is important to have data that makes sense. Here are guidelines to follow when conducting language assessment:

**Recognize the Variability of Language** It is helpful when classroom teachers have some general guidelines for assessing language. Shuy and Staton (1982) emphasize that oral language cannot thoroughly be assessed outside the students' natural environment. Oral language reflects great variability. How students talk to an adult may be different than how they talk to their peers. How they talk in classrooms may be very different from how they talk at home or on the playground. The importance of assessing language in these different contexts needs to be stressed.

exploring

# Children's Literature

## Books about School and Self-Discovery

### Grades K to 3

*Chrysanthemum*—Written and illustrated by Kevin Henkes, published by Greenwillow (1991).
Chrysanthemum loves her name—until she starts going to school and the other children make fun of it.

*David Goes to School*—Written and illustrated by David Shannon, published by Scholastic (2000).
David's activities in school include chewing gum, talking out of turn, and engaging in a food fight, causing his teacher to say repeatedly, "No, David!"

*First Day Jitters*—Written by Julie Danneberg, illustrated by Judy Love, published by Charlesbridge (2000).
Sarah is afraid to start at a new school, but she and the reader are in for a surprise when she gets to her class.

*First Grade Takes a Test*—Written by Miriam Cohen, illustrated by Lillian Hoban, and published by Greenwillow (1980).
The first grade is distressed by an intelligence test that fails to measure true aptitude.

*Higher on the Door*—Written and illustrated by James Stevenson, published by Greenwillow (1987).
James Stevenson remembers what it was like growing up in a village, taking the train to New York City, and waiting to get older.

*Little Vampire Goes to School*—Written by Joann Sfar and published by Simon and Schuster (2003).
In graphic novel format, this book tells the story of a lonely little vampire who yearns for a friend, gets permission from the other monsters to go to school, and makes the acquaintance of a boy who does not believe that vampires are real.

*Today Was a Terrible Day*—Written by Patricia Reilly Giff, illustrated by Susanna Natti, and published by Viking (1980).
This story follows the humorous mishaps of a second-grader who happens to be learning to read.

*Wemberly Worried*—Written and illustrated by Kevin Henkes, published by Greenwillow (2000).
A mouse named Wemberly, who worries about everything, finds that she has a whole list of things to worry about when she faces the first day of nursery school.

### Grades 4 to 8

*A Bad Case of Stripes*—Written and illustrated by David Shannon, published by Blue Sky (1998).
To ensure her popularity, Camilla Cream always does what is expected, until the day arrives when she no longer recognizes herself.

*A Fine, Fine School*—Written by Sharon Creech, pictures by Harry Bliss, and published by HarperCollins (2001).
When a principal loves his school so much that he wants the students to attend classes every day of the year, it is up to his students to show him free time is a good thing, too.

*Hooray for Diffendoofer Day!*—Written by Dr. Seuss (with some help from Jack Prelutsky and Lane Smith) and published by Knopf (1998).
The students of Diffendoofer School celebrate their unusual teachers and curriculum, including Miss Fribble who teaches laughing, Miss Bonkers who teaches frogs to dance, and Mr. Katz who builds robotic rats.

*The John Hancock Club*—Written by Louise Borden, illustrated by Adam Gustavson, and published by Margaret K. McElderry (2007).
Third-grader Sean McFerrin wants to be part of the good penmanship club, but it all depends on how well he learns the new cursive writing.

*Love That Dog*—Written by Sharon Creech and published by HarperCollins (2001).
A young student, who comes to love poetry through a personal understanding of what different famous poems mean to him, surprises himself by writing his own inspired poem.

*No More Nasty*—Written by Amy MacDonald, illustrations by Cat Bowman Smith, and published by Farrar, Straus and Giroux (2001).
When Simon's Great Aunt Matilda becomes the substitute teacher for his unruly fifth-grade class, her unique way of looking at things gives the students a new perspective on learning.

*American Born Chinese*—Written by Gene Luen Yang and published by First Second (2006).
In graphic novel format, this story alternates three interrelated stories about the problems of young Chinese Americans trying to participate in the popular culture.

**Recognize Dialectic Variations** Any assessment of language must also recognize dialectic variations. Often, teachers hear a dialect and assess that dialect in relation to Standard English. In these situations, students from linguistically different homes do not fare well. A good assessment will ask the question whether the student has learned the language of his or her community. Only by asking this question can teachers determine whether students have language problems. This is not to say, however, that students should not learn Standard English. Regardless of the dialect, normally developing children are capable of learning Standard English. Teachers who are aware of dialect variations, however, will know that these students have full and rich languages. They will know how to approach a running record or an informal reading inventory. They will not readily refer students using dialects for language therapy. Refer back to Chapter 2 and Chapter 4 for additional information on students who use dialects.

**Assess Language Production and Use** Observations and oral language checklists are helpful in assessing students' understanding, production, and uses of oral language. Look at Figure 5.9 for an example of an oral language checklist.

**Figure 5-9**

### Oral Language Checklist

Oral Language Pre–K

1. Begins to use different language functions
2. Listens to and enjoys stories
3. Enjoys rhyming and other word play
4. Knowledge of grammar and language conventions grows

Oral Language Grades K–1

1. Uses standard sentence construction
2. Participates in discussions
3. Facility with oral language
4. Uses standard sentence construction

Oral Language Grades 1–2

1. Use of standard English grows
2. Ability to use language in variety of settings
3. Interest in words grows

Oral Language Grades 2–4

1. Use of standard English continues to grow
2. Learning to differentiate between standard and nonstandard English
3. Use of all language functions grows
4. Speaking and listening vocabulary growing
5. Aware of language techniques used by speakers

Oral Language Grades 5–6

1. Uses language in a variety of functions
2. Uses language with a variety of audiences
3. Able to move between formal and informal modes of talking
4. Vocabulary continues to grow

## engaging in Oral language

### Standardized Tests

Standardized tests for assessing oral language are also available. Some tests assess all aspects of language; others look at only one. Many of the tests can be administered by classroom teachers, but others require special training. Here is a list of standardized tests that teachers can use with their students along with the age level and language focus of each test.

| Test | Age Level | Language Focus |
|---|---|---|
| Expressive One-Word Picture Vocabulary (Academic Therapy, 2000) | 2–18.11 years | Semantic |
| Peabody Picture Vocabulary (American Guidance Services, 1997) | 2–18 years | Semantic |
| Preschool Language Scale-4 (Harcourt, 2002) | Birth–6.11 years | Semantic, syntactic, phonetic |
| Test of Language Development-Primary (PRO-ED, 1997) | 4–8.11 years | Semantic, syntactic, phonetic |

**Assess Listening Skills** Three kinds of listening can be assessed in the classroom. Students listen to appreciate or enjoy stories, poetry, or music. They listen to learn from lectures, discussions, and other activities designed to help them learn. They also listen to evaluate. As students listen to a presentation, for example, they evaluate the factual content, bias of the speaker, or persuasive techniques used by the speaker. Listening assessment can occur during classroom observations, conferences, and checklists. Checklists that reflect the developmental nature of language growth in the classroom are particularly useful. Figure 5.10 and Figure 5.11 present checklists that can be used in the classroom. They can also be models for checklists that you develop based on the language skills assessed in the grade level you are teaching. In addition to the areas identified on the checklists, observe your students to detect any problems with hearing or difficulties with understanding English. For a look at standardized measures of oral language, read the Engaging in Oral Language feature.

## Reading Assessment

These specific reading assessment techniques look at behaviors that students use when reading:

## Figure 5.10 Listening Assessment Checklist for the Primary Grades

| Listening Behaviors | Yes | No | Comments |
|---|---|---|---|
| While listening, the student can: | | | |
| • Understand when spoken to | | | |
| • Understand statements | | | |
| • Understand questions | | | |
| • Understand and retell stories | | | |
| • Understand intonation | | | |
| • Recognize words in sentences | | | |
| • Recognize phonemes in words | | | |
| 1. at the beginning of words | | | |
| 2. in the middle of words | | | |
| 3. at the end of words | | | |
| • Recognize rhymes in words | | | |
| • Recognize repeated words in poems | | | |
| • Listen carefully to others | | | |
| • Follow simple two-three step directions | | | |
| • Listen to stories and: | | | |
| 1. Make predictions | | | |
| 2. Recall events in order | | | |
| 3. Recall important details | | | |
| 4. Tell what is liked or disliked about the story | | | |
| • Recognize the difference between fact and fantasy | | | |

*Source:* Adapted from Sample Emerging/Early Developing Phase Listening Checklist (Regina, Saskatchewan: Saskatchewan School District).

**Running Records** An important consideration, especially in the beginning of the school year, is to find out the level of reading material each of your students is able to read. To check this, conduct a *running record,* in which students read brief, hundred-word selections from books while the teacher determines whether they recognize 90 to 95 percent of the words. Running records can be done in small groups or with individual students. They require a small amount of time, but they yield helpful information about the level of material that your students can comfortably read. See Chapter 6 for more information about conducting running records (a documented

Figure 5.11

## Listening Assessment Checklist for Intermediate Grades

| Listening Behaviors | Yes | No | Comments |
|---|---|---|---|
| While listening, the student can: | | | |
| • Follow more complex sets of directions | | | |
| • Recognize the differences between fact and opinion | | | |
| • Listen to stories and: | | | |
| 1. Make and support predictions | | | |
| 2. Recall events in order accurately | | | |
| 3. Make and support inferences | | | |
| 4. Understand cause-and-effect relationships | | | |
| 5. Recognize imagery in stories and poems | | | |
| 6. Respond to mood and atmosphere expressed in stories | | | |
| 7. Evaluate stories heard | | | |
| • Listen to nonfiction presentations and: | | | |
| 1. Recognize details | | | |
| 2. Recognize structure | | | |
| 3. Recognize persuasive words | | | |
| 4. Draw conclusions | | | |
| 5. Evaluate ideas | | | |

*Source:* Adapted from Sample Developing Phase Listening Checklist (Regina, Saskatchewan: Sasketchewan School District).



running record is shown in Figure 5.12). See the Exploring Diversity feature on page 167 to read how Mr. Bergen uses running records with his class.

**Informal Reading Inventories** Another informal assessment that helps identify students' instructional reading levels is the informal reading inventory, or IRI, which is comprised of graded word lists and reading passages that progress from lower to higher grade levels. Three reading levels can be obtained:

Figure 5.12

## Running Record.

Name Robert    Date 2-15-06

Reading Selection: Fun with Leaves*

| | | | | | | | | |
|---|---|---|---|---|---|---|---|---|
| Line 1 | ✓ | ✓ | ✓ | ✓ | ✓ | ✓ | ✓ | ✓ |
| Line 2 | ✓<br>rack | ✓ | ✓ | ✓ | ✓ | ✓ | ✓ | ✓ |
| Line 3 | than<br>then | ✓ | ✓ | ✓ | ✓ | ✓ | ✓ | ✓ |
| Line 4 | ✓ | ✓ | ✓ | ✓ | ✓ | ✓ | ✓ | ✓ |
| Line 5 | ✓ | ✓ | ✓ | jump<br>jumped | ✓ | ✓ | ✓ | ✓ |

*"Fun with Leaves" from J. Johns, *Basic reading inventory*, 8th Ed. (Dubuque, IA: Kendall/Hunt, 2001).

- Independent Reading Level (95 to 100 percent accuracy, 90 percent comprehension): Student reads fluently and comprehends fully. At the intermediate level, independent reading moves to a higher criterion of 98 to 99 percent word accuracy.
- Instructional Reading Level (90 to 95 percent accuracy, 75 percent comprehension): Student reads fairly fluently and comprehends fairly well. At the intermediate grades, an accuracy level of 95 percent is a more secure guideline for instructional level.
- Frustration Reading Level (below 90 percent accuracy, 50 percent comprehension): Student reads with difficulty and comprehends poorly.

**Simulation Homework Exercise**

*Classroom Assessment*

Go to the Homework and Exercises section of Chapter 5 of MyEducationLab and view the Simulations Video, "Classroom Assessment (Part 1): An Introduction to Monitoring Academic Achievement in the Classroom," which includes a discussion between a first-year teacher and her mentor regarding children who are struggling in reading. Complete the activities that follow, and save your work or transmit it to your professor as assigned.

The results of administering the graded word lists help determine how strong a student's sight vocabulary is and what word attack skills the student possesses. Oral reading of passages indicates how fluently a student reads and how context is used to figure out unfamiliar words. Silent reading comprehension can be compared with the oral reading comprehension. IRIs are time consuming and must be administered individually to students but provide detailed information about students' reading behaviors while reading. There are a number of published informal reading inventories (Johns, 2001; Woods and Moe, 2003; Silvaroli, 2000), and some commercial reading programs have IRIs that accompany their programs. The scoring grid obtained from an informal reading inventory given to a fourth-grader can be seen in Figure 5.13.

**Read and Retell** Another way to informally assess reading comprehension is to perform read-and-retells with your students. To prepare for read-and-retells, you or your students select a story to read. Once you know the story, create a retelling outline that includes the story elements of setting, characters, problem, plot, solution, and ending. Have the student read the story orally or silently depending on his or her reading ability and then retell the story. When the student stops the retell, you can

## exploring diversity

### Using a Running Record

A group of Mr. Bergen's third-graders are about to begin reading a new novel. To make sure that the book is not above their instructional level, he decides to do a running record with each student using a selection from the book. He counts out a 110-word selection near the beginning of the book and marks it in his copy. He meets with the group and explains that he wants to make sure the book they are about to read is not too difficult, so he sends all but one student back to their seats and gives the book to the remaining student. Sitting next to the student, Mr. Bergen produces a blank sheet of paper and a pencil with which to fill in the running record. He shows the student where to begin reading and where to stop, and he writes a check for each word the student reads correctly, all the while writing down any errors the student makes while reading. He repeats this process with the remaining five students. Later, he lists the errors each student made and the correct form of the word. The error lists indicate that the word accuracy score for the students ranged from 92 to 96 percent, which are acceptable scores for the reading instructional level. He also noticed that two of his students, Michael and Raymond, regularly left off endings when using plural and past tense verb forms, but none of the omissions had a significant effect on the meaning of the selection (see chart). Both students are African American, and Mr. Bergen realizes that these oral reading errors are a reflection of their dialect. He will watch to see whether the errors come up in their writing, but for reading, Mr. Bergen is satisfied that they, as well as the other four students, can begin reading the book he has selected for them.

| Word | Error |
|---|---|
| houses | house |
| rested | rest |
| stopped | stop |
| started | start |
| stories | story |
| cars | car |
| looked | look |

prompt the student to talk about any omitted story elements. Keep track of the ones given with and without prompts. You can even check students' understanding of story elements before they are actually reading by having them listen to a story that you read out loud. Follow the same retell format used with students who read the story. Figure 5.14 provides an example of a read-and-retell done by a second-grade student. This particular retelling took place as part of an informal reading inventory done with the student.

## Writing Assessment

The best way to assess student writing is to look closely at the writing the student has produced. This allows you to see how the student is progressing and to discern the areas of writing that may warrant additional support and instruction.

Figure 5.13

## Informal Reading Inventory Scoring Grid

| Grade | Word Recognition (Isolation) Timed | Word Recognition (Isolation) Untimed | Word Recognition In Context | Comprehension Oral | Comprehension Silent | Comprehension Listening |
|---|---|---|---|---|---|---|
| PP | | | | | | |
| P | | | | | | |
| 1 | | | 100 | 90 | 90 | |
| 2 | 90 | 95 | 100 | 80 | 70 | 55 |
| 3 | 75 | 80 | 97 | 80 | 45 | 50 |
| 4 | 75 | 90 | 95 | 80 | 55 | 40 |
| 5 | 60 | 65 | 93 | 30 | 20 | |
| 6 | 60 | 60 | | | | |

**Writing Samples** By obtaining student writing samples early in the year, you can get an overall impression of the writing abilities of your students and can determine the instructional needs that their writing reveals. These needs can include the use of writing process steps, content development and organization, sentence structure, and writing conventions. Because the writing itself yields the most information, every effort should be made to encourage students to write freely and often. Once you have reviewed students' writing, you can better determine how best to teach them how to become better writers. Writing samples also help create instructional groups (based on their writing abilities and needs) and allow you to work with students in smaller groups on building specific writing skills in writing workshops. For additional information about assessing student writing, see Chapter 7.

**Holistic Assessment** This type of evaluation seeks an overall picture of the completed writing assignment or final draft. Holistic assessments are administered quickly, and they call for the writing to be given a brief examination for the purpose of seeing how successfully students responded to a writing assignment. They are not intended to be a close analysis of every element in the writing, but rather to give a general impression. The procedure for using holistic evaluations is quite simple and involves the following steps:

1. Review the writing requirements for students' final drafts.
2. Read the final drafts quickly to see whether they meet the requirements.
3. Place in a pile the papers that successfully meet the requirements.
4. Place in another pile the papers that somewhat successfully meet the requirements.
5. Place in a third pile the papers that less successfully meet the requirements.
6. Place in a fourth pile the papers that clearly did not meet the requirements.

Grades can be assigned to the papers in the four different piles, but it is probably more appropriate to use the paper groups to find out which students need additional help with the assignment or which ones need help in future assignments. It is best to

**Figure 5.14**

## Retelling Notes on a Second Grader's Read and Retell

**A 8224** (Grade 2)
Comprehensive Questions

| Comprehensive Questions | Retelling Notes |
|---|---|
| T 1. T What is this story about? (a boy at camp; Bill's walk in the woods) | boy 1st time to camp explore / went to find animals |
| F 2. T Did Bill enjoy going to camp? How do you know? (yes, the story said he was happy there) | yes its says he was happy |
| F 3. T Why did Bill go walking in the woods? (to look for leaves) | to see more animals and more leaves |
| F 4. T What kind of leaves did Bill find in the woods? (maple and oak leaves) | oak, maple |
| F 5. T What else did Bill see besides the mouse? (a bird nest; animal tracks) | tracks |
| F 6. T Where did the mouse go? (into a small hole by or in a tree) | small hole by the tree |
| F 7. T What other animals did Bill see? (none; he didn't see any) | it didn't have another animal |
| I 8. T Do you think Bill went on this walk by himself? What makes you think so? (any logical response) | yes, it doesn't say another persons name |
| E 9. 1/2 What other animals might Bill see if he goes for another walk? (any logical response) | monkey, snakes |
| V 10. T What are "tracks"? (footprints made in the dirt; something made by animals when they walk or run) | footprints |

*Source:* Johns, J. (2005). *Basic Reading Inventory* (8th ed.). Dubuque, IA: Kendall/Hunt, p. 230. Used by permission.

use holistic assessment to make statements about groups of students rather than individual students. An example of a holistic assessment rubric is found in Figure 5.15.

**Classroom Artifact Homework Exercise**

*Snow*

Go to the Homework and Exercises section of Chapter 5 of MyEducationLab and examine the artifact, "Snow," which is a sample draft of a student's writing. Complete the activities that follow, and save your work or transmit it to your professor as assigned.

**Analytic Assessment** One of the most widely used summative assessments of writing is analytic assessment. The purpose of analytic assessment is to analyze each of the basic elements in a piece of writing. Weights can be assigned to each element and may vary from writing assignment to writing assignment. A popular type of analytic writing assessment is the six-trait writing assessment. The six traits assessed are: content, organization, voice, word choice, sentence fluency, and conventions. An example of an assessment rubric with the six traits (as the Jordan school district defined them) is found in Figure 5.16.

# Spelling Assessment

A spelling assessment is another language arts assessment that can be given to the entire classroom. There are several ways to accomplish this. Examine the writing

**Figure 5.15**

## Holistic Assessment Scoring Rubric

**Score of 4**
These papers choose a single subject and describe it with concrete, clear language. They contain considerable details and are written in a well-organized manner. There are few grammar, mechanics, or spelling errors.

**Score of 3**
These papers usually choose a single subject and describe it clearly but with less detail. The papers are organized but less so than the 4 papers. Grammar, mechanics, and spelling errors are relatively minor.

**Score of 2**
These papers are less focused and organized than 3 and 4 papers. They tend to be more like lists of details but still describe something. There is greater evidence of errors in grammar, mechanics, and spelling than in the 3 and 4 papers.

**Score of 1**
These papers tend to be brief and confused. It is not always clear what is being described. There are few details and many errors in mechanics, spelling, and grammar.

**Score of 0**
These papers do not respond to the writing topic at all.

**Figure 5.16**

## Six Writing Traits and Assessment Rubric

| **Six Writing Traits Found in Good Writing** | **Six Trait Writing Assessment Rubric** |
|---|---|
| 1. IDEAS AND CONTENT<br>• clarity and details<br>• showing not telling<br>• central theme controls the idea<br>2. ORGANIZATION<br>• structure (skeleton) of the piece<br>• strong lead (beginning)<br>• good ending<br>• using transition words<br>• effective sequencing | IDEAS AND CONTENT<br>________5 Sticks to main idea throughout, uses supporting details and examples.<br>________4<br>________3 Occasionally wanders from main idea, lacks supporting details.<br>________2<br>________1 Has no main idea, does not support idea, limited information.<br>*(Continued)* |

3. VOICE
   - author's personality
   - writer-reader interaction
   - audience awareness
   - changes voice for different types of writing
4. WORD CHOICE
   - clear and precise
   - words that reflect attitude and meaning
   - using strong verbs
   - minimal repetition
5. SENTENCE FLUENCY
   - easy to read aloud
   - sentences have power
   - sentences are a variety of lengths
6. CONVENTIONS
   - spelling
   - punctuation
   - grammar
   - capitalization

ORGANIZATION

________5 Has clear beginning focus, strong ending, uses natural transitions.

________4

________3 Generally writes with a clear sequence, weak transitions.

________2

________1 Has no clear beginning and ending, sequence and details confused.

VOICE

________5 Strong individualistic style, sincere, and suits author's purpose.

________4

________3 Style and enthusiasm inconsistent.

________2

________1 Flat, dull, lifeless.

SENTENCE STRUCTURE

________5 Paper is easy to read and understand, fluid and varied sentences.

________4

________3 Sentences are understandable but tend to be mechanical.

________2

________1 Sentence flaws make paper hard to read and understand.

WRITING CONVENTIONS

(Punctuation, spelling, grammar, etc.)

________5 No glaring errors, paper easy to read and understand.

________4

________3 Noticeable errors that begin to impair readability.

________2

________1 Numerous errors, paper difficult to read.

WORD CHOICE

________5 Uses varied words, fresh, original, and fit the author's purpose.

________4

________3 Offers general or ordinary words, only some variety.

________2

________1 No new or different words, weak, repetitive language.

*Source:* Left column, R. Culham (2003). 6 + 1 traits of writing: The complete guide. Portland, OR: Northwest Regional Educational Laboratory. Right column, created by teachers from Jordan School District Elementary Literacy, Sandy, Utah. Thanks to Kathy Ridd, Sara Andreason, Linda Peterson, and Gerri Hixnebaugh. Used by permission.

samples that you gather from your students, paying specific attention to the spelling in the writing. Look for common spelling errors among individuals and across the classroom. Examine the spelling errors to determine the developmental spelling stage they represent. Once you know this level, you can select specific spelling instructional strategies (located in Chapter 9).

# When Do You Assess Language Arts?

We have talked about national, state, and school language arts standards and developmental benchmarks to determine language arts performance and what may need to be assessed. With the discussion of various assessment techniques, ranging from norm-referenced tests to teacher observations in the classroom, we have answered the question of how to assess the language arts. Now we turn to the question of when to implement language arts assessment.

## Beginning-of-the-Year Assessment

Before school begins in the fall, you can begin the language arts assessment process by looking at students' cumulative folders and progress reports. Learning about students' performance in the language arts during the previous year can give you some insights into the instructional needs of your students for the upcoming year. Results of state-mandated language arts assessments (standardized norm-referenced, criterion-referenced, or both) should also be available for you to review before the school year begins. Keep in mind that three to four months may have passed since teacher comments were made and tests were taken. Students can change over the summer, so this information is not always entirely reliable, especially when it is used to place students in language arts programs.

You need to begin gathering your own assessment information about your students' language, reading, and writing abilities at the beginning of the school year. Get language, writing, and spelling samples from your students in the first few weeks of the school year. If you are a teacher in kindergarten, first grade, or second grade, you might assess student understanding of concepts of print, word, and story elements. Also, find out which students are prereaders, emerging readers, and readers. Observe and note how students use the writing process. For teachers of second grade to fifth grade, take running records of students' reading out loud to determine the independent and instructional levels of reading material for your students. These records can also be used to find out which students are fluent readers and which ones need additional support to become fluent readers. Have students do read-and-retells or administer parts of an informal inventory to determine how accurately students read and comprehend. Use graded word lists from the same informal reading inventories to determine whether students need help with sight vocabulary development or word recognition skills.

With this beginning-of-the-year information, you can form instructional groups and decide on the language arts instruction that will move each student forward in the new school year.

By performing beginning-of-the-year assessments and collecting information, you can form instructional groups and decide on the language arts instruction that will move each student forward in the new school year.



## Continuous Monitoring of Student Performance

Once the school year is underway, language arts assessment continues throughout the year. With an eye on state and school district standards of learning, you can monitor the progress of your students in all the language arts. This continuous assessment becomes the most important tool in helping you decide who gets what language arts instruction and when they get it. Periodic tests or end-of-unit tests may be used to see whether students have mastered concepts and material covered during language arts instruction. Observations, anecdotal records of student responses to instruction, checklists, conferences, and portfolios are assessment techniques that can be used for monitoring continuous progress. Revisiting beginning-of-the-year assessments helps to determine whether students have acquired knowledge or skills such as concepts of print, reading fluency, and story elements. Writing assignments and reading experiences can be assessed with rubrics that indicate how successfully students respond to both. Students' periodic self-reflections about their own work and progress can add to your own language arts periodic assessment. Regular review and interaction with students about ongoing and finished products in their language arts portfolios provide additional assessment information during the year. See the Engaging in Visual Literacy feature to read more about using visual representations to monitor student understanding.

## End-of-the-Year Assessment

As the school year comes to an end, many states have specific language arts standards of learning assessed through standardized criterion-referenced or norm-referenced tests. These may take considerable time to administer in the classroom, and they often require time spent in preparing for the tests. Additionally, many of the assessment techniques used for continuous monitoring of student progress can be used in the final collection of assessment data. End-of-the-year assessment can include final conferences, writing and reading samples, running records, read-and-retells, checklists, and self-reflections. The end of the year is also an excellent time to review and organize the final set of students' work that will go in their language arts portfolios. These final portfolios should also contain students' reflections on their work over the course of the year and final comments by their teachers. In many school districts, portfolios are a permanent authentic assessment record of a student's progress in the language arts and go to the student's teacher for the next school year.

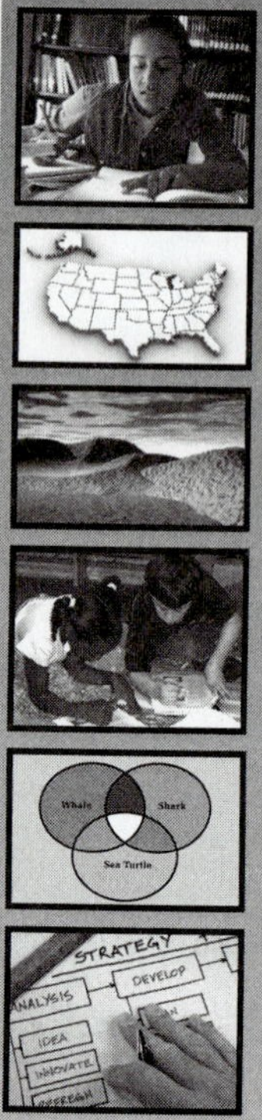

## Using Diagrams

To assess her fourth-graders' knowledge of electricity before beginning her electricity unit, Mrs. Meekins wants her students to visually represent this knowledge. She hands out a sheet for each student with a list of vocabulary terms that are key to understanding the electricity concepts in her unit. She instructs her students to arrange and organize the vocabulary in ways that demonstrate their understanding of the relationships among the concepts of electricity. She also includes three diagrams of objects that the students are to label with appropriate vocabulary (a flashlight battery, a light bulb, and an insulated wire with insulation removed from the ends of the wire). Students are to put a check mark in their graphic organizer next to vocabulary they know and use, and they are to put a question mark next to vocabulary they are unfamiliar with or unsure about. In addition to the graphic organizer and labeled diagrams, students are to write a brief description of how to use the three objects to light the bulb. Here is the list of vocabulary and one student's response to the assessment tasks:

Electricity
Electrons ?
Atoms ?
Reaction
Electric cell
Negative charge
Positive charge
Open circuit ?
Closed circuit
Conductor
Insulator
Resistance ?
Heat

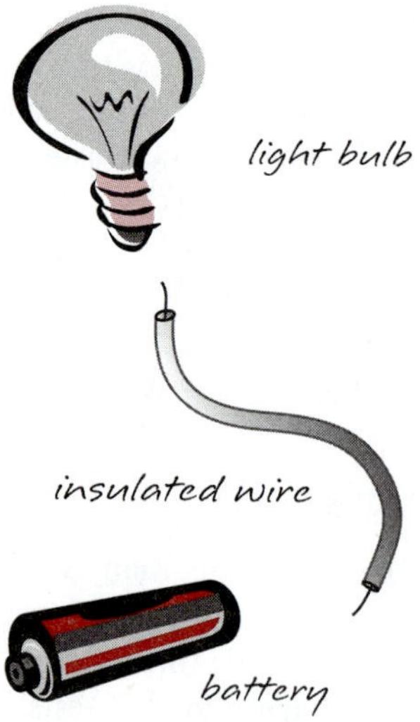


To make the light bulb go on, place the bottom of the bulb on the top of the battery. Then take one end of the wire and put it on the bottom of the bulb. Put the other end on the top of the bulb. I'm not sure about the wire. The electrons in the battery will go up through the top of the battery to the filament in the light bulb making it glow to make it light.

**Directions:** Arrange and organize your vocabulary words to show the relationships among the concepts of electricity. Then place a check mark next to those you know and use, and a question mark next to those that you are unfamiliar with or are unsure about.

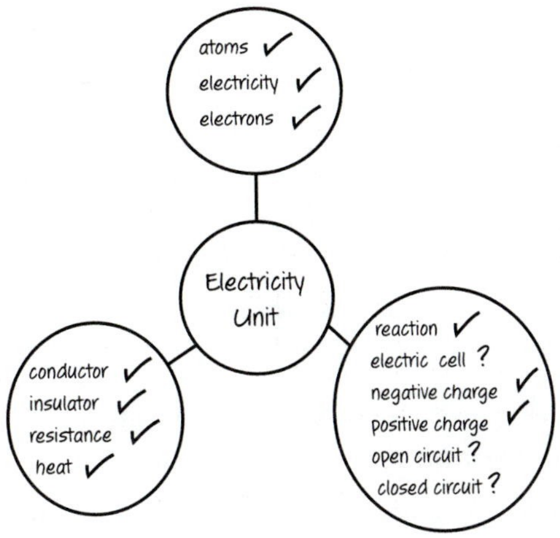


When Mrs. Meekins looks at her students' graphic, she learns that many do not fully understand how electrons work to produce light. There is confusion over the direction that electrons flow to make a closed circuit. She turns this visual representation into an instructional guide for her students by having them return to it as they go through the electricity unit. It also alerts her to concepts and understandings that she will be sure to address in her instruction as the electricity unit progresses. This is an example of assessment informing instruction.

## revisit the classroom challenge

Now that you have come to end of this chapter, how would you answer the three questions about Mr. Bergen and language arts assessment in his classroom? Take a few minutes and write your own answers to the three questions:

1. What language arts assessment information can you obtain early in the school year?
2. What ways can you monitor students' progress during the year to ensure that your instruction will advance your students in the language arts?
3. What language arts assessment should be carried out at the end of the school year to see how students have progressed?

# chapterreview

Language arts assessment has many facets that can disperse information in many directions when placed under the light of national, state, and school district language arts standards. When the standards are aligned, the resulting instruction and assessment will serve national, state, and local constituencies without sacrificing quality or quantity. In the final analysis, you the teacher are able to best assess the language arts instructional needs of your students. Standardized norm-referenced tests and standards-based criterion-referenced tests can yield general information about students, but your informal observations, conferences, reading and writing instruction, and portfolios will supply the most effective, authentic assessment for the language arts instruction that benefit your students.

## Why Is Language Arts Assessment Important?

Through language arts assessment, you learn about the language, reading, and writing abilities of your students. The results will guide you as you make instructional decisions about your students.

## What Are Different Perspectives on Language Arts Assessment?

National standards and their assessment focus on general language arts performance by students across the country. State standards assessments compare language arts performance across school districts in a state. Language arts standards assessments allow districts to see how students in local schools are performing. Developmental language arts benchmarks overlap all three levels of language arts standards.

## What Are Principles to Follow in Language Arts Assessment?

Language arts assessment is ongoing, part of instruction, authentic, and a collective and reflective process. It is multidimensional, and it accommodates cultural, developmental, and learner factors. It identifies students' strengths and needs to reflect an understanding of how students use language and acquire literacy.

## How Can You Assess Language Arts?

Language arts assessment identifies language arts objectives to be taught, informs instruction to meet the objectives, assesses learning based on the instruction, evaluates student performance (as well as instruction), and identifies subsequent learning objectives based on the evaluation. General language arts assessment techniques can be used for any of the language arts, and specific language arts assessments exist for evaluating oral language, reading, writing, spelling, and visual literacy.

## When Do You Assess Language Arts?

Language arts assessment begins in the fall and includes students' cumulative folders and progress reports, as well as student samples from all the language arts. Using this early assessment information, important decisions can be made about instructional groups and instruction. Once the school year is underway, continuous monitoring of students' progress in the language arts occurs. At the conclusion of the school year, state-mandated language arts assessments take place as well as the collection of final classroom language arts data. Often, this data goes into students' language arts portfolios.

PEARSON

**myeducationlab™**

Where the Classroom Comes to Life

Now go to www.myeducationlab.com to take a Pretest to assess your initial comprehension of chapter content, study chapter content with your individualized Study Plan, take a Posttest to assess your understanding of chapter content, practice your teaching skills with Building Teaching Skills exercises, and build a deeper, more applied understanding of chapter content with Homework and Exercises.

chapter 6

# Reading in the Primary Grades

## classroom challenge

**Mrs. Santos** has twenty students in her first-grade classroom this year. To help her find out what emergent reading skills her students have, she conducts informal emergent literacy assessments with her students early in the school year. To accomplish this, she uses language experience stories with small groups of five students.

On Tuesday, she meets with each group to discuss the topic for a language experience story. She has learned that nearly all her children have pets or want to have pets, so that becomes the topic for discussion. Following the discussion, Mrs. Santos asks the children in each group what they would like to say about pets so she can write it down on the experience chart paper. After she writes down every contribution made by the students, she completes the following tasks:

She reads aloud while pointing to each word in the entire story.

She has children choral read the story with her.

She has children come up and read their own contributions.

She has children come up and read other students' contributions.

She has children come up and read the entire story on their own.

She has children draw a picture to go along with their favorite part of the story.

During this first day with the language experience story, she jots down observations about her students' emergent reading skills.

On Wednesday, Mrs. Santos has each group come back up to their group-dictated experience story that has been covered with a blank sheet of chart paper. She begins by having the students discuss what was in the story they dictated on Tuesday. After the discussion, she completes the following tasks:

With the story covered, she has students recognize words taken from the story.

With the story uncovered, she has students read the story together.

She has students come up and read the story alone.

She points to a word and has students find it in the story.

She points to a word and has students say a word that begins the same way.

She points to a word and has students say a word that ends the same way.

During this second day, she jots down her observations about her students' emergent reading skills. By the end of the week, she has identified students who are prereaders, beginning readers, and readers. Over the weekend, she decides on the kinds of literacy instruction that will benefit each group of students in her classroom.

## Questions for Reflection

1. What do you know about emergent reading skills?
2. What emergent reading skills is Mrs. Santos assessing?
3. How can she use her assessments to guide her literacy instruction?

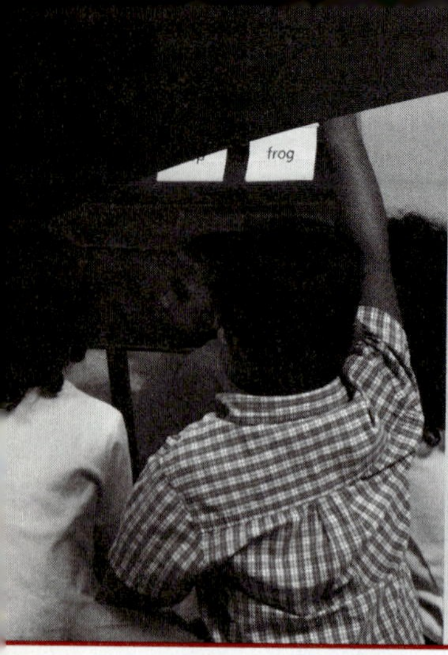


## anticipating this chapter

This chapter focuses on reading development and instruction in the primary grades by answering the following questions:

What are important factors for successful beginning reading?

How does beginning reading develop?

How can you support reading development?

How can you assess early reading development?

# What Are Important Factors for Successful Beginning Reading?

As students begin their journey from spoken to written language, a number of factors support their progress toward literacy, including motivation, language, metacognitive awareness, and orthographic knowledge.

## Motivation

Students who enjoy books and are curious about signs, words, and other aspects of language are motivated to learn to read and write. They experiment with written language through drawing and writing attempts. They enjoy playing with magnetic letters, markers, crayons, and other implements for writing. They constantly request favorite stories and books to be read to them. They actively participate in the reading and rereading of these favorites and cannot be fooled when a reader tries to skip pages or characters during a reading.

## Language

Students who have developed all aspects of their spoken language are prime candidates for success in early literacy development. They have developed extensive spoken vocabulary and can use it freely as they speak. They have also engaged in much oral language interaction with parents, siblings, and other primary and secondary caregivers. Their language is rich not only in vocabulary but also in the complexity of the syntactic structure they use while speaking. This is especially important as they learn to apply their understanding of vocabulary and syntax to the reading material they listen to and begin to read. They also have the ability to substitute words in sentences and further reveal their understanding of context, which combines syntactic and meaning awareness. This same skill is important as they learn to use context as they read. Much of what they have been doing with oral language will serve as rehearsal for what they will do with written language.

## Metacognitive Awareness

Young students who are able to monitor their own learning demonstrate early aspects of metacognitive awareness, which will later be essential as they learn to read and write. For example, a four-year-old playing with wooden blocks is trying to build a bridge. If we listen carefully, we can hear him say the following:

> I put these two short ones here. Now put the long one on top. Oops! One short one fell over. Try again with them not so close. Better. Now put another short one next. Put a longer one on top. Fell again!

What we are witnessing is a child using language to think through bridge-building challenges. He also monitors his learning as he tries to extend the bridge, which is a precursor for metacognitive awareness, or learning how we learn. This allows the child to make predictions about the outcomes of his bridge-building techniques and encourages problem-solving and the use of imagination and creative thinking. Why is this important for literacy development? It will support reading comprehension and the construction of meaning through writing.

## Orthographic Knowledge

Another important factor that can enhance or impede reading development is **orthographic knowledge** (Adams, 2001; Ehri, 1991). Students use this knowledge in a number of ways. It shows them that written stories are dependent on the print in a text. It reveals that text is comprised of words that are read left to right and that the words progress from the top of a page to the bottom. Spaces between written words signal word boundaries, and the letters in the words are related to sounds in spoken words. Students also come to realize early in their exposure to print that there are acceptable spelling patterns in words they encounter and other letter combinations that are not.

See the Exploring Technology feature for website resources to support early literacy.

### exploring technology

### Early Literacy Websites

**Professor Garfield (www.professorgarfield.org)**
Professor Garfield, a site created by the makers of the Garfield the cat cartoons in association with Ball State University, provides educational games for students in grades K–8 that cross the curriculum. Early literacy games promote reading comprehension, sequencing, and phonemic awareness.

**Learning the Alphabet (www.starfall.com/n/level-k/index/play.htm?f)**
This site hosts a number of interactive games that engage students in learning letter-sound relationships.

**Between the Lions (pbskids.org/lions)**
Sponsored by the PBS television series *Between the Lions,* this site has 250 interactive games and stories all focusing on the development of early literacy skills.

# How Does Beginning Reading Develop?

To help explain how early reading development occurs, it is helpful to distinguish between prereaders, beginning readers, and readers with respect to three areas: *concept of word, concept of spelling,* and *concept of story.* When students have **concept of word,** they recognize that there is a one-to-one correspondence between spoken and written words. Beginning readers understand that words are read from left to right in a line of text and that lines of text go from the top to the bottom of a page of text. With **concept of spelling,** they realize that words are composed of letters and that letters represent sounds in words. It also includes phonemic awareness, or the ability to identify, isolate, separate, and combine sounds in words and to recognize acceptable spelling patterns in words. **Concept of story** includes an understanding of story elements common to all stories, such as characters, setting, plot sequence, problem, and problem resolution. To better understand these literacy concepts, a look at the characteristics of prereaders, beginning readers, and readers can help.

## Stages of Early Reading Development

### Stage I: Prereader

A. Concept of Word

- Recognizes no left-to-right direction or word as a unit
- Begins to move in left-to-right direction
- Focuses on letter, stress, or syllable as the unit in a text
- May self-correct while reading memorized text
- Is moving toward more accurate tracking of words in the text

B. Concept of Spelling

- Makes random marks, letterlike forms, and letters
- Begins to use beginning consonants with or without letters
- Moves to using beginning and final consonants
- Shows some recognition of vowel elements in the middle of a word

C. Concept of Story

- Randomly recalls events when retelling a story
- Begins to demonstrate story sequence
- Begins to demonstrate awareness of key elements

### Stage II: Beginning Reader

A. Concept of Word

- Able to track memorized text
- Can track less familiar text with support
- Able to find similar or related words in text

B. Concept of Spelling

- Uses initial and final consonants
- Begins to spell using letter names
- Begins to use short vowels
- Begins to use long vowels without silent *e*
- Begins to use endings spelled phonetically

C. Concept of Story

- Shows awareness of sequence
- Shows awareness of key elements
- Can accurately retell story

**Stage III: Reader**

A. Concept of Word

- Is reading at primer level
- Has growing sight vocabulary
- Shows more fluency in oral reading
- Makes fewer context errors with appropriate material

B. Concept of Spelling

- Begins to use short vowels
- Begins to use long vowels with silent *e*
- Begins to use endings spelled correctly when root unchanged

C. Concept of Story

- Makes predictions and reads to confirm
- Reads for meaning
- Begins to deal with interpreting stories

## Overlap of Characteristics

It is important to remember that there is some overlap in the three areas described in each stage. The overlap demonstrates that young students do not march lockstep through the stages; rather, they proceed in individual ways that vary from student to student. Examples of each concept for a prereader, beginning reader, and reader can be found in Figure 6.1. All three of these students were given three tasks. For concept of word, students were asked to point to each word in the Jack and Jill nursery rhyme while reading it. For concept of spelling, they were given twenty words to spell. For concept of story, a brief story about birds flying south for winter was read to the students. After the story was read, the students were asked to retell the story in their own words. A review of the characteristics of the three stages of early reading development reveals that Travis is a prereader, Angela is a beginning reader, and Joey is a reader. In particular, notice the spelling responses of all three students. We will explore more about the characteristics of early reading development as we turn to how to support early reading development in students.

**Figure 6.1**

## Concepts of Word, Spelling, and Story in a Prereader, Beginning Reader, and Reader

### Stage I: Prereader

| Writing sample | Concept of Word | Concept of Spelling | Concept of Story |
|---|---|---|---|
| Initial sounds: b - but, b - bench, k - kicked, d - drive, s - sink<br>Internal sounds: s - is, t - get, s - wasted, t - faster, c - tack<br>Incorrect: and - no response, did - k, wet - no response, man - i, jump - E, late - no response, little - c, fell - s, trip - c, washed - c<br>S B K T C I E<br>B C S S T C K C D S | When tracking Jack and Jill nursery rhyme, Travis moves continuously left to right without stopping at the words. | Travis usually spells the first letter of each word. He is an early phonetic speller. | When retelling a story, Travis can sequence some of the story. He knows the character and setting. |

### Stage II: Beginning Reader

| Writing sample | Concept of Word | Concept of Spelling | Concept of Story |
|---|---|---|---|
| BUT but ✓<br>dId did ✓<br>GET get ✓<br>TAC tack<br>WET wet ✓<br>MAN man ✓<br>LAT late<br>JUP jump<br>BECH bench<br>LITL little<br>WESdI wasted<br>FL fell<br>FASTR faster<br>TRIP trip ✓<br>KICT kicked<br>WOSHT washed<br>dRIV drive<br>SIC sink | Angela can track Jack and Jill accurately matching each written word with the correct spoken word. | Angela sounds out all the words when she tries to spell them. She is a phonetic speller. | Angela's retelling was somewhat sequential. She recalled the characters but had to be probed for much of her retelling. |

### Stage III: Reader

| Writing sample | Concept of Word | Concept of Spelling | Concept of Story |
|---|---|---|---|
| Incorrect: tack = tak, late = lat, bench = binch, little = littl, wasted = wastid, fell = fel, faster = fastr, kicked = cikt, washed = whosht, drive = droiv, sink = singc<br>Correct: is, and, but, did, get, wet, man, jump, trip<br>is and but did get tack wet Man Lat Jump Binch Litl Wastid FeL Fastr trip Cikt Whosht droiv Zingc | Joey read Jack and Jill fluently while pointing to each word. | Joey spelled almost half of the words correctly. His spelling is very phonetic. | Joey recalled all of the story events in sequence. |

## How Can You Support Reading Development?

When students are learning to become readers, they need to know about letters, sounds, and words. They also need to learn about text and how it conveys meaning to readers who actively engage it. Following are a number of instructional strategies that can help students become readers:

# Learning Letters of the Alphabet

One of the strongest predictors for early success in reading is the students' knowledge of the letters of the alphabet (Scarborough, 1998). Young students need to learn that English is an alphabetic language because letters represent sounds heard in spoken words. This important link helps students learn to pronounce and identify words as they begin to read and write (Adams, Foorman, Lundberg, and Beeler, 1998). Children learn the letters of the alphabet when they engage in a variety of reading, writing, talking, and listening activities. Here is a list of activities designed to help students learn and use the letters of the alphabet:

### Reading Activities

- Read alphabet big books with the students and point to the words. Have students come up with other words that begin with the letters.
- Read other big books with the children. Have them identify both the words in the books and letters in the words.
- Have children match the beginning letter for pictures on picture cards.
- Have children sort picture cards according to the first letter.
- Read pattern stories and point out words that are repeated.
- Read rhyming poems and have children identify the letters and words that create the rhymes.

### Writing Activities

- Place an alphabet strip with all the letters (in order) at the top edge of each child's desk.
- Encourage students to use these letters in their writing.
- Have children draw their own alphabet book and write the first letter of the name of each picture they draw. Later, they can write words that begin with each letter.
- Help children label parts of the classroom with the first letter of each part.
- Help children create their own pattern stories and rhyming poems.
- Have children write letters of the alphabet using paint on an easel, chalk on the chalkboard, or markers on a whiteboard.

### Talking and Listening Activities

- If students do not know the "Alphabet Song," teach it to them. Have them point to the letters on their desk as they sing it. Have them pick another tune, such as "Row, Row, Row Your Boat," and put that tune to the letters of the alphabet. It helps with the l-m-n-o letter sequence.
- Play a game with picture cards. Have students show cards to other students who have to say the name of the letter that goes with the picture.

The Exploring Children's Literature feature presents a number of books that can be used to support students in learning and using the alphabet as well as other concepts students learn in kindergarten and first grade.

**Video Homework Exercise**

*Matching Sounds*

Go to the Homework and Exercises section in Chapter 6 of MyEducationLab and watch the video, "Matching Sounds," which demonstrates children who are sorting objects that rhyme. Complete the activities that follow, and save your work or transmit it to your professor as assigned.

# Developing Phonemic Awareness

Another important prerequisite for successful beginning reading is phonemic awareness (Juel, 1988; Snow, Burns, and Griffin, 1998; Neuman and Dickinson, 2001). **Phonemic**

# exploring Children's Literature

## Alphabet Books and Concept Books

### Grades K to 2 Alphabet Books

*The Accidental Zucchini: An Unexpected Alphabet*—Written and illustrated by Max Grover, published by Harcourt (1993).
Each letter of the alphabet is represented by an unusual combination of objects, such as "fork fence," "octopus overalls," and "umbrella underwear."

*Alphabet Adventure*—Written by Audrey Wood, illustrated by Bruce Wood, and published by Scholastic (2001).
On their way to school, the little letters of the alphabet have to rescue little "i" and find his dot before they can proceed.

*Alphabestiary: Animal Poems from A to Z*—Selected by Jane Yolen, illustrated by Allan Eitzen, and published by Boyds Mills (1995).
This collection of poetry celebrates animals from A to Z. Poems by William Blake, Theodore Roethke, Isak Dinesen, and others are included.

*The Alphabet from Z to A (with Much Confusion on the Way)*—Written by Judith Viorst, illustrated by Richard Hull, and published by Atheneum (1994).
Verses running backwards through the alphabet take note of some anomalies in English spelling and punctuation.

*Chicka Chicka Boom Boom*—Written by Bill Martin Jr. and John Archambault, illustrated by Lois Ehlert, and published by Simon and Schuster (1989).
An alphabet rhyme/chant relates what happens when the whole alphabet tries to climb a coconut tree.

*The Disappearing Alphabet*—Written by Richard Wilbur, illustrated by David Diaz, and published by Harcourt (1997).
A collection of 26 short poems pondering what the world would be like if any of the letters of the alphabet should disappear.

*G Is for Goat*—Written and illustrated by Patricia Polacco and published by Philomel (2003).
This book is a rhyming celebration of goats and their antics, from A to Z.

*The Z Was Zapped*—Written and illustrated by Chris Van Allsburg, published by Houghton Mifflin (1987).
This story depicts how A was in an avalanche, B was badly bitten, and C was cut to ribbons, with the other letters of the alphabet suffering similar mishaps.

### Grades K to 2 Concept Books

*Grouchy Lady Bug*—Written and illustrated by Eric Carle, published by Crowell (1977).
Time of day.

*The Very Hungry Caterpillar*—Written and illustrated by Eric Carle, published by Putnam (1969).
A small hungry caterpillar nibbles his way through the pages of a book as he grows into a beautiful butterfly (includes the days of the week).

*Chicken Soup with Rice: A Book of Months*—Written and illustrated by Maurice Sendak, published by Scholastic (1962).
A boy enjoys chicken soup through all the months of the year.

*26 Letters and 99 Cents*—Written and illustrated by Tana Hoban, published by Greenwillow (1987).
Color photographs of letters, numbers, coins, and common objects introduce the alphabet, coinage, and the counting system.

*Close, Closer, Closest*—Written by Shelley Rotner and Richard Olivo, published by Atheneum (1997).
This book introduces perspective and scale through pictures of objects taken from three different distances.

*The Jacket I Wear in the Snow*—Written by Shirley Neitzel and published by Morrow (1997).
This book presents the concept of seasons as a child is bundled into layers of winter clothing that are then removed piece by piece.

*Black? White! Day? Night! A Book of Opposites*—Written and illustrated by Laura Seeger, published by Roaring Brook (2006).
Pairs of opposites are explored in die-cuts that lead from one element to another in a parade of happy contradictions.

*Over Under*—Written by Marthe Jocelyn, illustrated by Tom Slaughter, and published by Tundra (2005).
This book shows cut paper images that introduce color, form, and design as tall giraffes and short mice, squares and circles, and light day and dark night are explored.

*Actual Size*—Written and illustrated by Steve Jenkins and published by Houghton Mifflin (2004).
This book discusses and gives examples of the sizes and weights of various animals and parts of animals.

**awareness** is the recognition that words are comprised of sounds that can be identified, separated, and joined together to form words. Other aspects of phonemic awareness allow students to hear and identify rhymes in words and to indicate whether or not words rhyme. As Pressley (2002) points out, there are several levels of phonemic awareness:

- Match simple rhyming words (s*ing*-r*ing*).
- Identify words with the same beginning sound (*c*an-*c*ar).
- Identify words with the same ending sound (ca*n*-pa*n*).
- Blend sounds together (/h/-/o/-/p/ into *hop*).
- Remove the beginning sound in a word (*stop* becomes *top*).
- Replace the beginning sound in a word with a different one (*m* for *h* in *hop*> *mop*).

The challenging part of teaching phonemic awareness is to get students to see how individual sounds operate in spoken words. This awareness of individual sounds is something they did not have to attend to as closely when they were learning to speak. Identifying, isolating, separating, substituting, and blending sounds are tasks that students do not do naturally and need to be taught how to do. Why? The road to rapid word recognition begins with phonemic awareness that is supported by phonics and other word recognition skills. Learning about sounds in words is also challenging because sounds are invisible and have no meaning unless they are part of a word (/d/ in *dog*). Add letters to sounds and students face the additional task of mapping these sounds onto written words. Is it any wonder that students may be confused with all the sounds and all the letters? This is why we need to teach phonemic awareness and, later, phonics in an orderly and systematic way with attention paid to using these skills in a meaningful context. Here is a set of instructional strategies that focus on each of the levels of phonemic awareness.

**Rhyming Strategies** Ericson and Juliebo (1998) divide rhyming strategies into three levels of difficulty. The easiest level focuses on students' knowledge of rhyme (K), the second level on students' ability to discriminate rhymes (D), and the most challenging level is students' ability to produce rhymes (P). The following rhyming strategies have a (K), (D), or (P) attached to each to indicate the level that the strategy is intended to support. In some instances, a strategy may support more than one rhyming level.

1. Say pairs of words to students and have them say whether or not the pairs rhyme (K).
2. Read a poem with rhyming words to students. Have students recognize and say the rhyming word at the end of each line (K, P).
3. Have students dictate their own rhyming poem using a familiar poem as a guide. See the example of work using the Jack Prelutsky poem "No, I Won't Turn Orange" in Figure 6.2 (K, P).
4. Play rhyming riddles. "This word rhymes with *two* and it's what cows do (*moo*)" (P).
5. Gather picture cards that rhyme and have students group them by the rhyming sounds (D).
6. Have students draw pictures of objects that rhyme with the object in a picture (D, P).
7. Have students circle or cut out magazine pictures that rhyme with a given word or picture (D, P).
8. Play matching rhymes. In pairs or small groups, students give words that other students match with a rhyming word, such as *man*/*fan* (D, P).

**Figure 6.2**

## A First-Grade Class Dictated Poem Based on a Jack Prelutsky Poem

**No, I Won't Turn Orange***
**by Jack Prelutsky**

No, I won't turn orange if I eat this orange,
so don't you give me that!
No, I won't turn orange if I eat this orange,
you're talking through your hat!
No, I won't turn orange if I eat this orange,
that's just a bundle of stuff!
No, I won't turn orange if I eat this orange,
I'm going to call your bluff!
No, I won't turn orange if I eat this orange,
so who are you trying to kid?
No, I won't turn orange if I eat this orange,
Well, what do you know,
I DID!

**First-Grader's Dictated Poem Based on *No, I Won't Turn Orange***

No, I won't turn green if I eat this bean,
so don't you give me that!
No, I won't turn green if I eat this bean,
you're talking through your hat!

No, I won't turn purple if I eat this gerbil,
that's just a bunch of stuff!
No, I won't turn purple if I eat this gerbil,
I'm going to call your bluff!

No, I won't turn blue if I eat this shoe,
so who are you trying to kid?
No, I won't turn blue if I eat this shoe,
well, what do you know,
I DID!

**Beginning and Ending Sound Strategies** Drawing students' attention to the beginning and ending sounds of words is important because the greatest letter-sound regularity in written words is located at the beginning and ending of words. When students are able to determine whether words begin with the same sound or end with the same sound, they are better prepared for phonics instruction. Also, when students begin to write, they attempt to represent the first and last parts of the words they want to write (Beers and Beers, 1991). We offer one word of caution here: Students have to break away from the rhyming concept in order to focus on the beginning and final sound in words. They often overgeneralize about rhyming when they begin to listen for similar beginning

*"No, I Won't Turn Orange," *The New Kid on the Block,* by Jack Prelutsky. © 1984. Used by permission of HarperCollins Publishers.

or ending sounds. For example, it is common for five- and six-year-olds to state that two words have the same beginning sound when the two words do not, but they do rhyme (*sand/hand*). The converse of this also occurs frequently with these students when they indicate that two words rhyme when they only begin with the same sound (*hand/hope*). What we learn from these students' mistakes, or overgeneralizations, is that the language of instruction can be confusing to them. We need to carefully explain words such as "beginning, ending, rhyming, same, different, sounds, and rhyme" with much "thinking out loud" to help students attend to sound features in words. We also need to recognize that our young students will apply sound knowledge correctly one day and misapply it another day. With this in mind, here are some helpful instructional strategies that support students' understanding of beginning and ending sounds in spoken words:

- Gather picture cards that begin and end with common consonants. Choose a card and have students pick out pictures that begin with the same sound as a card you chose. Do this several times to make sure your students understand the task. Begin with words that have distinct beginning sounds (/s/, /t/, /f/, /h/, /m/, /p/, /sh/, /ch/, /th/), then go to other consonant sounds (/b/, /d/, /j/, /l/, /n/, /r/).
- With the same set of picture cards, choose a card and have students pick out pictures that end with the same sound as the card you chose. Do this several times to make sure they understand the task.
- Show students an object and have them look around the room for objects that begin or end with the same sound as the object you chose.
- Show students picture cards and have them produce a word that begins or ends with the same sound as the picture card. Have students cut out pictures from magazines that begin or end with the same sound as one you present to them.
- Read the "Jack and the Beanstalk" tale to students. Draw attention to the "fee, fie, foe, fum" expression used by the giant. Have students make up different expressions with the same beginning sound (e.g., "he, hi, ho, hum").

**Blending Sound Strategies** Sound blending is another important prerequisite skill for successful beginning reading, because it draws students one step closer to the alphabetic

Drawing students' attention to the beginning and ending sounds of words is important because the greatest letter-sound regularity in written words is located at the beginning and ending of words. This teacher is using a sorting activity to help students identify ending sounds.

nature of written English (Snow et al., 1998). There are three important aspects of sound blending for students to develop: blend by syllables, by onset and rime, and by individual phonemes (Ellery, 2005). Phonemes are the smallest pronounceable unit in a spoken word, such as /c/ in *cat.* Syllables are pronounceable units larger than a phoneme, such as *kit* in *kitten.* Onsets are consonants that appear before a vowel in a syllable, such as *c* in *cat* or *st* in *stop.* Rimes are the vowel and subsequent consonants in a syllable, such as *-at* in *cat* or *-op* in *stop.* Students often are able to separate words into syllables before separating syllables into individual phonemes. Many of the same picture cards, stories, and poems used for rhyming and beginning/ending sound activities can be used for teaching all three of these blending tasks. In the following list, (S) refers to syllables, (OR) to onset and rime, and (IS) to individual sounds. These letters appear next to the sound blending strategies to indicate the type of sound blending that the activity supports:

- With several one-syllable picture cards, say each word and clap once. With two-syllable words, say each word and clap for each syllable. Have students do this with you. Say other two-syllable words and have students clap for each syllable (S).
- Say the onset (first sound) and rime (rest of the word) followed by the entire word for several picture cards. For example, use /c/ then /ar/ to form *car.* Have students do this with you with other words (OR).
- Just say the onset and rime for words and have students put them together to create the words (OR).
- Have students look around the room for objects. Have them say the onset and rime for the object and identify the object (OR).
- With three sound words, say each sound and put them together to form the words. Have students do this with you (IS).
- Go around the room and say the sounds of the names of several objects in the room. Have students try to identify the objects (IS).

**Removing and Replacing Beginning Sounds** Once students have become familiar with these sound blending tasks, it is time to turn to the last category of phonemic awareness—removing and substituting the beginning sounds in words.

- Using picture cards or spoken words, say the word then say the word without the first sound. Have students do this with you. Point out that you have taken the first sound away. Use names of students as example words.
- Using the same picture cards or spoken words, add a new sound to the beginning of the word. For example, for the word *cat,* remove the /c/ sound and replace it with the /h/ sound to form *hat.* Have students do this with you and practice it in their own words with each other.

## Word Recognition

IRA/NCTE 3

Knowing letters and developing phonemic awareness are significant predictors for beginning reading success, but students have to connect the two to understand the alphabetic nature of English. When that occurs, students are not only able to learn written words, but also, they are able to learn *about* them. **Word recognition** is a necessary prerequisite for understanding what one reads. If we do not recognize enough of the words in a text, we cannot understand or appreciate fully what the author of the text has written. It is true that word recognition can come about through the use of context while reading or through closer analysis of structural features in words (Cramer, 2004), but at the emergent literacy stage, three aspects of word recognition are particularly important. These are phonics, spelling, and sight vocabulary. This book devotes an entire chapter to spelling, so we will focus here on phonics and sight vocabulary at this stage of your students' literacy development. Even within this focus, however, we will discuss spelling as an indicator of phonemic awareness and word recognition.

**Phonics Instruction** We like the definition of phonics instruction that Stahl (2001) provides. He defines **phonics** instruction as anything that a teacher does to help students decode words or recognize them. This might include teaching letter-sound relationships, common spelling patterns in words, or "anything else which helps students learn about orthographic patterns in written language" (p. 335). Students' understanding of the link between the sounds or sound patterns in spoken words and the spelling patterns that represent them in written words helps them recognize words while reading and helps them spell words when writing. The National Reading Panel (2000) concludes that phonics understanding is particularly helpful to students in kindergarten and first grade regardless of the approach used in teaching phonics. With this in mind, we do not see phonics instruction as the controversial topic that it may have been in the past (Tompkins, 2005). Rather, we view phonics as a helpful vehicle for students on the road to word recognition.

**Phonics Instruction Sequence** Is there a magical sequence to follow in teaching phonics to students? Well, not exactly, but a brief look at developmental spelling research provides some guidance. When students begin to spell using letters that represent sounds in their words, they start at the beginning of words, go to the end of words, and eventually approach the middle of words. This suggests that when developing phonics instruction for emerging readers, we should consider the following instructional sequence:

- Beginning consonants in words students use
- Onset and rime that link these consonants with simple spelling patterns
- Ending consonants found in words students use
- Consonant blends and digraphs
- Short vowels
- Long vowels

Keep in mind that we are only talking about the kind of phonics instruction that is helpful for beginning readers and not phonics for older students. For definitions and examples of the phonics terms just mentioned, review Figure 6.3.

**Phonics Strategies** There are as many instructional strategies for teaching phonics as there are phonic elements. Fortunately, useful guidelines do exist for selecting and using the strategies presented:

***Phonics Instruction Guidelines*** Learning about sounds of words and phonics can help students improve their spelling and speech skills.

- Use students' letter, sound, and spelling knowledge to determine the phonics to teach. One size does not fit all students.
- Use the same picture cards for phonics instruction that were used for phonemic awareness instruction. They reinforce both.

Figure 6.3

## Phonic Terms and Examples

| | |
|---|---|
| Consonants: | 21 letters of the alphabet *(b, c, d, f, g, h, j, k, l, m, n, p, q, r, s, t, v, w, x, y, z)* |
| Consonant Blends (Clusters): | Two or more consonant letters whose sounds are blended together *(s + t = st)* |
| Initial Consonant Blends: | *r* blends *(br, cr, dr, fr, gr, pr, tr,* and *wr)*<br>*s* blends *(sc, sk, sm, sn, sp, st, sw)*<br>*l* blends *(bl, cl, fl, gl, pl, sl)*<br>3-letter blends *(sch, scr, squ, str, spr, spl, shr)*<br>Other initial blends *(dw, tw, thr)* |
| Final Consonant Blends: | *l* blends *(ld, lm, lp, lt)*<br>*m* and *n* blends *(mp, nc, nch, nd, nk, nt)*<br>*r* blends *(rd, rt)*<br>*s* blends *(sk, sp, st)*<br>*t* blends *(ct, ft, pt)* |
| Consonant Digraphs: | Two consonant letters that represent one sound that is different from either consonant sound *(ch, gh, ph, sh, th, wh)* |
| Vowels: | 5 letters of the alphabet *(a, e, i, o, u)* and sometimes *y* |
| Long Vowels: | Vowel letters that say their name *(**a** as in **cake, e** as in **eve, i** as in **hide, o** as in **hope,** and **u** as in **tube**)* |
| Short Vowels: | Vowel letters that make the short vowel sound *(**a** as in **hat, e** as in **pet, i** as in **sit, o** as in **hot,** and **u** as in **cut**)* |
| Vowel Digraphs: | Two vowel letters that represent one vowel sound *(**ai** as in **paid, ay** as in **say, eat** as in **meat, ee** as in **meet, oa** as in **boat, ow** as in **grown, ew** as in **new**)* |
| Vowel Diphthongs: | Two vowel letters whose sounds are blended together *(**oi** as in **boil, oy** as in **toy, ou** as in **shout, ow** as in **cow**)* |
| *R* Vowels: | Vowel letters whose sound is influenced by the *r* sound *(**ar** as in **car, er** as in **her, ir** as in **shirt, or** as in **fort,** and **ur** as in **purse**)* |

- Provide opportunities to learn the names of common phonic elements (consonants, short vowels, etc.) and examples of words that have them. Knowing the names makes it easier to talk about them.
- Play onset and rime games during which students change the first letter of a word and say the new words (*cat, hat, sat, pat, mat*).
- Label parts of the room using different colors to highlight onsets and rimes.
- Using big books or experience chart stories, have students find words with the same beginning, ending, or rhyming sounds by identifying the letters that represent the sounds.
- When students write, encourage them to spell words phonetically.

**Spelling Strategies** Learning about common spelling patterns and the relationship between sounds and how they are spelled can also help students recognize words. Encouraging students to spell words the way they sound allows them to apply their developing letter and phonemic awareness knowledge in the spelling of words. This developmental, or *invented,* spelling as it has come to be called can reinforce phonics instruction and phonemic awareness (Adams, 1990).

***Invented Spelling*** **Invented spelling** is the term used to describe students' efforts at spelling sounds they hear in spoken words they wish to write. When teachers and parents support students' invented spelling, they help students see one of the connections between spoken and written language. Their support also promotes students' writing fluency and confidence. When students are encouraged to spell words as best they know how, they are more likely to write longer pieces and write more often. It is the best response to a student who says he cannot write because he cannot spell. This freedom to spell can also provide teachers with valuable information about their students' developing understanding about a written word or concept of word (Morris and Slavin, 2003). One way to promote invented spelling in students' writing is to model it for them. For example:

- Make a long "word" by writing lots of letters in a row (*cbcbcbcbcbbc*).
- Make a short "word" by using just a few letters (*cbcb*).
- With initial consonants, have students sound out the beginning part of a word and write the corresponding letter (*hippo-h*).
- With initial and final consonants, take a word and show how the first and last consonant sound could be spelled (*hat-ht*).
- When students show the beginning of vowel awareness in their spelling, model the phonetic spelling of a word (*enormous-enrmis*).

Keep in mind that invented spelling is used to encourage writing and to give teachers a window into students' knowledge of words. It is only temporary and should be accepted but not ignored. Be informed by students' invented spelling and use the information to decide on appropriate word study instruction. For additional instructional suggestions related to these emerging reading stages, see Chapter 9 (Spelling Development).

***Spelling Patterns*** Thirty-seven important spelling patterns are found in a surprisingly large number of words students encounter in their early school years (Wylie and Durrell, 1970; Adams, 1990). The common spelling patterns listed show several examples of each pattern in parentheses:

| | | | | |
|---|---|---|---|---|
| ack (back, pack) | ank (sank, thank) | eat (meat, seat) | ill (fill, will) | ock (clock, sock) |
| ail (pail, tail) | ap (clap, map) | ell (bell, shell) | in (chin, win) | ke (joke, woke) |
| ain (main, pain) | ash (flash, trash) | est (best, nest) | ine (fine, line) | op (hop, stop) |
| ake (bake, make) | at (bat, cat) | ice (ice, nice) | ing (ring, sing) | ore (more, store) |
| ale (sale, stale) | ate (gate, plate) | ick (pick, sick) | ink (sink, think) | ot (hot, pot) |
| ame (came, same) | aw (draw, saw) | ide (hide, ride) | ip (hip, ship) | uck (stuck, truck) |
| an (can, man) | ay (say, stay) | ight (light, fight) | it (hit, sit) | ug (bug, rug) |
| ump (bump, dump) | unk (junk, sunk) | | | |

When students do word sorts and word family activities with words having these common spelling patterns, they are more likely to use them as part of their word recognition strategies. This helps them increase their sight vocabulary (Wagstaff, 1994). Another useful way for students to reinforce these spelling patterns is by word analogy (Gillet, Temple, and Crawford, 2004). For example, if a student knows *cat* and *hat*, he or she can learn *sat* and *pat*.

> **Case Study Homework Exercise**
>
> *Greg*
>
> Go to the Homework and Exercises section in Chapter 6 of MyEducationLab and read the Level A-Case 3 about Greg, a first-grader who is experiencing difficulties with learning sight words. Complete the activities that follow, and save your work or transmit it to your professor as assigned.

**Sight Vocabulary Strategies** **Sight vocabulary** is made of individual words that can be recognized automatically when encountered while reading. A large sight vocabulary is necessary for readers to be able to move through text rapidly and efficiently. Beginning readers do not have a large vocabulary, which accounts for their need to read slowly and often to stop and figure out words. As beginning readers increase their sight vocabulary, they become more fluent in their reading and are better able to comprehend what they read. To help students begin to acquire a large sight vocabulary, teachers should keep several factors in mind:

- Students acquire sight vocabulary through repeated reading of familiar texts.
- Reading texts in which high-frequency words appear repeatedly reinforces sight vocabulary growth.
- Reading support, such as choral reading or echo reading, helps students learn words.
- The use of dictated stories helps to develop sight vocabulary.
- Reading fluency and sight vocabulary reinforce each other.
- Word study and writing activities give students strategies for recognizing words while reading.
- Teaching sight words in isolation is the least effective way for students to learn the words.

> **BUILDING TEACHING SKILLS: Lesson Planning Exercise**
>
> *The Language Experience Approach*
>
> Go to the Building Teaching Skills section in Chapter 6 of MyEducationLab and read the lesson plan ideas for using the Language Experience Approach. Complete the activities that follow, and save your work or transmit it to your professor as assigned.

**The Language Experience Approach** An effective instructional approach that promotes reading for meaning, word recognition, and sight vocabulary development is the **Language Experience Approach**, or **LEA** (Stauffer, 1980; Hall, 1981; Gillet et al., 2004). LEA promotes learning words and learning about words within the meaningful context of written stories that are dictated by students themselves. This is valuable because no matter what phase of the approach a teacher uses, students can always return to the original text because they created it. LEA can help students transition into their own writing and is a helpful source of reading material for students. We are focusing, however, on a set of LEA procedures outlined in Figure 6.4 that supports reading words in context, word recognition, and sight vocabulary growth. The procedures include a set for group-dictated stories and a set for individually dictated stories.

The language experience approach is useful for assessing early reading abilities in students. An excerpt from a group dictation using the language experience approach can be seen in Figure 6.5. The Engaging in Assessment feature on page 197 points out why Mrs. Santos used it with her students.

**Managing Word Banks** Using students' dictated stories helps students develop sight vocabulary and increase their word recognition skills. Many of the most frequently used English words that are more difficult to decode appear again and again in students' dictations. Words such as *said, come, there, they,* and *the* can be learned through their repetition in experience stories. As for word recognition skills, what better way to develop them than through words students are using and learning in their experience stories?

Words that students learn from their dictations can be put in their own **word banks.** The word banks become a resource for word study activities that explore similarities and differences among words students know. Students can apply this word knowledge to words they encounter that have similar features as words they know. Word banks are helpful in teaching students about words. They can be used to help students learn about



**Figure 6.4**

## Language Experience Approach Routines

**I. Group-dictated stories**

1. Day one
   a. group discusses and reacts to topic or experience
   b. children decide what story title will be
   c. teacher asks for volunteers to contribute dictated sentence
   d. writes down what children say
   e. reads back aloud the story
   f. choral reading with group
   g. sees who can choral or independently read part or all of story
   h. sees who can recognize words or parts of words—similarities or difference among words
   i. children create illustrations for the story
2. Day two
   a. teacher reviews the topic or experience
   b. sees who can choral and individually read the story
   c. continues word recognition activities from words in story
   d. puts words on cards next to the story to see who can match the words in the story
3. Day three
   a. teacher covers the story
   b. sees who can identify individual words shown on cards
   c. those who do keep the words for their word banks
   d. sees who can then independently read the story or part of it

**II. Individually dictated stories**

1. Day one
   a. pupil dictates own story and teacher writes down what is dictated in a composition book
   b. teacher reads back story to see if child wants anything added or changed
   c. child illustrates story right in the book
2. Day two
   a. individual/choral read story
   b. do word recognition activities with the story
   c. see who can find same words or similar parts of words
   d. children underline known words in own stories
3. Day three
   a. teacher shows student-known words in isolation
   b. words that are identified are placed in word bank
   c. child reads story one more time

**Figure 6.5** **Excerpt of a First-Grade LEA Group Dictation**

What I like About the Fall

Sammy said, "I like the Fall because it starts to get cooler."

Shonay said, "I like the Fall because of the colored leaves."

Robert said, "Football is why I like the Fall."

Sharon said, "I like Fall because of Halloween and Thanksgiving."

Chris said, "I like Fall because I go back to school."

Miguel said, "I like Fall because my birthday is in September."

sound-spelling patterns in words, understand the syntactic functions of words in reading and writing, and learn how affixes influence the meaning of words. For this learning to occur, however, it is important for students to be able to manage word banks in an efficient way. Here are some suggestions for managing word banks:

- Having a permanent word bank container is important. Small boxes, food storage containers, coffee cans, or manila envelopes are appropriate. Metal shower curtain rings can be used as word banks by punching a single hole in each word card.
- Sturdy cards are best for making word bank cards.

## *engaging in* Assessment

### Using LEA Routines to Support Assessment

By using various language experience approach (LEA) routines, Mrs. Santos identifies a number of emergent literacy skills in her students. She knows who has a beginning concept of word and who has a strong concept of word. She knows who has some phonemic awareness and who is ready for phonics. She knows who can read a text without support and who can make a one-to-one match between spoken and written words. After she administers a brief spelling test, she knows who has a beginning and advanced concept of spelling. By putting her observations together, she knows who are prereaders, beginning readers, and readers in her classroom. This knowledge helps her in making decisions about reading material and instruction for all of her students.

- As soon as students can alphabetize their cards, alphabetic index cards should be used in the banks.
- Place students' names or initials on their word bank cards so they can use them with other students' cards without having them get mixed up or lost.
- As word banks grow, classroom word banks can begin to be used. These can start as soon as enough students have the same words in their word banks; say, approximately fifty. Whenever students learn the same word, that word can be added to the class word bank. Newly learned words can still be added to students' word banks, but when they are recognized quickly, they can be added to the class bank. Different words that are not learned by all students can still be placed in the student's own bank.
- Another way to keep individual banks from getting too large is to create word bank pages, similar to dictionary pages. These can be made of sturdy tag board paper or regular paper that is laminated. A hole can be punched on the page and hung on a line with a ring. Word sorts can be done with these pages by having students write the words under the categories that they are working on.
- When students are using their word banks, make sure enough space is available for them to spread out their word cards so they can see all of them. To keep the word cards being used to a manageable number, specific word sort categories given to the students ahead of time will have them bring only the words that they need. For example, when doing initial/final consonant sorts, have them pull out their words that begin with *b, f, t, m, p.*

See the Engaging in Oral Language feature for an example of how Mrs. Santos uses the LEA routine to help her students speak in complete sentences.

**Reading Aloud to Students** Another important way to increase students' awareness of language structures and vocabulary is to read aloud to them daily. With the wonderful variety of fiction and informational books available, teachers can find books to help introduce students to a wide range of new vocabulary words and ways of expressing

## engaging in Oral language

### Using Complete Sentences

One Monday, Mrs. Santos decides to have her students create an LEA chart story that focuses on an upcoming trip to the local zoo. Her students have looked at picture books that contain pictures of animals they will see at the zoo. She asks her students to pick out the favorite animal that they would like to see and tell why they want to see it. As students dictate sentences for the experience story about the animals they want to see at the zoo, she realizes that several students are not giving her complete sentences. One student says "the spots" when asked why he wants to see the leopard. Another responds "stripes" when asked why she wants to see a zebra.

To help these two students with their dictation, she replies," You want to see the leopard because of its stripes?"

The student replies, "Yes, I want to see the leopard with all of his stripes."

She asks him for permission to write that down as his sentence, and he agrees. She tries to do that with the student who wants to see the zebra but still gets, "Yah, the stripes." So, she writes "Anita said, Yah, the stripes."

In both cases, Mrs. Santos honored the initial contribution but helped each student by expanding what the student said into a complete sentence. In time, she knows that these two students will volunteer complete sentences as they learn the differences between spoken and written language.

ideas. When doing read-alouds, it is important to remember to select books carefully, to practice reading them aloud, and to engage the students during and after your reading so they attend to the particular elements that you want to emphasize.

**Support Reading** In addition to reading experience stories together and reading to students, there are other kinds of **support reading** that can reinforce students' sight vocabulary. Choral reading of familiar stories and poems with students is one example. Teachers can read a poem or a story with pattern writing to students and have them choral read the material. Echo reading is another example in which teachers read a sentence aloud and students repeat the sentence. Both examples are especially helpful when used with big books, so students can readily see the text as they read it together.

**Shared Reading** A third kind of support reading that is helpful for concepts of print, word recognition, and comprehension is **shared reading.** Using a big book, a teacher engages students in many of the same activities used in the LEA. Typically, some or all of the following elements may come up in a shared reading experience:

- After introducing the big book, the teacher stimulates interest by having students make predictions and share their own experience with the subject of the book.
- While reading the book aloud, the teacher points to each word. Sentences may be repeated as students choral read them; some students may echo read with the teacher, and some may reread a sentence by themselves.

- To see whether students can find other similarities and differences with other words in the story, the teacher points out similarities and differences among the words.
- Throughout the reading, the teacher provides opportunities for students to make predictions, to reflect on their predictions, and to construct new ones as the story unfolds.
- Depending on the needs of the students, the teacher may spend time reinforcing concepts of print with the big book. For example, students might be asked where to start reading when a page is turned.
- The teacher and students may return to the same big book several times, and students themselves can be encouraged to read the big book by themselves.

When shared reading experiences are done in conjunction with experience stories, students receive the support needed to go from self-generated text to text written by others. This support not only leads to reading fluency but also writing fluency.

**Video Homework Exercise**

*The Second Rereading in a K–3 Multilingual Classroom*

Go to the Homework and Exercises section in Chapter 6 of MyEducationLab and watch the video, "The Second Rereading in a K-3 Multilingual Classroom," which demonstrates how a teacher conducts shared reading to enhance fluency. Complete the activities that follow, and save your work or transmit it to your professor as assigned.

**Reading and Writing Fluency** The best way to promote **reading fluency** is for students to frequently read material that is easy for them to read (i.e., when they recognize at least 95 percent of the words in a text). The best way to help students develop **writing fluency** is to provide support that allows them to write down their ideas easily and frequently. The goal in both instances is to promote reading and writing fluency and to instill confidence in students regarding their ability to read and write.

**Reading Fluency** Two strategies to encourage reading fluency are support reading and repeated reading. Support reading can include one or more of the following:

- Shared book reading in which students do many of the shared reading routines discussed earlier
- Choral reading in which students read the same text in unison with each other or with the teacher and may also include echo reading
- Read-alongs using prerecorded text that students listen to as they read along with their own copy of the text, such as big books and experience stories that provide material teachers can prerecord

Repeated reading is helpful for students because the number of oral reading errors decreases and their reading fluency increases when they read the same text a few times (Samuels, 2002). It is best to select a text for younger readers of approximately one hundred words. Gillet et al. (2004) describes the steps for doing repeated readings with a fluency monitoring feature. We have modified these steps here:

1. Choose (or help each student choose) a fairly comfortable, interesting selection of approximately one hundred words to practice reading.
2. Make up a chart for each student that includes the number of repeated readings, words per minute read (wpm), and oral

> The best way to promote reading fluency is for students to frequently read material that is easy for them to read.

reading accuracy (percentage of words read correctly) for each reading selection (see an example of one student's chart in Figure 6.6).

3. First, determine their beginning reading rate and reading accuracy by having students read the text aloud. Record their efforts on the chart.
4. Then, encourage students to read and reread the text aloud as many times as they like. They may practice in pairs, independently, or at home.
5. On another day, have students read their text out loud again and mark the chart for Timed Reading 2. Show the students how to mark their own charts.
6. Continue timing at intervals of several days. As their rate increases for the first passage, help each student set up a new rate goal.
7. When the reader reaches the goal set, begin a new passage of equal (not greater) difficulty. Successive portions of a long story are excellent choices. Repeat steps 3 through 6.

IRA/NCTE 12

**Writing Fluency** Because one of the greatest challenges for young writers is making the transition from spoken to written language, the following suggestions are intended to help them meet this challenge and to promote writing confidence and fluency at the same time:

- ***Talking Thoughts*** Students need to use their oral language by talking and listening with teachers and other students. This provides models for language structures and vocabulary that can be used by students in their "writing." The external speech that students generate forms the basis for internal speech that helps them when they think about things.

- ***Expanding Talk*** Students' vocabulary and sentence structures grow through this activity. Students who use single words or brief phrases need to have their oral responses expanded by teachers. This can occur during discussions, dictations, and

**Figure 6.6**

**Repeated Readings Chart**

**Student:** T'Ayanna

**Grade:** 2

**Overall Grade:** 100 WPM

| Reading Selections | Readings | Reading Fluency (WPM) | Reading Accuracy (WPM) |
|---|---|---|---|
| 1 | 1 | 67 | 92 |
| | 2 | 74 | 93 |
| | 3 | 87 | 97 |
| 2 | 1 | 78 | 93 |
| | 2 | 81 | 95 |
| | 3 | 89 | 96 |
| | 4 | 99 | 98 |
| 3 | 1 | 87 | 96 |

even writing. By expanding the student's responses, the teacher provides a more elaborate vocabulary and sentence model that can later be used by the student in his or her own speech, dictations, or writing.

- ***Draw Write*** Because the goal of writing is to convey ideas and transmit thoughts to others, drawing is an effective means of communicating for students who have few letters or signs to use. Have students "talk" their drawing as though that were reading it. Volunteer to write a word, phrase, or sentence that can label the drawing. To help organize a story told through drawing, draw lines that create sections in the paper that can be numbered 1, 2, 3, 4 to help with sequencing the story.

- ***Sign It*** Encourage students to think of interesting signs or symbols that they can use to represent ideas in their writing, especially when they lack the concept of word. They can be encouraged to arrange the signs from left to right so that they give the appearance of "writing." Even with students who have letters, invented spelling, or even words, a sign for an unknown word is helpful.

- ***Pattern Writing*** By listening to pattern books or poems, students can be given parts of the pattern that makes writing a story or poem easier for them. The pattern could be a repeating sentence or word. The pattern could a repeated action in a story or poem.

- ***Story or Poem Maps*** These focus on key elements found in poems and stories that students have listened to or read. The maps can be as simple as beginning-middle-end (or more elaborate) and can help students organize their ideas. Modeling the use of maps with poems or stories that students know can help them see how the maps work.

- ***Sentence for Sentence*** Students who are concerned about length of writing or spelling can be encouraged by agreeing to match their writing sentence for sentence. Always have the student write the first sentence; then, write what the child says as the next sentence. The child writes the third sentence, followed by the teacher's sentence, and so on.

- ***Word Walls*** When students are thinking and talking about topics for dictations or writing, significant words that they mention can be written on the chalkboard or bulletin board. This provides some of the key words that they wish to use in their writing. Students are still encouraged to use other strategies for "writing" their ideas, but word walls can give them additional support for their writing.

- ***Give Me Five*** For students who are reluctant writers because they are afraid to use invented spelling, agree to give them five words for their writing *if* they use invented spelling for at least five other words. Encourage them not to "waste" their request for words that they can "invent" by spelling. This encourages students to try more invented spelling because they know they will get some words from the teacher.

- ***Modeling Invented Spelling*** Follow the steps for modeling invented spelling outlined earlier (in the section on invented spelling on page 193).

## Reading for Meaning

IRA/NCTE 3

The goal of good reading instruction in the primary grades is to help students become independent readers for meaning regardless of the nature of the text they are reading. Developing a sight vocabulary and learning about words is helpful in achieving this goal, but there is also need for instructing students on how to comprehend what they read. Reading comprehension requires students to:

- Activate their prior knowledge about the topic and structure of the text they are reading (Is it a story or poem? What do they know about stories or poems?)
- Make predictions about the text to help guide their reading of it
- Monitor their understanding of the text as they read and adjust their reading accordingly
- Support their predictions and understanding with direct reference to the text itself
- Review and summarize what they read based on their understanding of the text
- Apply to future reading the knowledge and understanding acquired while reading the text

To successfully accomplish these reading comprehension goals, reading instruction must engage students before, during, and after the reading. Three comprehension strategies relating to this engagement sequence are: (1) directed listening-thinking activities (DLTAs) and directed reading-thinking activities (DRTAs), (2) story/content impressions, and (3) predict-o-grams. Each strategy activates prior knowledge before students read, promotes interaction with the text as they read, and helps students review and summarize after they read. All three can be used with fiction or nonfiction texts but are used more frequently with story reading in the primary grades. Figure 6.7 shows how all three comprehension strategies might be used with a story. The Engaging in Visual Literacy feature illustrates other ways students can review and summarize stories they read.

**Directed Listening-Thinking Activity (DLTA)** To begin developing comprehension in younger students, have them participate in a directed listening-thinking activity, or DLTA. This activity is designed to help students link their prior knowledge and experience to a story that they listen to through a series of predicting-listening-proving cycles. Here are the steps to follow for successful DLTAs:

- **Establish the purpose for listening: Making predictions about the story**
  1. Read the title aloud and have students listen to the first paragraph or page of a story or look at the pictures to predict what the story will be about.
  2. Take words from the story and ask the students to predict what story might have those words in it.
- **Let students listen to the story: Confirming or adjusting the predictions**
  1. Have students listen to the story to see whether their predictions are on target.
  2. Reach an appropriate place to stop, then have students discuss their predictions in light of what they have heard.
  3. Ask the question: Did it happen the way you thought? Why or why not? What did you find out to change your mind?
  4. After discussing their predictions, have students summarize where the story is now.
- **Set listening purposes again: Making predictions again**
  1. Once the students have summarized, have them make predictions about the next segment of the story.

Figure 6.7

## A DRTA, Story Impression, and Predict-o-gram used with *Flight: The Journey of Charles Lindbergh*

**DRTA**

Predicting Question (Beginning of the story): What do you think a story entitled *Flight: The Journey of Charles Lindbergh* will be about? Why?

Predicting Question (page 157): Do you think that Charles Lindbergh will get above the huge storm cloud? What if it gets too cold?

Predicting Question (page 160): How do you think Lindbergh can get through the night without any lights?

---

**Story Impression**

Charles Lindbergh
Airplanes
Atlantic Ocean
Compass
Paris
Storm Cloud
Fog
Paris
Hero

Think of a story where these vocabulary words appear in this order. What would it be about? What might happen? Write your story.

---

**Predict-o-gram**

| Characters | Setting | Problem | Events | Solution | Outcome |
|---|---|---|---|---|---|
| | | | | | |

Charles Lindbergh, Airplane, Atlantic Ocean, Compass, Paris, Storm Cloud, Fog, Paris, Hero

Place the words taken from the story under the story element where you think they go. Then make a prediction about what the story might be about.

*Source:* Burleigh, R. (2002). Flight: The Journey of Charles Lindbergh. From *Picture This!* Scott Foresman Reading. Glenview, IL: Scott Foresman. Used by permission.

2. These predictions can be based on what the students think about the story at this point or they can be in response to a predicting question(s) raised by the teacher.
3. Once again, students listen to confirm or change their predictions and follow the process just outlined.

## engaging in Visual Literacy

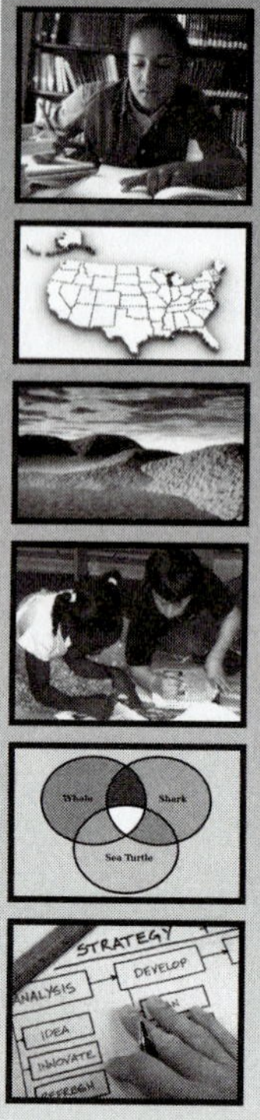


### Story Maps

An effective way to assess students' understanding of stories is with story maps. For example, students in Mrs. Sharpe's third-grade classroom have been reading Aesop's fables as part of her folk tales unit. She has introduced Story Steps to help students plot the story sequence in the fables. The story steps depicted the various characters, setting, and events in the fables. One of her students used story steps to illustrate his understanding of "The Fox and the Grapes." Another student climbed the story steps with information about "The Lion and the Mouse." When the students had completed their story steps, they shared them with one another. Mrs. Sharpe found this to be a very effective way for students to check their understanding of the fables they had read. She also learned that visual displays of students' reading comprehension helped students remember fables for a longer period of time and with greater detail. Here is a story steps map that she created for the two students:

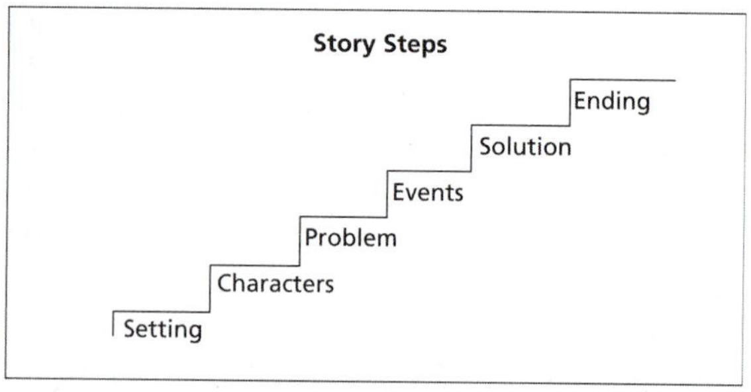


4. Students repeat the predict, listen, and discuss steps for the rest of the story.
5. At the conclusion of the story, students may discuss story elements, characters, or similar stories they have heard before.

IRA/NCTE 3

**Directed Reading-Thinking Activity (DRTA)** Developed by Stauffer (1976), a DRTA is quite similar to a DLTA, except students *read* the text rather than *listen* to it. For prior knowledge to surface, students make predictions before reading, they read to confirm or change their predictions, and they make predictions again. Not only do students make predictions, but they must also refer to the text in supporting their predictions and other opinions about the text. This proving from the text reinforces self-monitoring as students read, and it provides support for subsequent review and summarizing at the conclusion of the reading. Steps and hints for successful DRTAs include:

- **Establish the purpose for reading: Making predictions about the story**
  1. Students examine the title, listen to the first paragraph or page of a story or look at pictures to predict what the story will be about.
  2. The teacher may initiate discussion by asking the students a predicting question.
  3. Vocabulary may be taken from the story and the students asked to predict what story might have these words in it.

4. As students make predictions, they should be encouraged to discuss their reasons for their predictions.
5. There are no right or wrong predictions but rather reasons for reading to find out about the story.

- **Let students read the story: Confirming or adjusting the predictions**

1. Have students read to check out their own predictions.
2. When students have completed an appropriate amount of text, have them return to their predictions.
3. Ask: Did it happen the way that you thought? Why or why not? What did you find out to change your mind?
4. Encourage students to refer to actual lines or passages in the text to support their thinking.
5. If a student changes a prediction, have him or her go to the text to show you why.
6. It is also appropriate after discussing their predictions to have students summarize where the story is now.

- **Set reading purposes again: Making predictions again**

1. Once the students have summarized, have them make predictions about the next segment of the story.
2. These predictions can be based on what the students think about the story at this point, or they can be in response to a predicting question(s) raised by the teacher.
3. Once again, students read to confirm or change their predictions and follow the process just outlined.
4. Students repeat the predict, read, discuss steps for the rest of the story.
5. At the conclusion of the story, students may discuss story elements, characters, or other possible outcomes of the story.

- **Hints for successful DRTAs**

1. Use stories that have interesting characters and plots.
2. When selecting points for stopping in a story, look for changes in characters, setting, or plot action. Avoid stopping at every three pages. Have a specific reason for stopping in a story.
3. When developing predicting questions, come up with questions that get students to think forward in the story and beyond what they have already read.
4. Review with students ahead of time what they do when they encounter an unfamiliar word in a story (Do they skip it, sound it out, use context clues, etc.?).
5. Encourage students to use their word attack strategies. If they still cannot get the word, have them raise their hands and you give them the word.
6. As students become familiar with DRTAs, the number of stops during a story should be reduced. This is especially important for students who are eager to read more of the story between stops.

Take a look at Figure 6.8 for an excerpt of a DRTA conducted with a group of fourth-graders. Look for parts of the DRTA structure just outlined.

IRA/NCTE 11

**Story/Content Impressions** As with DRTAs, story impressions (McGinley and Denner, 1987) encourage students to make predictions and to read to confirm, and they help in reviewing and summarizing the text. More attention is given, however, to vocabulary and the story sequence or structure that the vocabulary provides for

Figure 6.8

## Excerpts from a DRTA based on *Flight: The Journey of Charles Lindbergh*

| | |
|---|---|
| Mrs. Litz: | If the title of this story is *Flight: The Journey of Charles Lindbergh,* what do you think this story might be about? |
| Suzanne: | I think the story will be about an airplane ride that Charles Lindbergh takes. |
| Mrs. Litz: | Why do you think that? |
| Suzanne: | There is a picture of an old plane on the first page and Charles Lindbergh is named in the title. I don't know who he is. |
| Lisa: | I don't know who he is either, but I think he goes on a long trip because a journey is a long trip. |
| Mrs. Litz: | Where do you think he will go? |
| Miguel: | Across the country? Around the world? |
| Henry: | Yeah, I think he's going around the world. |
| Mrs. Litz: | What do you think, Albert? |
| Albert: | I agree with Henry. |
| Mrs. Litz: | OK, I'm going to write down these ideas on the board to help you remember your predictions as you read the first two pages of the story to find out what it's about. |

[Students read the first two pages.]

| | |
|---|---|
| Mrs. Litz: | Well, Lisa and Suzanne, were you right? What did you find out? |
| Lisa: | He is going on a very long trip. Over 3,600 miles between New York and Paris. |
| Suzanne: | And he has to do it without stopping because he is crossing the Atlantic Ocean. |
| Miguel: | So he's not going across the country or around the world. |
| Henry: | I agree with Miguel and Lisa. |
| Mrs. Litz: | Do you think this will be a difficult journey for Lindbergh? |
| Henry: | Yeah, it's back in 1927. He doesn't have radar or a radio like planes have today. |
| William: | How is he going to know where he is going? |
| Mrs. Litz: | That's a good question, William. Did it say anything about that? |
| William: | No, here on page 152, it just said "He climbs into the boxlike cockpit that will be his home for many, many hours." |
| Mrs. Litz: | So, how do you think he will be able to see where he is going? |
| Suzanne: | We use a compass to find our way in camp. |
| Henry: | What's a compass? |
| Suzanne: | If you have a map, you can use it to find your way. |
| Henry: | Did Lindbergh have a map? |
| William: | How long will his flight take? How will he stay awake all that time? |
| Mrs. Litz: | These are really good questions. I have written them on the board. Go ahead and read the next ten pages to see if you can find the answers to these questions. |
| Albert: | I have a question. |
| Mrs. Litz: | OK, Albert, what do you want to find out about? |
| Albert: | How does Lindbergh know where he is going? |
| Mrs. Litz: | Good one, Albert. I'll add that one and you look for that one as you read. |

predicting what the story is about or the content of a nonfiction text. Here are the steps to follow when conducting a story impression:

1. Select 8–12 vocabulary words from the text. For nonfiction, select words that are related to the concepts in the text. For fiction, select words that are related to story elements, such as setting, characters, problem, plot, and solution.
2. Present the words in the same order in which they appear in the text.
3. In pairs or small groups, have students create a text based on the words in the list. For nonfiction, students can write a paragraph that summarizes what they think the text is about. For fiction, they can create a story based on the words.
4. Students then share their writing with one another.
5. After sharing their writing, students read the text.
6. After the reading, students compare and contrast what they wrote with the actual text.

Not only does a story impression support students as they read stories, but it also provides an excellent prewriting activity for writing stories.

**Predict-o-Gram** A predict-o-gram is a graphic organizer that focuses on key story elements in a similar way as a story impression. The elements are depicted in the graphic organizer, and students place vocabulary from the story with the elements with which they predict the words will go. This reinforces the connection between vocabulary and story structure, just as the story impression does. Here are the steps to follow for using predict-o-grams:

1. Create a predict-o-gram that contains key headings for a text. For nonfiction, they can be related to the key headings or concepts in the text. For fiction, they can be story elements.
2. Select 10–20 vocabulary words from the text that are related to the concepts or story elements included in the predict-o-gram.
3. In pairs or small groups, have students place the vocabulary words under the appropriate headings on the predict-o-gram.
4. Students read the text.
5. Once the text is read, students return to their predict-o-grams to make changes based on their reading.
6. Have students explain their predict-o-grams and summarize what they learned from the text.

Once again, this comprehension strategy provides opportunities for activating prior knowledge, self-monitoring while reading, and summarizing at the conclusion of reading.

Now that we have looked at ways to support reading development in the primary grades, what reading instruction helps to create independent readers? Read-alouds and guided reading are two effective strategies to use in your classroom.

## Read-Alouds

All students need to hear written text read out loud to them. This is especially important for younger students. **Read-alouds** develop appreciation for good literature. They help promote vocabulary development while revealing similarities and differences between spoken and written language. In developing readers, read-alouds also instill an understanding of basic story elements and the ways that stories develop. By having students make predictions, listen to a story, and discuss their predictions, students rehearse with spoken text what we want them to be able to do when they read. Finally, read-alouds are shared experiences that have psychological value. A bond develops between the teacher, the students, and the book being read. Students suspend their disbelief, enter new worlds, and laugh and cry with the characters. Just read E. B. White's *Charlotte's Web* to a class of third-graders to see this bond at work. Guidelines for selecting books for read-alouds and for conducting successful read-alouds can be seen in Figure 6.9.

## Guided Reading

For students to become independent readers, they need to read. In the primary grades, providing support while students are reading helps to ensure they become successful readers. In a similar way as the language experience approach and shared reading mentioned earlier, **guided reading** (Fountas and Pinnell, 1996) provides an instructional setting that supports young readers. Guided reading is an instructional approach used with a small group of students who are reading on the same level or have the same strategy need. It is designed to have students focus on meaning while reading and learn how to use strategies to help with unfamiliar words, sentence complexity, and new concepts. Guided reading occurs before, during, and after the reading of a text similar to the steps in a DRTA. Before the reading, the teacher introduces the story or unfamiliar vocabulary and addresses predictions or questions raised by students about the story. During the reading, students read aloud or silently (depending on their reading level) while the teacher listens to students individually and observes their reading. After the reading, students discuss their predictions and other aspects of the story. The teacher may direct their attention to a particular segment of the story, discuss any problem words, or reinforce a reading strategy used in

**Figure 6.9**

### Guidelines for Selecting Books and Conducting Read-Alouds

**Selecting Books**

- Keep in mind the age and interest of the students to be read to
- Select books that you like
- Include picture books, story books, and poetry books
- Choose books or sections of chapter books that can be read during the allotted read-aloud time
- Refer to *The Read Aloud Handbook* by Jim Trelease for examples of good read-alouds

**Conducting Read-Alouds**

- Set aside a special time for read-alouds each day
- Select a special place to do your read-alouds
- Practice! Practice! Practice! reading the book you select
- While reading, use your voice, pacing, gestures, and facial expressions to bring the book to life
- An occasional prop or piece of clothing can add dramatic effect to your reading
- With picture books, make sure all students can see the pictures clearly
- For poetry, clearly enunciate and read in the rhythm of the poetry
- For story books, have students make predictions and listen to see if they are correct
- Look at your students as you go through the book

the reading. Running records or other informal reading assessment may occur during the guided reading period. The primary goal of all this reading activity is the development of independent silent reading by the students.

The best way to support students in guided reading is to make sure that they are reading material on appropriate reading levels. Remember from Chapter 5, the independent level (95 to 100 percent accuracy) is best for free or recreational reading that does not require support from a teacher, and the instructional level (90 to 95 percent accuracy) is best when conducting guided readings, DRTAs, story impressions, and other instructional reading activities. A simple running record with a text can help determine these levels for individual students. The students' levels then can be matched with materials for them to read. Stories and other texts provided by basal reading programs are assigned to levels that approximate the first or second half of a grade level. For example, stories in the *Picture This!* book (from Scott Foresman Reading) are written at approximately the 3.2 grade level, or the second half of third grade. Many commercial reading programs have several levels of books for the first grade. If your school uses a set of these materials, check its basic developmental sequence and the materials provided for students who need easier materials. Fountas and Pinnell (2005) have a guided book list that levels books for students in grades kindergarten to fourth grade, and that considers interest, book length, vocabulary, and sentence structure to determine whether a book is a kindergarten, first-grade, second-grade, or third-grade book. Regardless of the leveled text approach you use, it is important to provide students with interesting texts that they can read independently and confidently in a small group instructional setting.

All students need to hear written text read out loud to them. This is especially important for younger students. Read-alouds develop appreciation for good literature, promote vocabulary development, and instill an understanding of how stories develop.

Now that we have provided instructional strategies that help students develop into successful readers, how can we find out whether our reading instruction has been successful?

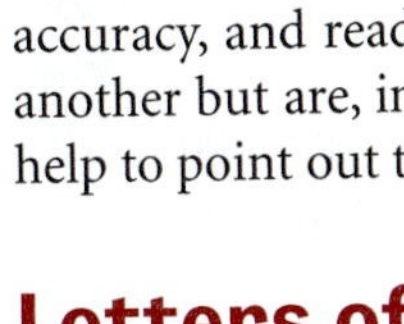

## How Can You Assess Early Reading Development?

Important reading skills that early reading assessment can measure include alphabet letters, concepts of print, phonemic awareness, phonics, spelling, reading fluency and accuracy, and reading comprehension. These skills do not stand independent of one another but are, in fact, very much related. A brief look at the assessment of each will help to point out these relationships.

### Letters of the Alphabet

Two areas of letter identification are important for students to be able to do. Students should be able to identify the names of the letters in alphabetic order as well as in random order. Alphabetic order helps reinforce the names of the letters, and random recognition indicates that they can use letters to help identify written words. It also demonstrates that students can begin to distinguish words by beginning letters (onsets) and the subsequent cluster of letters (rimes). Letters in alphabetic and random order that can used for this assessment can be found in Figure 6.10.

## Concepts of Print

As Marie Clay (1993) and others have pointed out, students need to learn certain concepts of print to maneuver through books. Some of these concepts are book orientation, what is printed is read, left to right, top/bottom, words, letters, and punctuation. Students who have been read to a great deal before entering school have already acquired many of these print concepts. Teachers can develop these concepts in classrooms by reading books aloud to their students. Print concepts are important road signals that help young readers get on the road to reading. Assessment of print concepts can be accomplished with a favorite picture book that has printed text. While going through the book and asking simple questions, teachers can discover what print concepts their students know. These could include:

1. Where do I start the story? (book orientation)
2. What do I read? (the printed part)
3. When I finish this page, where do I go next? (page orientation)
4. Where is the top (and bottom) of the page? (top/bottom)
5. What is this mark for? (punctuation)
6. If I start at the beginning of this page, where do I go? (left to right)
7. Can you show me a word, a letter? (concept of word, letter)

These questions can be woven into a shared book experience with a group of students or during a smaller book read with one child. This assessment informs early reading instruction about concepts of print. If a student does not move left to right, return to the left, or repeat the same movement down the printed page, the teacher can model this for

**Figure 6.10**

### Letter Identification Assessment

**ABC's in order**

| | | | | | | | | | | | |
|---|---|---|---|---|---|---|---|---|---|---|---|
| A | B | C | D | E | F | G | H | I | J | K | L |
| M | N | O | P | Q | R | S | T | U | V | W | X |
| Y | Z | | | | | | | | | | |
| a | b | c | d | e | f | g | h | i | j | k | l |
| m | n | o | p | q | r | s | t | u | v | w | x |
| y | z | | | | | | | | | | |

**ABC's out of order**

| | | | | | | | | | | | |
|---|---|---|---|---|---|---|---|---|---|---|---|
| A | L | T | B | M | U | C | N | V | D | O | W |
| E | P | X | F | Q | Y | G | R | Z | H | S | I |
| J | K | | | | | | | | | | |
| a | j | r | b | k | s | c | l | t | d | m | u |
| e | n | v | f | o | w | g | p | x | h | q | v |
| i | z | | | | | | | | | | |

the student with any printed material (e.g., books, charts, or experience stories). By instructing the student on this concept, he or she will also come to realize that the same movement is done in writing. Asking students to write a story or write on the chalkboard can reveal whether students are transferring print concepts from reading to writing.

## Phonemic Awareness

The ability to recognize that spoken words are comprised of sounds (phonemic awareness) and that these sounds can be represented by letters in written words (phonics) is a strong predictor of early reading success (Byrne and Fielding-Barnsley, 1995). There is also a growing body of evidence that phonemic awareness, phonics, and spelling development are linked and are sharpened by each other as students learn to read (Adams, 1990). Phonemic awareness points to the sounds in words, and phonics attaches letters to those sounds as letter-sound patterns. These patterns, in turn, become recognizable spelling patterns in many words. Recognizing and using this connection leads to increased reading vocabulary and reading fluency in young readers. The assessment of phonemic awareness can be done with the following activities:

1. Show paired pictures or say word pairs; students decide whether or not they rhyme.
2. Have students clap syllables in words.
3. Show paired pictures or say word pairs; students decide whether they have the same beginning or ending sound.
4. As students learn letters of the alphabet, have them try to match letters with beginning sounds in words.

Students' responses to these phonemic awareness tasks can direct teachers toward instruction that concentrates on the beginning, ending, or rhyming sounds in words.

## Phonics and Spelling

Phonics and spelling knowledge can be assessed by giving students a short list of words and asking them to spell the words. The students' spelling effort can reveal important information about their knowledge of phonics and spelling. A sample of misspellings from their writing or spelling attempts of words with key phonic elements can provide reliable measures of students' phonics or spelling ability. The following list of words can be given to students to determine their early phonic or spelling abilities:

| | |
|---|---|
| but | fell |
| and | faster |
| did | trip |
| jump | kicked |
| bench | washed |
| little | drive |
| wasted | sink |

Examine the students' responses by answering these questions:

1. Are all the phonic elements spelled phonetically? (*DD/did*)
2. If not, are the beginning elements spelling phonetically? (*KEFG/kicked*)
3. Are the ending elements spelled phonetically? (*KIKT/kicked*)
4. Are vowels spelled correctly or by letter names? (*GAT/get*)

By analyzing students' spelling attempts, a picture will emerge of their knowledge of letters and sounds and how these elements work together to spell words. It is also helpful to realize that this knowledge develops in stages and that teachers can use these stages to plan effective instruction. For additional information about analyzing student spelling, turn to Chapter 9 on Spelling Development.

## Reading Fluency

One of the traits of a successful reader is reading fluency. A fluent reader rapidly recognizes words in print, observes the phrasing or structure of the text, and comprehends the text easier and quicker than a less fluent reader (Samuels, 1994). As students begin to recognize more words in their reading, they rely less on their need to sound out words to identify them. Recognizing words quickly helps readers focus more on the structure and the meaning of the text. Decodable text, predictable text, or pattern writing provides support for easy recognition of the words while reading. Other instructional strategies that can develop or improve reading fluency include having students do repeated readings of the same text (Samuels, 1988) or pairing up for shared reading (Juel, 1991). Regardless of the instructional techniques used by students, reading fluency is achieved ultimately through frequent opportunities to read and reflect upon meaningful text (Lipson and Wixson, 1991).

To assess whether young readers are developing reading fluency, teachers may have them read aloud text that is on their reading instructional level (when they can recognize close to 95 percent of the words in a selection). While listening to a student read the text, teachers note the actual reading behaviors in three areas: (1) the smoothness of the reading, (2) the pace of the reading, and (3) the attention being paid to the phrasing and punctuation. The following scales, which are modifications of the Multidimensional Fluency Scale (Zutell and Rasinski, 1991), can be used to rate these three aspects of reading fluency:

1. Smoothness
   - Frequent hesitations, breaks, and repetitions
   - Periodic hesitations, breaks, and repetitions
   - Smooth reading with some breaks
2. Pace
   - Slow and labored
   - Somewhat slow, uneven, or both
   - Natural and expressive
3. Phrasing
   - Word-by-word reading
   - Inappropriate phrasing, intonation, punctuation
   - Appropriate phrasing, intonation, punctuation

By assessing these three aspects of reading fluency, teachers can determine which students are fluent readers and which ones need help to become fluent readers.

## Reading Accuracy

An important correlate to reading fluency is reading accuracy. Rapid recognition of words while reading (with a minimum of miscues) signals that the reader is reading text at the appropriate difficulty level. For example, when a student is reading with 95 to 100 percent accuracy, the material would be considered easy for the student. If, however, the student's oral reading of the text is less than 90 percent accurate, the material would be considered difficult for the student. When reading material is read with accuracy close to 95 percent, the text is considered to be on the student's instructional level. In addition to determining the accuracy of the reading, teachers can also determine a young reader's word recognition strategies while actually reading: phonics, sentence structure, and/or meaning.

To assess word recognition accuracy and strategies, teachers can make running records of their students' oral reading (Pinnell, 1987; Clay, 1993). Using a blank sheet of paper, the teacher makes a check mark for each word that students correctly identify as they read a text on their instructional level. A running record can also be done on a copy of the text that the child is reading. An example of each is found in Figure 6.11. Whenever a student omits, mispronounces, or substitutes a word while reading, the teacher makes note of it on the blank sheet of paper.

When the student read this text of forty-six words and only made three errors, a reading accuracy rate of 93 percent would be obtained. Whenever the student reads a word correctly, add a check mark. With any error, write a line with the correct word below the incorrect response. In this running record, the first oral reading error, *pay* for *play,* signals that the student may need help with the pl blend. The check mark above *play,* however, indicates that the reader self-corrected and said *play.* The second error, *walks* for *walked,* points out that the reader may ignore past tense verb endings while reading. In either case, occasional errors such as these are not significant. When errors are more numerous, however, and they point toward a pattern of similar responses, teachers should be alerted to the possible need for instructional intervention. For example, if a young reader frequently ignores the second letter in beginning consonant blends while reading (*set* for *step, bank* for *blank, tip* for *trip*), additional instruction that helps him or her differentiate single consonants from consonant blends would be helpful. Four questions that can help in analyzing oral reading errors are:

1. Are the errors frequent (more than 5 percent of the words)?
2. Do the errors change the meaning of the text?
3. Do the errors suggest problems in phonics?
4. What patterns emerge from the errors?

**Figure 6.11**

## Two Examples of a Running Record

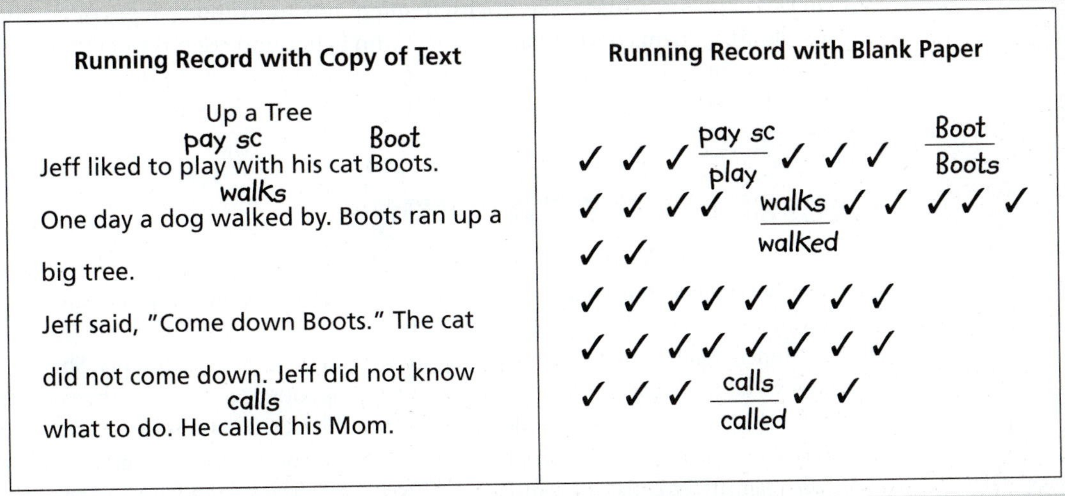
Running Record with Copy of Text
Up a Tree
pay sc
Boot
Jeff liked to play with his cat Boots.
walks
One day a dog walked by. Boots ran up a
big tree.
Jeff said, "Come down Boots." The cat
did not come down. Jeff did not know
calls
what to do. He called his Mom.
Running Record with Blank Paper
pay sc
play
Boot
Boots
walks
walked
calls
called

*Source:* Johns, 2005, p. 231.

Answers to these questions can guide teachers in making instructional decisions about the word recognition strategies used by their students when they are reading text.

## Reading Comprehension

IRA/NCTE 3

The ultimate goal of all reading instruction is to have students become independent readers who can read successfully and comprehend a variety of reading material. As young readers develop word recognition strategies that allow them to read text fluently and accurately, they are able to turn more of their attention to the meaning of what they read (Snow et al., 1998). Because young fluent and accurate readers may think that error-free rapid reading is all there is to reading, teachers need to help them focus on comprehension as the ultimate end of reading. Too often, students believe they can comprehend by simply reading a text accurately. Comprehension research over the past twenty years suggests, however, that comprehending narrative (a story) or expository (nonfiction) text requires active engagement of the text by the reader. This involves the use of prior knowledge and awareness of the text structure, which helps students better understand what they read (Dymock, 1999).

Because narrative text accounts for much of the reading done by students in the primary grades, it is important that much of their comprehension instruction center on story structure (Irwin, 1991). Common elements found in stories that students read or hear read aloud are: Who are the characters? Where does the story take place? What happens in the story? How does the story end? See the Engaging in Visual Literacy feature earlier in the chapter for several ways that students can demonstrate reading comprehension as well.

**Retelling** One way to help students recognize these story elements is to point them out when retelling a story and to have students retell the stories themselves. To acquaint students with oral retelling, teachers read several stories aloud and retell the stories in their own words. Included in the oral retellings are the important story elements presented in the correct sequence. Using teachers' retellings as models, young readers can retell stories that they have read. As a comprehension assessment technique, retellings can reveal whether a student can identify the setting, characters, and events in a story and present them in an organized manner. If an element is omitted in a retelling, the student can be prompted with a question. For example, if the setting is essential to the plot, a question such as "Where did the story take place?" or "Where did all this happen?" can be asked. With frequent retellings and changes or additions to the retellings, students develop into readers who better understand what they need to do to comprehend what they read. Refer to the Engaging in Visual Literacy feature earlier in this chapter for ideas on assessing students' understanding of stories.

## revisit the classroom challenge

In Mrs. Santos' first-grade classroom, what emergent literacy skills did she find in her first-graders? She learned who can read the experience story without any help from her or her students. She learned who can read the story with support from her or her students through choral reading. She saw what students can accurately track words while reading the experience story. She found out the students who can recognize the beginning and ending sounds of words in the experience story. She sees the students who recognize identical words in different locations in the experience story. She knows the students who can recognize words taken out of the story. All this information, as well as what her students do with words in their writing attempts and their story retelling, helps her determine which students are prereaders, beginning readers, or readers in her first-grade class.

We have tried to uncover the variety of factors that students bring with them as they begin to learn to read. We have also endeavored to explore the stages of literacy development and the literacy skills and instructional strategies needed in learning to read. Students embark on a wondrous journey when they set out to learn to read. We encourage you to let your students instruct you about where they are along this journey. Your skillful observations and informed conclusions will help you assist students in becoming literate. They need guidance and support along the way, and we have tried to describe both for you in this chapter.

Here is a summary of the questions raised at the beginning of the chapter and the answers to them:

## What Are Important Factors for Successful Beginning Reading?

Students who are motivated about reading and writing and have developed all aspects of their oral language are prime candidates for success in beginning reading instruction. Being able to monitor their own learning, including their awareness of spelling and print features, is also helpful.

## How Does Beginning Reading Develop?

As students develop concepts of word, spelling, and story, their ability to read develops. The concept of word leads to the recognition that they can match written words with spoken words, the concept of spelling helps them recognize the alphabetic nature of written words, and the concept of story helps them recognize common story elements. Students progress through three stages: prereaders, beginning readers, and readers as they develop and use these concepts.

## How Can You Support Reading Development?

For students to learn to read, they need support in learning the alphabet, developing phonemic awareness, learning how to recognize words through phonics and spelling awareness, and developing a sight vocabulary. In addition, students benefit from activities that promote reading and writing fluency and reading comprehension.

## How Can You Assess Early Reading Development?

In assessing early reading development, a number of areas should be included: knowledge of letters, concepts of print, phonemic awareness, phonics, spelling, reading fluency and accuracy, and reading comprehension. There are informal assessment techniques for each of these reading areas.

PEARSON **myeducationlab**™

Where the Classroom Comes to Life

Now go to www.myeducationlab.com to take a Pretest to assess your initial comprehension of chapter content, study chapter content with your individualized Study Plan, take a Posttest to assess your understanding of chapter content, practice your teaching skills with Building Teaching Skills exercises, and build a deeper, more applied understanding of chapter content with Homework and Exercises.

chapter 7

# Writing Development

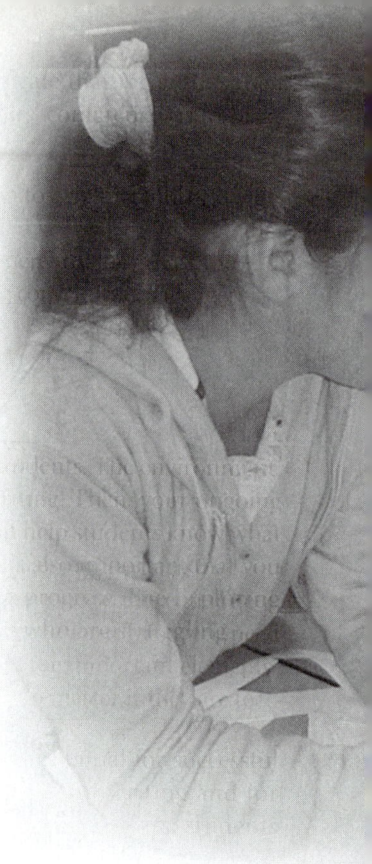

## classroom challenge

**Raymond,** a first-grader, chews the end of his pencil as he stares at the picture he drew in the illustration portion of his experience writing paper. The picture he has carefully drawn depicts a Halloween scene he has imagined. The sky is dark with a large, white moon. The trees are bare. He has drawn a cat with raised hair and a dog howling at the moon. He has also placed a witch on a broom in the sky and two small children dressed as ghosts at the base of the picture. This young writer fidgets with the corners of the paper as he chews his pencil. He is having trouble getting started on his story. He raises his hand for help from his teacher. Mrs. Ramos walks over to his desk.

Mr. Harris, a third-grade teacher, develops a poetry writing assignment for his students. He wants his class to try writing some haiku poetry. He reads haiku poems to his students and talks about the characteristics that are common to all haiku poetry. The

class goes over the definition of syllables because there are important syllabic constraints in haiku poetry. The class discusses scenes or experiences in nature because nature is the common theme in haiku poems. The class is then given thirty minutes to construct a haiku poem on some aspect of nature. As the teacher walks around the room, he realizes that his students are not writing haikus. The task of writing haiku poems is more difficult than he had anticipated.

## Questions for Reflection

1. What do these two classroom examples have in common?
2. How could Mrs. Ramos have helped Raymond before he tried to write?
3. What could Mr. Harris have done to help his students write haiku poems?

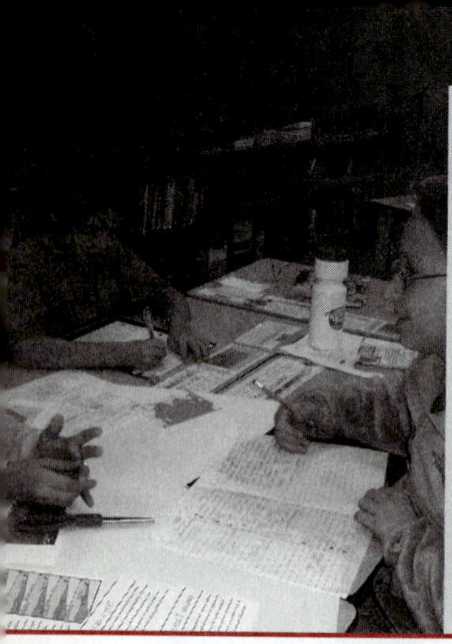

## anticipating this chapter

To help you answer these and other questions about writing, this chapter will address the following questions:

How do students develop into writers?

What is the writing process?

How can you help students become writers?

How can you assess students' writing?

# How Do Students Develop into Writers?

Writing development in elementary school students is a process that touches virtually all aspects of child development. Learning to write is learning to recognize that there are important similarities and differences between oral and written language. As students grow as writers, they gradually gain control over the conventions of written language. These include sentence and paragraph structure, spelling, punctuation, and mechanics. If children's cognitive development influences how they think, then that same influence can be seen in their written thoughts. This will be especially true when students realize that writing can be used to identify and clarify those thoughts. Once thinking is down on paper, students can reflect on it, modify it, confirm it, or reject it.

If learning to write is a journey, the journey is one that takes students from their private inner world to the public outer world of school and beyond. As we shall see later in this chapter, the young writer's road is a bumpy one and can bring joy, anxiety, trust, or mistrust to the student who travels it. To help students become confident writers eager to write, we need to know about writing development in children, understand the process of writing, and recognize the strategies that will help students write.

## The Influence of Oral Language

IRA/NCTE 6

Children develop into writers as the result of a number of important factors that begin to influence them at a very early age. Oral language and oral language experiences form the basic language foundation for developing writers. Oral language plays an important role in the early stages of writing development in children of preschool and elementary school age (Dyson, 1989). In the beginning, children make squiggles and other marks that "look" like writing but have no relationship to real words. In Example 1 in Figure 7.1, the child's marks have no relationship to "We went to the bus garage," which was what the student said in his writing. These preliterate writers, however, are eager to explain what their "writing" says

**Figure 7.1**

## Preliterate to Emergent Literate Writing

**Example 1**

**Example 2**

**Example 3**

*Source of Example 2:* "Daddy Painted the House" spelling example, p. 58 from *Spelling Research and Information: An Overview of Current Research and Practices.* © 1995 by Scott Foresman and Company. Used by permission of Pearson Education, Inc.

(Dyson, 1993; Teale and Sulzby, 1986). Oral language at this stage is primary in explaining the writing, while the writing remains secondary. As students become partially literate (see Example 2 in Figure 7.1) in their writing, the beginnings of actual writing begin to appear (*DDPTDHS* turns out to be *Dad Painted The House*). Many of the features of the writing may not be understandable, but enough of them are so that the beginnings and endings of words are recognizable. With the emerging literate writer (Example 3 in Figure 7.1), his or her writing can begin to speak for itself (*I Love Lag Riss N a Car* becomes *I Love Long Rides in a Car*). As students continue to grow as writers, however, they begin to realize that written language has its own structure and conventions; consequently, their later writing begins to read more like written discourse than spoken discourse (Kroll, 1981).

In addition to the supportive role that oral language plays with children's early writing, it also acts as a rehearsal for written language. When young children have opportunities for conversations and discussions with their peers, older siblings, and adults, they generate many of the language structures and meanings that they will later use in their writing. Bruner (1986) refers to this as *external dialogue*, while Britton et al. (1975) term this interactive language activity *external speech*. It is used in expressing or explaining ideas as well as solving problems. As children mature, the external language for these cognitive activities becomes internalized; that is, it forms the basis for the thought processes that older students and adults use. When we think about something or try to think through a solution to a problem, we are using language and thought processes that originated in childhood oral language experiences. This language/thought rehearsal becomes even more important to young writers as they think about writing topics, what they want to "say," and how they want to "say" it in their writing. Language fluency affects the words and grammatical structures used by youngsters in their writing. When we encourage children to use their oral language, they actually rehearse many of the language patterns that they later use their writing. We have seen that the ability to talk and discuss provides a necessary support for the youngest writers who have not yet mastered the basic conventions of written language. As they acquire these conventions for writing, the need to "talk" their writing is replaced by more understandable writing. Spoken language is also important to the young writer because it allows for the feedback that all writers need if they are to progress in their writing.

## Cognitive Development Influences

In addition to oral language influences on writing development, we have seen that cognitive ability also has an impact on what students write and how they write. As children progress through stages of cognitive development, their writing changes. For example, four-, five-, and six-year-olds who use preoperational thought produce writing that is highly subjective, lacking description, organization, and writing conventions—and seeming to ignore the reader (Figure 7.2). Often, these young writers will not include sufficient context for their writing, which makes it more difficult for an external reader to understand. As Mayher, Lester, and Pradl (1983) have pointed out, these youngest of writers seem to be unaware of the audience for their writing.

**Figure 7.2**

### Cognitive Development Influences on Writing

We paly basball. He hiots it it braks trhe windo. Thay look at it. he cms out and shouts becuz thay brok it. so thay ran away and he tels them off.

Four boys were playing baseball. One boy hits the ball so hard it gos across the street and hits a window on the house. A man comes out and shouts at the boys for playing baseball in front of his house. He tells the boys that he will call there parents. So they run home.

Older students who function at the concrete operational level of thought create writing that is quite different from their preoperational-thinking counterparts. Their writing tends to be more objective and focused. Descriptions are more full, and ideas appear in some logical or sequential pattern in the writing (see an example of this in Figure 7.2). These student writers demonstrate a growing awareness of conventions of written English and supply ample context in their writing for their readers. These writers *do* recognize the limits of their readers and are developing a sense of audience in their writing. The primarily egocentric writer is replaced by the older decentered writer (Graves, 1983). Once young writers become less centered and more logical in their writing, they are able to separate themselves from their writing. This separation or distancing allows young writers to come back to their writing not as writers but as readers. Once students are able to respond to their own writing as readers, they are more apt to understand the value and need for revision in writing. It may even be the case that until students have attained Piaget's cognitive level of concrete operational thought, it will be difficult for them to revise their own writing.

These cognitive abilities also correlate with the emerging concept of audience. As very young writers, children are less conscious of the audience for their writing. As they mature, however, they begin to see that beyond themselves there exists a world of audiences whose opinions, feedback, and limitations are instrumental in helping students shape their writing. Cognitive development also helps to determine what kinds of writing, forms, topics, and audiences are appropriate for students and when the students are best able to handle them.

## Print Development in Writing

Based on her observations of young children as they begin to write, Marie Clay (1975) identified several characteristics of their early writing. These include recurring, directional, generating, and other graphic features. These principles, or features, become embedded in preschoolers and kindergarten students as basic concepts of print.

**Classroom Artifact Homework Exercise**

*The Bear and the Horse*

Go to the Homework and Exercises section of Chapter 7 of MyEducationLab and view the artifact, "The Bear and the Horse," which illustrates a young child's rough draft of a story summary. Complete the activities that follow, and save your work or transmit it to your professor as assigned.

**The Recurring Principle** Parents at one time or another have encountered a child joyfully scribbling on the floor, the wall, the bed, the door, or their favorite magazine. This scribbling is often accompanied by giggling or outright laughter from the child. The first example in Figure 7.3 shows this kind of "writing." Notice that the scribble has a repeating feature to each as though you were looking at a series of small peaks. Clay (1975) refers to repeating features in children's early writing as the **recurring principle.** When this type of activity is initiated by a child, quite possibly it serves the same function in preliterate writing as does lolling for infants in their precommunication speech. Both are simply done as self-stimulating activities for the amusement of the child. The recurring marks do not represent anything meaningful at this point except when a parent voices approval or disapproval of the activity. This response, of course, would probably depend on the surface the child had chosen to mark.

As children mature, the recurring principle continues to be at work in their writing. Instead of just marks, however, single letters, letter clusters, and words are repeated in their writing. As children learn more about letters and words in writing and reading, they come to recognize that while letters and words may be repeated in writing there are limits to the acceptability of their recurrence. As Clay points out: "When he is older the pupil will learn the limitation that two but never three consecutive repetitions of letters are allowable and only in rare instances can three words be repeated in English" (p. 22).

**Figure 7.3** Print Development in Writing

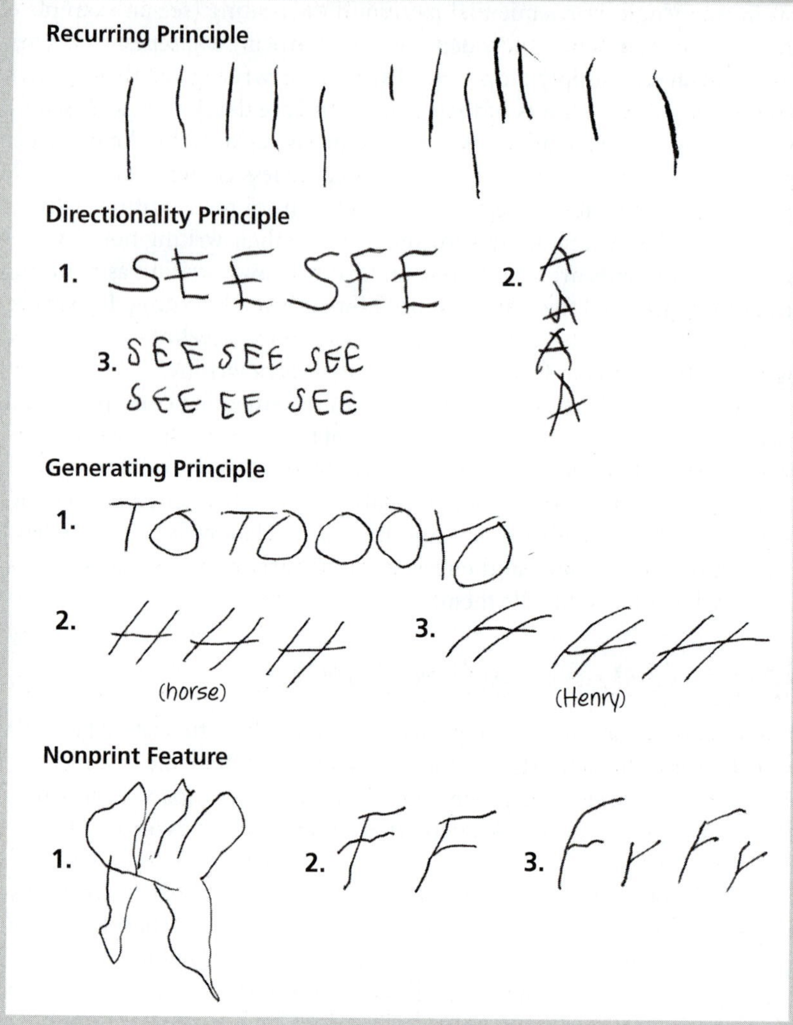


**The Directionality Feature** A second graphic feature that Clay identified in young developing writers is the **directionality feature.** Eventually, writers of English learn that in extended writing beyond one line of text, they start at the top left of a page, write across to the right side of the page, return to the left side but lower than the last line, and proceed again to the right. Examples on preliterate "writing" by four- and five-year-olds show the development of these directionality principles (see Figure 7.3). In the second example, we can see the downward movement but not the return to the left. In the third example, not only is the left-to-right movement seen in this older child's writing but the return movement to the left and down is as well. Notice in all of these examples that directionality can also refer to the correct formation of letters and words.

**The Generating Principle** The **generating principle** is another graphic feature that develops in the writing attempts of preschool and primary grade students. The generative principle allows us to create a seemingly endless number of sentences using a finite number of letters or words. Preliterate writers will combine a set of letters in several different arrangements, and these arrangements, when strung together, begin to look like long "sentences." Of course they are not sentences (Figure 7.3) but rather a series of wordlike letter combinations rearranged in different ways to create new "words." When young students employ the recurring and generating principles together, their graphic effort begins to look like writing. As students create this pseudowriting, they also explain or "talk" their writing. This "talking" was described earlier in this chapter as an important use of oral language in the early stages of preliterate writing.

## Nonprint Features

One other interesting feature that Clay discovered in preschool writers was the use of drawings, signs, or nonprint graphics in their writing. Drawing is an important print substitution for preliterate writers as Graves (1983) and Dyson (1989) point out. Clay finds that drawing, for these students, is necessary in providing the context for what they say about their early writing. The students begin to move away from a visual representation of what they write and toward a more symbolic representation; they begin to write signs in their writing. In the fourth example in Figure 7.3, several signs are presented. Signs can include drawings that stand for words, a pattern of letters that stand for words, or, of course, words used in writing. Notice that the first sign was the student's sign for *french fries*, the second sign was two letters that represented *french fries*, and the last sign was quite close to the actual word.

When preliterate writers begin to use signs in their writing, they begin to realize that written language is an organized, arbitrary set of symbols and marks that represents something. Only those who use and understand these symbols and marks are able to communicate in writing with one another. Fortunately, most students have arrived at this understanding of written language by the time they reach the age of seven. It should come as no surprise that the recognition that writing uses symbols to represent meaning seems to occur at the same time students realize that reading uses the same symbols. In fact, Clay (1975) believes that as children become readers they have a need to put these symbols (letters and words) into a structure that closely resembles the structure of their reading.

## Other Graphic Principles

Several other graphic concepts or principles seem to show up in the writing of children who have become readers. Early writing in which letter or word forms are strung together, later becomes separated by spaces. Early readers also seem to follow Clay's flexibility principle as they produce a variety of forms for the same letters. This same principle, however, can account for students not seeing letters as being different even when the letters are reversed. Young students eventually learn that even though letters look alike in different positions, the letters are actually different. For example, if *p* is turned upside down it looks like *b*, if *n* is turned upside down and reversed it looks like a *u*, and if *Z* is turned on its side it looks like *N*. One other important principle that accompanies beginning reading is Clay's message concept that states that messages that can be thought or spoken can be written. At first, nonreaders use drawings and other graphic devices to present their messages, but the messages have to be explained. Later, when young readers gain some understanding of the features in written language, they use more conventional graphics (letters and words) to present their messages.

## Writing Functions

IRA/NCTE 4

We see another aspect of writing development that parallels cognitive development in the functions or purposes for which children write. Britton et al. (1975) reduced these functions or roles for writing to three, but the three are significantly different to account for most of the writing that students do.

**Expressive Writing Function** **Expressive writing** is the label given by Britton to writing that is personal, informal, and conversational in tone and form. This writing function is widely used by younger children as they write about immediate concerns, observations, and feelings (see Figure 7.4). The young writer using this writing function is very much a part of the writing and may assume that the teacher knows about

**Figure 7.4**

### Britton's Writing Functions

**Expressive Writing**

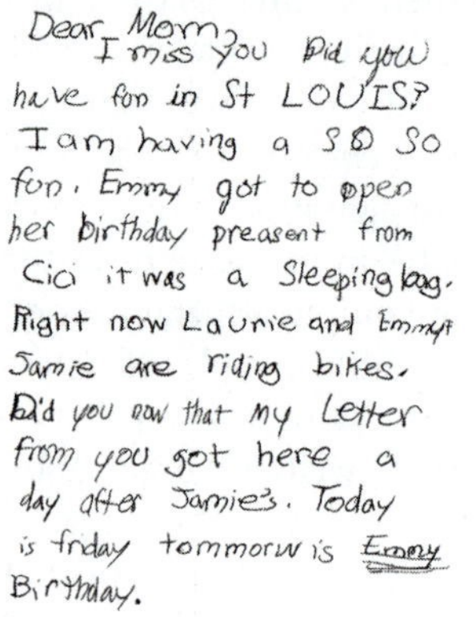
Dear Mom,
I miss you Did you
have fon in St LOUIS?
I am having a SO So
fon. Emmy got to open
her birthday preasent from
Cici it was a Sleeping bag.
Right now Laurie and Emmy&
Jamie are riding bikes.
Did you now that my Letter
from you got here a
day after Jamie's. Today
is friday tommorw is Emmy
Birthday.

**Transactional Writing**

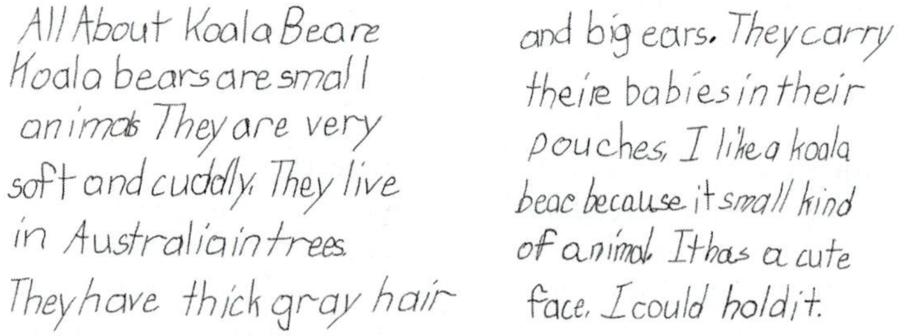
All About Koala Beare
Koala bears are small
animals They are very
soft and cuddly. They live
in Australia in trees.
They have thick gray hair
and big ears. They carry
theire babies in their
pouches. I like a koala
bear because it small kind
of animal. It has a cute
face. I could hold it.

**Poetic Writing**

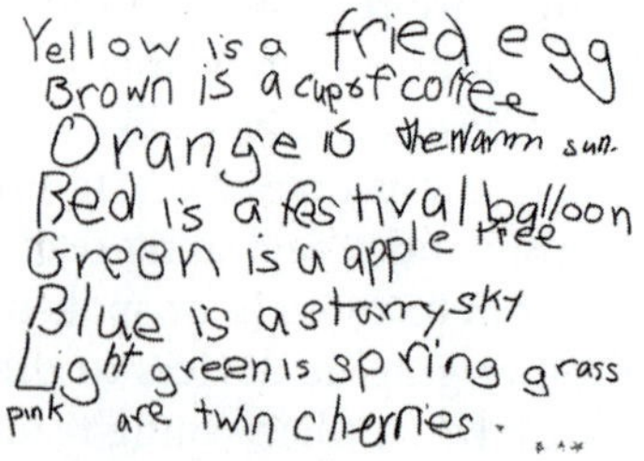
Yellow is a fried egg
Brown is a cup of coffee
Orange is the warm sun.
Red is a festival balloon
Green is a apple tree
Blue is a starry sky
Light green is spring grass
pink are twin cherries.

everything he or she is writing. This makes some expressive writing hard to follow because it does not include sufficient context for understanding. This can explain why the expressive writer omits details or other information that can make the writing more clear and more complete for a teacher. It is this same lack of clarity that Kroll (1985) sees in the early writing attempts of children. The writing often reads and sounds more like a conversation between two friends. Like a conversation, it moves from topic to topic, jumps around, and often digresses without bothering to define the context for each remark or statement in the writing (shown in Figure 7.4). The trusting nature of young expressive writers also comes across in their writing because they are willing to share their personal feelings and ideas with the teacher. We would also think that through expressive writing, young students identify and explore their own voices as writers.

**Transactional Writing Function** The most common function for writing used by students in school is **transactional writing** and includes the forms of explanation, description, and persuasion. As youngsters grow and develop as writers, their writing becomes less private and more public. Young writers use transactional writing for accomplishing something between themselves and their readers. For example, students may write to explain how thunderstorms are formed, to describe the natural materials used in constructing early colonial houses in Massachusetts, or to persuade the principal to extend recess on days that the temperature exceeds 85 degrees. The writing is usually more focused, more detailed, and more objective than expressive writing, as we see in the writing about koala bears (Figure 7.4). The writer tends to be the mastermind controlling the writing rather than being the subject of the writing and begins to realize that the purpose of the writing—to describe, explain, persuade—dictates the form of the writing and how it is developed. Even so, this young writer expresses her own feelings about how "small . . . and cute . . ." a koala bear is.

**Poetic Writing Function** The poetic function for writing seems to evolve at the same time as the transactional function. **Poetic writing** is writing done for its own sake and is to be enjoyed more for its own sake. The forms of poetic writing include poetry, plays, stories, novels, scripts (for radio, television, or movies), or any other literary form that can stand on its own. Rather than focus on the points being made in transactional writing, poetic writing focuses on language as the primary mover of the reader. The words, phrases, rhythm, rhymes, pictures in the minds, and feelings generated by the writing are the basis for poetic writing. Look at the examples in Figure 7.4 to see how different poetic writing is from transactional writing.

**Supporting Writing Functions** Britton et al. (1975) and Emig (1971) encourage teachers to stimulate students to write for all three functions. *Expressive writing*—with its personal tone and feeling in letters, journals, opinion pieces, and firsthand accounts—can help students find their own voices. *Poetic writing* will foster growth in imagination and interesting use of words and phrases whether in stories or verse. *Transactional writing* is still held in high regard by Britton because it is the writing that helps writers think and learn. It is the mode of writing that passes on information, explains ideas or phenomena, or persuades through reasoned arguments. When the expressive voice is encouraged, it will give heart to the transactional writing and feeling to the poetic writing. The poetic writing will give rise to words and phrases that paint vivid pictures in transactional writing. In the next chapter of this book, we discuss writing experiences that encourage students to explore all three functions of writing.

**Figure 7.5**

## Growth in Sentence Maturity

1. He has a dog. Her name is Maggy. Maggy has long hair.
2. He has a dog, and his name is Charlie.
3. he likes to run, and he like to jump.
4. He has a brother whose name is Carlos.
5. Sitting on the bench, Mark called his dog who was barking.
6. What he said was what everyone remembered
7. Moby Dick was a dangerous white whale who had a crooked jaw.

# Growth in Sentence Maturity

Young writers' growing control over their writing is also reflected in the sentence structures that they choose to use in their writing (Hunt, 1965; Christensen, 1967). The chart in Figure 7.5 provides sentence samples that point out the growth in sentence maturity in student writers. Here is a description of this growth:

- Sentences are short with one or two main clauses.
- Sentences include subordinate clauses with main clauses.
- An increase occurs in the use of subordinate clauses with a main clause.
- A gradual increase occurs in the use of specific kinds of clauses, including noun, adverbial, and others.
- Noun clauses appear as the result of the writing topic.
- The increase in adverbial clauses peaks at the fourth grade.
- Adjectival clauses continue to increase through the grades.
- Increase in adjectival clauses coincides with an increase in descriptive writing.
- Main clauses are combined into one.
- Greater use of prepositional phrases is seen.

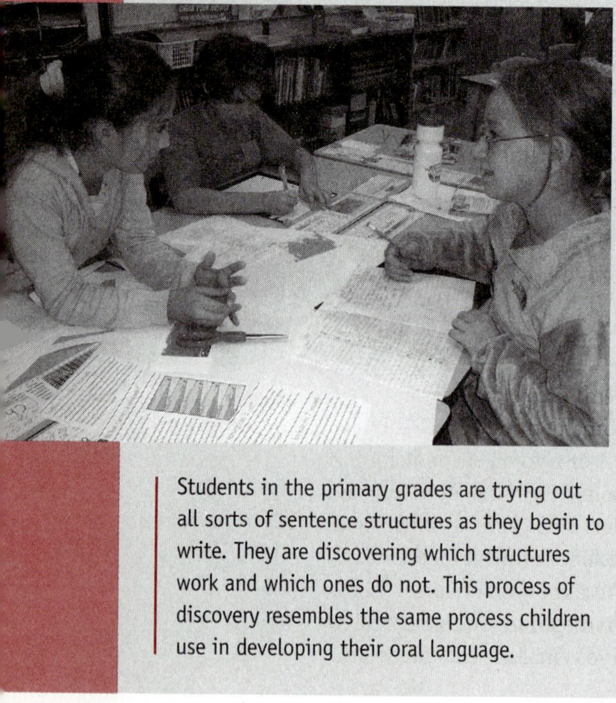

Students in the primary grades are trying out all sorts of sentence structures as they begin to write. They are discovering which structures work and which ones do not. This process of discovery resembles the same process children use in developing their oral language.

The remaining examples in Figure 7.5 illustrate these other changes in the sentence complexity of student writing.

We hasten to add one additional point about sentence maturity in student writing. Hunt admitted that when he looked at the writing of students in the primary grades, he found that measuring sentence complexity or structure was difficult. This was the case because students in these early grades used such a variety of sentence structures in their writing that it was difficult to identify a recognizable sequence of sentence structures. As one second-grade teacher put it, "my kids' sentences are all over the place. Some days they write short sentences. Some days they write longer ones. I can't tell how they will write them [the sentences] next." Students in the primary grades are trying out all sorts of sentence structures as they begin to write. They are discovering which structures work and which ones do not. Sound familiar? This process of discovery resembles the same process that students use in developing their oral language. It can also be that until students have the concept of audience, they do not have to attend very closely to the sentence grammar in their writing. Concept of audience is much more apparent in young students as they seek to find the right words in the right order to effectively use their oral language.

# What Is the Writing Process?

When we think of the writing process, we think of the steps that writers go through in developing a piece of writing. These include prewriting, drafting, revising, editing, and publishing. Although we discuss each of these steps in this order, research has shown that writers move across and back and forth through these writing process phases rather than follow a strictly linear progression (Dyson and Freedman, 1991).

IRA/NCTE 5

## Step 1: Prewriting

We think of prewriting as an initial effort to discover a writing topic or as the first step in responding to a topic. Prewriting may include time spent planning a response to a nonfiction topic taken from social studies or science. It may require thinking and organizing of ideas related to the topic. This may lead to brainstorming, mapping of ideas, and organizing them before writing. Prewriting may include talking or reading about a topic to recall known information or to discover new information. In addition to the gathering of ideas for writing, prewriting can include narrowing or expanding what might be included in the actual writing.

Two important activities generally associated with prewriting are *planning* and *organizing*. Here are a few strategies that students can use to help them plan and organize a response to a writing topic:

**Art Activities** Elementary school teachers have known for some time that many students enjoy working in a variety of visual art media as a creative means of expressing themselves and their ideas. A six-year-old may do a crayon drawing of a remembered personal experience or favorite television episode or movie. Other students find using the larger easel paper and poster paints to be more conducive to their artistic efforts at portraying recalled or imagined scenes. Still other students find sculpting with clay or papier mâché to be a stimulating medium for tapping into their feelings and ideas about a topic or theme in social studies or science. Students can use art media as the basis or starting point for writing ideas. Drawing, painting, sculpting, and other art media can help students with writing in several important ways. When a student draws a picture, a visual record of ideas has been created. When a teacher or classmate encourages the student to talk about the picture, the student can translate the visual, but nonverbal, expression into a nonvisual, but verbal, recording. This language record, in turn, can be used as the basis for writing about the picture. See the Engaging in Visual Literacy feature for an example of art used for writing.

**BUILDING TEACHING SKILLS: Video Exercise**

*Interview Student POV*

Go to the Building Teaching Skills section of Chapter 7 of MyEducationLab and view the video, "Interview Student POV," which is about how students in a classroom tackle prewriting skills. Complete the activities that follow, and save your work or transmit it to your professor as assigned.

## engaging in Visual Literacy

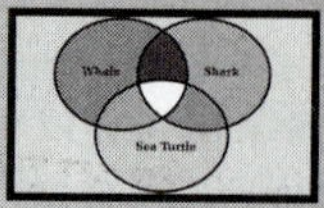

### Using Art to Support Writing Development

Mrs. Cho has her fourth-graders writing folk tales that include three events or occurrences, such as Jack going up the beanstalk three times in "Jack and the Beanstalk." To help her students visualize their folk tales, she has them make drawings that depict the beginning of the story, the three events, and the ending of the story. They do this by folding a blank piece of paper into fourths. Each quadrant of the paper is the frame for one event. The ending of the story is depicted on the reverse side of the paper. She encourages her students to refer to their pictures as they write to help them include details or other information depicted in their pictures. In this way, they transfer visual literacy onto their written literacy.

**Freewriting Strategies** Freewriting is the writing students do to help discover a topic or to focus on a topic before beginning an initial draft. Elbow (1983) considers freewriting a valuable tool for the writer because it gets the writer to just write. Even if the writer begins with "I can't think of anything to write about," it is still a beginning for the writing. As Elbow says, "The goal of freewriting is the thinking process, not the product" (p. 13).

■ ***Unfocused Freewriting*** The primary purpose for unfocused freewriting is to get students to open their minds so that thoughts and ideas can be written down in a nonstructured manner. Unfocused freewriting has students take several important steps in this topic-generating stage of the writing process.

1. Students write continuously for five, ten, or fifteen minutes. They should write freely with no concern for what is coming out of their heads and onto the paper. Students should think of this step as a search for a topic.
2. Students stop the freewriting and read over what they wrote.
3. Encourage students to identify the main idea or key point. Get them to write down that point or idea in a sentence or two.
4. Starting with this main idea, students freewrite for another five, ten, or fifteen minutes. They may stay on the main idea or begin to develop another one.
5. After this second freewriting, students stop again, identify the important idea, and freewrite once more.
6. This freewriting process should be repeated until students arrive at a topic on which they wish to write.

Once students have established a topic, they may choose to include any portions of their freewriting in their subsequent writing.

**■ *Focused Freewriting*** This type of freewriting is best suited for those students who have a writing topic in mind but need to narrow or broaden the scope of the topic. Focused freewriting can also be an opportunity for young writers to write down the important ideas or points that they wish to include in their actual writing. It is not important during these focused freewriting episodes for students to be concerned about the order or completeness of their ideas but to use this technique to get closer to and more specific about their writing topic.

There are many ways to do focused freewriting, and they are particularly helpful for elementary or middle school students. We present them in the form of questions that students can use to begin focused freewriting. The questions help students think about different ways to approach their writing topic.

- **What do you know?** Students write down as quickly as they can anything that comes to mind that relates to their writing topic and what they might wish to include in their writing.
- **How do you feel?** Students write down what they like or dislike about a position on a particular issue that they have chosen to write about. This question helps students express their views or opinions about a topic that may require further analysis or substantiation. This is particularly helpful for students who are writing about issues in social studies or science.
- **Can we talk?** Students create a running conversation between or among characters in the fiction they may be writing. These conversations can also be imagined ones between historical figures and themselves or between themselves and the writer.
- **Who's the reader?** Students direct their freewriting toward a real or imagined reader to help them determine what needs to be included or discarded from their actual writing. For example, if students are writing about the dangers of nuclear power plants and the reader is a nuclear physicist, the information and point of view for the writing will be different than if the reader is a fisherman whose livelihood is dependent upon the fish that live in the waters near a nuclear power plant.
- **What's the story?** Students write down incidents, experiences, or situations that they have known or know from others that relate to their writing topic. For example, if they are going to write about the significance of an upcoming political race for social studies, they can jot down discussions, conversations, even arguments they have heard that deal with the upcoming election. This question can also help students put more "real life" into their social studies writing.
- **Who's the writer?** This question can be used to encourage students to adopt the voice of someone other than themselves as the writer. For instance, rather than write about Martin Luther King Jr., a student might write from the perspective of a bus driver in Selma, Alabama, before, during, and after the bus boycott in the 1960s.

Other questions, of course, can be generated to help students focus on their own writing topics. By trying out different questions, students can discover how point of view or changes in audience influence their own writing. The Exploring Technology feature lists websites that support students during the writing process.

**Reading as Prewriting** As students learn about their written language, reading and writing reinforce each other (Dobson, 1989). Students can learn about the structure of fiction and nonfiction *writing* as a result of their fiction and nonfiction *reading* (Mason, Peterman, Powell, and Kerr, 1989). Students not only can use the structure of their reading for their writing but also can take the content of their writing from their reading.

exploring technology

## Websites to Support the Writing Process

**Picture Books for Teaching Literary Devices (http://iuswp.com/mentor-texts)**
The Indiana University Southeast Writing Project website offers a list of approximately 50 picture books that can be used to teach multiple crafting techniques for writing.

**Kid's Space (www.kids-space.org)**
Kids' Space provides opportunities for kids to communicate with other kids around the web through publication of pictures, stories, music, and webpages. Students can also collaborate to write a picture book, or they can find e-pals—the online versions of pen pals.

**Teaching Writing as a Process (www.learner.org/channel/workshops/readingk2/session5/index.html)**
The Annenberg Foundation provides several programs for teacher professional development. This video program examines how to teach writing as a process. Dr. Jeanne R. Paratore of Boston University begins her lecture by distinguishing between the different forms of writing and the various purposes for writing. She reviews the stages of the writing process and outlines the classroom practices that develop students' writing.

***Reading for Structure*** Stories, poetry, plays, and other forms of literature can be used with students as models for their own writing structures (Dahl and Freppon, 1995). For example, folk tales such as "Goldilocks and the Three Bears" or "The Old Woman and the Rice Thief" provide a repeating (predictable) action that can be imitated by students in their own writing. In "The Old Woman and the Rice Thief" (Bang, 1978, p. 19), the old woman is on her way to the Raja's palace because "Every night a thief [a rat] steals my rice." She meets five characters on her way to the Raja's castle who ask her the same question: "Old woman, where are you going?" She, in turn, repeats the complaint: "Every night a thief steals my rice, so I am on my way to tell the Raja." Each replies in turn: "On your way home take me with you and you will be glad that you did." This repetitive language and action pattern can be used as the basis for a pattern story. To generate this story, the folk tale was read to the students, the pattern was discussed, and students created their own story using a similar pattern.

Stories, folk tales, and fables can also be read and discussed with respect to the overall structure or organization of each form. For example, stories have a setting, characters, a beginning incident or episode that begins the story, the presence of a problem or conflict, events that lead to the elimination or resolution of the problem or conflict, and the story ending. By reading familiar stories and discussing these common elements, students can begin to realize the important elements that need to be included in their stories. For example, by looking at the structure of "Jack and the Beanstalk," students find that there are several settings, four major characters, one minor character, several problems, one ultimate solution, and an ending in which Jack and his mother live happily ever after. By discussing *Charlotte's Web*, which is a longer and more complex story than "Jack and the Beanstalk," students can still see that many of the same story elements are found in both stories. A graphic that can be used as a model for the discussion of story structure can be seen in Figure 7.6.

***Reading for Content*** Stories and poetry have long been known to evoke strong feelings and creative ideas in the students who read them. It is not difficult to get fifth-graders to talk about their fears and concerns in their own lives once they have read Shel Silverstein's poem "What If." It is a poem that mirrors students' concerns and can also generate other poems, stories, and even plays by students once discussion of the poem has begun. The same thing happens when fourth-graders discuss what it means to be a fourth-grader like Peter Hatcher in Judy Blume's *Tales of a Fourth-Grade Nothing*. Students go on to write about fifth-grade nothings or second-grade nothings or third-grade somethings or fourth-grade somethings. It is just as important to encourage students to write their

**Figure 7.6**

**Story Structure Discussion Questions**

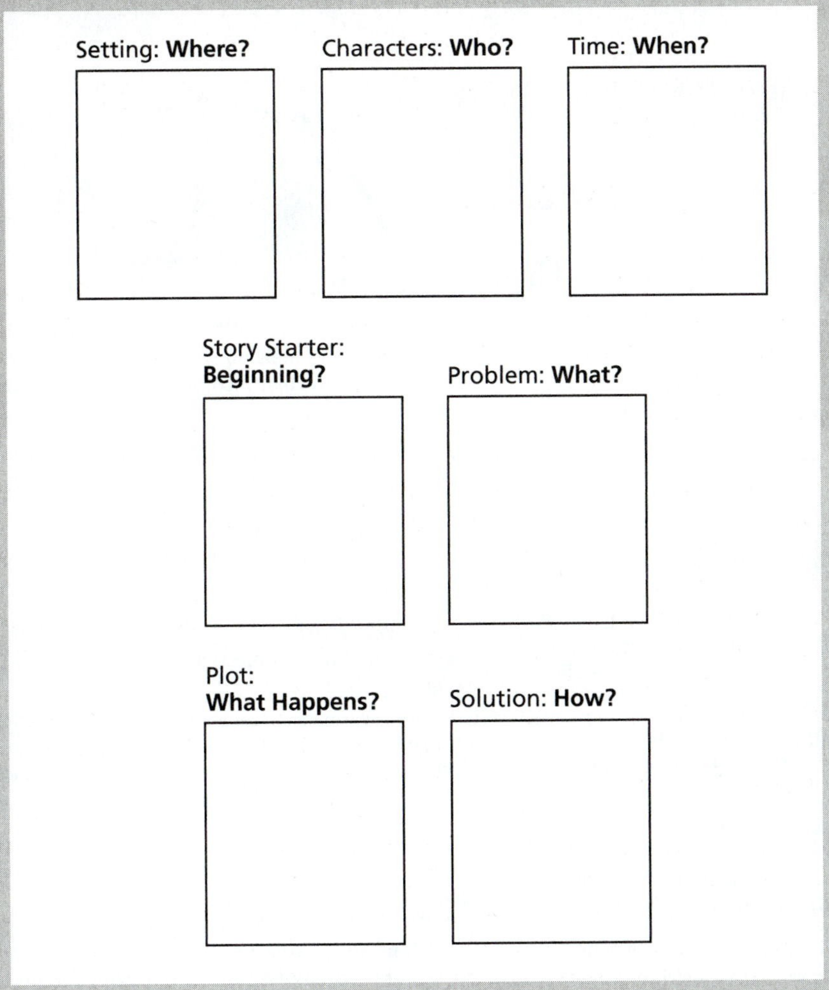

own stories that are triggered by their own reading as it is to get them to write about that reading. The first is poetic and just as valuable as the second, which is transactional.

One way of helping students make connections between their reading and their own lives is to ask questions that help them think about the connections. Questions might include the following:

1. Have you ever had an experience like the one this character had?
2. What was it about the character(s) that you liked? Disliked?
3. What would you change in this story if you had written it?
4. Did you think of anyone you know as you read this story? Who? Why?
5. What kind of a situation could you write about that would make you think of this story?

IRA/NCTE 12

These and other questions that encourage students to discuss the similarities between their lives and the lives of story characters can help generate other characters and episodes that they can use in their own stories. See the Exploring Children's Literature feature for additional ideas on texts that will mentor young writers.

## exploring Children's Literature

### Mentor Texts for Teaching the Craft of Writing

#### Grades K to 3

*A Kick in the Head*—Edited by Paul B. Janeczko, illustrated by Chris Raschka, and published by Candlewick (2005).

This collection presents examples of twenty-nine poetic forms to demonstrate the rules of poetry.

*Amber on the Mountain*—Written by Tony Johnston, illustrated by Robert Duncan, and published by Dial (1994).

Isolated on her mountain, Amber meets and befriends a girl from the city who gives her the determination to learn to read and write. Example of using rich description.

*Bat Loves the Night*—Written by Nicola Davies, illustrated by Sarah Fox-Davies, and published by Candlewick (2001).

Bat wakes up, flies into the night, uses the echoes of her voice to navigate, hunts for her supper, and returns to her roost to feed her baby. Example of narrowing the topic to one specific kind of bat.

*Chameleons Are Cool*—Written by Martin Jenkins, illustrated by Sue Shields, and published by Candlewick (1998).

This book describes different kinds of chameleons and examines their physical features, behavior, and ability to change color. Example of narrowing the topic.

*Hey, Little Ant*—Written by Phillip and Hanah Hoose, illustrated by Debbie Tilley, and published by Tricycle (1998).

This is a song in which an ant pleads with the kid who is tempted to squish it. Example of different points of view.

*Lilly's Purple Plastic Purse*—Written and illustrated by Kevin Henkes and published by Greenwillow (1996).

Lilly loves everything about school, especially her teacher, but when he asks her to wait a while before showing her new purse, she does something for which she is very sorry later. Example of a powerful beginning.

*Milo's Hat Trick*—Written and illustrated by Jon Agee and published by Hyperion (2001).

Milo the Magnificent needs a new trick or else he will never perform again. Maybe pulling a very clever bear out of a hat can save Milo and his act. Example of a satisfying ending.

*The Painter*—Written and illustrated by Peter Catalanotto and published by Orchard (1995).
Her father is busy working as an artist at home, but he still finds time to spend with his daughter. Example of show not tell.

*Shortcut*—Written and illustrated by Donald Crews and published by Greenwillow (1992).
Children taking a shortcut by walking along a railroad track find excitement and danger when a train approaches. Example of establishing a beginning, middle, and end.

## Grades 4 to 8

*Aunt Flossie's Hats (and Crab Cakes Later)*—Written by Elizabeth Howard, illustrated by James Ransome, and published by Houghton Mifflin (1991).
Sara and Susan share tea, cookies, crab cakes, and stories about hats when they visit their favorite relative, Aunt Flossie. Example of using rich description.

*Charlotte's Web*—Written by E. B. White, illustrated by Garth Williams, and published by Harper & Row (1952).
Wilbur, the pig, is devastated when he discovers that he is destined to be the farmer's Christmas dinner until his spider friend, Charlotte, decides to help him. Example of a powerful beginning.

*The Memory String*—Written by Eve Bunting, illustrated by Ted Rand, and published by Houghton Mifflin (2000).
While still grieving for her mother and unable to accept her stepmother, a girl clings to the memories represented by forty-three buttons on a string. Example of show not tell.

*Owl Moon*—Written by Jane Yolen, illustrated by John Schoenherr, and published by Philomel (1987).
On a winter's night under a full moon, a father and daughter trek into the woods to see the Great Horned Owl. Example of using the senses.

*Pictures of Hollis Woods*—Written by Patricia Reilly Giff and published by Wendy Lamb (2002).
When a troublesome twelve-year-old orphan stays with an elderly artist who needs her, she remembers the only other time she was happy in a foster home with a family that truly seemed to care about her. Example of developing a small moment in time.

*Read a Rhyme, Write a Rhyme*—Poems selected by Jack Prelutsky, illustrated by Meilo So, and published by Knopf (2005).
Segmented into ten subjects, this collection of "poemstarts" provides amusing beginnings to poems to challenge readers to complete the tale in their own special way.

*Voices in the Park*—Written and illustrated by Anthony Browne and published by DK (1998).
Lives briefly intertwine when two youngsters meet in the park. Example of different points of view.

**Graphic Organizers** Another successful prewriting strategy that can help students plan and organize their thoughts around a writing topic is the use of graphic organizers or schematics. These visual graphics can be used to help students discover a writing topic or help them structure information or ideas around the topic. Many of these writing techniques are used to help students prepare for content area reading (Richardson and Morgan, 2003), but they have also been found to be helpful for preparing students for writing assignments (Heimlich and Pittelman, 1986). For example, semantic webbing or mapping has been suggested as an aid in improving reading comprehension (McLaughlin and Allen, 2002) and can also be used to help students identify important information related to a nonfiction writing topic. Although a number of these visual schematic techniques exist under various names, the ones that follow are named according to their overall function or purpose for student writers.

**Video Homework Exercise**

*Prewriting in 6th Grade*

Go to the Homework and Exercises section of Chapter 7 of MyEducationLab and view the video, "Prewriting in 6th Grade," which demonstrates how a sixth-grade teacher implements graphic organizers as a prewriting activity for biography writing. Complete the activities that follow, and save your work or transmit it to your professor as assigned.

■ ***Topic Cluster*** This graphic presentation is designed to get students to think about a topic by encouraging students to think of as many ideas as they can that might be related to the topic. Topic clusters are more similar to loosely focused brainstorms. Emphasis is on generating ideas rather than organizing them around a topic. The topic can be determined by the teacher, students, or by teacher and students together. The key to the cluster lies in the free-flowing discussion that occurs as the brainstorming occurs. Students are encouraged to bring out whatever ideas they can think of that they feel are connected to the topic. No idea is rejected nor is any effort made to organize the ideas during the initial brainstorm for the cluster. To help students generate a topic cluster, follow these steps:

1. Identify the topic in a word or phrase and write it down on a chalkboard, chart paper, or transparency.
2. As students begin to discuss the topic, the teacher jots down a word or phrase that represents each idea presented.
3. As students respond, locate the students' ideas according to their proximity to the cluster. For example, if a student is sitting on the right side of the room, his or her idea(s) would appear on the right side of the cluster. This helps to stimulate students around the room to volunteer ideas for the cluster.
4. Accept all ideas during the creation of the cluster so that students will not hesitate to present ideas that come from them spontaneously.
5. Encourage student participation.
6. The number of ideas generated is more important than the correctness or completeness of the ideas.

An example of a topic cluster can be seen in Figure 7.7. The cluster topic is frogs, and the ideas presented by third-graders represent the information they believed was

**Figure 7.7**

## Topic Cluster on Frogs

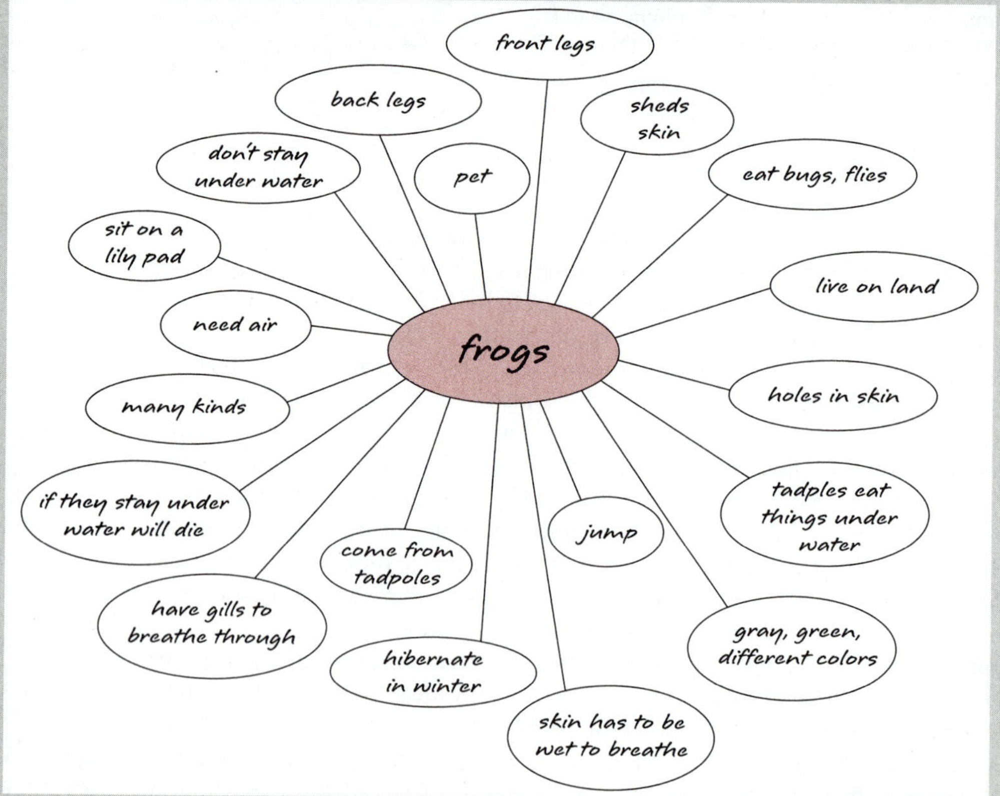

important to connect to the topic. Students used this particular cluster as they prepared to read and write about a frog. Often, subsequent reading or discussion by students can lead to additions, modifications, or deletions to the cluster.

***Semantic Maps*** Maps, by their definition, are more structured and organized than clusters. They act as blueprints or designs that not only help students identify important information related to a writing topic but also represent an organizational scheme for the information. The teacher, students, or both can decide what and where information should be located on the map according to the structure of the map. This grouping of ideas around the map can form the bases for paragraphs or stanzas or any other organizational writing pattern that might be used in writing on the topic. The teacher or students can map the main ideas, and the students can supply the important details for the ideas that appear on the map. An example of a teacher-designed map can be seen in Figure 7.8. The teacher identified the four important features related to snakes that students would be reading and writing about with this simple semantic map. After much discussion, reading, and continued mapping, the students ended up with the elaborate map seen in Figure 7.8.

***Story Maps*** These maps are designed to help students generate ideas for stories that they might write and also to draw their attention to important elements found in most stories. These elements include setting and time, character(s), beginning event, conflict or problem, plot, and resolution of the problem or conflict. These elements are found in the simplest folk tale or most complex novel. They are also in most stories that students hear from parents, other relatives, teachers, and other students. Although some research indicates that knowledge of these story features is helpful in writing stories (Fitzgerald and Teasley, 1986), other studies have shown that knowledge of these features alone does not lead to successful story writing (Dreher and Singer, 1980). In fact, students often use basic story elements in their own stories even when they are unable to identify these elements themselves (Galda, 1984). The use of story structures or maps, however, does seem to help students when creating their own stories (Fitzgerald and Spiegel, 1983).

Students can use a variety of story maps to help them think about and prepare for story writing. When using story maps with students, especially students in the primary grades, it is important to model the maps with familiar stories. This modeling makes it easier for students to understand the story elements that you want them to use in their own story. To help illustrate this point, different story maps are presented in Figure 7.9 using "Jack and the Beanstalk."

***Cubing*** This particular prewriting graphic organizer encourages students to explore writing topics from a number of perspectives (Neeld and Kiefer, 1990). The term *cubing* refers to the fact that students think of a topic as being a cube, which has six sides. Each side of the topic cube represents one perspective on the topic or one way of exploring the topic. To cube a topic, students carry out six steps: describe it, compare it, associate it, analyze it, apply it, and argue for or against it. These steps are somewhat similar to Bloom's six levels of comprehension. Each step in this thinking process can be considered one side of a cube; hence, all sides of the topic are accounted for in the cube. With younger students, actual cubes can be constructed with each step located on one side of the cube. The sides of this type of cube used with a class of second-graders can be seen in Figure 7.10 on page 238. The cube was filled in based on the topic "my favorite animal."

IRA/NCTE 5

## Figure 7.8 Semantic Map on Snakes

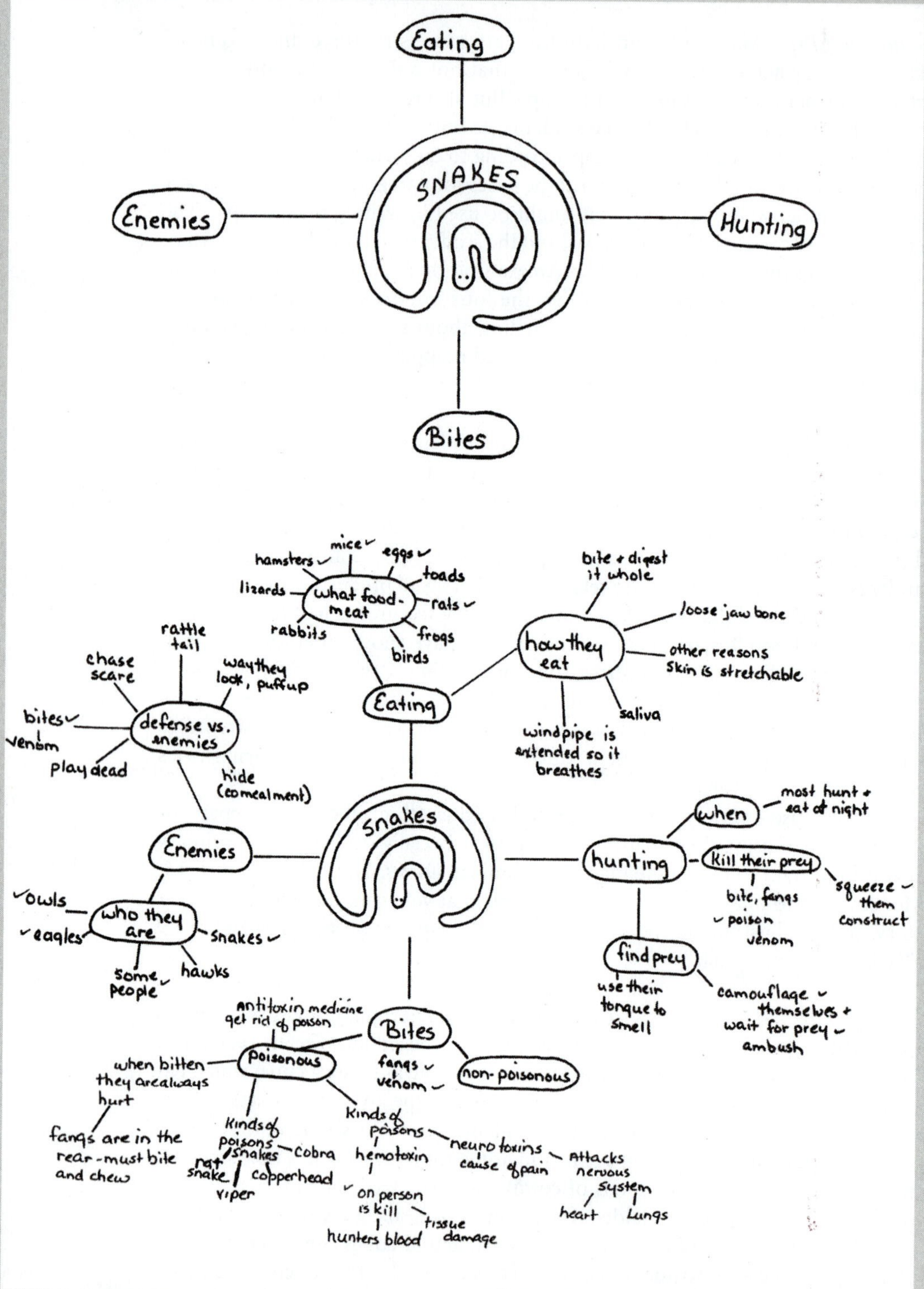

**Figure 7.9** Two Different Story Maps on Jack and the Beanstalk

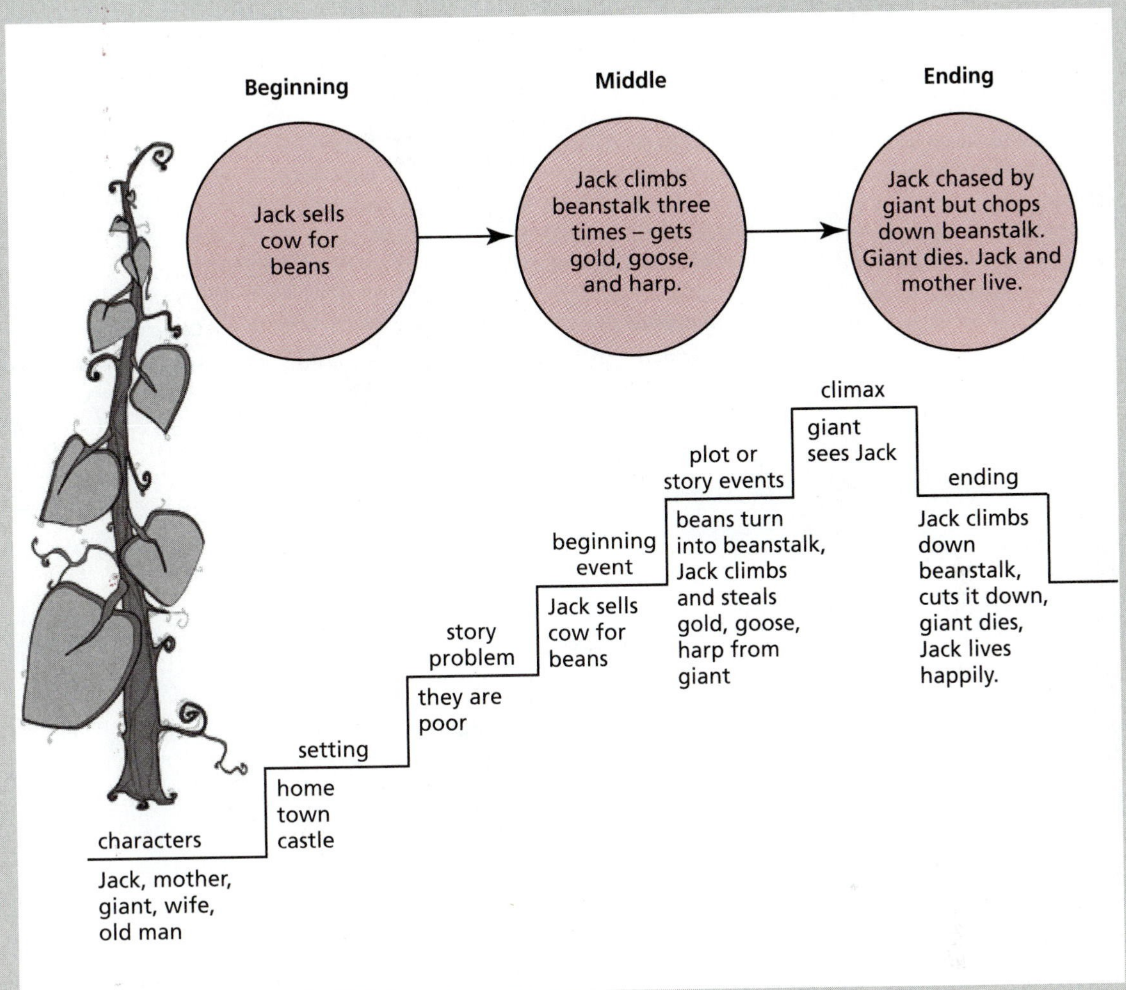


**Journals and Learning Logs** "Let me tell you what I think" might be an appropriate title for journals and learning logs because this is the primary purpose for this prewriting strategy (Fulwiler, 1987). Journals can be used for a variety of reasons and can take different forms, but their greatest value is in getting students to put their first thoughts about their world and themselves into the journal. To keep a journal is to keep a regular record or accounting of thoughts and observations. For journals to be successful as prewriting sources for subsequent writing topics, students need to see the value in this regular and ongoing prewriting activity.

How can students find value in the time they spend writing in their journals? Journals allow them to discuss their feelings and personal observations without fear of others seeing the entries. Students should be allowed to decide what entries can be made public and which ones are to remain private. To help students understand the importance of this journal requirement, discuss with students the book *Harriet the Spy*

**Figure 7.10** My Favorite Animal Cube

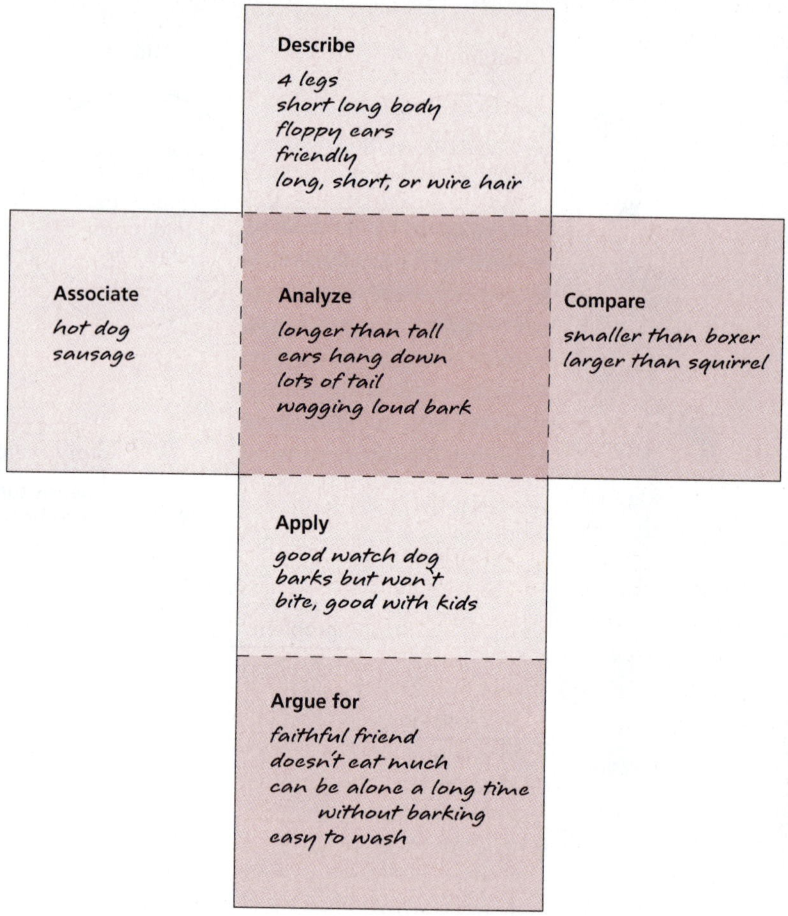


by Louise Fitzhugh. Questions, concerns, and observations about classroom learning can also be recorded by students in their journals. Teacher response to the journals is very important because the responses set up a dialogue between student and teacher. This periodic feedback will stimulate students to continue making entries in their journals. These frequent entries, whether personal or informational in nature, will yield a variety of potential writing topics and prewritings for students to use in the future. With guidance from a teacher, for example, students might take a personal experience from their journal and use it to form the basis of a fictional story.

Describe
4 legs
short long body
floppy ears
friendly
long, short, or wire hair
Associate
hot dog
sausage
Analyze
longer than tall
ears hang down
lots of tail
wagging loud bark
Compare
smaller than boxer
larger than squirrel
Apply
good watch dog
barks but won't
bite, good with kids
Argue for
faithful friend
doesn't eat much
can be alone a long time
without barking
easy to wash

Learning logs serve some of the same functions as journals but are generally more subject-oriented. Students can use them to respond to questions raised by their teacher about a science demonstration or a social studies reading assignment. Students can also use logs to explain what they learned in class, what they did not understand in class, what they liked, or what they disliked in class. By raising questions in their learning logs, students do not have to face the potentially embarrassing situation of asking the "dumb" question in class. The logs are less public and more apt to contain more realistic indications of what students do not understand in their class. Teachers should respond to these learning logs frequently to determine whether students are learning what is being taught and to assist those who are having difficulty. As students write frequently about what they are learning in class, they may discover an interest in a subject that can lead to a writing topic. For example, students who have been raising questions in their logs about acid rain and deforestation in their state might take one of those questions and use it for a writing topic in science.

The list of prewriting strategies presented here is not a complete one. Many variations of every approach are mentioned, and an effort was made to include many different ones that have been used by teachers in their classrooms. Certain prewriting techniques will be discussed more fully in subsequent chapters because they are particularly suited for specific kinds of writing. Let's assume, however, that students in any elementary school classroom have used some prewriting strategy to identify and focus in on a writing topic. The talking, the reading, the mapping, the planning, the organizing, the interviewing, even the "percolating" (Mayher et al., 1983) has to give way to the actual writing. Now is the time for writing.

## Step 2: Writing

To help students begin their writing, there are guidelines to follow that can make this a more fruitful and enjoyable time for both teacher and students. This is the time when students seem to hold their breath, need to go to the bathroom, require pencils to be sharpened, stare out the window, twitch and squirm, pull or twist their hair, exhibit an inability to sit directly in a chair, crumple paper, and even come up to the teacher for help. Teachers need to be aware that every writer, whether student or professional, child or adult, exhibits these and many other equally interesting anxiety-related behaviors as they begin to write. Hopefully, some of the prewriting will reduce some of the behaviors, but others will remain. The guidelines that follow are designed to help teachers help their students get started on their writing.

**Let Them Incubate** It may be difficult, but you should let the writing begin without you. Students need to try to begin on their own without an adult hovering over them. Students who do not need help can be distracted or may start to believe that perhaps they do have a problem with their writing. Less able students who may need the teacher's help will learn to rely on it too frequently if it is available before it is asked for. Keep in mind that students should already have some indication of what they are going write about because of some preceding prewriting activity with their writing topic. Let them try to get off the writing runway by themselves, but do not let them go entirely solo when they need you, which brings us to the next guideline.

**Circulate and Comment to Stimulate** After about ten minutes or so, walk around the room looking for signs of stalled or winded writers. Remember, young writers often write in a rush during those first ten or fifteen minutes and begin to run out of gas, steam, or ideas about this time. Offer an encouraging smile, nod of the head, or pat on the shoulder to spur on the students. With stalled students, look quickly at the writing and offer a comment or question related to the topic that can help them get back on track. Some comments might include:

- Where are you trying to go?
- What might be some other reasons?
- Look back at your last idea.
- Take another look at your picture.

- You might begin with this instead of that.
- What might be another example?
- How do you want your reader to feel?
- Do not worry about the spelling.

These are only a few of many other comments that could be made to a student during the writing of an early draft. The nature of the student, the purpose and audience for the writing, and the student's success with writing dictate what comments might be made and to whom. The more writing the student can do at this stage without interruption the greater the chance for him or her to develop writing fluency or ease in writing drafts.

**Spell or Tell** When students ask about spelling during their early drafts, get them to spell the word in a way that will help them remember it after the draft is complete. If you tell them the word, you will reinforce in them the idea that writing halts when you come to a new word. The spelling of words in the early drafts needs only be sufficient so that the writer can read back what was written. Constant stopping for spelling only interrupts the flow of ideas from their brains to their paper.

**Group or Individual Dictations** For students in kindergarten and first grade (where the physical demands of writing are greatest), it is perfectly acceptable to take group or individual dictations instead of the actual writing. The same care should be taken in discussing writing topics that lead to dictations as those other children write about. This includes opportunities to generate ideas, organize them, and prepare responses for the dictations.

## Step 3: Revising

IRA/NCTE 6

The need to reexamine or reevaluate initial drafts in terms of the purpose, content, and form of the writing leads to what Sommers (1980) calls the heart of the writing process: revising. Revising is the most important step in writing according to Murray (2004) because it helps writers look at their drafts not as writers but as readers.

This is one of the most difficult steps for young writers to take because it asks them to drop one perspective (the writer's) and pick up an entirely different one (the reader's). As was pointed out earlier in this chapter, there are cognitive and language reasons why this is difficult for young writers. Revising requires rethinking, refining, reorganizing, and rewriting of early drafts until students are confident that their writing means what they have intended it to mean for their intended readers. Revision focuses on content and the organization of that content as well as the words used by the writer with an eye on the purpose and audience for the writing.

Revising brings up a recurring principle in the writing process. Students may look back at their drafts to see whether they used the "right words" or whether they have explained something fully or whether their poem is an extended metaphor. They can also look back at their prewriting plan or notes and revise them according to what they wish their writing to accomplish. Revising does not necessarily fit into a neat linear step but can occur at any step in the writing process (even during the early discussion of a possible writing topic). Revising as a recurring principle in the writing process can also occur in a forward direction or take the form of "projective structuring" as Perl (1979) describes forward revising. Forward revising occurs when students think about the intended audience for their writing and make revisions based on that thinking. For example, when sixth-graders who are writing a fable for second-graders check to see that the words in their fable can be read by second-graders, they are engaged in forward revision. When third-graders write a class letter to their principal requesting more time in the school's computer center and revise their request by changing the word "demand" to "respectfully request," they are revising in a forward direction. Whenever students revise their writing as a result of thinking of the impact or consequences of their writing on someone outside the writing, they are participating in forward revising.

So what is revising? It is young writers going backward and forward to see whether what they had in mind to write has appeared on the paper. Revision is the link in the writing process between the intentions (purpose and audience) of the writer and the outcomes of their writing efforts (content and audience response). It is the most difficult step in the writing process because it requires students to change from writers to readers and to decide what will remain and what will change in their writing. The euphoria of creation that rises during drafting must be dismissed during revision to rise again, hopefully, with the publication of an even better writing piece. See the Engaging in Oral Language feature for a partnered reading activity that supports student revising.

The following guidelines can help students understand what revising is and how to best use it to improve their writing.

### Revision Guidelines for the Classroom

- All writing does not need to be revised. It may be reviewed, discussed, and even evaluated but it need not be revised.

## engaging in Oral language

### Partnered Reading to Support Writing

Students need to recognize the differences between spoken and written language if they are to progress as writers. Words or phrases can be omitted when someone tells a story, or incomplete sentences may occur as a natural part of telling a story. When writing a story, these very words, phrases, or complete sentences are needed so the reader can better follow and understand the story. Story*tellers* can use props, gestures, and voice to convey setting, character, or events in a story, while story *writers* have to use words and punctuation to convey the same things. One way to help students with this is to group them in pairs. Have one student read a story while the other student reads it out loud. Students note whether words are added or omitted from the oral reading of the story. This helps student writers see when they need to make changes in their writing so that their writing will be more complete and better understood by the student as reader. This is particularly helpful for students in the primary grades whose thoughts often get ahead of their writing or whose writing sounds more like talking written down.

- Revision should focus on the quality and organization of ideas in the writing, not on surface errors such as spelling and punctuation.
- Revision responses to student writing by teachers and students should encourage students to write again.
- When appropriate, revising efforts by students should consider audience and purpose in their writing.
- Students are better able to revise their writing in assignments when the expected content is clearly stated as well as how the writing is to be developed.
- Let students know whether writing is to be evaluated and what criteria will be used. Preferably do this before they begin an assignment.
- Recognize that all students in the same grade do not necessarily write on the same level nor are they capable of the same level of revision in their writing.
- Adjust writing and revising expectations of your students according to their level of writing maturity.
- Avoid giving overly general comments such as "That's nice"; or if you do, then follow them up with a related but more specific comment such as "This paragraph reminds me of how cold winter can be in Michigan."
- Revising skills are recursive. Students go backward and forward in their ability to use these skills just as they do in learning any complex, difficult, cognitive strategy.

**Revising Techniques and Strategies** Keeping these revising guidelines in mind, we now turn to revising techniques and strategies that can be used with students in the classroom. Some of these revising activities are helpful in focusing on specific revision skills while others are useful in getting students to revise their own writing or to work with other students in solving one another's revising needs. Any of these revision activities can be used at any point in the development of a writing assignment. Keep in mind that the closer the revising goals in a writing assignment are to the purpose, audience, and content of the assignment, the more useful the revising efforts will be.

■ ***Author Conferences*** These informal conferences focus on the students as authors and address needs or concerns students have about a writing assignment in progress, the writing process in general, or how they are developing as writers. The conferences can take place between the student and the teacher or the student and other students, and they can occur during any stage of a writing assignment (Graves, 1994, Calkins, 1994). The key to the success of author conferences is that the student receives feedback that encourages the author to want to write again. Figure 7.11 is a list of comments and questions that you can use during an author conference to support revision at different steps in the writing process.

■ ***Writing Groups*** Once students realize that they can help one another become better writers, they should be encouraged to work in groups. These writers' groups (or writing groups) can be extremely helpful in shifting the responsibility of revising from the teacher to the students themselves. When used effectively, writing groups can provide a supportive audience for student writers with revising needs regardless of when those needs arise. Suggestions can be made in helping students narrow or define a writing topic. They can also be made in a writing group to help students manage new writing forms or organize a response to a writing assignment. Writing groups help students get "unstuck" during their writing. Important feedback is available to students from their writing groups to help them revise their writing. Working cooperatively

Figure 7.11

## Questions to Use in an Author Conference

**Prewriting/planning questions and comments**

What is your topic?

What do you need to find out?

How do you think you'll start?

Do you need a plan for your writing?

Who will you write this for and how will you write it?

Can I help you as you begin to work on this topic?

Do you think you'll need all of this material?

What have you learned about planning for an assignment like this?

**Writing/drafting questions and comments**

How are you coming?

You have really got a lot of stuff here!

Are you sticking to your topic?

I noticed that you stopped writing. Need any help?

Why not check your plan to see if that can help?

Sometimes I forget what I'm writing. Why not go back to the beginning of this draft to help remind you where you were trying to go in your writing?

What have you learned about writing this piece?

**Revising questions and comments**

Have you found places that need to be changed?

What about the purpose for the writing?

What might be another way to write this?

Do you need to take anything out of your writing?

Do you have enough details for your audience?

Why not share this with your writing group?

What did you learn from revising this piece?

**Editing/proofreading questions and comments**

What proofreading problems do you have?

Did you find any punctuation/capitalization errors?

What words were hard for you to spell?

Read the word as you wrote it to check its spelling.

Read what you wrote out loud to check for missing words.



within a writing group, students create a shared responsibility for each member's writing efforts. To ensure that each member of a writing group gets the benefits of being in the group, each member of a writing group should:

- *Listen* carefully to the writing when it is read.
- *Think* about what the writing says to you about the topic, the ideas expressed, and the purpose of the author.
- *React* to specific features in the writing—content, organization, vocabulary, images, etc.
- *Remember* what makes you uneasy about writing.
- *Respond* in ways that will encourage the writer to write again.

***Writing Group Responses*** To help reinforce the role of reader/responder in a writing group, we offer an adaptation of Rosenblatt's responses to literature. When students think of others' writing as though it were literature, it raises the student writer to the level of author. Responses to writing include personal, analytic, and creative. They offer a natural sequence or structure for a writing group to talk about a member's writing.

***Personal Response*** After a student has read a writing piece to a writing group, members of the group should be encouraged to respond to the piece on a personal level. They can begin to do this by trying to answer these questions or ones similar to these:

- How does the writing make you feel? ("I felt really sad when I got to the part in your story about the day you came home and found your cat by the side of the road.")
- What does it remind you of in your life? ("Your 'used to be/but now' poem reminds me of how hard it was to learn how to ride a bicycle.")
- What do you especially like about this piece? ("My favorite part of your story is when the farmer's friends bring their tractors over to help him get in his hay before the rain came.")
- Why did you like it? ("Because it shows that when people are in trouble, there are others who can help them if asked.")
- Would I have reacted like one of the characters? ("I think I would have reacted the same way Henry did when he missed the bus.")
- What is the purpose or theme of this writing? ("This poem seems to be about how easy you forget how hard it was to learn how to ride a two-wheel bike.")

These questions with example responses and other similar questions and comments show that students' writing can have a personal impact on readers just like writing by professional authors. They also point out that when a writer makes a personal commitment to a piece of writing, there are readers who will give it the same kind of personal commitment.

***Analytic Response*** Once writing groups have shared their personal reaction to a student's writing, the next kind of response should be based on a close analysis of various elements in the writing. These analytic responses can include comments or questions that can help a writer improve the writing. The writing elements that are analyzed may include the purpose or intention of the author, the content, the organization of the content, paragraphs, sentences, words, even grammar, usage, and mechanics. These elements can be discussed using questions similar to the questions below. These analytic questions will vary according to the nature of the writing assignment, the writing level of the students, and the needs of the student whose writing is shared with the group. How teachers model the use of these or similar analytic questions will help determine how writing groups will use them with their writers. When the teacher participates as a writing group presenter and a responder, the students in the group can see how best to treat one another. Here is a list of analytic questions:

- Why did you decide to write this?
- Does this come through in the writing?
- Is there any part that does not make sense?
- Is the writing in a logical order?
- Does anything need to be added?
- Are there any sentences that do not belong?
- Are there better words that could be used?
- Has the writer given enough facts?

- Are there too many facts?
- Are sentences complete?
- Can sentences be combined?
- Do you have trouble with any part of your writing?
- Would it help if I read the part out loud?
- What about the beginning? What about the ending?
- Is there a beginning, middle, and end?
- Are there spelling or mechanics problems?

***Creative Response*** Analytic comments or questions that point out areas of a student's writing that might be changed should be followed by creative responses or suggestions that can help the student make those changes. These suggestions can come at any phase of a writing assignment. For example, if a student needs help in finding information about a particular science topic, the writing group can recommend sources for that information. Recommendations about the organization of the writing can be given at the prewriting or planning stage of an assignment or after an early draft of the assignment. Strategies for changing an introduction or tightening up a paragraph or changing words in a poem are creative responses. They are creative because they can actually be used in the writing by the student. They are helpful because they may provide writing strategies to a student who may not have come up with them alone. Sometimes, however, a writing group may see the need for changes in a student's writing and not be able to think of ways to change it. These occasions reinforce the need for teachers to be able to guide writing groups as the need arises. Here are examples of creative responses that might be given by writing groups:

- It might help to tell why you feel this way.
- Why not begin the introduction with this sentence?
- Did you think of looking this up in . . . ?
- This needs an introduction. What about . . . ?
- What about some other things you like to do?
- Why not tell us where this came from?
- What if you described it like . . . ?
- How about this for an ending . . . ?
- What if you added this sentence . . . ?
- Take these out. They don't belong.
- I think this part in the story should go first.
- "Said" is used so much. Try these words instead.
- What if you didn't rhyme the lines?
- Maybe the title could be . . . or . . . .
- If you are writing to . . . maybe you should say . . . .
- You decide. You're the author.

## Step 4: Editing

Editing is the final step in the writing process that comes after revising and before publishing. If revising addressed purpose, content, and audience, then editing finishes up with punctuation, correctness, and appearance. To help students edit their writing for these kinds of errors, get them to read their writing exactly as it appears on the page—with younger students, this usually means that they actually read their writing out loud. Otherwise, they will read what is in their minds rather than what is in their writing. Younger students are also more apt to find editing needs in the writing of other students because they will read the writing as it is actually written. While correctness is not as important as the quality or development of ideas in a paper, it is necessary to learn the writing conventions that make writing easier for readers to read. We devote an entire chapter to teaching these conventions (grammar, usage, mechanics, and punctuation), but we offer a few general comments about editing here.

Proofreading is at the heart of editing and focuses on writing format, such as business letter format, as well as paragraph indention, punctuation, capitalization, grammar and usage errors, spelling, and writing legibility (handwriting). Students should try to avoid attending to these kinds of errors while revising their writing unless the errors are so widespread as to make the writing difficult to read.

The same strategies used for revising are just as effective for helping students learn to edit their own writing. Conferences with students can focus on specific editing problems. Encourage writing groups to attend to editing needs of their members. Keep in mind, as with revising needs, students cannot identify all editing needs in their own writing. This is especially true with students in the primary grades. Develop realistic editing goals based on the local school division language arts curriculum or the state's language arts objectives. Often, these are minimum objectives but they at least give you a starting point with your students.

In helping students use newly learned editing skills, develop editing charts that highlight the editing skills your students are working on (see Figure 7.12). Encourage students to refer to the charts as they prepare to proofread their writing. Model the use of these editing skills with pieces of your own writing to show students that every writer makes editing errors. Try to instill in students that writing correctly is like cleaning up after a party or using manners when out in a restaurant. We do it so that others can more easily read our writing.

Writing needs to be more than just the process. It needs to be viewed as an opportunity to entertain, inform, or move to action those who read the writing. Poetry, stories, plays, editorials, reports, letters, journal entries, short stories, and even novels are the products of writing to be shared with an audience.

## Step 5: Publishing

The final phase in the process of writing is one of the most important reasons for writing. It is why writers toil; it is why students listen patiently to comments about their drafts; it is why they revise; and it is why students find the reason for careful handwriting. It is the big test, opening night, the final match for the championship, and the envelope that holds the name of the Academy Award winner. Webster defines *publishing* as making known, announcing, or proclaiming. It is a permanent record standing on its own in public for the first time. For writers—student and professional alike—publishing

**Figure 7.12**

## Editing Chart

Did I write complete sentences?

Did I indent my paragraphs?

Do my verbs agree with my nouns?

Do I use the correct verb tense?

Do I use correct punctuation?

Do I use correct capitalization?

Do I use correct spelling?

is very public but also very personal. Writing brings the exhilarating feeling of accomplishment and pride, but it also brings the anxiety of the expectant father. What will the public say? Will it understand? Will it appreciate? Will it be moved to laugh? Will it be moved to act? Young authors and their written works are tied inexorably to their readers once the writing goes public. Teachers need to celebrate this union by providing the best avenues for student publication.

One of the best ways for students to publish or share their writing is to read their finished writing out loud to their classmates. Young writers can use an Author's Chair (Graves and Hansen, 1983) to add to the read-aloud sessions. By bringing in a comfortable chair and designating it for authors only, you signal to students the importance of sharing their writing with others. Placing the chair in a special location in the room also emphasizes the value of writing and its publication. Although other furniture and equipment may have to be moved from time to time in the classroom, the Author's Chair in the Author's Place remains in a permanent, and important, location in the room. It is a visible reminder that students' writing and what they have to say is a central part of the classroom.

Another approach to publishing that also stimulates discussion about student writing is the young authors' conference. The young authors' conference is the culminating experience for students who have poetry, plays, stories, or nonfiction writing that they wish to share with other student writers. Because publishing at a young authors' conference is the final step in the writing process, all the preceding writing activity leading up to the conference occurs in classrooms. The planning and discussing of writing forms and topics, drafting and revising, as well as input from other students lead to a finished product. The published writing, however, is not the only thing shared at a young authors' conference. Students engage one another in discussion about how they get ideas, what helps or hinders them as they write, and what future writing projects they are considering. The student writers, in short, act like professional writers at these conferences.

Young authors' conferences can occur in individual classrooms, across grades in a school, across schools in one school division, or across school divisions. Often, an author of children's books will make a presentation at the conference and talk to the students about how a professional writer goes about coming up with writing ideas that lead to books that children read. Occasionally, time at the conference may be devoted to techniques for illustrating student writing. Young writers at these conferences participate in writing experiences that can help them refine or further develop their writing abilities. At most young authors' conferences, participants receive a certificate that recognizes their efforts as real writers. An important goal of these special writers' conferences is to make young writers feel special and to honor their writing efforts.

## How Can You Help Students Become Writers?

There are many ways you can nurture writing abilities in your students. The environment, with the Author's Chair, sets the tone for the importance of writing. Then, your ongoing responsibility will be to present good lessons and scaffolding that help students know what is important and how they can improve in their composing. It is also important that you keep listening to your students and keep assessing their works in progress. The Exploring Diversity feature includes a resource to use in helping writers who are struggling.

### Classroom Environment

A comfortable and trusting environment created by teachers is essential for successful writing development. This includes encouragement to take risks in writing and for teachers and peers to provide helpful feedback. During their school years, students need to write for a variety of purposes, use a variety of writing forms, and focus on a variety of audiences. Greater writing confidence and fluency should be the hallmarks

exploring diversity

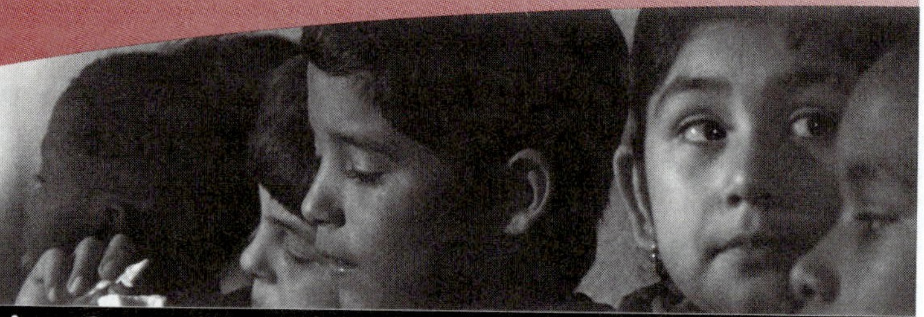

**Supporting Struggling Writers**

Classroom teachers can use several writing instruction strategies to help students with special needs and students who are English language learners. The language experience approach (LEA) is excellent for helping all student writers make the transition from spoken to written language. When students have the opportunity to talk about things in their own lives and then see the actual words they used written down by the teacher, their stories become the basis for their own reading and writing. Student-selected writing topics help students write about their own lives and can be shared with other students. Writing groups offer support to students by promoting discussion and providing other writing models for them. Scaffolding strategies such as graphic organizers, pattern writing, and dialogue journals help writers who are in ELL populations with vocabulary and grammar support. More discussion about all four of these instructional strategies can be found in *Reading, Writing, and Learning in ESL,* fifth edition (Peregoy and Boyle, 2008).

for writing experiences in the elementary grades. The value of content in student writing should precede the need for correctness in grammar, punctuation, and spelling. Young students need to believe early in their school experience that they have things to write about and things to share with others through their writing.

Writing needs to be viewed as more than just a process. It needs to be viewed as an opportunity to entertain, inform, or move to action those who read the writing. Poetry, stories, plays, editorials, reports, letters, journal entries, short stories, and even novels are the products of writing to be shared with an audience. The writing process is just an empty assembly line without the thoughts and ideas of the young writer that need to take shape early in the process. What students write about should also excite them, interest them, and make them want to go down the writer's road toward publishing their final drafts.

## Standards-Based Writing Assignments

Good, standards-based writing assignments are an important element in a classroom that supports student writers. Langer and Applebee (1987) and Mayher et al. (1983) provide some guidelines for good writing assignments.

**Video Homework Exercise**

*Interview Presentation*

Go to the Homework and Exercises section in Chapter 7 of MyEducationLab and view the video, "Interview Presentation," which gives a comprehensive view of how one teacher encourages her students to write and share research reports. Complete the activities that follow, and save your work or transmit it to your professor as assigned.

**Writing Assignment Principles** We have adapted some of the guidelines from the research and added others in developing this set of principles for good writing assignments:

1. Writing assignments make students want to write because the students care about the assignments.
2. Writing assignments challenge students to acquire and provide information during the course of completing the assignment.
3. Students use the most appropriate writing form to convey their message to their readers.
4. Writing assignments consider the experiential background and writing skills of students.
5. Writing assignments follow the general framework of the writing process(es).
6. Writing assignments help students learn something, solve a problem, or develop new insights about what they write about.
7. Writing assignments need to involve readers at various points to provide valuable feedback and reaction to what is being written.
8. Writing assignments should also make very clear to young writers the criteria used when their writing assignment is to be evaluated.
9. To help your students prepare for a state-mandated, standards-based writing assessment, incorporate those standards into appropriate writing assignments.

## Writing Assignment Answers to Writer Questions

IRA/NCTE 12

Another way to consider writing assignments is to see how students can answer writer questions. We present the writer questions along with answers that a good writing assignment can provide.

**Question 1: What Do I Write About?** A good writing assignment should help students answer this question by identifying a topic or topics for the writing assignment. Sometimes, as Williams (1989) suggests, teachers have to make clear to students what they are to write about. This helps in identifying those writers who have mastered a particular writing form and those who are still developing the form. Other times, specific topics may be given to students to see whether they have learned and understood the content that is presented in other subject matter, especially in social studies or science. It is also appropriate for writing topics to be chosen by students themselves to strengthen their writers' commitment to the writing and sense of ownership (Graves, 1983). We suggest that opportunities for both kinds of writing topics be available to all students.

**Question 2: Why Am I Doing This Writing Assignment?** Students want an answer to this question as often as they want an answer to the first question. It is an appropriate question for students because it gets to the heart of any writing: its purpose. There are two different categories of writing purpose that must be united to produce writing assignments that have "beyond the classroom" meaning and reality. One set of purposes focuses on the modes or kinds of writing and the other on the forms of writing that can be used by a writer. Writing modes refer to the intentions of writers or what they expect to accomplish through their writing. To persuade a reader to support the writer's point of view is one kind of intention. Another kind of intention might be to explain or describe a concept such as gravity to assure the reader that the writer really understands the concept. A writer who intends to move a reader through imagery in a poem exhibits still a third different mode or intention for his or her writing. Recall Britton et al. (1975), who categorized these and other writing modes as the expressive, transactional, and poetic functions of writing.

Another way to think about writing modes or intentions is to return to the Joan Tough's language functions (1982) discussed in Chapter 2. If language functions were replaced with writing functions, they would look like this:

1. Self-maintaining—Used to satisfy a need or get something for the writer through journals, letters, and persuasive writing
2. Directing—Writing that presents steps in following directions or completing tasks such as recipes or science notebooks
3. Reporting—Writing done to report, describe, compare, or contrast information using informational writing
4. Reasoning—Writing that uses cause-effect relationships, draws conclusions, and offers reasoned solutions to challenges or problems, often in the form of informational writing
5. Predicting—Writing that makes predictions about future events or actions based on prior knowledge of associated events or actions in the past
6. Projecting—Writing that projects the writer's feelings onto people or events as a way of identifying with the people or the topic being written about
7. Imagining—The poetry, plays, and stories that draw upon the imagination of the writer

**Question 3: Who Am I Writing This For?** Students need to learn to adjust their content and purpose for writing by taking into account the nature of their readers. Take the letter written to persuade someone to give you something. When a child responds in a letter to a favorite grandfather who has asked the child what he wants for her birthday, that letter in tone and language will be very different from the letter that a student writes to a teacher in hopes of getting a grade changed. The purpose or function of the letters may be identical, but the difference in audience will influence how the writer uses that function. If students have an audience for writing but no real purpose for the writing, how will they know how to address their writing topic? If they have a real purpose but no identifiable audience, how will they know what language to use or what content to include in their writing? Audience and purpose, though not synonymous, are certainly dependent on each other, and both should be considered when responding to a writing assignment.

**Question 4: How Should I Write This?** This question leads writers to decide what writing form or forms to choose to fulfill their purposes for writing. To convey the intent or purpose for a piece of writing successfully, students need to become familiar with the variety of writing forms available to them. Writing forms such as haiku, extended metaphors, shape poems, cinquains, short stories, letters, essays, plays, and the like provide helpful structure for the content of writing. Without a discernible structure, it is not only difficult for writers to convey their thoughts and feelings to their readers, but their readers will also have difficulty following or responding to the writing. Experience with writing modes and forms will help students learn which forms to use with which writing modes. It can also help them learn that, depending on the audience and writer's purpose, any form can be used. For example, poetry can be just as informative as a research paper, and poetic imagery can be used successfully in essays to move an audience to consider the argument presented in the essay.

**Question 5: What Will I Include in This Writing?** As young writers consider the topic, purpose, audience, and form for their writing, they will also have to decide what to put in their writing. Suppose their writing topic was to create a travel brochure for a favorite vacation to be written for prospective travel agencies. Decisions will have to be made about the nature of the vacation, what facts to include, and which ones to ignore. Certain adjectives that would appeal to potential vacationers would have to be chosen and used to make the vacation truly inviting. These content decisions will likely be made through the writing process for the brochure and not just at the beginning of the assignment. Once again, the purpose and audience, along with the brochure form, will help writers make these decisions.

**Question 6: How Will This Writing Be Developed?** The answer to this question is tied closely to the answers to the questions of writing form and content. It is rather difficult to organize a piece of writing without considering what is important to include and what writing form to use. The order of ideas or the organization of major portions of a writing can be seen as matters of structure or form, but it is possible to follow a writing form without cohesion among the various components of the form. For example, an essay that contains an introduction, three supporting paragraphs, and a conclusion may have the form of an essay but have enough disjointed sentences so as not to fully develop important points made in the essay. Writers must be cautious not to overdevelop ideas in their writing. This leads to digression and tangents in their writing that confuse their readers. Not surprisingly, this expressive kind of writing is most common in young children and, later, in young adolescents. Initially, students can check their writing to see whether the important ideas are presented in a structure understood by readers. As these writers mature, the questions of transitions from sentence to sentence or verse to verse or paragraph to paragraph can be addressed. How the writing develops is a less tangible question than what form to use or what topic to choose. All the writing processes come into play for students as they attempt to respond to this question.

**Question 7: How Will This Writing Be Assessed?** This is an important question particularly for young writers who will be challenged and stretched over their school years as they develop as writers. Assessment of writing is important for students and teachers. Students need to know the criteria that will be used to evaluate their writing, not just in terms of grades, but in terms of helping them see whether they have accomplished what they set out to do with their writing. Teachers need to know whether what they do in the name of writing instruction is helping their students become better, confident writers. Writing assessment should not only be seen as the culmination of student effort and learning but also as a measure of teacher effort, guidance, and instruction. By making sure that students know long before their final draft how their writing will be assessed, they will recognize what they are responsible for in their own writing.

For some assignments, teachers can decide what is included in each part of a writing assignment. For other assignments, students can be responsible for determining what occurs at each stage of the assignment. Teachers and students can also negotiate the elements of a writing assignment. A mix of all three kinds of assignments permits choice for students, emphasis and reinforcement for teachers, and collaboration between both.

In addition to the actual writing assignment, the writing process should also be included to help students successfully complete writing assignments. Actual instruction and feedback involving these processes will help students learn how to use them effectively when writing. Keep in mind that the processes of prewriting, writing, and revising are recursive and can occur at various times throughout the writing process. With young or inexperienced student writers, however, it is helpful for teachers to refer to prewriting, writing, and revising as steps in the writing process. As students mature, they identify the writing process that best suits them.

## Writing Workshops

An ideal instructional format for dealing with all aspects of writing assignments and the writing process is the **writing workshop** (Atwell, 1998; Calkins, 1994; Fletcher and Portalupi, 2001). The success of writing workshops is predicated on five principles:

- Students need time for all aspects of writing.
- The writing process is as important as the writing product.
- Students need feedback and response to their writing.
- Students are taught about writing through their writing.
- Students form a community of writers in their classrooms.

How do writing workshops support these principles? The principles are supported through a 60–90 minute time frame each day that includes writing, sharing, and teaching.

**Writing** Students spend 30–45 minutes each day working on writing assignments. They may work individually or in pairs or small groups on any aspects of their writing at any stage of the writing process (prewriting, drafting, writing, revising, editing, or publishing). This is also a time for conferences and feedback sessions by teachers and students. Brief conferences can help students consider writing topics, prewriting strategies, revising and editing suggestions, and publishing ideas. The purpose of feedback sessions is to support students' writing efforts and encourage further writing. Many of the questions identified earlier under author conferences or writing groups lend themselves well to writing workshop conferences and feedback sessions.

**Sharing** Time is set aside each day at the end of the writing workshop for students to share their writing with one another. One or more students might "publish" a finished piece of writing while sitting in a special Author's Chair. Other students might share writing that is not at the finished stage to get suggestions for possible changes in their writing. This is where the three types of responses to writing (personal, analytic, and creative) can be especially helpful. The primary purpose of this sharing time is to raise the value and importance of writing and its publication.

**Teaching** Mini-lessons are the primary teaching vehicle in writing workshops. Teachers focus on any aspect of writing during a 5–15 minute time frame using students' writing as a guide for the types of mini-lessons to do. Teachers also use mini-lessons to acquaint students with all aspects of the writing workshop, including writing workshop behavior. Steps in a mini-lesson include:

Step 1: Share topic or reason for the lesson.

Step 2: Model think-aloud about the lesson.

Step 3: Call upon prior knowledge of students.

Step 4: Use examples to illustrate the skill being taught.

Step 5: Have students summarize what they learn and how to use it.

Step 6: Have students write the new learning into their writer's notebooks.

Examples of mini-lessons include how to decide on a topic for writing, how to provide more details in writing, writing complete sentences, and noun-verb agreement. The key to successful mini-lessons is linking them directly to student writing. For example, when students are writing about an experience in the past, a mini-lesson on verb tense can be done before as part a prewriting mini-lesson or after the writing as part of an editing mini-lesson.

Because writing is the focus in writing workshops, here are some guidelines to go along with students' writing.

- Do not erase; instead, draw a line through it (you can see the change).
- Write on one side of the paper, so you can cut and paste (helps in revising).
- Double-space drafts to leave room for revision (you can write over/under).
- Write drafts in pencil (makes it easier to line through).
- Revise and edit in a different color ink (to show changes easily).
- Date and label all writing: draft 1, final edit (shows writing development).
- Save your writing and all its phases (preserves a record of your writing).

These guidelines, along with the writing workshop guidelines, help to instill in your students the value and enjoyment that writing brings to writers.

## How Can You Assess Students' Writing?

We present the following writing assessment guidelines so that assessment provides helpful feedback to students and teachers. Students need not fear assessment and can share in the responsibility for it with their teachers.

## Writing Assessment Guidelines

1. *Assessment of student writing should be continuous.* Students need to see assessment as a way of providing them with helpful feedback on their writing.
2. *Assessment is not synonymous with grading.* Formative assessment is probably more useful than summative assessment when it comes to instructional strategies.
3. *Students need to share in the assessment of their writing.* This allows students to take more responsibility for their writing. If all assessment is done by the teacher, then authorship is taken out of the hands of the students.
4. *Look for common writing problems when assessing students' writing as the basis for subsequent writing instruction.* Students' writing needs tend to cluster, so looking for the clusters can indicate which students need what kind of instruction. This allows for group instruction and interaction among students who experience similar writing difficulties. The clusters also indicate which students have mastered a particular writing skill and who might be asked to help those students who have not.
5. *Build assessment criteria into the writing assignments.* This will help students keep in mind how their writing will be evaluated as they complete the assignment.
6. *Stick to the assessment criteria that have been selected for a writing assignment.* This prevents confusion for students and frustration for teachers.
7. *Not all writing done by students has to be graded, so have students select their best one or two pieces of writing for grading.* This grading policy recognizes that students will have varying success with different writing topics and forms and should not be penalized as they develop as writers. By allowing them to select their best writing effort for purposes of a writing grade, they will feel more ownership toward the grade they receive.

## Writing Assessment Strategies

Authentic writing assessment means taking a closer look at students' writing. Here are three informal ways to conduct authentic writing assessment:

**Direct Observations** One of the difficulties that students can have is the inability to write while being closely watched by their teachers. To reduce this difficulty, spend time talking to your students about your need to keep your ears and eyes open while they are working on writing assignments. Let them know that by watching them as they write, you can see which students need help. Remind them, however, that at times you will want to do your own writing while they are doing theirs. This comment reinforces in students that even the teacher needs time to write without interruptions. These discussions are especially important with primary grade students because they need continuous support as they begin to write. Explaining why you need to watch your students write can also lessen anxiety in students who think you watch them to see their mistakes. Let them know that you watch to see all they can do and to look for times to help if they need you.

### What to Look for as You Watch Your Students

- Which students have trouble finding a topic and which ones do not?
- How do students respond to writing topics?
- What prewriting strategies do students use?

- Who needs to be closely monitored as they write and who does not?
- Which students reread their drafts carefully and which ones ignore what they have written as they reread their writing?
- What students will accept constructive feedback on their writing and which students will not?
- Who works well in writing groups and who does not?
- Which students are listened to by other students when suggestions are made? Who is reluctant to revise or edit their writing?
- Who is eager to share their writing and who prefers a less public forum for presenting their writing?

These are just some of the many questions that can guide your observations as you watch your young authors. Your best guide for watching is to look for those things that impede student writing so that you can offer suggestions to keep the writing process going.

**Writing Folders/Portfolios** Writing folders are a valuable source of information about a student's writing for teachers, students, and parents. They should contain writing efforts that occur at each phase of a writing assignment, writing topics, readers' comments, and the student's responses. This running record of student writing can help teachers see how a student is progressing. You can find evidence of success or difficulty with a particular writing skill in a student's writing folder. With constant referral to students' writing folders, teachers can decide which students need help with specific writing skills and which ones do not. Teachers can better guide writing conferences or writing groups when they have access to the writing record from student folders (Graves, 1983). Writing folders can contain questions or checklists that students can respond to as they review their writing before they meet with their teacher or other students (see Figure 7.13 for an example of writing folder assessment questions). The contents of a student's writing folder can be used to explain to the student's parents how the student is developing writing skills.

To effectively use writing folders as part of a formative writing assessment approach, keep in mind the following guidelines:

1. Make sure that students take responsibility for creating and maintaining their writing folders. Encourage students to make the folders their own by having them design the covers.
2. Show them how to organize their folders into topics, prewriting plans, writing drafts, revised writing, and final copies.
3. Include students when decisions are made about the checklists to be placed in their folders. Writing skills that are reflected in checklists should be taught before the checklists are used.
4. Encourage students to review their writing using the appropriate checklist before going to a writing conference or writing group.
5. Regularly respond to students' writing folders. It is important that they realize that you take enough interest in their writing to comment on their assessment sheets, to put response notes in their folders, and, generally, to let them know how much you look forward to opening their writing folders.
6. Above all, use writing folders and have students use their writing folders interactively with you and with themselves. The folders should be viewed as a source of writing topics and writing pieces to be shared and discussed.

Figure 7.13

## Writing Folder Assessment

Name: ______________________ Date: ______________

Portfolio Grading Period: ______________________

Since your last writing folder assessment:

- What topics have you written on? ______________________
- What writing forms have you used? ______________________
- Who have you written for? ______________________
- What writing pieces do you like the most? ______________________
- Which ones did you not like as much? ______________________
- How has your writing improved? ______________________
- What do you need help with in your writing? ______________________
- What writing have you shared with others? ______________________
- What comments or suggestions have you found helpful? ______________________

**Student Self-Assessment** In addition to writing assessment by teachers and other students, students can also learn to assess their own writing. They can look at the writing in their folders and review comments made by their writing groups to see how they are developing as writers. Students can also assess a specific writing assignment with questions that students can ask themselves about the assignment. See Figure 7.14 for an example of writing assignment questions. By including regular student self-assessment, students more readily take ownership of their writing and the progress they make as writers.

**Figure 7.14**

## Writing Assignment Questions

Name: ______________________________ Date: ____________

Assignment: ______________________________

| | |
|---|---|
| Purpose: Why did you write this?<br><br>Audience: Who did you write for?<br><br>Writing Genre: What writing form did you use? | Prewriting: How did you prepare for this writing?<br><br>Drafting: How did you develop your writing?<br><br>Revising: What revising did you do to your writing?<br><br>Editing: What editing corrections did you make? |
| What was easier for you to do in this writing assignment?<br><br>What was harder for you to do in this writing assignment? | What do you need help with in your writing? |



Writing assessment can seem overwhelming for new teachers. By observing and talking to many elementary teachers who have found ways to successfully address this concern, the following guidelines can help:

### Guidelines for Reducing Time Spent Evaluating Student Writing

- Refrain from grading your students' writing the first two or three weeks of school to determine the writing abilities of your students.

Authentic writing assessment can seem overwhelming at first. Using a variety of methods (such as direct observations, writing folders/portfolios, and student self-assessment) and strategies can make writing assessment less time consuming.

- Grade one in every three or four papers and allow students to select the paper to be graded.
- Use and have students use assessment checklists or guides.
- Develop a set of assessment questions that can be used with any paper. Write the number of the question in the appropriate place in a paper's margin.
- Help students assess one another's writing in writing groups to reduce the amount of assessment you must do.
- Always include assessment criteria in students' writing assignments so that the students know the criteria from the beginning.

See the Engaging in Assessment feature for an example of how to use storyboards as assessment guides.

## *engaging in* Assessment

### Storyboards as Assessment Tools

After Mrs. Cho's fourth-graders complete their folk tale storyboards, they start to write their folk tales. She walks around observing and encouraging her students as they write. As they finish their first drafts of the folk tales, she notices that students have left many interesting features in their storyboards and have not included them in their writing. The next day, she groups the students in pairs. Each student looks at the other student's storyboard and compares it to the student's folk tale. Students notice things in the storyboards that could make the folk tales more interesting with more details and description. Students make suggestions to their partners, which leads to revision of the folk tales. The students engage in assessing each other's folk tales by using the storyboards as a helpful assessment guide when reading the folk tales.

## revisit the classroom challenge

Now that you have read this chapter, what suggestions can you make to Mrs. Ramos and Mr. Harris to help their students get started with their writing? You might suggest to Mrs. Ramos that she go over to Raymond's desk and ask him to tell her about his picture. Who is in his Halloween picture? Where are the two children going? She might even help him begin his story with the line: "One Halloween, two children saw a witch on a broomstick going . . ." She could encourage him to take the things in his picture and include them in his story. Mr. Harris could decide to have his students stop writing their own haiku poems. He might have the class write a haiku poem together so that he can model and guide the construction of a haiku poem with them. His students could brainstorm haiku topics. In smaller groups, students could pick a topic and come up with different ideas or phrases to go with it. Mr. Harris could walk around helping students count syllables in their haiku lines. In both cases, you can offer suggestions that make writing easier, not harder, for their students.

# chapterreview



We hope that you have enjoyed the learning to write journey presented in this chapter. We have observed how students develop as writers, the writing process, and strategies that you can use to support students as they write. The classroom environment you create for writing and the instructional strategies you use to help students with their writing play a large role in developing writing confidence and competence in your students.

This chapter answered the following questions about writing development and how to teach writing.

## How Do Students Develop into Writers?

Language and cognitive abilities influence students' writing development. Writing development includes gaining control over print features (recurring, directionality, and generating principles). Students' writing reflects their knowledge of sentence structure and spelling development. The functions or purposes for students' writing are expressive (personal), transactional (informational), and poetic (stories, poems, plays). Over time, students learn to write for a variety of audiences, on a variety of topics, and using a variety of writing forms.

## What Is the Writing Process?

Process writing includes prewriting, drafting, revising, editing, and publishing. Writers go back and forth across these writing processes as needed. Prewriting strategies include art, freewriting, reading, and graphic organizers. While drafting, teachers can encourage incubating, comment to stimulate, spell or tell, or have students dictate. To help students revise, author conferences and writing groups are helpful. Editing benefits from author conferences and writing groups. Publishing gives value to writing and can be done in a variety of ways.

## How Can You Help Students Become Writers?

When writing is an integral part of a classroom with a trusting supportive environment, students find great value in it. The content in students' writing should be valued above the correctness of their writing. Good writing assignments help students answer writer questions. Writing workshops provide opportunities for dealing with all aspects of writing.

## How Can You Assess Students' Writing?

Writing assessment should provide helpful feedback to students and teachers. Writing assessment should be continuous, shared with students, focus on common writing challenges, and built into writing assignments. There are ways to reduce the time spent assessing students' writing.

PEARSON **myeducationlab**™
Where the Classroom Comes to Life

Now go to www.myeducationlab.com to take a Pretest to assess your initial comprehension of chapter content, study chapter content with your individualized Study Plan, take a Posttest to assess your understanding of chapter content, practice your teaching skills with Building Teaching Skills exercises, and build a deeper, more applied understanding of chapter content with Homework and Exercises.

chapter 8

# Writing Conventions

## classroom challenge

**As Mr. Johnson** looks over his fifth-graders' memoir pieces about a special relative, he marvels at the fathers, mothers, uncles, aunts, granddads, grandmothers, cousins, brothers, and sisters that his students wrote about. He spent time with his students helping them focus on past experiences with their special relative and encouraged them to use specifics: How did granddad look? How did he talk? What did he wear? What did he do that made him special? What experiences did the student share with granddad? The focus was on the past, so Mr. Johnson addressed the need for using past tense words and their correct form. As he reads the students' papers, he sees a lot of evidence of past tense verb forms. After reading the memoirs for content and organization, he goes back to read for correctness. This is when he notices examples of noun-verb agreement errors. He decides to have a lesson on noun-verb agreement the next day. He prepares examples of correct and incorrect noun-verb agreement. He checks a grammar practice software program for exercises that students can practice. The next day, he conducts his noun-verb agreement lesson and has students follow it up

with the grammar practice exercises at the computers in his room.

Four weeks later, he looks over another set of papers by the students who, this time, had taken the memoir piece and turned it into a story of fiction. Once again, the content of the stories and the way his students crafted them impresses him. Once again, however, he finds more examples of noun-verb agreement errors. He feels a little frustrated because he thought the noun-verb disagreements were a thing of the past. He is not sure how to proceed at this point.

## Questions for Reflection

1. Why do you think the noun-verb disagreements show up again?
2. How could Mr. Johnson have helped his students with this the first time?
3. How can students help one another with this in the future?

## anticipating this chapter

These questions get to the heart of teaching about the writing conventions of English, which is the focus of this chapter. To help you answer these questions and other questions about grammar, word usage, punctuation, and capitalization, this chapter addresses the following questions:

- What are writing conventions for English?
- What do we know about teaching writing conventions?
- How can you teach writing conventions?
- How can you assess writing conventions?

# What Are Writing Conventions for English?

Writing conventions are the standard rules that we use to make writing comprehensible for readers. English writing conventions include grammar, parts of speech, sentences, usage, and punctuation and capitalization. We will examine each of these, in turn, in this section.

## Grammar

We describe **grammar** in the language development and instruction chapter as one of the important language systems that students acquire as they develop oral language. In this chapter, we turn more specifically to grammar as an important feature of written language. One way to define grammar is to describe the functions of words in sentences. Another way to describe grammar is to identify the grammar rules that control the written order of words in sentences. A third way is to identify and describe the relationships between words, phrases, clauses, and sentences in written English. Perhaps the most important way to describe grammar is that it is an arrangement system for words, phrases, and sentences used by a reader and a writer to communicate with each other. This gets to the primary purpose for grammar in writing. It facilitates the transfer of meaning from a writer to a reader who is familiar with the grammar used by the writer. Grammar alone is not sufficient for writers to communicate with readers. Readers need to know something about the topic of the writing, the meaning of the words, and the context in order to fully understand the writer. For example, look at these two sentences:

Racing cars can be dangerous.
Visiting relatives can be exhausting.

The first sentence can mean that racing cars as a category of cars can be dangerous because they go so fast. It can also mean that racing them on the road can be dangerous and you can get hurt. The second sentence can mean that relatives who come to see you can tire you out, or it can mean that going to see them can tire you out. How can you be sure of the meaning of these sentences? You need to know more about the context in which the sentences are being used. Even when you know the meaning of all the words in each sentence, you can still be unsure of their meaning. Although you have several meaning options for each sentence, imagine if the writer arranged them like this:

Using writing conventions, such as correct grammar, facilitates communication between readers and writers.

> Dangerous can racing be cars
> Relatives be visiting exhaustive can

These sentences create greater meaning challenges because they are not grammatical. In fact, they are not really sentences. This brings us back to the value and importance of grammar for writing. Correctly used, grammar facilitates communication between readers and writers who share an understanding of the grammar. See the Exploring Technology feature for grammar websites to explore with your students and to use as a reference for your teaching.

IRA/NCTE 6

## exploring technology

### Grammar Websites

***Maggie's Earth Adventures: Grammar*** **(http//:teacher.scholastic.com/activities/adventure/index.htm)**
Developed by Scholastic, this site has five interactive games on English grammar including: nouns and verbs (also in Spanish), punctuation, prefixes and suffixes, word ending, and homophones.

***Grammar Gorillas*** **(www.funbrain.com/grammar)**
Grammar Gorillas is an interactive game in which students can identify parts of speech. The game has a beginner level (nouns and verbs) and advanced level (all parts of speech).

***Writing*** **(www.learner.org/channel/workshops/teachreading35/session4/index.html)**
The Annenberg Foundation provides several programs for teacher professional development. In this video, Professor Nadeen Ruiz of Stanford University discusses components of an effective writing program, types of strategies that teachers can use to help students improve, and effective assessment practices.

## Parts of Speech

If grammar controls the order of words in sentences, the words are also part of grammar. Each word in a sentence serves a specific function in conveying the meaning of a sentence. We refer to them as **parts of speech,** even though they are more often discussed in the context of writing. Knowing the names or functions of parts of speech does not correlate highly with correct grammar in writing, but it is useful to know the names when talking about parts of sentences. The eight parts of speech and their functions are:

1. **Nouns** name persons, places, or things (*dog, toy, courage*).
2. **Pronouns** stand in for nouns (*she, he, it, they*).
3. **Verbs** tell what a person, place, or thing does (*run, stop, laugh*).
4. **Adverbs** describe verbs, adverbs, and adjectives (*sing loudly, well-behaved dog*).
5. **Adjectives** describe nouns or pronouns (*happy people, he was happy*).
6. **Prepositions** show words in relation to others (*under the rug, beside the tree*).
7. **Conjunctions** connect words or groups of words (*hot or cold, he jumped and caught the ball*).
8. **Interjections** show emotion or strong feelings (*Whoops! Wow! Ow!*).

## Sentences

**Classroom Artifact Homework Exercise**

*I Slammed My Finger in the Door*

Go to the Homework and Exercises section in Chapter 8 of MyEducation Lab and examine the artifact, "I Slammed My Finger in the Door," in which a child writes about an episode in his/her life. Complete the activities that follow, and save your work or transmit it to your professor as assigned.

If parts of speech identify the functions of words in sentences, **sentences** determine their functions by controlling the order of the words. For sentences to be a set of words that express a complete thought, they have to have a subject and a predicate. The subject is a person, place, or thing and is usually a noun, and the predicate tells what the subject does and is usually a verb. In the sentence, *Happy cows jump over full moons*, *cows* is the subject, and *jump* is the predicate. By looking at the order of the words in the sentence, we see that *Happy* is an adjective (describes the cows), *cows* is a noun, *jump* is a verb (tells what the cows do), *over* is a preposition (describes the position of the cows in relationship to the moons), *full* is another adjective (describes moons), and *moons* is a noun (the object over which the cows jump). This sentence is a relatively simple statement that describes what a person, place, or thing is doing. Sentences come in many structures and sizes, and they perform other functions besides making statements. As students develop as writers, they learn to use a variety of sentence structures for a variety of reasons. Knowing the names of the structures and functions of sentences may not be essential to using them correctly and effectively, but teachers can help their students by knowing what structures and functions are.

**Sentence Structures** One way to describe sentences is to examine the complexity of sentence structures. The number of clauses determines the complexity of the sentence. A clause has a noun and verb and can be either an independent or dependent clause. An independent clause (also called a main clause) can exist as a sentence on its own. *The dog barked* is an independent clause and a complete sentence. A dependent clause (also called a subordinate clause) is a set of words that cannot exist as a complete sentence but needs to be attached to an independent clause to form a complete sentence. The dependent clause, *when its owner walked into the room,* is not a complete sentence. When it is attached to *The dog barked*, however, it forms a complete sentence: *The dog barked when its owner walked into the room.* It is the use of dependent clauses with independent clauses that determines a sentence's level of complexity.

■ ***Simple Sentences*** A sentence that has only one independent clause is a simple sentence with a subject and verb: *The cat meows.* Simple sentences can have numerous subjects and verbs, but the sentence structure remains the same: *Cats and dogs meow and bark.*

■ ***Compound Sentences*** When writers create sentences by connecting two or more independent clauses, they write compound sentences. The connection occurs with the use of a conjunction such as *and, or, but*: *The dog barks, and the cat meows.* Often, a comma appears before the conjunction to signal the presence of a second independent clause. Sometimes, writers join independent clauses with a semicolon: *Dogs bark; cats meow.*

■ ***Complex Sentences*** When an independent, or main, clause hooks up with a dependent or subordinate clause, the result is a complex sentence: *Dogs bark when they see cats.* The subordinate clause, *when they see cats*, supports the main clause, *Dogs bark.* How? It acts as an adverb and tells when dogs bark. Words that signal adverbial subordinate clauses include *if, before, when*, and *since.* Dependent clauses can also act as adjectives: *The dog that looks like a hotdog is a dachshund.* Adjectival dependent clauses begin with words such as *who, which*, and *that.* They can also act as nouns: *What cats do always interests dogs.* Signal words for noun dependent clauses are *what, that*, and *who.* With all these examples of complex sentences, the role of the dependent or subordinate clause is to add information about the information contained in the independent or main clause.

■ ***Compound-Complex Sentences*** As sentence complexity grows, so does the number of main clauses and subordinate clauses. A compound-complex sentence has at least two main clauses and one subordinate clause: *If you open the door, the dogs will bark and the cats will meow.*

As students mature as writers, they increasingly want to use more complex sentence structures. Why? It is more efficient to combine main clauses or add subordinate clauses. This reduces the number of sentences while increasing the information or meaning in the sentences. Look at these sentences:

*The dog has long ears. He has short legs. He wags his tail. He gets a treat.*

Now look at this one sentence:

*The dog with the long ears and short legs wags his tail to get a treat.*

The same information found in the first set of four sentences is contained in this one sentence. The sentence is more complex, more efficient in conveying the same information, and more interesting to read.

**Sentence Functions** There are four basic functions for writing sentences: statements, commands, questions, and exclamations. Statement sentences supply information to the reader: *Some dogs like cats.* Question sentences ask for something: *Why do dogs bark at cats?* Command sentences make requests or give orders: *Please eat your food. Stop barking.* Exclamation sentences emphasize strong feeling or surprise: *Watch out for the dog! You'll step on him!* It is also possible to write sentences that are two or more types at the same time: *Where have you been?!* The biggest challenge for student writers is to learn how to correctly punctuate these kinds of sentences. The punctuation section of this chapter will provide suggestions for helping with this.

## Usage

If parts of speech refer to the functions of words in a sentence, *usage* refers to the appropriate forms of the words in sentences. For example, *I have three dogs and cats* uses the appropriate Standard English (SE) plural noun forms. The sentence, *I sleeped for eight hours*, does not use *slept* for the past tense verb form of *sleep*. Another example, *Run quick to the store*, does not use the SE adverb form, *quickly*. In addition to noun and verb usage errors, other SE usage errors include double negatives, incorrect subject-verb agreement, and incorrect pronoun forms. Why are these word usage errors? They do not conform to the generally accepted word usage standards of Standard English. Why do they not conform? They are more reflective of nonstandard English dialects spoken by millions of students in the United States. As students go through school, they learn to use a variety of dialects or language registers. For conversation, more informal language is appropriate. For discussion or oral presentations, a more formal language, closer to SE is expected. Some refer to this difference as "out of school language" and "in school language" or "home language" and "school language." Both are the right language because there is an acceptable context for each. The same can be said about written language. There are times when informal language is well suited for certain kinds of writing: personal letters, poems, plays, short stories, and novels. Other times, formal language reflective of SE is required in business letters, essays, scientific reports, business proposals, and other kinds of formal writing. While recognizing the importance and value of students' nonstandard English dialects, it is equally important that all students learn Standard English word usage to be successful in school and beyond.

IRA/NCTE 4

**Word Usage Challenges** For each of the eight parts of speech, there are different forms depending upon the meaning conveyed by the writer. To appreciate the variety of forms that present usage challenges to elementary school writers, Figure 8.1 presents the nine parts of speech with questions that identify usage challenges for each. In addition

**Figure 8.1**

## Parts of Speech Word Usage Challenges

| | |
|---|---|
| 1. Noun: | Does it use the single or plural form? Is it a possessive form? |
| 2. Verbs: | Does it use the correct tense form? |
| 3. Pronoun: | Is it the correct form for an adjective or noun? |
| 4. Adjective: | Is it the correct form for its noun or pronoun? |
| 5. Adverb: | Is it the correct form for its verb, adverb, or adjective? |
| 6. Preposition: | Is it the correct word used to show the correct relationship between two or more words? |
| 7. Conjuction: | Is the correct word used between two words or groups of words? |
| 8. Exclamation: | Is the appropriate one used? |
| 9. Articles: | Is it an or a before the noun? |

**Additional Word Usage Challenges**

| | |
|---|---|
| 1. Adjective and Adverbs: | Is the comparative or superlative form correct? |
| 2. Verbs: | Is the irregular form correct? |
| 3. Subjective-Verb Agreement: | Do noun or pronoun forms agree with their verb forms? |
| 4. Subject-Object Pronouns: | Are subjective and objective pronoun forms correct? |
| 5. Negatives: | Are double negative forms absent? |

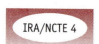

to these parts of speech usage challenges, several other word usage challenge questions are listed. Students can use these questions as they reread their writing to identify any word usage errors that may be present.

## Punctuation and Capitalization

Why is it important to know how to use punctuation? Effective use of grammar helps a writer communicate better with readers.

Why include **punctuation** and **capitalization** under grammar? Punctuation and capitalization are important signals in sentences and are key grammatical structures in writing. Punctuation signals when a sentence ends (period), how to separate a series of items or ideas in a list (comma), how to separate two main clauses or subordinate and main clauses (comma or semicolon), and it tells when to pause while reading (comma or semicolon). Punctuation signals when a question is being asked (question mark) and when strong feeling is being declared (exclamation mark). It tells when someone is speaking (quotation marks), and it shows ownership—it can also consolidate two words into one (apostrophe). Punctuation signals when a sentence is beginning (capitalization) and identifies proper names, places, and things. These and other punctuation and capitalization features in written language help writers express their ideas in ways that are easier to read than were the features absent. They reduce possible confusion or misunderstanding by the reader. We know, for example, that students who ignore punctuation and capitalization while reading have difficulty comprehending what they have read (Gillet, Temple, and Crawford, 2004). To assist their readers, therefore, writers need to learn about capitalization and punctuation and use both correctly.

What is grammar? It is all the above when it comes to writing. It is the structure of sentences. It is the parts of speech with their individual roles to play within sentences. It is the word usage forms of the parts of speech. Finally, it includes the punctuation and capitalization that signal the key elements in sentences. Why is it important to know how to use punctuation? Effective use of grammar helps a writer communicate better with readers.

# What Do We Know about Teaching Writing Conventions?

In the 1980s, the National Council of Teachers of English (NCTE) adopted the following resolution regarding grammar instruction:

> Resolved, that the National Council of Teachers of English affirm the position that the use of isolated grammar and usage exercises not supported by theory and research is a deterrent to the improvement of students' speaking and writing and

that, in order to improve both of these, class time at all levels must be devoted to opportunities for meaningful listening, speaking, reading, and writing; and that NCTE urge the discontinuance of testing practices that encourage the teaching of grammar rather than English language arts instruction (NCTE, 1985).

Predicated on the NCTE's examination of fifty years of grammar research, this resolution concluded that grammar instruction by itself did not result in grammatical improvement in students' writing. Hillocks's (1986) analysis of grammar research data supported the NCTE resolution. With the rise and popularity of the National Writing Project (1974) and process writing, grammar instruction that had been a steady fixture in the language arts curriculum of elementary schools began to receive less emphasis. Does this mean there is no place for grammar instruction in the classroom? No. What we have learned since the NCTE resolution is that students can benefit from grammar instruction when the instruction is given within the context of students' writing (Noguchi, 1991; Weaver, 1996; Bromley, 2003; Nagin, 2003). What does the context of students' writing mean? Rather than learning grammar elements and doing grammar exercises that include the five grammar areas (discussed earlier) as ends, students focus on grammar as a means to clearly and effectively communicate with readers. Graves (1994) echoes this belief that grammar instruction provides a helpful tool for students to better understand their own writing and convey that understanding to their readers. Baker, Gersten, and Graham (2003) refer to this as concentrating on the function of the writing and the role that grammar can play in supporting that function. Noden (1999) would add that grammar is what writers use to create an image for their readers. The more grammatical brushstrokes available to the writer, the greater the visual image the writer creates in the mind of the reader. Another important aspect of effective grammar instruction is that it needs to be included in the assessment of students' writing as it enhances or detracts from the content of the writing (Allen, 2003).

## How Can You Teach Writing Conventions?

IRA/NCTE 4

**Video Homework Exercise**

*Peer Editing*

Go to the Homework and Exercises section in Chapter 8 of MyEducation Lab and view the video, "Peer Editing," about two students who are editing their work by checking their spelling, grammar, and punctuation. Complete the activities that follow, and save your work or transmit it to your professor as assigned.

A variety of strategies can be used to teach writing conventions. In this section, we will explore activities and lessons to use in teaching a grammar workshop and creating a grammar toolbox.

### Grammar Workshop

If students benefit from learning and using grammar in the context of their own writing, grammar workshops are ideal settings for this to happen. A grammar workshop provides the opportunity for teachers and students to identify grammar challenges observed in students' writings. These challenges can fall into any of the five grammar categories identified earlier: sentences, parts of speech, word usage, punctuation, or capitalization. It is best to limit these challenges to one, although several may naturally occur simultaneously. For example, the topic might be sentence fragments, coupled with ending sentence punctuation. Gradually, students can develop a checklist in the form of questions for each grammar category. These questions can come out of the discussion that occurs in grammar workshops. See Figure 8.2 for steps to follow in conducting a grammar workshop.

Figure 8.2

## Grammar Workshop

- Identify or have students discover the grammar problem found in their writing. Use an actual piece of writing that contains the problem, and place it on an overhead transparency, or give students a copy of the writing.
- Have students discuss the nature of the grammar problem in the writing. The discussion can include what the writer might have been trying to do in the writing, as well as the effect of the grammar problem in the writing. Comments should be written down by the teacher or volunteer students and summarized.
- Have students talk about possible solutions to the grammar problem and record them on the chalkboard. Students may be working in small groups and record their own solutions or ones mentioned by other members of the class.
- Make changes in the actual writing piece, or have students in groups, or individually, make the appropriate revisions on their copy of the writing. Students can compare and discuss with each other the revisions they have made.
- It may be appropriate to go to grammar exercises in a commercial language arts program to reinforce the grammar solution before students revise the actual writing piece.
- At the conclusion of the revision discussion, have students identify a grammar principle or goal they can use to help them review their own writing for the grammar problem.
- Place their grammar statement on a chart so that it can be referred to in the future by the teacher or the students.
- After the grammar workshop, have students go back to one of their earlier or current writing pieces, and have them apply the grammar principle to their own writing.

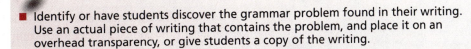

Grammar workshops can also occur before students begin work on a writing assignment. They can also be used to introduce correct usage or punctuation guidelines for student writing. In these instances, writing with well-crafted sentences or appropriate word usage can serve as models for students. This would be particularly helpful when students were writing about events in the past for a social studies paper or a fictionalized account of a past experience in their lives. Attention paid to past tense verb forms is helpful to convey clearly to readers that something happened in the past. Grammar workshops can also be opportunities for students to explore sentence structure and to create and control their own sentences.

**BUILDING TEACHING SKILLS: Lesson Planning Exercise**

*Frameworks for Skills Development*

Go to the Building Teaching Skills section in Chapter 8 of MyEducationLab and read the mini-lesson plans that provide a framework for developing skills-based mini-lessons. Complete the activities that follow, and save your work or transmit it to your professor as assigned.

## Grammar Toolbox

We have adapted the writer's toolbox concept developed by William Strong (1996) to go along with the grammar workshop. Students should think of sentence structure,

Grammar workshops create opportunities for students to explore sentence structure and how to create and control their own sentences.

parts of speech, word usage, punctuation, and capitalization as tools in a grammar toolbox. As young writers, students start with a small set of tools that grows in number and complexity as students grow as writers. What goes in the grammar toolbox?

**Sentences** Students need clear, concise sentences that vary in length and complexity. **Sentence-composing strategies** are just the grammar tools to help students do this. Killgallon (1998) identified four of these strategies: sentence imitating, sentence combining, sentence expanding, and sentence unscrambling. At the heart of sentence-composing strategies is modeling and imitation. If these two terms sound familiar, they should, because both are essential for students to successfully acquire and use oral language. Just as young students listen to oral language models, imitate them, and use them in their speech, we believe that young writers benefit from hearing and seeing well-written sentences and begin to construct the same kinds of sentences in their writing. Sentence composing is also an excellent way to draw students' attention to excellent literature.

**Classroom Artifact Homework Exercise**

*Two Moves in One Week*

Go to the Homework and Exercises section in Chapter 8 of MyEducation Lab and examine the artifact, "Two Moves in One Week," which is a true story written by a seven-year-old about a life-changing event. Complete the activities that follow, and save your work or transmit it to your professor as assigned.

***Sentence-Imitating Strategy*** Pick a sentence from a favorite children's book that illustrates a specific sentence structure. Using the sentence as a model, write several sentences that imitate the same structure. In this example from *Frog and Toad Are Friends* (Lobel, 1970, p. 6), the sentence "Frog walked into the house" could be followed by "Toad ran into the house, Frog sneaked into the house, and Sparrow flew into the house." Have students notice the similarities among the sentences. Encourage students to compose a sentence that imitates the structure of the sentences and write it under the model sentences. Lined chart paper is an excellent material for group-constructed sentences that students can dictate to the teacher. When deciding on sentences to imitate, use students' writing and reading material as a guide. Sentence models can be simple or complex, depending on the students' writing development. Keep in mind that in the primary grades, students try a variety of sentence structures in their writing. Use their sentence writing efforts to help them master the basic and more complex sentence structures they are trying to learn. Remember the language tenet mentioned in the language development chapter: Comprehension always precedes production. The same holds true for written language: Students understand complex sentence structures before they are able to produce them.

***Sentence-Combining Strategy*** Young writers often write a series of short sentences that do not differ at all in structure, such as these:

*I have a dog.*
*Her name is Maggie.*
*She has short legs.*
*She has a long body.*

To help students learn to write fewer sentences with more information in them than individual small sentences have, use sentence-combining activities, which have proved successful in promoting more complex sentence structures (Cooper, 1981; Daiker, Kerek, and Morenberg, 1985; Strong, 1996). Using the sentences just listed, combine them into: *My dog, Maggie, has a long body with short legs.* To introduce sentence-combining to students, select an interesting complex sentence that illustrates a complex structure that students could use. Why not find a sentence that embeds information in a subordinate clause attached to a main clause? Use this one from Katherine Paterson's *Bridge to Terabithia* (1977, p. 39–40): "Leslie named their secret land 'Terabit,' and she loaned Jess all of her books about Marina, so he would know how things went in a magic kingdom—how the animals and the trees must be protected and how a ruler must behave." If you were using this sentence, you could turn it into the small sentences:

*Leslie named their secret land "Terabit."*
*Leslie loaned Jess all of her books.*
*Her books were about Marina.*
*He would know how things were in a magic kingdom.*
*He would know how the animals must be protected.*
*He would know how the trees must be protected.*
*He would know how a ruler must behave.*

Have students combine these sentences into two or three and try to combine those into one to get back to the original sentence. Three sentences might look like this: "Leslie named their secret land 'Terabit.' She loaned Jess all of her books about Marina so he would know how things were in a magic kingdom. He would know how animals and trees must be protected and how a ruler must behave."

Students can look for other sentences in their reading, break them down into small sentences, and combine them back into longer sentences. Sentence combining activities, when done in small groups, encourage students to create different versions of the same sentence. They can help student with parts of speech, word usage questions, and even punctuation and capitalization. More about this is discussed as the grammar toolbox fills up.

■ ***Sentence-Expanding Strategy*** Another approach to helping students increase the complexity of their sentences is to show them how to expand sentences. This is useful to illustrate the role of subordinate clauses and phrases. Select a sentence that illustrates an element in a sentence structure with which students are working. Why not try the participle phrase that often leads to sentence fragments? Here is an example of a sentence with such a phrase taken from Alexandria LaFaye's *Dad, in Spirit* (2001, p. 122):

> Watching Samuel mush his ring-macaroni salad into the shape of a fish instead of eating it, I thought about how Dad did everything in a whirligig fashion.

After introducing this sentence to students, have them discuss the connection between the opening phrase and the rest of the sentence. The opening phrase describes what the son, Ebon Jones ("I"), was doing as he thought about his dad. After the discussion, write only the opening phrase: "Watching Samuel mush his ring-macaroni salad into the shape of a fish instead of eating it . . ." and have students create their own expansion of the sentence. You could begin with just "Watching Samuel . . ." A group of fifth-graders who had read *Dad, in Spirit* created this expanded sentence: "Watching Samuel mush his ring-macaroni salad into the shape of a fish instead of eating it, Ebon remembered how his Dad jumped around from place to place trying to be everywhere at the same time." The fifth-graders had thought back on what had happened in the book and remembered just as Ebon had.

■ ***Sentence Unscrambling*** This technique helps students focus on the best order or arrangement of words in sentences. It can also be used to highlight punctuation at various points in a sentence. Find a sentence that includes a sentence element that the students are working with. Here is an example from Cynthia Rylant's *The Relatives*

*Came* (1985, p. 11): "You'd have to go through four different hugs to get from the kitchen to the front door." Divide the sentence into a list of phrases:

*You'd have to go*
*through four different hugs*
*to get from the kitchen*
*to the front door*

Now, scramble the phrases so they are out of order:

*to get from the kitchen*
*through four different hugs*
*to the front door*
*You'd have to go*

Then have students unscramble the phrases to come up with the original sentence or a sentence that conveys the same meaning. For example, "To get from the kitchen to the front door, you'd have to go through four hugs" does convey the same meaning as the original sentence. If students are working on punctuation in sentences, leaving punctuation marks or capitalized letters in the scrambled phrase can help signal the order of the phrases and reinforce the signals.

Other challenges in sentence writing that are common in student writing are run-on sentences, sentence fragments, and the incorrect use of parts of speech in sentences. Here are some suggestions for helping students with these sentence challenges.

IRA/NCTE 6

***Run-On Sentences*** A common occurrence in student writing is the presence of run-on sentences. The most common type is a series of main clauses joined by a series of ands. Here is an example from a second grader: "I have a stuffed koala bear and he is furry and he is small and his name is Koko and stays in my room and I go to school." There is no grammatical problem with this sentence, but it is somewhat monotonous in its structure. First, take the sentence and have students identify its main parts:

*I have a stuffed koala bear*
*and he is furry*
*and he is small*
*and his name is Koko*
*and he stays in my room*
*and I go to school*

Have students combine sentence parts into two sentences with no more than one *and* in each sentence. Examples of these combined sentences are:

*I have a stuffed koala bear that is furry and small.*
*His name is Koko, and he stays in my room when I go to school.*
*I have a furry stuffed koala bear named Koko, and he is small.*
*When I go to school, he stays in my room.*

In addition to combining two or more run-on sentence parts, students can also take run-on sentences and add appropriate punctuation to eliminate the run-on sentence.

***Sentence Fragments*** Sentence fragments are the result of students omitting words in their writing or in trying to write more complex sentences. Younger writers may omit words in sentences when their thinking gets ahead of their writing, especially when the students are writing by hand. When students attempt to use dependent clauses with independent clauses, they often treat the dependent clause as a complete sentence. Look at these pairs of sentences:

*When she opened the door. The dog barked.*
*After the game was over. We went home.*
*If you get there first. Open the door.*

The first sentence in each pair is a dependent clause that is a sentence fragment because it is not connected to its subsequent independent clause. Sentence combining can help eliminate the sentence fragment. The first one would be: "When she opened the door, the dog barked." How would you rewrite the other sentence pairs? When sentence fragments occur in students' writing, the best way to help eliminate them is with sentence combining activities.

The grammar workshop is an ideal vehicle for focusing on sentence structure challenges that appear in students' writing. The sentence composing strategies can be easily incorporated into the grammar workshop. Remember to use excellent examples of sentences from excellent literature for the sentence models. Models lead to imitation, which leads to better sentences.

**Parts of Speech** The function of parts of speech is to help convey meaning from a writer to a reader. Sometimes, a sentence only needs a verb: "Stop!" Another sentence may need nouns, verbs, prepositions, adjectives, and adverbs: "The cow jumped quickly over the big yellow moon." Choosing the parts of speech to use and the best words for each is one of the challenges facing young writers as they craft a piece of writing. Teachers can help students meet this challenge, all the while exposing them to literature that explores the eight parts of speech in informative and entertaining ways. The Exploring Children's Literature feature identifies several excellent books on the parts of speech that can be used. *The Amazing Pop-up Grammar Book* (Maizel and Petty, 1996) looks at adjectives, adverbs, nouns, and verbs, and *Fantastic! Wow! And Unreal!* (Heller, 2000) focuses on interjections and conjunctions.

IRA/NCTE 6

Identifying overused or weak words from students' writing can happen during grammar workshops. When sixth-grade students focused on words that came up frequently in their writing, they came up with the stronger nouns, verbs, adjectives, and adverbs seen in Figure 8.3. Armed with these new words, the students began to incorporate them into their own writing.

Good writing does more than just use adjectives and adverbs. In addition to replacing words for the same parts of speech, students look for words that paint a stronger visual image when attached to verbs, adjectives, and adverbs. For example, "He ran quickly," does not paint a picture of how quickly, as does this sentence: "He ran as quickly as a squirrel running from a dog" or "He ran so quickly you could almost see smoke coming off the soles of his sneakers." During a grammar workshop on adverbs, this question can be raised: How quickly was he running? When students go beyond adjective and adverbs, they add more details and give more information to enlighten their readers. Take a look at the Engaging in Visual Literacy feature on page 276 for another way to reinforce stronger parts of speech with concrete poems.

**Word Usage** If selecting the right words for conveying a writer's message is important, the appropriate form of the word helps the reader stay focused on the message. Inappropriate noun or verb forms can mislead or confuse readers. To help students with word usage questions, we turn to their favorite literature again. Many books

# exploring Children's Literature

## Books about Writing Conventions

### Grades K to 3

*Amelia Bedelia*—Written by Peggy Parish, illustrated by Fritz Siebel, and published by Harper & Row (1963).

A literal-minded housekeeper causes a ruckus in the household when she attempts to make sense of some instructions. Examples of words with multiple meanings.

*The King Who Rained*—Written and illustrated by Fred Gwynne and published by Windmill (1970).

Confused by the different meanings of words that sound alike, a little girl imagines such unusual sights as "a king who rained" and "the foot prince in the snow."

*Max's Words*—Written by Kate Banks, illustrated by Boris Kulikov, and published by Farrar, Straus & Giroux (2006).

When Max cuts out words from magazines and newspapers, collecting them the way his brothers collect stamps and coins, they all learn about words, sentences, and storytelling.

*Nouns and Verbs Have a Field Day*—Written by Robin Pulver, illustrated by Lynn Rowe Reed, and published by Holiday (2006).

When the children in Mr. Wright's class have a field day, nouns and verbs in the classroom make their own fun.

*The Perfect Pop-Up Punctuation Book*—Written by Kate Petty, illustrated by Jennie Maizels, and published by Dutton (2006).

This is a pop-up book for learning the proper use for commas, semicolons, colons, exclamation points, dashes, and more.

*Babymouse: Beach Babe*—Written by Jennifer Holm and Matthew Holm and published by Random House (2006).

It looks as though Babymouse's summer fun is not shaping up quite the way she expected. Will she become the surfing star she dreams of being . . . or sharkbait? Graphic novel format.

*Punctuation Takes a Vacation*—Written by Robin Pulver, illustrated by Lynn Rowe Reed, and published by Holiday (2003).

When all the punctuation marks in Mr. Wright's class decide to take a vacation, the students discover just how difficult life can be without them.

*Yo! Yes?*—Written and illustrated by Chris Raschka and published by Scholastic (1993).

Two lonely characters, one black and one white, meet on the street and become friends. Examples of interesting use of punctuation.

### Grades 4 to 8

*The Amazing Pop-up Grammar Book*—Written by Jennie Maizels and Kate Petty and published by Dutton (1996).

This pop-up book is for learning the proper use of nouns, verbs, adjectives, adverbs, and prepositions.

*Dearly, Nearly, Insincerely: What Is an Adverb?*—Written by Brian P. Cleary, illustrated by Brian Gable, and published by Carolrhoda (2003).

Rhyming text and illustrations present numerous examples of adverbs and their functions.

*Eats, Shoots & Leaves: Why, Commas Really Do Make a Difference!*—Written by Lynne Truss, illustrated by Bonnie Timmons, and published by Putnam Juvenile (2006).

This book takes a clever look at how misplacing or leaving out a comma can change the meaning of a sentence completely.

*Fantastic! Wow! and Unreal!: A Book about Interjections and Conjunctions*—Written and illustrated by Ruth Heller and published by Putnam (2000).

This book introduces and explains various interjections and conjunctions, including "awesome," "alas," and "yet."

*The Girl's Like Spaghetti: Why, You Can't Manage without Apostrophes!*—Written by Lynne Truss, illustrated by Bonnie Timmons, and published by Putnam (2007).

This book shows how apostrophes make a difference in meaning and understanding.

*The War between the Vowels and the Consonants*—Written by Priscilla Turner and published by Farrar, Straus and Giroux (1999).

## exploring Children's Literature

The vowels and the consonants fight each other until they realize that if they work together they can create marvelous poems, plays, and memoirs.

*Why Did the Chicken Cross the Road?*—Written and illustrated by Tedd Arnold, Harry Bliss, David Catrow, Marla Frazee, Jerry Pinkney, Chris Raschka, Judy Schachner, David Shannon, Mo Willems, and Jon Agee and published by Dial (2006).

Each contributor offers a new, illustrated punch line to the title question. Examples of interesting use of punctuation.

*Scholastic Dictionary of Synonyms, Antonyms, and Homonyms* (2001).

This dictionary contains 12,000 synonyms, 10,000 antonyms, and 2,000 homonyms and is the perfect reference tool for student writers. Not only will it help students expand their vocabularies, but this lightweight volume will help young people pick the perfect words to express their thoughts and feelings.

contain excellent examples of correct word usage. Sentences can be taken from the books and used as models during a grammar workshop. There are four steps to follow:

1. Read a book that contains the word usage model sentence.
2. Students identify the word usage feature in the sentence.
3. Students write their own sentence, using the word usage sentence as a model.
4. Students return to their writing to see whether they need to apply the word usage model to their own sentences.

Students develop an awareness and appreciation for correct word usage when they encounter it on a regular basis, such as in favorite stories and poems. Once again, the instructional emphasis is the impact that word usage has on the message or meaning that writers try to convey to their readers. For example, *The Very Hungry Caterpillar* (Carle, 1984) and *Goodnight Moon* (Brown, 1991) are excellent books for teaching plural nouns. A strategy for using *Goodnight Moon* for helping diverse language learners with the plural form can be seen in the Exploring Diversity feature.

**Figure 8.3**

### Stronger Words

| | | |
|---|---|---|
| (Noun) | house: | shack, cottage, cabin, apartment, dwelling, duplex, townhouse, condo |
| (Noun) | car: | minivan, van, pickup truck, sports car, convertible, SUV, camper |
| (Verb) | say: | growl, scream, whisper, laugh, shout, declare, exclaim |
| (Verb) | walk: | hike, saunter, stroll, march, meander, skip, race, roam, ramble, scuffle |
| (Adjective) | bright: | glistening, glittering, shiny, dazzling, intense |
| (Adjective) | surprised: | astonished, amazed, stunned, flabbergasted |
| (Adverb) | slowly: | reluctantly, gradually, leisurely, steadily |
| (Adverb) | fast: | quickly, rapidly, speedily, swiftly |

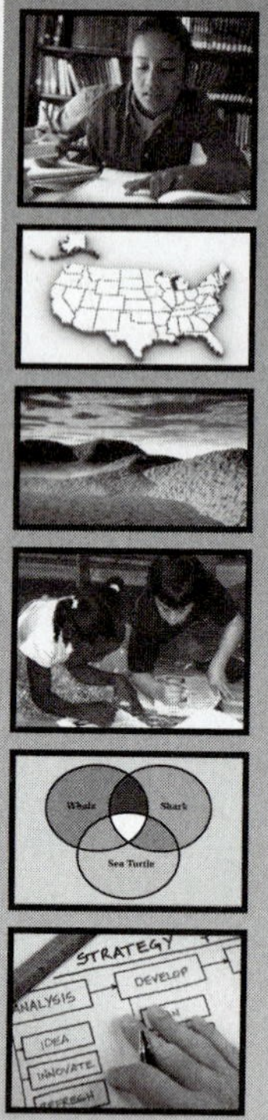

## Concrete Poems

Students can focus on stronger nouns, verbs, adjectives, and adverbs by depicting them visually in concrete poems. To engage students in writing a concrete poem that emphasizes stronger words, have students come up with a place, person, thing, or activity that they like. Students then brainstorm two to five strong nouns, verbs, adjectives, and adverbs that describe what they came up with. Next, students draw an outline of a shape or object that depicts the place, person, thing, or activity. Once they have the shape of the poem, students arrange the words they have written to fit the shape of the poem. For example, a student who chose fishing might make the shape of a fish with the words and phrases. A student who chose playing soccer might make the shape of a soccer ball. The concrete shape of the poem creates a visual picture while the strong nouns, verbs, adjectives, and adverbs create the poem. Here are the fishing and soccer examples from a third-grader and a fourth-grader after they brainstormed the words.

**Soccer**

passing
zigging
zagging
facing
kicking
racing
blocking
head
chest

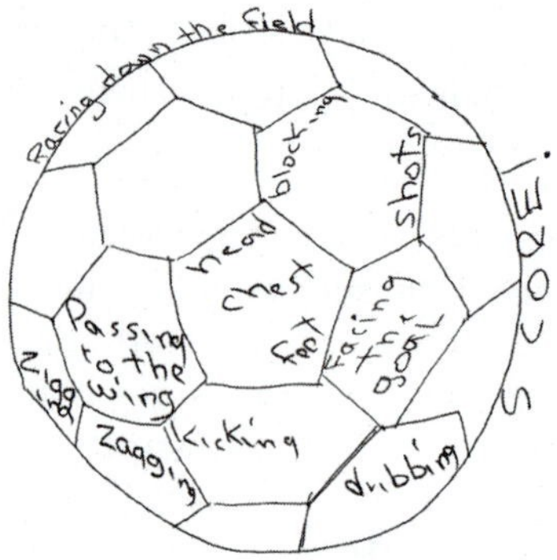


**Fishing**

bait
reeling
hooked
strike
slam
striped bass
swim
line
pulling

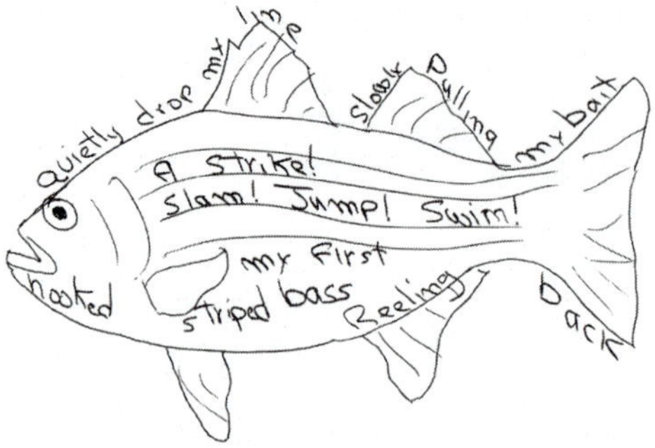


**Punctuation and Capitalization** If you can use literature to teach students about sentence structure and word usage, can you use it to teach punctuation and capitalization? Of course. If sentence structure and word usage are important for writing to convey meaning, so are punctuation and capitalization. Without proper punctuation and capitalization, you cannot tell when a sentence ends or another begins. It can be confusing for the reader. Look at the paragraph taken from Natalie Babbitt's *Tuck Everlasting* (1975).

## exploring diversity

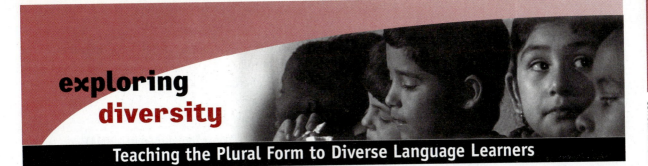

### Teaching the Plural Form to Diverse Language Learners

For students whose spoken dialect omits plural forms of nouns (such as *two car* or *three dog*), you can use *Goodnight Moon* by Margaret Wise Brown to teach students the plural form of regular nouns. In this story, a little bunny is getting ready for bed and says goodnight to many of the things in his room. Some of the things are single nouns (*room, moon, cow, mouse*) while others are plural nouns (*bears, chairs, clocks, socks, mittens, and kittens*). The pictures in the book also illustrate which nouns are singular and which are plural. Read the story out loud to students asking them which things are one and which things are more than one. After reading the story, write the nouns in two columns with one for single nouns and one for plural nouns. Have students say them and note that nouns that include an *s* at the end denote plural nouns. Then have students create their own good night or good morning stories using single and plural nouns. A group of third-graders wrote this story and called it *Good Morning, Mrs. Dawson* after their teacher.

> Good Morning, Mrs. Dawson.
> We get off the bus and walk to Mrs. Dawson's classroom. She waves at us, and we go inside. Good morning Mrs. Dawson. Good morning girls and boys. Good morning chalkboard and ceiling. Good morning door and floor. Good morning pencils and markers. Good morning lights and walls. Good morning desks and chairs. Good morning books and windows. Good morning chalk and paper. We are ready to go to work.

With younger students, you can have students dictate their own stories and check their single and plural nouns. It is just as important for students to hear the sounds of plural nouns as it is for them to see their written representation.

---

> ". . . it was a good supper flapjacks bacon bread and applesauce but they are sitting in the parlor instead of around a table Winnie had never had a meal that way before and she watched them carefully at first to see what rules there might be that she did not know about but there seemed to be no rules jesse sat on the floor and used the seat of a chair for a table but the others held their plates in their laps there were no napkins it was all right then to lick the maple syrup from your fingers winnie was never allowed to do such a thing at home but she had always thought it would be the easiest way and suddenly the meal seemed luxurious."

You find yourself reading slowly and sometimes rereading to construct the meaning of this text. To help students understand the value of punctuation and capitalization, take a passage such as this one from any example of children's literature and have students read it. Then have students insert punctuation and capitalization and read the passage again. Get students to discuss what made the first passage harder to read than the one they edited. Often, students will punctuate the passage in different ways, which leads to a difference in meaning. This reinforces the value of punctuation, when done by the writer, because the reader does not know what the writer wanted to write.

Can you use children's literature to teach or point out punctuation and capitalization?

Of course. Here are some children's books that highlight certain punctuation marks and capitalization:

> Capitalization and Periods: You can use just about any book to point out examples of capitalization and punctuation.
> Quotation Marks: *Sally Dog Little* (Richardson, 2003)
> Commas: *I Like Me!* (Carlson, 1990)
> Exclamation Points: *Meow!* (Arnold, 1998)
> Question Marks: *How Many Kisses Do You Want Tonight?* (Bajaj, 2004)

The same steps with punctuation and capitalization literature models should be used as the ones for word usage or sentence-composing literature models. For additional literature resources for teaching students about writing conventions, refer to the Exploring Children's Literature feature earlier in the chapter.

## How Can You Assess Writing Conventions?

Writing conventions can be assessed using the writing assessment techniques discussed in Chapter 5. Because some of the writing conventions are closely linked to the purpose and meaning of a piece of writing (such as word usage and sentence structure), formative assessment helps students during the writing process. Other conventions (such as punctuation and capitalization) can be part of the summative assessment of the writing. The content and organization of a finished writing piece should receive greater weight in its final assessment, and the writing conventions should receive less emphasis. When writing conventions significantly impede the meaning of a writing piece, it may be necessary to reassign assessment weights. A good example is the presence of enough sentence fragments so that the writing is difficult to follow and understand.

Students can learn to assess their own use of writing conventions by using editing checklists. Encourage your writers to use the checklists after their initial drafts have been completed and substantive revision has taken place. This helps to ensure that students do not agonize over punctuation or word usage until they have written down their ideas. It gives priority to writing content over writing correctness. An editing checklist can include the following questions:

1. Does each sentence have a subject and predicate?
2. Are there any sentence fragments?
3. Are there any run-on sentences?
4. Did you use the correct form of each word?
5. Does each sentence begin with a capital letter?
6. Does each sentence end with the correct punctuation mark?
7. Do you notice any comma errors?

These questions can vary according to the age and writing maturity of students. They can also come from the grammar principles identified by students during grammar workshops. For additional information about assessing writing conventions, see the Engaging in Assessment feature.

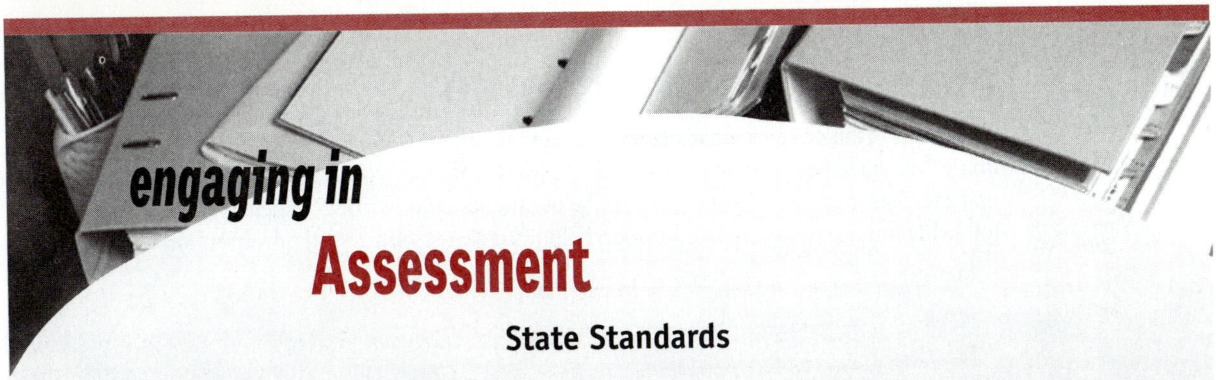

# engaging in Assessment

## State Standards

All states have language arts standards of learning, so the best way to determine the writing conventions that are assessed for a particular grade is to go directly to the state standards. In this example, typical standards for first and second grades are listed. The ones shown in italicized lines are the first and second grade standards for writing conventions.

### First Grade

Students must be able to communicate ideas in writing. To do this they must:

a. Formulate ideas.
b. Remain on topic.
c. Describe events, things, places, and people.
d. *Use complete sentences in final drafts.*
e. *Use capital letters in beginning sentences and end punctuation correctly in final drafts.*

### Second Grade

Students must edit writings for error-free grammar, spelling, capitalization, and punctuation. To do this they must:

*a. Write in complete sentences.*
*b. Capitalize proper nouns.*
*c. Correctly punctuate declarative, interrogative, and exclamatory sentences.*
*d. Correctly spell high-frequency sight words.*
*e. Use singular and plural nouns.*
*f. Use apostrophes in contractions.*

Notice the increase of writing convention standards from the first grade to the second grade. Statewide assessments of these writing conventions differ from state to state. However, teachers in all the elementary grades have to introduce and teach writing conventions beginning in the first grade. As you prepare to teach writing to students at your grade level, the attention you pay to state writing convention standards will help students prepare for the writing assessment required by your state.

## revisit the classroom challenge

After reading this chapter, what suggestions can you make to Mr. Johnson to help his students with noun-verb agreement problems? How can he use a grammar workshop? How can he use the grammar exercises in the workshop? How can he use the students' writing? Where would you use the following four verbs to help Mr. Johnson help his students with a writing convention challenge?

Identify________________________

Model________________________

Practice________________________

Apply________________________

## chapter review

In this chapter, we have presented the conventions of writing as necessary tools that writers and readers use in creating and understanding text. They all must work together toward this end. The structure of sentences relies on the parts of speech and their roles in sentences. Parts of speech need the correct word usage forms. Punctuation and capitalization help identify the important elements in every sentence. All of the conventions are important for student writers to master if they are to communicate effectively with their readers.

### What Are Writing Conventions for English?

Writing conventions include grammar, sentences, parts of speech, word usage, punctuation, and capitalization. They are important aids in writing to ensure that writers communicate clearly to their readers. Sentences have subjects and predicates. They can have different structures and functions. There are nine parts of speech: nouns, verbs, adjectives, adverbs, pronouns, prepositions, conjunctions, interjections, and articles. Word usage includes noun and verb forms, subjective-verb agreement, and negatives. Punctuation and capitalization signal sentence beginnings and endings, pauses in sentences, exclamations, and questions.

### What Do We Know about Teaching Writing Conventions?

Students learn writing conventions best when the conventions are linked directly to their own writing. Grammar workshops provide opportunities for making this link and for emphasizing the value of writing conventions for clear communication between writers and readers. Grammar toolboxes include sentence composing activities and cures for run-on sentences and sentence fragments. They also include strategies for incorporating stronger words, appropriate word usage, punctuation, and capitalization in student writing.

### How Can You Teach Writing Conventions?

By using grammar workshops and helping students create grammar toolboxes, students learn to use their own writing to help them master the writing conventions of sentence grammar, word usage, punctuation, and capitalization

### How Can You Assess Writing Conventions?

Use writing assessment techniques that include attention to correctness and content in the writing. Students can learn to use grammar and editing checklists with their own writing.

PEARSON myeducationlab™
Where the Classroom Comes to Life

Now go to www.myeducationlab.com to take a Pretest to assess your initial comprehension of chapter content, study chapter content with your individualized Study Plan, take a Posttest to assess your understanding of chapter content, practice your teaching skills with Building Teaching Skills exercises, and build a deeper, more applied understanding of chapter content with Homework and Exercises.

chapter 9

# Spelling Development

## classroomchallenge

**As a way to learn** about her students, first-year teacher Angela Franklin has her twenty-eight third-grade students introduce each other to the rest of the class. She pairs them up and gives them a series of questions they can use to learn about each other. These include: Who is in your family? Do you have pets? What is your favorite subject in school? What is your hardest subject? What do you do for fun? What's your favorite book? TV show? Students also ask their own questions to find out more about the student they will introduce. After twenty minutes, the room becomes quiet as students begin to write their introductions. Students write for about another twenty minutes.

The room becomes noisier again as student pairs share their introductions with each other. Students are encouraged to check with each other for accuracy and also to see if the student to be introduced wants anything changed. After students edit their work, they begin to introduce other students to the rest of the class. Ms. Franklin learns who likes to read; who has trouble with math; who has brothers and sisters; who has dogs, cats, turtles, and mice; and what her students like to watch on TV. When students have finished the introductions, Ms. Franklin collects the papers.

Later, that evening, she takes out the introductions and starts to read them. She notices early on that misspelled words abound in many of them. While she reminded the students that these were more like notes and not final papers, she is still surprised to see so many misspelled words. Some students have left out letters. Others had doubled letters that are not supposed to be doubled or had not doubled letters that should be doubled. Some students have similar misspellings while others have more unique misspellings. She spreads the papers out on a table. After a quick count, she finds forty-six pages with many spelling mistakes! "Where do I begin?" she asks herself.

## Questions for Reflection

1. What do you know about learning to spell?
2. What are common spelling errors? How should Ms. Franklin help her students identify these errors?
3. What spelling instruction would help Ms. Franklin's class?

## anticipating this chapter

To help you answer these and more questions about spelling and spelling instruction, this chapter is organized around the following questions:

Why is spelling important for reading and writing?
What do we know about English spelling?
What do we know about learning to spell?
What else do we know about spelling development?
How can we teach spelling?
How can we assess spelling?
How can we help English language learners learn to spell?
Why teach handwriting?

# Why Is Spelling Important for Reading and Writing?

IRA/NCTE 5

While spelling has always been thought to be important for writing, over the past thirty years research has also demonstrated that it is just as important for learning to read and to recognize words while reading. It is spelling that helps students recognize words and recall words that they have learned.

## For Reading

As children learn to read, they gradually come to understand that English is an alphabetic language in which letters represent sounds. One important prerequisite for this understanding is phonemic awareness, or the ability to identify, separate, and combine sounds in a spoken word. Phonemic awareness is not sufficient for learning to read, because reading requires making the connection between sounds and letters in written words. Spelling helps children make that connection. In fact, learning to spell actually sharpens phonemic awareness (Adams, 1990) and strengthens young readers' understanding of the alphabetic nature of the English language. The link between phonemic awareness and spelling also supports the understanding and use of phonics by young readers.

One of the characteristics of a successful reader is the ability to rapidly recognize words in text without having to decode or sound them out. An important key to this automatic word recognition is recognizing common spelling patterns in the words. Children use these spelling patterns to quickly match them to words already known as they read (Stahl, 2001). By using the spelling patterns in the words, readers avoid having to sound out or pronounce every letter or letter combination in each word. For example, knowing the word *house* can help a child recognize the word *mouse.* Recognizing that words can be spelled similarly and have identical rhymes also correlates highly with early reading and writing success (Gaswami, 2001).

Reading also supports spelling. As children become fluent readers and expand their reading experiences, they recognize more and more words with similar pronunciations, spellings, and meanings. These readers, in turn, use this growing knowledge about words to spell words in their writing and to recognize words in their reading. In fact, every time a teacher highlights any aspect of written words during reading instruction (such as word recognition, phonics, and comprehension), attention is drawn to the spelling of words. This attention may not always be explicit, but invariably it occurs. Perhaps, the attention should be more explicit during phonics, structural analysis, or context analysis instruction. For example, when teaching about comparatives (such as *faster, higher, slower,* or *lower*), wouldn't it be helpful for students to see that all the words end in *er*?

## For Writing

What first-grade teacher has not marveled at his or her young charges when they write up a storm with the help of invented spelling and spelling awareness? It is children's developing understanding of the role of spelling that supports their writing efforts (Richgels, 2001). This understanding coupled with children's realization that as writers they share the same language as their readers reinforces the link between reading and writing. The shared aspect of written language, in turn, leads to expanded writing and increased audiences for these young writers. Sharing writing also entails greater responsibility on the part of the writer. Readers can best read writing when the words are spelled correctly. Students have an obligation to strive for the correct spelling of words in their writing so that readers recognize these words and focus on the meaning rather than on the misspelled words.

There is another reason related to writing that explains why spelling is important. Judy Jones, a fifth-grade teacher, best expressed this reason to her students many years ago by comparing writing to a party. You get excited while you plan the party: Who will you invite? When will you have it? What kind of food and drinks will you have? What games will you play? Once the planning is complete and the special day arrives, your friends show up and you have a great party. Once the party is over, to make it complete, you have to clean up all the dishes, put away the food and games, and straighten up the room where the party took place. Judy equates checking spelling, grammar, and mechanics to these final steps after the party to impress on her students how important these steps are in producing a finished piece of writing. It's what writers do to recognize and honor their readers. Just as they wouldn't leave a messy house after a party, they wouldn't leave writing without cleaning it up for others to read.

You might ask the question, what about spell checkers? "If my students can all do word processing on a computer, won't the spell checkers correct their misspelled words?" At first glance, you might answer *yes* to this question. Before you do, take a look at this sentence written by a second-grader: *I left the hows to go to school in the morning.* The second-grader was not using a computer at the time he was writing. Had he been doing so and a squiggly red line appeared under *hows,* he would have seen that the word was misspelled. Upon hitting the spell check key, he would have been given the following possible words to choose from: *haws, hews, howls, how's, how, hoes, chows, hobs, hog,* and *hops.* Even if he eliminated *howls, chows, hobs, hog,* and *hops,* he is still left with five choices that don't even include the correct spelling. He would have to know more about the correct spelling of *house* to reject all these choices and try a different spelling for *house* in his writing. The point we are making is that children need to learn to spell and understand enough about English spelling in order to choose the correct spelling for a word that is caught by the spell checker.

Now that we have made the case for including spelling instruction in your language arts curriculum, we'll turn to a brief discussion of English spelling and what we know about it.

# What Do We Know about English Spelling?

Is English spelling a chaotic, confusing spelling system that lacks regularity or order? On the contrary, there is a great deal of consistency and regular patterns to be found in the English spelling system.

## Overview

The English spelling system has evolved over the past 1,500 years, and it continues to evolve. A myriad of languages have played a role in its development. These include French, German, Greek, and Latin—in its earlier years. In more modern times, we have seen the impact of other languages from other parts of the world including Japanese, Arabic, and Spanish to mention a few. One thing the English spelling system can say is that it never met a word from any language it didn't like. While some nations strive to restrict the invasion of words from other languages into their own (France, for example), the increase of words in American English over the past two hundred years proves that the United States has no such word restrictions. See the Exploring Diversity feature for an example of how using etymology can help students understand the multicultural influence that has shaped standard English. As Ed Henderson points out in his eloquent book, *Teaching Spelling* (1990):

> This may be one reason that English today is read as a first or second language by over half the literate population of the world. At all events history makes it clear that English is not a narrow, restricted language, but one that is rich in vocabulary and well suited to a diverse country such as ours. (p. 9)

Henderson also points out that to teach children how to spell, we need to know something about the English language. By learning more about the relationships between letters and sounds, spelling patterns, and meaning, teachers are better able to spark children's interest in words and in how they are spelled. Henderson also cautions us to accept English spelling as it exists today and not be swayed by arguments that some spelling reform will make it better or easier to learn. This is why we address three of the most important regular features of English spelling that you can teach to your students. See the Exploring Children's Literature feature for resources that model spelling strategies.

IRA/NCTE 5

## Spelling and Pronunciation Consistency

A common complaint about English spelling is that it "does not have a one-to-one correspondence between sounds and letters" (Fischer, 1993, p. 2). Years ago, however,

# exploring diversity

## Look for Etymology

To help students with different language backgrounds, have them look at the etymology, or origin, of words in the English language. Explain that etymology refers to the history of a word and that many words in English come from many other languages. Sometimes, the spelling of the words comes into English with little change but the word may be pronounced differently. Other times, the spelling may change but the pronunciation changes very little. For example, *tycoon* comes from the Japanese, *taikun,* meaning "mighty lord"; *barbecue* comes from the Spanish, *barbacoa*, meaning "a framework of sticks used to smoke, dry, or cook meat"; and *alligator* comes from the Spanish, *el lagarto,* meaning "lizard." This same etymological journey can also occur when students volunteer to identify and describe foods from different countries that are now found commonly in the United States. For example, *tacos, nachos,* and *frittatas* come from Mexico. These and similar etymology activities broaden students' understanding of the multicultural influence on English words, and they also honor and validate the importance of other cultures and languages. This is especially important for English language learners, so they can recognize the value and influence of their first languages.

# exploring Children's Literature

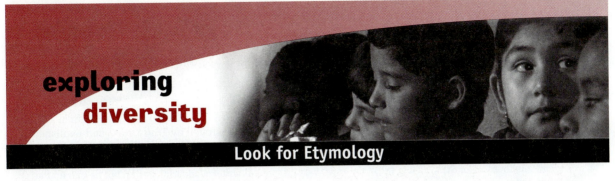

## Books to Model Spelling Strategies

### Grades K to 3

*Abby Cadabra, Super Speller*—Written by Joan Holub and published by Grosset and Dunlap (2000).
Abby is the best speller in the class until a new witch shows up at school and the two of them compete in a spelling bee to see who will win a new broomstick.

*Alphabet Soup*—Written by Kate Banks, illustrated by Peter Sis, and published by Random House (1989).
A boy's ability to spell words with his alphabet soup comes in handy during the magical journey he takes in his mind with a friendly bear.

*The American Heritage Picture Dictionary*—Published by Houghton Mifflin (2006).
In this dictionary for students in preschool and early elementary grades, each word is defined by a sentence using the word to describe the object or activity portrayed in the accompanying illustration.

*Andy (That's My Name)*—Written and illustrated by Tomie dePaola and published by Prentice Hall (1973).
Andy's friends construct different words from his name: *an* words, *and* words, and *andy* words.

*(Continued)*

## exploring Children's Literature

*Antics!*—Written and illustrated by Cathi Hepworth and published by Putnam (1992).

Alphabetical entries from A to Z all have an "ant" somewhere in the word: There's E for Enchanter, P for Pantaloons, S for Santa Claus, and Y for Your Ant Yetta.

*Bug Off!: A Swarm of Insect Words*—Written and illustrated by Cathi Hepworth and published by Putnam (1999).

This book presents vocabulary words relating to insects, including bees, moths, and ants, that are found in other words such as *moth* in *smothered*.

*Sparkle and Spin: A Book about Words*—Written and illustrated by Ann Rand and Paul Rand, published by Chronicle (2006).

Lyrical text explores what words are and how they are used, highlighting such characteristics as the fact that some words are spoken softly, some are shouted, some sound like their meaning, and some evoke certain feelings.

*There's an Ant in Anthony*—Written and illustrated by Bernard Most, published by Morrow (1980).

After discovering an *ant* in his own name, Anthony searches for the word *ant* in other words.

*Word Wizard*—Written and illustrated by Cathryn Falwell, published by Houghton Mifflin (1999).

Using her magical spoon to make new words by changing letters around, Anna embarks on a series of adventures with a lost little boy.

### Grades 4 to 8

*Arthur's Teacher Trouble*—Written and illustrated by Marc Brown and published by Atlantic Monthly Press (1986).

Third-grader Arthur is amazed when he is chosen to be in the school spell-a-thon.

*In Trouble with Teacher*—Written by Patricia Demuth, illustrated by True Kelley, and published by Dutton (1995).

Third-grader Montgomery draws great pictures and writes wonderful stories, but he's afraid that his teacher only cares about his terrible spelling.

*Miss Alaineus: A Vocabulary Disaster*—Written and illustrated by Debra Frasier and published by Harcourt (2000).

When Sage's spelling and definition of a word reveal to her classmates her misunderstanding of it, she is at first embarrassed. But then, she uses her mistake as inspiration for the vocabulary parade.

*Mom and Dad Are Palindromes*—Written by Mark Shulman, illustrated by Adam McCauley, and published by Chronicle (2006).

When Bob realizes that he is surrounded by palindromes—from his mom, dad, and sis Anna to his dog Otto—he discovers a way to deal with the palindrome puzzle.

*Phoebe and the Spelling Bee*—Written and illustrated by Barney Saltzberg and published by Hyperion (1997).

While participating in her class spelling bee, Phoebe uses her wonderful imagination to remember tough word spellings.

*Scholastic Dictionary of Spelling*—by Marvin Terban (2006).

Sections include "The Four Longest Words in the English Language" and "The Spelling Words That Made Kids Champions." The introduction gives instructions for looking up a word the reader does not necessarily know how to spell, offers more than 150 memory tricks to correct commonly misspelled words, and clearly explains general spelling rules.

Hanna, Hanna, Hodges, and Rudorf (1966) analyzed the spellings of the 17,000 most commonly used words in English and found that a surprisingly large number of those words did have consistent letter-sound spelling patterns. In fact, when they looked more closely at the syllables in these words, they discovered an even greater percentage of letter-sound spelling consistency. The words listed in Table 9.1 are examples of English words that have a consistent letter-sound pattern or regular phoneme-grapheme correspondences.

**Table 9.1**
**Common Spelling and Letter-Sound Patterns**

| | | | | |
|---|---|---|---|---|
| sat | boat | matter | stack | rent |
| hat | float | patter | stick | splash |
| mat | goat | flatter | stock | jump |
| pat | coat | shatter | stuck | chance |

If you look at the first column of words, each word has a different beginning letter or onset, but all words have the identical rime—*at*. The second column contains words with the identical rime *–oat,* which is pronounced the same way. The same holds true for the third list of words. The rime is identical and represented by the same group of letters in each word. The fourth column may appear somewhat different from the first two because the vowel letters are different in each word. If we look closer, however, the words all have that same sound-letter spelling pattern. Each word contains a short vowel sound followed by *ck*. The words, therefore, do have a regular letter-sound pattern if we focus on the type of vowel sound that precedes the *ck*.

The last column of words poses the greatest challenge to letter-sound consistency. Two begin with a single consonant /r/, /j/; one begins with a consonant digraph /ch/ and one with a consonant blend (*spl*). They all end differently as well (*nt, sh, mp, nce*). Each has a vowel letter that represents a short vowel sound, and this feature helps identify the regular letter-sound pattern revealed in their spelling. All four words have the same spelling pattern found in the third and fourth column of words: The short vowel sound is followed by two consonants. We find this pattern in even greater numbers of words than those in the first four columns because words that contain this pattern are not limited to words with the same ending letters like *stack—stick* or *matter—patter.*

## Spelling and Structural Consistency

To see if letter-sound consistency can be found in other types of words, look at Table 9.2. The first column has words with inflected endings that represent the past tense form of a verb. These words have a letter-sound pattern that is determined by the last sound of the root word. If you say *miss, pack, slip,* and *wash,* you will find that all the words end in a voiceless sound—a sound produced by not vibrating the vocal cords. So as not to get too technical or linguistic, put two fingers on your throat and say each word. You will notice that as you pronounce the last sound of each word, your vocal cords are silent. Now put

**Table 9.2**
**Spelling and Structural Patterns**

| | | | |
|---|---|---|---|
| missed | paved | hated | matches |
| packed | scrubbed | landed | wishes |
| slipped | rolled | waited | passes |
| washed | showed | needed | fences |

the *ed* ending back, and do the finger test as you say the words. You should see that the endings are also voiceless. If you follow the same procedure with the second list, you will find that the root words end in a voiced sound, as do the words when the ending is added.

Young children discover this regular sound feature in their spoken language long before they come to school. Berko (1958) discovered that preschoolers could produce the correct past tense form of nonsense words when given the present tense form. For example, if a present tense verb ended in a voiceless sound, a child would say the past tense verb form with a /t/ sound at the end. She found similar correct matches for plural forms and comparatives. Later, Beers and Beers (1991) found a similar pattern with first-graders when they spelled words with these endings. For example, when asked to spell the past tense of the nonsense word *tike,* first-graders ending the word with a *t,* given the same task for *rin,* they ended it with a *d.* What is important to realize is that there is a regular sound-spelling pattern in both columns and children recognize it.

The last two columns also contain a consistent sound-spelling pattern that might not be readily apparent. Both sets of words have a sound feature different from the first two. In the third column, the past tense /ed/ ending becomes an additional syllable as it is pronounced. The same is true for the plural forms seen in the last column. Why do these words require an additional syllable to represent their respective forms? To answer that question, we return to features of our spoken language as we did with the first two lists of words. If you pronounce the present tense forms of *hate, land, wait,* and *need,* you will find that they end in a /t/ sound or a /d/ sound. Remember the voiced and voiceless feature in past tense verb forms? If you simply add a /t/ or /d/ sound to their respective voiced or voiceless sound partners, you would be unable to distinguish between the present and past tense form of the verb. Take *hate.* Put a /t/ sound at the end. There is no sound difference between the present or past tense forms. Do the same with *land* but add a /d/ sound instead. Notice that there is again no difference. Do the same thing with the plural forms. You either can't distinguish the singular from the plural form, or it is difficult to pronounce the plural forms. Try to say *passs* or *matchs.* Once again, we have encountered a regular sound feature in the spoken form of words that has a regular sound-spelling pattern when we look at their written forms. Words such as *matches, wishes,* and *passes* will always have the plural form spelled with an *es* ending. Do you still believe English spelling needs more consistency?

## Spelling and Structural Change Patterns

Let's turn to Table 9.3. These words have one thing in common. When you add an ending to the root word, the root word changes: the silent *e* drops, the final consonant

**Table 9.3**
**Spelling and Structural Changes Patterns**

| | | | |
|---|---|---|---|
| bite | biting | hop | hopping |
| hope | hoping | run | running |
| wade | wading | quit | quitting |
| bat | batting | berry | berries |
| slide | sliding | city | cities |

doubles, or the *y* changes to *i* and *es* is added. Another confusing irregular spelling pattern? Not really. Even when there are root changes in words, the changes themselves are consistent and they reveal yet another consistency in English spelling. All of the long vowel words (*bite, hope,* and *wade*) followed the identical spelling pattern. The silent *e* is dropped when *ing* is added. All of the short vowel root words have the final consonant doubled when the ending is added. Look at *city* and *berry.* The *y* is changed to *i* when the *es* is added. It isn't important to discuss the reasons for these changes but rather the consistent spelling in these changes. Even when the root word changes, the changes demonstrate once again a regular letter-sound spelling.

## Spelling and Meaning Consistency

Now let's look at another English spelling consistency in Table 9.4. This last table reveals a consistent feature in English spelling that might be overlooked if you relied solely on the pronunciation of a word. When you look at the first three words (*define, definition,* and *definitive*), you will notice three things: (1) they are variations of the same root word (*define*), (2) they have different pronunciations, but (3) they contain much of the identical spelling found in the root word. You can find these same features in the three other related sets of words (*accuse, know,* and *sign*). What is the spelling consistency found in all three sets of words? Even when the pronunciation and structure of related words vary, the key meaning element in each word is spelled consistently. This spelling consistency is not only important for writing but also for reading. Knowing the word *define,* for example, can help you figure out the meaning for *definition* when reading. It can also help you spell *definition* when writing.

### Table 9.4
### Spelling with Sound and Structural Changes

| | |
|---|---|
| define | know |
| definition | knowledge |
| definitive | acknowledge |
| accuse | sign |
| accusatory | signal |
| accusation | signature |

To summarize, consistency in English spelling is found in thousands of words when we look at three general principles.

1. There are sound spelling patterns in words.
2. There are structural spelling patterns even with changes in words.
3. There are meaning spelling patterns even with sound and structural changes.

What is especially interesting about these underlying principles that control much of English spelling is that children from a very young age gradually learn them and apply them in their own spelling.

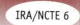

# What Do We Know about Learning to Spell?

IRA/NCTE 6

We know that learning to spell:

- Occurs over time
- Is developmental
- Reflects children's knowledge of words
- Occurs in stages

We also know that children gradually come to understand how pronunciation, structure, and meaning are related to the spelling of a word, and this understanding seems to occur in stages (Read, 1975; Beers and Henderson, 1977; Gentry, 1987; Beers and Beers, 2001). The evidence for spelling stages is best seen in children's spelling efforts in their writing as they progress through the school years. We agree, however, with Laminack and Wood (1996) that children do not progress through these stages in a lock-step manner. Children bring to any stage what they have come to understand about English spelling and may drop back to an earlier stage spelling strategy when faced with particularly challenging words.

## Prephonetic Spelling Stage

Long before children enter school, they provide us with examples of this early spelling stage. Children move from drawing to using letters as a means to express their ideas on paper. The stage is called *prephonetic* because the letters used bear no relationship to the sounds they represent. Children may also use the same letter or letters over and over again to represent different words in their "writing." How do we know this? Just ask a three- or four-year-old to tell you what they wrote, and it becomes very evident (Beers and Beers, 1991). By being read to and learning about alphabet letters, however, these very young "writers" already demonstrate their understanding that letters are used in writing. Sometimes, they will use letters in a particular way that shows the connection between groups of letters and meaning. In Table 9.5, you can see a long series of Fs and three short series of Fs. When asked what they were, the four-year-old said the long series was the mother cat and the short series was her kittens. This is an early spelling-meaning connection at the prephonetic stage.

### Table 9.5 Student Examples of Prephonetic Spelling

| | |
|---|---|
| AABBTTT (Random letters) | PTGOS (airplane) HHHOA (fireworks) |
| eEDD (stars) | XXFF (I like to go on the bus) |
| FFFF (kitten) | FFFFFFFFF (cat) |
| ghgh (puppy) | GHGHGHGH (dog) |

## Early Phonetic Spelling Stage

As four- and five-year-olds learn more about letters and sounds in words, they start to focus in on the beginnings of words and spell them phonetically by selecting letters that represent the beginning sound. They progress from using a beginning consonant letter, to a consonant with other unrelated letters, to the beginning and ending consonant letters. See Table 9.6 for examples of early phonetic spelling. Near the end of this stage, children make attempts at spelling vowel sounds in the middle of words (see Table 9.6). This stage represents the children's early understanding of the alphabetic nature of their language—that letters do represent the sounds in words. It also reveals their early phonemic awareness or the ability to segment or separate words into letter-sound units. Teachers and parents look at children's writing at this stage and see words spelled more and more like real words.

**Table 9.6**
**Examples of Early Phonetic Spelling**

| | | | | |
|---|---|---|---|---|
| F (four) | CR (car) | KT (cat) | DG (dog) | HS (house) |
| RIS (rides) | N (in) | BKS (because) | SPSHL (special) | HM (home) |
| FxxL (fell) | WL (will) | BK (book) | BSB (baseball) | KHN (keychain) |

## Phonetic Spelling Stage

As children move from the early phonetic to the phonetic spelling stage, they begin to spell everything phonetically. Not only are beginning and ending sounds represented phonetically but so are vowel sound in words. A characteristic of the vowel spelling is letter-name spelling. This is most prevalent with words with short *e* and short *i*. The letter A appears routinely for short *e* (BAD for *bed*), and the letter E appears for short *i* (STEK for *stick*). If you slightly exaggerate the short *e* sound in bed, you can hear the name of the letter A. For the short *i* sound in *stick*, you hear the letter name *e*. Children may also use a letter-name strategy for certain consonants such as *y* for *w* (YKIN for *walking*). Children at this stage ignore silent letters, especially silent *e*, when they spell. They also use phonetic spelling for one word to spell another. An example of this is CHEP for *trip*. Hear the /ch/ in the beginning of *trip*. Inflected endings are spelled phonetically (KIKT for *kicked* and SKARD for *scared*). See Table 9.7 for examples of these and other spellings at this stage.

What is impressive about this stage (usually acquired by the middle to the end of first grade) is that children demonstrate with their writing complete phonemic awareness. Remember that Adams (1990) and others recognized the value of spelling development as a means to support and strengthen phonemic awareness. The proof can now be

**BUILDING TEACHING SKILLS:**

**Artifact Exercise**

*We Clied*

Go to the Building Teaching Skills section of Chapter 9 of MyEducationLab and examine the artifact, "We Clied," which is a writing sample of a child with limited alphabetic word fluency. Complete the activities that follow, and save your work or transmit it to your professor as assigned.

**Table 9.7**
**Examples of Common Phonetic Spelling**

| | | | |
|---|---|---|---|
| GAT (get) | JUPT (jumped) | RID (ride) | KEP (keep) |
| HET (hit) | GAET (gate) | SKARD (scared) | WAN (when) |
| STOPT (stopped) | YAWK (walk) | GAMZ (games) | CHRE (tree) |

seen in the spellings made by children in this stage. The relationship between oral language and spelling becomes clear when the spellings of dialect speakers are analyzed.

## Structural Spelling Stage

In this stage, children go beyond pronunciation in their spelling and they focus on the structural elements in words that include the roots and endings. Also referred to as the *transitional* spelling stage (Beers and Henderson, 1977), *within word* spelling stage (Templeton, 1992), and the *syllable juncture* spelling stage (Cramer, 1998), the structural spelling stage presents several important spelling challenges for children:

- What are common short and long vowel spelling patterns?
- What are other common vowel spelling patterns?
- How do these spelling patterns affect the spelling of structural elements in words?

Children build upon their sound spelling knowledge of single syllable words by turning to two or more syllable words. They recognize common spelling patterns for short vowels and gradually learn the variety of patterns for long vowel words. Letter-name spelling is replaced by these spelling patterns. They look at how the syllables are joined (*lit* + *tle* = *little* but *ti* + *tle* = *title*). They add inflected endings to words and discover different patterns (*help* + *ing* = *helping* but *hop* + *ing* = *hopping* and *hope* + *ing* = *hoping*). They find similar challenges with comparative adjectives and adverbs (faster—no change, easier—change) as well as plurals (socks—no change, glasses and bunnies—change).

As children mature as writers, they use more elaborate language and vocabulary with more than one syllable. They write about experiences in the present as well as the past. This, in turn, leads to deciding whether to drop a letter, double another, or change a third (*run* + *ing* = *running, stop* + *ed* = *stopped,* and *try* + *ed* = *tried*). With exposure to these patterns, children realize that it's the sound of the vowel that helps answer the question: Do I add, subtract, or change the letter when adding an ending?

Students in these middle elementary grades are also beginning to apply the meanings of words onto their spellings. Homophones and compound words are common examples of how this meaning orientation leads to misspellings (*there* for *their, every one* for *everyone*). Table 9.8 contains examples of many of the structural spelling stage errors.

### Table 9.8
### Examples of Common Structured Spelling

| | | |
|---|---|---|
| runing (running) | hideing (hiding) | barryes (berries) |
| stickking (sticking) | strieke (strike) | raceve (receive) |
| lidle (little) | savved (saved) | our (hour) |
| riden (ridden) | sudenly (suddenly) | up on (upon) |

## Meaning/Derivational Spelling Stage

Students generally move through this final spelling stage as they finish elementary school and move into middle school. The nature of their reading and writing at this stage reflects the words they encounter in their content area subjects, including social studies, science, mathematics, and English. The vocabulary found in these subjects has two important things in common. Many of the words have their origins in Latin, Greek, and other languages, such as *telephone, television,* and *telepathy.* Words have alternate forms with different pronunciations but similar spelling, such as *define—definition, explore—exploration, ignite—ignition,* and *nation—nationality*). Spelling errors are still present at this stage but reflect the level of vocabulary used by students (Templeton, 1992). They have mastered most common spelling patterns, especially with words whose spelling changes but whose pronunciation does not. They now focus on the connection between words that also have pronunciation changes. For example, recognizing that *define* is related to *definition* helps reveal the correct spelling for the schwa sound of the first /i/. If students have been taught to only learn to spell by memorizing correct spelling, they may be diverted from looking for these important connections in meaning that provide keys to spelling correctly.

This brings us to another important feature in English spelling related to alternate forms of words. Everyone has trouble with schwa vowel sounds or the unaccented vowels in words. Often, however, the pesky schwa sound cries out its name when you turn to one or more of its alternate forms. Take *compose—composition* or *nation—national.* The schwa sound of the second syllable in *composition* becomes the letter-name /o/ in *compose,* and the schwa sound in *national* becomes the letter name /a/ in *nation.* This works with hundreds of words derived from Greek and Latin and is another important piece of information about English for these older students. Examples of spelling errors found at this stage can be seen in Table 9.9.

**Table 9.9**

**Examples of Meaning Derivational Spelling**

| | | |
|---|---|---|
| nashunal (national) | signiture (signature) | dafinition (definition) |
| financal (financial) | desperite (desperate) | admeration (admiration) |

## Spelling Stage Summary

As we examined these spelling stages, we hope you saw that they also reflected children's growing understanding of English spelling. Table 9.10 compares the English spelling consistencies with children's spelling stages. You can see that children begin by mastering the alphabetic principle reflected in letter-sound patterns as they go from early phonetic to phonetic spelling. Then, they turn to structural spelling consistency by exploring spelling patterns within words and between syllables. Finally, they expand their understanding of English spelling when they recognize the power of meaning on the spelling of words. All along the way, they build upon the basic foundation of their own language: sound, structure, and meaning. Their own language power supports their growing understanding of English spelling just as it does as they learn to read and write.

**Table 9.10**

**Spelling Principles and Spelling Stages**

| | |
|---|---|
| Letter-Sound Spelling Principle | Prephonetic Spelling Stage<br>Early Phonetic Spelling Stage<br>Phonetic Spelling Stage |
| Structural Spelling Principle | Structural Spelling Stage |
| Meaning/Derivational Spelling Principle | Meaning/Derivational Spelling Stage |

# What Else Do We Know about Spelling Development?

In addition to the stages of spelling development, there are several other things that we have learned about what students do as they progress through these stages.

**Children Vary in Spelling Development Rate** As with other aspects of language development, we know that children progress through stages of spelling development at different rates. The two examples of first-graders' writing in Figure 9.1 can help to confirm this. One first-grader wrote "Being Skard" in November and another first-grader wrote "Lost" in March. The spelling of both students reflects the early phonetic spelling stage. Many of the consonants are being spelled phonetically with some attempt to represent vowels. Now look at the third example, which was also written in March. This example written by the November first-grader has clearly moved into the phonetic spelling stage. Is one student more advanced and the other behind? No. They are simply developing their understanding about English spelling at different rates as they did learning to talk or walk.

**Figure 9.1**

## Different Spelling Development Rates

**November 19**
Being Skard

Wn I gow to school frs tm I waz skard
When I go to school first time I was scared
Wn my sadrz coz ta dr I m skard!
When my sister close the door I am scared!

**March 17**
Lost

I fat cod in the wuz.
I felt cold in the woods
It wuz cod and dn it gt codr.
It was cold and then it got colder
I wz frttnd Bacz av the owd
I was frightened because of the owl
n the chrty.
In the tree.

**March 24**
The Pegwin
The Penguin

His Nim Waz Brrt But he wuz owz gidt in to tubol.
His Name Was Burt But he was always getting into trouble
Evrre Theg he did Evrre Bode Got Mad.
Every Thing he did Everybody got mad
So he srrtid to yawk a way an tal he hurrt hes mom kol hem.
So he started to walk away until he heard his mom call him

**Teaching Strategy Homework Exercise**

*Jeopardy Game*

Go to the Homework and Exercises section in Chapter 9 of MyEducationLab and read about the "Jeopardy Game," which describes a spelling strategy for words that follow a particular pattern. Complete the activities that follow, and save your work or transmit it to your professor as assigned.

**Children Use Known Words to Spell Other Words** Children also use information about words they have learned to help them spell other words. For example, a child who writes *rooler* for *ruler* when asked why, replies it reminds her of school. Another child when asked why he wrote the word *tree* as *chree* said it begins like his name Charles. This transferring of information from a known to an unknown word is especially apparent during the structural spelling stage as students deal with the variety of long vowel spellings. For example, a student who knows how to spell *eat* spells *greedy* as *greaty,* and another student who knows how to spell *ate* spells *wait* as *wate.*

**Importance of Frequent Writing** The expression "use it or lose it" can be applied to children's spelling. One of the ways to reinforce and make the correct spelling of a word automatic is for students to use words they are learning in frequent writing experiences. These writing experiences connect the meaning and function of the word, such as an adverb, verb, and the like, to the spelling of the word. As we have already seen, these are important connections to continually reinforce for students as they become writers and readers. Think of a time when you wanted to use a word in your writing and hadn't seen or written it for some time. How many *n*'s appear in the word that we frequently refer as MAYO? There are two—*mayonnaise.* Simply writing words in spelling exercises or on weekly spelling tests is not enough to reinforce the spelling of this and other words. Students need to write to reinforce the correct spelling of familiar words and to explore the spelling of less familiar words.

**Lesson Plan Homework Exercise**

*Collecting Individual Dictations and Group Experience*

Go the Homework and Exercises section in Chapter 9 of MyEducationLab and read the lesson, "Collecting Individual Dictations and Group Experience," which describes a way to model spelling during student dictations and LEA. Complete the activities that follow, and save your work or transmit it to your professor as assigned.

# How Can We Teach Spelling?

We will look at several approaches to teaching spelling that can be used separately or in concert with one another: a *spelling program approach* and *individualized spelling instruction.* A third approach that focuses on *developmental spelling* can be used with either approach.

## A Spelling Program Approach

As with most commercial instructional programs, spelling programs are organized around a five-day cycle. Each week, a spelling principle or lesson is introduced with a list of words. Several days are devoted to word study and writing activities with the words to reinforce the principle or purpose for the lesson. Adding *ed* and *ing* to verb forms is one example of a lesson. Near the end of the week, students may edit a piece of writing to correct misspelled words from the lesson. At the end of the week, students take a spelling test to see whether they have learned the words for the week. After a set number of weekly lessons, students take a week to review the words for the unit and take a unit test. This cycle is repeated approximately six times to provide spelling instruction throughout the school year. Figure 9.2 provides sample pages of the first two pages of a weekly spelling lesson from a spelling program.

While many spelling programs look alike, there are important differences. How can you determine if a spelling program has the most important features to help students in

**Figure 9.2**

## First Two Pages of a Weekly Spelling Lesson

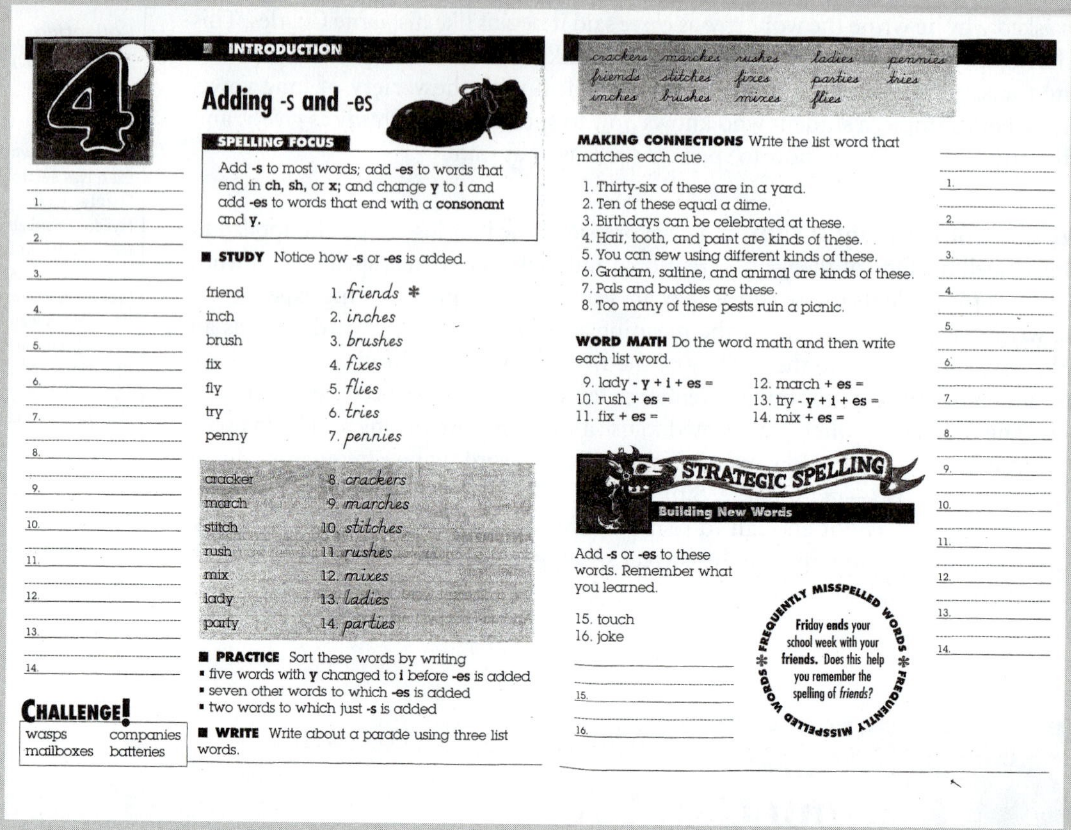
4

INTRODUCTION

**Adding -s and -es**

**SPELLING FOCUS**

Add **-s** to most words; add **-es** to words that end in **ch, sh,** or **x;** and change **y** to **i** and add **-es** to words that end with a **consonant** and **y**.

**STUDY** Notice how **-s** or **-es** is added.

| | |
|---|---|
| friend | 1. *friends* * |
| inch | 2. *inches* |
| brush | 3. *brushes* |
| fix | 4. *fixes* |
| fly | 5. *flies* |
| try | 6. *tries* |
| penny | 7. *pennies* |
| cracker | 8. *crackers* |
| march | 9. *marches* |
| stitch | 10. *stitches* |
| rush | 11. *rushes* |
| mix | 12. *mixes* |
| lady | 13. *ladies* |
| party | 14. *parties* |

**PRACTICE** Sort these words by writing
- five words with **y** changed to **i** before **-es** is added
- seven other words to which **-es** is added
- two words to which just **-s** is added

**WRITE** Write about a parade using three list words.

**CHALLENGE!**
wasps companies
mailboxes batteries

*crackers marches rushes ladies pennies friends stitches fixes parties tries inches brushes mixes flies*

**MAKING CONNECTIONS** Write the list word that matches each clue.

1. Thirty-six of these are in a yard.
2. Ten of these equal a dime.
3. Birthdays can be celebrated at these.
4. Hair, tooth, and paint are kinds of these.
5. You can sew using different kinds of these.
6. Graham, saltine, and animal are kinds of these.
7. Pals and buddies are these.
8. Too many of these pests ruin a picnic.

**WORD MATH** Do the word math and then write each list word.

9. lady - **y** + **i** + **es** =
10. rush + **es** =
11. fix + **es** =
12. march + **es** =
13. try - **y** + **i** + **es** =
14. mix + **es** =

**STRATEGIC SPELLING**
**Building New Words**

Add **-s** or **-es** to these words. Remember what you learned.

15. touch
16. joke

FREQUENTLY MISSPELLED WORDS
Friday ends your school week with your **friends.** Does this help you remember the spelling of *friends?*

*Source:* Taken from Beers, Cramer, & Hammond (2008). *Everyday Spelling.* Glenview, IL: Scott Foresman. Used by permission.

learning to spell? Table 9.11 has a set of instructional criteria to consider when examining spelling programs.

As with even the best instructional material, it may be necessary to modify the order of lessons or number of words that students can comfortably handle each week. Your students can give you the best source of information on their spelling developmental issues and types of modification needed.

## An Individualized Spelling Instruction Approach

Individualized spelling instruction or personal spelling instruction places greater demands on the teacher than traditional spelling programs do. Some of the demands include knowledge of spelling development, individualized spelling word lists, instructional activities, and assessment techniques.

While these challenges may require greater preparation for spelling instruction, the approach has several advantages over commercial spelling programs. Word lists and instructional strategies can be tailored to meet the needs of individual children. Students take more interest in learning about words they use in their own writing or

## Table 9.11
## Criteria for Evaluating Spelling Programs

1. Has a research base for word selection.
2. Words and lessons reflect developmental spelling stages.
3. Introduces and recycles words through the grades: Widely misspelled words.
4. Includes words widely used by students in their own writing.
5. Includes key spelling principles at appropriate grades.
   - Sound patterns
   - Structural patterns
   - Meaning patterns
6. Students work with words.
   - Onset and rime activities
   - Building words
   - Words by analogy
   - Word ladders
   - Word walls
7. Regular writing and editing activities each week.
8. Spelling assessment features
   - Pretests
   - Final test
   - Review tests
   - Placement tests

encounter in their reading. In selecting spelling words, students' writing is an ideal source with which to begin. While some words will differ from student to student, many words will be similar across students.

With a developmental spelling perspective, teachers can determine which words to select, how many, and what features to address with instruction. For example, if the misspelled words in the first column of Table 9.12 were taken from the writings of first-graders, instruction could focus on contrasting short and long vowel spelling patterns. The second graders' words in the second column would suggest that some instruction be conducted with contrasting words that change or not with endings.

## Table 9.12
## First and Second Graders' Misspellings

| First Grade | Second Grade |
|---|---|
| HAT (hate) | SITING (sitting) |
| STOPE (stop) | RESTTING (resting) |
| MACK (make) | STOPING (stopping) |
| STIKE (stick) | STIKKING (sticking) |
| GAT (get) | LICKING (liking) |

Spelling stage-appropriate instructional activities described earlier can be used once a stage analysis of students' misspellings has been done.

**Spelling Patterns** In an individualized approach, students should have opportunities to learn about patterns in words. There are a number of instructional strategies for doing this.

The Making Words (Cunningham, 1992) activity can be used to reinforce a spelling feature or pattern. For example, take the word *stick.* It could be used to strengthen a student's recognition of the short *i* vowel spelling pattern. Take the letters in *stick* and mix them up like this: *ickts.* Have students write words that have a short *i* sound that use these letters. When they come up with this list of words (*is, it, kit, sit, sick, tick, stick*), they can see short vowel spelling patterns in these words. Another example is with the short spelling pattern found in the word *batch. Abcht* leads to *bat, cat, hat, chat, cab, bath, batch.*

Making words helps in highlighting key spelling patterns found in many words. To successfully "make the words," students must actively look for spelling patterns in the words.

The Words-by-Analogy activity (Gaskins, Ehri, Cress, O'Hara, and Donnelly, 1997) also supports children's learning and recognizing common spelling patterns. Take the two words *speak* and *rain.* If you recognize these words, you can use them to recognize and spell the word *sprain.* If a teacher has the two key words written side-by-side, students can look and say the *sp* in *speak* and then the word *rain.* Underline the *sp* and all of *rain* to show what parts of the words to put together to say and spell *sprain.*

speak          rain
sp + rain = sprain

A second example can be seen with *saw* and *more.*

saw          more
s + ore = sore

As with the Making Words activity, the Words-by-Analogy activity reinforces key spelling patterns that are found in English words. Not only is this helpful for spelling, but it is also helpful for recognizing unfamiliar words in reading.

**Word Ladders** Word ladders are also helpful for reinforcing spelling patterns. Clues or synonyms can be included to help students build the ladder. You can also simply show the first and last word on the ladder to see if students can build the ladder like the one in Table 9.13. The key to building the ladder is to look for patterns that vary only by one letter as students go up or down the ladder. For example, *in* could be followed by *ink* but not *pink. Ink* could be followed by *pink* and then *rink.* Take a look at the word ladder found in Table 9.13. Variations of word ladders can include the words that have been used in Making Words activities. The end result of students' constructing word ladders is that they will become very familiar with the spelling patterns found in the ladders. This is especially important as students move beyond phonetic spelling and begin to focus on spelling patterns within and across words.

**Word Walls** Another way to help students with spelling patterns in an individualized spelling approach is to arrange words they are using as word walls. This means writing the words on large cards and creating a special section of the classroom wall for the Word Wall. The words included on the wall can be words students are using in their writing and words they use in their reading. The word wall can help them see similarities and differences among these words by the way they are arranged. For example, stu-

## Table 9.13
## Examples of Word Ladders

| | |
|---|---|
| i n | not out (in) |
| _ _ _ | in a pen (ink) |
| _ _ _ _ | a color (pink) |
| _ _ _ _ | where you skate (rink) |
| d r i n k | when you are thirsty (drink) |

dents confused by beginning consonants and consonant blends can have a word wall with examples of each spelling. Students having difficulty with words that change when endings are added can have a word wall with examples of these spellings. The key is to change the word walls as students move to different elements in their spelling.

IRA/NCTE 3

**Word Sorts** Students need to explore the similarities and differences among words across categories of pronunciation, structure, and meaning (Bear, Invernizzi, Templeton, and Johnston, 2004). An effective way to do this is with word sorts. The general format for word sorting activities is outlined below:

1. Gather a collection of words a child knows that conform to 2–3 patterns.
2. Ask the child to examine the words and sort them into groups or categories.
3. Identify the category based on your analysis of the student's spelling or encourage the student to discover the category for each set of words.
4. Examples include short vowel and long vowel words, one-syllable words, past tense verbs, words with prefixes, and others.
5. Word sorts can also be done with contrasting spelling patterns, such as short-long vowel words.
6. Once a word sort is completed, ask the following questions:
   a. Why did you put these words together?
   b. What similarities do you see in these words?
   c. What differences do you see in these words?
   d. Is this a helpful category for grouping words?
   e. How can it help you in spelling the words?

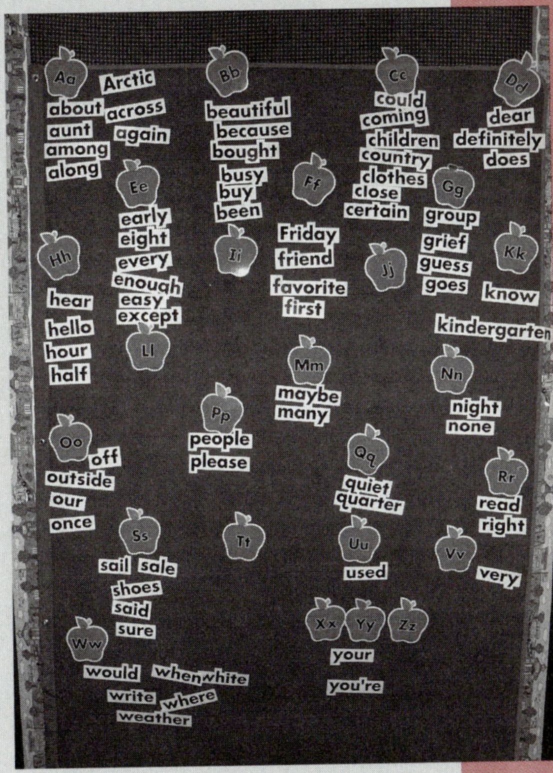


Word Walls help students to learn spelling patterns. Arrange words in a special section of the classroom wall for the Word Wall.

Through word sorts and the discussion they entail, children reveal their notions about spelling and may focus on aspects of words they may have previously ignored. The kind of word sort that helped Henry, a second-grader, can be seen in Table 9.14. The discussion he had with his teacher about the word sort can be seen in Table 9.15. See if you can figure out what spelling challenges he was having that prompted this particular word sort.

What has this word sort done for Henry? He was able to see real differences between sort and long vowel word spellings, especially in words with endings. He revealed his recognition of

## Table 9.14
## Henry's Word Sort

| Long Vowels | | Short Vowels | |
|---|---|---|---|
| **One Syllable** | **Two Syllables** | **One Syllable** | **Two Syllables** |
| boat | hoping | bet | hopping |
| wait | taping | wit | tapping |
| leaf | taking | bat | begging |
| late | lazy | bent | tipping |
| steel | | shelf | |
| | | lunch | little |
| | | truck | happy |
| | | | faster |

## Table 9.15
## Discussion of Henry's Word Sort

T: Why did you put these words together (short vowel word sort)?

H: They all have a long vowel sound.

T: What else did you see in these words?

H: Words with one syllable and two vowels have a long vowel sound.

T: Anything else?

H: One- or two-syllable words that have a single consonant before an ending have a long vowel sound.

T: Why did you put these words together (long vowel word sort)?

H: They all have a short vowel sound.

T: What else did you see in these words?

H: One-syllable words with one vowel have a short vowel sound.

T: How about the other two groups of two-syllable words?

H: The second group has double consonants in front of the ending.

T: How about the last group?

H: Same as the second group except Faster.

T: Is this a useful way to group words?

H: Yes, it helps me see how long vowel words are spelled differently than short vowel words especially with endings.

T: Anything else?

H: Yeah, there is something about the second consonant in the short words. I don't see that pattern in the long vowel words.

a relationship between the vowel sound in words and whether a final consonant is doubled before adding an ending. He knows words that end in two consonants seem to have a short vowel (*bent, shelf, truck*). His last comment to his teacher indicates that he is close to seeing why this group of words shares the same spelling structure as *hopping, tapping,* and *little.* As Henry does more word sorts with short and long vowels, he will see similar spelling patterns. Notice that the teacher does not end the word sorting activity by identifying a spelling rule. It is not always necessary to do this because the observations and conclusions drawn by the student are more important. He is observing, ordering, and classifying information about words much the way his does with all his learning.

Were you able to identify Henry's spelling challenges? He was having difficulty deciding when to double or not double a final consonant when adding an ending. This word sort helped him see the relationship between the vowel sound (short versus long) and structural features (one versus two consonants) in the words. It will help him understand that if *hit* did not double the *t* before *ing*, it would be spelled *hiting* and be pronounced like *biting.* It will also help him realize that the *k* in *stick*, like the *m* in *jump*, does not need to be doubled to maintain the correct pronunciation. How will he learn this and more about the spelling of words? By working with words in a variety of ways and using them in meaningful writing activity, he will be able to learn these important concepts. See the Engaging in Oral Language feature for word sorting activity ideas.

**Classroom Artifact Homework Exercise**

*Skyway*

Go to the Homework and Exercises section in Chapter 9 of MyEducationLab and examine the artifact, "Skyway," which is personal account written by a student at the "conventional" stage of writing. Complete the activities that follow, and save your work or transmit it to your professor as assigned.

**engaging in Oral language**

## Sorting Words in Pairs and Squares

When Mr. Garcia looks over the writing of his second-graders' favorite animal stories, he notices that the students are still having trouble with short and long vowel spellings. To help them with this spelling confusion, he creates word sorts that contrast long and short vowel spellings. To encourage his students to talk more about their spelling, he has them engage in a Think-Pair-Square cooperative learning activity. To do this, he divides the class into pairs of students. He gives each pair a collection of words with short vowels and contrasting long vowels (*hat—hate, hop—hope, set—seat, bit—bite, lick—like, lame—lamp,* etc). Each student is given the same words and told to think about how to arrange the words according to vowel sound (long vowel words go in one group and short vowel words go in another group). Students in each pair compare observations and determine what the sorts tell them about the short and long vowel spelling of the words. After sharing observations, each pair works with another pair to form a square. Each pair then shares its observation with the other pair. Each square summarizes its collective observations and shares them with the rest of the class. Mr. Garcia believes that students speak more freely about their observations when they are in a smaller setting of pairs and squares. He also finds that his students can discover and discuss patterns in the spellings of words as well as he can and that they remember what they share with others.

## A Developmental Spelling Approach

This approach identifies the spelling stage students seem to use in their spelling. By analyzing spelling errors they use in their writing or with a developmental spelling assessment, students can participate in stage-appropriate spelling activities to promote progress through the stages. It is an approach that can be used in conjunction with any spelling program or individualized spelling instruction. Instructional activities that use a developmental spelling approach are listed in Table 9.16.

### Table 9.16 Developmental Spelling Instructional Activities

| Prephonetic Spelling Stage Instructional Activities | Early Phonetic Spelling Stage Instructional Activities |
|---|---|
| 1. Read aloud and often to children using big books or experience story charts.<br>2. Teach the alphabet song with alphabet strips on each child's desk.<br>3. Use dictations and experience stories to develop one-to-one matches between spoken and written words.<br>4. Read poems and play rhyming games.<br>5. Label parts of the room and objects in the classroom.<br>6. Encourage children to draw and "write."<br>7. Write a sentence about the drawing on the drawing.<br>8. Have students listen to and create pattern stories and poems. | 1. Have students create picture/word banks from their stories.<br>2. Students match picture cards with beginning consonant letters.<br>3. After beginning consonant picture/word sorts, go to final consonant sorts.<br>4. Go to word families with different beginning consonants.<br>5. Begin consonant blend picture/word sorts.<br>6. Continue speech-to-print match with experience stories.<br>7. Encourage frequent writing and "invented" spelling.<br>8. Create simple word walls for writing. |
| **Phonetic Spelling Stage Instructional Activitiess** | **Structural Spelling Stage Instructional Activities** |
| 1. Children build their word banks.<br>2. Begin contrasting consonant/consonant blend word sorts.<br>3. Begin short vowel word sorts.<br>4. Go to consonant digraph word sorts.<br>5. Contrast consonant/consonant digraph word sorts.<br>6. Begin long vowel word sorts.<br>7. Have student do contrasting short/long vowel word sorts.<br>8. Encourage frequent writing. | 1. Continue with short/long vowel word sorts.<br>2. Turn to r-controlled word sorts.<br>3. Sort words with endings with no root change.<br>4. Sort words with endings with root change.<br>5. Contrast words with and without root changes.<br>6. Sort words with double consonants in the root word.<br>7. Begin simple word expansion activities (run, runner, running).<br>8. Have students develop personal dictionaries.<br>9. Help students find their own "challenge" word or parts of words.<br>10. Have students help as spelling editors for each other. |

## Table 9.16
## (Continued)

| Meaning/Derivational Spelling Stage Instructional Activities |
|---|
| 1. Review basic structural elements in words (prefixes, roots, suffixes, inflected endings).<br>2. Have students do words sorts that relate spelling changes in words:<br>a. No root change (nation/national)<br>b. Silent letters (sign/signal)<br>c. Dropping e (promote/promotion)<br>d. Long to short vowel sound (ignite/ignition)<br>e. Long to schwa (invite/invitation)<br>f. Schwa to long (central/centrality)<br>3. Review common words derived from Greek and Latin.<br>4. Have students create meaning maps or wheels using related/derived forms.<br>5. Explore interesting words in terms of their origin or history for sound, meaning, and spelling clues. |



## Challenges of Teaching Spelling

Regardless of which approach or combination of approaches for teaching spelling you choose, there are instructional challenges that await you. Are the spelling word lists appropriate for the ability and level of students? Can I adjust the number of words according to the needs of my students? Does my instruction focus on sound, structure, and meaning as part of spelling? Are my students using spelling strategies when spelling problem words? To answer these questions, we offer the following suggestions:

**Word Lists** In addition to words that students encounter in their reading, why not also include the most frequently misspelled words for your particular grade? Table 9.17

## Table 9.17
## The 25 Most Frequently Misspelled Words, Grades 1–8

**Grade 1**

| | | | | |
|---|---|---|---|---|
| because | too | with | was | were |
| when | said | have | would | people |
| like | there | very | are | about |
| they | house | friend | want | Christmas |
| went | know | my | friends | play |

**Grade 2**

| | | | | |
|---|---|---|---|---|
| because | went | friends | would | Easter |
| too | their | were | upon | once |
| they | Christmas | said | know | again |
| when | people | our | friend | didn't |
| there | favorite | a lot | outside | scared |

**Grade 3**

| | | | | |
|---|---|---|---|---|
| too | Christmas | favorite | upon | then |
| because | were | when | with | I |
| there | said | friend | our | always |
| their | went | know | really | finally |
| a lot | they | that's | friends | again |

**Grade 4**

| | | | | |
|---|---|---|---|---|
| too | favorite | they're | again | outside |
| a lot | that's | were | they | said |
| because | our | it's | Christmas | we're |
| there | when | know | went | different |
| their | really | finally | until | sometimes |

(Continued)

**Table 9.17 (Continued)**

| Grade 5 | | | | | Grade 7 | | | | |
|---|---|---|---|---|---|---|---|---|---|
| a lot | favorite | it's | until | through | there | it's | Easter | Christmas | until |
| too | that's | really | friend | were | a lot | because | they | off | buy |
| their | finally | different | they | believe | too | don't | you're | where | let's |
| there | our | where | you're | know | their | probably | finally | Halloween | really |
| because | they're | again | friends | something | that's | they're | our | didn't | then |
| **Grade 6** | | | | | **Grade 8** | | | | |
| a lot | their | everything | until | college | a lot | that's | don't | can't | didn't |
| too | there | finally | different | they | too | there | we're | usually | off |
| it's | you're | our | really | through | it's | they're | finally | doesn't | TV |
| because | favorite | probably | usually | where | you're | because | there's | really | until |
| that's | were | they're | beautiful | we're | their | probably | where | allowed | something |

*Source:* "25 Most Frequently Misspelled Words at Each Grade Level," pp. 26–27 from SPELLING RESEARCH & INFORMATION: AN OVERVIEW OF CURRENT RESEARCH AND PRACTICES. Copyright © 1995 by Scott, Foresman and Company. Used by permission of Pearson Education, Inc.

shows the twenty-five most frequently misspelled words in each grade according to an analysis of one-and-a-half million words from 18,599 compositions written by students in grades 1–8 across the country (Cramer and Cipielewski, 1995).

**Number of Words** How many words should you expect students to focus on each week? A good rule of thumb is to consider a number that accommodates a range of students. For first- and second-graders, the number of words could range from five to ten; for third- and fourth-graders from seven to fourteen words; and for fifth- and sixth-graders, ten to twenty words. If you are using a commercial spelling program, you can adjust the number of words on the weekly list to better support the range of students you have in your class.

**Sound, Structure, and Meaning** As we saw earlier, English has three important regular features in its spelling system. Be sure to highlight those when developmentally appropriate in your spelling instruction. For example, in the early grades special attention to the letter-sound relationships in English spelling should be given; in the middle elementary grades, structural features with words and between syllables should receive emphasis; and for the upper elementary grades, the connection between spelling and meaning should be addressed. Keep in mind that as children progress through the grades, they do not leave behind what they learn about English spelling, but rather they add to that knowledge as they move to higher levels of understanding. So when a child has mastered common letter-sound spelling patterns, the child adds to this knowledge when facing the challenges of doubling or not doubling consonants as endings are added.

**Spelling Strategies** Sometimes, students need additional strategies when dealing with particularly challenging words. Here are six that can help:

- Building words (*chop> chopping, chopped*)
- Helping rhymes (*try—fly, light—sight*)
- Say it right (*diffrent—different, suprise—surprise*)

## engaging in Visual Literacy

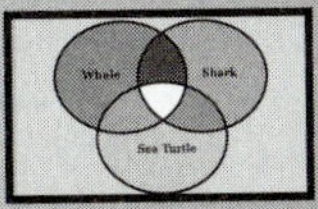

### Identifying the Challenge in Words

To help her third-graders with problem parts of their spelling words, Mrs. Gatton uses several strategies. One strategy is to have her students underline the problem parts of a spelling word. When a student spelled *friend* as *FREND,* he underlines the problem part *E.* He then writes the correct form of the word above the spelling word and underlines the correct part of the word: *ie.* The word looks like *friend.* This helps him to remember visually what the problem part of *friend* is and how to spell it correctly. Another strategy that also helps students remember visual clues to correct spelling is when she presents four words that are similarly spelled. Only one word is correctly spelled, and students have to circle the correct spelling and discuss why they circled that spelling. For example, the four words might be *hoose, house, howse,* and *hosh.* The word *house* is the only word spelled correctly and *ou* is the key pattern. To check this pattern, students can look up the words in the dictionary.

---

- Find the problem (*believe, friend*)
- Memory trick (*occasion—I can't come on that occasion*)
- Divide It Up (*million—mil/lion, letter—let/ter*)

See the Engaging in Visual Literacy feature for strategies to use when helping students identify the challenging parts of their spelling words. See the Exploring Technology feature to investigate websites that support spelling development.

IRA/NCTE 4

# How Can We Assess Spelling?

Spelling assessment is important because assessment results can help you decide what words or kinds of spelling patterns to teach as well as determining where a student is on a spelling development continuum. By looking at students' spelling attempts in the elementary grades, you can figure out which spelling stage a student is in. One way to do this is to gather up a collection of writings from students and do a spelling development analysis of the misspelled words. Another way is to select one or more lists from

# exploring technology

## Spelling Websites

**A Spell CHECKing Strategy for Students with Learning Disabilities (www.ldonline.org/article/6233)**
This article, published on LD Online, presents the CHECK strategy, which was developed to help students become more effective and independent in their use of spell checks. The acronym (Check, Hunt, Examine Changes, Keep) helps students remember a sequence that will assist them with selecting the desired word quickly.

**Flip-a-Chip (www.readwritethink.org/student_ mat/ student_material.asp?id531)**
In this interactive online activity by ReadWriteThink, students flip two chips to mix and match four word parts and make four words. Students then insert the four words into a paragraph, using context clues to determine where each word belongs. After each exercise, students can print their work to check whether they placed the four words in the paragraph correctly.

the Developmental Spelling Test, or DST (Beers, 2005) and use those results. The three word lists used for the test are found in Table 9.18.

To use the DST, select the list that best reflects the kinds of words that students encounter. For students in grades K–2, it would be the primary grade list; for grades

### Table 9.18
### Developmental Spelling Test

| Primary Grades | Middle Grades | Upper Grades |
|---|---|---|
| is | run | define |
| get | button | carried |
| jump | swimming | hesitate |
| bench | spatter | reverse |
| little | happily | separate |
| man | benches | definition |
| late | berries | special |
| wasted | running | alternate |
| fell | bombed | alternative |
| faster | saving | separation |
| did | watched | hesitation |
| kicked | biting | reversible |
| washed | jumped | occur |
| drive | crater | occurred |
| sink | bite | carry |

3–5, the middle grade list; and for grades 6–8, the upper grade list. Each list contains words with spelling elements that challenge students at different grade levels and reveal spelling stages found in those grade levels. The primary grade list has examples of regular letter-sound spelling patterns, the middle grade list contains words with structural elements that cause difficulty in the middle elementary grades, and the upper grade list has alternate forms of words that relate spelling to meaning. The nature of the misspellings generated by these lists is actually more important than the number of words spelled correctly because the misspellings signal the spelling stage strategy used by a student. If a student spells 60 percent or more of a list correctly, go to the next list.

If you look at the results of the spelling assessment done by three students, in Table 9.19 you can see what spelling stage each seems to be using.

## Student Responses on the DST

Emily is in the second grade. If you look at her responses on the primary grade list, her spelling errors indicate that she is very much in the phonetic spelling stage (*kicked—kect, drive—driv, wasted—wastid, washed—wacht*). Morgan is in the third grade, and his misspellings on the middle grade list reveal that he is focused more on the structural spelling stage as he deals with the doubling consonant challenges on this list (*button—buton, spatter—spader, biting—bitting*). Angela is a sixth-grader whose misspellings on the upper grade list point out that she is spelling at a stage higher than Emily or Morgan but is being challenged by alternate forms of words. For example, she can spell the word *define* correctly but she misspells *definition* (*defenition*) or gets *alternate* correct but misspells *alternative* (*alternitive*).

**Table 9.19**
**Developmental Spelling Assessment Results**

| Emily | | Morgan | | Angela | |
|---|---|---|---|---|---|
| **Word** | **Response** | **Word** | **Response** | **Word** | **Response** |
| is | + | run | + | define | + |
| did | + | button | + | carried | cared |
| get | + | swimming | + | hesitate | + |
| man | + | spatter | spader | reverse | + |
| late | + | happily | happly | separate | + |
| jump | + | benches | benches | definition | defenition |
| little | little | berries | berries | special | + |
| wasted | + | running | running | alternate | + |
| fell | + | bombed | bombed | alternative | alternative |
| faster | fastr | saving | saveing | separation | serperation |
| wasted | wastid | watched | watched | hesitation | hesatation |
| kicked | kect | biting | bitting | reversible | reversable |
| washed | wacht | bite | bite | occur | acur |
| drive | driv | jumped | jumped | occurred | acured |
| sink | seck | crater | crader | carry | + |

Each of these students requires different spelling instruction based on their individual spelling stage. Emily would benefit from activities that look at words which have past-tense endings that are spelled the same but pronounced differently to help stabilize her understanding of common past-tense endings (*like—liked, save—saved, paste—pasted*). Morgan needs to explore words that have consonants doubled and not doubled to learn the relationship between the spelling of the consonants and the vowel sound that precedes them (*biter, bitter, hater, splatter*). Angela, who is already familiar with this relationship with two syllable words, needs to work with words that show her how one form of a word can help with the spelling of another form (*alternate—alternative, define—definition*). For a closer look at how to use the DST as an effective assessment tool, see the Engaging in Assessment feature that focuses on the spelling of past tense verbs. Additional instructional activities for students are in Table 9.16 (p. 304), which lists spelling stage-appropriate activities.

## Spelling Placement Assessment

Spelling placement tests accompany most commercial spelling programs. Placement tests are designed to help establish a student's instructional spelling level. To use the spelling placement test, begin with the list of words that is two grade levels below the grade level of your students. Continue with grade level lists until students misspell half of a list. To determine the appropriate grade placement level, use the following criteria:

| Score | Placement Level | What to Do |
|---|---|---|
| 90–100% | Independent | Too easy. Go to higher level. |
| 60–80% | Instructional | Place students in this grade-level book. |
| 40–50% | Support | Place students but assign half the words. |
| 0–35% | Frustration | Continue testing until you reach instructional or support level. |

## Weekly Spelling Assessment

Once you have decided on the list of words to be taught each week, a pretest of the words will help determine the words and instruction to focus on during the week. Be sure that your students can spell at least 50 percent of the words on the list. You can always reduce the number of words on a list. Administer the pretest by giving each word. You may repeat each word several times and use it in a sentence or phrase. Be careful not to over-pronounce or under-pronounce the words as you administer the test. At the completion of the test, show your students the correct spelling of each word and have them write next to any word they misspelled the correct spelling. After students check their own spelling, have them discuss how their misspellings differ from the correct form and why. This discussion will give you insights into your students' spelling strategies. This, in turn, can help them in learning about the spelling of the words. The discussion can also promote spelling awareness in the students and add to their own "spelling conscience."

After students spend the rest of the week working with their spelling words in word study activities and writing exercises, they take the end-of-week spelling test. Once again, students should compare any misspelled words with the correctly spelled words and talk about how and why they spelled words as they did. You can also see if students have improved from their pretest results. The students, too, need to see evidence of their learning. With particularly troublesome words, a spelling strategy to help with particular words can be suggested and tried out.

*engaging in*
## Assessment

### Tailoring Instruction to Student Needs

Mrs. Schweitzer administers the Developmental Spelling Test (DST) to Luke, one of her third-graders. On the DST, Luke spelled 53 percent of the words on the primary list correctly. His errors indicated that he has not mastered common past tense endings (wastid—*wasted,* washt—*washed,* kict—*kicked*). On the middle elementary list, he was unable to spell any of the words correctly, and his difficulty with endings persisted (benchis—*benches,* wacht—*watched*). His spelling of short and long vowels were frequently correct, so she decided to do a series of word sorts that began with short and long vowel words that did not change with inflected endings (-s, -ed, -ing). Luke already knew the words: like—likes, stick—sticks, race—raced, wave—waved, pass—passed, jump—jumped, roll—rolled, reach—reached, hand—handed. As Luke put long vowel words in one group and short vowel words in another group, he began to notice that the past tense -ed ending was spelled the same way even though it was pronounced /t/, /d/, or /ed/. He concluded that if a word was a past tense verb, the ending is spelled with an *ed.* As Mrs. Schweitzer continued to have Luke do word sorts with words that did not change with endings, she introduced words that did (trip—tripped, stop—stopped, etc.). Luke still recognized that the past tense ending was spelled with an *ed.* He was also beginning to see the connection between vowel sounds and how they could signal whether or not to double a consonant. As Luke continued to learn about the spelling of endings, Mrs. Schweitzer saw a decrease in the number of past tense spelling errors in Luke's writing. Her instruction for Luke grew directly from her assessment and analysis of his spelling errors.

## How Can We Help English Language Learners Learn to Spell?

One of the challenges facing students who are English Language Learners and students who speak a nonstandard English dialect is that the English spelling system does not correspond to their oral language. Sounds in one language may not be found in American English, and AE may spell sounds that are not found in other languages. For example, the /th/ sound in English found in *think* or *smooth* is often pronounced as an /s/ by Latin American students and Asian American children (Owens, 2005). When saying words that begin with /th/ as in *though* and *these,* African American students may pronounce these words as *dough* and *dese* (Owens, 2005). A short vowel sound in English such as /a/ in *hat* and *tap* often is pronounced like the short /o/ sound in *hot* and *mop* by Latin American children (Owens, 2005). Another common challenge for Latin American children is dealing with the presence of consonant blends in English words such as the /st/ in *store* or the /nd/ in *band.* The /st/ blend, for example, does not appear in the beginning of Latino English words and the /nd/ blend does not appear at the end of Latino English words (Owens, 2005).

There are also grammatical differences between Standard English (SE), African

American English (AAE), Latino English (LE), and Asian English (AE). The endings that denote a past tense verb form or a plural noun form may be omitted by AAE, LE, and AE speakers (*run* for *ran* or *three car* for *three cars*). Pronouns used in Standard English are absent in Latino English (*it is round* in English but *es redondo* in Latino English).

Why is it important for teachers to know about these differences across languages and dialects used by children in the classroom? For the answer, we must go back to one of the language premises described earlier in the book. When you understand a child's language, you are more able to appreciate the fact that it is a complete communication system ideally suited for the community in which the child has been raised. It can help you recognize that a mispronunciation of a word or the omission of a past tense verb form is not a mistake or due to carelessness or ignorance. It is, however, a language difference, which explains why a Latino American student may use *sin* or *tin* to spell *thin* or why an Asian American student may use *sanks* when spelling *thanks.* The difference can also explain why LE, SE, and AAE children omit certain letters or leave off endings in words they spell. If you know something about language variation in children, you can provide models and examples that help them cross the bridge between their language and standard American English.

## Instruction That Helps Students Who Are ELLs Learn to Spell

IRA/NCTE 6

Maria Canado (2005) offers a number of guidelines for helping Spanish children learn to spell in English. These guidelines are also applicable for English Language Learners in the United States:

- Use explicit spelling instruction of English spelling.
- Spelling should be viewed as part of writing.
- Use a multisensory approach combining visual, auditory, and tactile activities.
- Vary the instructional activities when teaching English spelling.
- Teach developmentally appropriate words that are used by children in the classroom.
- Have students learn similarities and differences between their native language and English.
- Have students read and write pattern stories and poems.
- Have students dictate, write, and share experiences stories.
- Use words from their languages to compare them to SE words.
- Show how SE words have come from other languages.

# Why Teach Handwriting?

IRA/NCTE 4

Teachers write course papers on a computer, send text messages by cellular phone, and send and receive e-mails regularly each day. You fill out applications and other documents online and cut and paste information from hyperlinks, instead of writing down notes from your reading. You may still handwrite a shopping list to take to the supermarket or write down a message retrieved from your telephone voicemail. You might conclude, therefore, that handwriting is becoming an obsolete skill destined to disappear much like the typewriter or rotary telephone. You would be mistaken, however, if you thought that students need not learn to write legibly. On many occasions throughout their school years and beyond, students will be required to engage in legible handwriting. Illegible handwriting confuses readers and puts the writer at risk of being misunderstood. It is also true, though possibly unfair, that students are judged (and thus graded) as being careless or lazy by the degree of illegibility in their handwriting.

There are numerous occasions through students' school years and beyond that require text written in legible handwriting. Illegible handwriting confuses readers and puts the writer at risk of being misunderstood.

There needs to be a purpose for good handwriting, but all writing need not adhere to good handwriting. Let's say you are in a language arts course to learn about handwriting. Take out a piece of paper and in thirty seconds write the names of as many animals as you can. If you write the most animal names in the thirty seconds, you win a prize. When you have finished your list, take one of the animals and carefully write out three or four important characteristics that distinguish this animal from any other. You will be asked to make copies of your animal characteristics and hand them out to the members of your class. Compare your two pieces of handwriting. What do you see? The second piece is considerably more legible than the first. Why? You had to write as quickly as possible to name as many animals as you could in the first writing. You knew you would be making copies of the second piece that others would read. The purpose of the handwriting, therefore, has some bearing on how legible it should be. When writing for others, your handwriting has to be more legible than when writing for yourself.

## Manuscript and Cursive Writing

There are two basic types of handwriting that are taught in classrooms today. One is called *manuscript* writing, which is generally referred to as printed writing that uses letters formed individually and not connected to each other. The other type of handwriting is *cursive* writing, which is handwriting in which the letters are formed individually and *are* connected to each other.

**Manuscript Handwriting** Manuscript handwriting is taught in the early primary grades and looks most like the print found in trade books and textbooks used in classrooms. For many years, the most popular method used to teach manuscript handwriting was the Zaner-Bloser manuscript alphabet. Those who used this approach believed that writing individual letters using short separate strokes was easier for first- and second-graders to write. Some have referred to these short strokes as the "ball and stick" approach because many Zaner-Bloser manuscript letters are formed when a straight line (stick) is connected to a curved or circular line (ball). The letter *b*, for example, is made by drawing one short line down and adding a circle to the right side of the line. Notice the arrows and numbers associated with each letter. The numbers indicate the order in which each stroke is to be written, and the arrows point out the direction the stroke is to follow. While many teachers and parents have supported the use of the "ball and stick" method for teaching handwriting, others began to find the manuscript handwriting approach developed by Don Thurber in the 1970s more to their liking.

Don Neal Thurber called his manuscript alphabet the D'Nealian alphabet (see Figure 9.4). He believed that it was easier for younger students to write letters using a continuous motion once they had started writing a letter. There is also more of a slant to his letters, and many of them have hooks or curves at the end of the letters. Arrows

**Figure 9.3 Zaner-Bloser Alphabets**

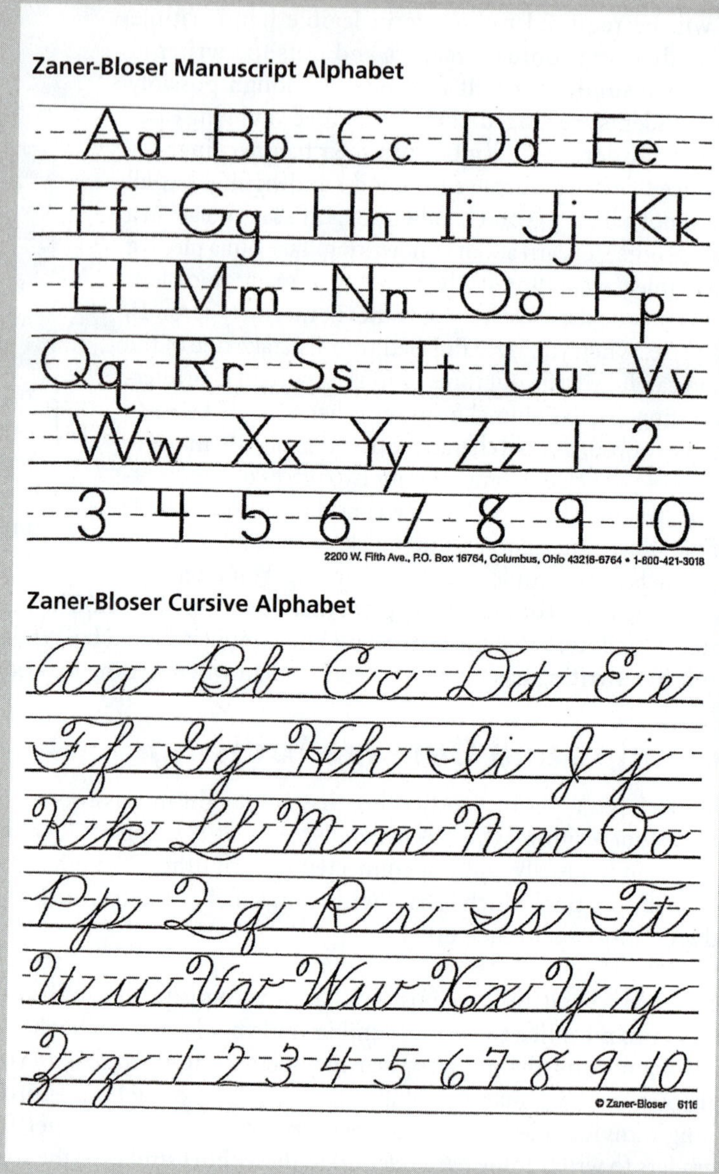


*Source:* From Zaner-Bloser Handwriting. © by Zaner-Bloser, Inc. Used with permission. All rights reserved.

associated with each letter show the continuous direction the young writer should use to form the letters. Although some have argued that the manuscript style developed by Thurber has students write letters that appear different from those encountered in books, the D'Nealian approach remains popular.

**Cursive Handwriting** Sometime in the second grade and into the third grade, students begin to switch from writing in manuscript to writing in cursive. Because letters are joined in cursive writing rather than separated as in manuscript writing, students gradually begin to write more swiftly. Another look at Figure 9.3 shows the Zaner-Bloser cursive alphabet

**Figure 9.4**

## D'Nealian Alphabets

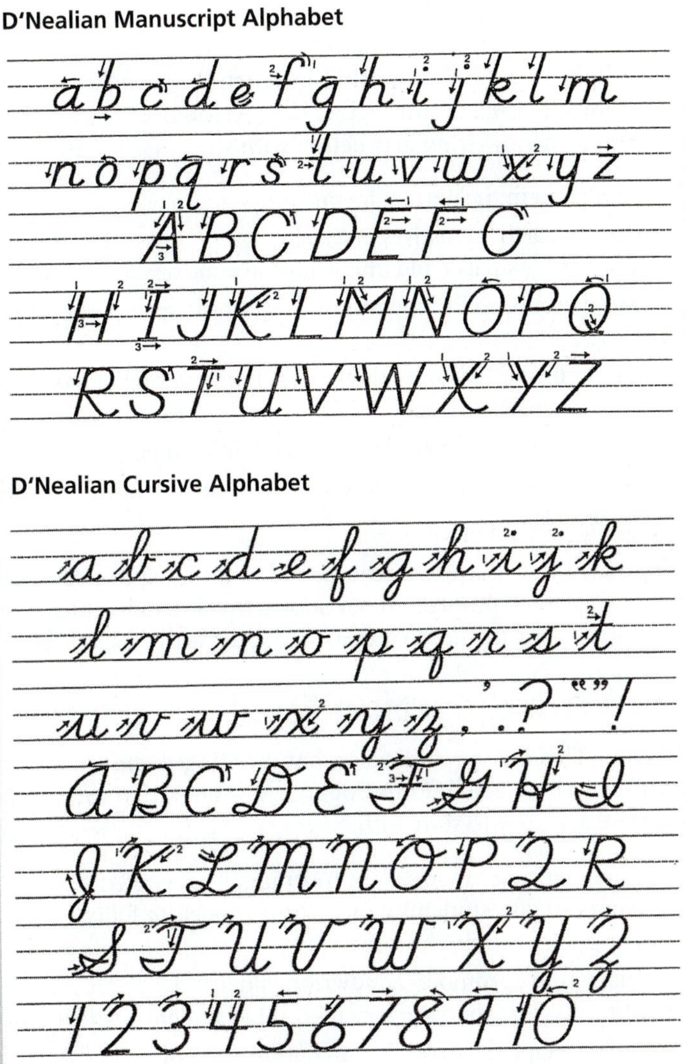


*Source:* From *D'Nealian Handwriting,* copyrighted by Pearson Education, Inc. All rights reserved. D'Nealian is a registered trademark of Donald Neal Thurber.

with arrows and numbers used to determine the order and direction of the strokes to form the letters. It also reveals that several cursive letters look quite different from the manuscript letters, which can make transitioning from manuscript to cursive difficult. A second look at Figure 9.4 illustrates several reasons why D'Nealian handwriting has been growing in popularity. Only five letters are different from their manuscript counterparts (*f, r, s, v,* and *z*), and many of the letters already have hooks or curves that makes learning how to connect letters in cursive easier than with the Zaner-Bloser cursive alphabet.

Each of these approaches to handwriting has its supporters and detractors. There is, however, little published research that definitively proves that one approach is any better for teaching handwriting in the primary grades. Personal preference, anecdotal stories, and school districts' instructional decisions largely determine which handwriting system classroom teachers use.

## Legible Handwriting

Regardless of the approach to handwriting instruction you take, you still have to answer the question: What makes for legible handwriting? Use the following list of questions to help guide handwriting instruction with students:

- Are the letters written in the correct form?
- Are letters proportional to themselves in terms of size? (Uppercase letters are larger, and lowercase letters are smaller and uniformly the same size according to their case.)
- Are letters spaced evenly apart in words and are words spaced one letter apart from each other?
- Are letters straight or slanted consistently, depending upon the handwriting form used? (manuscript versus cursive)
- Are letters aligned consistently on the lines used in lined paper?
- Are letters formed with consistent pressure so that the thickness and steadiness of the letters are uniform?

Daily writing activities that help students attend to these handwriting elements provide the necessary practice and purpose for developing legible handwriting. They also help students develop handwriting fluency to increase the speed with which they can write.

## Developing Handwriting Fluency

Write! Write! Write! This is how to develop handwriting fluency in your students. There are numerous writing activities throughout this book that can promote handwriting fluency. Here are a few to start with:

- Provide good handwriting models. Your morning messages written on the board or on chart paper can give students handwriting models to follow. Dictated experience stories or poetry can do the same.
- Frequent journal writing promotes handwriting fluency. Dialogue journals provide good handwriting models when teachers respond to students in their journals.
- Pen pals and other recipients of letters, invitations, or notes provide audience and purpose for good handwriting.
- By making editing an important step in the completion of a piece of writing, students learn that good handwriting makes it easier to read their writing.

This last point brings us back to the primary purpose for teaching handwriting stated earlier: Illegible handwriting confuses readers and puts the writer at risk of being misunderstood. Does the writing have to absolutely perfect? No. Does it have to be legible and easy to read? Yes. Understanding someone else's writing already has built-in challenges for any reader. Handwriting should not be one of them.

## Left-Handed Writers

As one of the authors of this book can attest, being a left-handed writer presents unique handwriting challenges that 90 percent of right-handed people may not appreciate.

While right-handed writers swing away from their bodies in a natural direction toward the right, left-handed writers encounter their left elbow pushing in from the left as they try to write across the paper to the right. It is only the peculiar nature of our written language that causes ease for right-handed writers and difficulty for left-handed writers. What if we read right to left? Right-handed writers would suddenly feel the pain experienced by the left-handed writer. But we don't read this way, so left-handers try several approaches to this left-to-right writing. They may use the "claw" method, in which they turn their paper so far to the right that they bend their hand and write over the top of lines. They may turn their paper even more so that it is perpendicular to their bodies and write from top to bottom on the line. If the paper is turned ever farther to the right, the left-hander writes toward his or her own body. Some of us, however, are particularly resistant to writing like right-handed writers and insist on holding the paper slightly to the right of perpendicular and slanting our writing decidedly to the left. Regardless of the approach, left-handers often have legibility issues with their writing, especially when the words are being read by right-handed people.

So while we offer you suggestions about how to help left-handed writers, they will generally create a hybrid technique that makes it easier for them, regardless of how you teach them to write.

- Have left-handers find a paper position that feels natural for them.
- Try to encourage them to write away from themselves to avoid the left elbow that cramps their hand and arm movement.
- Because left-handers push rather than pull a writing instrument across the paper, a softer lead pencil, a rollerball pen, or a felt-tip marker often will be easier to move across the paper.
- By virtue of their pushing the pencils and pens, left-handers tend to poke or dig into the paper. Hence, experimenting with different writing instruments is often necessary.
- Have patience with your left-handed writers. They live in a right-handed world and may become frustrated at your efforts to "improve" their handwriting.

## The Role of Word Processing

With the advent of desktop and laptop computers and word processing programs, an alternative writing instrument has become available in every school. This is particularly helpful for students who have handwriting challenges. In the primary grades, students should be encouraged to get familiar with the computer keyboard, including locating letters; making punctuation; understanding the shift key; using capital lettering; and using the backspace key, space bar, and return key. However, students should not begin to learn touch typing until the third or fourth grade, to allow enough time for their hands and fingers to grow sufficiently. Hand and posture positioning and learning to look at text rather than keys can commence in the fourth grade. With the introduction of touch typing, the emphasis on keyboard skills moves to speed and accuracy in typing.

With word processing comes spelling and grammar checkers. The more students learn about spelling and grammar through instruction, the better they will be able to make use of these word processing tools. The checkers won't replace the need for this instruction—they only support it.

With the advent of desktop and laptop computers and word processing programs, an alternative writing instrument has become available in every school. This is particularly helpful for students who have handwriting challenges.

## revisit the classroomchallenge

Let's return to the classroom challenge and the three questions posed:

1. What have you learned about English spelling system?
2. What have you learned about how children learn to spell?
3. What spelling instruction suggestions could you make to Angela Franklin?

Are any of the answers to these questions listed below? Which ones would you use to answer each question? Put the number (or numbers) of the question that is answered by the following statements:

____ Words come from many different languages and retain traits of the original language.
____ Administer the DST to your students to determine their spelling level.
____ Letter-name spelling is a characteristic of phonetic spelling.
____ See if any of the missed words are in the top 25 missed words in your grade.
____ Children progress through spelling stages at different rates.
____ See if groups of students cluster around specific spelling errors or spelling stages.
____ English is a pattern-oriented spelling system related to sound, structure, and meaning.
____ There are important criteria for evaluating a commercial spelling program.
____ Individualized spelling programs can be assisted with spelling software programs.
____ Knowing similarities/differences among ELL native languages helps with spelling.
____ Additional responses to question 1.
____ Additional responses to question 2.
____ Additional responses to question 3.

## chapter review

We hope that you appreciate the complexity but regularity in the American English spelling system and the remarkable way that children set out to master this system. They do it developmentally and systematically. They also require support from knowledgeable teachers who are skillful in determining how their students spell. Knowing about English and about your students is the best preparation for teaching children how to become proficient spellers. Whether you use a commercial spelling program or a more individualized spelling program, the key to successful spelling instruction begins with these two principles.

Here is a summary of questions introduced at the beginning of the chapter with brief answers for each.

### Why Is Spelling Important for Reading and Writing?

Young readers learn to use spelling patterns to quickly recognize words while reading. Young writers learn that spelling supports their writing efforts so that others can read and understand those efforts.

### What Do We Know about English Spelling?

There is a great deal of consistency and regular patterns found in English spelling. These include consistency and patterns in spelling and pronunciation, spelling and structure, and spelling and meaning.

CHAPTER REVIEW

## What Do We Know about Learning to Spell?

Learning to spell occurs gradually over time. As with oral language, it occurs developmentally and in stages that range from prephonetic to meaning/derivational stages. Children vary in spelling development rate, they use known words to spell other words, and they benefit from frequent writing opportunities that support and reinforce their spelling development.

## What Else Do We Know about Spelling Development?

Children progress through the stages of spelling development at different rates. They use information about the words they know to help them learn to spell new words. Children reinforce their growing knowledge of spelling through their writing.

## How Can We Teach Spelling?

A spelling program approach, an individualized spelling approach, and a developmental spelling approach can be used to teach spelling. Within the context of any spelling instruction approach, there are challenges: what words to teach, how many, the three key spelling features in English words, and the need for additional spelling strategies.

## How Can We Assess Spelling?

Spelling assessment includes developmental spelling assessment and spelling placement assessment in spelling programs. It can also include weekly spelling assessment. Informal word sorting activities give teachers indications of students' internalization of spelling patterns. Finally, looking closely at the writing that students produce is one of the easiest ways to gain insights into students' spelling development.

## How Can We Help English Language Learners Learn to Spell?

Allow English language learners to bring their culture and their language into the classroom so that they learn the differences and similarities between their primary language and English. This will make it easier for them to switch from one language to another without diminishing the importance of both languages.

## Why Teach Handwriting?

Legible handwriting is important for students because illegible handwriting confuses readers and puts writers at risk of being misunderstood. There are two kinds of handwriting (manuscript and cursive) and two approaches for each (Zaner-Bloser and D'Nealian). Legibility should be the goal when teaching handwriting. Frequent writing promotes handwriting fluency. Left-handed writers have unique handwriting challenges. Computers will not entirely replace legible handwriting.

PEARSON myeducationlab™ Where the Classroom Comes to Life

Now go to www.myeducationlab.com to to take a Pretest to assess your initial comprehension of chapter content, study chapter content with your individualized Study Plan, take a Posttest to assess your understanding of chapter content, practice your teaching skills with Building Teaching Skills exercises, and build a deeper, more applied understanding of chapter content with Homework and Exercises.

chapter 10

# Exploring Writing Genres

classroomchallenge

**The students in** Mr. Raymond's fourth-grade classroom have been studying animal habitats in their science curriculum for the past two weeks. The class has divided up into five groups based on each group's interest in a particular animal and in where the animal lives. The students have even gone to a living science center to observe and take notes on the various animals and their habitats at the center. Some of the students have gone to websites to gather more information about their animal's habitat. Each group has collected a considerable amount of information about their animal as they prepare to write a report. Mr. Raymond suggests to the groups that one way to understand and report on the animals is to answer the question, "How can we protect your animal's habitat?" The students begin to gather the information they have collected and try to organize it to make the case for protecting their animal's habitat. Some of the groups

have difficulty deciding which facts to keep and how to organize them in their report. Other groups have organized the facts by building a strong argument for protecting their animal's habitat. Mr. Raymond decides to stop the class and help them with two important skills: How to organize information and how to write a persuasive report using the information. Because it is the end of the last day of the week, he plans to help his students with their reports over the weekend.

## Questions for Reflection

1. What can Mr. Raymond do to help students write a persuasive report?
2. What can he do to help his students to organize information in their reports?
3. What other writing genres can his students use to make the case for their animal's habitat?

## anticipating this chapter

To help you answer these and other questions about writing genres, this chapter addresses the following questions:

- What is personal writing and how do you teach and assess it?
- What is story writing and how do you teach and assess it?
- What is informational writing and how do you teach and assess it?
- What is poetry writing and how do you teach and assess it?

# What Is Personal Writing and How Do You Teach and Assess It?

IRA/NCTE 3

Captain John Smith kept a diary of his experiences as he crossed the Atlantic Ocean and started the first settlement in the New World on Jamestown Island in Virginia in 1607. Henry Thoreau filled a journal of over twenty volumes with his observations and thoughts about the time he spent living in a hut along the shores of Walden Pond outside of Concord, Massachusetts. Thomas Jefferson and Samuel Adams wrote countless letters to each other discussing their views on government and why they disagreed during the early years of the United States. Scientists create notebooks filled with steps in experiments and the outcomes of the experiments so that the experiments may be confirmed and replicated by others. We call these and similar kinds of writing *personal writing* for several reasons. They may be hurriedly written with personal thoughts and observations as in the form of notes or brief statements. They express personal views or opinions about topics the writer feels strongly about. They may also be filled with observations completely devoid of feelings, such as the list of observations in the scientist's notebook. Sometimes, personal writing jumps around from topic to topic without a recognizable form, such as a letter between two old friends who do not need to provide extensive context for the writing contained in their letters. Personal writing has been around for a very long time and is a primary source of information about historical figures and events as well as providing insight into the motives and feelings of individuals from the past.

Personal writing is an important avenue for young writers to explore their own voices and express their thoughts and feelings. If a student is angry, surprised, or delighted about something that happened in school, the student can write about such feelings in a journal or diary. This writing will allow different voices to be expressed in writing in a private, rather than a public, arena. Personal writing in journals or learning logs allows students to explore their understandings or confusion about what they are learning. Students can write questions about their learning that can be shared with you and their peers. Often by writing about their learning, students better understand their learning. Regular personal writing in journals each week encourages writing fluency and writing confidence as it becomes an ongoing writing activity. Personal writing can also be an excellent source of writing topics that students can use. These can range from ideas for stories and poetry to topics for informational writing.

Personal writing, or *recounts* as Lewis and Wray (1995) refer to them, come in different forms and serve different functions. These include personal journals, learning journals, letters, autobiographies, and memoirs, to name a few. For a more complete list of types of personal writing see Figure 10.1.

## Personal Journals

Students need a safe, personal space to express and reflect on their own lives, experiences, and responses to what is going on around them at home and at school. Personal journals provide such a space. The audience for personal journals or diaries is the person writing in the journal. Students can record their thoughts and ideas about events in their lives as though they were talking to themselves. Their voices become an important part of the entries in a personal journal. Often, students arrive at a better understanding of their own feelings when they write them down and reflect upon them. When students have a concern about an issue in school or with a friend or teacher, by writing about it, the issue becomes clearer, as do possible solutions or responses to the issue.

Personal journal writing is safe and individual for several reasons. Because the audience for personal journals is the writer, the writer can allow others to read it or not. The goal of personal writing is to provide a space for reflection, not perfection. Misspelled words, dangling modifiers, or incomplete sentences can be ignored because revision is not the goal of personal writing. The value of personal journals is that ideas can be jotted down quickly so that they can be reflected upon more slowly at a later time. The writing in personal journals is individual because students decide what they want to write about and how they want to write it. They can write dialogue between themselves and their teachers or a poem that starts every line with "I need help with. . . ." The choice is up to the student. Often, the topics that students pick for their personal journal writing become the basis for longer writing assignments out-

**Figure 10.1**

### Types of Personal Writing

| | |
|---|---|
| Autobiographies | Memoirs and personal stories |
| Biographies | Pen pal letters |
| Dialogue journals | Personal letters |
| Diaries | Picture and illustration captions |
| Double-entry journals | Scrapbook captions and comments |
| Get well cards and letters | Sympathy cards and letters |
| Learning logs | Thank you cards and letters |

side of the journal. For personal journals to be helpful to students, they must be a safe place for students to visit every day.

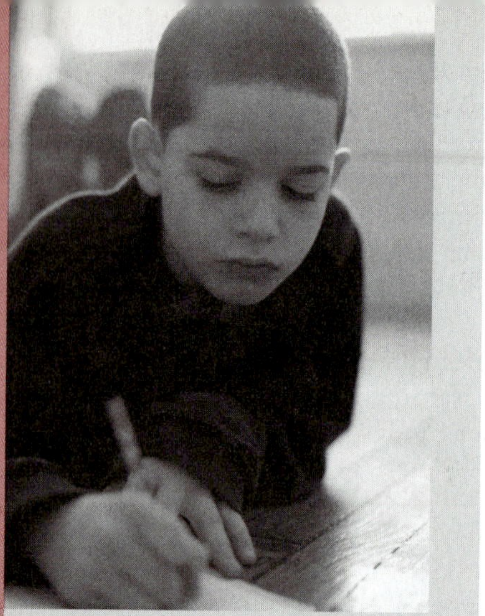

Students need a safe personal space to express and reflect on their own lives, experiences, and responses to what is going on in their lives both at home and at school. Personal journals provide such a space.

## Learning Journals

While personal journals focus on experiences and events in students' lives, learning journals or learning logs are places where students respond to what they are learning in school. Entries that students put in learning journals can identify, analyze, or question what they learn in any subject. A learning journal is also a place where students can organize their thoughts about what they are learning in any subject; students can summarize what they have learned about a topic in science or math. Learning journals allow students to track their own understanding about a particular subject by preserving a record of that learning. The act of writing about their learning helps students to reinforce new learning as well as link it to students' prior knowledge about a subject. Writing in learning journals helps children to assimilate what they have learned and accommodates the new learning that happens as they learn more about a subject.

IRA/NCTE 1

**Learning Logs** Students can use learning logs to write down what they are learning in a particular subject by summarizing, asking questions, or relating it to prior learning. Learning logs are a daily record of student learning that can help students keep track of important concepts and make connections among them. Learning logs provide opportunities for students to answer questions about a subject and to ask questions themselves. Students can refer to their learning logs when they discuss concepts or topics covered in their reading.

**Double-Entry Journals** Another type of learning journal is a double-entry journal (Macon, Bewell, and Voight, 1991) in which students create two parallel columns on a page that contains related information about what students are learning. The source of the first column can be the reading they have done in a subject or notes in response to a class demonstration or lecture. For example, students in a third-grade classroom are reading *The Women Who Outshone the Sun: The Legend of Lucia Zento.* Their teacher wants the students to create a story impression with a list of vocabulary words taken from the story. Using their double-entry journals, students wrote their impression or predictions of what the story would be about based on the vocabulary and its sequence given to them by their teacher. The words were:

| | | | |
|---|---|---|---|
| Lucia | bathing | angered | sun |
| elders | afraid | dignity | cruel |
| river | leaving | quiet | advice |
| sun | village | hair | |

**BUILDING TEACHING SKILLS: Simulation Exercise**

*Providing Instructional Supports*

Go to the Building Teaching Skills section of Chapter 10 of MyEducationLab and view the simulation, "Providing Instructional Supports," about a teacher who attempts to engage her students in journal writing about their science projects. Complete the activities that follow, and save your work or transmit it to your professor as assigned.

After students wrote their predictions, they read the story and wrote their understanding of the story in the second column of their double-entry journals. In the double-entry journal entry in Figure 10.2, you can see one student's response to the story. In the first column, the student wrote her predictions based on the vocabulary the teacher presented from the story. In the second column, you can see that the student's understanding of the story was based on her reading. Notice that some of her predictions were accurate while others were modified or changed based on her reading of the story.

Figure 10.2

## Example of Double-Entry Journal That Goes with *The Woman Who Outshone the Sun: The Legend of Lucia Zento*

| My predictions | What my reading told me |
|---|---|
| Lucia is a special person. She goes bathing in the river. The people in the town are afraid of her and want her to leave town.<br><br>They get angry at her and she leaves the village. The sun gets really hot and the people suffer.<br><br>Maybe they try to get Lucia to come back to the village to help. | Lucia is a special person. When she went bathing in the river, fish would come out of her hair. The river loved her. People were afraid of her and drove her from the village. The river and fish went with her so there were no more fish and water for the village. After time went by, the people saw how cruel they had been to Lucia. They go out and find her. She forgives them and comes back bringing the river with her. |



Double-entry journals can be used with classroom observations and demonstrations, and with fiction, nonfiction, and poetry. To help students begin to use double-entry journals, give them prompts in the form of questions:

- What did you learn? What questions do you have about your learning?
- Did you hear or read any new vocabulary words? What do they mean?
- Did you meet any new characters in your reading? How do they change the story?
- How does the story end? Do you like the ending? Why or why not?
- How do you describe the author's writing style? Does it remind you of another author?

The point of the guiding questions with double-entry journals is to help students summarize their learning while at the same time reflecting on the learning.

**Dialogue Journals** Another excellent journal format is the dialogue journal (Bode, 1989), in which a teacher and one or two students communicate with each other by means of a journal. When time is at a premium in the classroom, dialogue journals encourage students to jot down thoughts or ideas directed to the teacher. The teacher, in turn, reads the entries and responds in writing in the student's journal. Entries can focus on questions or concerns about what students are learning or what the teacher is teaching. Students can also address personal issues or topics so the teacher can respond to them in writing. Dialogue journals can often address topics that students are more comfortable writing down instead of asking or commenting out loud. There is a degree of privacy as teachers write directly in a student's own journal. The point of the dialogue journal is two-way communication between individuals to encourage open and authentic communication. The greatest challenge presented by dialogue journals is that students are eager to share their thoughts, and the teacher should respond in a timely manner. Setting up a daily or weekly schedule to ensure that all students receive written responses is important.

For dialogue journals to be successful, teachers need to respond in ways that encourage students to write entries and respond to teacher comments. Teacher responses should be brief and specific, recognize students' comments and ideas, supply new information, and find out what other information students would like from you (Staton, 1987). The whole point of dialogue journals is to create a setting and atmosphere similar to that of a good conversation.

## Guidelines for Teaching Journal Writing

You can help students be successful with journal writing if you remember to follow these five important guidelines:

1. Students should have notebooks or other permanent forms of writing material for their journal writing. Personal journals include dated entries, while learning journals may have double-entry columns or other formats that work best for the subject area.
2. Select specific times of the day for journal writing. Students can write in personal journals at the beginning or end of the school day. Learning journals lend themselves to the time of day when students are reading or learning about a specific topic. If students are using dialogue journal entries, responses to these entries need to occur on a regular basis each week.
3. Help students develop a list of topics for writing in their personal journals as well as topics for their learning journal writing. Topics can come from brainstorming activities with students or from discussion of questions or ideas about the subjects they are learning. Freewrites (Elbow, 1973) or quickwrites are other strategies for identifying a journal writing topic. These 5- to 10-minute entries encourage students to jot down quickly any ideas that come to mind. Often, writing topics emerge from these quickwrites.
4. To help students begin to do journal writing, model how to write in and use journals. For personal journals, this modeling includes providing the date, an entry about something happening in your life, and a possible illustration. Using a personal journal entry, teachers can build trust for personal writing while showing how everyday events or activities in one's life are idea material for personal journals. For double-entry journals, show students how to create and use two columns for these entries. For dialogue journal entries, start with one entry, have a student respond to it, then respond to the student's response.
5. Respond to student journal entries in a timely manner. Sometimes, students respond to students' entries; other times, the teacher should respond to the journal entries. Responding to learning journals can also occur when instruction in a particular subject area takes place.

## Letter Writing

One of the oldest and frequently used forms of personal writing is **letter writing.** Even though e-mailing, instant messaging, and blogging have given us abbreviated forms of personal writing, letter writing is still an important practice for students to learn. Think about your own personal correspondence. Who has written to a favorite aunt or grandparent or a sister or brother in some faraway place? What about the obligatory thank-you letters that you wrote after every birthday? We pour over letters of famous writers, explorers, politicians, and other historical figures and marvel at the care they took in crafting letters to friends, relatives, and others. Effective letter writing also sets up an avenue for ongoing communication between two people. In letters, you want to share ideas and information while seeking reaction and response from the receiver of the letter. This encourages the recipient to write back until the need to send and receive letters becomes second nature to us. Letter writing requires clear purpose and organization which are valuable writing skills to encourage in students. The two basic forms of letter writing are the **personal letter** and the **business letter.**

We write personal or friendly letters to people we know or want to get to know. These include relatives and friends or individuals with whom we want to be friends. The letters are characterized as informal or conversational and friendly in tone and include "news" about the writer and requests for information or "news" about the recipient of the letter. Grandparents, aunts, and uncles are frequent letter recipients who learn about the adventures and exploits of their grandchildren and nieces and nephews, respectively. To reach less familiar audiences, students can write to pen pals in other classes or other schools for the purpose of sharing information about subjects and topics familiar to the pen pals. This can become a very helpful means of gathering or sharing information about a subject two third-grade classrooms are studying on opposite coasts of the United States.

We write business letters to inform, explain, or express an opinion about a product, event, or experience in a more formal way. Often, the recipient of a business letter is unknown to the writer. Where do business letters go? They go to newspapers, magazines, politicians or government offices, and businesses. The tone and language used in business letters are more formal than in letters written to friends or relatives. We often write business letters to express a point of view or to agree or disagree with the recipient's point or view. Letters to the editors are good examples of this kind of business letter. The formats for business letters and friendly letters are quite similar. If you look at the two formats in Figure 10.3, you will see that both have a return address, date, greeting, body, and closing. The one difference between the two letter formats is that the business letter has the full name and business address of the recipient of the letter.

## Guidelines for Teaching and Assessing Letter Writing

The best way to help students with letter writing is to model letter writing and reinforce the value and purpose for letter writing. An amusing book filled with excellent examples of all kinds of letters is *Messages in the Mailbox: How to Write a Letter* (Leedy, 1994). The book includes addressed envelopes with letters written to storybook characters in "Jack and the Beanstalk," *Alice in Wonderland,* and four other favorite children's stories. Another source of information that includes letter writing, envelope addressing, postage, and mailing is the U. S. Postal Service's *Wee Deliver Program.* This instructional unit helps students set up a post office complete with students acting as real postal workers. The students are responsible for the delivery of student-generated mail within the building. The unit provides letter writing practice and builds interest in letter writing.

What should students include in their letters? Personal letters to relatives, friends, or pen pals-to-be can include information about activities happening in the writer's life and questions to find out about the person receiving the letter. This encourages the recipient of the letter to write back. The purpose for a business letter helps determine what to include in the letter. For example, if students want to communicate their opinion about an issue with a government official, they identify the issue, why it is important, and the

**Figure 10.3**

## Formats for Business and Friendly Letters

| Business Letter Format | | Friendly Letter Format | |
|---|---|---|---|
| Name<br>Organization Name<br>Street<br>City, State, ZIP<br>Date | (Return Address) | Street<br>City, State, ZIP<br>Date | (Return Address) |
| | (Date) | | |
| Dear ____________ | (Greeting) | Dear ____________ | (Greeting) |
| ______________________<br>______________________<br>______________________<br>______________________<br>______________________<br>______________________ | (Body) | ______________________<br>______________________<br>______________________<br>______________________<br>______________________<br>______________________ | (Body) |
| Sincerely yours, | (Closing) | Your pal, | (Closing) |
| Signature | | Signature | |

reasons for the recipient to support it. If students want to seek information about a topic or issue from a company or organization, they identify the information they want and why, and they determine where to send the information. The practice of requesting information is especially important in subject areas because so much printed and online information is available on so many topics. Figure 10.4 includes a set of questions that students and teachers can use to assess both types of letters.

> **Video Homework Exercise**
>
> *Prewriting in 6th Grade*
>
> Go to the Homework and Exercises section of Chapter 10 of MyEducationLab and view the video, "Prewriting in 6th Grade" that demonstrates a teacher's guidelines for writing biographies and includes students' examples of how they accomplished the teacher's assignment. Complete the activities that follow, and save your work or transmit it to your professor as assigned.

IRA/NCTE 1

## Autobiographies, Memoirs, and Biographies

Autobiographies and memoirs are natural extensions of personal journals and letters. These life story recounts provide opportunities for students to expand and reflect upon experiences or observations taken from their journals or letters. **Autobiographies** tell about the life of the writer with events or experiences presented in a sequential timeline. They give students an opportunity to write about important events in their lives and the people with which they experience them. See Figure 10.5 for excerpts from two fourth-graders' autobiographies. **Memoirs** focus on a specific person, event, or experience in the writer's life that has special meaning to the writer which is revealed by the writer. An example might be "My First Camping Trip" or "How We Won Our Soccer Game." **Biographies** tell about the life of an individual written by a different person and allow students to write about a favorite relative or person in their lives and the influence the person had on them. Students can also write biographies about important people encountered in any of their school subjects. These include famous scientists, historical figures, writers, and poets to name a few.

**Figure 10.4**

## Letter Writing Assignment

**Friendly Letters**

Did you tell about yourself?

Did you ask questions about your friend?

Did your letter include:

- Return address
- Greeting
- Salutation
- Sender's name

Did you check for complete sentences, grammar, spelling, and punctuation?

**Business Letters**

Did you state your opinion or ask for information?

Did you give reasons for your opinion or why you want the information?

Did you thank the receiver?

Did your letter include:

- Return address
- Receiver's address
- Greeting
- Salutation
- Sender's name

Did you check for complete sentences, grammar, spelling, and punctuation?

**Figure 10.5**

## Excerpts from Two Fourth-Graders' Autobiographies

Anna Reames

Hi' my name is Anna Reames. One of my favorite things to do after school is play outside with my friends. My friends and I play on our heelys, we also go on bike rides every were. My friend Savannah has a piano and I have guiatar so we made up a band called B.F.F. (Best. Friends. Forever). Savannah plays the piano, Maggie my little siter sings, I play the guiater. We've written a cople songs. My Dad works at Warick Air Conditing, My Dad helped work on Matoaka, right now he's working at Warick forest. My mom is a house mom she takes very good care of me and my little sisters. thats all about me.

Trish Webb

I love to play softball, I love to hang out with my friends', I love my puppy, I have a collectin of arrow heads and thimbles, I was born in Suffolk 1998, I am 9 years old. This is a little something about me.

## Guidelines for Writing and Assessing Autobiographies and Memoirs

First, students learn about autobiographies by listening to and reading autobiographies and memoirs and talking about the elements in both as well as how they are different. Some excellent examples of autobiography include *Marianthe's Story: Painted Words and Spoken Memories* by Aliki (1998) for the primary grades and *Once upon a Time* by Eve Bunting (1995) for the upper elementary grades. Excellent memoirs are *Hattie and the Wild Waves: A Story from Brooklyn* by Barbara Cooney (1990) for the primary grades and *Calling the Dove: El Canto de las Palomas* by Juan Felipe Herrera (1995) for grades 3–6. Then, using an autobiography or memoir as a model, students write their own autobiographies or memoirs. Here are some additional guidelines and strategies to help students write their life stories (autobiographies) and life episodes (memoirs):

- ***Life Graphs*** Students create pictures depicting special events in their lives, and they use the pictures to help them write their life stories. In the early grades, these pictures can form the basis for Me Stories written by students. A student not able to write can dictate to the teacher what the picture tells about the student, and the teacher can write that below the picture.

- ***My Bag*** Students gather important objects, pictures, and other physical reminders of a special event or time in their lives and bring them to school in a bag, box, or basket. By selecting, thinking about them, and sharing their importance, students can use them in telling their own stories.

- ***Me Maps*** To help in organizing their life stories, students create a visual representation of stages or periods in their lives and add events around the **Me** center of the map, such as the one in Figure 10.6. It also could look like a ladder with the top of the ladder representing the most recent event—the bottom represents the earliest event, and the ladder rungs represent the events in between.

**Figure 10.6**

**Me Map**

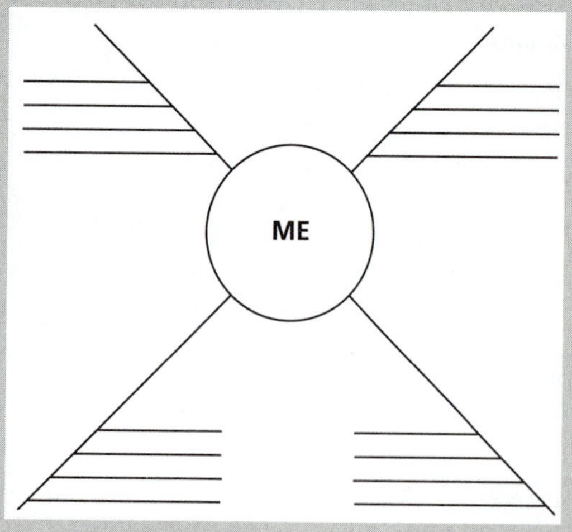


- ***Lifelines*** Students array key events along a timeline that depicts the sequence of events. Lifelines can be drawn with events written on the line or created out of string and objects, or pictures symbolizing the events can be attached to the string in the order that the events occurred.

Students derive several important benefits from writing their life stories or writing about episodes that have special meaning to them. They share and learn about their backgrounds and cultures. They cause students to reflect upon common experiences and challenges in the lives of their fellow students. Teachers get to know more about their students, and a sense of community is shared and strengthened by all in the class.

Students can use checklists to help them develop their life stories and episodes and to check and revise them. Teachers can use the same checklists to assess how successfully students have written them. Here is a checklist for autobiographies and one for memoirs:

| **Autobiography Checklist** | **Memory Checklist** |
|---|---|
| Do I introduce myself in an interesting way? | Do I introduce myself in an interesting way? |
| Are events presented in the order in which they happened? | Do I answer **who, what, where, when,** and **why** about the experience I write about? |
| Do I support my facts with correct information? | Do I sequence the events correctly? |
| Do I have an interesting conclusion to my life story? | Do I have an interesting conclusion that explains the importance of the experience in my life? |
| Did I check my writing for grammar, usage, spelling, and punctuation errors? | Did I check my writing for grammar, usage, spelling, and punctuation errors? |

## Guidelines for Writing and Assessing Biographies

Begin helping students write biographies by exploring biographies with them. Read biographies to students pointing out their common elements. All the biographies by Jean Fritz (Paul Revere, Samuel Adams, George Washington, etc.) are great for the primary grades. Russell Freedman's biographies (Martha Graham, Abraham Lincoln, the Wright Brothers, etc.) are appropriate for the upper elementary grades. Many of the characteristics of biographies are similar to those found in autobiographies, although accuracy of information about another person is especially important. Many of the guidelines and strategies for writing autobiographies are applicable for memoirs.

■ ***Biographs*** Students create visual scenes representing different periods in a person's life that become the basis for that person's biography. Pictures and photographs can be used much the same way as drawings in life graphs. Paper folded to make four or more sections can help to sequence the scenes.

■ ***Biobags*** Students collect things that refer to a person's life. These can be objects, pictures, maps, and the like that are significant reminders of the person. If the person is a family member, family mementos can be put in the biobag. Sticky notes about each item placed in the biobag can be attached to the item and can become the basis for statements made in the biography.

■ ***Lifelines*** As with lifelines for autobiographies, lifelines can be constructed to point out significant events in the life of the person who is the subject of a biography.

An especially valuable source for biographies is the special grandmother or aunt, father or mother, neighbor or friend. To write these kinds of biographies often requires students to interview this special person or friends and family of the special person. Questions that students ask might include the following:

- What is your full name?
- Where were born?
- Where did you live?

- Do you have any brothers and sisters?
- Where did you go to school?
- What kinds of jobs have you had?
- What do you like to do to relax?
- What things are different from when you were a boy (girl)?
- What things are the same?
- Who was your favorite relative and why?

Interviewing a special family member or friend is a great experience for all students at any grade level. By asking adults some of these questions, memories start to pour out and note-taking or tape-recording becomes very helpful. In writing a biography about the special person, students often discover things about themselves and other friends or family members. See also the online resources in the Exploring Technology feature.

In helping students write their biographies, try using the following checklist. Teachers can also use it to assess the completed biographies.

- Do you introduce the person in an interesting way?
- Do you identify the person and include important information about the person?
- Do you explain why the person is important and what the person has accomplished?
- Do you write a conclusion that tells why the person is important for others to know about?
- Do you tell where or how you got the information about the person?
- Do you check for grammar, spelling, and punctuation errors?

## exploring technology

### Sites for Writing Genres

**The Biography Maker (www.bham.wednet.edu/bio/biomaker.htm)**
Hosted by Bellingham Public Schools in Bellingham, Washington, the biography maker takes students through four steps of writing an engaging biography: questioning, learning, synthesis, and storytelling.

**The Poetry Foundation (www.poetryfoundation.org/features/children.html)**
The children's section of the poetry foundation's website has interviews with children's poets, such as Nikki Grimes, Janet Wong, Bruce Lasky, and many others. A video of children's poet laureate Jack Prelutsky provides tips for introducing children to poetry.

**Writing with Writers (http://teacher.scholastic.com/writewit/index.htm)**
The website of the book publisher Scholastic hosts the "Writing with Writers" workshop series, in which students learn from authors, illustrators, and editors to develop their skills in writing certain genres. Workshops focus on biography, fairy tales, folk tales, description, mystery, myth, news, poetry, and book reviews.

# What Is Story Writing and How Do You Teach and Assess It?

Story writing is an extension of the longstanding oral tradition of telling stories. What we learn from this tradition is that good stories come from real people and real events. They come from life experiences that can be funny and silly or sad and painful. It is the connectedness that stories have between the teller and the listener or the writer and the reader that demonstrates the power and value of stories. What better motivation to tell or write a story than the recognition that the story you listened to or read reminds you of your own life and stories you have to tell. It is the telling and the writing of the story that can give meaning to the simplest event or most ordinary experience.

IRA/NCTE 2

## Story Structure Elements

Every story has structural elements and ways that the author uses language to engage the reader. Story structure can be as simple as beginning, middle, and end or as elaborate as initiating event, setting, conflict, plot, conflict resolution, and conclusion. Children become aware of story elements by listening to many different kinds of stories read out loud to them and by reading just as many different kinds of stories themselves.

Story structure comes in as many different shapes and sizes as there are different types of stories. What are the different types? Folk tales, fairy tales, fables, legends, and myths make up one group of stories. Realistic fiction and historical fiction comprise another group. Personal narratives or memoirs make up a third group. For a list of story genres and their story elements, see Figure 10.7. By exposing students to all story genres, teachers can help students learn to write their own stories using any one of these genres.

## Guidelines for Teaching Story Structure

To help your students write stories using the genres identified in Figure 10.7, follow the steps outlined in this section. These instructional strategies can help students move from listening to, talking about, and reading stories to writing their own. There are three basic components of this story writing plan: First, students learn about the genre's story structure by listening to and reading stories and talking about their story structure. Second, using the story genre structure as a model, students create a group- or class-constructed story. Third, students write their own stories using the same story genre structure as a model. These three phases of story writing are similar to those advocated by Rebecca Olness (2005): Shared Writing is done by students and the teacher using a model provided by the teacher, Guided Writing happens when teachers assist students in their writing, and Independent Writing is done by students without help from the teacher. These scaffolding strategies support young writers as they gain understanding of a story genre and move toward writing their own individual stories. These steps can be expanded to include some or all of the following:

- Read aloud excellent examples of a particular story genre.
- Create charts or other kinds of graphic organizers that depict the story structure.
- Draw a picture or pictures to depict the story structure.

Figure 10.7

## Story Genres and Their Story Elements

**Fables**

Short tales whose characters are usually animals although humans can be in them. The story illustrates a moral based on the action of the characters. Examples: *Tortoise and the Hare* and *The Boy Who Cried Wolf.*

**Folk Tales**

Tales about heroes and heroines who overcome evil and adversity. There are often repeated actions or responses in folk tales as well as magic or supernatural action. Folk tales can be cumulative tales, talking animal tales, realistic tales, or pourquoi tales and come from every country in the world. Examples: *The Gingerbread Man, Rapunzel, How the Zebra Got His Stripes.*

**Historical Stories**

Realistic stories that have historical settings so that readers can understand the historic past. The plot or story line uses an accurate historic setting to do this. Examples: *Lyddie* (1991), *My Brother Sam Is Dead* (1974).

**Legends**

Stories that have humans perform extraordinary acts that form the basis for the legend. Examples: *Paul Bunyan, John Henry.*

**Myths**

A traditional story that explains some natural occurrence or natural phenomenon. Characters can include animals, gods and goddesses, fanciful creatures like dragons and unicorns. Examples: *Saint George and the Dragon* (1984), *The Bronze Cauldron—Myths and Legends of the World* (1998).

**Modern Fantasy**

Modern-day fantasy stories that resemble traditional folk tales or fanciful stories where whole new worlds and characters are created. These can include magical transformations of time and characters that enable characters to do extraordinary or impossible tasks. Examples: *Tuck Everlasting, A Wizard of Earthsea, Charlotte's Web, Harry Potter books, Winnie the Pooh,* and *The Lion, the Witch, and the Wardrobe.*

**Realistic Stories**

Stories set in contemporary times with realistic characters faced with real life challenges and conflicts. These include the trials of growing, losing family or friends, coping with disabilities, ethnic or racial conflict, and the impact of divorce or loss of jobs. Examples: *The Great Gilly Hopkins, Heaven, Cousins, Belle Prater's Boy,* and *Rainy*.

**Science Fiction Stories**

Stories that depict the world as it might be in a different time or era in the future. These stories also include journeys back in time or into the future through some scientific phenomenon or invention. The role of science is prevalent in many of these science fiction stories. Examples: *The Green Book, Harriet's Home, Journey to the Center of the Earth, A Wrinkle in Time, The Secret Under My Skin,* and *The Giver.*

- Have students identify and discuss the function of the story structure elements.
- Have students listen to or read another story in the same genre.
- Help students create a group or class constructed story graphic organizer or picture depicting the story elements.
- Have students act out or dramatize all or parts of the story.
- Have students draw pictures to go with the story.
- Have students create a class story that follows the story genre structure.
- Have students create their own story in the same genre.
- Encourage students to create drawings before writing their stories.
- Encourage students to write their stories before creating drawings for the story.
- Give students graphic organizers to help organize their story ideas and story elements.

Look at Figure 10.8 for examples of story structure organizers and other story structure plans.

Something to keep in mind when introducing story genres to children is to use familiar stories whenever possible. For example, the number three used in folk tales is easily demonstrated with "Jack and the Beanstalk" or "Goldilocks and the Three Bears." Models for cumulative folk tale story patterns in which one event builds upon another

**Figure 10.8**

## Story Structure Graphic Organizers

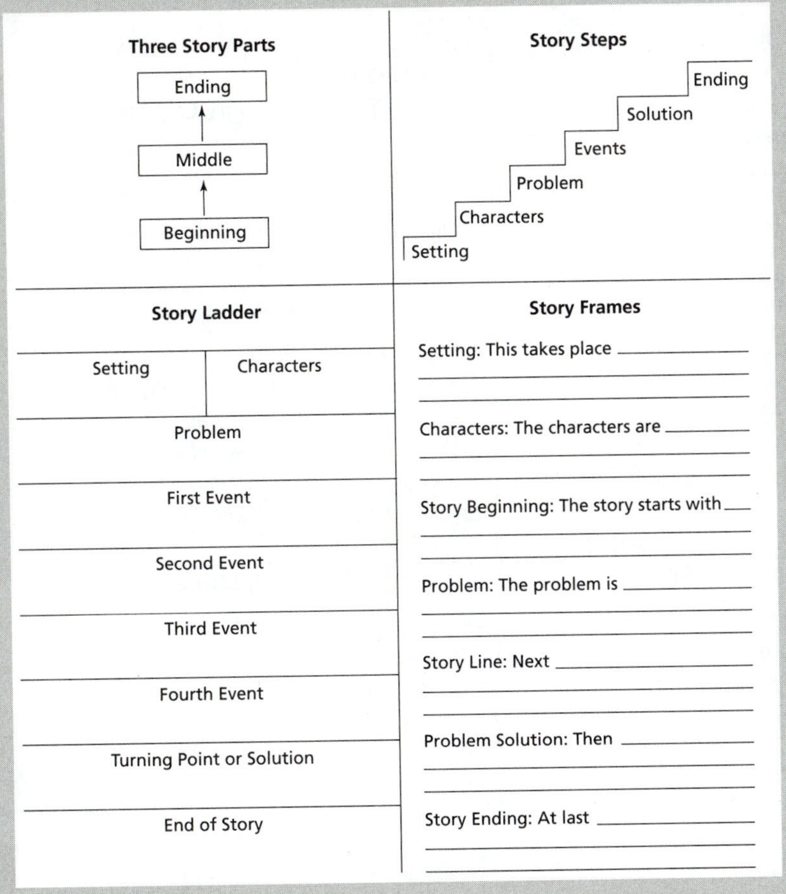

can be seen in *The Mitten* by Jan Brett (1987) or *The House that Jack Built.* Circular story models can be seen in *Where the Wild Things Are* by Maurice Sendak (1963), while *Brown Bear, Brown Bear, What Do You See?* by Bill Martin (1995) follows a question/answer story structure model. *The Old Woman and the Rice Thief* by Betsy Bang (1978) depicts a repeating story structure as the old woman repeats her reason for going to see the Raja to each character that she meets on her journey to the Raja's palace. See Figure 10.9 for a list of stories and the story patterns they use. Wordless picture books are also an excellent source of story material to help students generate written stories.

Story starters and story frames can provide additional scaffolding in helping students write stories. Students can use a one-sentence story starter to help them begin to write a story. Story frames can provide a structure for students to identify setting, characters, and plot for a story they can write. Students should be encouraged to use these techniques as a way to get started. They should also be encouraged to move away from these techniques as their stories begin to unfold. A typical story frame might look like this:

> The story happens in _______.
>
> _______ is one character in the story who _______.

**Figure 10.9**

## Story Patterns with Story Examples

| Circular Stories | Repetitive Stories |
|---|---|
| Aardema, Verna. *Why Mosquitoes Buzz in People's Ears*<br>Brett, Jan. *The Umbrella*<br>Brown, Marcia. *Stone Soup*<br>Lester, Helen. *It Wasn't My Fault*<br>Martin, Bill. *Barn Dance!*<br>Numeroff, Laura. *If You Give a Mouse a Cookie* | Aardema, Verna. *Why Mosquitoes Buzz in People's Ears*<br>Carle, E. *The Very Hungry Caterpillar*<br>Galdone, P. *The Gingerbread Boy*<br>Martin, B. *Brown Bear, Brown Bear, What Do You See?*<br>Williams, S. *I Went Walking* |
| **Cumulative Stories** | **Sequential Stories** |
| Arnold, T. *No Jumping on the Bed*<br>Brett, J. *The Mitten*<br>Carle, Eric. *Today Is Monday*<br>Lobel, Arnold. *The Rose in My Garden*<br>Neitzel, S. *The Bag I'm Taking to Grandma's*<br>Ward, J. *The Seed and the Giant Saguaro* | Bang, B. *The Old Woman and the Rice Thief*<br>Carle, E. *The Very Hungry Caterpillar*<br>Carle, Eric. *Today Is Monday*<br>Galdone, Paul. *The Three Billy Goats Gruff*<br>Bucknall, Caroline. *One Bear All Alone*<br>Sendak, Maurice. *Chicken Soup with Rice* |
| **Question & Answer Stories** | **Rhyming Stories** |
| Janovitz, M. *¿Es Hora? Is It Time?*<br>Kraus, R. *Whose Mouse Are You?*<br>Martin, B. *Brown Bear, Brown Bear, What Do You See?* | Ackerman, K. *This Old House*<br>Chandra, D. *Miss Mabel's Table*<br>Hennessy, B.G. *Jake Baked the Cake*<br>Janovitz, M. *¿Es Hora? Is It Time?*<br>Leuck, L. *Sun Is Falling, Night Is Calling*<br>Shaw, N.E. *Sheep on a Ship* |

# Visual Literacy

engaging in

## Storyboards

To help her third-graders write stories, Ms. Kryscio shows them how to create simple storyboards with one sheet of drawing paper. To demonstrate, she takes a large sheet of chart paper and folds it in half then folds it again. When she opens the paper again, it has four sections, which she labels 1, 2, 3, and 4. Using "The Three Little Pigs," she tells the story as she draws a picture of the first pig, the straw house, and the wolf (in section 1); the second pig, the stick house, and the wolf (in section 2); the third pig, the brick house, and the wolf (in section 3); and the three little pigs dancing together at the end of the story (in section 4). Sometimes, Ms. Kryscio folds her paper into three sections and labels them beginning, middle, and end and draws a picture depicting each section of a familiar story. She encourages her students to use the same technique to help them visually represent what they want to put in their stories when they write them. The pictures help to remind students of details they can include in their stories. On other occasions, Ms. Kryscio reverses the process and encourages her students to write their stories and create pictures that portray different scenes in their stories. Here is an example of one of her third-graders' storyboards (next to the storyboard is the actual story that the student wrote):

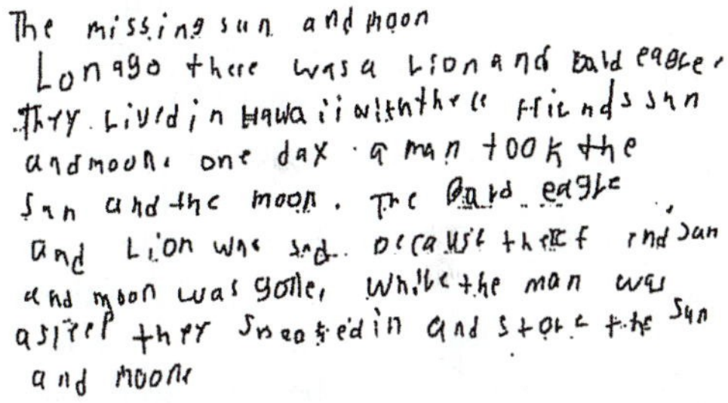


Another character in the story is _______ who _______.
A problem that happens in the story is _______.
When that happens, _______ happens.
The problem gets solved by _______.
The story ends with _______.

IRA/NCTE 6

For another approach to story structure, see the Engaging in Visual Literacy feature showing how students can create storyboards to depict different parts of a story.

## Elaboration and Description in Stories

IRA/NCTE 5

To bring stories to life, authors elaborate on characters, setting, or events of the story through extensive descriptions and adding details to the story. Two important ways to make stories interesting and understandable is by providing enough relevant details and description at various points in the stories. By elaborating with greater details in a story, the story become fuller and more interesting to readers. Description helps to paint vivid pictures of the characters, setting, and action and draws readers into the story.

## Guidelines for Teaching Elaboration and Description in Stories

Hughey and Slack (2001) identify six questions that students can use to add more details to their stories. By reading their stories and answering these questions, students can see what they can add or remove from their writing. The six questions are: Who, What, When, Where, How, and Why? Here is each question with additional information that students can use to check for details in their stories:

- **Who** is in the story? What do they look like? How do they act?
- **What** happens in the story? What do the characters do? What events take place?
- **When** does the story happen?
- **Where** does the story happen? How would you describe where it happens?
- **How** does action in the story take place? How is the problem solved? What ends the story?
- **Why** does the story take place? Why do the characters do what they do? Why does the story end as it does?

Students can use these same questions when they read other students' stories to provide helpful feedback as readers for their fellow student writers.

When helping students with description in their writing, keep in mind that strong nouns and verbs are as important as adjectives or adverbs. More specific nouns are more descriptive than general nouns. For example, *cottage, apartment, brownstone, rancher, bungalow, shack,* and *mansion* are more descriptive than *house.* With specific verbs such as *laughed, shouted, sneered, murmured, wailed,* or *whispered,* there is more description of how someone spoke than with the general verb *said.* Adjectives can add detail to strong nouns so that the *cottage* can be *gray, white, weathered, abandoned, Cape Cod,* or *beach.* Adverbs can add to strong verbs as *whispered* becomes *whispered quickly* or *wailed* becomes *wailed uncontrollably.* The combination of good nouns and verbs with adjectives and adverbs makes for better descriptive writing.

To help students include more description and detail in their story writing, follow the same sequence of steps outlined under **Guidelines for Teaching Story Structure.** First, help students learn about details and description by listening to and reading stories that have excellent examples of each. Second, using the examples as models, have students create group or class constructed stories with details and description modeled after the stories. Third, encourage students to write their own stories incorporating details and descriptions they learned from the model stories. This approach is also useful when helping students write dialogue or write from different points of view.

Another way to help students recognize the importance of details or description in stories is to have them read or listen to two different versions of the same story. Pick a story or part of a story that students enjoy and remove key details or descriptions from the story. Have students read the abridged version first and then the complete version. Encourage them to discuss the difference between the two versions. Which one seems more interesting? What is missing in the shortened version? What is added in the complete version? What are the interesting nouns used? What interesting verbs, adjectives, and adverbs are used? Which version would students choose to read? The point of this exercise is to help students see the importance of remembering what readers like to find in stories. It helps to reinforce the importance and value of an audience for writing.

When assessing student stories, you must consider the nature of the student, the story genre being used, and the success of the story.

## Assessing Story Writing

When assessing the stories that students write, the *nature* of the student, the *story genre* being used, and the *success* of the story should be considered using the following questions as a guide:

- What is the age or grade level of the student?
- What is the story genre used by the student?
- How familiar is the student with the story genre? (similar stories read/listened to?)
- Does the student include all of the elements of the story genre?
- How successful (interesting) is the story?

Additionally, questions about content, organization, grammar, usage, spelling, and mechanics can be included. For these questions and formative assessment techniques on how students use the writing process, refer to Chapter 5 (Assessing Language Arts).

# What Is Informational Writing and How Do You Teach and Assess It?

When you pick up a newspaper, thumb through a catalog, glance at a brochure at a car dealer or highway rest area, read the back of a cereal box, read a map, or flip to the inside of the book jacket on a new novel, what are you reading? Informational text. People read more informational text than any other kind of text. Why? It informs, explains, describes, defines, lists, compares, contrasts, analyzes, synthesizes, or summarizes for us all manner of facts and other information that we can use to make decisions about much of what we do as we go about our daily lives. It is also the most common kind of writing that students do in school, college, and beyond. Book reports and science reports are later replaced by research papers and term papers. More importantly, in the informational age we live in, many professions and businesses require clear and concise informational writing to remain informed and competitive. Information has become the currency for commerce as well as an important tool for teachers.

Another important reason to introduce and support informational writing in the classroom is that it provides an important learning medium for your students. When children write about what they are learning they can best answer the question: How do I know what I know? This can be as brief as an account of what a student learned about electricity in science or as elaborate as a detailed lab report explaining how a flashlight, a battery, and a bulb combine to create light. Teachers use these writings to see how their students are learning, and students use them to inform themselves about their own learning

What are the hallmarks of good informational writing? When you pick up a brochure, article, or any other kind of informational text of interest to you, these features should be present:

1. Factual, accurate, and up-to-date information
2. Information that is organized in a clear way based on the purpose of the text
3. Helpful visual information
4. The form of the text fits the purpose of the text (e.g., a brochure)
5. Additional resources, references, or contacts for further information

Think of something you are interested in, say, where to stay in Orlando if you are going to Disney World or how to use a wok for cooking. Maybe you go online to read about hotels in Orlando or perhaps you visit a bookstore to look at a book on woks. Online, you can click Orlando, click on hotels, and look at them in some detail. There is information about rooms, rates, restaurants—complete with photographs. At the bookstore, you flip through pages with colorful photographs and detailed instructions on how to use a wok along with numerous recipes for cooking food in a wok. If the information in both instances is not accurate or informative or is not presented in a way that helps you in your search, you might be disappointed or even annoyed. Even if the information is accurate but is not presented in a clear or interesting way, you may ignore it. Worse, the information may be presented in a visually attractive way that piques your interest but the information is out of date or even false. Neither scenario is attractive.

This is the challenge of informational text. We want it to be interesting, and we want it to be accurate.

## Types of Informational Writing

To better prepare students for informational writing, you need to know the different types of informational writing and the form or structure of each type. Lewis and Wray (1995) divide informational writing into six types: discussion, explanation, persuasive, procedural, recount, and report. Buss and Karnowski (2002) reduce the types to four in their treatment of nonfiction genres: recount, procedural, informational, and persuasive. We are focusing on procedural, informational, and persuasive writing here because we have discussed recounts under personal writing earlier in this chapter.

**Procedural Texts** Everyone has had some experience with procedural texts. They are as simple as directions on how to make a peanut butter and jelly sandwich to steps to follow in completing an elaborate science experiment. Writing and understanding directions that may include diagrams, a list of parts, or grainy photographs of difference phases of construction can be difficult. Have you ever put together a computer desk or other "needs assembly" items? At least today, pieces of pressed lumber are labeled with numbers or letters that correspond to numbers or letters in the diagrams that accompany the assembly directions. How about those quick reference diagrams that show you how to connect your digital camera to your computer or printer? Often, there are no words at all but a series of sketches with arrows pointing to key connection locations. The key words missing might be: "Plug in here, dummy!" What about those ". . . for Dummies" books? There are many different kinds of procedural texts, including ABC books, counting books, and seasonal cycle books. Figure 10.10 includes a list of common types of procedural texts with examples from children's literature.

What are the important elements in any procedural text? Each procedural text contains key vocabulary, steps to follow using the vocabulary, and a final product achieved with the successful completion of the steps. Here is an example to illustrate these common elements:

**Making a Peanut Butter and Jelly Sandwich**

| | |
|---|---|
| Vocabulary: | A jar of peanut butter, a jar of jelly, two pieces of sliced bread, one knife |
| Step 1: | Put two pieces of bread next to each other (see picture 1). |
| Step 2: | Open the peanut butter jar. |
| Step 3: | Open the jelly jar. |
| Step 4: | Take the knife, put it in the peanut butter jar, and remove some. |
| Step 5: | Spread the peanut butter on one slice of bread (see picture 2). |
| Step 6: | Clean the knife and repeat steps 4 and 5 for the jelly and other bread slice. |
| Step 7: | Carefully, put the jelly and peanut butter slices of the bread together. |
| Step 8: | Your sandwich should look like the one in picture 3. |

**Figure 10.10**

## Types of Procedural Texts with Examples

**ABC Books**

Brown, P. (1995). *African Animals ABC*. San Francisco: Sierra Club.

Chin-Lee, C. (1997). *A Is for Asia*. New York: Orchard.

Knox, B. (2003). *Animal Babies ABC: An Alphabet Book of Animal Offspring*. Mankato, Minn: Capstone.

Raczka, B. (2007). 3-D ABC: *A Sculptural Alphabet*. Minneapolis: Millbrook.

**Counting Books**

Carle, E. (1996). *1, 2, 3 to the Zoo*. New York: Philomel.

Numeroff, L. (2006). *When Sheep Sleep*. New York: Abrams Books for Young Readers.

**Life and Seasonal Cycle Books**

Allan, J. (2000). *Are You a Butterfly?* New York: Kingfisher.

Allan, J. (2000). *Are You a Ladybug?* New York: Kingfisher.

Numeroff, L. (1996). *If You Give a Mouse a Cookie*. New York: HarperCollins.

**How to Do Something Books**

Charles, O. (1988). *How Is a Crayon Made?* Englewood Cliffs, NJ: Prentice Hall.

Jones, G. (1995). *My First Book of How Things Are Made: Crayons, Jeans, Peanut Butter, Guitars, and More*. New York: Scholastic.

Thompson, L. (2004). *Little Quack's Hide and Seek*. New York: Simon and Schuster.

**How to Play Games**

Jaffe, E., Field, S., & Labbo, L. (2002). *Games Around the World: Hopscotch*. Minneapolis: Compass Point.

Gryski, C. (1998). *Let's Play: Traditional Games of Childhood.* Buffalo, NY: Kids Can Press.

Perez, E. (2000). *100 Best Games*. Hauppauge, NY: Barron's.

**Recipe Books**

Cobb, V. (1994). *Science Experiments You Can Eat*. New York: HarperCollins.

Jones, J. & Jones, E. (1998). *Knead It, Punch It, Bake It: The Ultimate Breadmaking Book for Parents and Kids*. New York: Houghton Mifflin.

Key vocabulary for procedural texts can fall into different categories depending on the purpose of the text, including:

- Tools and materials for completing a project
- Things used in a game (e.g., dice, play money, balls, hoops, etc.)
- Ingredients and utensils for completing a recipe
- Directional words and locations of places for getting to a destination
- Words that depict time, direction, temperature, and distance

In short, key vocabulary is any set of vocabulary that one must understand and follow in a particular sequence in order to successfully complete the task set forth in the procedural text. Games, experiments, directions, and recipes all require knowing and using the vocabulary required for any of these tasks.

The careful sequencing of steps or commands to complete a task successfully is also essential in procedural texts. These steps can be presented in one or more of the following ways:

- Rules for playing a game (dodge ball)
- Steps in completing a recipe that may include time frames (making stone soup)
- Timed steps as part of an experiment (colored water and celery stalks)
- Pictures numbered to signify a sequence of actions (story sequence)
- Illustrations or photos that signify a sequence over time (leaf changes over four seasons)
- A visual or verbal depiction of a cycle (tadpole to frog)

IRA/NCTE 1

The success of these procedural steps rests with the use of specific vocabulary and visual cues and the identification of the essential steps needed to follow to complete the assigned task. See the Exploring Diversity feature for an example of integrating cultural lessons with your lessons on procedural writing.

**Guidelines for Teaching Procedural Writing** Keeping in mind the need for specific vocabulary and the sequential order of information presented in procedural texts, how should you proceed with helping students write procedural texts? Follow the same instructional steps for writing stories.

1. Students listen to and read good examples of procedural texts appropriate for their age and grade level.
2. The teacher guides discussion of the use of vocabulary and the sequence of tasks in the text with particular attention paid to nouns (peanut butter jar), verbs (open, spread), and sequence words (first, next, last).
3. Students explain why the sequence is important and what happens if a step is omitted or the sequence changed.
4. Using the model of one of the procedural texts, students collaborate on a procedural text.
5. Students identify important vocabulary and the steps needed to complete the task described in the text.
6. Students create visual support for the text (pictures, diagrams, etc.).
7. Students create their own procedural text using collaborative procedural texts as models.

See Figure 10.11 for an example of a third-grader's procedural text that was written to describe how to play Hot Spot Basketball.

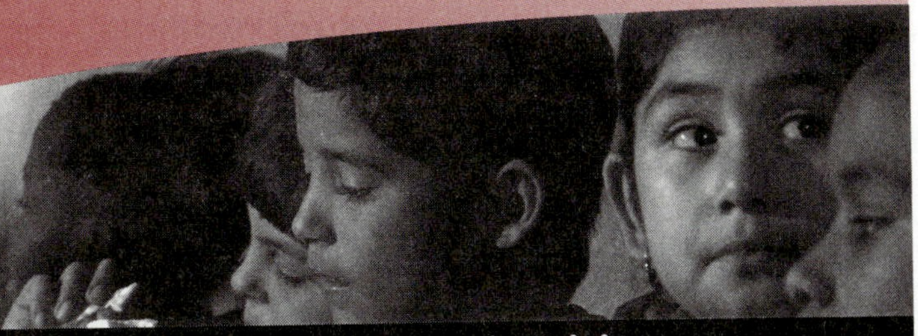

# exploring diversity

## Integrating Cultural Lessons with Procedural Writing

To promote procedural writing and foster appreciation for the diverse cultures represented in her fourth-grade classroom, Mrs. Diaz asked her students to write recipes of their favorite meals. She instructed her students to spend time at home talking with their parents to discover the ingredients, cooking utensils, and steps to follow to create the meal. She modeled a recipe for tacos to show the students how to arrange the information in their recipes. The taco recipe began with a list of the ingredients and cooking utensils, followed by the steps for making the tacos.

The following week, students brought in recipes that included Chinese, Japanese, Korean, Mexican, and Italian meals. Students also included drawings or photographs depicting the finished meals. Students shared their recipes with one another, checked on the ingredients and cooking utensils, and discussed the steps in the recipe. Interestingly, students found gaps in recipes or steps that were out of sequence. For example, instructions to turn off the oven were missing from one recipe and directions for draining the rigatoni were absent from another. Her students chose a recipe from each cultural category to use, and on the Friday of the next five weeks, Mrs. Diaz (with the help of her students) created a meal from one of the recipes. Students talked about the different flavors and ingredients and discussed the textures and shapes of food in the meals. The experience helped students learn the importance of precise and accurate writing in procedural texts. It also allowed them to share some of their own cultural heritage. Many also learned to appreciate the culinary results from other heritages. Here are two of the recipes:

**Italian Recipe:**
**Baked Rigatoni (Enough for 10)**

*Ingredients:*

1 ¼ lb extra lean ground beef
4 ½ cups hot cooked rigatoni
1 32 oz jar of tomato and herbs pasta sauce
1 ¾ cups mozzarella cheese, shredded
¼ cup (1 oz) fresh grated Parmesan cheese
cooking spray

*Preparation:*

1. Preheat oven to 350°F
2. Spray a 12x9" baking pan with the cooking spray
3. Brown ground beef in a large skillet or pot. Drain well.
4. Combine beef, rigatoni, pasta sauce, and 1 cup mozzarella cheese; toss well.
5. Pour the beef/rigatoni, pasta mixture into the baking pan.
6. Spread the ¾ cups of mozzarella cheese, and the Parmesan cheese on top.
7. Bake for 20 minutes or until thoroughly heated.

Serve in bowls with fresh Italian bread.

**Chinese Recipe:**
**Wonton Soup (Enough for 8–12)**

*Ingredients:*

¾ lb ground or shredded pork
1 diced green onion
½ teaspoon of cornstarch
¼ teaspoon of ground ginger
2 teaspoons of soy sauce
24 wontons
5 Cups of water
3 cans (8–10 ounces) condensed low sodium chicken broth
3 soup cans of water
1 tablespoon of low sodium soy sauce
1 Cup of chopped or torn fresh spinach

*Preparation: The wontons*

Spread the wontons out on a baking sheet or flat surface.
In a skillet, cook pork and green onion until pork is brown. Drain.
Put 2 teaspoons of the pork and green onion mixture in center of each wonton.
Moisten the edges of each wonton with water.
Fold each one in half to form triangle and overlap.
Moisten one corner with water.
Pinch the edges to seal the wonton.

*Preparation: The wonton soup*

Heat chicken broth, 3 cans of water, and the soy sauce in a small pot.
Bring to a boil.
Add the spinach and simmer.

In a large pot, bring 5 cups of water to a boil
Add the wontons and bring to a boil again.
Simmer the wontons uncovered for 2 minutes

Place 2 or 3 wontons and 1 cup of broth in a small cup or soup bowl.

Figure 10.11

## Third-Grader's Procedural Text

Playing Hot Spot Basketball

Vocabulary: Basket ball, Basketball Goal
Basketball court, Poly Spots, cones

Step one: Spread Poly Spots on
Court

Step two: Put Students in Four teams
behind the cones
Step three: Give each team a
basketball.

Step Four: the First Person in
each line Stands on a Spot and
Shoot the basketball.

Step Five: if the Player Makes the
basket Pick up the Poly Spot and
Place it under the cone. Pass the basketball
to the nest Person in line

Step Six: if the Person Misses
the basket, Pass the ball to the nest Person
in line.

Step Seven: all Players shoot until
the last Spot is gone the team Who earned
the Most Spots Wins!

**Assessing Procedural Writing** When assessing procedural texts, the nature of the student, type of procedural text, the vocabulary, and the accuracy of the text should be considered. Use the following questions as a guide:

- What is the age or grade level of the student?
- What is the type of procedural text the student wrote?
- How familiar is the student with this type of procedural text? (directions for a game or steps in an experiment)
- Does the student include the important vocabulary for the text?
- How accurate are the steps in presenting the task to complete in the text?
- If you follow the steps, can the task be successfully completed?

Additionally, questions about content, organization, grammar, usage, spelling, and mechanics can be included. For these questions and formative assessment techniques on how students use the writing process, refer to Chapter 5.

## Informational Writing Structures

If you were a third-grade science teacher looking for a book that discusses the differences between poisonous and nonpoisonous snakes or a fifth-grade teacher going to the Internet to read more about the benefits of writing workshops or a first-grade teacher reading an article explaining the importance of phonemic awareness, you would be using informational texts. These texts provide information through cause-effect, chronological, comparison-contrast, definition, description, and explanation writing patterns. They can also include analysis and synthesis of factual information and summarize it for the reader. Students read informational texts in gaining new knowledge, and write informational texts to demonstrate and use this knowledge. Figure 10.12 contains examples of informational texts.

The challenge of teaching students how to write informational texts is to have them understand the various organizational writing patterns that writers use. The purpose for the writing determines which organizational or text structural patterns a writer uses. What are the common text structures in informational texts?

> **Video Homework Exercise**
>
> *Collecting and Using Data*
>
> Go to the Homework and Exercises section of Chapter 10 of MyEducationLab and view the video, "Collecting and Using Data," in which students are engaged in a science exploration about worms and should be recording their scientific observations. Complete the activities that follow, and save your work or transmit it to your professor as assigned.

**Description** Authors use attributes, details, and characteristics when they describe something. They may also use examples in describing a person, place, or thing. One of the characteristics of good description is that it calls upon the reader's five senses by describing how something looks, sounds, smells, feels, or tastes. Writers will also label visual information in expanding their description of something. Description can be a simple as a labeled illustration or as elaborate as a multiple paragraph description. Often, writers use key signal words to alert the reader of an elaborate description (such as *examples of, features are, types of*).

**Chronology** A common writing pattern used by authors to convey a sequential time element to the information they present in their writing is chronology. Social studies texts often use this pattern in presenting the sequence of events during a particular period in history. It is also common in writing that presents a sequence of steps to follow for completing a task. Signal words (such as *first, second, next,* and *finally*) inform the reader of this organizational writing pattern.

**Cause and Effect** This structural pattern examines the cause-effect relationship between two or more things, events, or people. It explores the consequences of actions

## Figure 10.12 Examples of Informational Texts

**Informational Books**

Arnosky, J. (1996). *All about Turtles.* New York: Scholastic.
Gibbons, G. (1998). *All about Penguins!* New York: Holiday House.
Maass, R. (1997). *Tugboats.* New York: Holt.

**Question-and-Answer Books**

Berger, M. & Berger, G. (2001). *How Do Bats See in the Dark? Questions and Answers about Night Creatures.* New York: Scholastic.
Chinnery, M. (1999). *Questions and Answers about Polar Animals.* New York: Kingfisher.

**Travel Books**

Krull, K. (1997). *Wish You Were Here: Emily's Guide to the 50 States.* Ill. A. Schwartz. New York: Doubleday.
Peterson, D. (2001). *A True Book: National Parks.* New York: Children's Press.

**Guidebooks**

Hamilton, K. (1997). *The Butterfly Book: A Kid's Guide to Attracting, Raising, and Keeping Butterflies.* Santa Fe, NM: John Muir.
Lambert, M. (1997). *DK Pockets: Reptiles.* New York: Dorling Kindersley.

or the outcomes of events in an effort to explain how things happen. Signal words for this cause-effect writing pattern are *if . . . then, as a result, because, consequently,* and *impact.*

**Comparison and Contrast** When writers wish to show that two or more things are alike or different, they use the comparison-contrast writing pattern. They may begin by telling how two things are alike (such as toads and frogs) followed by how they are different. Sometimes, writers alternate a similarity and a difference as they compare and contrast two things. They may use visual cues such as Venn diagrams to illustrate the comparison-contrast pattern in their writing. Signal words in this writing pattern include *like, unlike, similarly, looks like, in contrast, faster, slower, taller,* and *shorter.*

**Problem and Solution** When writers want to explain how to solve a problem, get out of a predicament or situation, or how to avoid a problem, they use the problem-solution writing pattern. Writers also use this pattern when explaining or describing how conflicts can be resolved. Key signal words for this pattern are *problem, as a result, question . . . answer,* and *solve.*

As students read and listen to informational texts, they become familiar with these basic organizational writing patterns. Teachers can help students understand informational texts by showing how the writing patterns present the information and why they are used by writers. As they learn about the writing pattern, students can begin to use them in their own informational writing. Figure 10.13 presents informational books that represent the five organizational writing structures.

**Figure 10.13**

## Five Informational Writing Structures with Examples from Children's Literature

**Cause and Effect**

Gibbons, G. (1995). *The Reason for Seasons.* New York: Holiday House.

**Comparison and Contrast**

Simon, S. (1999). *Crocodiles and Alligators.* New York: HarperCollins.

**Description**

Stewart, M. (2001). *Fishes.* New York: Children's Press.

**Problem and Solution**

Schanzer, R. (2003). *How Ben Franklin Stole the Lightning.* New York: HarperCollins.

**Sequence**

Brandenberg, Aliki (1992). *Milk: From Cow to Carton.* New York: HarperCollins.

# Guidelines for Teaching and Assessing Informational Text Writing

To help students create their own informational texts, they need to understand the purpose for the writing and the best organizational writing structures to fulfill the purpose. How can they achieve both? Follow the same steps presented earlier for learning to write in any genre. First, students learn about purpose and writing organizational structures by listening to and reading nonfiction texts and talking about their purpose and structure. Second, using purpose and writing structure as a model, students create a group or class constructed informational text. Third, students write their own information texts using the same purpose and writing structure as a model. Specific steps might include:

1. Children listen to and read good examples of informational texts appropriate for their age and grade level.
2. The teacher guides discussion of the purpose of the text with particular attention paid to the organizational writing structure and key signal words in the structure.
3. Students explain why the structure is important as it relates to the purpose for the writing.
4. Using the model of the informational text, students collaborate on an informational text (such as a book report, science report, brochure, etc.).
5. Students identify the purpose for the writing and what writing to use and why.
6. Students can create visual support for the text (such as pictures, diagrams, etc.).
7. Students create their own individual informational writing using the collaborative informational text as a model.

For two examples of students' informational writing, look at Figure 10.14.

When assessing informational texts, the purpose for the text, the choice of the

**Figure 10.14**

## Students' Informational Writing

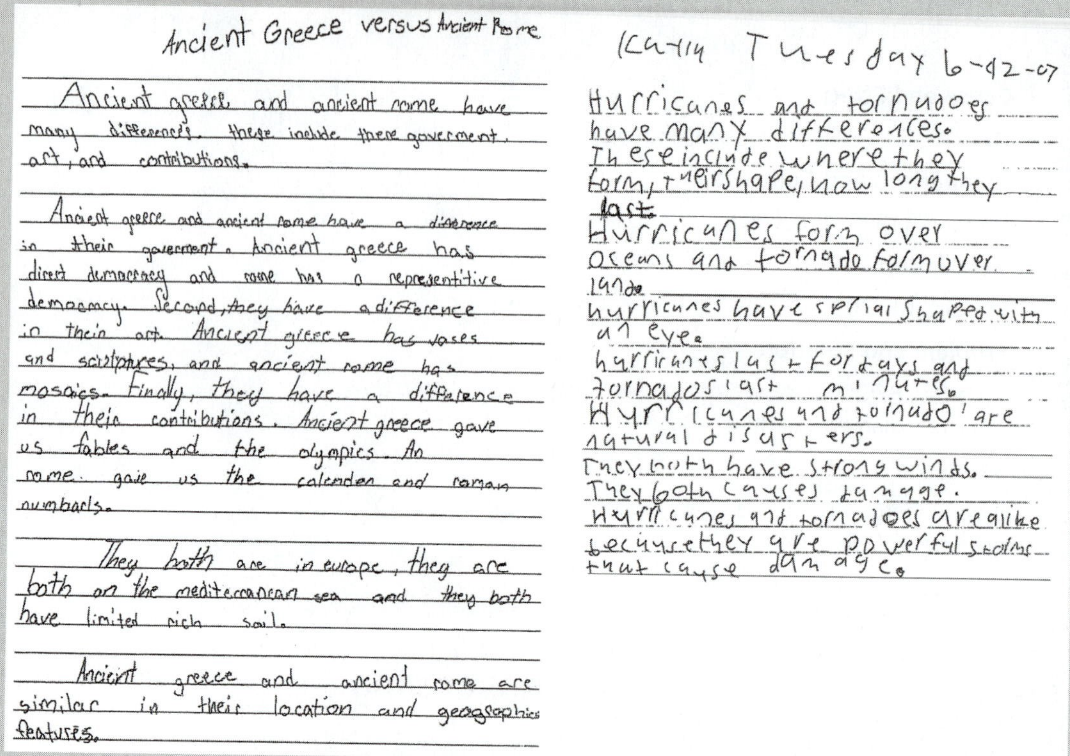

Ancient Greece versus Ancient Rome

Ancient greece and ancient rome have many differences. these include there goverment, art, and contributions.

Ancient greece and ancient rome have a difference in their goverment. Ancient greece has direct democracy and rome has a representitive democracy. Second, they have a difference in their art. Ancient greece has vases and sculptures, and ancient rome has mosaics. Finally, they have a difference in their contributions. Ancient greece gave us fables and the olympics. An rome gave us the calender and roman numbers.

They both are in europe, they are both on the mediterranean sea and they both have limited rich soil.

Ancient greece and ancient rome are similar in their location and geographics features.

Katia Tuesday 6-12-07

Hurricanes and tornadoes have many differences. These include where they form, thershape, how long they last. Hurricanes form over oceans and tornado form over land. hurricanes have sprial shaped with an eye. hurricanes last for days and tornados last minutes. Hurricanes and tornado are natural disasters. They both have strong winds. They both causes damage. Hurricanes and tornadoes are alike because they are powerful storms that cause damage.

writing structure, and the accuracy and completeness of the text should be considered. Use the following questions as a guide:

- What is the age or grade level of the student?
- What is the purpose for the text the student wrote?
- How familiar is the student with this type of text?
- Does the student select the appropriate writing structure(s) for the writing?
- Is the writing structure(s) used correctly?
- Is the informational text accurate and complete?
- Does the writing achieve its purpose?

Additionally, questions about content, organization, grammar, usage, spelling, and mechanics can be included.

## Persuasive Writing

Trying to persuade others to do something or accept another point of view begins early in students' lives. As infants, children cry to persuade someone to feed them, change their diapers, put them to bed, or get them up. Recall from Chapter 2 that, as they get older, children use the self-maintaining language function (Tough, 1982) to try to stay up past their regular bedtime, get a parent to purchase a desired toy, or avoid having to eat their vegetables. As they mature, children add the reasoning language function (Tough, 1982) to the self-maintaining function in hopes of persuading someone to do what they want or to support their views on some issue. "I need new basketball shoes because (1) my feet have grown, (2) my old ones don't have any springs, and (3) all my friends have them." Children recognize that simply saying *because* does not carry the persuasive power that reasons do when they are presented in an organized and polite way. Further along in their development, children gain the ability to step into someone else's shoes as they learn to empathize. The basic tools for persuasive writing, therefore, already exist in most children by the time they come to school.

Think of a piece of persuasive writing (editorial column, essay, poem, or political speech) that you have read. You will find that all three language functions described next are regularly used. Politicians try to persuade you to vote for them (self-maintaining) because they point out how much alike they are to you or how much they feel your pain or anger (projecting). They also include reasons for not supporting their opponent (reasoning). Think of an advertisement that persuaded you to buy a particular product. Did it make you feel good about yourself or imagine how it would make you look or feel good? Did it give several reasons for why you should purchase the product? Did it convince you that this product was better than other similar products? Did you buy the product? Chances are one or more of the three language functions identified here helped you make the decision to buy the product. For a list of different types of persuasive writing, look at Figure 10.15. See the Engaging in Oral Language feature for an example of how to integrate oral language with your persuasive writing lessons.

IRA/NCTE 3

Students can learn how to write any of the persuasive writing forms identified in Figure 10.15, if you help them understand three things about persuasive writing. Persuasive writing focuses on a specific audience, has a specific purpose, and uses specific writing techniques in making a case or influencing the thinking or actions of those who read it. Writers appeal to the beliefs, attitudes, and interests of the intended audience when creating a persuasive writing piece. For example, if some students want all students to recycle paper and plastic drink containers after lunch each day, they consider what would appeal to students: raising money for field trips, keeping the school cleaner, or helping the environment. The purpose for the recycling request is to collect paper and plastic drink containers and recycle them to avoid having them go to a landfill. It might also be to instill pride in the appearance of the school and protect the environment. Once the students have identified the audience and purpose for recycling paper and plastic, students have to decide on the appropriate writing techniques to convince their audience to recycle paper and plastic.

**Persuasive Writing Techniques** Carolyn Piazza (2003) identifies six writing techniques that writers use to argue their position in trying to get their audiences to support it. Continuing with the recycling topic as an example of persuasive writing:

- They might give reasons in support of recycling (reduces energy use, makes money, etc.).
- They might present different perspectives on recycling (landfill operator, plastics manufacturer, energy environmentalist).
- They might present two opposing sides of the position (reasons for recycling and reasons for not recycling).
- They might use analogies in support of recycling (recycling is like replanting every spring in the same soil).
- They might use the power of authority to support their position (the EPA, Sierra Club, etc.).

engaging in
# Oral language

## Integrating Oral Language with Persuasive Writing

An excellent way for students to use their oral language in conjunction with persuasive writing is through discussion webs (Alvermann, 1991). A discussion web gets students to look at both sides of a challenging issue or a thought-provoking question that arises from informational material they have read. As the discussion web grows, students can visualize and listen to others' responses to the issue or question and can express their own views. The position that a student takes and the argument that the student makes can be the basis for subsequent persuasive writing in response to the issue or question. Mr. Raymond's fourth-grade class participated in a discussion web after reading *Global Warming: Threat of Earth's Changing Climate* (Pringle, 2003). Here are the steps followed in the discussion web:

1. Mr. Raymond wrote a question in the middle of the chalkboard with a series of lines on each side of the question.

| Yes | | No |
|---|---|---|
| _______ | To reduce gas emissions in the United States, should | _______ |
| _______ | we support the reduction of the size of cars | _______ |
| _______ | and greatly increase our support of rail and other | _______ |
| _______ | forms of mass transportation? | _______ |

2. Each pair discussed and listed four or five reasons why the question could be answered yes or no and recorded their reasons.
3. Each pair talked with another pair to compare lists. They modified the lists as they talked.
4. Each square of four talked with another square to consider all their arguments and tried to reach consensus on their answer to the question.
5. The groups of eight then reported out to the whole class including dissenting views.
6. At the end of the discussion, students wrote their own persuasive arguments in support of their own positions.

Discussion webs encourage students to actively listen as statements are made by others and to prepare responses to those statements. Students learn the power of their own persuasive language as they elicit support for their positions. The success of discussion webs depends on the acceptance of different points of view that surface in any discussion. The acceptance leads to more give-and-take, which is the hallmark of good discussion. For additional information, models, and examples of discussion webs, go to www.justreadnow.com/strategies/web.htm.

**Figure 10.15** Types of Persuasive Writing

| | |
|---|---|
| Advertisements | Essays |
| Book reviews | Letters |
| Campaign speeches | Movie reviews |
| Debates | Political cartoons |
| Editorials | Travel brochures |

- They might combine one of more of these writing techniques in their writing (different perspectives and citing authorities).

It should also be noted that writers use many of the organizational writing structures identified earlier in the informational writing section of this chapter (cause and effect, comparison and contrast, etc.) with these writing techniques. With the recycling example, students might use cause/effect to support the argument for recycling, or they might compare and contrast the two opposing views on recycling. See the Engaging in Assessment feature for an example of how to use student-created rubrics to assess persuasive reports.

## Guidelines for Teaching and Assessing Persuasive Writing

To help students prepare for writing persuasive text, follow the same steps in preparing students to write any informational text. Students read and listen to different types of persuasive writing to understand the relationship between audience, purpose, and writing techniques used in persuasive writing. Students then collaborate on a small group or whole class persuasive writing text using these texts as models. Finally, students write their own pieces of persuasive writing with the shared writing as a model. Instructional steps to follow include:

1. The students listen to and read persuasive writing texts with particular focus on the purpose, audience, and writing techniques used by the authors.
2. The teacher guides discussion of the text with respect to purpose, audience, and writing techniques (e.g., reasons, perspectives, etc.) as well as the organizational writing structures (e.g., comparison/contrast, problem/solution, etc.).
3. Students explain how the author uses purpose, audience, and writing techniques in the text and why they work. They look at how the author gets readers' attention (speaks to the audience, begins with questions, or gives a vivid example).
4. Using the persuasive text as a model, students identify the topic, audience, purpose, and writing technique to use for a collaborative piece of persuasive writing.
5. Students in small groups or the whole class create the persuasive text.
6. Students write their own individual persuasive writing pieces.

Because there are a variety of persuasive writing forms (see Figure 10.15), different ones should be used as models for students. Other writing forms not identified in Figure 10.15 that students can use include poems and songs. As long as students keep their focus on the purpose and audience for their persuasive writing, they can experiment with any writing form they wish.

# *engaging in* Assessment

## Student-Created Rubrics

To further help his fourth-grade students write their group persuasive reports on animal habitats and how to protect them, Mr. Raymond decides to have the students construct the assessment rubric that he will use to assess their reports. He wants to have them involved in the creation of the rubric because they will come up with language that pertains specifically to their habitat report. He knows his students are familiar with six-trait writing assessment because he has used it with them in the past to assess their biographies and poetry. The six traits or elements of their reports that he will assess include: ideas and content, organization, voice, sentence fluency, word choice, and conventions. To help them get started, he asks the class to think about the purpose of the report—to persuade people to protect their animal's habitat—and how their writing will support that purpose. After discussing the six traits of the report within their groups, each group offers statements that Mr. Raymond puts on this chart.

Once Mr. Raymond has written his students' description of each writing trait, the class decides what would be a 5, 3, or 1 rating for each trait. By having his students construct their own rubric, Mr. Raymond believes that his students will not only own their reports but also the assessment rubric he will use to assess their reports.

**Habitat Report Six-Trait Writing Assessment Rubric**

*Content and Ideas*
Identifies the animal and its habitat
Presents a strong case for the habitat
Has good reasons for saving the habitat
Has good ideas for protecting the habitat

*Voice*
Strong voice throughout the report
Speaks directly to the reader
Really cares about the animal

*Word Choice*
Strong nouns and verbs
Strong visual picture presented
Clear and accurate words used
No clichés
Good use of literary techniques

*Organization*
Has a strong beginning about the habitat
Uses good strategy for building the case
Makes logical sequence of ideas
Supports case with research on habitat
Memorable ending about the animal

*Sentence Fluency*
Sentences vary in length
Create a dramatic pace to the ideas
Ideas flow easily in the report

*Conventions*
Correct sentences
Correct punctuation
Correct grammar and usage
Correct spelling
Paragraphs indented

Two additional features found in good persuasive writing are also found in other informational writing: description and details. Encourage students to provide strong visual images with their description and use strong nouns and verbs in the details they include in their persuasive texts. Description often includes comparative adjectives or adverbs to make a stronger case for a position in the text. Details can also make an emotional appeal to the reader by depicting the outcomes of a position or outcomes if the position is not taken (such as floating plastic bottles in streams, shore birds getting caught in the plastic handles, etc.). Questions to help students focus on description and details in their writing include:

- What details will appeal to my audience?
- What description should I use in my reasons for taking this stand?
- What is my strongest argument and how do details support it?

When students talk about the persuasive writing models used in class, they can highlight the description and details used by the author to determine where they are used and how they are used effectively. For an example of a student's persuasive writing trying to persuade his principal to allow students to have cell phones in school, look at Figure 10.16. When assessing persuasive writing, the nature of the student, purpose, audience, form, and writing technique used, along with the strength of the argument presented, should be considered, using the following questions as a guide:

**Figure 10.16**

**Example of Persuasive Writing**

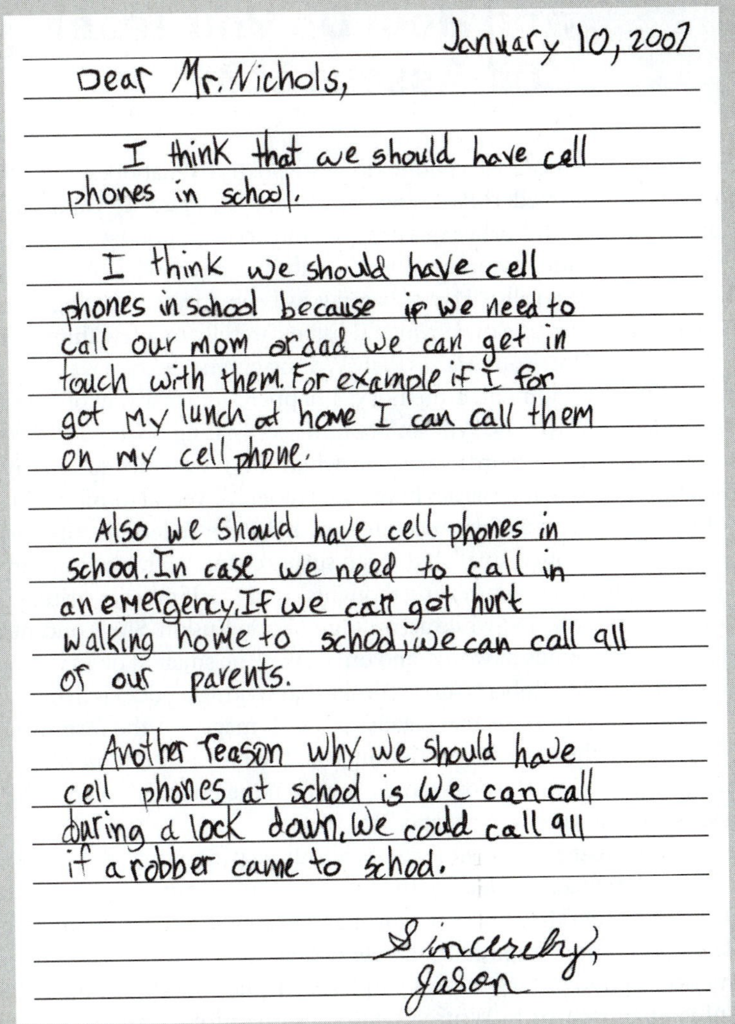
January 10, 2007

Dear Mr. Nichols,

I think that we should have cell phones in school.

I think we should have cell phones in school because if we need to call our mom or dad we can get in touch with them. For example if I for got my lunch at home I can call them on my cell phone.

Also we should have cell phones in school. In case we need to call in an emergency. If we can get hurt walking home to school, we can call all of our parents.

Another reason why we should have cell phones at school is we can call during a lock down. We could call 911 if a robber came to school.

Sincerely,
Jason

- What is the age and grade level of the student?
- How familiar is the student with this type of persuasive text?
- What is the purpose of the text?
- Who is the audience for the text?
- Does the student present a logical argument in support of the topic?
- Is the appropriate persuasive writing form used successfully?
- Is the appropriate writing technique(s) used successfully?
- Is the appropriate organizational writing structure(s) used successfully?
- Are there sufficient details included in the writing?
- Does the writing achieve its purpose?

Specific questions about content (depending on the models used), organization, grammar, spelling, and mechanics can be included.

# What Is Poetry Writing and How Do You Teach and Assess It?

> **Classroom Artifact Homework Exercise**
>
> *Song of Myself*
>
> Go to the Homework and Exercises section of Chapter 10 of MyEducationLab and examine the artifact, "Song of Myself," which is a poetic piece of writing by a child about himself. Complete the activities that follow, and save your work or transmit it to your professor as assigned.

Why write poetry or encourage children to write poetry? What does it do for the writer? What does it do for the reader? Paul Janeczko's book, *The Place My Words Are Looking For* (1990), answers these and other questions about writing poetry. In this collection of poetry, Janeczko includes comments by a number of poets who reveal why they write poetry. As Naomi Nye recalls: "Poetry has always been a way of paying attention to the world . . . a poem makes us slow down and listen carefully to a few things we have really heard" (p. 7). Lillian Morrison believes that "Writing poems can be a way of pinning down a dream; capturing a moment, a memory, a happening; it's a way of sorting out your thoughts and feelings" (p. 11). William Stafford sees writing poetry as "Talk with a little luck in it . . . just let the words take you where *they* want to go" (p. 59). For Paul Fleischman, the poems that he writes have "two voices . . . Verbal music, making use of the sounds of words as much as their meaning" (p. 103). Siv Cedering writes that a poem is "Like the blue bird . . . often small, but it can surprise you. With words it can paint a picture . . . that leads to other pictures and thoughts" (p. 117). If prose is writing in color then poetry is writing in black and white according to Karla Kuskin. She "concentrate[s] more on the rhythms and sounds of words, and on details. The smallest observations can be the start of a poem" (p. 138). Robert Currie admits that writing a poem is demanding because the poet has to "select the concrete details . . . vivid images . . . the form from which the poem can grow . . . the sounds and rhythms . . . the best possible words . . . in the best possible order" (p. 141). If the poet can do this, then the poem is "touched by an indefinable magic as it's preserved on the paper" (p. 140).

What can we learn from these poets about writing poetry? A poem explores a moment, an experience, or a feeling in time. It sharpens our senses as it promotes the power of close observations of the world around us, even the smallest part of that world. The observations require "concrete details" that lead to "vivid images," which are hallmarks of good poetry. It puts emphasis on the sounds in our words as well as the meaning of those words. Writing poetry also requires conscious control over the words, structure, and the form chosen for the poetry. What else can poets do? Play! Play with sounds. Play with words. Play with images. Play with forms.

## Guidelines for Teaching and Assessing Poetry Writing

To help students write poetry, follow the same steps in preparing students for any writing. Students read and listen to different kinds of good poetry to understand the form and nature of the poetry. Students then collaborate on small group or whole class poetry writing using these poems as models. Finally, students write their own poetry with the shared poetry writing as a model. Instructional steps to follow might include:

1. The students listen to and read poems about people, friendship, sports, or other themes.
2. The teacher guides discussion of the poem with respect to purpose, meaning, and writing techniques (rhyming words, etc.) as well as how the poem is organized.
3. Students explain how the poets use language and writing techniques in the poems and why they work.
4. Using a poem as a model, students identify the topic and writing technique to use for a collaborative poem.
5. Students in small groups or the whole class create poems.
6. Students write their own individual poems.

Since there are a variety of poetic forms and techniques, different ones should be used as models for students. Also, students should be exposed to ways of finding the words they want to use in their poems. Here are ways of helping students with words, forms, and literary techniques. Along with instructional steps and strategies for teaching poetry, the teacher's interest and enthusiasm for reading and writing poetry are essential. There is a bit of mystery and wonder about poetry that children can learn to understand and appreciate with the help of their teachers. Help make it easier, not harder, to write it. A list of books with poems to use as models for writing poetry can be found in Figure 10.17.

**Sharpen Senses** In his book, *Development through Drama*, Brian Way (1967) urges teachers to encourage their students to use their senses to stimulate their imagination through a series of sensory activities. Poetry writing can also begin with students thinking about what their senses tell them about the world around them. What their senses tell them can be put into words that provide details and ideas for poetry. A preliminary activity that sharpens students' senses can begin with questions that activate sensory memories:

- What does the ground feel like at different times of the year? (Touch)
- What does cake frosting taste like right off the beater? (Taste)
- What do burning leaves smell like in the fall? (Smell)
- What do you see the first cold, windy day when leaves fall? (See)
- What sounds do you hear on a hot August night? (Hear)

As students think and respond to these questions, encourage them to go a step beyond their sensory memories and to think about what their answer reminds them about the memory.

Figure 10.17

## Poetry Books with Poems to Use as Models for Writing Poetry

**Alliteration Poems**

Edwards, P. (2001). *Clara Caterpillar.* New York: HarperCollins.

**Color Poems**

O'Neill, M. (1989). *Hailstones and Halibut Bones.* New York: Doubleday.

Yolen, J. (2003). *Color Me a Rhyme: Nature Poems for Young People.* Honesdale, PA: Boyds Mills.

**Haiku Poems**

Gollub, M. (1998). *Cool Melons—Turn to Frogs!* New York: Lee and Low.

Prelutsky, J. (2004). *If Not for the Cat.* New York: Greenwillow.

**Onomatopoeia Poems**

Moss, L. (1995). *Zin! Zin! Zin!: A Violin.* New York: Simon and Schuster.

Yolen, J. (2000). *Off We Go.* Boston: Little, Brown.

**Rhyming Poems**

Franco, B. (2000). *Shells.* Danbury, CT: Children's Press.

Merriam, E. (1986). *Fresh Paint.* New York: Macmillan Child Group.

Yolen, J. (Ed) (1982). *Street Rhymes around the World.* Honesdale, PA: Boyds Mills.

**Parallel Poems**

Koch, K. (2000). *Wishes, Lies, and Dreams: Teaching Children to Write Poetry.* New York: Harper.

**Sensory Poems**

Dotlich, R. (1998). *Lemonade Sun and Other Poems.* Honesdale, PA: Boyds Mills.

Fletcher, R. (1997). *Ordinary Things: Poems from a Walk in Early Spring.* New York: Atheneum.

Fletcher, R. (1997). *Twilight Comes Twice.* New York: Clarion.

Moore, L. (1997). *Poems Have Roots.* New York: Atheneum.

**Simile Poems**

Hopkins, L. (Ed.) (2004). *Wonderful Words: Poems about Reading, Writing, Speaking, and Listening.* New York: Simon and Schuster.

Norton, J. (1998). *As: A Surfeit of Similes.* Morrow.

Peters, L. (2003). *Earthshake: Poems from the Ground Up.* New York: Greenwillow.

**Word Picture Poems**

Grandits, J. (2004). *Technically, It's Not My Fault: Concrete Poems.* New York: Clarion.

Roemer, H. (2004). *Come to My Party and Other Shape Poems.* New York: Holt.

Solt, M. (1980). *Concrete Poetry: A World View.* Bloomfield, IN: Indiana University.

**Word Play Poems**

Steig, J. (1992). *Alpha Beta Chowder.* New York: HarperCollins.

| | |
|---|---|
| Question: | What sounds do you hear on a hot summer night? |
| Answer: | I hear lots of noisy insects. |
| Question: | What do the noisy insects remind you of? |
| Answer: | The clicking sounds on a rollercoaster ride. |

By having students think about what something sounds like, looks like, feels like, tastes like, or smells like, they begin to use the language of poetry. Students can pick any place or event or time of the year and sharpen their senses on any one of these types of memories to write sensory poems. Here is an example of a third-grader's poem about watching someone swinging on a swing during recess in the spring.

Swinging
Going up,
legs are bending,
arms are closing,
hair is blowing.
I see a smile.
Stopping at the top,
Legs are stretching,
arms are stretching,
coming down.

To help students write poetry, follow the same steps in preparing students for any writing. Students begin by reading and listening to different kinds of good poetry to understand the form and nature of the poetry.

Known poems can provide a scaffold or structure for the third-grader's poem, but the sensory moment gives the student the words that make up the poem.

**Word Play** Another avenue for helping students write poetry is through word play. Poets often play with words and the sounds in words. Look at how Mary O'Neill plays with words in "Sound of Water" from her book of poetry, *What Is That Sound!* (1966):

**Sound of Water**

The sound of water is:
Rain,
Lap,
Fold,
Slap,
Gurgle,
Splash,
Churn,
Crash,
Murmur,
Pour,
Ripple,
Roar,
Plunge,
Drip,
Spout,
Slip,
Sprinkle,
Flow,
Ice,
Snow.

What fun to think of a whole series of nouns and verbs that remind us of the sounds of water. What about the sounds of other things? Look what this fourth-grader came up with:

**Sounds of Dogs**

Lick,
Scratch,
Wag,
Bark,
Sniff,
Yelp,
Yawn,
Snore,
Thump,
Whine,
Gulp,
Splash,
Lap,
Pant.

Children can play with words just like this using their senses. What about sounds of school, sounds of riding the school bus, sounds of other pets, or sounds of the seasons? This is only a partial list for sounds. What about Sights? Tastes? Textures? Smells? Any topic can work. The key is to use good examples of poetry, such as Mary O'Neill's, to show students how poets play with words.

Other word play includes rhymes, alliteration, and onomatopoeia. For rhyming, teach children to write hink-pinks and couplets. Hink-pinks are two single-syllable words that rhyme and are responses to a riddle or question. Here are two examples:

| | |
|---|---|
| Question: | What is a dachshund? |
| Answer: | Log dog. |
| Riddle: | Where do mice live? |
| Answer: | Mouse house. |

Students can also write hinky-pinkies (two-syllable words) or hinkity-pinkities (three-syllable words).

Alliteration is when a series of words begin with the same sounds. Students can begin to play with alliteration using their own names. Here are several examples:

Jim jumps for joy

When he joins the band.

Donna starts the day

With a dozen donuts.

Onomatopoeia is when poets use words whose sounds convey their meaning. O'Neill's poem has examples of onomatopoeia (*gurgle, churn, splash, crash*). Other examples would be *hiss, boom, bang* or *woof, bow wow, yelp.* Using this device, O'Neill, Spier, and Bacmeister have written many poems that are good models for students. Take a look at Rhonda Bacmeister's famous poem "Galoshes" (Bacmeister, 1969) as a great example of this:

**Galoshes**

Susie's galoshes
Make splishes and sploshes
And slooshes and sloshes
As Susie steps slowly along in the slush
They stamp and they tramp
On the ice and the concrete
They get stuck in the muck and the mud:
But Susie likes much best to hear

The slippery slush
As it slooshes and sloshes,
And splishes and sploshes
All around her galoshes!

Students can play with onomatopoeia by inventing new words with sounds that convey meaning. They can also add letters to existing words to extend the sound of a word. For example, the school bus might sound like "crankyplop!" as it drives away. "Owwwwww!" lets us know that something really hurt. Students can also combine two or more kinds of word play in their poetry.

■ ***Word Pictures*** Also known as concrete poems, word pictures are poems in which the writer arranges the letters, words, or phrases to form shapes or pictures that depict what the poem is about. For example, if a student is writing a poem about playing baseball, the shape of the poem can be a baseball with words inserted on the baseball. Look at the two examples of students' word picture poems in Figure 10.18.

**Parallel Poems** One of the best ways to help students write poetry is to provide forms or structures that students can use in constructing their poems. Kenneth Koch (2000) includes a variety of poem structures that have been used successfully with students. These include parallel poetry in which the lines are alike in a particular way. Lines might begin with the same word or phrase or might use a repeating form. Some of these repeating forms include:

| | |
|---|---|
| I wish: | Every line begins with "I wish." |
| Colors: | Every line includes a color. |
| I remember: | Every line begins with "I remember." |
| Not poem: | Every line begins with "I am not a ________ because." |
| I used to be: | Every line begins with "I used to be ________ but now I'm ________." |
| Comparison: | Every line begins "________ is like ________." |
| Senses: | Each line refers to one of the senses. |

Some of these parallel forms are particularly useful in helping students compare something about themselves in the past with how they are today. For excerpts from students' parallel poems, see Figure 10.19.

**Found Poems** Another approach to poetic forms is to get students to write found poems. A found poem derives its name from words that come from other sources of writing, including textbooks, trade books, newspapers, brochures, advertisements, magazines, menus, and even songs. The topic for the poem can come from looking through writing sources or students can look through them with a topic to help them select

**Figure 10.18**

## Examples of Word Picture Poems

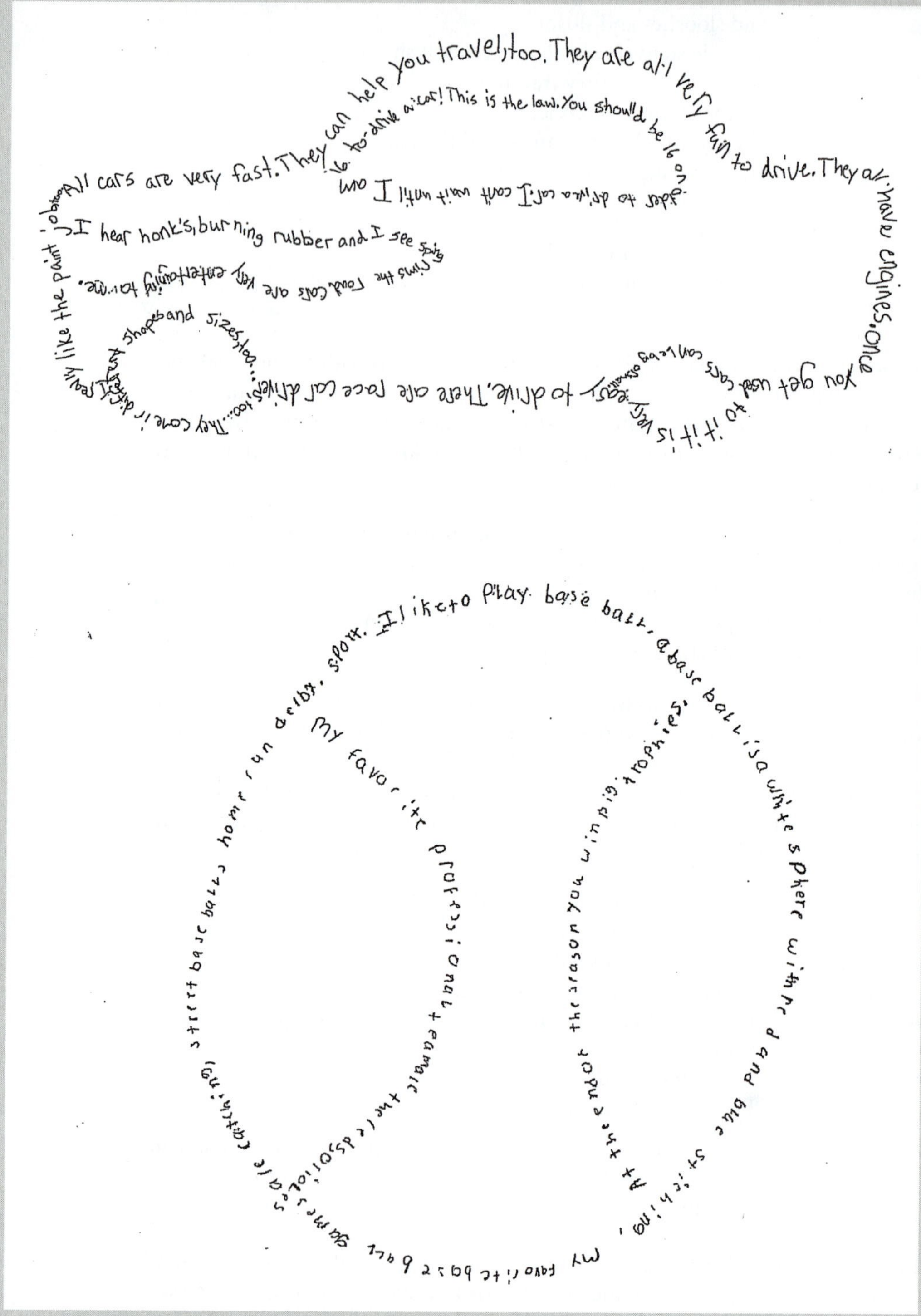

**Figure 10.19** Excerpts of Parallel Poems

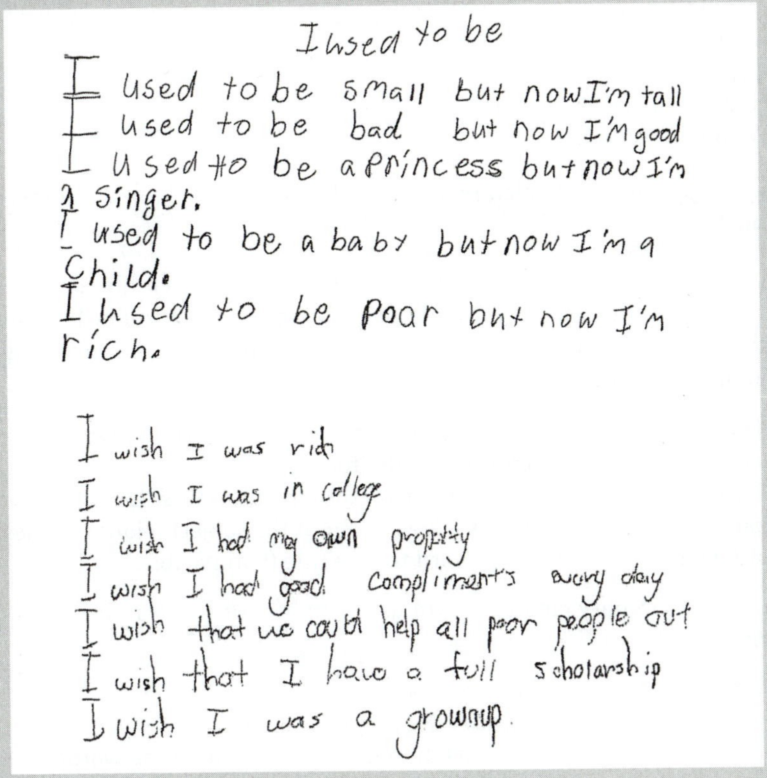

I used to be

I used to be small but now I'm tall
I used to be bad but now I'm good
I used to be a princess but now I'm
a singer.
I used to be a baby but now I'm a
child.
I used to be poor but now I'm
rich.

I wish I was rich
I wish I was in college
I wish I had my own propetty
I wish I had good compliments every day
I wish that we could help all poor people out
I wish that I have a full scholarship
I wish I was a grownup.

words and phrases to go with it. Here is a found poem written by sixth-graders about a weekend in the country. The source for the phrase used was a series of summer advertisements in a magazine.

**A Weekend at the Beach**

United,
Like a couple of relaxed vacationers
Who kick up their heels!
The great escape tells them,
See all the sights!
Make your tan glow!
Start fresh in the morning!
It will make you happy!

What's great about found poems is that students can add or remove words or lines as they create their own poem out of someone else's writing.

**Haiku Poems** This ancient poetic form from Japan focuses on a special time or place in nature. The Japanese version contains a total of seventeen syllables—the first line has five, the second has seven, and the third has five. A somewhat easier form of haiku has three lines but does not have the syllable restrictions. After students have determined a topic in nature, encourage them to make the first line describe what is happening, the second line tell where, and the third line describe when. Here is an example written by as fifth-grader:

A star-lit night
A sparkling tent
Hovering above the Earth
Waiting for sunrise.

The student paints a vivid picture of what a star-lit night looks like to someone looking up from the Earth.

**Cinquain** A cinquain poem is a five-line poem with each line telling something about the topic of the poem. Adelaide Crapsey created this form in 1911 and used the French word, *cinq*, which means five, to name this type of poem. Her formula for writing cinquains uses the following pattern:

| | |
|---|---|
| First line: | Title or subject of the poem (two-syllable word) |
| Second line: | Describes the title (four syllables) |
| Third line: | Shows action related to the title (six syllables) |
| Fourth line: | Describes a feeling about the subject (eight syllables) |
| Fifth line: | Another word for the title (two syllables) |

A more contemporary cinquain form uses numbers of words rather than syllables in its formula and goes like this:

| | |
|---|---|
| First line: | Title (one word) |
| Second line: | Describes the title (two words) |
| Third line: | Shows action related to the title (three words) |
| Fourth line: | Describes a feeling (a four-word phrase) |
| Fifth line: | Synonym for the title (one word) |

Here is an example of a contemporary cinquain written by a fourth-grader:

Flying
Taking off
Rising, Soaring, Landing
Leaving your cares behind
Airborne

**Diamante** The diamante was created by Iris Tiedt (2002) to focus on contrasting ideas. When complete, it forms the shape of a diamond. The seven lines in the poetic structure are arranged in the following way:

| | |
|---|---|
| First line: | Subject (one noun) |
| Second line: | Describes the subject (two adjectives) |
| Third line: | Tells about the subject (three *-ing* participles) |
| Fourth line: | Contrasting words about the subject (two similar and two opposite nouns) |
| Fifth line: | Tells about the opposite of the subject (three *-ing* participles) |
| Sixth line: | Describes the opposite of the subject (two adjectives) |
| Seventh line: | Opposite of the subject (one noun) |

As with other poetry forms, diamantes help students expand their use of vocabulary and parts of speech. Here is an example of a fifth-grader's diamante poem:

**Morning**

Early, rested
Waking, rising, leaving
Dawn, light, dusk, dark
Returning, setting, sleeping
Late, sleepy
Evening

You can see the contrasting words that describe the differences between morning and evening (**dawn, light** versus **dusk, dark**).

**Similes** Another literary device that students can use in writing poetry is the simile. Like the cinquain, similes compare one thing to another. For example, *The sky is as red as a glowing fire* or *The train is as loud as a hurricane.* Learning how to write similes helps extend students' language in one line or provides a line structure for an entire poem. The two basic simile forms are:

_______ as _______
_______ like _______.

Here is a series of similes that students in a fourth-grade classroom wrote about learning:

**Learning**

Learning is as hard as talking to a brick wall.
Learning is as hard as juggling three balls.
Learning can be as tiring as running in a marathon.
Learning is as surprising as finding a twenty dollar bill.
Learning is as rewarding as a smile.
Learning is as creative as building bridges.
Learning is as exciting as fireworks.
Learning is as illuminating as turning on a light.

Students could easily substitute *like* for the *as* _______ *as* structure in each line. As students experiment with similes in their poetry, they will begin to explore different comparisons and use vocabulary in more unique ways.

**Metaphor** Another literary technique that creates comparisons is the metaphor. A metaphor makes comparisons not by stating how something is like something else but how something actually *is* something else. For example, the first line of the earlier example, *Learning is as hard as talking to a brick wall,* becomes a metaphor when written as *Learning is talking to a brick wall.* The fourth-grade students who wrote the similes turned them into metaphors by removing the simile structure. This is the poem they came up with:

Learning is talking to a brick wall.
Learning is juggling three balls.
Learning is running in a marathon.
Learning is finding a twenty dollar bill.
Learning is a smile.
Learning is building bridges.
Learning is fireworks.
Learning is turning on a light.

This poem has a series of metaphors, while other poems can contain extended metaphors. By exploring metaphors in their poetry, students activate their imaginations while comparing things in their own world to other things they see. For example, in this poem, a student compares learning to read to learning to ride a bike.

**Learning to Read**

Training wheels keep you from falling
Blocks on the pedals keep you moving
Handlebars keep you straight in steering
My Dad keeps me steady by holding.
The training wheels come off
The blocks come off
I hold the handle bars
My Dad holds me
Running beside
I begin falling
He pulls me
I keep
Going.
It's like
learning
to read

This fifth-grader was able to sustain the metaphor—about learning to ride a bike—throughout the poem by thinking of his own experiences when he thought about learning to read. Every student has challenges when learning something new, such as roller-skating, swimming, drawing, and the like, which means every student can create a poem with an extended metaphor that compares two learning challenges or any other experiences they have. See the Exploring Technology feature for an example of how keyboarding skills can help students transition from prose writing to poetry writing.

IRA/NCTE 5

**Parachute Poetry** Another way to help students examine their own experiences for possible topics for poems is to try parachute poetry. This approach to poetry, designed by Ben Brunwin (2004), uses perspective to help students write poetry about important people, places, or events in their own lives. Like a parachutist jumping from an airplane, students gradually approach the subject of their poems (a favorite vacation place, for example). In their gradual descent, students' observations change as they get closer to the place of special meaning for them. Their poems reflect this change in what they see and how they describe it. To help them get started, Brunwin has students close their eyes and recall a special place using the phrase "In my mind I have a picture . . ." Brunwin has also identified five essential steps in this poetry writing approach:

- Unpacking a notion (look at a subject from a variety of angles and perspectives)
- Putting the right words in the right places (words that reflect different aspects of the subject)
- Putting the right phrases in the right spaces (each line reflects a changing perspective)

# exploring technology

## Using Keyboarding to Transition from Prose Writing to Poetry Writing

One of the challenges that students have when writing poetry is learning how to use words and phrases as lines in poems rather than sentences. To help them transition from prose to poetry writing, the computer and a word processing program are part of the perfect solution. They can help with rhythm and word or syllable counts for haiku, cinquain, or diamante poems. Look at what third-grade students wrote about autumn and the changes they observed. In the first column, you can see the sentences they wrote. In the middle column, they broke the sentences into smaller phrases using a word processing program and the Enter key. In their final version (right column), they deleted some words and changed others to create the poem.

The computer may have made the creation of this poem easier, but the third-graders still made the decisions about phrases and omissions in their sentences. By reading the phrases aloud, they discovered the rhythm of their poem.

We see days get shorter and nights get longer.
We feel cooler days and cooler nights.
We hear birds chatter and geese honking.
They are getting ready to fly south.
Crickets are chirping less as it gets colder.
Squirrels gather acorns and seeds for the winter.
Leaves turn from green to red, yellow, and orange and begin to fall.
We stop swimming and start raking.
We jump in piles of leaves instead of jumping into swimming pools.
We put away our summer clothes and put on our sweaters and jackets.
These are ways that fall changes.

We see
days get shorter
and nights get longer.
We feel cooler days
and cooler nights.
We hear birds chatter
and geese honking.
They are getting ready
to fly south.
Crickets are chirping less
as it gets colder.
Squirrels gather
acorns and seeds
for the winter.
Leaves turn to red, yellow, orange
and begin to fall.
We stop swimming
and start raking.
We jump in piles of leaves
instead of jumping
into swimming pools.
We put away
our summer clothes
and put on our sweaters
and jackets.
These are ways
that fall changes.

Autumn
days get shorter
nights get longer.
cooler days
cooler nights
birds chattering
Geese honking
getting ready
To fly south
Crickets chirp less
Squirrels gather more
As Fall continues.
Leaves turn orange,
Red, and yellow
And fall.
Swimming stops
Raking begins.
We jump
In piles of leaves
Instead of
swimming pools.
Our shorts and tees
Become sweaters
And jackets.
Fall changes
And changes us.

- Creating a unique rhythm (establishes a pace for the poem)
- Arranging the words on the page (enables the reader to say the poem as the writer has written it)

Here is an example of how a sixth-grade student used the parachute process to create a poem about going to the beach every summer. Notice the difference between the two versions. The first draft of the poem has scaffolding devices that are absent in the final version.

**The Beach**

In my mind I have a picture of
a beach
It looks like a squiggly line
of sand
Being drawn and erased by the
waves
I see people lined up lying down
Blotting out stripes, colors, and
pictures
On their towels
I see Dad digging a hole in
the sand
That fills with water from the
waves
Like a sandy bathtub.
He smiles and says the water
is fine.
I jump in the tub.
I am happy to be back
At the beach

**The Beach**

The beach is
Like a squiggly line of sand
Drawn and erased by waves.
People sitting and lying down,
Blotting out
Stripes, colors, and pictures
On their towels.
My dad,
Digging in the sand,
Makes a tub that fills
With ending waves.
The water's fine he laughs.
I am happy to be back
At the beach
Again.

What is interesting about this approach to poetry is the ease with which students write down their ideas about the subject of their poems. Often, their first attempts are more like sentences without the restriction of formula poems. This approach does have a formula based on a parachute drop, a subject (favorite person, place, or event) and the feeling associated with the subject. The crafting of the poem comes with the application of Brunwin's five steps (unpacking, finding the right words, finding the right phrases, etc.) that help students remove the scaffolding to reveal the final version of the poem.

When assessing poetry writing, the nature of the student, type of poetry, poetic techniques used, and the development of the poetry should be considered. Use the following questions as a guide:

- What is the age or grade level of the student?
- What is the poetry type (form) the student uses? (haiku, cinquain, limerick, etc.)
- How familiar is the student with this type of poetry?
- Does the student use the poetic form correctly?
- Does the student use poetic techniques successfully?
- Does the student use words and phrases effectively?

Additionally, questions about content, organization, word choice, voice, spelling, and mechanics can be included. For these questions and formative assessment techniques on how students use the writing process, refer to Chapter 5. See the Exploring Children's Literature feature for a list of titles that provide different examples of writing structures.

IRA/NCTE 2



## exploring Children's Literature

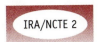

### Mentor Texts for Teaching Writing Structures

#### Grades K to 3

*26 Fairmont Avenue*—Written and illustrated by Tomie de Paola, published by Putnam (1999).
Children's author and illustrator Tomie De Paola describes his experiences at home and in school when he was a boy (memoir text structure).

*Bringing the Rain to Kapiti Plain: A Nandi Tale*—Written and illustrated by Verna Aardema, published by Dial (1981).
A cumulative rhyme relating how Ki-pat brought rain to the drought-stricken Kapiti Plain.

*Diary of a Worm*—Written by Doreen Cronin, illustrated by Harry Bliss, and published by Joanna Colter (2003).
A young worm discovers, day by day, that there are some very good and some not so good things about being a worm in this great big world (diary/journal text structure).

*I Love Animals*—Written and illustrated by Flora McDonnell, published by Candlewick (1994).
A girl names all the animals she likes on her farm, from Jock the dog to the pig and her piglets. The tale contains a repeated refrain structure, "I love . . ."

*The Relatives Came*—Written by Cynthia Rylant, illustrated by Stephen Gamball, and published by Bradbury (1993).
The relatives come to visit from Virginia and everyone has a wonderful time (circular text structure).

*The Seashore Book*—Written by Charlotte Zolotow, illustrated by Wendell Minor, and published by HarperCollins (1992).
A mother's words help a little boy imagine the sights and sounds of the seashore, even though he's never seen the ocean (story-within-a-story text structure).

*Tough Boris*—Written by Mem Fox, illustrated by Kathryn Brown, and published by Harcourt Brace Jovanovich (1994).
Although he is a very tough pirate, Boris von der Borch cries when his parrot dies (seesaw text structure).

*Wallace's Lists*—Written by Barbara Bottner, illustrated by Olof Landstrom, and published by Katherine Tegen (2004).
Devoted to making lists about everything in his life, Wallace the mouse discovers the joys of spontaneity and adventure when he becomes friends with his neighbor Albert (list structure).

#### Grades 4 to 8

*All the Places to Love*—Written by Patricia MacLachlan, illustrated by Mike Wimmer, and published by HarperCollins (1994).
A young boy describes the favorite places he shares with his family on his grandparents' farm and in the nearby countryside (memoir text structure).

*Ashanti to Zulu: African Traditions*—Written by Margaret Musgrove and Diane Dillon, published by Dial (1976).
This book explains some traditions and customs of twenty-six African tribes beginning with letters from A to Z (alphabet structure).

*My Mama Had a Dancing Heart*—Written by Libba Gray, illustrated by Raul Colon, and published by Orchard (1995).
A ballet dancer recalls how she and her mother would welcome each season with a dance outdoors (circular text structure).

*Nettie's Trip South*—Written by Ann Turner, illustrated by Ronald Himler, and published by Macmillan (1987).
A ten-year-old northern girl encounters the ugly realities of slavery when she visits Richmond, Virginia, and sees a slave auction (letter text structure).

*(Continued)*

*Starry Messenger*—Written and illustrated by Peter Sis, published by Farrar, Straus Giroux (1996).
This illustrated biographical treatment of Galileo describes the life and work of the courageous man who changed the way people saw the galaxy by offering objective evidence that the earth was not the fixed center of the universe (diary/journal text structure).

*Up North at the Cabin*—Written by Marcia Chall, illustrated by Steve Johnson, and published by Lothrop, Lee & Shepard (1992).
Summer vacation up north at the cabin provides memorable experiences with the water, the animals, and the other faces of nature. This book contains a repeated refrain structure, "Up north at the cabin. . . ."

*The Wright Brothers*—Written by Pamela Edwards, illustrated by Henry Cole, and published by Hyperion (2003).
Cumulative text in the style of "The House That Jack Built" describes the series of events that led to the Wright Brothers' historic flight (cumulative text structure).

*Iron Wok Jan*—Written by Shinji Saijiyo and published by ComicsOne (manga series).
Jan is a talented, arrogant young chef on a nonstop quest to become the world's greatest cuisine master. Mr. Otani, the famous food critic is in for a huge surprise when he is served his own head on a platter.

## revisit the classroomchallenge

How did Mr. Raymond help his students write their persuasive reports? Over the weekend, he downloaded several models of reports published by the Environmental Protection Agency (EPA) that focused on protecting the habitats of animals. Using these reports as models, he had students discuss the writing techniques used by the authors and the organizational writing structure. For example, one report presented a view that supported protecting a habitat while another view opposed it. Students also commented that one report used a comparison-contrast writing structure while the other used the problem-solution writing structure. Once students became familiar with the writing techniques and structures used in the reports, they began to organize their information and arguments. Mr. Raymond showed them how to use graphic organizers to help with this. Later, he showed them how other writing genres (including poems, plays, etc.) could be used to persuade audiences about an important topic or issue.

## chapterreview

Learning to write in all genres is both rewarding and challenging. The keys to helping students master these genres include reading and talking about the genres, collaborating on group and class writing, and supporting students as they use the genres in their own writing. Quite often, the writing skill developed in one genre will spill over into other genres that students explore. For example, the imaginative use of words in poetry can lead to effective analogies and metaphors in persuasive writing. Students should be encouraged to engage in all writing genres to stimulate their imaginations, clarify their own thinking, and reveal to themselves the power of their own language.

### What Is Personal Writing and How Do You Teach and Assess It?

Personal writing includes personal journals, learning journals, and letter writing. For journal writing, students need notebooks or other permanent forms of writing material, models for journal writing, and reader responses to their journal writing on a regular basis. Assessment should focus on frequency, honesty, and sincerity of student effort.

Personal letters are for friends and family members; business letters are for less familiar audiences. Teaching letter writing involves explaining the purposes for letter writing, modeling letter writing, sharing information from the letters, and choosing the appropriate format. Assessment should include the correct letter format, correct writing conventions, and quality of the content.



## What Is Story Writing and How Do You Teach and Assess It?

Stories come in a variety of forms and share some common elements: plot, setting, characters, problem (conflict), resolution of the problem, and point of view. The teaching of story writing should address story structure and elaboration. Story elaboration includes details and description. Follow the same procedures for teaching story elaboration as the ones used for story structure. Assessment includes elements of the story structure used, elaboration, and how successful (interesting) the story is.

## What Is Informational Writing and How Do You Teach and Assess It?

Informational writing explains, describes, defines, compares, contrasts, analyzes, synthesizes, or summarizes information. In teaching informational writing, students need to read and listen to different types of information text and discuss the type, writing, structure, and techniques used by the writer. When assessing informational writing, consider the nature of the student, the purpose, type, and techniques used in the informational text, and how successful the student has been in achieving the purpose of the writing.

## What Is Poetry Writing and How Do You Teach and Assess It?

Poetry is writing that has a rhythm, form, and sound all its own and explores a moment, an experience, or a feeling in time. It comes in many shapes, sizes, and forms. Instruction has students read and listen to poetry, discuss different kinds of poetry, collaborate on writing poems, and write their own poems. One technique for poetry writing is parachute poetry, which focuses on the senses, observations, and perspectives. When assessing student poetry, consider the nature of the student, type of poetry, poetic techniques, and the words and phrases used by the student.

PEARSON myeducationlab™
Where the Classroom Comes to Life

Now go to www.myeducationlab.com to take a Pretest to assess your initial comprehension of chapter content, study chapter content with your individualized Study Plan, take a Posttest to assess your understanding of chapter content, practice your teaching skills with Building Teaching Skills exercises, and build a deeper, more applied understanding of chapter content with Homework and Exercises.

chapter 11

# Engaging with Literature

**Denise Johnson,** College of William and Mary

## classroomchallenge

**The students in** Miss Hall's classroom are starting a study of westward expansion of the United States during the early 1800s as part of the social studies curriculum. Though the social studies textbook provides coverage of the major events, the students do not have adequate background knowledge to fully understand these events. Miss Hall also believes it is important for students to understand and appreciate westward expansion from the multiple perspectives of the different races, ethnicities, and classes involved. Miss Hall decides to supplement her social studies textbook with children's literature. Each day during the reading/language arts block, she reads aloud a nonfiction picture book that provides the class with additional background information on the westward expansion. She has also divided the class into several groups and assigned each group a different historical fiction book to read that presents the period from different

perspectives. As the students read and discuss the historical fiction books, they have questions about whether certain events in the stories actually happened or whether certain characters really existed. Sometimes, the book discussions become more of an argument than a thoughtful conversation. Miss Hall decides to conduct a lesson on two important skills: determining the difference between fiction and nonfiction and learning how to have a meaningful book discussion.

## Questions for Reflection

1. What can Miss Hall do to help students understand the difference between fiction and nonfiction?
2. What can Miss Hall do to help students engage in meaningful book discussions even when students disagree about aspects of the text?
3. How can Miss Hall assess whether students have learned the differences between fiction and nonfiction and have learned to engage in meaningful book discussions?

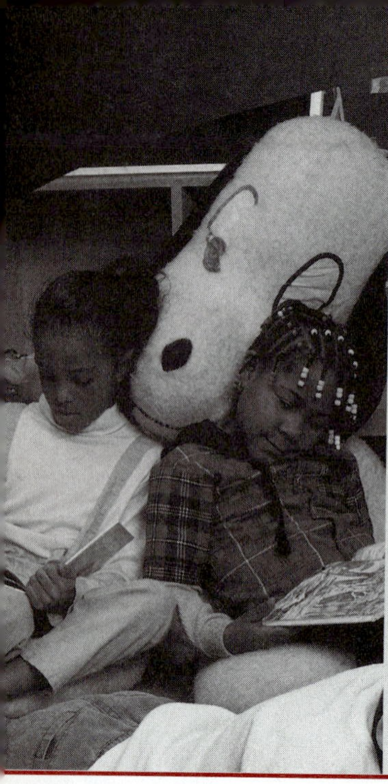

## anticipating this chapter

To help you answer these and other questions about engaging with children's literature in the classroom, this chapter addresses the following questions:

Why is children's literature important for reading and writing?
What do we know about children's literature?
What do we know about how children learn about literature?
How can we teach children's literature?
How can we assess students' understanding of literature?
How can we support diversity and differentiated instruction in the classroom?
How can we support technology use and children's literature?

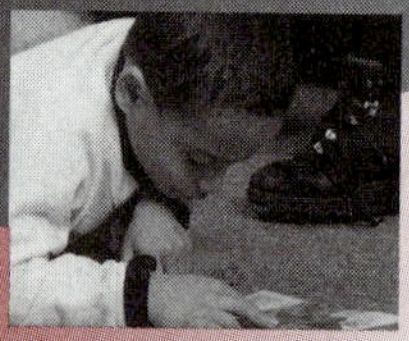

# Why Is Children's Literature Important for Reading and Writing?

IRA/NCTE 1

Do you remember your favorite book as a child? Perhaps it was the crazy adventures of Dr. Seuss's *The Cat in the Hat* or Maurice Sendak's *Where the Wild Things Are*. Maybe you were drawn to the friendship between Wilbur and Charlotte in E. B. White's *Charlotte's Web*? Or, did you prefer the mysteries of Donald J. Sobel's *Encyclopedia Brown* or the magical worlds in C. S. Lewis's *Chronicles of Narnia* or Madeleine L'Engle's *A Wrinkle in Time?* These books bring back fond memories and are a tribute to how stories resonate in the minds of students and leave a lasting impression. The power of stories to captivate students will endure forever as long as adults help students experience children's literature.

Reading children's literature not only provides enjoyment, but it can lead to an increase in language acquisition, reading comprehension, reading vocabulary, understanding story patterns, reading fluency, and writing. Additionally, reading a balanced selection of good literature offers students many other benefits.

- Good literature provides students with points of reference for understanding their personal experiences as well as providing a broader perspective on the world.
- Good literature develops the imagination, piques curiosity, and stimulates problem solving.

- Good literature helps students develop insight into human behavior and motivations, such as morality, relationships, empathy and compassion, and the universality of these emotions and experiences among diverse people all over the world.
- Good literature is a means of handing down a culture's literary and cultural heritage to the next generation, and it validates for students their own culture as it opens doors to other cultures.
- Being familiar with good literature is included in the *Standards for the English Language Arts* (IRA/NCTE, 1996). Students need to become familiar with a variety of genres, have experiences discussing and interpreting literature, and develop their own tastes and preferences.
- The National Assessment of Educational Progress (NAEP) and state assessments measure reading for literary purposes and understanding of literary conventions.

Books can play an important role in students' lives. Yet, students do not come into the world with a natural affinity for books. They internalize the pleasure that literature brings into their lives from caring adults who share the delight of books with them. Therefore, teachers play a significant role in the extent to which books are a part of students' lives. Indeed, it is passion and enthusiasm for reading that separates effective from ineffective teachers (Bohn, Roehrig, and Pressley, 2004). Harvey and Goudvis (2000) write, "There is nothing more powerful than a literacy teacher sharing her passion for reading, writing, and thinking. Passion is contagious. Kids will respond" (p. 4). The goal of this chapter is to help you to gain valuable information that will prepare you to evaluate, select, and share with students the kinds of quality literature that will help them develop a love of reading. Many considerations must be made when choosing books to be read aloud to students (or to be read by students) to ensure the best possible reading experience for every child.

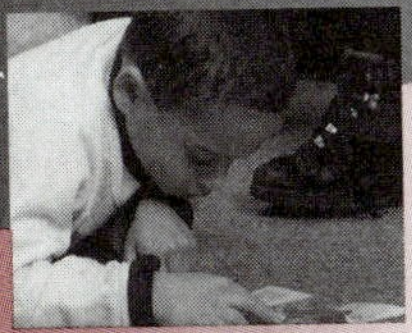

# What Do We Know about Children's Literature?

**Children's literature** comprises an immense collection of prose and poetry written over the past 250 years for children from birth to adolescence. Literature for children and young adults covers a broad range of topics from nursery rhymes and concept books to novels and informational books. Children's book sales have grown at such a rapid rate over the past few decades that the publication of children's books now accounts for the majority of many book publishers' sales. Currently, more than 180,000 children's titles exist in print and more than 8,000 new titles are published annually in the United States.

Children's literature includes books such as Jonathan Swift's *Gulliver's Travels* and Daniel Defoe's *Robinson Crusoe* that were originally written for adults but are now read by children and young adults. Conversely, many books written for children and young adults appeal to adults such as J. K. Rowling's *Harry Potter* series and J. R. R. Tolkien's *Lord of the Rings* trilogy. The manner in which content is handled helps to delineate children's books. Some books *about* children and young adults may not be *for* them, such as Tony Earley's *Jim the Boy* and Harper Lee's *To Kill a Mockingbird.* Stories that are nostalgic or overly sentimental, such as Robert N. Munsch's *Love You Forever* (about the assumption of responsibility for an aging parent) and Shel Silverstein's *The Giving Tree* (about the passing of childhood), reflect adult themes and are beyond the psychological and emotional realm of children and young adults. Cynicism and despair are also inappropriate content for children's books. Theodor S. Geisel (Dr. Seuss), wrote many books early in his career that continue to delight students today, but his later titles such as *The Lorax*, *The Butter Battle Book*, and *Yertle the Turtle* reflect adult themes of pollution, war, and ambition.

## Elements of Quality Literature

A book is said to have "high" quality when it has **literary merit** and appeals to the reader. A few accepted criteria for looking at the literary features of children's books can serve as guidelines for selecting high quality literature, such as:

- The protagonist is usually the age of the target audience.
- The theme appropriately reflects the emotions and experiences of children today.
- The language is specific and clear.
- The literary elements consist of a believable plot and characters, engaging writing style, and compelling themes that unite into a satisfying whole.
- The book doesn't blatantly teach or moralize and tells the truth about the human experience.
- The book broadens understanding and perspective on the world and opens up new possibilities and the capacity for empathy.
- Books for younger students usually include engaging pictures, fast-paced action presented in a straightforward manner, a single setting, and a satisfying ending.
- Books for older readers may not include pictures and, therefore, include more description to assist readers with visualizing the characters, setting, and dialogue to provide insight into the characters' motives and intentions. Books may or may not have a happy ending, but the ideas are important and meaningful.

It is important to note that the quality of a book as deemed by an adult may or may not be liked by a child just as books that you enjoy now as an adult may not have been your favorites as a child.

**BUILDING TEACHING SKILLS: Video Exercise**

*Literary Elements*

Go to the Building Teaching Skills section of Chapter 11 of MyEducationLab and view the video, "Literary Elements," in which a teacher carries on large and small group discussions about the literary element of flashbacks. Complete the activities that follow, and save your work or transmit it to your professor as assigned.

## Literary Elements in Children's Literature

Literary merit for narratives is measured by evaluating the literary elements of characterization, setting, plot, style, and theme (see Table 11.1). When the **elements of literature** are skillfully woven together by an author, then the book is said to have literary merit.

## Table 11.1

## Literary Elements and Selected Examples of Children's Literature

| Element | Description | Example |
|---|---|---|
| *Style* | *Style* refers to the author's distinctive way of writing. The author's word choice and arrangement and sentence construction come together in a unique way that makes the characters, setting, and plot come alive. The author's writing style also creates the mood or atmosphere of the story, the tone, and the pacing. | The writing style in *Sarah, Plain and Tall* by P. MacLachlan reflects the straightforward manner of the main character, Sarah, a mail-order bride who has come to live on the prairie.<br><br>Summer, the main character in *Missing May* by C. Rylant, reflects the language of a child and the natural sound of dialogue. |
| *Point of view* | *Point of view* is also an aspect of style and is the position the narrator takes in telling the story. Most stories are written from the first person (I) point of view, third person (he/she) point of view, or omniscient (all knowing) point of view. | *Bull Run* by P. Fleischman presents many points of view from different participants in the Civil War.<br><br>*Encounter* by J. Yolen is the story of Christopher Columbus's arrival in the New World told from a Taino child's point of view. |
| *Setting* | The *setting* is when and where the story takes place. The story can be set in the past, present, or future and can be very generic or detailed and specific. When and where a story takes place affects the plot, characters, and theme of the story. | *Julie of the Wolves* by J. George is set in Alaska's harsh wilderness, which serves as the antagonist, as the main character, Miyax, struggles to survive.<br><br>*Midwife's Apprentice* by K. Cushman is set in medieval England and accurately reflects the historical era, which plays a prominent role in the story. |
| *Character* | It is important for the *characters* in a story to be well developed and believable. Authors must create characters in such a way that we become involved with them and care about them. | Stuart Little, Wilbur, Madeline, Olivia, Ramona, Amelia Bedelia, Peter Rabbit, Cassie Logan, Gilly Hopkins, and Bilbo Baggins are just a few characters from children's books that have left an indelible impression on us. |

*(Continued)*

**Table 11.1**
***(Continued)***

| Element | Description | Example |
|---|---|---|
| *Plot* | *Plot* is the action of the story usually consisting of a beginning, rising action, climax, and falling action or resolution. The plot must have a conflict, and the resolution of that conflict carries through to the conclusion. The *pacing* of the plot, or how quickly the action moves, can be steady throughout the story or move faster or more slowly at times.<br><br>*Suspense* and *tension* create interest in the plot. It is important for the plot to be natural rather than contrived or coincidental for the story to be believable. | *Holes* by L. Sachar employs dual plots: the story of Stanley Yelnats' crime and punishment at Camp Green Lake, a juvenile detention facility; and the other experienced by the reader through flashbacks when Stanley reflects on the story of his no-good-dirty-rotten-pig-stealing great-great-grandfather. The two plots come together in the end to reveal how the past comes to fruition in the present. |
| *Theme* | *Theme* is the central idea of the entire story that lies beneath the story's surface. Enduring themes of friendship, growing up, overcoming fear, and acceptance of self do not overpower the characters or plot and are not didactic or preachy. | *Bridge to Terabithia* by K. Paterson includes themes of friendship and death. In *Heart of a Chief* by J. Bruchac, the theme is "growing up." *Project Mulberry* by L. Park has the themes of friendship and finding oneself. The themes of these books emerge and evolve throughout the story, are treated honestly, and do not override the plot and characterization. |

*Source:* Johnson, Denise. *The Joy of Children's Literature.* Copyright © 2009 by Houghton Mifflin Company. Reprinted by permission of Houghton Mifflin Harcourt Publishing Company.

## Genres of Children's Literature

IRA/NCTE 2

A **genre** is a category of writing that has defining characteristics such as the type of characters, setting, action, and an overall form or structure. As shown in Table 11.2, the genres of children's literature include traditional literature, poetry, fantasy and science fiction, realistic fiction, historical fiction, informational books, biographies, and digital text. Picture books cross all genres but are usually classified separately because of their unique picture/text format. Each genre has its own defining qualities of excellence that help the reader recognize the organization of the discipline of literature, provide a framework for talking about books, and help to guide book selection.

Each genre is unique and requires unique strategies for reading; therefore, it is not safe to assume that students who are competent reading one genre will automatically master another. Students must be exposed to a variety of genres across the grades. Students learn about particular genres through implicit experience reading indepen-

## Table 11.2
## Categories and Selected Examples of Genres

| Genre | Categories | Selected Examples |
| --- | --- | --- |
| *Traditional Literature*<br>Oral and literary heritage of humankind—no known author | Folk tales<br>Fairy tales<br>Myths and legends<br><br>Tall tales<br>Fables | *The Rough-Faced Girl* by Rafe Martin<br>*Little Red Riding Hood* by the Brothers Grimm<br>*The First Strawberries: A Cherokee Story* by Joseph Bruchac<br>*Swamp Angel* by A. Isaacs<br>*The Ant and the Grasshopper* by Aesop |
| *Poetry*<br>Condensed language, imagery, expression of imaginative thoughts and perceptions | Mother Goose nursery rhymes<br><br>Lyric<br><br><br><br>Narrative<br>Limericks<br>Haiku<br><br>Free verse<br>Concrete | *The Random House Book of Mother Goose* by Arnold Lobel<br><br>*A Child's Garden of Verses* by R. Stevenson<br>"Stopping by Woods on a Snowy Evening" by Robert Frost<br><br>"Paul Revere's Ride" by Henry Longfellow<br>*The Book of Pigericks* by Arnold Lobel<br>*Haiku: The Mood of Earth* by Ann Atwood<br><br>*A Light In the Attic* by Shel Silverstein<br>*Seeing Things: A Book of Poems* by Robert Froman |
| *Fantasy*<br>Imaginative worlds; make-believe story settings, people, and creatures, or events that could not happen | Animal fantasy<br>Miniature worlds<br><br>Time warps<br>Unreal worlds<br>Magic | *The Tale of Despereaux* by Kate DiCamillo<br>*The Family Under the Bridge* by Natalie Carlson<br>*A Wrinkle in Time* by Madeleine L'Engle<br>*Phantom Tollbooth* by Norton Juster<br>*Tuck Everlasting* by Natalie Babbit |
| *Science Fiction*<br>Stories about what might occur in the future based on extending physical laws and scientific principles | Mind control<br>Life in the future<br>Survival | *The Giver* by Lois Lowry<br>*The Ear, the Eye, and the Arm* by Nancy Farmer<br>*The Golden Compass* by Philip Pullman<br>*Phoenix Rising* by Karen Hesse |
| *Realistic Fiction*<br>"What if" stories, illusion of reality, characters seem real; contemporary setting | Adventure stories<br>Mysteries<br><br>Animal stories<br>Stories about growing up<br><br>Families<br>Peers<br>School<br>Sports | *Hatchet* by Gary Paulsen<br>*From the Mixed-up Files of Mrs. Basil E. Frankweiler* by E. L. Konigsburg<br>*Shiloh* by Phyllis Reynolds Naylor<br>*Are You There God? It's Me, Margaret* by Judy Blume<br>*Yolanda's Genius* by Carol Fenner<br>*Wringer* by Jerry Spinellli<br>*The Wheel on the School* by Meindert Dejong<br>*Skinnybones* by Barbara Park |

*(Continued)*

**Table 11.2**
***(Continued)***

| Genre | Categories | Selected Examples |
|---|---|---|
| *Historical Fiction*<br>Set in the past, could have happened—story reconstructs events of past age, things that could have or did occur | Fictionalized memoir<br>Fictionalized family history<br>Fiction based on research | *Little House on the Prairie* by Laura Ingalls Wilder<br>*Roll of Thunder, Hear My Cry* by Mildred Taylor<br>*A Single Shard* by Linda Sue Park |
| *Biography*<br>An account of a person's life or part of a life history | Authentic biography<br>Autobiography<br>Memoir | *Lincoln: A Photobiography* by Russell Freedman<br>*Knots in My Yo-Yo String! The Autobiography of a Kid* by Jerry Spinelli<br>*The Lost Garden* by Laurence Yep |
| *Informational*<br>Facts about the real world | | *Sea Turtles* by Gail Gibbons |
| *Picture Books*<br>Interdependence of art and text—classified by format rather than genre | Alphabet books<br>Concept books<br>Wordless books<br>Beginning readers<br>Picture storybooks | *The Z Was Zapped* by Chris Van Allsburg<br>*Cubes, Cones, Cylinders, and Spheres* by Tana Hoban<br>*The Red Book* by Barbara Lehman<br>*Frog and Toad Are Friends* by Arnold Lobel<br>*Where the Wild Things Are* by Maurice Sendak |

*Source:* Johnson, Denise. *The Joy of Children's Literature.* Copyright © 2009 by Houghton Mifflin Company. Adapted with permission of Houghton Mifflin Harcourt Publishing Company.

IRA/NCTE 2

dently and discussing literature with peers and through modeling, demonstration, and explicit instruction by their teacher. See the Engaging in Visual Literacy feature for resources to use in analyzing picture books.

## Evaluating and Selecting Children's Literature

Narrative literature is usually evaluated according to the literary elements just defined. Nonfiction, especially informational text, follows a different organizational structure than fiction and is evaluated according to a different set of criteria. Additionally, it is important to consider the accuracy and authenticity of the content and the authority of the author for both fiction and nonfiction. Table 11.3 provides a set of questions for evaluating fiction and nonfiction.

The best way to determine the quality of literary elements is to *read* children's literature. Donald Graves writes: ". . . to encourage literacy among students, attention to teachers' literacy has to come first" (1990, p. 21). Reading, discussing, and analyzing books increases our ability to recognize and recommend excellent literature in a way that simply reading a textbook about children's literature cannot.

## engaging in Visual Literacy

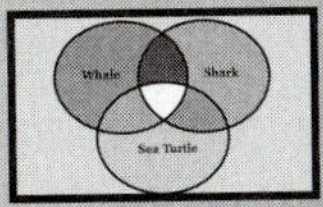

### Analyzing Picture Books

To assist his fourth-graders with analyzing the ways images make meanings, Mr. Porter has collected several of David Wiesner's wordless picture books, including *Flotsam, Sector 7, Free Fall, Hurricane, Tuesday,* and *June 29, 1999*. Because pictures are the text in wordless picture books, everything in the images contributes to the advancement of the plot and character development. It is in the "reading" of the pictures that the reader interprets and recounts the narrative. Readers must actively participate, bringing their own personal responses to the book and guiding themselves through it. Mr. Porter divides the students into groups, giving one of the wordless picture books to each group. He instructs the groups to carefully "read" the pictures first and then discuss their interpretation. Because the students will have some similar and different interpretations, students will begin to recognize how visual images can mean different things to different viewers. Once the students in each group have analyzed the pictures, they write the text to accompany them. When the groups have finished writing the text for their book, they share the stories with the class.

## Censorship in Children's Literature

Until the 1960s, the subjects of children's books didn't include controversial or sensitive issues, and the characters were mostly European American. The emergence of contemporary authors such as Judy Blume, Eve Bunting, Katherine Paterson, and Betsy Byars introduced issues such as divorce, death, abuse, and homelessness to young readers. Their books are highly praised by critics and they continue to be popular with children, though not so popular with families, librarians, and teachers. Some families or organizations prefer education that favors their particular worldview or refrains from exposing students to certain ways of life that are topics of some books and, therefore, they may seek to remove books from a school or public library. When a book is **challenged** by an individual or group, it is an attempt to ban or restrict materials in a public library or schools, based upon the objections of a person or group. A successful challenge results in materials being banned or restricted. During 2005, the American Library Association's (ALA) Office for Intellectual Freedom received a total of 405 challenges. Seven of the top ten most frequently challenged books of 2005 published by the ALA (www.ala.org) fell in the genre of realistic fiction. Sexual themes, sexual content, and offensive language are the most frequently cited reasons for seeking removal of books from libraries.

## Table 11.3
## Evaluation Criteria for Fiction and Nonfiction

| Fiction | | |
|---|---|---|
| **Element** | **Criteria** | **Description** |
| *Characterization* | Do the characters consistently act like real people within their age group and cultural background? Do they grow, change, and develop over the course of the story? | Characters act like real people: credible, authentic, not stereotypical, and fully developed as multidimensional human beings who show change and development throughout the story. |
| *Setting* | Does the setting seem real and appropriate to the story? | The historical or contemporary world as we know it supports the events of the story or fantastical world made believable through the use of rich detail consistently throughout the story so that the reader can see, hear, and feel the story. |
| *Plot* | Is the action consistent with problems that are developmentally appropriate for the intended age group? Does the author avoid manipulative devices such as sentimentality and sensationalism? | Action deals with familiar problems that are understood and believed by the target audience and solved in authentic ways that are logically consistent with the story. |
| *Theme* | Is the theme relevant and engaging to the reader? Does the story allow the reader to make his or her own moral judgments based on the insights in the book? | Reflects important issues of contemporary society that are applicable to students' lives and tied intrinsically to the plot, characterization, and setting. |
| *Style* | Is the writing style engaging and imaginative? Does the author's use of figurative language and dialogue help the reader to understand the complex nature of human relationships? | Engages the reader with vivid descriptions, believable dialogue, and language that reflects today's dialect, slang, and figures of speech. |
| *Accuracy and Cultural Authenticity* | Does the story accurately present historical information and cultural details? Does the story authentically reflect the culture depicted? | Model source notes are provided for citing sources in novels and picture books. |
| *Authority* | Is the author an insider writing about his/her own culture or an outsider? | If the author is an insider, he or she must have good credentials and local community endorsement; if the author is an outsider, he or she must include source citations, notes, and critical reviews. |

*(Continued)*

## Table 11.3 (Continued)

| Nonfiction | | |
|---|---|---|
| **Element** | **Criteria** | **Description** |
| *Organization* | Is the book clearly organized in a way that shows the relationship between concepts? Does it organize the information in a way that aids in the understanding of the concepts? | There should be a clear pattern and sequence. Headings and subheadings can help organize the information. The organization needs to be logical and should relate to the intended audience. |
| *Style* | Is the writing interesting? Does it show the author's enthusiasm for the topic? Does it draw the reader in by the use of language? | The information should be presented in a way that encourages the reader's involvement. The author's enthusiasm and relationship to the topic should be made evident by the tone of the work. A good work is precise with descriptive language. |
| *Design and Illustrations* | Is the design visually appealing? Does it support and add to the content? Do the illustrations help solidify the reader's understanding of the topic? | The illustrations should relate to the topic on the given page and enhance the reader's understanding of the subject matter. Illustrations should be explained through captions or in the text. The format should be clear and appealing. |
| *Accuracy and Authority* | Is the information current and accurate? Is the author an expert on the topic? | The information needs to be up-to-date and verified by individuals in the field. The author should be qualified to write about the topic. Facts should support generalizations. Biases and stereotypes should be avoided. |

Teachers must be knowledgeable of controversial and sensitive issues in children's literature. By following the guidelines for evaluating books for literary quality and involving the school faculty and community in discussions about children's literature, teachers and librarians can do much to avoid challenges of children's literature. Table 11.4 provides actions, questions, and resources for handling challenges to children's books.

## Table 11.4
## Handling Challenges to Children's Books

| Action | Questions | Resources |
|---|---|---|
| Keep current in the field. | • What elements in literature are offensive to censors?<br>• What happens when personal and community standards conflict?<br>• To what extent are school materials censored by the selection of administrators, librarians, and teachers?<br>• Which books are you personally willing to fight for? Why?<br>• What biases do you have? How do they influence you? | Maintain a file of material on censorship, including newspaper clippings, reference sources, and policy statements from various organizations (partisan and nonpartisan). Reference book reviews by relevant sources such as:<br>*Horn Book* magazine<br>*School Library Journal*<br>*The Bulletin of the Center for Children's Literature*<br>*Booklist*<br>*Children's Literature Review*<br>*Kaleidoscope: A Multicultural Booklist for Grades K–8*<br>*Adventuring with Books*<br>*Jewish Children's Books: How to Choose Them, How to Use Them* |
| Obtain selection criteria from national professional organizations. | • What professional organizations offer support in the form of policies, online information, or advocacy? Is your school aware of these policies?<br>• How can these policies assist you in selecting books for the classroom? | Assemble support from professional organizations such as:<br>American Library Association<br>The Council on Interracial Books for Children<br>The National Council of Teachers of English<br>The International Reading Association |
| Communicate with families. | • Have you held open conversations about children's literature with families?<br>• Have you provided families with the information they need to make informed choices about their children's reading material?<br>• Have you discussed the value and appeal of books that may be considered controversial with families? | Provide an opportunity to have an open discussion with families about children's literature during a special event (such as an open house). Invite families to read the books that might be in question. Discuss changes in children's books over the years, as well as the value and appeal of these books for children and young adults. Share written responses from students about these books or have students join in the discussion. |

*(Continued)*

## Table 11.4 (Continued)

| Action | Questions | Resources |
|---|---|---|
| Evaluate books with students. | • Are the students in your class able to critically evaluate books? If not, how can you engage them in judging books for quality?<br>• How can you assist students in understanding the concept of censorship and how it affects them? | Engage students in comparing/contrasting various versions of folk/fairy tales as a way to thinking about quality in books. In this way, you will provide students with tools of the mind to begin thinking critically about books. For older readers, have honest conversations about books that have controversial language/issues connecting to the criteria for quality literature. |
| Prepare a school policy statement. | • Does your school have a policy in place for selecting books for school and classroom libraries? | With the participation of the school's faculty, librarian, administration, and community members, construct a selection policy that establishes reasons for including a book in the school or classroom library. Keep everyone in the school and community informed of new acquisitions. Draft a policy for dealing with book challenges. |
| Adopt a formal complaint procedure. | • What support will you have from the school administration for book challenges?<br>• Does your school have a policy in place for handling book challenges? | The National Council of Teachers of English (NCTE) provides guidelines for coping with censorship. These guidelines suggest that the individual objecting to a book fill out "The Citizen's Request for Reconsideration of a Work" form. This form assumes that the individual has read the work in its entirety, which alone may discourage minor objections. Completed forms should be reviewed by a committee that will report on their findings and recommendations. |

*Source:* Adapted from Jalongo, M. and Creany A. 1991. Censorship in children's literature: What every educator should know. *Childhood Education*, *67*(3), 143–148. Used by permission.

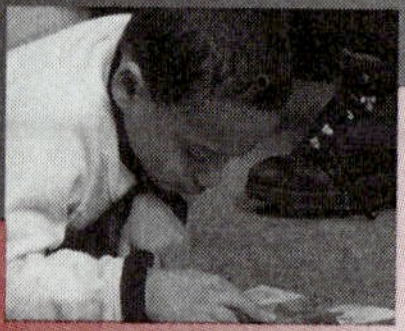

# What Do We Know about How Children Learn about Literature?

The pleasure of literature for students is bound with the nature of their development. Linguistic, social, emotional, and cognitive development are complementary processes that ultimately work together to shape a child's literacy growth. A child who is not developmentally ready for a particular book will gain less meaning from it and will respond differently to it. Lev Vygotsky, a twentieth-century Russian psychologist, theorized that social interaction shapes intellectual development and stressed the importance of language in the development of thought. Sociocognitive theory posits that social interaction is the primary means by which students arrive at new understanding.

The selection of literature is key to providing an experience that promotes enjoyment, literacy development, and a lifelong reading habit for students. Choosing books for students requires a general knowledge of child development, knowledge about the students for whom you are selecting children's literature, and an in-depth knowledge of children's literature. Based on the knowledge of each child, teachers can select texts that are interesting, engaging, and accessible; build background knowledge and experiences through teacher-led and student-led discussions; and provide instruction and support as needed so that students continually learn about literature.

## Students' Response to Literature

At the heart of literacy and literature instruction is what Louise Rosenblatt (1978) termed a **transaction** or "lived through" experience. We each make connections to a text that are unique because readers bring their own background knowledge and previous experience to a text which determine how they interpret the text and what they take from it. If a reader has difficulty reading the text, is not interested or engaged in the text, is distracted—or if the text is about situations, issues, or characters that are beyond the reader's experiences or development—he or she will not actively participate with the text. The reader may read the words on the page, but transaction or "lived through" experience will not take place. Teachers can do much to ensure that students are able to actively participate with texts if they consider the reader, the text, and the context.

**The Reader** The value of a book lies in the opinion of the reader. A good book to one child may not be good to another, depending on the child's interests, age, background experiences, or culture. Each reader, in the process of experiencing a literary work, brings meaning to and takes meaning from that book (Rosenblatt, 1978). The meaning made from experiencing a book is personal and idiosyncratic and is based on all that the reader has known and experienced outside that book.

**The Text** Characteristics of different genres also affect how a reader responds to a particular book. The structure of informational text, for example, is very different from the structure of narrative text. Students who are unfamiliar with how to read informational text may find it challenging. Students typically have more experience with narrative text and approach it with the expectation of becoming emotionally involved with the characters, the events, or the theme of the book. This doesn't mean that some students will not experience difficulty reading or becoming engaged in the narrative text. Students who have no experience or knowledge of the topic may be unable to make sense of narrative text. Whether or not a student has self-selected the book to read or has been assigned the book by someone else also makes a difference in how students respond. Reading a book to complete an assignment is quite different than selecting a book to read for pleasure or your own purposes.

**The Context** Teachers play a pivotal role in encouraging, nurturing, and deepening response. Teachers can ensure that students are given ample opportunities to engage in conversation with each other about the books they are reading. Research has shown that through conversations with peers students become involved in understanding and negotiating ideas and perspectives that promote reflection and insight. Peers also influence each other in powerful ways.

When considering what teachers know about their students as readers, what they know about the texts available in the classroom, and what they know of the context for teacher and peer conversations, teachers can create an environment that encourages students to have transactional experiences with texts. Teachers will be supporting the development of personal, sincere, reflective, and insightful responses from students by providing them with a well-stocked classroom library that includes a variety of book genres, magazines, comics, audiobooks, and Internet resources; by allowing them to read books of their choice; and by providing opportunities for them to share their reading with each other and to talk about books with each other in a nonthreatening atmosphere.

## The Role of Engagement and Motivation

Reading is more than a cognitive process; it is becoming **engaged**—deeply involved, captivated, absorbed, and immersed—in a text. Teachers must focus their attention not only on *how* students read, but also *why*. Reading engagement involves the cognitive, motivational, and social dimensions of reading and reading instruction (Baker, Dreher, and Guthrie, 2000) and can occur at all levels of development. In fact, engagement at a younger age predicts achievement at an older age (Baker et al., 2000). The engaged reader is capable of overcoming obstacles of low parental education and income, as well as preferences and abilities associated with gender. Guthrie and Anderson (1999) explain that "motivations and social interactions are equal to cognitions as foundations for reading" (p. 17). They believe that reading can be seen as engagement because "Engaged readers not only have acquired reading skills, but use them for their own purposes in many contexts" (p. 17); in fact, "an interested reader identifies with the conceptual context of a text so fully that absorbing its meaning is an effortless activity" (p. 19). Engaged readers are involved, interested, and constantly learning from their text. A child who is engaged in reading employs both his mind and his heart and is well on his way to becoming a lifelong reader.

**Motivation** is a critical factor of engagement. As motivation increases, students want to spend more time reading. Therefore, motivation plays a dual role; it becomes a part of both the process and the product of engagement. Engaged students read widely for a variety of purposes and create situations that extend opportunities for literacy. In the classroom, promoting reading engagement requires a coordinated emphasis on competence and motivation in reading instruction. Yet, research has found that teachers have little

Teachers can create supportive, nurturing environments that encourage reading engagement by providing appropriate literature experiences that support all students' reading levels, interests, and instructional needs.

knowledge of practices that facilitate motivation and interest (Pressley, Wharton-McDonald, Mistretta-Hampston, and Echevarria, 1998). Teachers and other adults in students' lives can create supportive, nurturing environments that encourage reading engagement by providing appropriate literature experiences that support all students' reading levels, interests, and instructional needs.

## Choice and Self-Selection

Olsen (1959) believes that students are "self-seeking, self-selecting, and self-pacing organisms" (p. 402) who will seek and select experiences that are consistent with their developmental level. Enjoyment of a book cannot be forced on a child; it must come about naturally. What adults may view as high quality literature might differ considerably from what students believe is a good book (Chatton, 2004; Worthy, Moorman and Turner, 1999). Even with a teacher's caring guidance and a parent's well-intended recommendation, students turn to books that reflect their own interests and preferences. When given the chance, students will make positive selections based on both interest and ability. Research suggests that students can, and do, make choices that increase their awareness and extend their growing knowledge of literacy (Fresch, 1995; McLaughlin and Allen, 2002; Schlager, 1978; Worthy, 1996). Hidi and Harackiewicz (2000) write, "Investigations focusing on individual interest have shown that students as well as adults who are interested in particular activities or topics pay closer attention, persist for longer periods of time, learn more, and enjoy their involvement to a greater degree than individuals without such interest" (p. 153).

The ability to make choices positively affects the educational development of students. Self-selection of books assists students in becoming both independent and responsible. Students learn to deal with differing difficulty levels of books, they understand that there are different and varying purposes for reading, and they learn to assess their progress by gauging their choices against their own standards and against the choices of others. When real-world readers choose a text, they are reading to learn and to enjoy. They accomplish these tasks by selecting a text that fulfills their needs. Selecting what to read is a major part of becoming a reader (Ollman, 1993).

## Time to Read Independently

IRA/NCTE 1

Krashen (2004) reviewed extensive research on free voluntary reading (FVR), which he defined as "reading because you want to . . . no book report, no questions at the end of the chapter, and no looking up every vocabulary word. . . . It is the kind of reading highly literate people do all the time" (p. x). Krashen's review of research indicated:

- Those who say they read more, read and write better.
- Those who recognize more authors' names have read more and have superior literacy development.
- In school, FVR results in better reading comprehension, writing style, vocabulary, spelling, and grammatical development.

- FVR is nearly always superior to direct instruction on tests of reading, vocabulary, writing, and grammar.
- The richer the print environment, the better the literacy development.
- Students who are read to at school or at home read more and show better literacy development.
- Reading itself promotes reading.
- Students read more when they see other people reading and when they have time to read.
- Students who are readers will develop at least acceptable levels of literacy. Without a reading habit, students simply do not have a chance.

It is critical that students be given ample time for reading every day. Ample time for reading is defined as "more time to read than the combined total allocated for *learning* about reading and *talking or writing* about what has been read" (Fielding and Pearson, 1994, p. 63) and supports the adage "practice makes perfect" by allowing students the opportunity to orchestrate the skills and strategies that are important to skillful reading. It also allows for the acquisition of new knowledge. Allington (2006, p. 35) states:

> In learning to read it is true that reading practice—just reading—is a powerful contributor to the development of accurate, fluent, high comprehension reading. In fact, if I were required to select a single aspect of the instructional environment to change, my first choice would be creating a schedule that supported dramatically increased quantities of reading during the school day.

Allington recommends a minimum of ninety minutes of in-school reading per day. This may seem impossible, given the curriculum that must be taught each day. But, by making a few improvements in organizational efficiency, including how much of the school day is spent on noninstructional activities such as opening and ending procedures, intercom announcements, and paperwork, it is possible to find thirty to fifty additional minutes for reading every day.

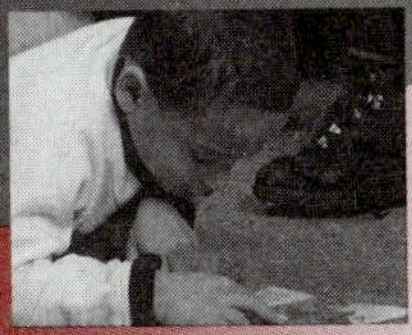

## How Can We Teach Children's Literature?

Barbara Rogoff (1990) considers students to be apprentices as they acquire a diverse repertoire of skills and knowledge under the guidance and support of more knowledgeable persons. In an apprenticeship setting, adults model the significance of written language as an important tool for documenting and communicating information. In an apprenticeship role, the teacher models, scaffolds, and demonstrates during a literacy event when the child is unable to complete a task on her own or when she needs a model of expertise. If the child is not engaged in the literacy event, then the child is not likely to gain knowledge or understanding from the experience. As adults and students engage in discussions about books, students gain important "tools of the mind" for literacy acquisition (Bodrova and Leong, 1996).

## Storytelling

Children's literature provides rich models of language and is an excellent resource for storytelling in the classroom. To encourage students to retell stories, teachers should model these storytelling approaches:

- Select stories with good plot structures.
- Be sure you know the story thoroughly so you can retell it in your own words without relying on the book itself. Include any rhythmical or repetitive phrases.
- Be expressive, changing your voice to reflect dialogue, intonation, and inflection.
- Tell the story slowly and with animation of body, hand gestures, and facial expressions.
- Use props and other creative storytelling techniques such as puppets, stuffed animals, cut-out characters and settings, a felt-board, and dolls.

Prior to modeling storytelling for students, be sure to let them know they will be given a turn to tell the story. Model telling a story many times before asking students to tell it. Students can take turns telling stories to each other during share time, during scheduled center time, or they can tell their story into a tape recorder to be listened to by other students, their families, or the teacher at another time (adapted from Strickland and Morrow, 1989).

## Reading Aloud

Ample research over that last two decades supports reading aloud to students in all grade levels. In the early 1980s, the *Becoming a Nation of Readers* report (1984) from the Commission on Reading found, "The single most important activity for building the knowledge required for eventual success in reading is reading aloud to students. There is no substitute for a teacher who reads students good stories. It is a practice that should continue throughout the grades" (Anderson, Hiebert, Scott, and Wilkinson, p. 51). Laminack and Wadsworth (2006, p. 2) summarize the following benefits of reading aloud to students:

- Provides models of language in use
- Builds interest in language
- Increases awareness of words
- Builds vocabulary
- Aids in the development of new insights and understandings
- Extends and layers on existing knowledge
- Aids in overall comprehension
- Creates a risk-free zone in which all listeners have more equal access to knowledge
- Has the potential to spark a love of reading
- Can have a positive influence in reading attitudes
- Provides models of fluent reading
- Provides a living demonstration of the act of reading

- Can model how readers think in the process of reading
- Demonstrates the nature and purpose of reading
- Shows the range of topics, styles, and genres available in written language
- Helps develop tastes in reading and in selecting literature
- Improves listening skills
- Aids in the development of imagery
- Offers multiple perspectives
- Broadens a listener's worldview
- Makes the rhythms of written language familiar
- Provides demonstrations of the various ways stories can be developed

Reading aloud to students can be a very important factor for providing motivation for reading, building critical concepts about reading, and developing an understanding of literature. Yet, just because a teacher reads aloud does not mean that the benefits just listed happen automatically. Morrow and Brittain (2003) state, "Reading stories does not in itself necessarily promote literacy; however, the research suggests that certain methods, environmental influences, attitudes, and interactive behaviors apparently enhance the potential of the read-aloud event for promoting literacy development" (p. 144). Reading aloud must be an intentional act in which the teacher considers his or her goals and objectives based on student assessment and curriculum standards.

The choice of what texts to read aloud to students is one that requires careful thought. Once a book or article has been selected, it is important to prepare for the oral reading so the reading is smooth and inviting. Remember, always preview materials before reading them orally to students; while reading aloud sounds so simple, it takes careful planning.

## Thinking Aloud

How does a good reader figure out unknown words while reading? How does a good reader make inferences between what the author states and what the reader knows? These are complex processes that take place while reading text. Thinking aloud during reading aloud can make the invisible processes of reading visible. Thinking aloud is when the teacher models his or her thinking by voicing all the things they notice, see, feel, or question as they process the text. "Think-alouds allow all students to hear how others sleuth out and make sense of all these text clues so that they can recognize and adopt these strategies as their own" (Wilhelm, 2001, p. 19). According to Wilhelm, think-alouds can be used to model:

- General processes of reading, such as predicting, monitoring, and summarizing
- Task-specific processes, such as symbolism, irony, and bar graphs
- Text-specific processes, such as understanding the structure of an argument and evaluating its effectiveness (2001, p. 28)

Think-alouds can be conducted with a variety of genres and texts including newspaper articles, magazines, and Internet sites. Teachers can record think-alouds on chart paper or overhead transparencies to have a record of the strategies modeled for students to refer to later and to make connections to other texts. Routman (2003, p. 138) provides a helpful list of language to use for thinking aloud:

**Reading Homework Exercise**

*Tips for Effective Think-Alouds*

Go to the Homework and Exercises section in Chapter 11 of MyEducationLab and read the strategy recommendations, "Tips for Effective Think-Alouds," in which the authors share important points regarding "think alouds" that teachers should consider. Complete the activities that follow, and save your work or transmit it to your professor as assigned.

- I'm thinking that . . .
- From the title and cover illustration, I'm going to predict that . . .
- You know that made me think about . . .
- And I'm now thinking . . .
- The illustrations help me to . . .
- I have a picture in my mind . . .
- I'm going to read that again. I'm a little confused about . . .
- In this next part . . .
- What was going through my mind was . . .
- Let me rethink this.
- One of the good things that readers do is always think . . .
- I'm predicting that . . .
- Good readers are always thinking about their reading.
- I'm connecting this to when [such-and-so] happened to me.
- I think this character is . . .
- If I stop, that means I'm waiting for somebody's attention.

Once students have observed the think-aloud process with a particular strategy numerous times, turn the process over for them to practice on their own. Students can use sticky notes to record their thinking and share it with the teacher in conferences or with a peer. Teachers can help students unlock the secret to engaged reading by lending their expertise to students through think-alouds.

## Literature Response: Reflecting on Books

Writing in response to literature can be a great way for students to develop meaning. Lucy Calkins (2001) writes, "We write—we put our thinking onto the page—so we can hold onto our fleeting thoughts. When we write, we can hold our thoughts in our hand, we can put our thoughts in our pocket, and we can bring out yesterday's thoughts" (p. 372). Sticky notes can be an effective way to encourage students to think as they read. Such notes actively involve readers in monitoring their own thinking by serving as a way to question, predict, or talk back to the text. Students' understanding of how to use sticky notes will progress over time. Some students enjoy the novelty and use sticky notes abundantly. Modeling how to use sticky notes from your own reading will help students understand the types of things you might put on a sticky note. Sticky notes can be removed from texts when students are finished reading and placed in reading journals that can be referred to later. One or two sticky notes can be left in the book for other students to read. It is like leaving tracks of thinking on the pages of books.

Reading response journals in which students write their thinking about the texts they read can also be used. Students can respond to questions such as:

- Was there a part in the book you really liked or disliked?
- Do you have a favorite character or event?
- Was there a part you didn't understand or were confused about?

- Was there a part of the book in which you make a strong connection?
- Did the author use memorable words or phrases that painted a picture in your mind?
- Draw your favorite event or character.
- Did you have questions about any parts of the book?

It is important to establish guidelines for journal entries and to model and demonstrate for students many examples of journal entries over several weeks so they understand your expectations. Often, teachers write back a response in the students' journals, which can include questions or other comments that prompt students to expand the breadth or depth of their thinking. Routman (2005) writes, "Many students, especially culturally and linguistically diverse students, substantially improve their writing—content, quantity, form, fluency—as a result of keeping these journals" (p. 125). In addition to deepening students' understanding of their reading, responses to reading assist teachers with ways of knowing how students respond to the books they read in order to provide meaningful instruction that continues to extend their understanding of literacy and literature. See the Exploring Technology feature for additional ideas for extending student understanding of literature.

IRA/NCTE 1

## Literature Conversations: Book Clubs and Literature Circles

Based on thirty years of teaching experience, Ardith Cole (2003) writes, "Literature conversations provide a platform for deep, rich comprehension of text. By developing these classroom structures for talk, teachers can help students collaborate, substantiate their ideas, and negotiate" (p. xiv). Several recent studies have found that in the classrooms of highly effective teachers, real conversations take place regularly between students and students and teachers (Allington, 2006; Ketch, 2005; Taylor and Pearson, 2002). Allington's (2006, p. 111) description of the differences between real-world literacy interactions and in-school literacy interactions points out why providing an environment for genuine classroom talk is so important:

> When you consider the richness of the talk about texts that occurs outside of school, the typical pattern of school talk about texts seems shallow and barren. Outside school we rely on the richness of a person's conversation about texts to judge how well they understood it. Their literateness. In school we typically rely on the flat recitation of events or information to make that same judgment. Outside of school settings we engage in conversations about the adequacy of texts and authors to inform, engage, and entertain us. In school we engage in interrogations about what was "in the text."

**Case Study Homework Exercise**

*Literature Circles Open the World of Literature*

Go to the Homework and Exercises section in Chapter 11 of MyEducationLab and read the case study, "Literature Circles Open the World of Literature," which discusses how a fourth-grade teacher introduces literature circles to his class. Complete the activities that follow, and save your work or transmit it to your professor as assigned.

You might ask why teachers need to teach students how to talk about texts. Don't students participate in conversations at home and in their community? Family book sharing is not a universal practice across cultural, linguistic, and social lines; some homes do not have books; and some families are so busy they don't have time to discuss books. Of course, many families do have conversations about books with their children. The bottom line is that many students come to school without knowing what a real conversation—deep, reflective talk—looks like. Yet, with high expectations, time to read, teacher modeling, scaffolding, direct instruction, and a supportive classroom community, all students can learn to engage in deep, reflective conversations about books (Kong and Fitch, 2003).

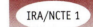

## exploring technology

### Online Literature Resources

***The Nightmare Room*** **by R. L. Stine (www.thenightmareroom.com)**
This site houses an online story *Dead of Night* by the master of scary books for children, R. L. Stine. Twelve-year-old David and his friends attempt to rescue their friend Keith from the hospital for one last night of total freedom until night turned into nightmare.

***The Neddiad*** **by Daniel Pinkwater (www.pinkwater.com/theneddiad)**
This story, also sold in print, is available in its entirety (without illustrations) online. When shoelace heir Neddie Wentworthstein and his family take the train from Chicago to Los Angeles in the 1940s, he winds up in possession of a valuable Indian turtle artifact whose owner is supposed to be able to prevent the impending destruction of the world . . . but he is not sure exactly how.

**The Moonlit Road (www.themoonlitroad.com)**
The Moonlit Road is a website that houses ghost stories and other strange Southern folktales, told by the region's best storytellers.

Ketch (2005) writes, "Conversation is a basis for critical thinking. It is the thread that ties together cognitive strategies and provides students with the practice that becomes the foundation for reading, writing, and thinking" (p. 8). Students need opportunities to practice the use of cognitive strategies in order to internalize them and strengthen their comprehension. Students who engage in conversation in the classroom become intellectually engaged with text (Kucan and Beck, 2003). One way to engage students in conversation is through literature discussion groups—self-selected group conversations about self-selected books.

**Video Homework Exercise**

*Before and During Reading Strategies*

Go to the Homework and Exercises section of Chapter 11 of MyEducationLab and view the video, "Before and During Reading Strategies," in which a teacher models for students how to engage with nonfiction text. Complete the activities that follow, and save your work or transmit it to your professor as assigned.

**Providing a Model for Students** Because many students come to school without having models of what meaningful literature discussion looks like, it is important to provide them with a model. If you have a colleague who implements literature discussion groups, ask if one of the groups could conduct a session in front of your class. This is sometimes called a *fish bowl* because the class is observing outside of the discussion group. As observers, they can jot down notes about what they noticed. Afterward, the teacher and students can discuss what the class noticed and how the actions observed supported the group discussion. Professional videos can also be used in the same way. The result might be a set of initial guidelines for conducting a good book discussion that the students can use as they start their own book clubs and find what works for them.

Developing rich discussion takes careful planning and support from teachers. Daniels (2002) provides a very useable elaboration on the different kinds of roles participants play in **literature discussion** groups. Someone needs to direct the discussion, and all members can make connections, illustrate ideas and images, highlight vocabulary and literary passages or effects, and, at other times, serve as interrogators and summarizers. By highlighting each of these roles, and at times assigning roles to students, they can become more aware of the different ways contributions can be made in discussion groups.

McMahon and Raphael (1997) suggest a different format in their **Book Club** model. Students keep response logs or think sheets as they read. A variety of responses are introduced to students, and they select which form to use for particular sections of text they read. They may do a sequence chart, build a character map, create a compare-contrast chart, arrange a story graph, write questions for the author, or involve themselves in other activities that the teacher first models and explains. The group brings their logs to the discussion group and uses what they have written as a foundation for their shared oral explorations (Raphael, Pardo, and Highfield, 2002).

**Selecting the Books** The selection of literature for discussion groups should be based on the teacher's knowledge of quality literature and of students' literary personalities, cultures, reading strengths and needs, independent reading levels, and cross-curricular goals. McMahon and Raphael (1997) suggest developing units with theme-related books. A set of four or five books for each title will be needed. Some of these books might be a part of the classroom library and others might be borrowed from fellow teachers, the school, or public libraries. Teachers can also send home a note requesting families to donate titles. Having enough text sets is always a challenge and collecting books takes time.

Though students should always have a choice when selecting books, the selection can be limited to a certain number of books ranging in reading levels that fall within a certain theme, content connection, author/illustrator study, or genre study. The teacher conducts a brief book talk on each of the books and then allows students to choose the book they want to read. A sign-up sheet can be used in which students indicate up to three different books they are interested in reading. Then the teacher decides who gets to read which books based on interest and reading level. The teacher should explain to students that not all students will get to read their first choice every time.

There are many other ways in which books might be selected:

- Student interests or topic (such as snakes, fantasy books, or Marc Brown's *Arthur* books)
- Author/illustrator study
- Genre study
- Content connections
- Thematic study (such as friendship, appreciating differences, or taking responsibility)
- Books with multiple character perspectives
- Books with global perspectives
- Student-suggested books

Interesting and relevant texts enhance discussions. Narrative and informational books should be used. Consideration should be given to gender and cultural differences. Certain books may be more interesting to girls than boys, and vice versa. Certain cultural groups may find certain perspectives in some books offensive. The guidelines presented at the beginning of this chapter for book selection should be taken into consideration before selecting books for literature discussion groups so that the best possible selections are made to promote rich conversations for all students.

**Forming Groups and Routines** Literature discussion groups are heterogeneous and should consist of no more than five or six members based on books the students have chosen to read, though students who read different books on the same topic could form a discussion group. Students may have different reading abilities but are still able to engage in high level discussion about topics they care about. Once a group has finished reading and discussing a book, the group disbands and students join a different group when new groups are formed.

Once students have decided on a book and a group is formed, an initial meeting is held with the teacher. Though the teacher has given a brief book talk, there is still a need to build background knowledge, to set a purpose for reading, and to decide how much to read before the first group discussion. The teacher might create a chart documenting students' prior knowledge, questions, and predictions that could be revisited during the first discussion group. Additionally, sometimes groups might get excited about reading a book and may assign an unrealistic number of pages to be read before the first group meeting. The teacher can model how to judge an appropriate number of pages based on the number of days before the group meets and where a good stopping point might be in the book.

Over the next week, students read the assigned pages during independent reading time. The students should be used to jotting down their thoughts on sticky notes and writing in response journals at this point, though students are reading with a new mindset—questions, thoughts, predictions, critiques—that will be shared with discussion group members, and this can open up a whole new way of thinking. The notes are critical to meaningful, thought-provoking discussion. The teacher meets with each group once a week—one group a day—during independent reading time. On the day they meet, students should come to the group with their books and journals, prepared for the discussion.

## Children's Literature across the Curriculum

Teachers can supplement textbooks with fiction and nonfiction trade books that can provide motivation, enthusiasm, caring, and insight into just about any aspect of the curriculum and inspire students to do their own research or further reading to learn more. For example, in the opening scenario, Miss Hall chose several picture books and chapter books written from different perspectives on the westward expansion, such as the picture book *I Have Heard of a Land* by Joyce Carol Thomas and illustrated by Floyd Cooper, which centers on the migration of African American pioneers to Oklahoma. The chapter book *The Birchbark House* and the sequel *The Game of Silence* by Louise Erdrich capture everyday life and the devastating effect of the Westward Expansion in the mid-1800s from the point of view of Omakayas, a young Native American girl. The sole survivor of a smallpox epidemic, Omakayas is adopted by a family in the Ojibwa tribe who lives on an island in Lake Superior when a white man brings smallpox to the community. A nonfiction or fiction trade book has the potential to be a magnifying glass that enlarges and enhances the reader's personal interaction with a subject.

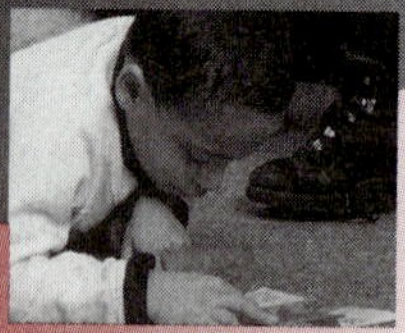

# How Can We Assess Students' Understanding of Literature?

Assessment is essential when looking at students' progress over time and determining next steps in instruction. Creating a system for organizing and maintaining documentation of each student's assessment information is critical.

## Interest/Attitude Surveys

Jill Cole (2003), a second-grade teacher, conducted a classroom study of her students' motivations to read. Jill found that her students had their own beliefs, purposes, and reactions. In short, each one had a unique literacy personality. When Jill discovered that her students were motivated to read by very different factors, she became more responsive by "providing a classroom culture that fostered their strengths, honored their voices, and met their needs" (p. 334).

Teachers can use a variety of methods to discover their students' literacy personalities. Reading inventories are designed to assess students' reading interests, preferences, habits, and attitudes. Existing inventories such as the *Garfield Reading Attitude Inventory* (McKenna and Kear, 1990) can be used or teachers can create their own inventories. Questions might include:

- How would you describe yourself as a reader?
- What are you currently reading?
- What kinds of books do you like to read?
- Do you have a favorite author? If so, who?
- What are you going to read next?
- How do you choose the books you read?
- What do you do when you start to read each day?
- How do you keep track of the characters in the books you read?
- What kind of reading is easy for you?
- What kind of reading is hard for you?

Observations of students when they are reading or writing independently, in pairs or small groups, or during one-on-one conferences can reveal important information about how students interact with and respond to texts, other students, and the teacher in instructional and independent settings. Reading response journals and other written products provide insight into how students connect with texts. By using different sources of information, many facets of a student's personality can be discovered.

As students change over the course of the school year, so will their personalities, and thus, too, should the classroom environment that supports their learning. With so many personalities in the classroom, teachers may feel overwhelmed at the thought of providing an environment that supports all of their learning needs. Yet, by providing a rich and evolving classroom library and providing a variety of supported and independent literacy contexts, all students can become motivated, engaged readers and writers.

## Assessing Literature Response Journals

Some teachers develop rubrics with scoring criteria that students can use as a guideline for journal entries that reflect evidence of thinking about texts. Students can also participate in generating criteria after many opportunities to observe the teacher model writing a response to reading. For example, the following criteria might be included:

Did the student:

- Respond personally to the text?
- Respond to the theme and/or author's purpose?
- Offer his/her opinion of the text?
- Ask questions?
- Make predictions/inferences?
- Respond to the author's writing style and language?

- Respond to the characterization or plot?
- Share connections?
- Respond to how the text is organized or other supportive features, such as diagrams?
- Respond to the accuracy of the information in the text?

You can periodically meet with students individually or in small groups to discuss journal entries to point out strengths and to provide additional instruction as needed. Positive development in students' journal writing over time is a good way to observe reading growth. See the Engaging in Assessment feature for an example of using reading response journals as assessment tools.

## *engaging in* Assessment

### Reading Response Journals

Mr. Moore has just finished looking through his third-grade students' reading response journals. He noticed that the students were making personal connections to the stories they were reading—a strategy he has been working on with them since the beginning of the school year. Most of the journal entries indicated that the students had made relevant connections that assisted them with understanding the story by sparking questions, predictions, or inferences that lead to a deeper level of comprehension. But Mr. Moore was concerned about Amber's journal entries:

Franklin's Halloween

> It reminded me of when I went trick-or-treating on Halloween.

Franklin and the Tooth Fairy

> It reminded me of when I lost my first tooth.

Sheila Rae the Brave

> It reminded me of when we had a thunderstorm and I was scared.

The Three Little Wolves and the Big Bad Pig

> It reminded me of when my cousin was knocking down my castle.

From her journal entries, Amber seems to be making superficial and limited connections to the stories she is reading and does not reflect further on the story. Mr. Moore decides he needs to conference with Amber about her journal entries. The next day, Mr. Moore meets with Amber and asks her a few questions about one of the books in her journal. She is able to recall the story in detail and answer all the questions Mr. Moore asks. When he inquires as to why her journal entries are not reflective of the depth of her understanding of the story, Amber states that she has so many thoughts in her head about the story that she is not sure what to write down. She seems to be overwhelmed with the task. Mr. Moore takes the opportunity to model his own response to one of the books in Amber's journal and asks Amber to extend one of the other entries. With some prompting from Mr. Moore, Amber is able to successfully add to her original response. Mr. Moore encourages Amber to continue to expand her journal entries to be more reflective of her thinking about the stories she reads. He assures her that he will check with her each day to see how she is progressing.

## Assessing Literature Conversations

Assessing the quality of literature conversations must include both the process necessary for literature circles to operate effectively and the content necessary for the conversations to be meaningful, insightful, and thought provoking. Fountas and Pinnell (2006) suggest the checklist in Table 11.5.

Students can experience using the checklist when observing another group of students during literature circles or from watching a video. In this way, students can

### Table 11.5
### Checklist for Literature Conversations

| Aspect | Name(s) |
|---|---|
| *Preparation* | _______ Read the assigned pages |
| | _______ Made notes and/or identified pages or parts in the text |
| | _______ Completed a writing or drawing assignment if assigned |
| *Discussion—Process* | _______ Came to the group prepared |
| | _______ Attended to and looked at the speaker |
| | _______ Spoke clearly, loudly enough for others in the group to hear |
| | _______ Spoke to other members (not just the teacher) |
| | _______ Contributed an appropriate amount, taking turns with others |
| | _______ Asked others for clarification when needed |
| | _______ Asked follow-up questions |
| | _______ Built on the comments of others |
| | _______ Encouraged others to share their thinking |
| *Discussion—Content* | _______ Contributed accurate information from the text |
| | _______ Showed familiarity with the text by providing specific examples to support thinking |
| | _______ Used prior knowledge to extend understanding of the text |
| | _______ Recognized and discussed examples of the writer's style or craft |
| *Discussion—Strategies* | _______ Provided evidence of literal understanding of the text through summary and important information |
| | _______ Went beyond the text in thinking to make inferences |
| | _______ Went beyond the text to make personal, world, or text connections |
| | _______ Went beyond the text to make predictions |
| | _______ Went beyond the text to incorporate or synthesize new information and ideas into their thinking |
| | _______ Noticed aspects of the text such as language, structure, or writer's craft |
| | _______ Provided evidence of critical thinking about the text |
| *Assessment* | _______ Noticed aspects of the discussion that were productive |
| | _______ Identified areas of needed improvement, providing specific examples from the discussion as evidence |
| | _______ Assessed self as individual participant |

*Source:* Adapted from Fountas, I. and Pinnell, G. *Teaching for Comprehending and Fluency: Thinking, Talking, and Writing about Reading, K–8*. Portsmouth, NH: Heinemann, 2006: 304. Used by permission.

observe what is expected of them and discuss ways to engage in certain aspects of the process or content of the conversations which they do not understand or find difficult.

## Assessing Independent Reading

When students are reading independently, you can meet one-on-one with a few students every day in conferences to monitor their reading and to provide specific feedback. By working with students individually, you not only provide individualized feedback, but also gain an understanding of how students are applying the skills and strategies previously taught, thus informing future instruction. During conferences, the teacher's role is to:

- Have authentic conversations with the child about the texts they are reading
- Assist the child with understanding aspects of the routines of independent reading (i.e., self-selecting "just right" books, reading for a sustained period of time)
- Teach the child effective reading skills and strategies
- Observe students' oral reading to ensure the use of fluency and phrasing
- Occasionally discuss students' journal responses

Students can also learn to assess their own use of independent reading time after the teacher has modeled and discussed his or her expectations. A rubric or chart can be created in which the following suggested criteria might be included.

Did the reader:

- Read for the entirety of independent reading?
- Stay in one good reading spot the entire time?
- Pick a "just right" book?
- Respect the readers around him/her?

By working with students individually, you not only provide individualized feedback, but also gain an understanding of how students are applying the skills and strategies previously taught, thus informing future instruction.

- Read for meaning and engagement?
- Read quietly?
- Stop and reread when the text did not make sense?
- Use sticky notes to help with his/her thinking?

When given the opportunity to self-assess their own use of independent reading time, students become aware of their own reading processes as well as classroom expectations. During reading conferences, teachers can then discuss areas in which the child excels or needs more support.

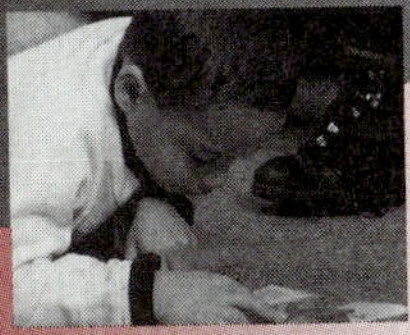

## How Can We Support Diversity and Differentiated Instruction in the Classroom?

IRA/NCTE 9

Au (1998) states, "Educators who wish to make literacy personally meaningful to students consistently draw on students' interests and experiences. By making literacy activities rewarding in an immediate sense, they provide students with the situational rationales for staying in school and engaging in literacy learning" (p. 309). Through an awareness of *each* child's path of development and by providing opportunities for scaffolded learning and shared activities designed to exemplify each child's strengths, teachers can use books successfully to promote "ownership of literacy" by all students. This is especially important for students from diverse cultures. Multicultural and international literature can enhance the education of students and have a profound effect on individual beliefs and understandings of the values of others.

### Multicultural and International Children's Literature

**Multicultural literature** is defined as "a group of works used to break the monopoly of the mainstream culture and make the curriculum pluralistic" (Cai, 2002, p. 4). This definition of multicultural literature characterizes books about those most excluded and marginalized people of color as well as books that represent children from underrepresented socioeconomic backgrounds, religions, genders, and exceptionalities. Research has shown that the use of multicultural literature that accurately depicts the experiences of diverse groups may improve the literacy achievement of students of diverse backgrounds. Multicultural literature does this by increasing students' motivation to read, encouraging their appreciation and understanding of their own language and cultural heritage, helping them to value their own life experience as a topic for writing, and promoting cross-cultural understanding (Au, 1998; Jordan, 1988; Lee, 1991; Louie, 2006; Spears-Bunton, 1990). See the Exploring Children's Literature feature in Chapter 4 (Supporting Diverse Learners) for a list of multicultural books to use in your classroom.

**International literature** has one or more of the following features: (1) It was originally written in a language other than English and subsequently translated; (2) it was originally written in English, but in a country other than the United States; or (3) it was written for students of another culture by a long-term member of that culture. International books must adhere to standards of literary quality, accuracy, and authenticity just as any other children's book.

Jacobs and Tunnell (2004, p. 216) offer three ways in which books about specific cultures and nations can offer positive experiences to young readers:

- Foster an awareness, understanding, and appreciation of people who seem at first glance different from the reader.
- Present a positive and reassuring representation of a readers' own cultural group.
- Introduce readers to the literary traditions of different world cultures or cultural groups in the United States.

Research has shown that the reading of multicultural books can be an effective tool for helping students embrace diversity (Wham, Barnhart, and Cook, 1996). Educators must ensure that students have regular, meaningful engagements with high-quality children's books that are culturally authentic and accurate. Authenticity is very important in the selection of literature that depicts the values, beliefs, and cultural backgrounds of various groups. Barrera, Liguori, and Salas (1993) point out "authenticity of content and images in children's literature is essential because inauthentic representation subverts the very cultural awareness and understanding that such literature can build" (p. 212). Critical evaluation of multicultural literature for authenticity and literary quality is essential to effective book selection.

Efforts have been made in recent years to increase the publication and recognition that multicultural children's literature deserves. Several awards for multicultural children's literature have been established to highlight outstanding books and their creators. The American Library Association (ALA) bestows several awards including the Coretta Scott King Award "given to an African American author and an African American illustrator for an outstandingly inspirational and educational contribution. The books promote understanding and appreciation of the culture of all peoples and their contribution to the realization of the American dream" (from: www.ala.org/ala/emiert/corettascottkingbookawards/corettascott.htm). The Pura Belpré Medal is presented to a "Latino/Latina writer and illustrator whose work best portrays, affirms, and celebrates the Latino cultural experience in an outstanding work of literature for children and youth" (from: www.ala.org/ala/alsc/awardsscholarships/literaryawds/belpremedal/belprmedal.htm). The Mildred L. Batchelder Award is given to an American publisher of a children's book considered to be the most outstanding of those books originally published in a foreign language in a foreign country, and subsequently translated into English and published in the United States. More information about all of the ALA awards can be found on their website (www.ala.org).

## Cultural Response to Children's Literature

IRA/NCTE 9

It is important to note the influence of cultural context in book sharing and literacy acquisition. As van Kleeck and Stahl (2003, pp. vii–viii) note:

> Family book sharing with young preliterate and early literate children is by no means a universal practice across cultural, linguistic, and social lines. Where it is practiced, it may be negotiated in a variety of ways, many of which are quite different from those favored in middle-class White families. As such, interven-

tions based on research among middle-class White families may be inappropriate, and hence less effective, for families from other backgrounds.

According to NCES (2003), 84 percent of public elementary and secondary classroom teachers are white, while 40 percent of elementary and secondary students are African American, American Indian, Asian American, or Hispanic American, and 5 percent of these students are English Language Learners. Students' difficulties in achieving adequate literacy can emanate from the mismatch between the teacher's narrow view of literacy and the reality of multiple literacies in today's society. As Au (1998) states: "To overcome barriers of exclusion proposed by conventional literacy instructional practices, educators must work with an expanded vision of literacy strategies and concepts in school, so that school definitions of literacy are transformed" (p. 308). Through their actions, both explicit and implicit, teachers relay, sometimes unwittingly, vast amounts of cultural information. For example, in selecting children's books to read aloud, a teacher may consciously or unconsciously choose books to share that reflect his or her culture and values to the exclusion of others. If a child's culture matches the culture of the teacher, then the child is more likely to get positive feedback about his or her ideas and responses. Educators' recognition of these inequalities depends on an understanding of their own cultural identities as well as the cultural identities of their students. Cross-cultural understanding can lead to identifying ways in which culture and school settings interact effectively and ineffectively in bringing students of diverse backgrounds to high levels of literacy (Au, 1998).

## Building a Classroom Library

School libraries and librarians continue to play an important role in students' lives, but as research has repeatedly shown, there is a high correlation between the amount students read and their reading achievement. Students must have access to many, many books and other media every day in their classrooms along with instruction on how to select, read, write, and talk about books with other students. Therefore, it is critical for teachers to have a classroom library. Reutzel and Fawson (2002) offer five major functions of the classroom library:

1. Supporting literacy instruction—Build an adequate collection of fiction and nonfiction materials at enough different levels to accommodate the many interests, cultures, and abilities of students desiring to check out books for take-home reading.
2. Helping students to learn about books—The small size of the classroom library is ideal for teaching students how to select "just right" books and how to take care of books.
3. Providing a central location for classroom resources—The classroom library can be used as a central storage location for instructional resources such as science equipment, CD and audiotape players, VHS tapes, DVDs, computers, games, magazines, and other materials.
4. Providing opportunities for independent reading and curricular extensions—Every good reading program provides students daily time to read independently. The classroom library is

The well-stocked classroom library allows easy access and must also reflect the range of student interests, preferences, genres, and curricular resources. Designing and stocking a classroom library around your students' literacy personalities takes time and careful consideration.

typically the resource that supports students' daily independent reading of self-selected books that meet their personal, recreational reading interests.

5. Serving as a place for students to talk and interact with books—The classroom library also provides a place for students to have book discussions with peers or the teacher. It is an area that makes books exciting and that kids cannot wait to get to so they can talk about their reactions to books.

A well-stocked classroom library allows easy access to books and must also reflect the range of student interests, preferences, genres, and curricular resources. Designing and stocking a classroom library around your students' literacy personalities with these five functions in mind takes time and careful consideration. For example, if you organize your library according to reading levels, students are only allowed to choose books within a certain level. Though you many have many books within each level, the topics, authors, and genres may not match the literacy personalities of your students. Moreover, how will they learn how to choose "just right" books on their own? If instead, books are organized by authors for instance, students will start to discuss authors, recommend books by various authors, and discover favorite authors. How you organize your classroom library sends a message as to what you want students to learn about book choice. Sibberson and Szymusiak (2003, p. 14) offer the following list of questions to ask when setting up a classroom library at the beginning of each year:

- How can the classroom library support good book selection habits? How can it support students as they think about themselves as readers, find favorite authors, and read for different purposes?
- Will the entire classroom library be located in one area of the room or will different sections be in different parts of the room?
- Will nonfiction be in a different area from fiction? How will this help students learn why they read different genres?
- What type of reading materials will students have access to during reading time? Will they be encouraged to read magazines, news articles, comic books, or poetry?
- How will I find space to display books face out?
- Which displays will be permanent? Which will include rotating titles?
- Will I use baskets to organize books with the same authors, topics, and genres?
- How will I highlight less popular books to make them appealing to students?
- How will I make room to highlight books throughout the year based on student need?

Book baskets or tubs can be an effective and flexible way to categorize books. They can be easily labeled, and with the books facing out, tubs create an attractive display that students can browse through. Tubs that are of medium size can be easily moved from shelves for browsing and later replaced. Tubs make it convenient to display books in a variety of ways to maximize students' exposure to new authors, genres, and topics. A few ways to categorize books:

- Alphabet books
- Concept books
- Pop-up books
- Number books
- Favorite characters
- Books with memorable language
- Wordless books
- Curriculum topics
- Authors
- Genres and subgenres, such as mysteries, sports, and memoirs
- Students' recommendations
- Award-winning books
- Humorous books
- Favorite series books
- Books read aloud by the teacher
- Newspaper and magazines
- Comics and cartoons
- Books written in a specific format, such as journals
- Books written by students in the class

Awards given for outstanding children's literature are excellent sources for finding books for the classroom library. The Newbery, Caldecott, and Coretta Scott King Awards given by the American Library Association are among the most prestigious in the United States (www.ala.org). The International Reading Association's Children's Choices, Young Adult's Choices, and Teacher's Choices awards are also great sources for book recommendations because these books are chosen by students, young adults, and teachers themselves. These books are voted on annually, and the winners are listed in *The Reading Teacher* or are available online at www.reading.org.

Unfortunately, most of the time teachers must spend their own money to buy books and other media for their classrooms. Other sources for obtaining books for your classroom library include book clubs and fairs (such as Scholastic), yard sales, donations from families, contributions from the school's Parent Teacher Organization, and local grants.

IRA/NCTE 1

See the Exploring Diversity feature for an example of one teacher's experience with building a sixth-grade classroom library.

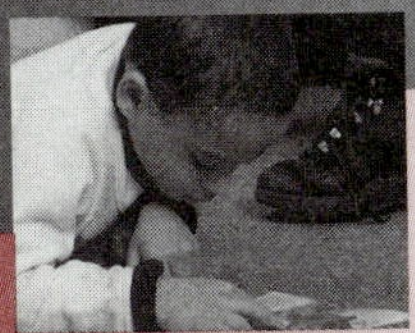

# How Can We Support Technology Use and Children's Literature?

"Throughout history, story has transformed lives. At the same time, we have also transformed story through the manner in which we present it and through the technology we have used to exchange it" (Leu, Grace, and Bevans, 2000, p. 4). New technologies challenge us to broaden our definition of *story*. The Internet and other new forms of information and communication technology (ICT) challenge us to broaden our definition of story even further. These resources enable us to appreciate stories in new and powerful ways.

The Internet provides us with many resources that are immediately available at our fingertips and helps in creating powerful new ways to enrich our understanding of authors and their stories. The Internet makes it possible for students anywhere in the world to have access to stories they may not otherwise have. These vast resources provide new opportunities for expanding our responses to literature, helping us to understand story in more extensive ways (Leu et al., 2000). CD-ROM books and e-books also offer new ways to access and interact with literature.

Just as it is essential that students understand the unique structure and expectations of the traditional genres of fiction and nonfiction, students must also learn about digital texts in order to live, learn, and work successfully in our society. It is vital that students have opportunities to use technology in meaningful ways that support the literacy and literature goals of mindful, knowledgeable teachers.

## Reading Online

Table 11.6 looks at each aspect of the reading transaction and focuses on the features or issues important to consider for optimal engagement and comprehension. In order to prepare students to successfully interact with ICT, teachers can do much to scaffold their acquisition of the new literacies required to comprehend and compose online.

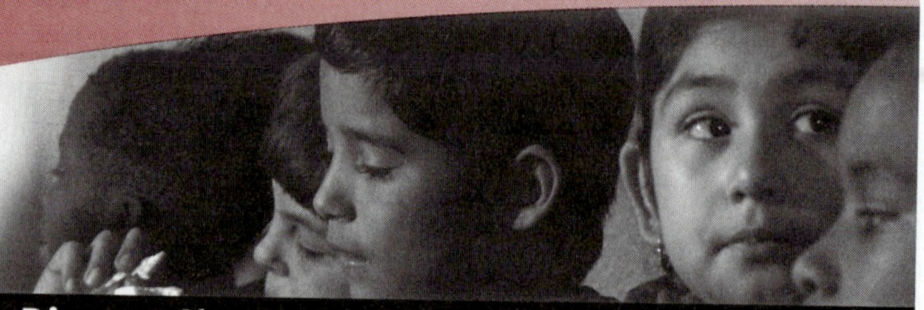

## exploring diversity

### Building a Diverse Classroom Library

Miss Quay is a sixth-grade teacher in an older school with small classrooms and no budget for providing teachers with funds to buy books. As a first-year teacher, Miss Quay has not had the opportunity to collect books for her classroom library, but she knows it is critical for her students to have access in the classroom to a variety of books of interest to them. As the first day of school quickly approaches, Miss Quay creates a book nook in the corner of her small classroom. Because it is her first year of teaching, her knowledge of sixth-graders' reading interests is limited. She decides to talk with the school media specialist who fills her in on the interests of the sixth-grade classes she has worked with in previous years. Miss Quay checks out several of the recommended books, but she notices that most of the books are realistic fiction. Without a variety of genres or reading levels to share with her students, Miss Quay visits the local public library. The children's librarian is very helpful and recommends numerous nonfiction titles including those that correlate with the science and social studies curriculum. The librarian also suggests several titles that represent a variety of genres and reading levels. But, Miss Quay notices that she still does not have many books that represent diverse cultures. On the recommendation of the assistant principal, Miss Quay decides to submit a proposal to the Parent Teacher Organization (PTO) to purchase a small collection of multicultural books. She consults several sources to find the best books to include in her request, such as *50 Multicultural Books Every Child Should Know*, which is a list by the Cooperative Children's Book Center at www.education.wisc.edu/ccbc. If she receives the funding to purchase these books, Miss Quay believes she will have a small, but adequate, collection for her classroom library with which to start the year. She realizes that as she gets to know her students and as the curriculum changes, she will replace books throughout the year. She also realizes that she will begin to collect books of her own and find various other resources to adequately stock the library.

The term *new literacies* (Leu, Kinzer, Coiro, and Cammack, 2004) has been defined as follows:

> The new literacies of the Internet include the skills, strategies, and dispositions necessary to successfully use and adapt to the rapidly changing information and communication technologies and contexts that continuously emerge in our world and influence all areas of our personal and professional lives. These new literacies allow us to use the Internet and other ICT to identify important questions, locate information, crucially evaluate the usefulness of that information, synthesize information to solve problems, and communicate the answers to others. (p. 1,572)

Acquiring the skills and strategies of the new literacies required to read, write, view, navigate, and communicate is critical to successful use of ICT.

## Table 11.6
## The Reading Transaction as It Relates to Digital Texts and ICT

| Category | Features/Issues in Reading on the Internet | Implications for Comprehension |
| --- | --- | --- |
| *Text* | • Hyperlinks<br>• Multimedia formats (animation, audio, video clips)<br>• Interactive nature | Because the text format is interactive, students have control over which direction they want the text to go. They must sort through and manipulate different media formats to create meaning. |
| *Reading Activity* | • Purpose not always clear<br>• Potential for propaganda, bias, and inaccurate information<br>• Potential for more engagement and personal applications | It is important that the teacher create a purpose for reading the text. Teachers also need to show students how to tell whether information on the Internet is accurate and unbiased. The nature of the Internet is interactive, so students can become more engaged in the reading activity. |
| *Reader* | • Experience with the Internet<br>• Motivation | As with conventional print matter, the readers' previous experience with the Internet can affect how successful they are in manipulating the different aspects of the World Wide Web to create meaning. In addition, teachers can use the different features of online data to motivate students. |
| *Social Context* | • Provides opportunities for collaboration | The social context influences the text, reading activity, and the reader to affect comprehension. The Internet provides opportunities for students to work together. |

*Source:* Excerpt adapted from "Reading Comprehension on the Internet: Expanding our Understanding of Reading Comprehension to Encompass New Literacies," by J. Coiro. *The Reading Teacher, 56*(6). Copyright © 2003 by the International Reading Association. Reprinted by permission.

## revisit the classroomchallenge

How did Miss Hall help her students understand the difference between fiction and nonfiction? She created a T-Chart—a chart shaped like a "T" providing two sides for which information can be compared. On one side, she recorded the characteristics of the nonfiction books she was reading aloud, and on the other side, she recorded the fiction chapter books the students were reading. The chart provided a visual guideline for understanding the different genres, and it remained posted in the room for students to use as needed. As new or additional information about nonfiction and fiction came up, it was added to the chart. Miss Hall was able to assess the students' understanding of the differences between the genres from their reading response journals, from their participation in class discussions, and from her own observations of students during book discussions.

How did Miss Hall help students engage in meaningful book discussions? She shared discussion strategies with the students and asked another middle-grade teacher to come to the class, and together they modeled for the students how they handled a discussion in which they disagreed on a particular aspect. She also gave students the opportunity to model for each other. Miss Hall used the literature conversation check sheet to assess the students' engagement in book discussions.

## chapterreview

This chapter answered these questions about children's literature:

### Why Is Children's Literature Important for Reading and Writing?

Children's literature broadens perspectives, imagination, insight, and cultural understanding. Reading children's literature also increases language acquisition, comprehension, vocabulary, knowledge of story patterns, fluency, and writing. Most importantly, however, children's literature brings enjoyment to young readers.

### What Do We Know about Children's Literature?

Literature that is specifically designated for children spans a broad range of genres and topics of interest to children from birth to adolescence. Children's literature is distinguished by characters, plots, themes, and language that typically reflect the emotions and experiences of children and is not overtly moralizing, cynical, or sentimental. High-quality children's literature has literary merit as measured by the literature elements of character, setting, plot, style, and theme. When selecting literature for children, teachers should consider the literary merit of books, including authenticity and accuracy. Teachers must also think about what issues might be considered controversial or sensitive by families and community members.

### What Do We Know about How Children Learn about Literature?

Children respond to literature that is interesting, engaging, and accessible to them. When students are able to actively engage with a text then they will have a meaningful transaction or "lived through" experience. Teachers can ensure that students become engaged and motivated readers by providing access to books within their experience and developmental levels, allowing students to self-select books, providing time for reading, and engaging students in conversations with each other in a nonthreatening environment.

### How Can We Teach Children's Literature?

To assist students in understanding children's literature, teachers can model, scaffold, and demonstrate effective ways of reading to their students and engaging them with a variety of texts. Oral storytelling, reading aloud, and thinking aloud are effective strategies for understanding literature that teachers can model and then slowly release responsibility to students for using on their own. Literature response journals and literature conversations are ways of engaging students in reflecting on their own thinking about the texts they are reading. Teachers can also incorporate children's literature into the content areas as a supplement to textbooks to provide a more in-depth look at a particular subject and to give students a personal connection to the subject.



## How Can We Assess Students' Understanding of Literature?

It is essential for teachers to provide books for students that reflect their experiences, development level, and interests. Interest and attitude surveys can help teachers assess this information. Assessment of literature journals, literature conversations, and independent reading assists teachers with determining students' understanding of children's literature and making effective decisions about instruction. The key to assessment of literature journals, literature conversations, and independent reading is evidence that reflects students' thinking about texts.

## How Can We Support Diversity and Differentiated Instruction in the Classroom?

Multicultural and international literature can positively affect students' beliefs and understandings of the values of others. Teachers must ensure that children have regular, meaningful engagements with high-quality children's books that reflect a multiplicity of cultures. Also, these books must be authentic and accurate. Several awards for outstanding multicultural and international children's literature have been established that can serve as a resource for teachers when selecting books for a classroom library and for instruction.

## How Can We Support Technology Use and Children's Literature?

The Internet and other digital technology have broadened our definition of reading, genre, and story. The interactive nature of texts on the Internet, CD-ROMs, and e-books has changed the strategies we use to read, the path we follow in our reading, and the way we engage in reading and writing stories from around the world. As with traditional texts, students must have a successful transaction with online text before it is meaningful. Students must be taught strategies for reading, comprehending, and responding to the unique structure and expectations of text online in order to live, learn, and work successfully in our society.

PEARSON **myeducationlab**™
Where the Classroom Comes to Life

Now go to www.myeducationlab.com to take a Pretest to assess your initial comprehension of chapter content, study chapter content with your individualized Study Plan, take a Posttest to assess your understanding of chapter content, practice your teaching skills with Building Teaching Skills exercises, and build a deeper, more applied understanding of chapter content with Homework and Exercises.

chapter 12

# Reading Beyond the Primary Grades

## classroomchallenge

**Tanya Arina** was upset; it was her first day as a certified teacher. She had been so excited to attend the opening staff development day in the district. Now she has to rethink all she had planned to do for her literacy curriculum. At the meeting, the director of curriculum made it clear that a "novel-based" program would not meet their expectations. The director spent most of the day explaining how the focus would be on "informational reading and writing" this year. In analyzing the district data from the last two years, it had become clear that students were not getting enough exposure to nonfiction, informational reading materials. Both the scores on the state reading test and on the content area tests indicated that students weren't well prepared. The district was below average in both areas. The director explained that on the fiction section of the state test, their students had been at grade level; on the informational reading, they were more than a grade lower on average.

Part of the development day was spent in grade-level teams exploring the state standards so all teachers would understand what was expected. On that list were objectives for activating background knowledge, previewing texts (noting the table of contents, chapters, glossary, index, and headings), identifying key content vocabulary, and using graphic information. Ms. Arina recalled that her group had some heated discussions about how students in the middle grades were to learn to identify informational text structures and to map them graphically. She didn't recall any of

her preservice training being devoted to identifying paragraphs or whole articles organized by compare/contrast, thesis and supporting details, problem/solution, chronology, or cause/effect. How was she ever going to be able to create a good, interesting curriculum now?

Luckily, the one good part of the day came when the Director invited new teachers to sign up for a mentor program. She explained that because there was a big push on literacy in the district, senior teachers had volunteered to work with the new ones and help ease them into the program. What a relief Tanya had felt, both at the suggestion of mentoring, and when she actually met her mentor. Mr. Walter seemed to be a very knowledgeable and helpful mentor. At least with his ideas, she could find a place to begin.

## Questions for Reflection

1. Why might Ms. Arina need to modify her novel-focused curriculum?
2. What should students in the middle grades learn about reading and language arts?
3. How can teachers use informal assessments to determine what students know so they can differentiate instruction?
4. How can Ms. Arina organize her instruction to build students' informational literacy?

## anticipating this chapter

To help you better understand issues related to reading beyond the primary level, this chapter addresses the following questions.

- What are goals for literacy beyond the primary grades?
- What instructional strategies are supported by research and best practices?
- How can students be encouraged to read for literary purposes?
- How can literacy be developed across the content areas?
- Why is visual literacy important?
- How can visual literacy be developed?
- How can you organize classroom instruction to accomplish your goals?
- How can integrated units of instruction enhance learning?

# What Are Goals for Literacy Beyond the Primary Grades?

IRA/NCTE 1

**Video Homework Exercise**

*The Research Process*

Go to the Homework and Exercises section of Chapter 12 of MyEducationLab and view the video, "The Research Process," which captures the essence of the goals teachers have for students as they read informational text. Complete the activities that follow, and save your work or transmit it to your professor as assigned.

One of the most important shifts in priority as students gain competence in basic reading is the expansion of the range of materials and purposes for reading. Students now use reading for their personal enjoyment, to learn new information, and to become more analytical and critical thinkers. The variety of text types expands and students need to use visual media and technology. They also learn to engage in more extended inquiry and research projects that combine reading, visual forms, and writing.

Reading beyond the primary grades becomes increasingly more differentiated at each grade level, and teachers need to plan ways to develop both students' understanding of literary texts and the variety of forms of informational materials they encounter.

Developing strategies for the variety of types of informational texts that become a major part of students' reading both in and beyond school is a key priority beyond the primary grades. Students need to be taught how to read textbooks, magazines, websites, and trade books. With your guidance, they will become familiar with the range of texts, learn how informational texts are structured, how concepts and vocabulary are elaborated, and how to engage with them so ideas can be learned and retained. This kind of careful reading represents a shift in emphasis for young readers. Each year, students need to be guided in increasingly sophisticated aspects of informational reading and writing leading to their ability to engage in self-directed inquiry and research projects.

This expanded range in the types of materials students need to read is reflected in the International Education Assessment, which was administered in 2006 to fourth-grade students in schools across the world. The reading test included an equal emphasis on reading literary texts and informational texts. In the introduction to the Progress In Reading Literacy Study (PIRLS, 2006, p. 3), this broad conception of reading literacy is explained as:

> . . . the ability to understand and use those written language forms required by society and/or valued by the individual. Young readers can construct meaning from a variety of texts. They read to learn, to participate in communities of readers in school and everyday life, and for enjoyment.

## Reading Practices Outside of School

What we read outside of school also underscores the importance of knowing how to read and use informational materials. Recent research studies on the reading habits of adults reflect the shift away from fiction to informational reading and using nonfiction sources (Smith, 2000; RAND 2002). We read the newspaper and magazines to find out about the world around us and about our favorite activities. We browse the World Wide Web to gain in-depth information and alternative points of view. We read self-help books and books on health and fitness because we want to improve our health and lifestyle. We read spiritual and religious books to reflect and deepen our quality of living.

As a society, we are shifting from a nation of fiction readers to a people who read a preponderance of informational texts. We want to know as much as possible—about ourselves as well as the rest of the world. Publishers know this shift in interests and are publishing more informational texts, both print and electronic. One of the real transformations in the last decade is the explosion of materials available for us to read on an enormous range of topics, on the Internet and also in more traditional publishing like books and magazines.

As children grow as readers, they will experience a variety of different informational materials—from the inviting trade books found in libraries to small, topically specific texts that support classroom units of instruction, to newspapers and magazines, Internet sites, electronic texts, histories, science books, travel guides, biographies, how-to books, textbooks, and many others.

## Reading Practices in School

Because so many sources of information are available in print formats, it is important for teachers to prioritize helping young readers develop the joy in and ability to read a wide range of materials. Central to achieving this goal is knowing every student and being able to help them find material that is of interest to them. Students need to be encouraged and given time to engage in self-selected choice reading in school. As a new teacher, one of your tasks will be to read and be able to recommend just the right book or source for each student. Chapter 11 introduced you to many books and materials, and you will want to continue to read children's literature so you can make informed recommendations and talk with your students about their reading.

To be successful learners, students must also learn to read and study about concepts that society considers important, sometimes in spite of their personal interests. Students need strategies that can help them effectively navigate course content in their school curriculum. This content is generally elaborated on in literature anthologies, content area textbooks, and other reference materials. With guidance, they can become confident and flexible readers empowered with the variety of strategies essential to making sense of the wide range of materials and formats used in the variety of materials they encounter regularly.

Introduce students to informational text structures by using the external graphic headings and subheadings in textbooks and informational articles. These often provide a key to how a text is organized internally.

**Instructional Priorities** Despite the priority being placed on informational reading in society and in tests, data collected in studies of classrooms (Duke, 2000; Taylor and Pearson, 2002; Pressley, Allington, Wharton-McDonald, Block, Morrow, 2001) indicate that primary teachers have not shifted their teaching to reflect these higher expectations. While some changes are being noted, especially with the increased availability of good, inviting informational materials for elementary children, responsible teachers need to ensure that students have a broad range of instruction in reading strategies and purposes and that they become comfortable negotiating a variety of text types (Blachowicz and Ogle, 2008). All students deserve this support so they can become successful learners for life. Most middle and secondary teachers also expect students to engage in independent research and to be able to write informational essays and reports. Guiding students through the inquiry and research process is another priority in the intermediate and upper elementary grades. The more classrooms can be places where students pursue questions important to them, the more they will grow intellectually and personally (Guthrie, 2003).

**Knowledge Standards** The current national focus on standards and measuring what students learn each year is putting more pressure on teachers to provide focused and content-rich units of instruction. Reading is still one of the most used tools for building student knowledge and understanding across the curriculum. Social studies, science, mathematics, and fine arts are natural contexts for teaching students strategies for reading and learning. Even when electronic technology is used, reading is essential. In fact, use of the Internet and other electronic resources puts additional demands on readers to evaluate materials that are appropriate to their needs and levels of reading and then combine ideas from a variety of sources. Instead of becoming less essential, the demands on learners as readers are increasing. Many states include in the professional teaching standards for each content area the expectation that teachers know how to help students read and learn from content materials. Teachers need to know how to make the most of the learning experiences they provide students. Therefore, it is the responsibility of all teachers to help students develop good active reading and learning strategies. Students need to learn to ask critical questions as they read from unedited sources: Who has written the text or website information? What point of view is being expressed? When was the information written? What evidence is presented to support the ideas? What do other authorities say? These critical questions lead students to use multiple sources of information and evaluate those sources as they compare various texts. This form of reading and thinking is stimulating and can, in itself, often develop high levels of engagement from curious students.

**High-Stakes Assessments** Another implication of the current accountability climate for teachers is that the large-scale assessments of students' reading abilities are now balanced between reading for literary purposes and reading to learn. These assessments reflect the fact that, for students to be successful as readers throughout schooling and life, they need to read for a variety of purposes in a variety of materials. Reading fiction for pleasure is only one of many forms reading takes. Equally important for school success across the curriculum is the ability to read informational texts and learn from them. It is also important that students know how to think about what they read and be able to compose responses to texts. Standardized tests, state performance assessments, and the current international tests (PIRLS, 2006; PISA, 2001; NAEP, 2009) all incorporate a variety of materials and purposes. Reading for information has as much importance as reading for literary purposes. Yet, on the 2001 PIRLS study, U.S. students showed the biggest discrepancy in their reading of fiction and informational passages. The U.S. came out near the top in fiction but was seventeenth in informational reading (Organization for Economic Cooperation and Development, 2003). This large discrepancy may be due to the fact that most primary reading programs have focused almost exclusively on fiction. Many elementary teachers love to read fiction and, therefore, fill their classrooms with books they like. Newer basal reading programs now include a balance of fiction and informational materials so there is more support for teachers committed to preparing students for a wide range of reading purposes and texts.

Many state standards tests balance fiction with informational passages. Standardized tests also include a range of reading passages and expect students to read for literary purposes, for information, and to perform tasks. Many assessments also add this third form of reading—reading to perform a task—a kind of reading that requires careful attention to text resulting in a concrete goal (performing a science experiment, creating an origami object, following steps in a math problem, etc.). These reading tasks are included under the general heading of "reading to learn" although it is a kind of reading that does not require long-term memory, rather careful attention to steps in completing the task. Learners often need to follow precise steps in completing processes in an incredibly wide range of activities—from taking medicines to putting together new technological equipment, to engaging in sports and games. Again, studies show that students are not good at this kind of reading and need much more experience in using procedural materials well (Hegarty, Carpenter, and Just, 1991; Albers, 2006).

The current awareness that reading involves a wide range of engagements with a variety of text types has led to more emphasis on informational reading with attention to expository and persuasive texts and on the need for students to both enjoy and learn from what they read. Research has also indicated that how students read, how they conceive of their roles as readers, is also important. The more students know about the act of reading, the more successful they can become.

## What Instructional Strategies Are Supported by Research and Best Practices?

There is much teachers can do to help children become balanced readers, able to navigate a wide variety of text types and purposes. Beginning with our own reading, teachers can share their strategies reading many kinds of materials. Thinking about the skills needed to read a wide range of texts and how to introduce and build children's knowledge and experience is important. Then, knowing how to scaffold for all students, those who embrace informational reading and those who embrace fiction, those who have large vocabularies and those with limited English, and those with and without confidence as learners is another level of challenge.

## Reading Is Social

One of the most important aspects of reading development is that it is social, grounded in the cultural expectations and habits of the community (Snow, 2002; Blachowicz and Ogle, 2008). From their earliest years, children either learn the value of reading from parents and extended family and friends or they don't. Those who have family who read to them from their earliest days are inculcated into a "literate" world and expect that they will learn to read and enjoy sharing those experiences. From the earliest experiences of sharing books together, parents focus their children's attention on aspects of written texts and guide them in forming interpretations of what is important in the texts. This process continues throughout life; readers talk with others about what they read and often find that through conversation they deepen their understanding of what they have read or viewed.

Our friends also help shape our tastes in what we read; most studies show that the easiest way for a book to become popular is for it to be recommended by friends (Temple, Martinez, Yokota, and Naylor, 2002, p. 19). We have known for a long time that teachers' and other classmates' recommendations of a book is one of the best ways to ensure that it will be read. The global Harry Potter phenomenon is one indication of the power of social connectedness in reading. At a national level, Oprah Winfrey has had an enormous impact on the book market; if Oprah recommends a book, it becomes a bestseller almost overnight. Reading is a very social activity!

## Reading Comprehension Is Constructive

A second important aspect of reading is that comprehension is a constructive process. Making sense of text requires the reader to activate his or her prior knowledge, to make associations between what has been known and the words and ideas being read, and to form hypotheses as the text unfolds (Pearson, 2003). Readers predict, visualize, form interpretations, and make connections as they breathe life into the words on a page (Pressley et al., 2001). Many research studies have demonstrated that much of interpretation is determined by the readers' prior knowledge and experiences (Anderson and Pearson, 1984; Steffensen, Joag-Dev, & Anderson, 1979). Readers continually call on their prior experiences to build meaning from the words in texts; creating an interpretation is what reading is all about.

## Reading Is Shaped by Our Purposes

Reading is also heavily influenced by the purposes for which readers approach texts (RAND, 2002). Someone who wants to find the name of the character they remember from a novel only needs to skim over a few pages in a chapter to recall the ideas and to locate the name. Someone reading that same text for the first time will enter the text fairly slowly, trying to develop a sense of the whole—where the story takes place, who the characters are, and what themes or issues are being developed. The new reader will also attend to the author's style and use of language. If the reading proceeds smoothly and the reader is able to construct ideas from the author's text, the journey will probably continue through the whole book. If the reader finds the author's text difficult and confusing, the reader may never finish the text—unless it is an assigned text in some course or a favorite of someone the reader wants to impress. If it becomes a real "favorite," then a reader may return to a book several times. Purpose is important in determining how and how much engagement a reader will commit to a particular text.

## Reading Is Strategic

IRA/NCTE 3

With a variety of texts and purposes for reading, another important aspect of maturing readers is that, with teacher help, they develop a range of strategies they can use flexibly when needed to meet their purposes. Among the most important strategies that lead to good comprehension are:

- Activating prior knowledge
- Making predictions
- Inferring
- Visualizing
- Asking and answering questions
- Attending to the text structure (both in stories and expository texts)
- Monitoring the developing meaning
- Engaging "fix-up" strategies if needed

As Pressley et al. (2001) explained, good readers use these strategies flexibly as needed and continually monitor their own comprehension processes.

Reading is a **transaction** between the reader and the text that requires monitoring and continued renegotiation. Where the reader and text author share experiences and assumptions, the reader can proceed easily, automatically; where there are differences and the reader cannot immediately interpret the author's intentions, then the reader needs to slow down, reread and retrace parts of the text interpretation he/she has constructed, and look more deeply at possibilities for what was intended. This often involves conscious use of strategies as the reader must keep revising a "text" that is emerging in the reader's head and develop a new interpretation. Less secure readers often find it hard to release their predictions and images and, instead, work with the information the author has provided to create a more shared interpretation.

**An Example of Strategic Reading: Reading Mysteries** There is no easier setting in which to follow this process than when one is reading a mystery. The ongoing purpose of many readers is to figure out the solution to the mystery before the author reveals it. The reader knows that the author sometimes leads readers down dead-end trails, and at other times embeds clues that may seem unimportant at the time, yet in rereading take on major significance. Those who love to read mysteries enjoy this play between author and reader and know that they must be ready to revise their interpretation with each potential turn in the trail of the unfolding mystery. The reader regularly predicts, reads to confirm, and then adjusts his/her predictions to the unfolding ideas.

Mystery readers draw on their knowledge of the text form and conventions, their experiences in looking for clues that connect pieces of the puzzle, and their sense of what is possible or plausible. Some stop periodically in their reading to think about the unfolding situations and to try to put the pieces together. Some draw diagrams and maps to see if they have constructed clear mental pictures of the scenes and actions. Others make marginal notes where they think important ideas or clues are introduced. This active engagement of readers with texts is characteristic of readers who enjoy reading mysteries. Therefore, this genre provides a good entry point for modeling the kinds of thinking and involvement teachers want to stimulate in students. See Figure 12.1 for ideas of mysteries that lend themselves to being read aloud with students. It is helpful to copy some short sections from a mystery being read orally on transparencies so students can see the exact text and reread silently to ponder possible clues. When this isn't possible, teachers and students can write on the board their predictions, questions, and significant clues provided by the author.

## Negotiating a Variety of Reading Contexts

This discussion of readers being strategic and engaged needs to include a summary of the larger set of strategies that researchers have confirmed as being important. The intermediate grades and beyond are when children expand their repertoire of strategies and learn to adjust their approaches depending on the text genre, the author, and their purposes for reading. In addition to the basic strategies mentioned earlier, readers need to learn how to:

- Activate their background knowledge
- Note important vocabulary
- Make connections
- Utilize the internal text structure
- Monitor comprehension

**Figure 12.1**

### Mystery Stories to Read Aloud

**Model Engaged Reading with Mysteries**

Balliett, B. (2005). *Chasing Vermeer.* New York: Scholastic Paperbacks.

Balliette, B. (2006). *The Wright 3.* New York: Scholastic.

Hiassen, C. (2005). *Flush.* New York: Knopf Books for Young Readers.

Hiassen, C. (2002). *Hoot.* New York: Knopf Books for Young Readers.

Pullman, P. (Sally Lockhart Trilogy)

*The Ruby in the Smoke* (1988). New York: Laurel Leaf.

*The Shadow in the North* (1989). New York: Laurel Leaf.

*The Tiger in the Well* (1992). New York: Laurel Leaf.

Raskin, E. (1997). *The Westing Game.* New York: Puffin.

- Construct meaning for the whole text
- Reflect on and appreciate the theme
- Attend to literary techniques used
- Evaluate the author's purpose and point of view
- Compare the text to others with similar themes and style



IRA/NCTE 2

**Expanding Genre Familiarity** The example of reading a mystery also raises another important component of reading development in the intermediate grades—the expanding range of genres that students are familiar with and the importance of knowing the particular characteristics of each. Students deserve to know if the short story they will read is realistic fiction, fantasy, or mystery. The genre both provides a structure and also sets limitations for what the reader can expect. For example, the title "The Little Boy's Secret" does not in and of itself give the reader any information about the characteristics of the story, nor does the picture of a little boy walking through the woods carrying a backpack. If a reader assumes the story is realistic fiction, none of the unfolding events would be anticipated or predicted. However, if the reader knows this is a folk tale, then a whole different set of possibilities can be considered. In fact, as a folk tale, the story is charming in revealing how this little boy, who was sent home early because he had contracted chicken pox, is able to escape from three giants who capture him in the woods. Without an awareness of the genre, readers are left not knowing what potential the story holds, nor will readers think of the message communicated by the tale.

**Attending to Characters and Plot** Intermediate and middle grades are opportunities to introduce students to new genres and to help them attend to the structure of each. Teachers can check to see if students are attending to the plot structure by having them create story maps. Many students start in on chapter books in third grade and love these longer, more complicated plots. Teachers can help them hold the various strands of the plot together by having them make visual maps as they read.

This is also the time to introduce students to careful attention to character development and ways in which characters respond to and learn from adversity. Teachers need to help students identify character traits and use examples from the actions and talk of those characters to make the inferences clear.

## Vocabulary

Another component of good reading is the development of one's own vocabulary. Unless readers can immediately make connections between the words they see in print and some concepts and associations in their memory, their reading will either be very slow or they won't gain the meaning the author intends. Therefore, throughout the grades, students need to be encouraged to keep expanding their vocabularies. Researchers have demonstrated that teachers can't teach all the words students learn, but that through wide reading, children can continue to expand their vocabularies by more than a thousand words each year (Anderson and Nagy, 1992; Cunningham and Stanovich, 1998).

At the same time that children expand their vocabularies through wide reading, teachers also need to be part of this vocabulary growth by teaching specific words and by teaching students more about how words are formed and how they have come into our language. Teaching new words and teaching about words are both important. The next chapter in this book is devoted to developing students' interests in and knowledge of general and academic vocabulary because it is so important.

## Fluency

The earlier description of the different variables involved in how comprehension functions is related to another important aspect of reading—fluency. Unless readers can read rapidly and with ease, they can't focus on the construction of meaning. Students who stumble over pronunciation of words, those who can't create natural phrasing so the text sounds like language, and those who have developed bad habits of looking at words as stand-alone units of meaning can't get to the heart of what reading is all about—meaning. Therefore, automaticity in word recognition and phrasing is essential. The National Reading Panel described fluency in these words (National Reading Panel, 2000, p. 22):

> Fluency is the ability to read a text accurately and quickly. When fluent readers read silently, they recognize words automatically. They group words quickly in ways that help them gain meaning from what they read. Fluent readers read aloud effortlessly and with expression. Their reading sounds natural, as if they are speaking.

There is a difference in oral and silent fluency; in the intermediate grades, teachers need to be particularly focused on developing students' silent reading abilities. By this time, the children should begin to read more rapidly when they read silently than when they read orally. This is the goal; students must develop more rapid silent reading if they are going to enjoy reading long texts and manage the academic demands of text reading that come in middle and secondary school. Teachers can check their students' oral and silent fluency rates early in the year to identify those students who may need more focus on this component.

How do students become fluent readers able to identify the vocabulary and feel comfortable with the style of different authors and different genres? It is clearly by reading a lot, in different types of texts over time. An important study by Anderson, Wilson, and Fielding (1988) showed what a large difference there is in the amount of reading children do (see Figure 12.2). Those at the upper end of time spent reading

**Figure 12.2**

### Differences in Amounts of Independent Reading by 5th Graders

| Percentile rank among readers | Minutes of out-of-school reading per day | Words read per year |
|---|---|---|
| 98 | 65.0 | 4,358,000 |
| 90 | 21.1 | 1,823,000 |
| 80 | 14.2 | 1,146,000 |
| 70 | 9.6 | 622,000 |
| 60 | 6.5 | 432,000 |
| 50 | 4.6 | 282,000 |
| 40 | 3.2 | 200,000 |
| 30 | 1.3 | 106,000 |
| 20 | 0.7 | 21,000 |
| 10 | 0.1 | 8,000 |
| 2 | 0.0 | 0 |

*Source:* Anderson, Wilson, and Fielding, 1988. Used by permission.

outside of school (in the 90 percent range of amount of reading accomplished) read nearly two million different words in a year. Children who engaged in little reading outside of school encountered few words by comparison.

Students do a great deal themselves that creates different levels of competency in reading. The research makes clear that teachers and schools also make a difference. The amount of time spent instructing students in the important components of reading, modeling, guiding students to practice, and monitoring students until they become independent in their reading are all important (Pearson and Gallagher, 1983; Taylor and Pearson, 2004). Teaching students to identify and select particular strategies and combinations of strategies as they read has been shown over and over again in research studies to enhance students' comprehension and long-term learning (NRP, 2000; RAND, 2002). Providing stimulating, challenging classroom contexts and differentiating so all students can learn at their own instructional level makes a difference (Allington and Johnston, 2002). Schools where teachers work together across grade levels so students' progress is cumulative also show the most improvements. This is another reason to attend carefully to both district and state standards and benchmarks for students. The more teachers work toward common goals, using common language and expectations, the more students benefit.

# How Can Students Be Encouraged to Read for Literary Purposes?

The majority of reading instruction in the elementary grades has generally been during "reading" class. New core reading programs with their supplemental trade books provide a good foundation for reading. Their goal is for children to develop confidence and competence so they can also engage in more self-selected and self-directed reading in book clubs or literature circles. Teachers also want students to read independently on a regular basis; in fact, it is a good practice to support students' reading at least fifteen minutes a night so they can continue to grow in their reading abilities.

## Expand the Genres Students Read

It is in literature study that teachers and students can focus their attention on expanding students' familiarity with genres and strategies (see Chapter 11 for more elaboration on these ideas). One way to involve them is through the use of genre wheels. Teachers can create their own focused genre wheels and involve students in charting their exploration of the varied genres. Children can rate their enjoyment of these genres and also reflect on their different ways of engaging with each. See the example of an elaborated genre wheel in Figure 12.3.

## Share Responses to Literature

IRA/NCTE 6

The sharing of responses to literature is another important aspect of students' literacy development. This begins when students identify their own interests in particular texts and content. Chances to share what they find interesting and to draw or illustrate their responses help students think about their own engagement and learn to share it with others. As children read more, they also find particular authors and books that are their favorites. By the intermediate grades, they can learn to participate in book clubs or

**Figure 12.3** Genre Wheel

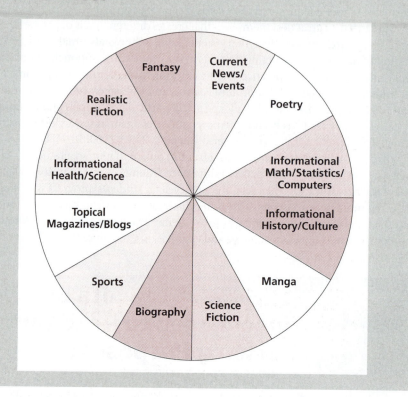

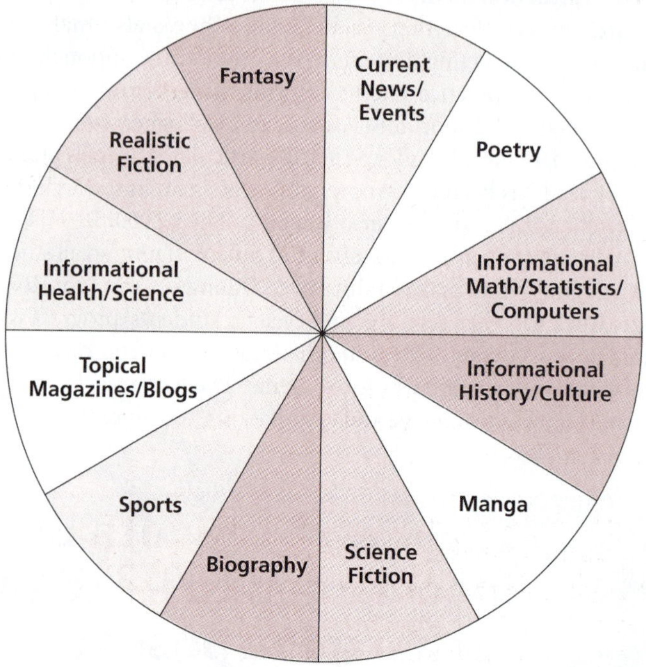


discussion groups. From the exchanges with others who have read the same text, students begin to understand that each person creates his or her own interpretation and finds personal meaning in a text. Teachers want students to learn to make connections to their own experience, to other texts, and to contexts beyond reading. These different ways of connecting have been identified by Harvey and Goudvis (2000) as text to self, text to text, and text to world.

IRA/NCTE 12

The group exchanges also help students expand their understanding of what an author created and even alter their interpretations and feelings. Formats such as Raphael and McMahon's (1994) **book club** and Daniels' (2002) **literature circles** provide starting points for students to learn how to deepen their enjoyment of books through sharing them with others. So, too, is the Sketch to Stretch activity already introduced in Chapter 2 and Mind Mapping. See the Engaging in Visual Literacy feature for an example of how Mind Mapping works.

The ways in which students respond to texts are also more elaborate as students mature—they can summarize the main ideas of a text and identify an author's point of view. This is also when teachers can encourage students to keep literature notebooks or response journals. After a period of silent reading or book discussion, students write in their own journals their ideas emanating from their reading and talk. Some good starters for writing include questions such as:

- Who did you connect with most in your reading and why?
- What do you think the characters could have done differently and what impact might that have on the development of the story?

- Where do you think the author is taking this story? What will most likely happen next?
- If this is an informational text, what did you find most interesting?
- Are there parts you want to check out in other references to be sure the author is accurate and current? Explain.
- What does this part of the book remind you of (other stories, real life, movies, etc.)?

All of these aspects of engagement and mental activity are part of what reading is all about. That is why teachers can't assume that students are aware of and using all the potential resources they have. It is important for both students and teachers to create ways of monitoring the extent of students' thinking and connecting. Later in this chapter, some of these tools will be explained. As already noted, a starting point is for the teacher to model his/her own thinking by engaging in structured times to read orally and "Think Aloud."

## engaging in Visual Literacy

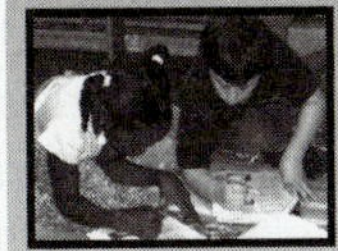
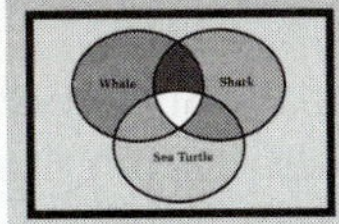

### Mind Mapping

Some students in Ms. Arina's class are reading "Thank You, Ma'am" by Langston Hughes in their literature discussion group. The teacher has asked the students to try a new approach to visualizing as they read. She instructs them to draw pictures that represent what they think at different points as they read the short story. She models how she first visualized the woman and draws a quick sketch of her. She is caught up with the boy and models by drawing a stick figure with a basketball. As the tension is created, she also draws a lightning bolt to indicate her concern. With this introduction, she turns the task over to the group of students and explains that when they have finished reading the short story, they will have a turn to share their visual map with the group and others will respond to it. They will use the procedure similar to what they do with the "Sketch to Stretch" activity. Each member of the group will have a turn to show the group his or her picture and ask the other students what was illustrated. Once each group member responds, the student who did the drawing will tell what he or she was trying to represent. The next student will then share the sketch he or she made, and the group will again take turns responding. Ms. Arina suggests that if they find this activity of mind mapping helpful, they can use it again with the other stories in this unit.

# How Can Literacy Be Developed across the Content Areas?

It is important that in the intermediate grades teachers extend students' knowledge of informational texts and build their interest in the rich array of materials available in print and electronic formats. Students should be able to identify expository forms of writing and use them to organize and summarize what they learn. The major ways authors organize information include:

- Sequence
- Compare/contrast
- Problem/solution
- Cause/effect
- Main idea and supporting details

Argumentative and persuasive texts also come into the curriculum at this time, especially in social studies.

## Explore a Variety of Genres and Presentations

Many sources exist now in magazines, books, online articles, and CD-ROMs, all of which are formats that invite children to explore the world around them and their own specific interests. Many of these sources are complex with information presented in a variety of ways—from text boxes to diagrams, charts, pictures with captions, and maps. Make sure that your classroom library has a selection of interesting and inviting informational books and magazines that students can explore as part of their independent reading. Even comics can be very engaging and full of information and rich dialog.

**Graphic Texts** Visual formats are increasingly a part of the presentation of informational materials and are more common in graphic novels and the Japanese manga that are popular with young adolescents. Students are very familiar with visual images, but often haven't taken time to look closely at the messages contained in cartoons and fast-moving images. Teachers have a great opportunity to help students become more visually attuned, to develop strategies for viewing and reflecting critically on what is presented, and for using visual and verbal data together in learning. Some research has pointed out that students don't move easily between visuals and narrative text information. Yet, this is exactly what is required in most textbooks, trade books, and magazines.

**Planning Together for Wide Reading** There are many formats and styles of information and content; students deserve an introduction to all and also need to learn to read and respond to them at a critical level. One way of getting started is for the teachers across grade levels to work together, analyzing what aspects of reading and learning in a variety of types of texts and genres are featured in the school and which need more attention. Specific aspects of reading lend themselves more appropriately to some content area learning than do others. If the school has a team-teaching model, then all teachers need to be involved to ensure that students have an introduction to the variety of text types and strategies needed to learn successfully. If teachers have self-contained classrooms, it is still important to map instruction in reading across the content areas.

# Learn to Read Textbooks

A major responsibility teachers have is introducing students to the structure of and the tools for content area textbooks. Students need to be introduced to the various features of informational texts and textbooks and learn how to use them. Looking at the Table of Contents is an important starting point. They also need to locate the glossary, index, chapter and unit divisions, and the ways key vocabulary terms are highlighted. Many young readers have never thought about how chapters are organized and how headings and subheadings function to give readers a guide to meaning. Readers who are aware of these aids can use the graphic features to guide their reading. In contrast to fiction, informational materials provide visual and graphic support to readers so they can get a preview of how a text is organized. The title, headings, subheadings, and boxed features are all provided so readers can have a road map of how the content is organized and what is highlighted. Most textbooks have subsections within each chapter so the amount of text to be covered is chunked with pre-reading supports, questions, and review features. These may be color coded to help readers. Teachers introduce new textbooks by having students do text "walk-throughs," so they can identify how a particular text is structured to help them learn. In this process, they can note how the key vocabulary in textbooks is generally identified—with boldface type, italics, or color. Pictures, diagrams, and charts are important components of the texts that readers should attend to before beginning to read each section.

One way to find out if students are aware of the important text features is to give them a pre-test and then a post-test after teaching them to identify and use the features. Renee Mackin, a literacy leader in Chicago, developed the assessment shown in Figure 12.4 to use with her students both initially and after taking time to help them locate and identify these features. She also uses a Scavenger Hunt to move this assessment into students' engagement with their textbook. Figure 12.5 shows the model she uses and adapts to particular textbooks and grade levels.

If students use three or four different textbooks during the day, help them compare and contrast the books so they won't be as confused when they have to negotiate several presentation styles. Making a chart of features is one way to do this. See Figure 12.6 for an example of a feature chart.

# Reading Development in Social Studies

Textbooks are generally used in social studies instruction and can be a good place to introduce students to the features of textbooks. At the beginning of the year, teacher modeling of how to use a textbook can be a starting place. It is also fun to give students a scavenger hunt guide for them to use with a partner to locate aspects of the textbook. Many students may have never looked to see how each chapter is introduced, how key terms are indicated, or when their textbook was published.

Social studies textbooks employ many photographs and pictures so helping students learn to read these visual "texts" can come naturally as the book is introduced. In addition, maps and charts are used heavily in social studies, so they also need to be taught. Without teacher guidance, many students simply ignore these important sources of information. On maps, the compass rose and key are important; on charts, the title and key or identification terms need to be noted. It is amazing how many children never attend to these pieces of information. Yet, these features are essential to accurate understanding and thinking about text ideas (Ogle, Klemp & McBride, 2007).

In social studies, it is important to develop students' ability to think sequentially and chronologically. Timelines and placement of events in order are basic to the expo-

**Figure 12.4**

## Text Feature Assessment

**Text Features Pre-test and Post-test**

Name ______________________________ Date ______________

Use the words to answer the questions about nonfiction text features.

| | | | | |
|---|---|---|---|---|
| Table of Contents | Glossary | Index | Pictures | Boldface Print |
| Caption | Text Box | Diagrams | Titles | Headings |

1. A list at the back of a book that gives definitions for new or difficult words. ______________________________
2. A title or short explanation that goes along with a picture or illustration. ______________________________
3. A list of chapters and the pages on which they start. ______________________________
4. Photographs that are used to clarify, illustrate, or explain what is in a book. ______________________________
5. The name of a chapter or of a book. ______________________________
6. Drawings that are created to explain or clarify what is written in a book. ______________________________
7. An alphabetic list of names, topics, or places from a book and the pages on which they are found. ______________________________
8. This provides extra information about the topic or subject. ______________________________
9. The title or topic that stands at the top of a paragraph. ______________________________
10. The letters in the word or words are darker than the rest. It is usually a new or important word. ______________________________

sition of content. Students must be able to use them as they develop knowledge and construct their own frameworks to interpret events. Many textbooks include timelines and charts of sequences of events. Young students will learn to use these tools with good instruction; without guidance they may lack understanding of these key organizing structures for their own learning. Asking students to create timelines is a good way of testing the development of this ability. Many state standards in literacy and social studies expect that students can think and construct visual representations across time.

Geography is also important in social studies, and students need to learn to read maps and compare different types of maps. This spatial ability is important as a tool for learning and making sense of content textbooks. It is also important that students be given guidance in reading and using maps before being expected to read them as part of a textbook presentation. If students are unsure about how to use the maps, these rich sources of information may be overlooked.

## Reading Development in Science

School districts vary considerably in their use of textbooks and printed materials in science. In districts where "hands-on" science is the major approach, teachers need to work with school librarians and collect books and magazines to support students'

Figure 12.5

## Textbook Scavenger Hunt

### Text Scavenger Hunt

Name ______________________________

Using your textbook, find each of the listed text features, give the page number, and tell why it is used and how it can help you better understand what you are reading.

| FEATURE | PAGE # | WHY IS IT USED AND HOW CAN IT HELP YOU BETTER UNDERSTAND WHAT YOU ARE READING? |
|---|---|---|
| Table of Contents | | |
| Index | | |
| Glossary | | |
| Pictures/ Illustrations | | |
| Boldfaced Print | | |
| Captions | | |
| Text Box | | |
| Titles/ Headings | | |

thinking. Because vocabulary is an important part of learning science, children need many opportunities to see and practice the key terms in the units they are studying. Especially for students who are ELLs, the ability to read more of the language they hear in classroom experimentation and exploration the more likely it is that they will be able to differentiate key terms and learn them.

Figure 12.6

## Student Chart for Comparing Text Features

| External Features | Unit/Chapter Organization (color coding) | Headings/ Subheadings Sections | Vocabulary | Questions and Review Aids | Index, Glossary, & Appendix |
|---|---|---|---|---|---|
| Content Areas | | | | | |
| Social Studies | | | | | |
| Science | | | | | |
| Mathematics | | | | | |

In addition, having good science texts available (books, Internet sites, and magazines) also helps children learn to read and use the visual information that is so critical to the way scientific ideas are explained. Both photographs and diagrams are important to the presentation of science. Students deserve teachers' guidance in learning to read these visual formats. By putting a diagram on a transparency or visualizer, teachers model for students how to make sense of these presentations: Highlight the title of the diagram, the key to interpreting it, and then take time to think aloud about what the diagram shows, including the perspective (cutaway, bird's-eye view, or flat). Follow this introduction with time for students to work with a partner in interpreting a similar diagram or two before asking them to read one independently. A more complex task is helping students locate the way the narrative text and a diagram are connected. Some books make the connection explicit, such as when they state: "Notice the Diagram at the bottom of this page that illustrates . . ." Or "See how these parts work together as shown in the diagram . . ."

A great way to help students understand the value of reading and writing is to show them scientists' diaries and working diagrams. Students themselves can also then create their own journals and diaries of what they are exploring in science. Some teachers keep a class diary as they deepen students' ability to observe and record data, for example, during units in which they watch chrysalises change, study the life cycle of meal worms, and monitor changes in plants (McKee and Ogle, 2005).

## Reading Development in Mathematics

Reading in mathematics textbooks poses a different set of challenges. Much of the text material is presented in numbers and mathematical symbols. Students need to be able to translate the numbers and signs into words (for example, $32x - 12x = ?$). As teachers analyze how information is presented in the more extensive paragraphs of directions and story problems, it becomes apparent that the order in which ideas are presented differs from other narrative texts. The details come first, and the main idea or problem is addressed at the end. Whereas students reading science and social studies would anticipate a heading or main idea to introduce a paragraph, that is not the case in mathematics.

Another difference in mathematics is that students have to use the three modes of presentation—visual, verbal, and mathematical—in all they do. There is not a choice. Most mathematics texts now have much more language in them—pages of number problems—than earlier books. Students must read and think about problems that have a lot of text. Although it is different from text in other disciplines, there is still a lot of reading to do. Teachers need to model their own thinking and visualizing for students so they can learn to use these texts well. They need to show how the book is laid out, how key terms are introduced and highlighted, and how the examples and pictures help students understand text ideas. The book *Integrating Instruction: Math and Literacy* (Fogelberg et al., 2008) provides a deep elaboration on how math reading skills can be developed.

## Why Is Visual Literacy Important?

IRA/NCTE 4

For many years, visual arts were considered quite separate from literacy. Research done during the past thirty years, however, has made it quite clear that visualization is part of both reading and writing: Readers create images and writers produce images to convey meaning. Textbooks, trade books, and websites are filled with visual presentations—from photographs and diagrams to short video clips and longer online resources. Therefore, it is important that we think seriously about how to build students' awareness of the impact and power of visual imagery and to develop their "visual literacy."

**Video Homework Exercise**

*A Visual Gallery Walk of Student Research Presentations*

Go to the Homework and Exercises section of Chapter 12 of MyEducationLab and view the video, "A Visual Gallery Walk of Student Research Presentations," which captures a variety of ways middle childhood students used visualization to demonstrate their knowledge about a topic. Complete the activities that follow, and save your work or transmit it to your professor as assigned.

## The Relationship Between Viewing and Reading

The relationship between visual imagery and reading is deep. Readers regularly create their own internal visual images as they read. When viewing visual texts, "readers" are also actively interpreting and making connections. Attention is focused differently depending on the type of visuals provided and the viewers' purposes and skills.

Psychologists have studied the impact of background knowledge and experiences on the way readers interpret and remember texts they read. Both in the initial stages of making connections with new texts and later as readers remember what they read, nonverbal mental associations of affect and imagery play a major role. Sometimes, our memories of events are actually more imagery-based than they are semantically or verbally based. Sadoski and Paivio (2001) call this understanding of how our brains work "dual coding." Many experiments on how we process texts demonstrate that our brain codes information in two ways, both verbally and in images and emotions. Even as we read a short text such as "The diver did a one-and-a-half into the pool," we as readers are creating visual images based on our experiences. (Think of what image comes to your mind. Did you see a particular diver? A particular pool?) Images are such an integral part of reading that, as Sadoski and Paivio explain, "imagery is an inherent part of the meaningful mental model of the event" (p. 115).

Several reading researchers (Pressley, 1976; Gambrell and Bales, 1986) have used this understanding of the power of visual images to store memories to help students improve their comprehension. They have shown that by just giving students instructions to create mental images as they read, students' retention is increased. This has led reading instructional programs to include the creation of mental images as one of the basic reading strategies (Harvey and Goudvis, 2007; Pressley, 2005; Blachowicz and Ogle, 2008).

Other research studies have demonstrated that it is easier to retain information that is presented in visual form, or in a combination of visual and verbal forms, than simply in words (Hegarty, Carpenter, and Just, 1991). The adage "a picture is worth a thousand words" does hold true in many studies of learning. The more that students are asked to study material that is beyond their personal experiences, the more valuable the visual displays can be in helping students build connections among the ideas and facts they study. However, the use of images is not always straightforward and students' ability to take advantage of visual images depends on their prior knowledge and skills in interpreting them. All of this means that readers need to learn how to monitor their own imagery, interpret the visual displays, and be able to orchestrate various forms of presentation to make meaning.

## The Relationship Between Viewing and Writing

Writing also involves mental imagery at many levels. At one level, what one writes is stimulated by experiences and memories. Young writers often describe events and emotions graphically from their memories. More accomplished writers and poets often express precise and vivid scenes and episodes they have experienced. The memories may be very sharp and clear; putting them into words takes skill and effort. Personal writing emanates from strong images and emotions we have stored in our memories. Miller (1994) studied college students' strategies while writing an expository essay. Over half reported that their main ideas occurred to them as images, 10 percent said that their ideas came both verbally and visually, and only 10 percent said words and language were their major focus.

Visual imagery also influences writing in another way. Writers often have intended audiences in mind as they compose, and teachers often help students create images of an intended audience. We may remember writing teachers who asked students to "think of the audience" and provide needed elaborations. This request doesn't so much involve creating a verbal description as it does calling up a picture.

Anne Haas Dyson makes a strong case for the connection between imagery and writing. Her research with very young children has led her to conclude that drawing is the precursor of writing (1982). Children often draw what they want to say. When teachers create the condition that they will transcribe the children's drawings, they find the children have been able to compose and rehearse their ideas in this way.

## How Can Visual Literacy Be Developed?

It may seem that looking at visual information is so easy that there is no need to include it in our teaching. Unfortunately, it is not quite that straightforward. Students need to learn to see more clearly, both what is before them and what is behind the images. As students are asked to handle increasingly diverse kinds of reading materials, it is important that they learn to interpret and create visual displays—from reading and interpreting the pictures and visual information in textbooks to understanding moving visual images in films and DVDs. In the language arts, we have a major responsibility to help students develop their abilities to use all of these forms of visual representations well. We need to help them both *interpret* visual images and *create* their own. Sometimes, depending on the grade and the class, it may be easier to focus on one of the visual formats by having students create their own. At other times, you may prefer a more directed approach to introducing the visual format included in published texts and on websites.

### Connecting Varied Types of Information

Students will regularly be asked to interpret visual displays in school and beyond. They will also need to be able to connect visual images with other ideas in the texts they encounter. It is becoming more common for text authors and editors to now present information in both visual and narrative forms, so attention to all visual displays is important. Therefore, it is important that students explore images for their own content, not just as examples of what is elsewhere in the written text (Pegler-Gordon, 2006). Particularly with informational materials, comprehending requires attending to all forms of presentation and making the connections between visuals and narrative text. A major literacy task is for students to combine the various types of presentations as they make their own interpretation of what they see and read. This is a complex interpretive activity to both interpret the visual and connect it appropriately with the narrative part of the text. One easy

**Figure 12.7**

## Three-Column Note Guide

| **Text ideas** (main ideas and important information) | **Visual information** (pictures, captions, tables, maps, charts, diagrams, etc.) | **My ideas, connections, questions, and reactions** |
|---|---|---|
| | | |

*Source:* Donna Ogle, 2001.



way to do this with intermediate-level students is to encourage the use of three-column notes. One column is for information from the text, the second is for information from the visual and pictorial information, and the third is for personal comments, summaries, questions, and connections. See Figure 12.7 for an example of a three-column note guide.

## Teaching Students to Read Visual Images

Students deserve help in learning to read and interpret visual images. Just as in the primary grades, where teachers often preview books with students by doing "picture walks" through a story using the pictures to create a discussion of the content, intermediate and upper-grade teachers can do the same. Both fiction and nonfiction books are often highly illustrated with pictures and paintings that contain the majority of the content. From teacher-modeling, students can learn to do their own partner picture or graphic walks through new magazines and short informational books.

**Focused Picture Walks** Select an attractive, visually rich information book to use with your students. As you introduce the new book, take students through the text page by page, attending to the pictures. By highlighting new vocabulary that is connected or shown in the pictures, you introduce young readers to text as meaningful and prepare them for the words. At the same time, you can focus attention on how important pictures and other visual illustrations are to the ideas presented in the informational texts. Rather than focus on single pictures, the relationship among a series of pictures is generally stressed. You can identify a key character and ask students where the character is and what he/she is doing from page to page. What is similar and what changes in the unfolding pictures? These early Picture/Visual Walks help students use visual information as an important source of meaning complementing ideas conveyed in words.

**Comparing and Contrasting Books** Picture books are now available on almost any topic discussed in school. Some of the best artists in our country now make their livings by illustrating children's books. As a result, the quality of the drawings and photographs is outstanding. These books make great sources to use in analyzing visual pictures, drawings, and diagrams. The informational books have continued to improve in quality and most now have outstanding photography. A good activity is to have children compare and contrast two books on the same theme or topic. In this way, they can see how different authors treat the same information visually. Techniques artists use can quite easily be demonstrated with current children's books. The styles can also be models for children's own artistic efforts. The list of Caldecott Award winners and Honor Books provides excellent examples of the best in children's book illustration. Modeling children's own book development from some of the professional texts can help them gain a better understanding of the relationship between visuals and text and determine what kind of visuals work with particular content.

Later, students can learn to use the same process of doing a walk-through of more detailed informational books, articles, and news magazines. The larger format big books and the enlarged teacher copy of *Time for Kids* can be used to model the attention to pictures and other visual features of informational materials. For example, we heard one teacher hold up the large book on frogs and exclaim, "What an amazing picture. I wonder how the photographer was able to photograph the frog underwater. It shows the habitat so clearly." She then continued showing the pictures and eliciting from students what they noticed on each page. By the time the picture walk was completed, the teacher and students all had a better idea of what they would be reading and learning. The teacher concluded the shared preview by reminding students to look for places where the pictures and written text connected. She periodically asked them to draw lines to the parts of the text that are most directly connected to the pictures.

A good starting place when developing content instruction is to examine the informational books that you will use with your students. In science materials, there may be several diagrams. In social studies, there are photographs, pictures, and maps. In mathematics, you note many mathematical formulae and steps needed to solve problems. It is also useful to consult the state guidelines for visual literacy and the district guidelines if they exist.

## Developing Understanding of Visual Images and Displays

IRA/NCTE 8

A part of language arts instruction includes helping students attend analytically to the wide variety of visual information they will encounter, from pictures and drawings to diagrams, maps, charts, tables, and film clips. Our suggestion is that you don't try to teach all visual forms to students. Rather select two to three visual forms that are commonly used in the class content materials. If you teach students how to interpret these focused visual displays well enough for them to develop the habit of carefully reading visual information, then it is easier to build to other visual formats later. For each type of visual, there are some common steps that can be followed so students will develop independence in interpreting visual information.

Four basic aspects of the teacher's responsibility in helping students learn to interpret visual images include:

1. Identifying the components of each type of imagery
2. Developing a strategy to help interpret the meaning of the image/s

3. Connecting the image with other aspects of the text content—such as relating pictures to the narrative text
4. Creating images, both as independent texts and as part of multimedia texts

The next section explains each of these aspects of developing visual literacy using the example of helping students learn to interpret photographs because that is one of the first types of visual literacy used widely in schools. Some basic ideas for developing other types of visual literacy will be provided.

**Identify the Components: Reading Pictures and Photographs** For each visual format, a helpful starting place in determining how to present it to students is to ask yourself these questions: What *aspects or components* of this visual art form are central to this presentation and permit us to discuss, analyze, and evaluate the quality of particular examples? What terms will help us discuss the visual form in depth? There is no one list of the components, but you can quite easily develop a set appropriate to your grade level of students. It is also useful to consult the state guidelines for visual literacy and the district guidelines if they exist to see if there are terms that students are expected to use.

In the case of photographs, some likely terms that you would put on a list to help describe and analyze their impact are:

- Central focus
- Quadrants (upper and lower, left and right)
- Black and white or color
- Contrast (especially in black and white images)
- Angles (frontal, distant, above or below)
- Camera shots—close up, medium, or long
- Purpose or intent for what they want the picture to "tell" the viewer

***Model Examination of a Photograph.*** Introduce the study of pictures by showing students a good example and talk about the features. Put a picture on an overhead projector, visualizer, or computer screen. Think aloud as you study the picture. "My eyes are first drawn to the center of this picture, to the _______. The photographer seems to want to get close to the subject and has caught the man looking right at the camera in a frontal shot. I notice that the background shows _______, _______, and _______. That makes me think this picture is from some years ago." (Let students know that there are aspects that may be unclear, questions that you have about the images.) "I'm not sure what this is. It seems strange that there was _______ in the corner." "What I see clearly is. . . . This makes me think that . . ."

***Compare Images.*** It is useful to show students one or two pictures and ask them to identify who or what seems to be the center of the picture, what feelings they have about the picture and how those are created by the art, and what they think the artist (i.e., photographer or artist) intended to communicate. If you can locate two photographs or pictures of the same place or people that illustrate different "views," students quickly learn how important the perspective and composition are. You might bring in two photographs from your own family—one where everyone is happy and engaged and another of the same gathering with people distracted or looking in several directions. Ask students:

- How does each image make you feel? What does each communicate?
- Why did the artist/photographer make/take this picture?
- What's at the center? Where do your eyes go?
- Is it a close-up, medium, or a wide-angle view? (Is the distance good?)
- What could have made this better?

Another good activity is to have students compare the photographs in two to three different texts connected to the same topic to enhance the meaning. Ask them to discuss which is most helpful, which are clearest, and what differences in perspective are evident or suggested. Do close-ups help more than broader, landscape views?

***Viewing and Thinking Critically.*** As you build students' ability to think about photographs and pictures from the perspective of composition and features, you may want to develop guide sheets to direct their attention. Having students work with a partner will help them attend more carefully to the aspects of the photographs that you consider important.

A good example can be connected to the study of American history. Look at photographs of social events from our past. Who is shown? Where are the minorities? How are children represented? Students are often critical of pictures that aren't in color; using historical documents can help students analyze the differences in black and white and color photography. It can also lead to a discussion of why painting was popular when there were no other means of indicating color.

As students progress in their interpretation skills in the upper grades (fourth to sixth), it is interesting to add to the general question set with questions such as:

- What did the artist/photographer leave out?
- What don't we see?
- How else could this picture or photograph have been focused?

**Develop a Strategy for Interpreting Visual Information** Moving beyond an orientation to the basic features of composition and content presentation, students mostly need to think of the meaning and purposes for the use of photographs and pictures related to their school text materials. The *interpretation of images is central and students need a strategic approach to images.* Students can learn to take time to think about pictures. Slowing down and looking carefully is the first step. "What do I see?" Asking about the focus of composition is, of course, the natural lead-in to the content. Just as authors have purposes for the stories they write, so, too, artists have purposes for the pictures they create. The editors who select these for inclusion with text materials also have purposes to illustrate ideas, present information, and establish contexts. If students know to think of the central focus of the picture, the frame, and the tone, they are on their way to building an interpretation.

***Active Reading Strategy.*** One strategy students can learn to use is to preview each two-page spread before they begin reading. This will ensure that all the visual information is considered. As they read, they ask: Is there a visual image that extends or explains this section? After reading the text, the students check the visual features again to see if the content contained in each is additional, redundant, or if the visual is explained within the text. Finally, if the text is important, creating notes using the three-column format or a text-mapping system may be needed.

Students benefit when we take time to analyze a few pictures in real depth using some basic questions they can then use regularly on their own. Look at the example in Figure 12.8. As part of a study of Chicago history, students learned to look carefully at

Figure 12.8

## Picturing Chicago

### Using Visual Literacy in the Classroom

**Introduction:**

This exercise involves using an inquiry model to read a photograph and write a four-line verse to describe its content.

**Reading the Photograph: What do you see?**

Please answer the following questions, writing your answers on the lines provided.

1. Who is in the photo? ______________________________
2. Describe these people (gender, age, dress, anything else?) ______________________________

   ______________________________
3. What are they doing? ______________________________

   ______________________________
4. Where are they? ______________________________
5. Using the answers to the above questions, in one word, describe the people in the photo and write your answer on the line to the right. ______________________________

**Exploring the Photo: What have you learned?**

On the lines, write a four-line verse that describes the photo as follows.

On line 1, write the one-word answer to question 5 above.

On line 2, write an action phrase that describes how these people feel.

On line 3, write an action phrase that describes what they hear and smell.

On line 4, write a one-word caption for the photo.

1. ______________________________
2. ______________________________
3. ______________________________
4. ______________________________

*Source:* Newman, Spirou, and Danzer, 2007. Used by permission.

photographs from the 1940s. The viewing guide shown in the figure (Newman, Spirou, and Danzer, 2007) helps students focus their attention. It asks students to identify the kinds of activities and transportation shown in the photograph. This background then helps them describe the people and what they are doing. From this close attention, students are asked to predict when they think the photograph was taken and what kind of place or location it represents. (The guide helps students with the basic orientation to a photograph: What, When, and Who are represented?) They can then connect this to what they are learning and add to their visualization of the city before they were born.

See the Exploring Diversity feature for a viewing guide to use with your students with special learning needs.

***Include Writing Activities.*** When working with students to develop their ability to look more carefully and critically at photographs and pictures, it is good to include writing activities. For example, place students in teams of three or four and give each a picture taken from a calendar that shows people in various parts of the world engaged in everyday living or doing interesting things. Begin by instructing each team to:

- Study their picture.
- Make a list of what they see.
- List the questions they have about the picture.
- Write a short story or description of what they think the picture is about.
- Have each group write a title or caption for the picture.

After each group is finished, pass the photos and stories from table to table and students will enjoy reading and viewing the work they all have done. Students may also come to appreciate how differently we see and interpret the same images.

***Label Picture Items.*** When working with children with special needs, starting with pictures can help them build their own connections with content more easily than if we do everything orally and from written texts. One activity that helps these students build connections to the content they are learning is to have them make labels for key items they see on pictures. Teachers can list terms that are illustrated on the pictures, give a photocopy of the picture to each student, and have them match the label to the aspect of the picture where it is shown. This activity works well with a transparency, too. Teachers can put the terms on colored small strips of transparency, and as a group, students can put the strips on the appropriate parts of a photograph.

Students need to learn to both study and analyze the pictures and look at the captions that the authors or editors of the material have used. In informational texts, the captions are often critical in helping readers determine what is important. What does the caption tell about the focus and purpose of the photograph or picture being included? Do the two parts cohere? (Sometimes editors add captions that don't seem to match the visual, and students can begin to think more analytically about these relationships, too.)

The third aspect of developing students' ability to use visuals thoughtfully is to help them make connections between the visual and the narrative, or connected, written text. Because so many of the fictional books students read beyond the first grade don't have many illustrations, students don't necessarily develop the habit of connecting information from pictures with the extended text writing.

It is when students read informational texts and magazines that they immediately need to connect different types of information. For example, in news stories and in

# exploring diversity

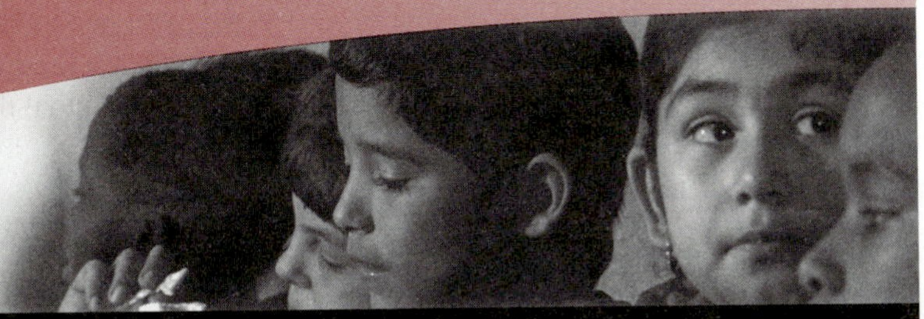

## Reading Photographs

To help students with special learning needs, Wu (2007) has developed some viewing guides to help students learn how to look more carefully at photographs. This supportive guide is one of a set available for students to use while their class engages in the Picturing Chicago study of the nineteenth century (Newman, Spirou, and Danzer, 2007).

**Picturing Chicago** — **Visual Literacy for All Learners**

**Reading for Content Visuals with Actions**

Based on the picture, when did this happen? — **When**

________________________________

**Where** — Based on the picture, where is this?

________________________________

Who is in the picture? — **Who**

________________________________

________________________________

________________________________

**Actions** — What are they doing?

________________________________

________________________________

________________________________

To whom or what are they doing this? — **Whom or what**

________________________________

________________________________

________________________________

________________________________

**How** — How are they doing these things?

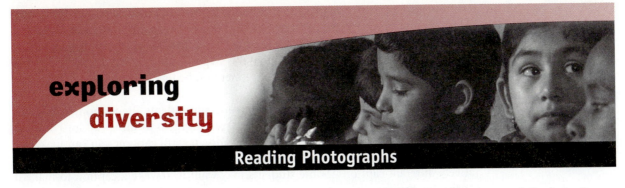

________________________________

________________________________

________________________________

Summarize the Picture or Write a Caption

| |
|---|
| |

Consult other sources if the information is not in the picture and its title.

history texts, a picture or map is often included to provide a context and image to help students get grounded in the content. Students need to learn the strategy of looking at the title and then attending to the pictures as they activate what they know about the topic. Reading the captions is important at this step. When students ignore the pictures and captions they miss an important component of the text information.

■ ***Attend to Captions.*** An interesting way to help students attend more to captions is to give them a set of two to three photographs and two to three captions and ask them to match those that go together. If you add an extra caption you can make the activity more challenging. This activity helps students understand that there are qualitatively different captions. Some students may want to rewrite a caption to make it more informative.

■ ***Use Arrows to Show Connections.*** It is also helpful to ask students to draw arrows or put sticky notes showing the relationship between pictures and the narrative text section connected to the illustration. Until teachers focus on the relationships among different types of presentations within a single text, students often ignore the relationships among the multiple types of information. Even in this text, you might want to stop for a moment and think through your strategy of using the visuals, the boxed examples, and examples we have provided. Draw arrows to show the connections among the different types of presentations.

■ ***Highlight Information in Assessments.*** Some teachers help students understand the value of attending to pictures and captions by including items from pictures and captions on reading assessments. It is not uncommon for state and national tests to do this, too. The visual aspects of texts are important; the more teachers and students can build a respect for and attention to the rich visual information available in print and electronic materials, the better they will become as viewers, readers, and thinkers.

■ ***Develop a Metacognitive Stance.*** Students need to be focused on the variety of ways information is presented in texts they read. They also need to consciously ask themselves to attend to all types of information on a regular basis. As a teacher you may direct students to create their own questions and make a bookmark of these to serve as a reminder. The set of questions might include:

- When and how do you link the visual/graphic image to the reading content of the narrative sections?
- Do you have a clear strategy you use?
- Do you preview each page or each section before reading and look for how the visuals connect to the section? (The headings and subheadings may provide a guide to the connections.)

**Create Visual Images and Supports** The fourth component of teaching about visual formats focuses on the students themselves using visuals in their own written work by creating visual forms. From kindergarten on children often learn that drawing can be a form of composing ideas.

With the rich resources on the Internet, young children can also learn to find and use clipart and images to support their writing. Many schools help children think about the ways to best illustrate their own writing with either personal or more general art available on the computer. Attention to layout and use of pictures in schools leads to some pretty sophisticated student texts.

**Import Photographs.** One school, for example, uses computer-assisted writing as part of a science. During a unit on plants, one group of students (when writing their report on types of roots) decided to use the school's digital camera to photograph plants with different kinds of root systems. The students located and pulled up some volunteer plants (weeds) that had taproots, veined roots, etc. They took photos of illustrative roots and then imported these pictures into their report. By using a publishing software program on their computers, the students were able to not only take photographs but also consider the best layout design and ways to highlight important information in their reports. The final products looked very professional.

**Create PowerPoint Presentations.** In the Pleasant Ridge School with its focus on technology, all students create PowerPoint presentations three times a year. An important part of these projects is learning how to create informative slides. Students learn to search online picture and graphic files so they can illustrate their main ideas with good visuals. The selection of when to use pictures and diagrams to highlight key ideas helps students think of the ways in which pictures and other graphics enhance the message they want to communicate (see examples online at www.MyEducationLab.com).

**Create Display Boards.** Another requirement of the projects at Pleasant Ridge School is that the children create a visual trifold board or triptych with information about their project. The format is clear. They need to use three photographs or illustrative diagrams as part of their presentation. In this way, the teachers help students think through what information is most important to show visually. They discuss how visuals convey meaning and how the selection of images influences content.

**Draw While Reading.** Asking students to draw images as they read informational texts is also a powerful way to get students to connect ideas and situate them in contexts. An easy way to get started is to give students sticky notes and ask them to create a drawing at the bottom of each page or each section of a text. You should model this process yourself a few times before asking students to try it. Then select a text that is quite visually translatable, so students can draw without too much trouble. If this idea works with your students, then spend some time developing "shorthand" images that can be shared. For example, if students are reading about tensions in the formation of America, create a logo or sign for conflict, process, groups, government, the king of England, etc. The idea of "Mind Mapping" (Margulies, 1991) provides some specific suggestions for ways to help students feel more free in creating icons for ideas and for regularly turning words into images as they read. See the Engaging in Oral Language feature for ideas on including second language learners during in-class read-alouds.

Sketch to Stretch, a strategy developed by Harste, Short, and Burke (1988), provides a context for intermediate and older students to use their visual images

In Pleasant Ridge School, with its focus on technology, all students create PowerPoint presentations three times a year. An important part of these projects is learning how to create informative slides. Students learn to search online picture and graphic files so they can illustrate their main ideas with good visuals. The selection of when to use pictures and diagrams to highlight key ideas helps students think of the ways pictures and other graphics enhance the message they want to communicate.

## engaging in Oral language

### Involving Second Language Learners during Read-Alouds

Reading aloud to students is a very popular activity in schools today. One easy way to help all students focus during these shared classroom events is to give them paper and drawing instruments and to ask them to draw key images that come to mind as they are listening. During the read-aloud time, stop frequently and ask students to draw what they are thinking. Pair up second language learners so they can talk about the text and draw together. This gives them time to clarify ideas they are hearing and also to move beyond just "translating" to thinking of meaning. It also helps them make the visual-verbal connection. When they lack words that are needed, they draw and use these as a way to reflect on the reading. Students do not have to explain what they drew; others are called on to interpret the images. This often gives second language learners a central role in the classroom without having to talk in front of the whole class. Often, with some success as artist/interpreters, these students learn that classmates are interested in their ideas and they become more willing to share in words as well as in visual images.

Some students are very able when it comes to drawing and putting a collection of classroom drawings on the bulletin board. These students can also help others begin to see how each reader brings his or her own ideas to text interpretation. Comparing and contrasting what students highlight visually makes a very tangible statement about the importance of listening to others and seeking out their responses to input—whether from read-alouds by the teacher or from what students themselves read.

as a way to discuss stories. This strategy has been introduced earlier in this book and is particularly appropriate as a part of building students' ability to create visual images. Students first read a story together. Then each creates a visual image in one focused drawing that captures the essence of the story for them. Once the drawings are complete, students gather in small groups to share their images. Each takes turns showing their drawing and asking the other members of the group what they see in the drawing. After all others have contributed, the "artist" explains what he or she intended with their image. This is a very effective strategy for helping students think visually and also more abstractly about theme and key ideas in stories. See the Engaging in Visual Literacy feature for visual brainstorming ideas.

This elaborated description of how teachers can help students attend more carefully to pictures and photographs has highlighted four aspects of helping students become more thoughtful and better viewers:

1. Students need to know what the key elements are of thinking about the composition and features of the visual form.
2. Then they need strategies for interpreting and thinking critically about the visuals.

## engaging in Visual Literacy

### Visual Brainstorming

Activating what students know before initiating inquiry units or any new topic of study can also be done effectively by asking them to draw what they know rather than put it into words. For example, when an urban group of students began their study of insects in the springtime one year, the teacher was concerned because she had several newly arrived second language learners. Instead of her usual KWL approach, she decided to put the word *spiders* on the board and showed students a jar that contained a live spider she had just collected from her basement. She explained that the class would be learning more about spiders of many kinds and wrote this objective on the board. She also included an objective that students would learn to visualize the body and home of some types of spiders. The next step was for each student to draw on paper what he or she knew about spiders. Questions included:

What do spiders look like?

What kinds of families do spiders have?

Where do spiders live?

How do spiders protect themselves?

3. Visuals are generally used in relation to larger units of study and making connections is a third key aspect of using visual inputs.
4. Finally, students also need to have many opportunities to create their own visuals, both as part of their writing and reading processes and as part of their creating compositions and interpretations to share with others.

## Extending This Process to Other Visual Features

Figure 12.9 provides some of the technical terms that can be used to describe each of the visual forms. Think about how you might develop a sequence of learning activities for one of the areas.

Each form of visual presentation, both still and moving, deserves attention at some point across the elementary grades. Students need to be aware of how each is constructed, be able to analyze and critically evaluate each, and use the various types of visual information in learning. This is a substantial task, and teachers need to work together across the grade levels to make sure that students have ample opportunities to engage with all forms. In textbooks and trade books, the purposes for visual and graphic materials are to inform and provide information. However, in mass media and on the Internet, students encounter much more material that is designed to persuade or influence viewers and that is not transparent. Learning to critically examine these displays is important. Students need to ask questions about the purpose and perspective of the

Figure 12.9

## Visual Literacy Technical Vocabulary

| Diagrams | Film | Maps |
|---|---|---|
| Labels<br>Sketch<br>Details<br>Key<br>Illustrations<br>Scale diagram<br>Cutaway diagram<br>Position<br>Orientation<br>Line drawing | Script<br>Story board<br>Camera angle<br>Shots (close-up, long, low angle, point of view, etc.)<br>Sound elements<br>Special effects (animation, split screen) | Perspective<br>Key<br>Color coding<br>Weather map<br>Political map<br>Historical map<br>Scale<br>Compass rose<br>Spatial relationships<br>Bird's-eye view |

constructors of the media. Chapter 15 on incorporating technology provides good ideas for helping students use a variety of technological tools.

The picture in Figure 12.10 shows how one teacher helped her students create a map of their community as a part of their study of maps and the use of the bird's-eye view perspective. The teacher was concerned that her students had very little "map reading" ability and wanted to begin with a concrete example. So, after studying different types of maps with the class and using appropriate language to label different features (compass rose, scale, bird's-eye view, direction) she guided the class in creating their own community map. Together, the class took two walks around their four-block area and made notes of all the physical features. They developed a scale and located the

Figure 12.10

## Community Map

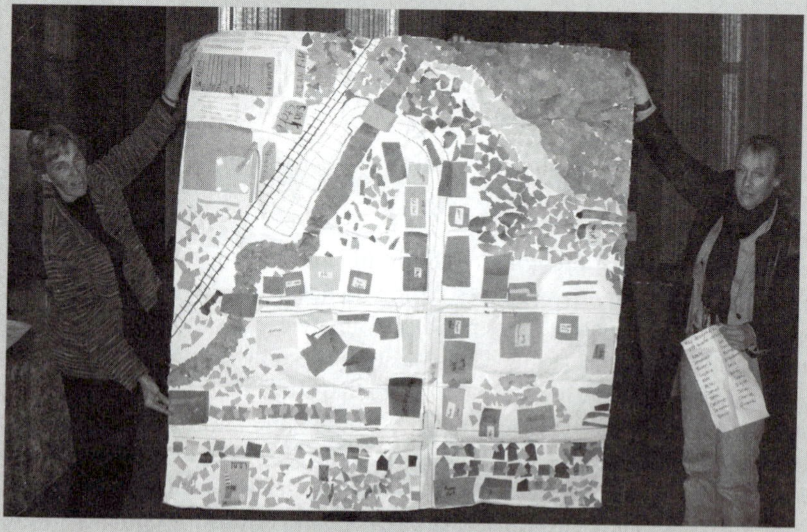

different types of buildings on the appropriate streets and their sides. By making a large and three-dimensional map, students gained a great deal of understanding of the mapmaking process and the major features of maps.

## Assessing Students' Abilities to Read Visuals

To learn which visual presentations your students can and do comprehend, develop some pre-assessments. You may start by putting one visual form (diagram, timeline, etc.) on the overhead projector or computer screen and ask students to "think aloud" about what they think it means. Another way to get individual student responses is to photocopy the visual and make a copy for each student. Write two to three questions about the visual and have all students respond. Another way to get a more general assessment of their ability to interpret visual information is to put several visuals on one sheet, one from each content area, and ask your students to read the visuals and answer one or two questions about each. You will quickly get an idea of how well your students can interpret information presented in these formats. Where students have problems reading and interpreting the visual presentation, create instructional lessons to develop their skills.

It is not difficult to construct a written assessment for visual displays. Begin by asking students to interpret a visual—either a picture, map, or whatever form you are going to focus on. On a sheet of paper ask them to write their answers to questions like these:

1. What do you see in this _______ (visual)?
2. What do you think this means?
3. What do you think is the most important part?
4. What part, if any, is confusing and why?
5. What does the phrase _______ mean?
6. How do you go about looking at and thinking about a(n) _______?
7. When you are reading a text, how do you use the visual information? Do you read it first? Do you ignore it?

Later, ask students to do a similar activity with a different visual. Adapt the questions to a particular text they are reading.

Another important aspect to assess is how well students can relate visual and verbal content. Provide students with a page of text with visual and narrative information. Make copies of one or two pages from a text students will be reading. Ask them to preview the page(s) and write down how they look at the page. Explain that they should write a number 1 beside whatever first draws their attention. Then they write a 2 beside the next aspect of the page to which they attend. They should continue in this fashion, marking with numbers each of the subsequent aspects they focus on. Then ask them to draw arrows between the visual boxed information, maps, pictures, and any other visual information connecting pieces that fit together. This activity provides a good piece of concrete evidence of how well students navigate and connect the multiple formats in which information is presented.

Activities that are described for student engagement during reading are also good formative assessments of how they can incorporate visuals into their writing pieces. Whatever activities the students are familiar with using may be evidence. For example, if students have learned to use Sketch to Stretch or mind mapping, the products they create can be evaluated by you or the class itself. Developing a rubric or description of what good visualizing entails may help students who have trouble using visualization to find more applications.

## Putting the Pieces Together

One of the best ways to think of putting together these components of informational reading is to think of the process of reading, before, during, and after reading. As we think of how we learn from reading, we know that this is an active, ongoing process. We can describe it by what we do before, during, and after engagement with an informational text just as we do with literature: We begin by anticipating what we want and need to learn. Then we build knowledge as we read and engage with authors. Finally, we must consolidate the ideas with what we previously knew, sometimes modifying and sometimes extending those ideas. (These are the simple ABCs of reading to learn—anticipating, building knowledge, and consolidating learning.) We also know that this process is an ongoing activity that is recursive. With each new set of ideas we read, we rethink what we knew, we ask new questions and set new purposes, and we build on the ideas that are freshly ours.

# How Can You Organize Classroom Instruction to Accomplish Your Goals?

As students move from the primary grades into the intermediate levels, the need for teacher guidance continues. Carefully planning the time that is available is important because time with the teacher is the most instructionally productive time (Barr, 1986). As has been pointed out already, the following need to be part of the planning and implementation of the literacy curriculum:

- Clear goals and expectations with diversified performance criteria so all students will be expected to grow—from those who struggle in readers to students who are gifted and fully engaged readers
- Assessments that are standards- and curriculum-based and that inform instruction so activities are most appropriate for all students
- Teacher modeling of engaged strategic comprehension
- Guided practice for students under the teacher's watchful diagnostic eye
- Independent practice and application in engaging activities

## Routines Lead to Productive Engagement

In arranging the times for all this to occur, teachers need to build in routines that permit some whole class time and some small group instruction, some small group independent teamwork, and some spaces for individual reading and response. One arrangement that provides a good starting place is to move from whole class to small group (parts) back to whole class (Strickland, 1998). In this way of organizing the class, the teacher can focus all the students on the theme, topic, or strategy under study. This is a particularly important setting for teachers to introduce students to vocabulary learning strategies and to encourage their explorations of words and language. With good teacher modeling and stimulation, students will be more ready for small group work and it is more likely to be productive. At the end of the class time, students can be reconvened to reflect on what they have accomplished and the teacher can lead them to both self-evaluation and new goal setting. Students need to be instructed by the teacher who models and provides direct coaching to students. This can happen during whole class lessons and during small, guided reading groups where students with similar needs are brought together to read through a text under the teacher's supervision.

One of our best starting places is to be a role model and share some personal reading interests with students. By reading aloud both from adult materials and from good texts at their level and discussing responses to some of the materials with students, they begin to see how "teachers" engage with ideas. A good guideline is to read daily from a variety of kinds of information materials—begin with something you enjoy exploring and learning about. For example, read interesting pieces from the newspaper, perhaps about how to raise special flowering plants, how to use computer programs, or how to choose the right foods to eat. You and your students can learn together. This is often one of the gifts of reading to learn—with the changing nature of our world we all can learn together. Read from some novel, biography, or literary text that connects with classroom themes. Later in the day, read aloud something related to a topic the class is studying—perhaps from a more difficult text than the students would be able to handle themselves (such as an essay or magazine article). This can be valuable in helping the students understand that their curriculum relates to what others know and care about and it can help them develop a broader vocabulary and sense of how content is structured by adults.

## Teacher-Guided Learning

Some particular ways teachers can model and guide the thinking they want students to develop are through:

- **Reading aloud**
- **Thinking aloud**
- **Modeling discussion with another teacher or aide**

Then teachers can help students implement the strategies they have modeled during small, guided reading groups. These groups can be useful so teachers can have an opportunity to work with a smaller group of students and listen to their enactments of active reading.

It is important to be a role model and share personal reading interests with students. By reading aloud both from adult materials and from good texts at their level and discussing responses to some of the materials with students, they begin to see how their teachers engage with ideas.

## Small Group Work

Students also need opportunities to practice their comprehension and responses with other students. This more student-directed guided practice can be accomplished through small group settings such as book clubs or literature discussion groups, which are important parts of the classroom. There are good guidelines for developing both of these small group structures in printed materials (see Raphael, Pardo, and Highfield, 2002; Daniels, 2002). As teachers develop integrated content units based around students' inquiry, students also can learn to work together and build knowledge while engaged in research for their projects. The I-Chart is a good concrete tool for young researchers as they start to use multiple sources to develop knowledge on particular topics. See Figure 12.11 for a sample I-Chart (Hoffman, 1992).

Working in several difficult urban schools led to the development of another intermediary format for students' ownership of their reading and response, Partner Reading with Content Too (PRC2). See Chapter 4 for a full explanation of this strategy. It permits students to work together in a less-involved context than the other small group settings just described.

## Independent Work

Finally, there also needs to be time in the reading structure for individual work. Students will vary considerably in their reading strengths and areas of needed development. There needs to be regular opportunity for them to work in targeted areas with appropriate materials. Fluency, vocabulary, and reading strategies are all areas that require regular practice. In addition, students need to read independently and respond to these readings in their logs or journals. Time needs to be set aside for some quiet periods of independent reading. Teachers can collect good information about students' engaged reading by reading and responding to their individual reading logs.

Figure 12.11

**I-Chart**

| Questions | What We Know | Text 1 | Text 2 | Text 3 | Summary |
|---|---|---|---|---|---|
| 1. | | | | | |
| 2. | | | | | |
| 3. | | | | | |
| Interesting new info./ New questions | | | | | |

# exploring Children's Literature

## Nonfiction Resources for Science and Social Studies

### Grades K to 3

*An Egg Is Quiet*—Written by Dianna Aston, illustrated by Sylvia Long, and published by Chronicle (2006).

This book introduces readers to more than sixty types of eggs and an array of egg facts.

*Celebrate Connections among Cultures*—Written by Jan Reynolds and published by Lee & Low (2006).

Photos explore the similarities among celebration rituals in several indigenous cultures around the world and compare them with celebrations in the United States (includes a map and an author's note).

*I Face the Wind*—Written by Vicki Cobb, illustrated by Julia Gorton, and published by HarperCollins (2003).

This book introduces the characteristics and actions of the wind through simple hands-on activities.

*Move!*—Written by Steve Jenkins, illustrated by Robin Page, and published by Houghton Mifflin (2006).

In this book, readers learn how different animals move.

*Our Seasons*—Written and illustrated by Grace Lin, published by Charlesbridge (2006).

This book provides an introduction to the seasons.

*Surprising Sharks*—Written by Nicola Davies, illustrated by James Croft, and published by Candlewick (2003).

This book introduces many different species of sharks and points out characteristics such as the small size of the dwarf lantern shark and the physical characteristics and behavior that make sharks killing machines.

*When Marian Sang*—Written by Pam Ryan, illustrated by Brian Selznick, and published by Scholastic (2002).

This introduction to the life of Marian Anderson presents an extraordinary singer and civil rights activist who was the first African American to perform at the Metropolitan Opera and whose life and career encouraged social change.

*Wild and Swampy*—Written and illustrated by Jim Arnosky, published by HarperCollins (2000).

This book describes and portrays the birds, snakes, and other animals that can be found in a swamp.

### Grades 4 to 8

*The American Heritage Student Science Dictionary* published by Houghton Mifflin (2002).

This dictionary defines terms used in a wide variety of fields, including chemistry, physics, biology, geology, meteorology, astronomy, ecology, and zoology. It includes more than 4,500 entry words; 425 full-color photographs and drawings; and 175 feature notes on important scientific concepts, the major discoveries of many scientists, and the usage and history of scientific terminology.

*The American Story: 100 True Tales from American History*—Written by Jennifer Armstrong, illustrated by Roger Roth, and published by Knopf (2006).

This collection contains one hundred brief stories about real people and occurrences in American history (arranged in chronological order by year from 1565 to 2000).

*Clan Apis*—Written by Jay Hosler and published by Active Synapse (2000).

The life cycle and natural environment of the honeybee are graphically explored (graphic novel format).

*Freedom Walkers: The Story of the Montgomery Bus Boycott*—Written by Russell Freedman and published by Houghton Mifflin (2006).

This nonfiction account explores the events surrounding and including the Montgomery bus boycott, which led to the end of segregation on buses.

*(Continued)*

*George vs. George: The Revolutionary War as Seen by Both Sides*—Written and illustrated by Rosalyn Schanzer and published by National Geographic (2004).

This publication explores how the characters and lives of King George III of England and George Washington affected the progress and outcome of the American Revolution.

*Team Moon: How 400,000 People Landed Apollo 11 on the Moon*—Written by Catherine Thimmesh and published by Houghton Mifflin (2006).

Culled from direct quotes from the people behind the scenes, NASA transcripts, national archives, and NASA photos, the whole story of Apollo 11 and the first moon landing emerges.

*Mapping the World*—Written by Sylvia A. Johnson and published by Atheneum Books (1999).

This history of mapmaking shows how maps reflect and change people's views of the world.

*The Snake Scientist*—Written by Sy Montgomery, photographed by Nic Bishop, and published by Houghton Mifflin (1999).

The work of Bob Mason and his efforts to study and protect snakes, particularly red-sided garter snakes, are discussed in this pictorial book.

# How Can Integrated Units of Instruction Enhance Learning?

**Video Homework Exercise**

*A Student Shares a Final Project*

Go to the Homework and Exercises section in Chapter 12 of MyEducationLab and view the video, "A Student Shares a Final Project," in which you will see how a middle school student presents her work that reflects an integrated unit of instruction. Complete the activities that follow, and save your work or transmit it to your professor as assigned.

Students need to understand that the skills and strategies they are taught in language arts are important for them across all content areas and in situations beyond school. One of the easiest ways to help them make these connections is to spend part of the instructional time integrating instruction (Ogle and McMahon, 2003). Some teachers do three to four integrated units a year. A good way to start is to plan to do one integrated unit with each of your content areas and language arts during the year. In the fall, the unit might be with science; in the winter, it might be with social studies; and in the spring with mathematics or careers. In one middle school, students study the twentieth century by studying a topic of their own choosing—from jazz, to comics, to microchips and lasers (Blachowicz and Ogle, 2008). In other schools, teachers plan an additional fourth unit in which students find their own topics and choose the kind of research they will do. At the upper levels, this often comes at the point where students learn to conduct a more formal research report.

An easy way to begin a new unit of instruction is to use the KWL (**K**now, **W**ant to Learn, **L**earn) framework (Ogle, 1986; 2008). Initially, teachers introduce a topic in some interesting way, establishing a purpose for new inquiry, and then ask students what they already know about the topic or issue. The teacher explains that he/she will be the scribe and that the students will brainstorm all ideas that come to mind without worrying if the ideas are right or not. The teacher may need to do a little "priming of the pump" if this is new for students; suggest associations and maybe ask questions such as, "I think I saw something on TV recently about. . . . ; Does anyone remember seeing the program, and remember something"; or "Who has visited or seen ________?" After some initial listing of ideas, the teacher turns to the students and asks them to think like experts in the field. How would they expect experts to categorize ideas on the topic; what are likely categories that are important? These are also listed on the K (what we Know) portion of the chart. As students discuss what they know about the topic, there are usually differences of opinion expressed. These are ideal times for the teacher to ask students to form a question that can be part of their study later. The teacher writes this and subsequent questions in the second column of the guide sheet under the W (what we Want to learn) column. As students think about their ideas and raise more questions, the chart is elaborated. If it can be placed in the room over time, the chart can be added to regularly as students have more questions and also think of what they knew already. The third part of the chart is where students add information they gain during their study, or the L (what we Learned) column. It is good to include a place for more questions—What We Still Want to Know—here, too. If the teacher has been successful, this initial chart stimulates students' interest in learning more and can lead to lots of exploration and contributions over an extended period of time. See an example of the KWL framework and student work in Figure 12.12.

In developing integrated units, it is helpful to use a planning framework so you can prepare students for as meaningful an experience as possible. Figure 12.13 shows a model of one way to conceptualize a unit. It begins with a thematic statement. For example, if students are going to study the influence of the environment on pond life the "theme" is not frogs or ponds but "the interrelationship of the physical environment and life in the pond." If students are studying the Bill of Rights, the theme statement might be "Individual rights and community welfare." Then a basic question for the unit might be, "What limits are there to individual freedoms?" "Should everyone have the right to bear arms?" This is different from a topical unit, but rather goes more deeply into a concept and gives teachers and students more avenues to pursue some deep thinking. After focusing the theme, then it is important to identify the standards in both language arts and social studies, or the other content areas, that will be developed. These can be listed in the initial planning frame.

There are many ways to build integrated units, and the instructional focus will vary depending on the standards and objectives that are central. Because

**Figure 12.12**

**KWL Chart**

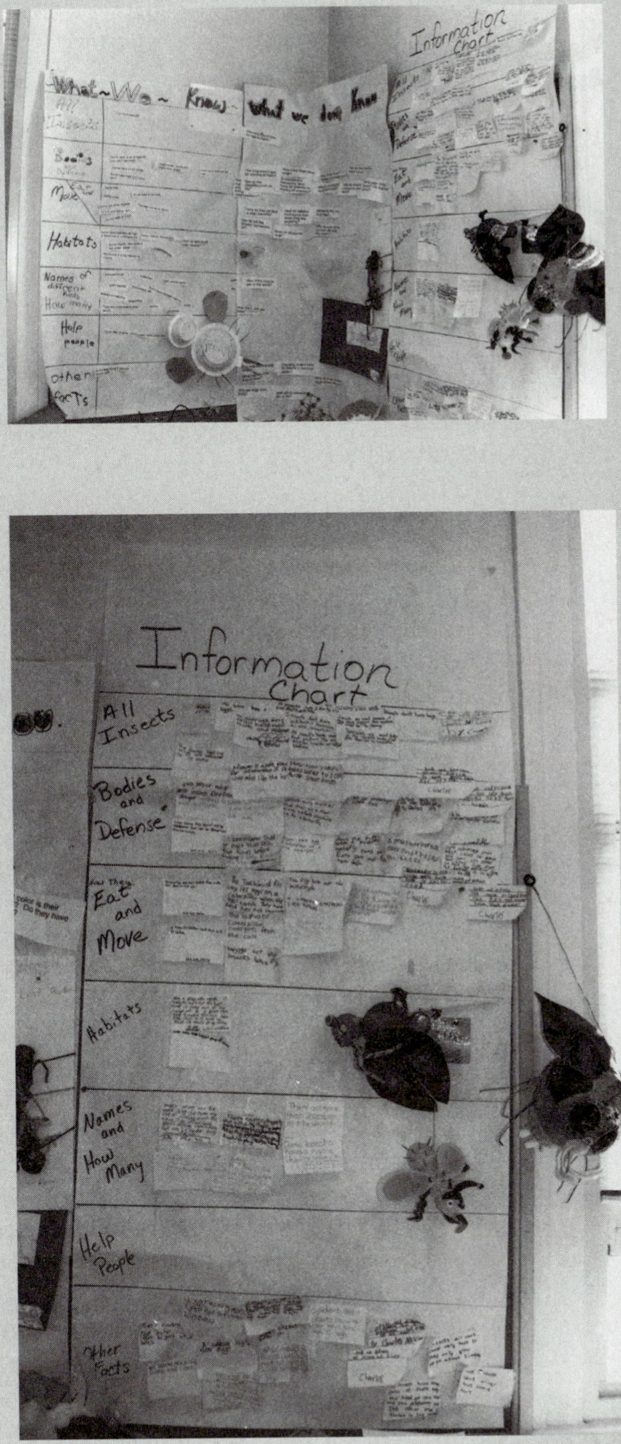

Figure 12.13

## Integrated Unit Planning Framework

| | |
|---|---|
| **Theme:** | |
| **Focus Questions:** | |
| **Language Arts Standards:**<br>(reading, writing, speaking, listening, viewing, and presenting) | Content Area Standards: |
| **Outcomes:**<br>Project:<br>Paper:<br>Oral presentation:<br>Other evidence of meeting the standards: | **Outcomes (rubrics to measure):**<br>Project:<br>Paper:<br>Oral presentation: |
| **Learning Activities:**<br>Anticipation:<br>Building knowledge:<br>Consolidating learning: | |
| **Resources/Materials:**<br>Easy reading:<br>Grade level:<br>Challenging:<br>Different text genres and types: | **Examples and Artifacts:**<br>Different points of view:<br>Different time periods:<br>Varied ethnicities and cultures (as appropriate):<br>Visual and graphic presentations: |

classes of children vary in their knowledge and interests, the length of units is often determined by the students' engagement. If the unit content seems to provide a sustaining interest and opportunities to build students' knowledge and skills, then it may be worth extending it. On the other hand, some groups don't get highly engaged in planned activities and it may be more valuable to shorten some units and create new contexts for students' learning.

The following section provides examples of how teachers use integrated units to teach both language arts and content knowledge. See the Exploring Technology feature for online resources to support informational reading.

The classroom examples that follow demonstrate how teachers use extended units of instruction to integrate literacy and content. The first example is from a class with a wide range of student diversity. See if you can visualize this experience and think about meeting the needs of students in this diverse group. In each example, think of how teachers can recognize students' particular strengths and needs and provide engaging instruction.

## Unit 1: Collaborative Inquiry—Native Americans

In their staff development meetings, Singer Elementary School teachers had been focusing on methods of inclusion for the diversity of their student population. Mrs. Kim had been thinking about what they were reading and discussing as she got to

## exploring technology

### Resources for Informational Reading and Content Area Reading Sites

Many good resources are available to help teachers and students learn about and work with informational topics and themes.

**Textmapping (www.textmapping.org)**
The Textmapping Project website explains a graphic organizer technique that can be used to teach reading comprehension and writing skills, study skills, and subject-area content. Using scrolls, or pages of a text affixed together into one long section of paper, students use textmapping techniques to mark the text for recording their thought process. The layout of the text and visual marking assist students, including those with learning challenges, with self-monitoring and metacognition.

**E-encyclopedia (www.dkeencyc.com)**
Dorling Kindersley and Google have teamed up to bring E-encyclopedia, which allows users to search for information in nine categories: space, earth, nature, human body, science and technology, people and places, society and beliefs, arts and entertainment, and history.

**Ultralingua Online Dictionary (www.ultralingua.com/onlinedictionary)**
This online dictionary provides a way to look up words in several different languages. It will also turn any website into a dictionary. Just type in the web address of any website and watch it become dictionary-enabled. The site also provides a grammar reference.

know her class of students in the fall. See the Engaging in Assessment feature for an example of a good assessment exercise to conduct when first starting a unit.

From Mrs. Kim's initial assessment, she knew that the reading levels varied across several grades for her English-speaking students. In addition, she had students who are ELLs who would need language support to tackle the new content, and she would still need to provide challenges for her few high-end students to keep them interested and moving forward in their own learning.

Mrs. Kim's class was beginning their study of Native Americans. To help students develop an understanding of the period in history, she was reading *Eagle Feather,* by Clyde Robert Bulla, to the class. They had pored over photos and pictures of the geographical sites they would be exploring to develop a mindscape for the new information. She had gathered a classroom library of books for students to use as they explored questions that had emerged from their K-W-L on the opening day. Interest was high as the students began finding out how homes were adapted to the varying environments, how nature was respected yet needed for survival, and how the cultural customs of the time were expressed. The children were trying out the new vocabulary that was inherent for this high-interest topic. There was time to research and time to discuss in small and large groups.

Mrs. Kim had been thoughtful in choosing trade books to bring into the classroom for this unit. Knowing the diversity in her classroom, she had collected picture books and nonfiction that included ample photographs and drawings with easy-to-read captions. She had also picked texts with varying readability levels, so that all of her students could access information as the study continued. She wanted her students to know that information could be found in an array of resources, not just the textbook provided by the

## engaging in Assessment

### One-Minute Fluency Measure

The challenge at the beginning of the year is to quickly assess students so they can be placed with appropriate materials and grouped for productive learning. Mrs. Kim knew that she would have to add and make adaptations to a unit she had used before to meet the needs of this year's class. For an initial assessment, she administers a one-minute fluency measure to each student using a passage from the social studies textbook (a variation on the running record sheet introduced earlier in this book). She selects a passage of about two hundred words from the beginning of a new section in the book. She then makes a copy of the page, marking the running total of words on the right margin. She photocopies this page and uses it to record students' responses as they read orally. When there is an error or skipped word, she makes a slash line (/), so she can have an accurate count of the total number of words read accurately at the end of one minute.

At the end of the one-minute reading, she asks the students to tell her what they find most interesting in the piece they just read. This permits her to listen to their level of English and their inclusion of the key vocabulary terms. She makes notes on what the students say and uses this data in subsequent planning.

school. The school librarian helped her to locate issues of student magazines with stories, articles, and lists of other resources that would round out the printed materials from which students could find answers to their questions. Several videos were identified for student viewing, which also added visual information and a setting for other learning.

As the body of knowledge began to grow, Mrs. Kim hung poster boards, each with a key question at the top to guide students in their explorations. As students found information linked to the questions, they wrote it on a sticky note, citing the source on the back, and adhered it to the appropriate board. As the boards began to fill, small groups categorized the sticky notes for each question and students were able to use the collaborative research in their own reports.

Mrs. Kim listened to her students and realized they needed to have support in thinking about points of view and what constituted *factual* information. She introduced questions to help students explore the more thoughtful issues facing the Native Americans in a historical perspective, such as "When the Europeans came to America, who had the right to the land? Why do you think so?" Students responded emotionally to the issues. Mrs. Kim realized that the class needed to separate fact from opinion. She decided to create a chart to record and value both, but to recognize the difference. The left side was for Facts and the right side for Opinions. With this visual tool, students looked for other examples of fact and opinion in student magazines and on TV to expand their understanding of how advertisements use both fact and opinion in their everyday lives. See Figure 12.14 for an example of a Fact and Opinion chart.

## Unit 2: Use of Simulations—Westward Expansion

Another teacher, Mr. Connolly, uses simulations as part of his integrated units to help students come closer to the experiences of those they study. In this example, the students become personally involved in the problems of traveling across the territories of the

Figure 12.14

## Fact and Opinion Chart

| Facts | Opinions |
|---|---|
| Native American tribes were part of larger groups called nations. | Native Americans were not very religious since they believed that nature and animals were spirits. |
| Native American children learned their history from the stories older people told them. | Native Americans weren't smart enough to learn to write books. |
| Native American children didn't go to school or learn to read. | Native Americans would have been better off if the Europeans had left them alone and let them have western lands. |
| Native Americans traded with the early explorers and pioneers. | Some Native Americans liked the new lifestyle the pioneers brought. |



West. His use of simulation came well into the study of Westward Expansion, after students had developed foundational knowledge of this period of American history. In the initial two weeks, they had been focused on their inquiry study and had added much to their bank of knowledge. Now it was time to do something with what they had learned to consolidate the factual information and actively put it to use. Mr. Connolly was careful to keep in mind the diversity of his whole class and wanted to provide opportunities for each student to participate successfully in a heterogeneous group. He made sure that both the activity and materials would make that goal a reality.

When the students arrived on Monday, they drew character cards that Mr. C. had prepared. Each card profiled a typical early American, including their age, occupation, and place in the family. Students stood together as their family photo was taken and put up on the bulletin board prepared to document the trip west. Later in the day, the families regrouped as they prepared to depart in their covered wagon. Several times a week, they got together to solve a problem that Mr. C. had created to give the students a clearer view of the hardships that were faced.

Initially, families had to negotiate what they would take with them. The wagons were small, so Mr. C. taped a rectangle to the floor to show how little space each family had to fill. Both needs and wants were discussed, and hard choices had to be made. Everyone in the family shared their ideas and a list of items emerged. During the next two weeks, students continued reading individual historical novels, and Mr. C. brought artifacts, maps, and photos into the classroom for discussion. Mr. Connolly shared Lewis and Clark's journal with the class as they considered the difficulties and wonders of such a trip in a simpler time. Each family member kept an authentic-looking journal, writing and illustrating incidents and insights about days on the trail and all that had happened during their trip west.

Mr. C. consulted with the special education teachers who work with his class and they collaborated to extend the westward expansion activities into the arts. Students learned songs from the period in music and studied the clothes and simple toys from that time in art. Students who struggle with reading and writing often flourish in other modes of expression. Given the opportunity, they may find an interest that stimulates them to increase the amount of reading and writing they do. Mr. C worked with the special education teacher to identify materials that were just right or that would reflect students' interests and stimulate them to increase their reading and writing. Interest-driven learning is a key to their success.

Mr. C. encouraged students to refer to the resource books he had collected for the unit and check the student sites on the Internet for information as they made decisions that affected the family or the wagon train community. Progress was marked on a U.S. map as the wagon train families worked together to problem solve their way across the country.

In these ways, Mr. Connolly was able to differentiate instruction for children with varying levels of knowledge, skill in English, and interest in history. His use of reading and writing permeated the activities in which the class was involved. He was also able to bring in multiple modes of expression and learning by teaming with the art teacher. His unit expanded as he engaged with his students and followed their interests and questions.

**Guidelines for Creating Units** Teachers build units in a variety of ways to deepen students' curiosity and help them move deeply into content. Often, units begin with visitors sharing their experiences. At other times, class guests can help to answer questions that have been raised through earlier study of particular topics. Helping students make the best use of the occasions when visitors come to class needs careful teacher attention.

**Hands-On Inquiry: Ask the Experts** This activity can take various forms to fit both the age and stage of the students. Experts can be visiting speakers, parents, and other adults in the school community, or the students themselves. The interview process and resulting written form give many opportunities to practice skills in an authentic context.

Inviting a speaker to discuss a topic being studied enhances both the content knowledge and connections your students will make to aid learning. Before attempting individual interviews, students will benefit from planning and participating in a class interview of the guest speaker.

**Setting the Stage** Students need some help in understanding the steps that will lead to a successful interview. If available, view an interview from author videos often available in school libraries. Another source, the popular Reading Rainbow series, is also available in both public and school libraries. The interview process can be introduced through viewing portions of these resources, watching for the process, and debriefing what students noticed. Another introductory lesson has students reading magazines that feature interviews to learn the format as they begin to plan their own. Many student magazines have useful interviews. Further preparation includes brainstorming ideas and organizing them into categories before meeting with the expert. Students should be mindful of the goal to learn about the person, his/her job, or area of knowledge. Planning the interview may have students doing some research on the person or job and writing questions to ask. Good questions lead to opportunities for discussion, not just yes and no answers. A small tape recorder can help in reviewing the information afterward as the students organize and write their interview for sharing with their classmates. A group discussion of what they learned will benefit all students and prepare them for a one-on-one as the next step. Having a real reason to craft and revise a written work from this type of activity makes some of the grammar and skill sets important and purposeful.

## Unit 3: Technology-Focused Inquiry and Research

IRA/NCTE 8

Pleasant Ridge School, housing grades three to five, is a place where technology has been an integral part of the classrooms for many years. The fourth- and fifth-grade pod is part of the Technology-Rich Educational Environment (TREE) where teachers have experimented with ways to best integrate technology into learning. The teachers on the team have focused much of their language arts instruction around students' extended inquiry projects that use technology on several levels. Because individual research is new to students at this level, the teachers have been careful to use the units to teach all the skills students need to identify good questions for inquiry, explore topics in varied sources, develop note cards, organize a report, develop a PowerPoint presentation, and finally, present what they learn to others.

**Scaffolded Units** The Pleasant Ridge teachers have developed a way to scaffold students' inquiry by concentrating on three major units each year. In the fall, the fourth-graders all complete a fairly structured inquiry under teacher guidance. Because the students are in the pod for two years, the project for one year revolves around the social studies unit on the United States. Each student is given one state to research for the individual project. In the other year, the science unit on the human body systems is the first unit. The mid-year and spring units provide experiences for students to take more ownership of their learning by self-selecting topics within a broader thematic umbrella determined by the teachers. These unit foci also rotate; the team has found eight different themes that work well by providing a common theme while still permitting a wide range of individual inquiry around them. For example, last year the winter theme focused on resolving conflicts, and in the spring, it focused on adapting to the environment. The teachers have evolved this scaffolded research process over several years; they have learned from the students what works best.

**Building Background Knowledge** The units begin by helping students find a good topic and then asking important questions. The students then are directed to print and electronic sources that can help them find answers to their background questions. The fourth-grade students work together with an older fifth-grade buddy as they go about learning more about their topic. Teachers introduce the importance of taking notes, and students learn to write note cards and include accurate citations. The shared work and discussion during this process of data collection help both sets of students grow in their interest and knowledge.

**Expert Interviews** A central part of the background building process is contacting a real-world authority, an expert. Students learn to write questions for the expert that will extend their own learning. They write a letter to the person and request a time to talk personally or via e-mail. After the interview, the students write a report on what they learned from their expert. This information is then incorporated into the final reporting by making the report part of the visual display each student creates.

**Current Events Connections** Students also need to watch for their topic in the news and include three articles from the press that deal with their topic. They write summaries of these articles and incorporate them in their reports and show them on their display. The articles are also part of the background information.

**Synthesizing and Sharing** A part of the energy that makes this inquiry project so successful is that students become "experts" themselves and share what they learn with other school students, parents, and community members. The sharing is an extensive process. It includes:

- Composing a written report
- Designing a large trifold board (three feet by five feet) showing each aspect of the process with a focus on creating an inviting visual display
- Preparing a PowerPoint presentation
- Presenting a culminating oral report to other classes, their parents, and community members

**BUILDING TEACHING SKILLS:**

**Video Exercise**

*Students Tell about the Research Process*

Go to the Building Teaching Skills section in Chapter 12 of MyEducationLab and view the video, "Students Tell about the Research Process," which illustrates how intermediate students understand the nature of conducting a research report. Complete the activities that follow, and save your work or transmit it to your professor as assigned.

Teachers focus on three components of giving talks. The first is finding a good "hook" to interest the listeners. Then there needs to be solid content (PowerPoint slides focus on this aspect) and, finally, a good conclusion. The presentations are often videotaped, so there is opportunity to return to the presentations and learn from them.

**Visit These Teachers and Students Using MyEducationLab** This whole process provides a rich learning context for students to learn the research process as well as learn how to share information in writing, speaking, and by representing it visually. You can visit the teachers and see their classrooms in action on MyEducationLab. Two student oral presentations are also included with views of their trifold visual presentations.

Students learn the inquiry research process very thoroughly by the end of the two years they are in the TREE pod at Pleasant Ridge School. One of the tools that helps in this process is the Assessment Rubric that all students receive a copy of in their individual research folders. By making the criteria explicit in each area of the process, there is no guessing game about what is important. Individual students, the class, and the teachers are part of the evaluation process. See Figure 12.15 for an example of the assessment rubric used at Pleasant Ridge School.

**Figure 12.15**

## Shared Evaluation Rubric

**Presentation Assessment**

Student ______________________ Topic: ______________________

Parent Signature: ______________________ Fall Winter Spring

Advisors: Hinton, Pattengale, Sainati

**COMPLETES WORK:**

____ INDEPENDENTLY ____ WITH MINIMAL ASSISTANCE ____ WITH EXTENSIVE ASSISTANCE

| | Exceeds Expectations | Meets Expectations | Working Toward Expectations | Needs Work |
|---|---|---|---|---|
| USES project time effectively | 4 | 3 | 2 | 1 |
| PRODUCES work of depth and quality | 4 | 3 | 2 | 1 |
| MEETS deadlines | 4 | 3 | 2 | 1 |
| **CURRENT EVENTS/REAL WORLD APPLICATION** | | | | |
| SELECTS at least three news articles | 4 | 3 | 2 | 1 |
| INCLUDES articles *currently* in the news | 4 | 3 | 2 | 1 |
| SELECTS articles which are relevant to the project topic | 4 | 3 | 2 | 1 |
| CHOOSES articles from a reputable news source | 4 | 3 | 2 | 1 |
| SUMMARIZES articles concisely and identifies key points | 4 | 3 | 2 | 1 |
| SELECTS an appropriate expert | 4 | 3 | 2 | 1 |
| GENERATES pertinent questions | 4 | 3 | 2 | 1 |

| | | | | |
|---|---|---|---|---|
| COMMUNICATES with expert effectively | 4 | 3 | 2 | 1 |
| EXPRESSES thanks to expert in writing | 4 | 3 | 2 | 1 |
| **POWERPOINT** | | | | |
| ENHANCES audience understanding of topic through information included on slides | 4 | 3 | 2 | 1 |
| CREATES attractive slides showing concern for color, design, uniformity, and layout | 4 | 3 | 2 | 1 |
| USES phrases with bullet points | 4 | 3 | 2 | 1 |
| MAKES slides clearly legible | 4 | 3 | 2 | 1 |
| INCORPORATES effective and relevant graphics | 4 | 3 | 2 | 1 |
| PROOFREADS slides and makes necessary corrections and revisions | 4 | 3 | 2 | 1 |
| **DISPLAY** | | | | |
| CREATES an attractive display showing concern for color, design, uniformity, and layout | 4 | 3 | 2 | 1 |
| DISPLAYS current events and summaries on a poster(s) | 4 | 3 | 2 | 1 |
| EXHIBITS Real World Application results on a poster(s) | 4 | 3 | 2 | 1 |
| **PRESENTATION** | | | | |
| DRESSES and grooms for a good impression | 4 | 3 | 2 | 1 |
| HOOKS audience at beginning of presentation | 4 | 3 | 2 | 1 |
| DEMONSTRATES poise through posture, eye contact, and facial expression | 4 | 3 | 2 | 1 |
| REFERS to notes; looks at Audience and does not read computer screen | 4 | 3 | 2 | 1 |
| SPEAKS with expression and proper volume | 4 | 3 | 2 | 1 |
| EXPLAINS topic clearly and thoroughly | 4 | 3 | 2 | 1 |
| INTEGRATES current events and RWA seamlessly into presentation | 4 | 3 | 2 | 1 |
| CONCLUDES presentation effectively | 4 | 3 | 2 | 1 |
| DELIVERS 10-15 minute presentation | 4 | 3 | 2 | 1 |

TOTAL POINTS: ____________________ GRADE: ______________

| | | | | | |
|---|---|---|---|---|---|
| 120-117 | A+ | 107-105 | B+ | 95-93 | C+ |
| 116-111 | A | 104-99 | B | 92-87 | C |
| 110-108 | A- | 98-96 | B- | 86-84 | C- |

*Source:* From the Pleasant Ridge TREE Team: Jan Hinton, Kathy Pattengale, and Deanna Sainati.

## revisit the classroomchallenge

Tanya Arina had been upset after her first day in the district. Several questions were raised by the district's focus on informational reading. These included:

1. Why might Ms. Arina need to modify her novel-focused curriculum?
2. What should students in the middle grades learn about reading and language arts?
3. How can teachers use informal assessments to determine what students know so they can differentiate instruction?
4. How can Ms. Arina organize her instruction to build students' informational literacy?

Although she felt lacking in vision for how to proceed, her mentor teacher and colleagues gave her a great deal of support and she found ways to extend her instruction to meet the direction of her district. One of the most important ways she was able to rethink her instructional organization was to create short two-week units of instruction around themes that she found in both her literature basal series and in her social studies and science curriculums. The mentor teacher suggested that she use one common text (sometimes from a news magazine and sometimes from the basal reader) to initiate the unit. Once she was into the routine and got to know the library media center director, she also found a wealth of videos and DVDs that she could use to start off her themes. With the help of her mentor, she also assessed her students immediately in August with a one-minute fluency snapshot and was able to begin differentiating the kinds and difficulty of materials she made available for her students to read.

By introducing easy texts and guiding students to both graphically represent and then write their own texts, Tanya led her students into a better understanding of ways in which texts are constructed and how important it is in retelling and writing with a structure. She felt satisfied that her students were well on their way to becoming flexible, informational readers.

## chapterreview

Intermediate- and middle-grade teachers have a big responsibility to extend children's reading in many ways. As children develop automaticity and fluency in reading, the instructional focus shifts to thinking about text ideas. Children learn to predict, connect, interpret, and critically respond. Teachers guide children to explore more genres and learn about new ways authors share ideas. Teachers also engage students in peer discussion as a way to deepen their thinking, share their personal responses, and build new interpretations together. Creating contexts in which students learn together and explore ideas in longer units of study helps them engage deeply and take ownership of their learning.

### What Are Goals for Literacy beyond the Primary Grades?

In addition to learning to use reading as a way of thinking and sharing ideas presented in a wide range of genres, after the primary grades, students need to develop their ability and confidence in reading a wide variety of informational texts. This learning includes understanding and navigating textbooks in social studies, science, and mathematics. It extends to reading a wide variety of informational formats, including newspapers, magazines, and Internet sites. Learning to critically think about and verify information has become increasingly important.

## What Instructional Strategies Are Supported by Research and Best Practices?

Teachers use strategies that model the active, constructive nature of reading. They help students approach learning with confidence by helping them *Anticipate* what they know and can bring to learning; they create guides to help students *Build* knowledge and understanding while reading and learning; and they provide time and support so students can *Consolidate* their learning and retain key information. These ABCs provide a framework for the selection of teaching activities. In addition, teachers take into account that learning is social and constructive. Partner and small-group activities help students deepen their interest and engagement. So, too, when teachers help students define their own purposes for learning, students are likely to become more involved and sustain interests longer.

## How Can Students Be Encouraged to Read for Literary Purposes?

Students should be encouraged to expand the range of genres they read individually and under teacher guidance once they have a firm grasp of the basic reading processes. Then they need regular opportunities to respond to engaging texts orally in discussion groups and in writing in literature notebooks or response journals. Teachers provide models of interested readers and can encourage students by reading aloud to them and sharing their responses and enjoyment.

## How Can Literacy Be Developed across the Content Areas?

Teachers can do a great deal to build students' literacy in content areas. They introduce students to the external features of textbooks and informational articles; they model and guide students in using these features to think about the text ideas. Teachers also take seriously the need to help students learn to read and interpret each of the graphic displays that accompany informational texts—including graphs, charts, maps, and diagrams. Because these graphic forms of information are important, they need to be taught, learned, and then woven together with the narrative textual information.

## Why Is Visual Literacy Important?

Both reading and writing involve visual processing. Studies of engaged readers indicate that they create visual images as they read. Writers, too, often begin the composing process by activating or creating images that guide their process. Creating visual images also helps learners retain ideas they read and study. Therefore, a foundation for comprehension and composing rests in visual imagery.

## How Can Visual Literacy Be Developed?

Four basic aspects of visual literacy need to be included as you help students interpret visual documents and presentations. First, it is important to have a vocabulary with which to describe each visual form. Then students need to spend time developing an interpretation of each format and comparing different visuals that are similar but that have different foci. Combining the visual forms in text materials with the narratives they accompany is another step that is very important so students see the relationships among elements. Finally, students need to be encouraged and supported in creating their own visual presentations.

## How Can You Organize Classroom Instruction to Accomplish Your Goals?

Teachers need to use a variety of instructional formats to provide new information and introduce strategies to students and then give them time to practice and gain confidence. The whole-part-whole model works well for instruction and practice. Students also need to be in settings where they can work collaboratively to discuss their reading and writing together. In building engagement with informational reading, integrated units within which students can explore their own level of interest and deepen their understanding are important. When teachers have self-contained classrooms, such integration is easiest; when teachers are on teams or they teach in different departments, finding time to collaborate and plan is important. There is much to be learned in the intermediate and upper grades, and effective use of time is important.

## How Can Integrated Units of Instruction Enhance Learning?

Creating opportunities for students to work over extended periods of time on the same content or themes gives teachers a way to differentiate instruction by responding to specific students' learning needs and their interests. Students gain by having more opportunities to nurture their own interests and learn ways to pursue learning from varied sources. Units provide rich opportunities to involve students in more extended reading and writing as they deepen their knowledge and concepts. With care, units can model the integration of content and processes in engaging and meaningful ways.

PEARSON

**myeducationlab**™

Where the Classroom Comes to Life

Now go to www.myeducationlab.com to take a Pretest to assess your initial comprehension of chapter content, study chapter content with your individualized Study Plan, take a Posttest to assess your understanding of chapter content, practice your teaching skills with Building Teaching Skills exercises, and build a deeper, more applied understanding of chapter content with Homework and Exercises.

chapter 13

# Developing Vocabulary

## classroomchallenge

**James Koburn** is preparing his first integrated unit for the fall on early Native Americans. He wants to ensure that his students will have a successful experience and come to enjoy exploring and learning together. He visited the Four Corners area of the Southwest during the summer, and he now has a collection of artifacts and books he wants to use with the class. He has also collected a number of trade books and new short informational texts from publishers such as National Geographic, Newbridge, and Rigby at a variety of reading levels so each student can have some successful reading experiences with books on Native Americans.

He introduced these informational books by using a big book so that all the students could see as he pointed out specific text features of the books including the table of contents, index, graphic information, and the glossary of terms. Then he showed the class how to use the index to find a specific piece of information, and he emphasized that they didn't have to read through the whole text from front to back. He then explained how the class would read their texts with partners so that they could share the building of knowledge as they read together.

However, as he listened to the students begin their partner reading in books at their reading levels, he realized there were many

words they did not know how to pronounce and that were unfamiliar to them. Even the names of the native tribes caused real trouble. As he moved around the room listening to partners read orally, he noted that many words were unfamiliar to them. What could he do? He didn't want students to stumble over key terms. He has already learned that this unit contained a large number of content-specific vocabulary terms. His students need to know them to participate actively and understand the content in the readings and activities he has planned. The beginning of the year is important; James wants his students to learn that they can be successful with content materials.

## Questions for Reflection

1. How can Mr. Koburn help his students access important academic vocabulary?
2. How much practice would students need with these terms to retain and use them?
3. How can he ensure that this learning will be enjoyable as well as productive?

## anticipating this chapter

This chapter discusses the major issues surrounding vocabulary development in the elementary and middle grades. It is organized around the following questions:

What do we know about vocabulary development during the elementary years?

What does a good instructional program include?

What role does the dictionary play?

How can students' word knowledge be assessed?

# What Do We Know about Vocabulary Development During the Elementary Years?

Our oral and reading vocabularies continue to grow throughout our lifetime. The most rapid expansion of language occurs during a child's first decade of life. By the time they enter school, children know several thousand words. Then, during their school years children add about three thousand words a year to their reading vocabularies (Nagy and Herman, 1987; Graves, 2006).

## Reading Vocabulary

Growth in children's vocabularies during the school years is stimulated and nurtured through wide reading experiences. The more children read and are read to, the more words they encounter and the more familiar these words become to them in appropriate contexts. This is true for students of all linguistic abilities and levels of reading development. From their work Nagy and his associates concluded that, on the average, students will learn about one of every twenty new words they encounter while reading. Cunningham (2005) summarizes this impact, "For example, the average fifth-grader reads approximately one million words of text a year and approximately 2 percent of these words are 'unfamiliar' to the child. If 1 out of every 20 of those unfamiliar words is incorporated into the child's lexicon then the average fifth-grader learns approximately 1,000 words a year through reading" (p. 48).

Even in preschool and kindergarten, children gain vocabulary through listening to and talking about books. These adult-led experiences provide important supports for language development. Primary-grade children love to hear interesting and "big" words and will engage in extended play with such terms as *pterodactyl, unobtrusive,* and *absorbent.* Several research studies have demonstrated how important the social experiences around books can be for vocabulary development (Zevenbergen and Whitehurst, 2003; Whitehurst, Falcon, Lonigan, Fischel, DeBaryshe et al., 1988; Biemiller, 2004; Beck, McKeown, and Kucen, 2002). Dialogic reading, interactive reading, and shared reading are terms used to describe variations on instructional routines that help teachers highlight new vocabulary and build students' concepts. Teachers help students build their vocabularies when we highlight important new words for children, explore their meaning, provide examples, and engage children in expressing their own ideas and feelings with words and concepts they are learning. Beck and McKeown suggest that teachers preview books they plan to read orally to a class and select three to five words that are interesting and have usefulness beyond the single book. Then during oral reading, these words can be emphasized, explained, and put on the board for further use.

Teachers help students build their vocabularies when we highlight important new words for children, explore their meaning, provide examples, and engage children in expressing their own ideas and feelings with words and concepts they are learning.

The nuances of how particular words and figurative expressions are used become clear to students when they hear them used in books or see them as they practice their own reading. When teachers highlight uses of language, students can reflect on them together and savor good language in print. Children build their understanding of the importance of using particular words to indicate precise meanings. Reading experiences are very important to students' continued language growth. In fact, vocabulary researchers (Cunningham and Stanovich, 1998; Nagy, Anderson, and Herman, 1987) credit reading with the rapid growth in vocabulary during the school years.

## English Is a Complex Language

Learning English is challenging for children who come from homes where languages other than English are spoken. One of the particularly challenging aspects of learning English is that the corpus of our vocabulary is so large and keeps growing.

With so many words from which to choose, words take on specific meanings and become associated with specific contexts; English-speakers can select particular words to reflect the connotations we intend. For example, we can indicate that something is attractive by using a wide variety of terms: *pretty, pleasing, appealing, lovely, gorgeous, smashing, sensuous,* and so on. It takes sophistication to learn that the word *pretty* generally connotes that someone or something is attractive but not beautiful. Learning which term to use in particular situations is a lifetime task. For English language learners, it often seems overwhelming. School support and rich instructional experiences are essential for their language growth. Teachers can make language learning and selection of just the right words a shared and enjoyable exploration with students.

Teachers can make language learning and selection of just the right words a shared and enjoyable exploration with students.

# What Does a Good Instructional Program Include?

**Reading Homework Exercise**

*Vocabulary Lessons*

Go to the Homework and Exercises section in Chapter 13 of MyEducationLab and read the article, "Vocabulary Lessons," about the importance of building vocabulary lessons that engage students in word learning. Complete the activities that follow, and save your work or transmit it to your professor as assigned.

Teachers can do a great deal to help students expand their vocabularies. Reviews of the research on vocabulary confirm that in addition to building a context in the school and classroom for interest in language, consistent and rich instruction is also beneficial and an important part of a comprehensive approach to vocabulary development. Vocabulary programs need to build both interest in words and word knowledge to enhance students' oral and written comprehension. In their review of the research on vocabulary instruction, the National Reading Panel (2000) concluded that teaching words directly and building strategies for word learning are parts of effective vocabulary instruction. Students need to possess strategies that develop their independence in building their vocabularies. They need to understand how words are formed, how to use word parts in determining new terms, and how to use context and resources (such as the dictionary) to clarify word meanings. All of these approaches are part of a comprehensive instructional program.

An important and often overlooked area of vocabulary development is content learning. Academic vocabulary is critical to learning in social studies, science, and mathematics, and teachers need to provide explicit instruction to help students deal with both the unfamiliar concepts and the new labels for those important ideas. A recent observational study of fourth- and eighth-grade classrooms found that teachers spent almost no time on teaching academic vocabulary (1.4 percent of the time), although about 12 percent of the time was spent in literacy activities focused on vocabulary (Scott, Jamieson-Noel, and Asselin, 2003).

IRA/NCTE 3

Good instruction includes attention to several dimensions of word learning (Blachowicz et al., 2006; Graves, 2006):

- Modeling and stimulating interest in words
- Creating a stimulating environment for language exploration
- Teaching about words and how to determine meanings through word parts, affixes, roots, and context, both verbal and visual
- Expanding deeper understandings of important terms in the lessons and units of study
- Providing regular opportunities for students to talk together and try out new ways of expressing ideas and feelings
- Developing students' metacognitive involvement in vocabulary learning
- Integrating vocabulary instruction across the curriculum and school
- Monitoring students' oral and written vocabulary growth

## The Teacher as Model

Students won't develop good vocabularies if they don't have opportunities to use language and to participate in lively discussions in which they can try out new words and explore ways of expressing ideas. Teachers who carefully establish environments in which children learn to talk with each other and respect each other's contributions create the context for vocabulary exploration and growth. One very easy way to do this is to teach children to Think-Pair-Share. The teacher can pose a question and then indicate to the students that they can use the Think-Pair-Share routine to respond. Each student writes or draws their ideas about the question. Then the students turn to their designated partners to tell how they respond to the question. After these partner discussions, the teacher calls the whole group back together to share good ideas coming out of the partner dialogues. The partner "rehearsal" and shaping of ideas helps students who may have been too shy or unsure of their ideas to initially share them with the whole class gain confidence. Sometimes, one partner shares the other's ideas. If children seem to create too much noise in the classroom during these exchanges, they can be taught to use "twelve-inch voices" or to talk "knee to knee." These easy suggestions and some modeling in the class by adults or partners who understand the ideas quickly can prepare the whole class for a productive framework for talk.

A major part of creating classrooms where students have opportunities to try new ways of talking with new vocabulary is the modeling that comes from the teacher. Students learn very quickly what teachers value and what they care about. Therefore, it is so important for teachers to share their delight in language and to consciously draw students' attention to well-expressed ideas. For example, a teacher might comment:

- "Listen to this sentence—the words are so perfect!"
- "What a beautiful way to express this idea; I can picture it in my mind! Jenny, you stated your idea so clearly!"
- Josh, thanks for sharing how you discovered that wounded kitten. You described your feelings of sadness and concern so vividly."
- "Karen just read this news article and learned about a new planet, so far away that it is called an 'exo-planet.' Isn't that an interesting new term!"
- "Juana, you get an added point today because you used two of our new vocabulary terms in your science journal as you wrote the explanation of the experiment."

Teachers also stimulate students' growth in language when they use language that is just beyond what students themselves use. This is the Vygotskyian idea of supporting students' learning at their zone of proximal development. If students don't hear language beyond what they can speak themselves, they won't build their vocabularies and flexibility with language.

Some teachers display a word-a-day calendar in the room or encourage students to use a website for new words each day. Others use their daily read-alouds as a way to reinforce the beauty of language and introduce students to new words. There are clever books about language that can stimulate students' interests and build their respect for language and words. Highlighting a few new words and phrases by putting them on the bulletin board so the class can return to them later makes clear to students how important our language is. See Figure 13.1 for a list of books about language that are good to read aloud. It also helps students make better use of the read-aloud time because, for many, new words simply float by them

**Figure 13.1**

## Good Books to Read Aloud

Eloise Greenfield. *Honey, I Love*. (HarperCollins, 1978).

Lulu Delacre. *Arroz con leche: Popular Songs and Rhymes from Latin America*. (Scholastic, 1989).

Debra Frasier. *Miss Alaineus: A Vocabulary Disaster.* (Harcourt, 2000).

Ruth Heller. *A Cache of Jewels and Other Collective Nouns; Kites Sail High: A Book about Verbs; Luscious Lollipops: A Book about Adjectives*. (Putnam, 1998).

Norton Juster. *The Phantom Tollbooth*. (Knopf, 1961).

Jon Scieszka. *The Frog Prince; The Stinky Cheese Man; The True Story of the Three Little Pigs*. (Various publishers).

Jack Prelutsky. *Read a Rhyme, Write a Rhyme*. (Knopf, 2005).

Donna Brook. *The Journey of English*. (Clarion Books, 1999).

unnoticed. Some teachers also go online and find a word for the day or a joke or word play. These can be displayed outside classroom doors or on the bulletin boards near where students spend time so that they can enjoy the stimulation of figuring out riddles and jokes and creating new words.

Finally, another aspect of the teacher's role as a model language user is to give positive affirmation to students for their verbal participation in class. With English language learners, students with language delays and word-retrieval issues, and students who are shy this is so important. Many will take risks when they learn that their teacher supports their efforts and doesn't require perfection.



## Select Words to Teach

Determining which words to teach is a question facing all teachers. Isabell Beck and her colleagues (Beck, McKeown, and Kucen, 2002) have helped by distinguishing three levels, or tiers, of words:

- Very frequent, everyday words = Tier 1
- Words used in written texts and found quite frequently so they have general utility if learned = Tier 2
- Words that are specific to particular contexts and content areas, more technical terms = Tier 3

Beck et al. argue that the words in the *second* tier are most worth highlighting and teaching to elementary students. Most children will hear and have opportunities to use Tier 1 words without teacher support. Tier 2 words, if taught, are most likely to enter children's receptive and expressive vocabularies, but without attention in school, they may not be learned. Both Beck et al. (2002) and Paynter, Bodrova, and Doty (2005) give teachers good guidance in selecting those words that will most likely be encountered in many contexts and can be learned and used frequently.

## Highlight Important Terms

One of the easiest ways for teachers to highlight those words they want to draw students' attention to is as they introduce new books. It is natural to preview new vocabulary with students and focus on words during the introduction of a new story or article to be read. The Reading Recovery practice of introducing books with a "picture walk" can be replicated by teachers at all levels. Teachers preview the text to anticipate unfamiliar terms. As the teacher leads students through the pages of the text, discussing the pictures and graphic features, the new words the teacher wants to ensure students hear and attend to, are introduced into the conversation. At upper levels, teachers can use the captions and highlighted words to reinforce how some authors help readers pay attention to key content terms.

**Use Text Talk** Beck and her colleagues have developed a process for highlighting new vocabulary as part of their discussion of books *after* they have been read, rather than *before*. In *Text Talk* (2003), designed for kindergarten through second grade, teachers and students collaboratively discuss their responses to the story they have read. The focus is on the shared meaning and students' initiative in asking questions about the text. After reading and discussing the story, two to four key terms are introduced and the teacher makes the connection to their use in the story and then explains their meanings. Children repeat the words orally with teacher guidance so that these longer terms are clearly segmented and all parts heard. Then the teacher gives other examples of where the words might be used to extend the association from the single context found in the book. Children create their own examples of the word and extend their understandings by thinking of examples, non-examples, and responding to teacher queries.

**Audiotapes for Listening** Most supports for new terms occur prior to students' engaging with a text. Because of the large numbers of second language learners in many schools, publishers are now providing short summaries of key texts on audiotapes or CD-ROMs in Spanish and sometimes in other languages, too. When students have gotten an idea of what a text is about in their first language, pointing out key terms in English can be particularly useful. Students can then create their personal lists of key terms using both languages.

## Intermediate Grade Priorities

For all students, and particularly for English language learners, teachers' awareness of the importance of vocabulary increases in the intermediate grades. How teachers recognize this need and provide guidance with important vocabulary will make a real difference in student learning. A key starting point is introducing highly useful terms. Plan carefully. There are several ways teachers can think and act strategically. Begin by listing words that are going to be significant. These include both content specific concepts and procedural terms.

**Procedural Language** Students may not understand terms for directions and will be helped if you provide meaning and clarification. For example, do students know what is involved in predicting, categorizing, providing support, etc.? The procedural language we expect students to follow can be easily checked for understanding. If students have trouble with some of these terms, the class can create their own dictionary with definitions or examples. These can then be made into bookmarks or a class dictionary/guide that can be posted in the classroom. Students may need to see these terms and hear them used frequently to gain understanding of them. Even adults seem to have trouble when asked to compare and/or contrast ideas. Arguing from a point of view and providing text-based evidence are other examples of how even mature learners need to be reminded of what the tasks entail. See the Engaging in Assessment feature for information on teaching procedural language.

**Pre-Assessments** Second, previewing the texts and content of instruction and listing key content terms are also useful. If you are not sure that students know all the terms, do a quick pre-assessment. There are several ways you can do this and make the precheck fun. One easy way is to make a list of the key terms you have identified and ask students directly to rate their knowledge of the terms. Figure 13.2 shows an example of a Before Reading Knowledge Rating Chart (Blachowicz and Fisher, 2006) activity completed by a fourth-grade class before reading about Jane Addams. With younger students, teachers can build in the practice of having students hold up fingers to indicate how familiar they are with the main vocabulary terms the teacher pronounces orally. For example, if students hold up a fist that indicates they don't know the term; one finger means some familiarity; all five fingers indicate the word is well known. By surveying the class, the teacher can get a quick indication of which words to spend more time with before the children read.

It is also easy to have students, either individually or with partners, connect two to three terms in sentences that reflect important uses of them. See Figure 13.3 for an example of the Connect 3 Prereading Activity. From a list of several content terms, students can select words they will use in their sentences. Reviewing the students'

**Figure 13.2**

## Before Reading Knowledge Rating Chart: Rate Your Knowledge

| Term | New to me | I've seen | I know | Definition |
|---|---|---|---|---|
| child labor | | | | |
| immigrants | | | | |
| settlement house | | | | |
| poverty | | | | |
| playground | | | | |
| Jane Addams | | | | |

contributions gives teachers clear ideas of which words are not selected by students, probably terms that are worth more attention. Another easy way to learn what students know about important vocabulary is to ask them to cluster or categorize words from a list you provide (see Figure 13.4 for an example). A variant on these prereading activities is to have students do an exclusion brainstorming activity (see Figure 13.5 for an

*engaging in*

## Assessment

### Procedural Language

Students who have learned English as their second or third language generally develop conversational English long before they learn the academic vocabulary they need in schools for social studies, science, math, and any specific area of content engagement—including art and physical education. Teachers need to be sensitive to their particular needs for more in-depth support as they learn to listen to and use academic terms. One of the first places to assess their readiness for learning is in the *procedural terms* we use: list, choose, above, compare, guess, check, draw, predict, analyze, sum, similarity, describe, etc. Many times, this basic language of instruction is not clear to these students; yet, with a little attention, they can perform the tasks asked of them much more easily.

At the start of the year, check to see how well your students understand the basic terms for instructional procedures. Give them a short task to complete and make notes of their responses.

If you find that some terms are not clearly understood, you can support your students by having the key procedural terms listed on the board with visual clues for each. For example, the word *list* is shown next to a drawing of a page with several items listed; the word *cut* is shown next to a pair of scissors, and *compare* is shown next to two concentric circles (a Venn diagram). Students can also participate in creating logos for instructional terms so that the entire class can be involved in attending to the precision with which directions are given. It is also helpful to group similar terms for older students. For example, the words *guess, predict, estimate, visualize,* and *hypothesize* are related. Explaining these words and how they are used is valuable for everyone.

example). From a list you provide, have them cross out words they think won't be in the content. In this way, students see new terms and are given time to think about their likelihood of being in the unit.

**Predicting ABC's** When they work in teams, students have more opportunity to explore the terms in depth and to draw on their associations. In more extensive units, students enjoy predicting what words they think they will encounter. "Predicting ABC's" (Allen, 1999) gives teachers and students a way to activate their ideas and think of words that are connected with the topic. See Figure 13.6 for examples of how students responded to the invitation to brainstorm words about their new unit on poetry.

**Prethinking a Story** Before students begin a new story, there are

**Figure 13.3**

## Connect 3 Prereading Activity

Connect 2–3 of the following words to make a sentence that you think might be included in the article we are going to read about "Plant and Animal Cells."

**Key Words**

**nucleus, cell wall, chloroplast, microscope, functions, mitochondrion, differences, plants, organisms**

Name________________________________________

Sentence: ____________________________________

______________________________________________

______________________________________________

**Figure 13.4**

## Create Categories

**Thinking about the Iroquois Indians**

Sort the list of words below into categories that make sense to you. Then label the sets of words that you have created so others will know why they are grouped together.

**Words:**

**longhouses, rivers, wampum, fur, culture, confederacy, food, trade, deerskin, crops, beaver, glass beads, middlemen, Europeans, treaty, groups, scarce**

**Figure 13.5**

## Exclusion Brainstorming

**Civil Rights**

We are going to read about the civil rights movement in the United States. Read over the list of words and cross out any you think DON'T BELONG. Then check the rest of the words and think about how they might be used when we read the article on "The Struggle for Equality in the U.S."

| | |
|---|---|
| **boycott** | **voting rights** |
| **activist** | **child labor** |
| **Mardi Gras** | **mass production** |
| **minority** | **Yalta Agreement** |
| **Native Americans** | **hemlines** |
| **Mason-Dixon line** | **women** |
| **Gold Rush** | **desegregation** |
| **desegregate** | **bilingual education** |
| **discrimination** | **Eleanor Roosevelt** |
| **reservation** | **Title 9** |

Figure 13.6

## Example of Ideas from One Partnership

| A-C | D-F | F-G | H-J | K-L |
|---|---|---|---|---|
| acrostic<br>couplet<br>Alice in Wonderland<br>anthology | diamante<br>Dr. Seuss<br>endings | | | |
| **M-N** | **O-Q** | **R-T** | **U-W** | **X-Z** |
| meter<br>nursery rhymes | poets | riddles<br>rhymes<br>Shel Silverstein<br>reader's theater | | |

also ways to engage them with important vocabulary. If they have fun thinking about the terms and being creative about how they may be related, the students will likely notice the words when they encounter them during reading.

**Vocab-O-Gram** One of the easiest strategies is to make a list of words that are associated with the elements of a story: characters, setting, plot/conflict, and resolution. Read over the words orally if the children may be unfamiliar with their pronunciation. Then ask students to put the terms in the box on the Vocab-O-Gram (Blachowicz and Fisher, 2006) where they fit. When children work with partners, they have more opportunity for oral language practice and for learning from each other. After they have determined where they think the words fit, the students then write out a sentence prediction. See Figure 13.7 for an example of a story Vocab-O-Gram.

IRA/NCTE 5

**Story Impression** A little more challenging is the Story Impression strategy (McGinley and Denner, 1987). The teacher creates a list of words and phrases that are essential in the story and lists them in the order they occur in the story itself. Students working with a partner or small group are asked to create their own "story impression" from this list. They write this as a short synopsis and then share with each other what they have created. Sometimes, these pieces are quite creative; in one class, the students preferred their creation to the actual story they read. See Figure 13.8 for an example of a Story Impression. See the Engaging in Oral Language feature for an example of how James Koburn used a variety of visual and oral formats to introduce new vocabulary to his class.

## Explicit Instruction in Word Structure and Meaning

IRA/NCTE 6

All children need to learn about how words are formed and how they can look for word parts to help them pronounce and understand new words. In the primary grades, students can be guided to look for compound words (*underground*, *upstairs*, *sandbox*),

Figure 13.7

## Story Vocab-O-Gram

**Directions:** All of the following words are from this story. See if you can predict how they are used. If you think the word describes a character, then put it in that box; if you think it is about the setting, write it in that box. If one word doesn't fit, there is a box for those words. Finally, see if you can make a prediction about the story, and write it in the bottom box.

**Words:**

| CHARACTERS | PROBLEM IN STORY | FEELING WORDS |
|---|---|---|
| SETTING | RESOLUTION | OTHER WORDS? |
| My prediction is that in this story: | | |

Figure 13.8

## Story Impression

Before reading this selection you and your partner can have some fun predicting what the story is going to be. You can be authors, yourselves!

Read through the words and phrases listed below. Then write a paragraph or two that includes all of the words in the same order in which they are listed here. Remember to tell a story.

**my friend**
**sick in bed**
**passed a store**
**I'll get him . . .**
**things I saw**
**some lace**
**a bone**
**a note**
**a kitten**

## engaging in Oral language

### Using Audio- and Video-Recorded Books to Teach Vocabulary

When academic vocabulary is unfamiliar to students, the introduction of new terms can occur in many different ways—by hearing the terms, by seeing them explained as they are discussed in visual formats, and by reading them. As James Koburn thought about the difficulty his class was having with pronouncing terms needed to discuss Native American life, he came up with the idea of creating an audiotape recording of one or two of the books so that students could hear the terms pronounced in the context of the texts themselves. By listening to the words pronounced correctly, Mr. Koburn hoped students would become more familiar with the terms. He decided to record the first books himself so that his students would make the connection between his voice and the written content. Then he went online and found a good source with a video of Early Americans that included many of the concepts he knew would be introduced in the unit.

Noting the students' increased attention to the words and their attempts to use them in their conversations, he realized that adding varied presentations was going to be useful to the class. What a great resource, he thought. Now students could see and thus establish better visual images of the context and actual concepts about which they would read and learn.

**BUILDING TEACHING SKILLS:**
**Classroom Artifact Exercise**

*Prefixes*

Go to the Building Teaching Skills section in Chapter 13 of MyEducationLab and examine the Artifact Prefixes in which there is a sample of a student's attempt to use prefixes in a writing sample. Complete the activities that follow, and save your work or transmit it to your professor as assigned.

words with suffixes such as "ful" (grace*ful*, hand*ful*), and endings such as "ed" and "ing" on verbs (want*ed*, runn*ing*). The children can then also notice words that have more than one meaning, giving part or morpheme. As they are reading independently, students often find that the longer words at first seem challenging. When they start looking for either syllables or word parts, they have a strategy that will help them figure out many unfamiliar words as they encounter them in print.

In the intermediate grades, students begin to look more specifically for prefixes and suffixes on words and identify root words. While there are many affixes, there are a few that occur so frequently that they can be the focus of instruction. The list in Figure 13.9 shows the most frequently occurring prefixes in English. For Spanish language speakers, Figure 13.10 shows how teachers can help students make the links between English and Spanish by sharing with them some of the common Spanish language prefixes. A natural place for students to explore roots and "combining forms" is during the learning of content topics in science and social studies. Many scientific terms come directly from Greek and some from Latin. When you point out these connections, students can learn more about the interesting evolution of modern English from a variety of contributing languages. For example, in a unit on photosynthesis teachers can use the opportunity to highlight some Greek roots. By writing **photo, therm, hydra,** and **bio** on the board or on graphic organizers for students, teachers can

Figure 13.9

## Affixes

| Prefixes | Meaning | Example |
|---|---|---|
| Un | not | *un*happy |
| In | not | *in*correct |
| Re | again | *re*pair, *re*move |
| Dis | not or away | *dis*agree, *dis*miss |
| Pre | before | *pre*school, *pre*pare |
| Ex | out | *ex*hale, *ex*port |
| Anti | against | *anti*freeze, *anti*war |
| Sub | under, below | *sub*way, *sub*marine |
| Super | over, more than | *super*sonic, *super*man |
| Com | together, with | *com*plete, *com*munity |
| Con | | *con*nect |
| Col | | *col*lection |
| Co | | *co*operate |
| Cor | | *cor*respond |
| Mid | in the middle | *mid*day, *mid*summer |
| Mis | wrong | *mis*behave, *mis*understand |
| **Number Prefixes** | | |
| Mono | one | *mono*tone |
| Uni | one | *uni*corn |
| Bi | two | *bi*cycle |
| Di | two | *di*alogue |
| Tri | three | *tri*cycle |
| Deca | ten | *dec*ade |
| Centi | hundreth | *centi*pede |
| Cent | hundreth | *cent*ury |
| **Suffixes** | | |
| s, es | plural | clock*s* |
| s, ing, ed | verb, time | sing*s*, sing*ing* |
| er, est | comparison | late, lat*er*, lat*est* |
| ly | how done | quick, quick*ly* |
| ful | full of | peace*ful* |
| ous | full of | fam*ous* |
| less | without | use*less*, sleep*less* |
| ist, ian | one skilled in | scient*ist*, physic*ian* |
| ness | state of being, having | sad*ness*, sick*ness* |
| ify, fy | to become, make | magni*fy*, dei*fy* |

*(Continued)*

*continued*

| Prefixes | Meaning | Example |
|---|---|---|
| en | make, cause, made of | soft*en*, wool*en* |
| able | can, able to, deserving | cap*able*, lov*able* |
| ible | | poss*ible*, vis*ible* |
| tion | action, process | comple*tion* |
| ion | | rebell*ion* |
| ish | have quality of | fool*ish*, child*ish* |
| ment | state of, action | fulfill*ment* |
| ry, ery, ary | product or action of, place where | bake*ry*, potte*ry* |
| ize | make, made into | dramat*ize* |
| ism | practice of, act of | hero*ism*, vandal*ism*, patriot*ism* |

*Source:* Dale and O'Rourke, *Vocabulary Building: A Process Approach.* Copyright © 1986. Reprinted by permission of Zaner-Bloser, Inc.

**Figure 13.10**

## Prefijos, Sufijos, y Raíces (Prefixes, Suffixes, and Roots)

| Prefijos | Significado | Ejemplos |
|---|---|---|
| *anti-* | *contra* [opposed] | *antiséptico* [antiseptic] |
| *co-* [co- or con-] | *junto con* [with] | *cooperar* [cooperate] |
| *re-* | *de nuevo* [repetition] | *reajustar* [readjust] |
| *sub-* | *debajo* [under] | *subterráno* [subterraneous] |
| **Sufijos** | | |
| *-able, -ible* | *digno de o se puede* [worthy to or able to] | *demonstrable* [demonstrable] |
| *-ción, -sión, -xión* | *acción o efecto* [action or effect] | *invención* [invention] |
| *-iento* | *parecido o tendencia* [resemblance, tendency to] | *crecimiento* [increase or increment] |
| *-oso* | *lleno de* [full of] | *luminoso* [luminous, shining] |
| **Raíces** | | |
| *bio* | *vida* [of living things, life] | *anfibio, biología* [amphibious, biology] |
| *geo* | *tierra* [earth] | *geografía, geología* [geography, geology] |
| *cracia* | *gobierno* [government] | *democracia* [democracy] |
| *hidro* | *agua, líquido* [water, liquid] | *hidrosfera* [hydrosphere] |

*Source:* From *Learning in Two Worlds: An Integrated Spanish/English Biliteracy Approach* by Bertha Perez and Maria E. Torres-Guzman. Copyright © 1992 by Longman Publishers. Reprinted by permission.

help students brainstorm lists of words with these roots. By analyzing a set of words with a common root, students can begin to identify the meaning of each root and look for it in further reading and learning.

From the four roots listed in the previous paragraph students might generate many words: *thermostat, thermal, thermos, thermometer, hydrangea, hydrogen, hydroxide, hydraulic, dehydrate, phototropic, photogenic, photography, photolysis, photometer, photon, biology, biography, bioluminescent, bionic, biomedical, biome, biopsy,* and *biorhythm.*

From this list, students can underline the common Greek roots and predict what each means. Then, returning to the words, they can also identify the meanings of the other combining parts and deepen their interest in how words are formed. Such an activity often leads students to identify even more words with these roots, words they hear on television or encounter on the Internet, or experience in conversations. Making a bulletin board or shared class space where students can add words to their lists solidifies such activities in memory much better than if the activities are just short-term, one- or two-day events.

With teacher guidance, students can also start to identify other roots and hunt for their origins. Making the study of word origins a part of "class detective work" can be enjoyable. It is important that classrooms have multiple copies of good dictionaries so students can be successful when they pursue word histories and meanings. If the class has second language students, then providing dual-language dictionaries is also important. Books about the English language and how it has developed extend students' interest and knowledge. See Figure 13.11 for some suggested resources.

**Case Archive Homework Exercise**

*Antonio*

Go to the Homework and Exercises section in Chapter 13 of MyEducationLab and read Level A-Case 1 about Antonio, a fourth-grader who needs help with vocabulary. Complete the activities that follow, and save your work or transmit it to your professor as assigned.



**Figure 13.11**

## Resources to Teach Language

Allen, J. (1999). *Words, Words, Words: Teaching Vocabulary in Grades 4–12*. Portland, ME: Stenhouse.

Bear, D., Invernezzi, M., Templeton, S., & Johnston, F. (2004). *Words Their Way.* Upper Saddle River, NJ: Merrill.

Blachowicz, C. & Fisher, P. (2006). *Teaching Vocabulary in All Classrooms.* Englewood Cliffs, NJ: Merrill Prentice-Hall.

Brook, D. (1999). *The Journey of English.* New York: Scholastic.

Bryson, B. (1990). *The Mother Tongue: English and How It Got That Way.* New York: Avon Books.

Graves, M. F. (2006). *The Vocabulary Book: Learning and Instruction.* New York: Teachers College Press.

Lederer, R. (1998). *Crazy English: The Ultimate Joy Ride through Our Language.* New York: Simon & Schuster.

Winchester, S. (2003). *The Professor and the Madman.* New York: Penguin Books.

## Deepen Students' Understandings of New Terms

Your work is just starting when new terms are identified and students are introduced to their meanings in the context of the classroom learning activities and reading materials. To make words their own, students need multiple opportunities to use the words in meaningful ways—both orally and in written formats. They also need to hear and see the words used in appropriate contexts.

**Vocabulary Notebooks** Teachers can help students expand their vocabularies by sharing with them the need to focus on and practice using unfamiliar terms. It is important to tell students to rehearse using new vocabulary; some students don't realize that retention takes effort. Teachers may introduce children as young as first grade to the practice of keeping vocabulary notebooks. These can be organized by alphabetical listings of new words—with one page for each letter of the alphabet—or by clustering words that are similar, such as the way they are in a thesaurus, or by the story and topic from which the words come. When keeping a record of new words, it is good to have students describe the new terms in their own words, not in definitions coming from dictionaries.

**Visualize and Draw Words** To retain words, students need to conceptualize the meanings in their own way. If they can visualize the term and draw an image or association, many students will be able to remember them more easily. Schwartz and Raphael (1985) developed a useful visual guide, the **Concept of Definition Map,** that helps students understand that word learning is ongoing and that definitions are ever expanding. On the Map, students think of the superordinate category to which the word belongs, several defining attributes and some examples, and then they draw the term. These types of maps are very useful, especially for students with word-retrieval issues. See Figure 13.12 for an

Figure 13.12

### Concept of Definition Map

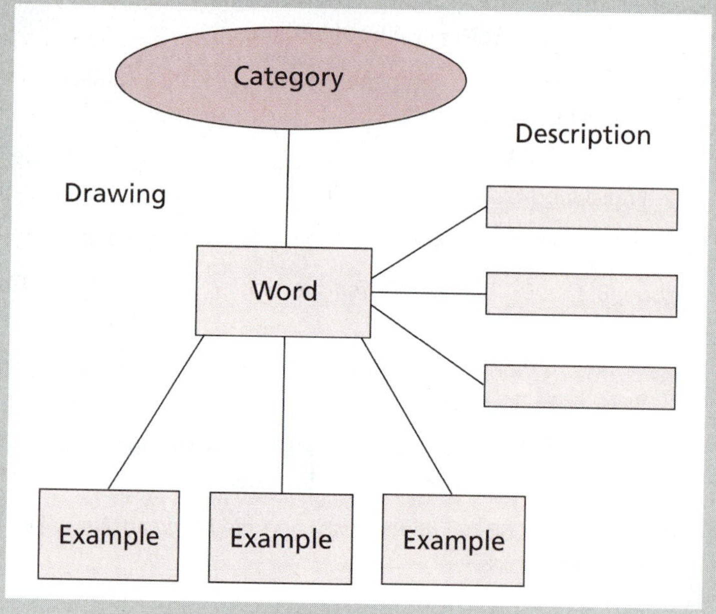

# engaging in Visual Literacy

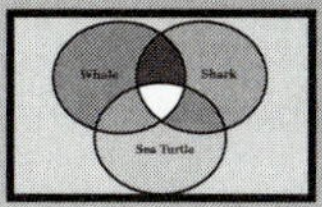

## Vocabulary Visuals

Students often learn new terms by visualizing them in their own ways. Mr. Koburn decided to include having students draw pictures of the terms they were most going to need to remember in the Native American unit. He made a list of the essential terms and asked each student to create a visual image of each one on one side of a four-inch-by-six-inch card. On the other side of the card, the students were to write a sentence using the term in an interesting way. On the first day, he introduced four terms and modeled for his students how he would think about each and then made a drawing for each one on his card (done on a transparency so all students could see). Students were concerned that they weren't artists, but Mr. Koburn was careful to explain that the quality of the art was not his interest; what he wanted was a drawing that each child could remember as a trigger for the academic term. As students got comfortable with this idea, they began to create interesting cards and share their illustrations with one another. As a result of their enthusiasm, Mr. Koburn decided to make a bulletin board where some of the students' illustrations could be visible and would remind the class regularly of the content terms they were learning.

---

RA/NCTE 3

example of a Concept of Definition Map. See the Engaging in Visual Literacy feature for an example of using vocabulary visuals.

Another visual tool for learning is creating a more concrete visual of a new concept or word. Because there are so many content terms students need to learn and because these take some practice to retain, helping students attend to these words regularly in an enjoyable and social activity can be very useful. Ask students to create vocabulary index cards with the word and explanation on one side of the card and a picture on the other that illustrates the word meaning. Then students can test each other on their drawings to see if they have associations with the new terms that are clear enough to trigger the key word in other classmates and significant enough to be memorable. We have watched science classes in which students take the first five minutes of the class period at least

Creating a concrete visual of a new concept or word is another strategy for teaching vocabulary. Because there are so many content terms students need to learn, and these take some practice to retain, helping students attend to these words regularly in an enjoyable and social activity can be very useful.

**Figure 13.13**

## Cloze Deletion Procedure

The invention of the wheel soon led people to new ways to adapt it. By ________________ a groove around the outside of the wheel and ________________ a rope around it, a new type of machine, the ________________ was made. A simple pulley changes the direction of a ________________.

(Words to use: force, cutting, putting, pulley)

two to three times a week to refresh their terms with each other as the teacher attends to procedural issues. Students can also check their own level of knowledge of the key terms weekly and pull the word cards they need to practice on so that they keep those words with them for more regular review.

**Watching for Words** While most of these ideas help students learn individual words, students always need to be on the lookout for interesting language and how it can be understood in the contexts in which it is encountered. Many times, meanings can be derived from the visual and verbal context as we see and hear language. Television ads are particularly engaging ways to identify new words—for example, commercials for absorbent towels provide great visual contexts for understanding what "absorbent" means.

**Using Context Effectively** Teachers who want to help students become attuned to how written context can be helpful often use a format called **cloze** in which either every fifth or tenth word is deleted or some particular words are deleted and a line is substituted where the word belongs. Students then use the surrounding context and their prior knowledge of both syntax and the content to supply a likely word replacement. For example, the same students who are learning science terms by rehearsing individual words can also review their awareness by filling in the missing terms in activities similar to the one found in Figure 13.13.

Sometimes, synonyms to the word are provided; sometimes, prior or following sentences give meaning clues; and sometimes, examples are also available either close to the unknown word or in nearby text or illustrations.

The old admonition, just use the context, has been proven to be not nearly as useful as it might seem. However, context is and can be important as a support for word learning and needs to be taught. Giving students some examples and asking them how the context can help them puts them into the inquisitor role and makes discovery of context supports more memorable. For example, look at the sentences in Figure 13.14 that are written to help students understand simple machines. Teachers can ask students to highlight the places in the text where the italicized words are defined. Then the students can share their highlighted words and see if they could write even better descriptions

**Figure 13.14**

## Science Textbook Definitions

When you turn the doorknob to open a door, you use a *wheel and axle.* A wheel and axle is made of two circular objects of different sizes that turn at the same time. Another simple machine is a *lever,* a bar that rests on a fixed point. A *wedge,* another simple machine, is made of an inclined plane that can move and push another object apart.

and explanations. By going to some science books, students can also check to see how authors have written descriptions of these tools.

## Approach Word Learning Metacognitively

Children come to school with such differences in their word knowledge that it is almost imperative that some differentiation in instruction be provided. One of the easiest ways to accomplish this is for the students themselves to help monitor their vocabulary learning. When teachers explain the importance of being attentive to words and continuing to learn new words through listening, speaking, and writing, children can become their own masters and monitor themselves. There are several ways teachers achieve this student ownership. A simple starting point is for students to get in the habit of *previewing* new materials they are going to read and *identifying* unfamiliar terms. Most informational books highlight key terms in some way—with **bold** type, *italics*, or definitions in marginal notes or boxes. Many have a glossary of terms or give a set of words as part of the introduction of a unit. Students can make a list of the words that are most unfamiliar and then attend to them during their course of learning. If they have vocabulary notebooks or word rings, students can keep track of their expanding understandings of the terms by jotting down new occurrences of the terms and the sentences in which they occur.

**Vocabulary Field Trip** Some teachers begin new units by asking students to take a **Vocabulary Field Trip** (Blachowicz and Obrochta, 2005). The teacher prepares a large picture or poster of the theme of the unit (i.e., a picture of a skeleton for a unit on the human body system or a photo from a pueblo as a way to introduce the Southwest Indian Unit Mr. Koburn planned). Then the students are invited to brainstorm words they think they will encounter as they learn about the topic. The teacher or students write those words and put them on cards around the large picture or poster. As the unit progresses, students continue to add word cards. By having the constant reminder of the unit theme on the visual chart, students are more likely to think of words that are central to their study and post them for each other. The teacher may have some important words that he or she notes that the students have overlooked and can add those to the class poster, too. This can become a visual grounding for the class as they talk about the topic and share activities. Giving students added points or recognition for using the terms in their talk and in writing helps extend this learning. Students can also keep their own list of words they have chosen to learn and monitor their success in learning them.

**Rate Your Knowledge** Another easy starting point is a **Rate Your Knowledge** chart. The teacher can identify key terms from a unit or selection and ask students to rate how well they know each term. Students then can set priorities on the words they need to learn by their level of familiarity at the start of the unit. Later, they can revisit this list and again rate their level of knowledge of the terms. Each student should see some improvement as several new words are added to their "know well" category. See Figure 13.2 on page 468 for an example of this activity.

**Individual Preferences** Students learn in different ways, and teachers can help students identify their own best ways to learn words. For some students, simply being avid readers means they will encounter words frequently and can look for those they have identified. Other students need word cards with reminders of how the words look graphically, then they need to use the words frequently in writing (Marzano, 2005). Teachers who provide time for children to experiment with writing and creating new poetry and graphic displays with the words that are central to the themes or stories being read will help these students. Some need to visualize terms and draw what the words look like (Pressley, Levin and Delaney, 1983). Still others learn best when they can physically create a movement linked to the concepts they are learning. Making personal connections to words by relating them to familiar people, places, and events is also a strong way for many students to learn new terms. Putting new words into rhymes and poetry is another strong associational device.

The essential ingredient is that teachers help students explore how to build their vocabulary and then encourage them to monitor themselves. Keeping a record in a vocabulary notebook of just how many times a word has been used in written form and how many times it has been spoken can develop children's understanding of how to learn new words (Lubliner and Smetana, 2005; Marzano, 2005). This way, they can also take more pride in what they accomplish!

## What Role Does the Dictionary Play?

Many teachers use the **dictionary** as their major tool for new vocabulary learning. However, research clearly indicates that this is not the best way for students to engage in learning words. That old lesson, "Write the list of words and look them up in a dictionary" just doesn't help much. As students look for unfamiliar words, they don't know which definition to select and often choose the first or shortest. Then, when they are asked to write sentences using the terms, they come up with strange meanings. For example, one student found the dictionary definition of *pregnant* and wrote "carrying a child." Her sentence was, "The fireman came down the ladder from the burning building pregnant." She had taken the words "carrying a child" to mean holding a child in his or her arms. This is clearly not quite the meaning this term actually has. Yet, when we don't know words, we can't know how terms are used until we have seen them several times and built an elaborated sense of how each word is used in different contexts. More helpful for learning new terms than the dictionary is a **thesaurus.** This resource presents words with their many connotations and connected terms. See the Exploring Children's Literature feature for books that use interesting language.

IRA/NCTE 1

Students need to learn how to use dictionaries and thesauri and how to find their way in them. In the primary grades, students need to learn the alphabetical organization, by first, second, third letter. They also can be guided to look for the core meaning and to link the terms with the pictures or illustrations that are often included in primary dictionaries. Intermediate students can compare dictionaries and find how different orderings of definitions are selected by the publishers (e.g., Merriam Webster, Scholastic, Thorndike, etc.). Dictionaries help students with pronunciations of unfamiliar terms, clarify the parts of speech and variant forms, and often include word origins. Students also need to be introduced to the many Internet resources for words. Guide students in going to online sources to model how easy it can be to get help with terms that are very new or used in specific contexts. Dictionaries of words in other languages are also readily available. At this level, students can begin to look for the word histories and see how many variations there are for clusters of related terms. Pronunciation keys become part of the tool kit of intermediate readers. Learning how vowels and stressed and unstressed syllables are represented is important. Students

# exploring Children's Literature

## Books That Use Interesting Language

### Grades K to 3

*Beach*—Written and illustrated by Elisha Cooper, published by Orchard (2006).
Women, men, boys, and girls spend a day at the beach enjoying a variety of activities on the sand and in the water.

*Come On, Rain*—Written by Karen Hesse, illustrated by Jon J. Muth, and published by Scholastic Press (1999).
A young girl eagerly awaits a coming rainstorm to bring relief from the oppressive summer heat.

*Hello, Harvest Moon*—Written by Ralph Fletcher, illustrated by Kate Kiesler, and published by Houghton Mifflin (2003).
Poetic prose describes a full autumn moon and the magical effect it has on the earth, plants, animals, and people around it.

*My Life as a Chicken*—Written by Ellen A. Kelley, illustrated by Michael Slack, and published by Harcourt (2007).
After escaping the frying pan, a chicken has an adventure that includes pirates, a typhoon, and a balloon ride before landing happily in a petting zoo.

*Nocturne*—Written by Jane Yolen, illustrated by Anne Hunter, and published by Harcourt Brace (1997).
A parent and child enjoy the nighttime world together before bedtime.

*Pieces: A Year in Poems and Quilts*—Written by Anna Hines and published by Greenwillow (2001).
These poems about the four seasons, as reflected in the natural world, are accompanied by photographs of quilts made by the author.

*Scarecrow*—Written by Cynthia Rylant, illustrated by Lauren Stringer, and published by Harcourt Brace (1998).
Although made of straw and borrowed clothes, a scarecrow appreciates his peaceful, gentle life and the privilege of watching nature at work.

*"Slowly, Slowly, Slowly," said the Sloth*—Written and illustrated by Eric Carle, published by Philomel (2002).
Challenged by the other jungle animals for its seemingly lazy ways, a sloth living in a tree explains the many advantages of his slow and peaceful existence.

### Grades 4 to 8

*All the Places to Love*—Written by Patricia MacLachlan, illustrated by Mike Wimmer, and published by HarperCollins (1994).
A young boy describes the favorite places that he shares with his family on his grandparents' farm and in the nearby countryside.

*An Angel for Solomon Singer*—Written by Cynthia Rylant, illustrated by Peter Catalanotto, and published by Orchard (1992).
A lonely New York City resident finds companionship and good cheer at the Westway Café where dreams come true.

*Arctic Lights, Arctic Nights*—Written by Debbie S. Miller, illustrated by Jon Van Zyle, and published by Walker (2003).
This book describes the unique light phenomena of the Alaskan arctic and the way animals adapt to the temperature and daylight changes each month of the year.

*The Boy Who Loved Words*—Written by Roni Schotter, illustrated by Giselle Potter, and published by Schwartz and Wade (2006).
Selig, who loves words and copies them on pieces of paper that he carries with him, goes on a trip to discover his purpose.

*Days to Celebrate: A Full Year of Poetry, People, Holidays, History, Fascinating Facts, and More*—Written and edited by Lee Bennett Hopkins, illustrated by Stephen Alcorn, and published by HarperCollins (2005).
This book lists events, births of famous people, and holidays, and includes information and poetry about the twelve months of the year.

*James and the Giant Peach*—Written by Roald Dahl, illustrated by Quentin Blake, and published by Knopf (1961).
A young boy escapes from two wicked aunts and embarks on a series of adventures with six giant insects he meets inside a giant peach.

*(continued)*

*One Green Apple*—Written by Eve Bunting, illustrated by Ted Lewin, and published by Houghton Mifflin (2006).

While on a school field trip to an orchard to make cider, a young immigrant named Farah gains self-confidence when the green apple she picks perfectly complements the other students' red apples.

*Stranger in the Woods: A Photographic Fantasy*—Written by Carl R. Sams II and Jean Stoick, published by C. R. Sams II Photography (2000).

Forest animals, awakened by the birds' warning that there is a stranger in the woods, set out to discover whether or not danger is coming. They instead find a wonderful surprise.

may add pronunciation keys to their own vocabulary notebooks as they encounter less frequently used words. Because much of the new vocabulary at the upper elementary levels is not often heard orally, having some pronunciation support can be valuable.

Many publishers now are making audiotapes of stories and content area textbook sections available in Spanish and, less frequently, in other languages so students can make their connections first in the language that is most familiar to them. This practice is strongly supported by research. Students should be encouraged to use their home language as a bridge to English when they need it. Encouraging students to listen to audiotapes also helps. Another way students can gain confidence with the content and expression of ideas is to work with a partner with the same home language so they can activate what they know about a topic first in their home language and then move to English. When students write down the concepts and ideas they already know, they can then locate those same ideas with English more easily.

Teachers have many good electronic and visual resources available. Beginning instructional topics and themes with these more accessible visual and language resources can be very helpful to students. Encouraging students to watch videos, to go online and find connections, and to share their ideas with classmates with the same language will help them gain confidence and independence in their language learning. See the Exploring Diversity feature for more resources to use with language learners. Also, see the Exploring Technology feature for websites that are resources for teaching vocabulary.

## How Can Students' Word Knowledge Be Assessed?

Knowing the size of students' vocabularies can be helpful in determining just how much attention to give vocabulary development and how to focus instruction. When there are second language learners in the classroom, it is even more important to be sure of their depth of English language. Many ELL students have developed proficiency with conversational language, yet they lack the depth of vocabulary they need for the content learning that is the heart of the intermediate and middle grades. It is very difficult to assess general vocabulary knowledge because there are just too many different words in English. The best standardized test of vocabulary knowledge is still the Peabody Picture Vocabulary Test (Dunn & Dunn, 1997). It is administered individually, so it takes time or some support staff to use.

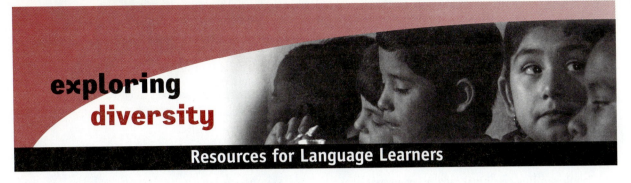

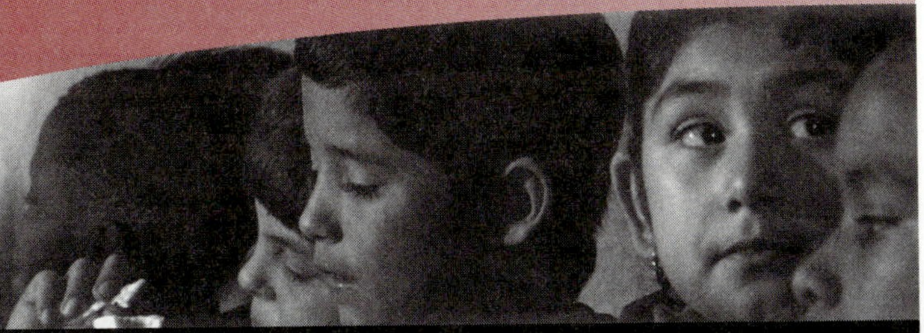

## exploring diversity

### Resources for Language Learners

If you have English Language Learners or students with language delays in your classroom, providing them with tools to help gain better understanding of English is important. There are a range of good dictionaries you will want to make available to students. Basic primary dictionaries can help students who need substantial language support. In addition, make sure you have intermediate bilingual dictionaries available for students who need them. Individual pocket dictionaries or small electronic dictionaries are also very useful to these students. Helping students find the dictionaries that are best for their level of language development is important. With more than one level of dictionary and numerous bilingual dictionaries in the classroom, students can become more critically aware of the variations. Online supports are also improving each year. Some online dictionaries provide oral pronunciations along with written pronunciation and definitions.

Websites we suggest:

**www.englishclub.com**—for language and vocabulary activities, pen pal listings, and teacher resources.

**www.yourdictionary.com**—for dictionaries of terms in most languages.

If you have trouble finding a good dictionary for your English language learners, check these out. The sites also have resources for students on audiotape, videotape, CD-ROM, and in traditional book form as well.

## General Vocabulary

The most available estimates of students' recognition vocabulary are on the standardized reading tests and state assessments. Most reading tests include a section on students' knowledge of words from passages or words presented in isolation. These can be helpful in giving a general range of the levels of word knowledge possessed by the students you have in your class. However, your observations of students' day to day functioning are even more important. Listening to students talk in class discussions and in informal settings can help you identify students who may need specific support in developing or using a broader range of language. Some teachers have also found that asking students to retell a short section of text after reading gives them a clear indication of how much of the text vocabulary they have grasped. If none of the more specific terms are used by the student, then the teacher can probe. Questions that can encourage more specific attention to the language of the text include "How did the author describe _______?" or "What details were provided to help you visualize _______?" If this doesn't work, the teacher can simply ask the student, "What does this word or phrase, _______, mean?"

exploring **technology**

## Websites as Resources for Teaching Vocabulary

**Online Graphical Dictionary (www.visuwords.com)**
With this online graphical dictionary, users enter a word in the search box and view a three-dimensional diagram that pops up with the word's meaning and associations with other words and concepts. Words are color coded according to their parts of speech. Simply place the cursor over a word in the diagram to see the definition or drag words to make connections with other words.

**Creative Word Study Activities (www.literacyconnections.com/WordStudyActivities.html)**
This site hosted by Literacy Connections provides links to online word study exercises and additional resources.

**Word Central (www.wordcentral.com)**
At Word Central sponsored by Merriam-Webster, students can look up a word in the student dictionary or in the rhyming dictionary. Students can also build their own dictionary, use the verse composer to create poems, or play a decoding game.

## Content-Specific Vocabulary

It is easier to assess students' knowledge of content-specific vocabulary (Marzano, 2005). Group activities during which students brainstorm words they know related to topics of study, and individual activities that ask them to list group words or rate levels of knowledge of terms, provide a window on students' instructional needs. A good tool to check students' familiarity with terms is a concept clustering activity. The teacher identifies three to four key concepts and then lists many words that are linked to those concepts. A few words should be known by all the students, so they can have some feeling of success. Other words should be those that will be needed during the unit. Then both before the unit begins and at the completion of the unit the students fill in the concept clusters. If students have learned the expected content, there should be substantial changes in their productions. This form of vocabulary assessment has the advantage that rather than just focusing on individual words, it helps students build associations of terms and key concepts.

revisit the

## classroomchallenge

As James Koburn thought about his options in answering the questions he had posed, he made some instructional decisions.

1. How could he help his students access the important academic vocabulary?
2. How much practice would students need with these terms to retain and use them?
3. How could he ensure that this learning would be enjoyable as well as productive?

As he thought more about the unit and how to help his students with the numerous content-specific words they needed to know, he first decided to be more proactive about introducing these terms and reinforcing them. He decided to look through the textbook and activity sheets and make a list of key terms. He wanted to get a good handle on the difficulty of this unit for his students and provide materials they could access independently and in small groups.

After looking at this list of words, Mr. Koburn was even more convinced of the need to provide more initial support for his students. He also realized that many of these terms might be difficult to pronounce, for instance the words *Anasazi*, *kiva,* and *kichina* are challenging for students to decode. He decided to make an audiotape of two books and found this very useful to the students.

James also decided to involve the students in collecting lists of words they felt they needed to know. He added a vocabulary section in their social studies journals so they could identify and keep an ongoing account of what they learned about the terms. As they found a term used in a new text or heard it in a video or discussion, each student could augment his or her own notes.

Rather than just focus on individual terms, he knew that students would more easily remember terms that were related to each other. One of the activities he created was on a graphic organizer so students would create clusters of words related to the same topic. For example, he realized that there were several terms that described the religious rituals of Native Americans including *kiva*, *ceremony*, *mound builders*, etc. On the graphic organizer, he made sections for rituals, economic system, and home life. He felt relieved as he reflected on what he could do to support his students' attention to the important vocabulary terms they would encounter as they read and enjoyed this unit.

James also decided that with all this work on helping his students handle the vocabulary in the unit, he should have some way of assessing its impact. He thought that the graphic organizer might serve this purpose. He could try assessing the effectiveness of this new attention to vocabulary by having students cluster terms on the graphic organizer both early in the unit and again as a post-assessment task. Then both he and the students could visually check their learning. With all this in place, James felt very ready to begin his unit.

chapter review

## What Do We Know about Vocabulary Development during the Elementary Years?

Children are constantly learning new words. During the early years of life, this learning comes from the stimulation of talk at home; later, teachers and the language of books extend the words children hear and see substantially. Children must read widely to develop vocabularies adequate to the challenges of school learning. English is a particularly difficult language to learn because it contains such a large corpus of words, many times larger than most other languages.

## What Does a Good Instructional Program Include?

Teachers can build strong instructional programs by creating a context in the classroom in which words and language are celebrated and explored. Teachers are important models and stimulators of students' interest in words. By reading aloud and talking about interesting words, teachers build students' attention to words. Then, teachers need to have a clear, explicit instructional program that includes the study of context, structure, and word origins. As students learn words, they can create their own definitions and illustrations and engage in activities that reinforce word learning.

## What Role Does the Dictionary Play?

The dictionary is an important resource for all students. Classrooms should have a variety of dictionaries at different instructional levels (primary, intermediate, and adult) so students can become familiar with them and begin to compare how dictionaries are set up and define words. English language learners and students with language delays also need to have resources appropriate to their language levels.

## How Can Students' Word Knowledge Be Assessed?

Teachers need to assess students' levels of general language development and their readiness for academic vocabulary in the content being taught. Then during each unit students' learning of key content terms and procedural directions also needs to be monitored.

PEARSON

**myeducationlab**™

Where the Classroom Comes to Life

Now go to www.myeducationlab.com to take a Pretest to assess your initial comprehension of chapter content, study chapter content with your individualized Study Plan, take a Posttest to assess your understanding of chapter content, practice your teaching skills with Building Teaching Skills exercises, and build a deeper, more applied understanding of chapter content with Homework and Exercises.

chapter 14

# Creating Classrooms for All Learners

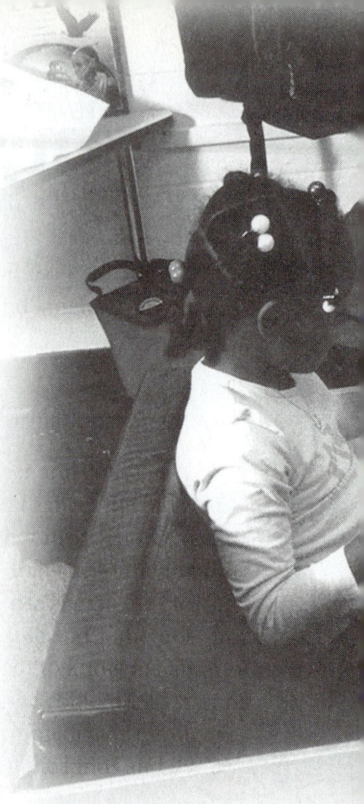

## classroomchallenge

**It was already** the third week of school and Janice Gordon knew things weren't going well in her fifth-grade classroom. She felt she had to keep the students together as a whole group because every time she gave them time for independent work, they wasted it; when she assigned a written response, whether in social studies or language arts, students seemed to procrastinate. None of the writing she wanted them to do was getting done. Her vision of students engaged in self-initiated writing, conferencing with other students, and revising their work seemed far off. In addition, she knew that the school reading program called for her to have her students in guided reading groups so they could have guidance while reading materials at comfortable reading levels. She hasn't even been able to find time to do the initial pre-assessments that would help her make initial groupings.

Janice also knew that if she didn't get a good set of routines going in her classroom soon she could be in trouble for the whole year. As she reflected she asked herself, "What is working? Have I created a workable schedule?" She thought to herself: Well, one part of the day is always good. That's the opening, the gathering of the class. She modeled sharing some news of the day, either from the local community, such as the progress on the park next to the school, or from national and international events. Students seemed interested in hearing about what was happening around them. She also liked the fact that some students were beginning to contribute to this time. Tanya and Pedro both actually brought in news articles—one from the newspaper and another from a news magazine that had an article about the Olympics and the fight for the next location. So, she had established at least one routine and students were getting actively involved. That gave her a little confidence! She also thought about the way students seemed to be

enjoying her reading nook. The bookcases she had used to create a separate corner of the room helped create a nice area, and the rug she had found at the outlet store worked well; kids were actually sitting on the floor and enjoying looking for books and magazines. But, what next?

Janice decided to analyze her planned schedule and see what different routines she expected from the students. Maybe she was expecting too much too soon. She really hadn't modeled how she wanted the children to work together with partners, she just spent one short period showing students how to draft a piece of writing and how to share it with another student. She recalled that she had gotten a book about cooperative learning groups—maybe she needed to explain, model, and give students more practice in how they could work and learn together. It felt like too much to do before she could have students involved in all the curriculum she needed to cover.

## Questions for Reflection

1. What do you notice about Ms. Gordon's classroom that you would like to include in your routines and activities?
2. What could she do to initiate her reading program and find more time for instruction?
3. Which of her concerns do you think would be most important to address right away?

## anticipating this chapter

This chapter addresses issues of organization and ways to develop a smoothly articulated classroom:

- How should I approach setting up my classroom? What work areas are needed?
- What priorities should I establish with limited space and resources?
- How do I set up a writing center?
- How can I develop a classroom library collection?
- What makes a workable schedule of activities?
- What is a good framework for creating integrated units of instruction?
- How can small group and partner routines be established?

# How Should I Approach Setting Up My Classroom? What Work Areas Are Needed?

One of the most exciting realizations for new teachers is that they have the ability to create their own classroom learning environment. Just as setting up your home is a creative and personal decision, so too, creating your own classroom will reflect what you consider important and will make a statement to all who enter your room. Classrooms clearly reflect the priorities and values of the teachers who create them.

**Simulation Homework Exercise**

Go to the Homework and Exercises section in Chapter 14 of MyEducationLab and complete the Star Legacy Module, "Accommodations to the Physical Environment," about how to set up a classroom for students with visual impairment. Complete the activities that follow, and save your work or transmit it to your professor as assigned.

The organization of the classroom needs to facilitate the kinds of learning experiences that you think are optimal for students. We argue in this book that several goals are important: incorporating active learning, using small group and collegial engagements, and providing choices through which students gain control over the processes of learning. If you share this understanding about optimal learning environments, then you will want to create spaces where students can work together, where small groups can convene, and where the whole class can gather as a unit, as well as providing spaces for private and quiet work. Careful planning is needed to ensure that these venues are made available. On the other hand, teachers who maintain a belief that teacher-directed, transmission-type learning is most effective can arrange classrooms where desks all face the teacher-focused instructional space at the front of the room without involving other group spaces. What you hold as commitments about learning should dictate how you arrange your limited space and furniture. At the most basic level, the placement of student desks says a great deal about what your priorities are. If, for example, all desks face the front, then student-to-student engagement is not encouraged. If you group student desks so that two or four are in clusters facing each other, you clearly honor the importance of student-peer collaboration. Talk and team problem-solving are encouraged by the physical arrangement of the desks.

## Curriculum-Centered Classrooms

IRA/NCTE 8

As you think about using your space well, be sure to think about your curriculum and the kinds of learning students will be involved in. Oral language development, writing and reading, science, social studies, mathematics, and arts all require areas where students can work together, access resource materials, and store and display their work. Computer space, books and other print materials, along with resources you will need for your teaching need to be readily available. Displaying print materials so that students will see the attractive books and magazine covers that invite them to read necessitates space. If your science program is built around hands-on materials, you will need more space reserved for these activities. If research and inquiry projects are part of your curriculum, then the resources and opportunities for developing projects are needed.

## Student-Centered Classrooms

In addition, consider the diversity of learning preferences of your students. Some will do better if there are quiet areas free of loud noises and distracting movements. Others need more opportunity for movement and physical involvement. Group activities require spaces where students can work together and yet not distract others engaged in more solitary work. Rug and table space can help them relax and engage. Most students are very visually attuned, so filling walls and bulletin boards with samples of student work, as well as reminders of key strategies and resources, enhances learning. However, some students are easily distracted by "noisy environments," so sensitivity is important in how "alive" the classroom is. You may want to check with the special education teacher if you have students with special needs so that you create places where they can be most comfortable and productive.

Therefore, in planning for your classroom design, there are many dimensions to consider. If you want to facilitate active, engaged learning, consider each of the following components:

- An area in which the whole class can gather—Morning Group, Morning Messages, etc.
- Small group gathering area for guided reading and discussion groups
- Writing table with resources for editing, conferencing, and storing folders
- Computer center and resources for research and printing
- Quiet area for individual work
- Conferencing area
- Science and activity areas
- Learning centers
- Storage area
- Library center with magazines and books
- Arts area
- Reference materials (dictionaries, thesaurus, maps, atlases, etc.)

**BUILDING TEACHING SKILLS: Case Study Exercise**

*Effective Room Arrangement*

Go to the Building Teaching Skills section in Chapter 14 of MyEducationLab and read the case study, "Effective Room Arrangement," which is about a third-grader who is distracted during independent work time. Complete the activities that follow, and save your work or transmit it to your professor as assigned.

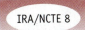

Careful planning is needed in order to create spaces where students can work together, where small groups can convene, and where the whole class can gather as a unit, as well as providing spaces for private and quiet work.

## Create a Graphic Design

With so many considerations, it will take some planning to create the classroom that will serve your needs. If you inherit a small classroom, then added care is needed. Get a piece of graph paper, measure your classroom, and represent it to scale on the paper. Then measure your furniture and cut out pieces of paper that are to the same scale for each piece. Try different arrangements until you find one that provides as much flexibility as possible. This will save your energy from moving pieces until you make a decision about what works best. If you are tight on space, you may want to purchase some moveable storage bins from a local discount store. They can help provide dividers for center areas as well as augment your storage space. Racks for displaying magazines and books can also become good storage places for materials; find some that really conserve space if your room is small. Think of the racks you see in airports and stores that are basically vertical and have multiple sides.

## Special Work Stations or Learning Stations

Centers don't have to take much space. You may need to find a hanging wall chart with pockets and create attractive visual displays with the stations of the center included in pocket holders. You can also put center activities and supplies on moveable carts and store them under counters until needed. Many teachers also find some comfortable lounge chairs and rugs if their space permits. Finally, remember to look in the classrooms of other teachers in your building. Some of them may have worked out clever ways to utilize space effectively. Study the classroom organization that is represented in Figure 14.1. What do you see in this layout that is important for literacy and students' activity?

Setting up a classroom requires thought and planning for the year ahead. What areas do you think will be important to create the vital workshop atmosphere to facilitate instruction and maximize learning of all sorts? We asked Susan Pierce, a reading specialist and assistant principal, to answer this question from her experiences in a vibrant elementary school. She responded:

> We know that learning takes place in a social context and areas need to be designated for students to hold book groups, have discussions about science and social studies topics, plan for collaborative projects, and come together for class meetings. If you are using a center approach to your community, areas for a listening post, small content focus areas, a writing center, and other workstations need to be designated. Of course, you'll need an area where you'll bring together small groups of students for guided reading instruction each day. Unlike the straight, solitary rows of desks of the past, the student's own desks or tables need to be situated in a way that encourages good talk and values each person's work space. Bookcases and tables need to be placed so that students have access to the resources and materials that support their learning. These will also provide the barriers to create the nooks and work areas for

Figure 14.1

## Room Arrangement

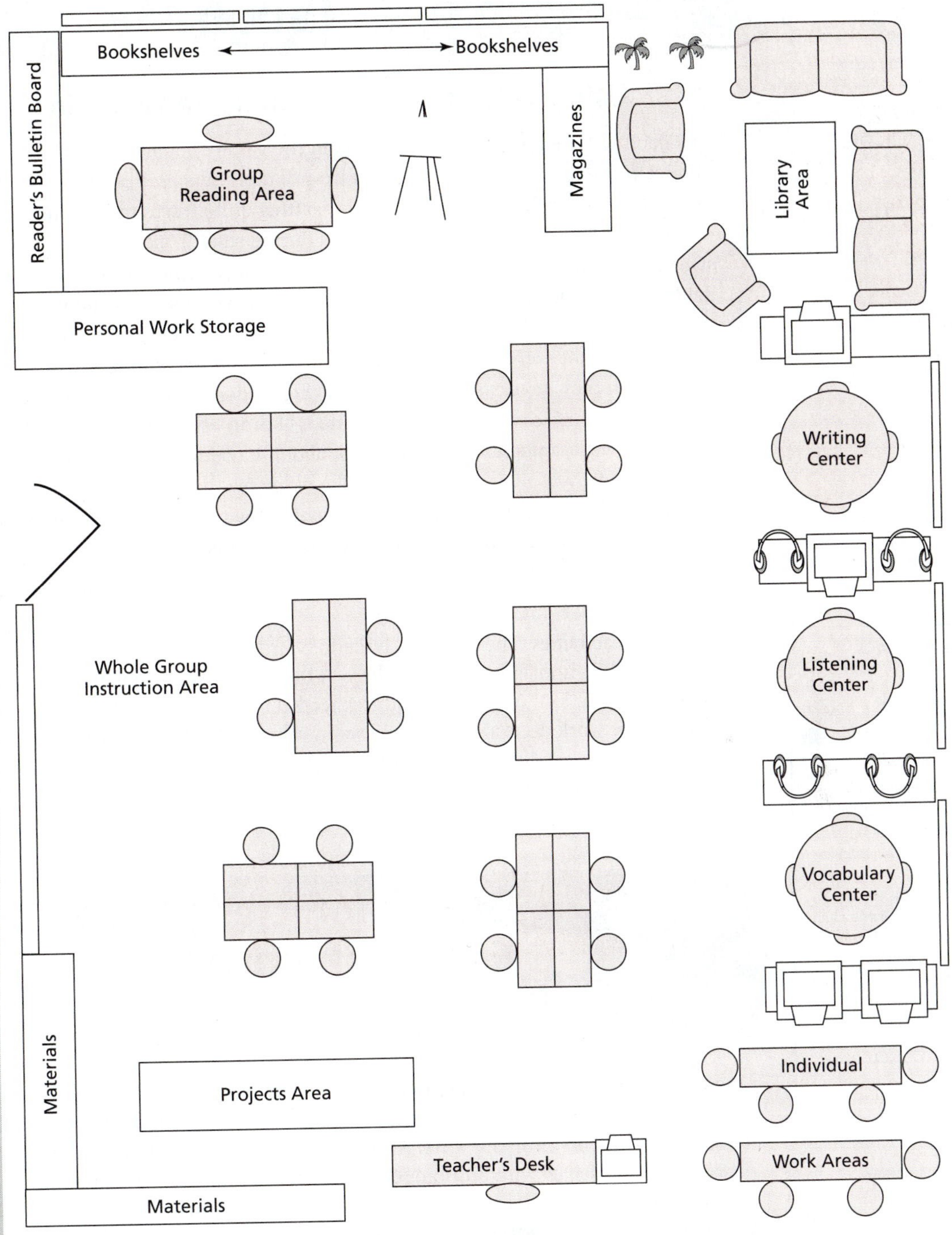

Bookshelves
Bookshelves
Reader's Bulletin Board
Group Reading Area
Magazines
Library Area
Personal Work Storage
Writing Center
Whole Group Instruction Area
Listening Center
Vocabulary Center
Materials
Projects Area
Individual
Teacher's Desk
Work Areas
Materials

## engaging in Oral language

### Using Video to Improve Group Participation

One good way to help students understand the value of focusing on oral communication skills is to let them see a mirror of their own group behavior. One middle-school teacher we work with was getting quite frustrated because her students talked so loudly and kept getting up during small book club sessions. We suggested the students videotape themselves during a typical session. The students then reviewed the tape and noted their positive behaviors and what they thought they could improve. As they looked at the video clip, they were amazed that they did not seem to show good listening skills or responses to one another. Some noted they never made eye contact. One student who seemed to fall out of his chair regularly saw this and commented, "I didn't think I looked like that. Wow!" He was immediately able to think about his body, and he adopted a more appropriate way of sitting at the table. The video feedback by the group was instrumental in improving their behavior. Later, the group made another video and was quite pleased with their improvement, as was the teacher.

**Classroom Artifact Homework Exercise**

*Self-Portrait*

Go to the Homework and Exercises section of Chapter 14 of MyEducationLab and view the artifact, "Self-Portrait," which is an example of how one child represented himself in a drawing. Complete the activities that follow, and save your work or transmit it to your professor as assigned.

each day's activities. The walls and bulletin boards set the tone as they chronicle and celebrate the important work done here. A thoughtful design enhances the possibilities for instruction, student-led and teacher-led interaction, and helps students realize that the work done at school is relevant, valued, and shared. See the Engaging in Oral Language feature for an example of using videotaped discussions to help students focus on their small group participation skills.

## What Priorities Should I Establish with Limited Space and Resources?

One of the most important statements classrooms make is the priority on students. Find ways to highlight students, their work, and your ongoing curriculum foci. You can honor your students in many ways. At the beginning of the year, have students create pictures of themselves with autobiographical sketches. Or take pictures with a digital camera and have students either write about themselves or interview each other and create poems or descriptions of each other. Some teachers have students create body-size drawings of themselves using butcher paper. These large forms are then filled with illustrations or words and take on personal identities. Others help students introduce themselves to others by sharing "All about Me Bags"—small brown paper bags that students fill with five to six artifacts that tell something about themselves. For example, students may bring a family photo, a favorite book, a magazine from their subscription, a DVD with favorite music, a baseball or hockey puck, and other pieces that help them introduce themselves to the class. See the Engaging in Assessment feature for an example of how to conduct an interest inventory.

## Celebrate Children's Work

During the year, it is important to highlight student work. The walls and bulletin boards should be celebrations of what the students accomplish. Be sure to spotlight

### engaging in Assessment

#### Interest Inventories

One of the most important initial assessments you need to complete is finding out what interests your students have and how you can create a classroom that reflects their interests with a library that provides inviting materials for them. There are many commercially available Interest Inventories. However, it is easy to create your own inventory that reflects your way of introducing reading to your students. Consider creating the inventory as a letter explaining to students that you want to ensure that the classroom has activities and materials they are interested in and want to share. You may include questions such as:

- What is the best thing about you?
- What do you most like to do?
- What is the best book you read last year?
- What sports are you interested in now?
- What activities do you like to do after school and in the summer?
- Do you have a magazine or author you choose regularly?
- What would you most like to learn this year?
- Do you have any things that bother you or that cause you to be afraid?
- What else would you like me to know about you?

To make this a more focused contemporary activity, ask your new students about their reading interests and create a computer-based classroom library. Explain to the class that you are going to let them take part in virtual book selection from an online bookstore. Each student can put books in their own book cart. You create a screen on the computer with the pictures of several book covers. Show these covers to the students and ask students to select the three to five they would most like to add to their personal "shopping cart." Then, ask them to explain why they have chosen those books. Be sure to have an array of selections available, including realistic fiction, biography, sports, animal and nature books, fantasy, and others.

These initial assessments of students' interests help you not only see which books are chosen but also to read the students' explanations of why they made the choices they did. The next step is to check the books available in the classroom library and the reading level of these books and resources. If any are missing, you can then plan your next steps to purchase or borrow the books you need to get started. Let the students know what is needed, and perhaps they can join in the effort to build the collection.

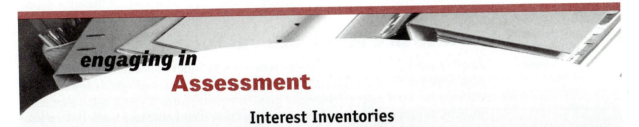

books, poems, and plays written by children. Some school districts have used the suggestion (Au, 2002) of posting **"I Can" statements** (Au, 2002) indicating what students are learning. For example, a fourth-grade class posted the following on sentence strips by the door to the classroom, "I can write a clear mathematical sentence." "I can identify the main idea in informational articles," "I can draw a picture of new vocabulary terms" and "I can introduce myself to adult visitors."

There are many ways to focus the room on students and their accomplishments. Make a list of what you see as you observe in schools. This list may get you thinking of how to honor the students you will have and create a visible celebration of student learning. Remember, too, that when your classroom includes student-written books and magazines in the library collection, you make a strong statement about the value of student authors.

IRA/NCTE 9

## Establish a Multicultural Focus

Another way to make your classroom personal is to honor the cultural backgrounds of your students. If you have some first-generation immigrants, highlight their homelands and cultures. Have maps of the world pinpointing the journeys that families have taken to arrive in your community. Include some texts in their home languages. If the school doesn't have any, ask the parents or community volunteers to help you acquire a few so that all students can learn about the other languages and some of the major authors. Find photographs of some special natural features of the other homelands and make all the children feel comfortable knowing more about each other.

## Create a Reading Corner

Making the importance of literacy clear is also important. An attractive **Reading Corner** with inviting displays of books and magazines can be a center for students when they enter the room each day. Classrooms with inviting print materials encourage children's inquiry and interest in literacy. The nature of the materials also tells students and visitors what you consider important. Current magazines, newspapers, and books that children are recommending displayed clearly and made easily accessible stimulate interests in learning.

Inviting students to select books and magazines of their choice is important. Helping them use the time for independent reading productively is also important. Some students can waste these valuable opportunities when there aren't structures in place that help them stay focused. Many teachers create student **reading logs** or recordkeeping folders of their reading. By having columns on the log for dates, books completed and pages read, and comments on special ideas and connections coming from the text reading, children are more likely to be responsible for their reading activity. See Figure 14.2 for an example of a student reading log.

See the Exploring Technology feature for websites that will help you set up your classroom library and establish a classroom environment that nurtures literacy.

## Create a Writing Center

The **writing center** is another student gathering place. Keeping a collection of different kinds of pens and markers, paper of many colors and types, and sticky notes invites students to explore not only their ideas but how they are presented. Having good organizational systems in place is also important. File folders in a plastic container next to the center can help students know where to keep their drafts and record pieces they are working on. Bulletin board space above can be used to display good writing and invite

**Figure 14.2**

### Student Reading Log

Reading Log

Name ______________________ Week ______________

| Date | Pages read | Book title | Comments |
|---|---|---|---|
| | | | |
| | | | |
| | | | |

students to read each others' creations. Some children like to copy special quotations and poetry for sharing, too. An interactive area brings writing to life in a shared way.

## Teacher as a Model Reader

As you make different kinds of printed materials available, remember, too, to make *your* personal reading visible in the classroom. Some children don't think of adults as readers; they may not see their own parents reading, especially if it happens after they are asleep. Keep two to three magazines and books that you are reading in a place that students will notice. Some time each day, read a bit to them from your adult reading (newspapers, magazines, poetry collection, literary book, etc.) so they build an under-

**exploring technology**

### Organizing for Instruction

**Organizing the Classroom Library (www.choiceliteracy.com/public/124.cfm)**
Sponsored by Choice Literacy, this article is written in dialogue format between two educators, Aimee Buckner and Franki Sibberson. This insightful conversation brings awareness to the important decisions teachers must make about how to arrange classroom libraries in a way that allows them to match books to their students' needs.

**Creating a Literate Community (www.learner.org/channel/workshops/readingk2/session1/index.html)**
The Annenberg Foundation provides several programs for teacher professional development. In this video session, Dr. Jeanne R. Paratore presents three research-based principles for creating an effective literacy environment—accessible materials, purposeful room and wall displays of print materials, and classroom routines that promote reading and writing.

standing of the range of materials that adults read and begin to appreciate the variety of information and ideas contained within them.

Then, invite students to enjoy the materials you have available in the classroom for their reading. Some teachers display books with their jackets showing, so students get the benefit of the great artwork that introduces the books. Magazine racks help students locate journals that match their interests and entice them to expand their curiosity. Marking books by reading difficulty and keeping books in easily accessible bins saves significant time when it is time for independent reading.

## How Do I Set Up a Writing Center?

Students need a space where they can write without interruption. They also need an area where they can conference with you, the teacher, and with partners. In the writing area, they need access to a good dictionary and thesaurus. Many teachers make writing inviting by providing options to students with a variety of kinds of writing resources. Include different utensils: pens, markers, colored pencils, and crayons. Even an old typewriter is enticing to young writers. Stock paper of all sorts for all types of writers: full blank sheets, full lined sheets, half and half for pages with writing and illustrations, and even large-format paper for young students. A box of colored construction scraps for collage pages and boxes of water color paints for students who get ideas for writing by putting their picture ideas onto paper. Once you start collecting, you'll be surprised by how many things you'll have that will find their way into a young writer's works.

If you have computers in your room that students can use for word processing they should be located here, too. They can either draft ideas on paper or keep all their work in computer folders. Students often respond to having choices that stimulate their creativity as they draft and create final versions of their pieces. It is helpful to have folders or bins for each student so they can keep copies of their works-in-process in the writing center. It can help them stay organized and not lose their texts.

### Organizing for Student Writing

Students need a place in the writing center to keep their writing notebooks, too. Some teachers have students create their own writing notebooks early in the year. If each student has a folder, it is important to also have a bin or file drawer that is easily accessible. Loose papers can easily be lost if there isn't a good location for them to be stored and retrieved regularly. An open notebook is useful if you want students to collect examples of good writing they want to keep. Some teachers encourage students to copy short pieces of well-written prose or good poems so they can have them as models in their own writing notebooks. If students like to sketch or write at home, then a folder that is expandable is a real asset. An alternative to open notebooks is for students to have their own spiral notebooks where they keep drafts of all they are working on. This doesn't permit the open expansion of types of materials to keep in the notebook, but is easier for management purposes. If students have one notebook for drafts and their collection of writing ideas, then the final forms of their pieces can be either done on the computer or in a class book.

## Show Student Work

Highlighting and celebrating the completed texts that students create is also important. One area of the wall can be for display of student work. Some of their writing can be made more appealing by creating covers or borders and posting these. Teachers who highlight "authors and poets of the week" help students stay focused on at least one audience for their work—their classmates. In addition, Don Graves has suggested (and many teachers have followed up on his idea) that that there be an Author's Chair in the room where children can sit when they share their pieces of writing. This special location makes clear the value of students as authors and the importance of having an audience for writing. A rocking chair, stool, or some chair that is distinct creates a special focus.

If you don't want your writing center to become a dusty place where no one has been in a while, think carefully about how you build it into the fabric of what your class is doing with writing in your day-to-day schedule.

## Getting Started with Your Writing Center

IRA/NCTE 5

Young writers need first to be filled with possibilities. If they are lacking experience with literature and with the richness of picture books, they won't have much to put on their own pages. Keep books that stimulate writing and that have clear patterns in your writing center. Reading to your students daily is necessary on many levels.

- Hearing about and seeing images in picture books for young and older readers help students build a schema for times and places that might otherwise be outside of their experiences.
- Reading just beyond the students' own reading levels gives them an auditory model of how more sophisticated text sounds, preparing them to try it out themselves. Asking students what phrases and words they hear that they really like adds to the level of listening that students do; these may also be written down in the students' own writing journals and savored for later use or as models.
- The value of literary vocabulary in context has been well documented in research as critical to building word acquisition. Attention to word use and vivid language is always helpful to budding writers. Keeping special words in their own journals helps children build their awareness of the varieties of ways ideas and images can be expressed.

A well-planned year of author/illustrator studies, read-alouds, and genre study will launch students as they try on the roles themselves. Many primary level teachers use author studies as a way of expanding children's interest in books and authors. For example, Eric Carle provides a rich introduction into both great text and the relationship between illustrations and writing. In upper grades, study of authors such as Katherine Paterson and Christopher Paul Curtis build bridges between authors and young readers.

## Instruction and Ownership

Time and reason to use the writing process are critical to make sure that your writer's center becomes a busy place. It is critical to block out portions of the week for writing and sharing as you build on the students' accomplishments with their own pieces.

Student-teacher conferences help you to keep track of each student's ongoing progress and differentiate instruction as needed. Student-student writer's conferences help authors at all stages of development take on the roles of audience and editor. As the year continues, you will find that writing becomes an integrated part of all you do.

## Writing across the Curriculum

The thread of students' writing will run throughout the curriculum. Beyond the personal writing of journals and fictional stories, students will be writing to learn by keeping science logs, math journals, and trying their hand at nonfiction with research reports. It has been said that we learn the most if we "read like an author, and write like a reader." In the classroom, reading and writing are mutually supportive and should be taught together so that students see the integrative aspects of both disciplines.

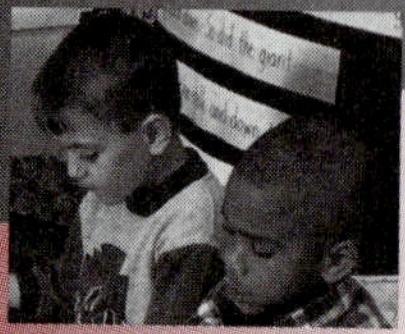

# How Can I Develop a Classroom Library Collection?

IRA/NCTE 1

Before students arrive in the fall, check to see what classroom collection is available; if there is no classroom book collection, check with the school administration immediately. Each classroom needs a good collection of books, magazines, and electronic resources that are at the students' interest and reading levels. Some library experts suggest that there should be five to eight books for each student in your class. If you don't have a good number of books, or if the books seem out of date and not immediately appealing to students, then it is important to start building a collection right away. Many times, the school librarian, reading specialist, or curriculum coordinator will help you. You may also want to check to see if the school's parent organization has small grants available to teachers through which you could create a good collection.

Students' interests should be central in determining what books and magazines to include. Remember that boys' interests are quite different from girls in reading. Comics and graphic novels are very appealing to many boys and often are an entry point in developing their self-selected reading habit. Plays and reader's theater collections can stimulate students' desire to produce their own renditions of dramatic pieces. Poetry is also a good introduction to oral presentation as well as a delightful form of literature.

## Match Books to Students

If you have books in the classroom, check through them to be sure that they are appropriate for the students' reading levels and interests. At every grade level, there are some students who will need easier books, the majority who will read at the grade level, and some who will savor more challenging books two to three grade levels beyond their age placement. Therefore, your collection needs materials at a variety of reading levels as well as interest levels. Books and magazines should also be fresh and inviting so children will be attracted to them. Including the new graphic novels and Japanese manga is also important because they represent what many children are reading outside of school. Collections filled with overused and old books need to be weeded and refreshed. You can do some of this before the year begins with your own knowledge or with the help of the librarian.

**Readability and Book Leveling System** Using a **book leveling system** is a valuable resource in organizing your classroom reading collection (Fountas and Pinnell, 2005). You want to ensure that books at students' instructional and independent reading levels are available. **Readability** checks can help. This enables you to mark books by level and to double check that you have ample books ready for all of your students. If you don't have enough at some reading levels and content themes in your room, check with the library and see if you can check out rotating sets of books. Some communities have public libraries that also permit teachers to check out sets of books for particular lengths of time. If your school library is limited, make friends with the librarians at your local public library. You may find help in selecting books and determining the possibility of checking out substantial numbers of good books for your classroom.

**Organize Books for Student Use** As you level the books, arrange some in plastic tubs so that students don't have to hunt through many books to find ones they can read during independent reading time. At the primary level this is particularly important. Students often seem to have difficulty finding the books they want to read; if they are already on their desks, they can focus then on reading, not on searching. It is also good to have sets of books on the various content topics you will be studying. Students need to read from a variety of sources to enhance their understanding of social studies, science, and mathematics concepts and to build their understanding of how informational content is written. As you initiate a new topic, arrange books in tubs so students can locate them easily. Marking them as "easy," "just right," and "challenging" can help guide students to appropriate starting places.

**Teach Students to Find the "Just Right" Books** Students need to learn for themselves how to select appropriate books. Using the idea of Goldilocks seeking the right porridge may be a fun connection for young children. First, Goldilocks tasted a bowl that was too hot, then one that was too cold, before she finally found the one that was just right. In selecting books to read, we need to do the same—look until we find a "just right" book. As children move into the second grade and beyond, one way to help them do this is to use the "Thumbs down" or "Five Finger Test." Model for students reading a page of text (usually ninety to one hundred words). Explain that you are going to read the page. Each time you come to an unfamiliar word or one that causes you to stumble and slow down, you are going to put a finger down. If you put all five fingers down, then you have probably found a book that is too hard. (This simple test is based on the guide for instructional reading level being when students can read words with 95 percent oral accuracy or at about 90 percent in the primary grades.)

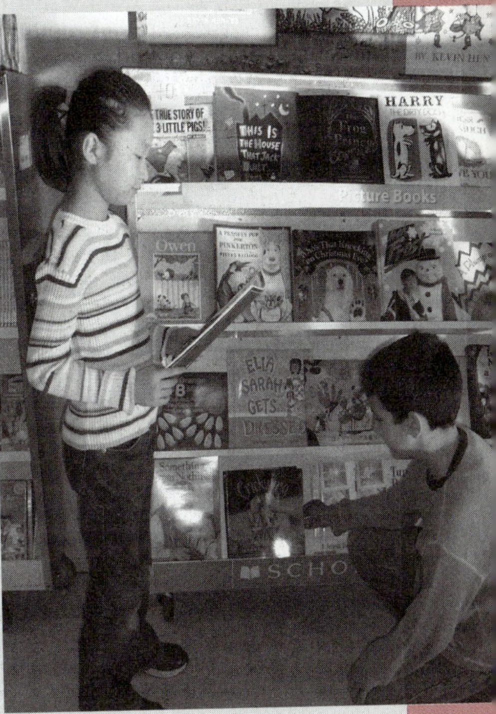


Every classroom needs a good collection of books, magazines, and electronic resources that are at students' interest and reading levels.

## Join Book Clubs

As you will want to keep adding to your classroom collection, check to see if there is a book club that teachers subscribe to. With these clubs, students can order their own books and you can build a collection from the bonus books that accrue. You can also suggest to parents that good birthday gifts are books that are donated to the classroom library. If you have book plates available, the books can be inscribed as gifts from the children and can become a legacy for subsequent classes.

## Books for Instructional Groups

In addition, you will want some sets of books that can be used in guided reading groups and perhaps one or two class sets of novels or informational books that will be central to units of instruction. As you develop topical and author-based units, you may want to create some text sets, collections of books on a single topic or by a single author, that are accessible to the full range of reading levels of your students. For instance, if you know that you will be studying the life cycle in a science-based unit, you can begin early in the year to collect books on the life cycle of butterflies and frogs. Some should be easy and clearly illustrated short books that your weakest readers can access; others should be more challenging and provide different text structures and features. A few may be ones that you select for their content but that you will use for read-alouds. For example, there is a beautiful book, *The Butterfly Alphabet* by Kjell Sandved that contains photographs showing each letter of the alphabet created from the scales on butterfly wings with accompanying poetry. It is both visually stunning and very informative, making it a great read-aloud for everyone in a class to enjoy.

## Audiotaped Books

Books students can listen to are also important. An audiobook collection is a good way to invite students into reading and becoming interested in authors and topics that may at first be beyond their reading levels. So many books are now available in audio format that you will want to include them in your classroom collection. Some schools still use the books on tape and have headphones sets for children. One of these makes a good listening center for a classroom. Audiobooks are good tools for struggling readers and second language learners, too. English language learners can be introduced to literate English by listening to books at their own levels. They can then be asked to read sections after listening several times. With experience hearing good readers, children can also develop their own taped books and make them available to other students who can benefit from hearing books read orally. At the upper grades students can help with programs for students who are visually impaired by recording books needed in the school curriculum.

## Resources for Teachers

There are several resources you can use to locate good books and audio materials for your students' ages, reading levels, and interests. If you have taken a college course in children's literature, use the textbook as a reference. Magazines such as the *School Library Journal, Book Links, Language Arts,* and the October issues of the *Reading Teacher* have regular reviews of good books and magazines for students. Both the school librarians and the public librarians are full of ideas and knowledge you can tap. Insure that getting an interesting and inviting collection of books and magazines for your classroom is one of your top priorities. We now have the international book collection available online, too. Make use of other online resources, too. They can expand your collection and your connection with authors and background materials significantly. See the Exploring Children's Literature feature for books that focus on creating communities.

**Video Homework Exercise**

*Collaborative Grouping*

Go to the Homework and Exercises section of Chapter 14 of MyEducationLab and view the video, "Collaborative Grouping," about a teacher who uses cooperative learning groups in his classroom. Complete the activities that follow, and save your work or transmit it to your professor as assigned.

## Putting Ideas into Action

Plan carefully for what you need to equip your room so you can facilitate all you want to accomplish. Make it easy for students to work in varied settings and to have access to the materials they need. Remember to look in other classrooms to get

## exploring Children's Literature

### Books for Creating Community, Making Friends, and Accepting Others

#### Grades K to 3

*Babymouse: Queen of the World!*—Written by Jennifer Holm and published by Random House (2005).

An imaginative mouse dreams of being queen of the world, but will settle for an invitation to the most popular girl's slumber party (graphic novel format).

*Ella Sarah Gets Dressed*—Written by Margaret Chodos-Irvine and published by Harcourt (2003).

Despite the advice of others in her family, Ella Sarah persists in wearing the striking and unusual outfit of her own choosing.

*Ira Sleeps Over*—Written and illustrated by Bernard Waber, published by Houghton Mifflin (1972).

A little boy is excited at the prospect of spending the night at his friend's house, but he worries how he will get along without his teddy bear.

*My Best Friend*—Written by Mary Ann Rodman, illustrated by E. B. Lewis, and published by Viking (2005).

Six-year-old Lily has a best friend all picked out for play group day, but unfortunately, the differences between first-graders and second-graders are sometimes very large.

*My Friend Rabbit*—Written and illustrated by Eric Rohmann, published by Roaring Brook (2002).

Something always seems to go wrong when Rabbit is around, but Mouse lets him play with his toy plane anyway because he is his good friend.

*Officer Buckle and Gloria*—Written and illustrated by Peggy Rathmann, published by Putnam (1995).

The children at Napville Elementary School always ignore Officer Buckle's safety tips, until a police dog named Gloria accompanies him when he gives his safety speeches.

*Pinduli*—Written and illustrated by Janell Cannon, published by Harcourt (2004).

Pinduli, a young striped hyena, is hurt by the unkind words of Dog, Lion, and Zebra, but her clever trick in return promotes her clan's survival and spreads harmony throughout the savannah (includes notes at the end of the book about hyenas and other animals of the African savannah).

*A Splendid Friend, Indeed*—Written and illustrated by Suzanne Bloom, published by Boyds Mills (2005).

When a studious polar bear meets an inquisitive goose, they learn to be friends.

#### Grades 4 to 8

*Apple Pie Fourth of July*—Written by Janet Wong, illustrated by Margaret Chodos-Irvine, and published by Harcourt (2002).

A Chinese American child fears that the food her parents are preparing to sell on the Fourth of July will not be eaten.

*Danitra Brown, Class Clown*—Written by Nikki Grimes, illustrated by E. B. Lewis, and published by HarperCollins (2005).

In this story told in a series of rhyming poems, Zuri faces her fears about starting a new school year with the help of free-spirited best friend, Danitra.

*Hot Day on Abbott Avenue*—Written by Karen English, illustrated by Javaka Steptoe, and published by Houghton Mifflin (2004).

After having a fight, two friends spend the day ignoring each other, until the lure of a game of jump rope helps them to forget about being mad.

*The Hundred Dresses*—Written by Eleanor Estes, illustrated by Louis Slobodkin, and published by Harcourt (1944).

Wanda Petronski, a little Polish girl in an American school, is laughed at because she always wears a faded blue dress, until her classmates learn a lesson.

*Miz Berlin Walks*—Written by Jane Yolen, illustrated by Floyd Cooper, and published by Philomel (1997).

Mary Louise gradually gets to know and love her elderly neighbor lady who tells wonderful stories as she walks around the block of her Virginia home.

*The Other Side*—Written by Jacqueline Woodson, illustrated by E. B. Lewis, and published by Putnam (2001).

Two girls, one white and one black, gradually get to know each other as they sit on the fence that divides their town.

*Weslandia*—Written by Paul Fleischman, illustrated by Kevin Hawkes, and published by Candlewick (1999).

Wesley's garden produces a crop of huge, strange plants that provide him with clothing, shelter, food, and drink, thus helping him to create his own civilization and to change his life.

IRA/NCTE 7

ideas. Then use the checklist shown in Figure 14.3 as another way to help you cover all the possibilities

See the Engaging in Visual Literacy feature for information on incorporating artifacts into your lessons.



**Figure 14.3**

## Classroom Checklist

### Checklist for Evaluating My Classroom Environment

**Time**—I have enough of it and use it well (minimum time, not including content reading):

________ K–3: I allocate 120 minutes.

________ 4–8: I allocate 90 minutes.

________ My students are engaged (involved in reading, writing, project work, instruction).

**Instructional organization** reflects the basic, research-established avenues to reading:

________ I do guided reading and instruction to develop comprehension and strategies (two to four per week) on developmentally appropriate material.

________ Students do independent reading practice (sustained silent reading, book clubs, lit. circles) in my class every day on independent-level material and are involved in response activities.

________ Students write every day, using a process model and doing appropriate editing (grammar, usage, mechanics).

________ I teach word study (phonics, spelling, vocabulary) three to five times per week.
(Note that half of the instructional time involves students in reading, both guided and independent.)

**Materials** are thoughtfully chosen for motivational and instructional value:

________ I have materials at students' developmental (instructional) levels to use for guided reading.

________ I have a wide range of independent-level materials (above and below grade level).

________ I use fiction and informational materials along with poetry, drama, newspapers, other print, references, electronic resources.

________ We have a classroom library that contains the material above, as well as magazines, guides, almanacs, and other motivating materials.

________ Materials are attractively displayed and available for students' independent use.

**Effective instruction and research-based practices** are used in my classroom:

________ I know the developmental level of each student in my class through quick, curriculum-based assessment.

________ I guide reading on an appropriate developmental level and jump-start students who need more help.

________ My main goal is helping students develop strategies that will make them independent readers.

________ I make the strategies and skills clear and explicit by combining discovery, modeling, and clear instruction, so students learn the "secrets" and the systems of language.

________ I motivate, guide, instruct, and facilitate during all instructional time.

________ I read aloud and/or discuss my own reading every day.

________ I believe I am responsible for helping each student in my class become a better reader.

*Source:* Blachowicz and Ogle, 2008. Reprinted with permission.

# engaging in Visual Literacy

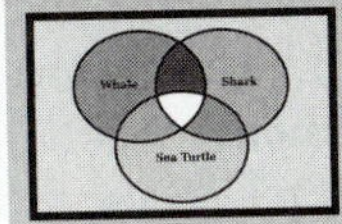

## Artifact Collections

Classroom collections that parallel your curriculum will be much more appealing to students when you include highly visual resources along with books and magazines. Posters, photographs, newspapers, maps, music, videotapes or DVDs, and CD-ROM resources related to your themes can invite students into explorations of topics and historical eras. Think, for example, of introducing the study of early Native Americans (a fifth-grade unit) with a set of pictures and a video clip. Having these resources collected in a box near the books you are using may provide a visual context that some students will need to make their reading come alive. Several museums will supply a collection of artifacts from Native Americans to complement this unit—these may include arrowheads, grinding stones, samples of the seeds and nuts early people survived on, and others. Display these beside the books you have available for students to read. Show a few video clips before having students actually read the texts because the context is so unfamiliar to most students in the intermediate grades. Helping students locate the early American groups on a map of North America can also help them orient their learning spatially and make connections to where they live. A time line illustrating the span of time from early American life until now can also help students build a better understanding of history.

For each theme or topic you want to highlight during the year, build a resource box of visual artifacts and resources. Encourage students to add to this collection. They may have some family history items they can give or loan to the class—photographs, letters, postcards, old books, clothing, political buttons and fliers, and music that relate to the curriculum or books your students will enjoy. Tangible, visual artifacts and items add life to literacy.

# What Makes a Workable Schedule of Activities?

Trying to schedule all the language arts creates its own challenge. You need to think carefully about what you know about how children learn. Especially keep in mind that the research on isolated skills teaching of spelling and grammar regularly shows that teaching skills in isolation does not produce long-term learning. Therefore, the more you can provide meaningful contexts for oral and written language development, the more likely it is that students will develop the skills they will need. Many teachers use the structure of large integrated units of instruction as the framework in which they then embed projects and assignments where they can guide students' skill development. Writing and spelling skills can be taught effectively when students are involved in constructing science journals and reports (McKee and Ogle, 2005); oral language skills needed in interviewing and then presenting information can be part of units in social studies (Ogle, Klemp, and McBride, 2007; Pennsylvania State Department of Education Local Community Project, 2000). Author and thematic studies provide good contexts for students to learn discussion skills and oral presentation; teachers often build in focused lessons on visual imagery and making personal connections as students read varied literary works. Poetry reading and reader's theater productions can be linked to any unit.

## Integrated Units

Many times, grade-level teams of teachers work together in creating integrated units, so it may not be necessary for you to start from scratch in planning your teaching. However, if that is not the case, an examination of the local standards and benchmarks in social studies, science, and language arts (genres of literature and particular works) will provide a good jumping off place. Some teachers choose to create integrated units by rotating the focus content area: the fall unit links literature with all the language arts, a winter unit is based in social studies, and a spring unit derives from science. All of these contents benefit from students learning to locate information, use visual sources, make notes and write for audiences, spell and use vocabulary appropriately, and communicate ideas and questions during the learning cycle (and afterward, in sharing their accomplishments).

Including all the priorities within the school calendar is challenging. One reviewer of the state and national standards concluded that it would take twice as much time to teach all the standards as is available during the school year (Marzano, 2005). Therefore, it is no wonder that many teachers feel overwhelmed at times. The demands keep growing, and little is removed from the curriculum. Some states and districts even mandate a particular number of minutes of instruction for particular subjects. Therefore, careful planning for how to use your time is essential. Most teachers think in weekly chunks and use the planning calendars provided by their districts. However, they often include larger time frames when doing inquiry or thematic units. Combining language with content standards in the lessons and units you teach is a powerful way to help ensure that you include all you can within your teaching cycle while you help students understand the importance of the language skills you are teaching.

## Weekly Planning

Within the weekly cycle, many teachers choose to either organize their instruction by content areas using standard textbooks and assessments (language arts, reading, science, etc.) or by integrated thematic units. Some combine the content areas of science and social studies into integrated units but teach mathematics and language arts/reading separately. Because many districts mandate a certain number of minutes of reading/language arts daily, this time is often the first morning time period blocked as the basic unit on the weekly calendar. Most districts have learned that to provide the full range of language arts instruction at least one and one-half to two hours are needed for the literacy block. Within that block, special time needs to be appropriated for the major activities: Whole group reading, guided reading, independent reading, writing and word study. At the primary level, time for fluency practice may also be added. Then you can also weave in times for more individualized help and meeting with special groups later as students work in other content. At all levels, some of your literacy instruction should be combined with science, math, and social studies so that you can develop your students' strategies in reading and using informational texts and in attending to content-specific academic vocabulary.

Some teachers and schools have found breaking the language arts/reading time into **four blocks** to be helpful. Cunningham, Hall, and Defee (1998) and Shanahan (Chicago Public Schools, Chicago Reading Framework, 2001) both suggest four components: guided reading, independent reading, spelling and word work, and writing. Within the writing block, skills of grammar and punctuation can be taught. What is missing from these frameworks is a focus on oral language and communication. They need to be built in at appropriate places. If you are conscious of the importance of providing regular opportunities for students to work together and to share both their thinking and their responses to what they read and what they write, you can begin by modeling and explaining the key aspects of oral communication.

At the upper grades particularly, you need to help students learn to use more informational materials and textbooks because they are a genre of material that will become increasingly important as students progress to middle and high school. Research skills are also part of the language arts standards; combining the teaching of these skills with content areas makes the most sense and gives students a shared content for exploration.

As you consider all that needs to be taught, planning time used carefully is essential. It is too easy to develop engaging activities but then neglect the important learning experiences that students need. Without shared planning, teachers have often ended up teaching the same "activities" in several grades. For example, while dinosaurs are an engaging topic, a unit around dinosaurs needs to be part of the science curriculum if it is going to be taught.

We have included some sample schedules for you to consider. As you visit classrooms, ask teachers about how they schedule their day. There are many ways to achieve a good schedule, but each way needs to be thought through and then followed or adjusted with your reflection. Consider the schedule one primary teacher established for her classroom (see Figure 14.4). It includes a lot of small group work and times to

**Figure 14.4**

### First-Grade Language Arts Schedule

| Monday | Tuesday | Wednesday | Thursday | Friday |
|---|---|---|---|---|
| 9:00–9:20 Whole group gathering and schedule setting | Read aloud and focus on strategies | | | |
| 9:20–10:00 Whole group lesson/reading or language arts | | | | |
| 10:00–10:40 Guided reading groups Center activities Writing | Guided reading/ small group | Guided reading/ small group | Guided reading/ small group | Cont. |
| 10:40–11:00 Word study/ phonics/choral reading | Word study/ poetry | Word study/ poetry | Cont. | Cont. |

**Figure 14.5**

## Fifth-Grade Language Arts Schedule

| Monday | Tuesday | Wednesday | Thursday | Friday |
|---|---|---|---|---|
| 8:45–9:10 Class focusing; independent reading and work checked; teacher read-aloud | Class focusing; indep.work; read-aloud | Class focusing; indep. work; read-aloud | | |
| 9:10–9:45 Teacher-guided lessons | Individual supported silent reading | Small group book discussions; journal reflections | Teacher-guided lessons – vocabulary and strategies | Silent reading discussion groups |
| 9:45–10:20 Small group and individual activities (some content intergration); writing workshop; reflections | Writing workshop | Writing workshop | Small group writing conferences; computer supports | Small group work class sharing of work done |
| 10:20–10:35 Project work (some content intergration); writing workshop; reflections | Reflecting planning time | Reflecting planning time | Reflecting planning time | Reflecting planning time |

meet with all students in reading two to three times a week. Also shown is a schedule from a fifth-grade teacher (see Figure 14.5).

Compare these two schedules and think about how you might create your own. Most teachers want the language arts blocks in the morning when children are freshest. However, some integration needs to occur across the day so that writing, reading, viewing, speaking, and listening are developed in meaningful settings.

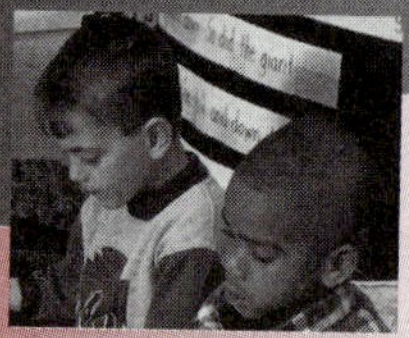

## What Is a Good Framework for Creating Integrated Units of Instruction?

Rather than starting out cold or, as some novice teachers do, with just a project or activity that you have known to be interesting for children, it is wise to start with the standards and benchmarks that students will be accountable for achieving. What will they be expected to know and be able to do as a result of being in your classroom this year? What science, social studies, and language arts outcomes are designated? How can you develop students' reading abilities through the instruction you provide in content units?

Make a list of the materials students will use and think about the skills and strategies they will need to possess to be effective learners with those materials. Then, create some diagnostic tools you can administer to assess the levels at which your students already function. Both their knowledge of the content and their literacy skills are important to assess.

## Assess Students' Abilities to Read across Genres

Reading fiction doesn't require as wide a range of skills and strategies as does reading and using informational material. Teachers need to be aware of students' knowledge of the basic features of informational texts—the table of contents, index, glossary, and chapters and the subdivisions with headings and subheadings. Do students know how to interpret maps, graphs, diagrams, charts, tables, and pictures? Are they aware of the different ways of organizing ideas and writing—description, cause/effect, compare/contrast, steps in a process, thesis and supporting arguments, and chronological order? Are students aware that, when reading for information, they don't need to start on the first page and read sequentially through the whole text? Can they read across different texts to find the information they need and can they also evaluate the accuracy and currency of what they read? Do they know how to summarize what they learn and also organize bodies of information into written and oral reports? There are so many aspects of reading and writing informational texts that need to be developed that assessing their knowledge early in the fall and then blocking out some special times during the year for units that permit you, the teacher, to model and develop these skills is important.

## Selecting Materials

Selection of just the right materials is another important planning step. With a basic understanding of your students' prior knowledge of the content and their level of skills in working with informational materials, you will have a better idea of how to scaffold the unit activities. The materials need to be within the range of the students' content knowledge, not too simple, but interesting and fresh in their presentation. Children love to learn about the world around them; with the beautifully illustrated books now available, it is quite easy to create a diverse and multileveled collection of materials. Including experiments, observations, research, and investigations, and other concrete activities whenever possible involves students "acting" on the content, not just absorbing it.

Selection of just the right materials is an important planning step. With a basic understanding of your students and prior knowledge of the content and their level of skills, you will be able to scaffold unit activities.

## Culminating Activities

An important part of unit planning is thinking of the final project or way in which students will consolidate what they are learning and share it. Here is where priorities in language arts can come to the foreground. Students need opportunities to create oral presentations, multimedia products, and visual displays as well as written summaries. These final products should permit children to develop a sense of accomplishment and an awareness of all they have learned. Involving them in self-assessment using rubrics or templates for the work extends their sense of efficacy and will carry over into later work they do. You may want to think through the example of the science/literacy unit overview that one group of teachers uses when developing new units that are more reading based than experimental based (see Figure 14.6). (Some of their other science/literacy units are grounded in experimentation and have more hands-on activities with journal keeping and drawing at their center.) How are the elements that were just explained included in this framework? What could you add to make it more complete?

IRA/NCTE 12



Figure 14.6

## Guide for Unit Planning

**Identify Standards (Language Arts and Content)**

Check on students' background knowledge and experiences.

Talk with other teachers to be sure your unit doesn't overlap other grade-level work or priorities.

Determine resources needed and available (books and magazines at varied reading levels, videos and other media, human, hands-on project materials, etc.).

Establish a plan for activities.

**Activation of Interest and Purposes**

Establish students' interests and connections.

Identify what is already known.

Highlight key content vocabulary and procedural terms needed (help ELLs make a list of terms in both their first language and in English).

**Building Understanding**

Develop mini-lessons, short lessons focused on skills needed for success (i.e. how to make note cards of important information).

Provide for whole group, small group, and independent activities.

Help students form working groups when appropriate for sharing their reading and viewing experiences, for writing and assisting others in drafting ideas, etc.

Create work forms so students keep records of their progress and activities.

Combine hands-on and text-based learning experiences.

Develop note-making formats so students can share their learning (i.e., a large KWL chart on the wall helps students add sticky notes of information to the class growing knowledge-base).

Prepare some read-aloud material so you, the teacher, contribute to the learning experiences of the class.

**Consolidating**

Provide activities where students create summaries of their learning (i.e., graphic organizers that connect all aspects and PowerPoint presentations).

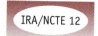

**Figure 14.6**

**(Continued)**

Compare and contrast ideas from different sources and experiences.

Discuss author's point of view and ways to present ideas in visual and verbal forms.

Take action on issues and share outcomes.

**Celebrating Achievements**

Create final products that can be shared with all students and other classes. Use this as an authentic setting for development of oral language skills and creating visual representations.

Have an open house for parents and the community to learn about this unit. Keep products in students' portfolios.

## How Can Small Group and Partner Routines Be Established?

Early in the year is the best time to attend carefully to oral communication and the social practices you want to develop in your students. Students are very eager and able to learn good communication skills if you make clear what your expectations are. The chapters you have read on oral communication (Chapters 2 and 3) go into depth explaining the importance of being able to use language well in varied contexts. Remember to establish among your first priorities the importance of letting your students know what you expect and how they can be good contributors to group activities. Provide a model of the skills you want them to exhibit. You can enlist another teacher to do a short discussion with you—ham it up and do examples of both good and bad behaviors. Or, ask two students to do examples of a good discussion. Seeing what it looks like is important. Teach them how to be active listeners—and be explicit about the characteristics of good listeners.

Teach them to learn small group roles and responses—and have a self-evaluation and group evaluation format. For example, you may work with the class to establish small group rules such as these:

- Everyone comes to the group prepared.
- Each person has a turn to speak and share.
- One person at a time is discussion leader or guide.
- Group members listen quietly and make eye contact with speakers.
- Members make a connection to what the previous person said before they share their own ideas. For example, "I like what Jamie said about. . . ." or "My experience was. . . ." Or, "Emma explained ________." "That was great, and I also want to share ________."

Involving students in partner activities is a valuable way for all students to learn to work productively and also to develop oral communication skills and abilities. Just as with small group work, students need to have specific guidelines for how to be productive and polite partners. Teach them some partner reading formats with self-evaluation criteria.

IRA/NCTE 10

Show them some video clips of good interactions among peers and let them describe and then evaluate good partner routines and behaviors. One of the guidelines even primary students easily understand is that when working with a partner twelve-inch voices should be used. Some teachers explain that students' voices shouldn't be louder than what can be heard knee to knee. See the Exploring Diversity feature for ideas on encouraging collaborative relationships in your classroom.

## exploring diversity

### Encouraging Collaboration

Your classroom can become an inviting place for students who come from homes where languages other than English are spoken with some added thought on your part. First, it is often easier for students who are less secure in English to have time to explore ideas with partners from their same linguistic background. Encourage ELL students to sit near each other in class so they can be resources for one another. When grouping students for partner work, consider making them partners, especially early in the year until you can assess their levels of English.

Explain to the students that you know they may find exploring some ideas in their first language helpful before using English and that it is OK for them to speak with each other in their first language. Then when they are ready to share in the whole class, they will have thought out their ideas and had time to translate what they want to say into English. Provide students dual-language dictionaries that can be at their desks to help when they need assistance with translation of difficult terms. It is also useful to have the students keep lists of terms that are central to the topic in both languages. Sometimes, if the directions are unclear, students can talk them over with a partner, and if needed, can then ask for your help in clarifying the task. Making a list of the "procedural" terms you use can be very useful. ELL students need to know what you mean by each of the directions you give. Making lists in both languages of terms they use may help them gain confidence in participating in the class activities. Having dual language content terms is an added support for their development of confidence in academic English.

As you set up your classroom, look to see how many audiotapes you can find that provide content you will cover. Second language students appreciate hearing the texts read over and over so they can learn the English better. Many textbook companies now have translations of their materials. Some computer programs are available in multiple languages. Helping students gain confidence with English by providing them with introductions and translations in their first language can be important to some students; others will thrive with the support of other students and your encouragement.

revisit the

# classroomchallenge



Janice Gordon sat back at the end of the day after completing the notes she made about activities from the day. She felt good; the students had been very productive and didn't need her help often in staying engaged. All the effort she had put into teaching them the routines they follow regularly had paid off. Her decision to focus on the routines she expected of students during the reading/language arts block for over a week in October had worked. She had just assumed too much of them at first! Posting the daily schedule and keeping cards on the board of which groups and activities the students were to complete each day had made a real difference. She now also understood how important it is to take time to work on each of the independent and small group routines so that students clearly knew what she expected of them.

The time she had spent working with students on establishing their independence in working in the different centers had paid off. She was very grateful to have help from Jody McKey, the reading specialist. When she had asked her for help, Ms. McKey not only talked through with her the language she could use to help students understand their roles, but she also made the great suggestion of creating a poster with the "rules" so they were visible for the children at all times. Ms. McKey's willingness to come and be a second adult in the classroom for a few days had also been useful. She had been able to work side by side with Kari and Jeremy to get them on track, while Janice was engaged with reading groups. Having two adults in the room at that critical point when the students were floundering had really helped.

Students now came into the room and, after settling into their desks, moved either to the writing corner to get their writing folders or took out their independent reading books and used the opening time for independent work. The schedule for the day written on the front board also gave students a way to think ahead. Her personal message to the class with some words of encouragement or a puzzle to be solved also helped set the tone for the class. Janice reflected on how easy now it was for her to work with the students in their guided reading groups. Her wall chart showed the times when partners would read together, when they would work on their writing, and when students would meet with her. Having students record the exact pages they read each day helped some remember that they had a real task to accomplish. The checklist in their writing folders also helped her know how students were progressing in their writing projects.

Adding the listening center had helped with the two students in special education and her three English language learners who benefited from hearing the literature selections read orally before coming to literature discussion times. The wall chart showing groupings and activities for the day was often referred to by a few students who seemed to need some external direction. Janice sighed. Finally, she felt she had the classroom working well. Now she could really focus on individual students' learning needs without having to always worry so much about behavior and management.

# chapterreview

All new teachers face a daunting task of determining how to manage the schedule for a classroom of diverse learners and establish routines so all can learn efficiently. Some routines must be established early in the fall so that students can begin learning and so that the teacher can provide some small group and individual attention to students. Using standards and an understanding of the basic components of good reading and language instruction, teachers can ensure there is time for whole group, small group, and individual and independent work time. The activities, routines, and use of space are all important.

## How Should I Approach Setting Up My Classroom? What Work Areas Are Needed?

Setting up your classroom takes thoughtful planning. Classrooms should have inviting work areas where students can find resources and space for the literacy activities that you design. That means you will want to create inviting desk arrangements and ways to bring groups of students together informally. Establishing a reading center or corner, a writing corner, and other work areas for projects are all important. Quiet work spaces and places for listening stations and computers also need to be available which means that setting up a classroom takes thoughtful planning. Thinking about and then organizing the classroom space so students can participate in a variety of group settings and can work individually in writing, listening, and reading (and also be part of whole class activities) is important. The more students can move from desks to varied settings, the more they will stay engaged. So, too, the more that students' work is represented in the classroom, the more pride they take as part of a community. In all of this time, the teacher is the model and guide.

## What Priorities Should I Establish with Limited Space and Resources?

Always think of your students first. Use your space with them in mind. Make sure their marks are clearly visible around the room; their work is on the walls and their personal belongings are respected. Then make sure your curriculum and standards priorities are also central. Having special boards with students' work examples and "I Can" statements and examples connects your students with your priorities in teaching content. Resources and activity centers that reflect those curriculum foci will help everyone in your classroom stay focused and engaged in learning.

## How Do I Set Up a Writing Center?

Students will enjoy writing when you create an environment that entices them into using writing instruments to share their thoughts. Keeping the writing center stocked with different kinds of writing instruments and paper as well as computers and older typewriters makes clear your value on student writing. Keeping folders for students' work-in-progress is important so students can easily access their drafts and projects. Showing finished products on the wall sends an important message that student work is valued and worth sharing.

## How Can I Develop a Classroom Library Collection?

One of your first priorities is to be sure you have a classroom collection of books and print materials that are just right for your students. As a new teacher, you may need to build a collection over your first few years of teaching. Consult the school librarian and administration to see if there are books you can bring to your room from other resources in the building. School parent groups can also help you build your collection. If there are few books available then going to garage sales, searching online, and looking through bookstores may be useful. And, remember the good online resources that are available; check the websites suggested earlier in this chapter.

## What Makes a Workable Schedule of Activities?

Your schedule needs to be carefully thought through so you have time to teach the key components of the curriculum and to do so in interesting and involving activities. Primary teachers generally need two hours of literacy instructional time. At the intermediate and upper levels, instruction can be partially integrated with content learning in science, social studies, and mathematics. There needs to be a regular schedule that may be based on a weekly cycle or may be extended over two weeks.

## What Is a Good Framework for Creating Integrated Units of Instruction?

Standards and benchmarks are an important starting place for creating integrated units of instruction. Then you need to assess what levels of proficiency are represented by your students. With this information, you can then begin to plan your unit. Be sure there are good materials available that your class can access, that students have both the skills to use the materials (online, visual, and print), and that materials match the appropriate reading levels for your class. Then, plan for the process of learning with engaging activities as students activate what they know, build their knowledge, consolidate learning, and celebrate the outcomes.

## How Can Small Group and Partner Routines Be Established?

A key to being able to create varied settings in which students can work together is ensuring that students know what is expected of them. Begin by modeling group interaction and identifying the behaviors that are productive. By developing clear rules for engagement and then posting them visibly in the room students will be reminded of what they need to do as group participants.

PEARSON **myeducationlab**™
Where the Classroom Comes to Life

Now go to www.myeducationlab.com to take a Pretest to assess your initial comprehension of chapter content, study chapter content with your individualized Study Plan, take a Posttest to assess your understanding of chapter content, practice your teaching skills with Building Teaching Skills exercises, and build a deeper, more applied understanding of chapter content with Homework and Exercises.

chapter 15

# Incorporating Technology

**Denise Johnson,** College of William and Mary

**classroomchallenge**

**The students in** Mrs. Henry's classroom have been studying the Revolutionary War. She had divided the class into five groups based on their interest in different battles during the war. Students were assigned to find out more information about each battle over the next two weeks and share the information with the class. She had been excited about this opportunity to use the social studies curriculum to involve students in the development of shared research papers and presentations.

Some groups were conducting their research in the library, and others used the Internet. Mrs. Henry notices that those students conducting searches on the Internet are having a difficult time finding the desired information. She observes one group as they search for information about the Battle of Trenton. The students type in "Battle of Trenton" in the search engine which returns 1,360,000 sites. The students click the first site but are overwhelmed with the amount of information. They go back to the original search results and click on the second link, which takes them to an unrelated commercial site. After clicking on four or five more sites

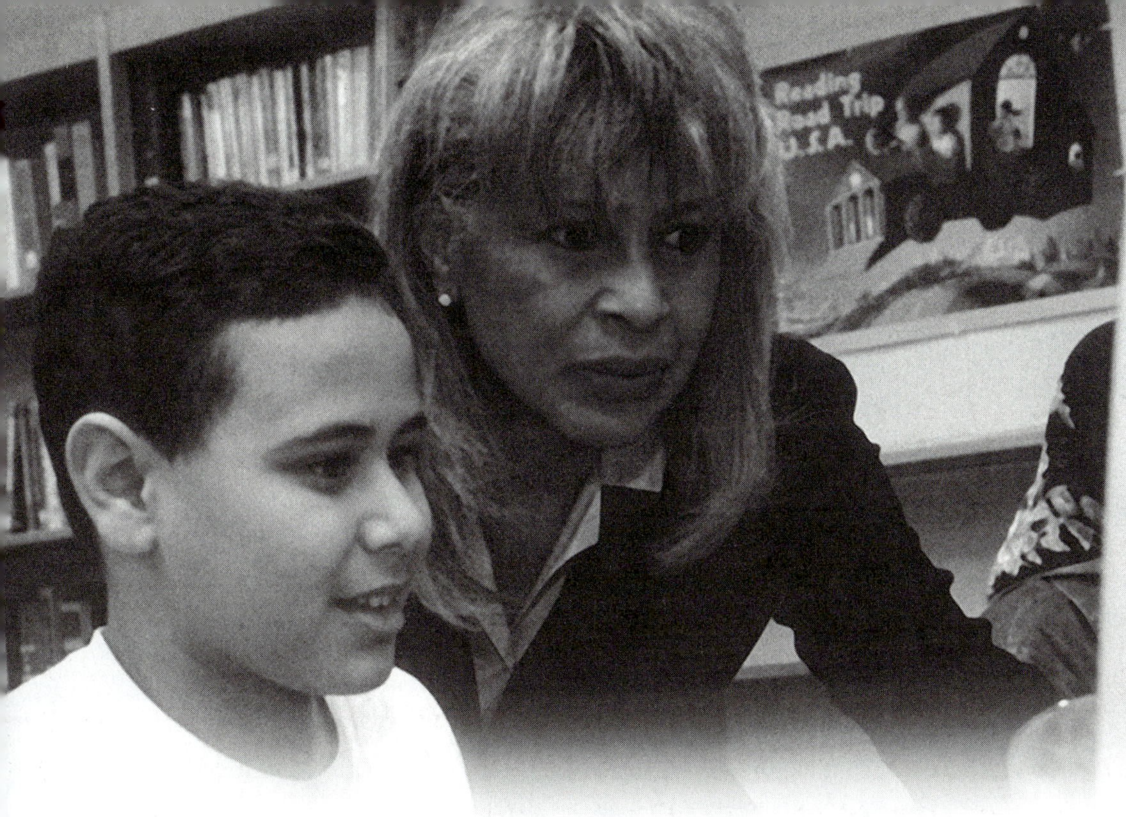



that don't lead the students to the needed information, the students become frustrated and begin to argue over who controls the mouse and who can do a better job of navigating the Internet.

Finally, Mrs. Henry intervenes. She determines that she will have to provide more support to help her students acquire the necessary strategies for conducting a successful Internet search. She had assumed they had learned how to use the Internet for research without doing much pre-assessment. However, her observations clearly told her otherwise.

## Questions for Reflection

1. What can Mrs. Henry do to help students conduct a successful Internet search?
2. What can she do to help students navigate the text once they find a site?
3. What other technology resources can students use to find information on their Revolutionary War battle?

## anticipating this chapter

To help you answer these and other questions about technology, this chapter addresses the following questions:

- Why is technology important for reading and writing?
- What do we know about technology?
- What do we know about learning and technology?
- How can we use technology in language arts instruction?
- How can we assess students' reading and writing with technology?
- How can we support diversity and differentiated instruction in the classroom?
- What professional development resources can help us learn about technology?

# Why Is Technology Important for Reading and Writing?

IRA/NCTE 4

Students today have never lived in a world without computer technology and will undoubtedly encounter unimagined new technologies before they graduate from high school. Rapid advancements in technology—computers, e-mail, fiber-optic networks, teleconferencing, and dynamic new software—have globalized the way the United States and other countries conduct business. Now, the phone call you place to get help with your computer might be answered by a person in China or your taxes might be prepared by someone in India. As the world becomes more globalized, middle-class jobs such as accountants and technical support staff will be digitized, automated, or outsourced to other countries that can do the work more cheaply. As students today enter the information-based job market of tomorrow, it is essential that they have the literacy skills necessary to acquire and use information from the extensive computer and **information communication technology** (ICT) that become available in a constantly changing networked environment.

It is important to understand that new literacies will not replace foundational literacies required by traditional books and print, but rather will build on and extend them. Yet, reading, writing, and communication will take new forms as text is combined with new media resources and linked within complex information networks requiring new literacies for their effective use. Thus, new literacies are necessary to fully engage with digital texts and ICTs.

Acquiring the skills and strategies of the new literacies required to read, write, view, navigate, and communicate is critical to the successful use of ICTs and to students' futures. The purpose of this chapter is to provide information on how the tools of technology extend students' understanding, motivation, and engagement with literacy skills and strategies and also how these tools extend opportunities to acquire the new literacies needed to live and work in the rapidly changing technological world. Think about your own use of technology both for personal use and for learning. There may be ways you can link areas of technology with which you are very confident with your classroom instructional program. This chapter provides many possible connections, too.

## What Do We Know about Technology?

There was a time when many people thought that computers would replace teachers. Now we know that computers are tools, like any other teaching material, and if used effectively they can supplement and enhance the literacy curriculum. Research has shown that use of computers and the Internet can have many benefits when teachers make appropriate decisions about their use. In such contexts, it can:

- Increase student motivation and engagement
- Improve reading and writing skills
- Expand classroom reading materials
- Expand response and collaboration opportunities
- Expand experiences and content area knowledge
- Promote imagination, critical thinking, and problem solving
- Promote multicultural understanding
- Support the learning of diverse students—those from low-income families, those with different cultural experiences, those who are English language learners, and those with physical, mental, and emotional challenges
- Increase understanding and use of the new literacies
- Promote professional development and collaboration

There are many software programs and Internet resources available to teachers to assist students in becoming independent readers, writers, thinkers, and communicators. Because a considerable variety exists in the quality of these programs and tools, they must be evaluated based on their potential for meeting the individual needs of the diverse learners in the classroom. For example, according to a meta-analysis of forty-two studies conducted between 1982 and 2000, the use of computer technology to teach basic literacy skills to beginning readers is only minimally effective and thus, not cost effective compared to teacher-based instruction (Blok, Oostdam, Otter, and Overmaat, 2002). Sometimes, the computer is not the best tool for the job.

The appropriate use of technology should be based on an understanding of how all students learn and develop literacy over time and across the curriculum. Cummins, Brown, and Sayers (2007, pp. 109–110) pose the following questions for consideration when evaluating and planning technology-supported projects or activities:

- Does the technology-supported instruction provide cognitive challenges and opportunities for deep processing of meaning?
- Does the technology-supported instruction relate instruction to prior knowledge and experiences derived from students' homes and communities?
- Does the technology-supported instruction promote active self-regulated collaborative inquiry?
- Does the technology-supported instruction promote extensive engaged reading and writing across the curriculum?
- Does the technology-supported instruction help students develop strategies for effective reading, writing, and learning?
- Does the technology-supported instruction promote affective involvement and identity investment on the part of the students?

Cummins et al. (2007) state, "The logic underlying the articulation of these principles is that if an educator can answer all or most of these questions affirmatively . . . then it is highly likely that this activity is promoting both engaged learning and literacy development" (p. 111).

## Software

A computer program used to accomplish specific tasks not related to the computer itself is called *software.* Examples are word processors, spreadsheets, and learning games. Software programs used in schools include drill and practice, tutorials, gamelike software, simulation software, multimedia software, and writing and publishing software.

**Video Homework Exercise**

*Presentation Software in Literature*

Go to the Homework and Exercises section of Chapter 15 of MyEducationLab and view the video, "Presentation Software in Literature," about a teacher who engages her students in a computerized game to review questions related to Hamlet. Complete the activities that follow, and save your work or transmit it to your professor as assigned.

**Drill and Practice, Tutorials, and Gamelike Software** **Drill and practice software** operates like a self-checking worksheet. The program presents a series of questions—if a question is answered correctly, the program moves on to the next question; if a question is answered incorrectly, the program provides feedback and usually presents another opportunity to respond correctly before giving the answer. These options can provide an opportunity for independent practice of literacy skills, but they should be used in moderation and in concert with teacher instruction.

**Tutorial programs** are more sophisticated than drill and practice programs in that they provide instruction and practice. The instructional component might be in the form of a presentation of a specific skill or concept, and then an opportunity is provided for the child to try the skill. As with drill and practice programs, feedback is provided and, based on the child's responses, may branch to more or less difficult material. Because tutorials provide a type of instruction, it is critical that teachers assure that the instruction is appropriate for the child in his or her reading development.

**Gamelike programs** capitalize on the popularity of video games with full-color graphics, sound, animation, and even video clips. Students can play against the computer or other students as they compete for the highest score. The appeal of certain aspects of gamelike software programs can lead to misuse. For example, a game in

Planning decisions are essential to the effectiveness of any educational material, but particularly for computer programs and Internet resources because these technologies will define the literacies of students' futures.



which getting the wrong answer results in graphics, sound, or animation may be more fun to experience than getting the right answer. Also, students may continue to play the game even though it has surpassed its educational value.

## Simulation Software

**Simulation software** presents a model of real-world events in which students must make decisions that will determine the next step in the scenario. Many times, the real-world events are based on social studies or science concepts but require reading, critical thinking, and problem-solving. Often, students can work in groups and collaborate on their decisions while participating in the program. For example, the program Kids and the Environment (Tom Snyder Productions) simulates a playground scenario in which students are presented with a series of events in which they must decide what to do based on a variety of resources available to them (see Figure 15.1). Most simulation programs use video content, graphics, sound, and animation, along with a recordkeeping program. Popular programs such as Where in the U.S.A. Is Carmen Sandiego? (The Learning Company) and Oregon Trail (also from The Learning Company) are examples of simulation software.

## Multimedia Software

CD-ROM storybooks transform traditional print stories by adding graphics, sound, animation, and video to create interactive texts. Glasgow (1996) examined CD-ROM storybooks at different stages in students' reading development and found that, in the emergent stage, they can be helpful in reducing dependence on text by integrating print, images, sound, motion, and color. In addition, students can track text from left to right and top to bottom because the text is highlighted as it is read. Older students can benefit from work with unknown vocabulary because some interactive storybooks have accompanying graphics that show the meaning of the word as it takes into account individual student differences. Further, the interactive nature of CD-ROM storybooks helps students become more personally involved as they learn skills and strategies presented in the storybook. Some CD-ROM storybooks, such as those in *The Living Books Library* (published by Riverdeep), are based on popular children's books

Figure 15.1

***Choices, Choices: Kids and the Environment***

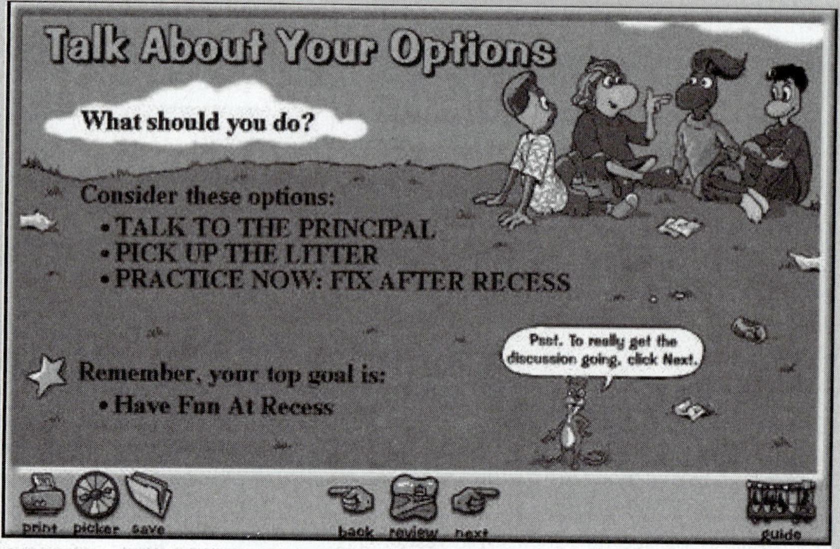


*Students, role-playing the team captain, must weigh how their choices will affect the team, school, and community.*

*Source:* Tom Snyder Productions. Used by permission.

by Marc Brown, Dr. Seuss, Kevin Henkes, Mercer Mayer, Janell Cannon, Tomie dePaola, and Aesop. These programs are also published in different languages and have some customizing capabilities.

Kahootz is a software program with a powerful set of three-dimensional multimedia tools that allows students and teachers to be creators, designers, inventors, and storytellers. Kahootz is also an interactive, online community in which students and teachers can publish their work and exchange, share, collaborate, deconstruct, and explore with other schools in the Kahootz community.

## Writing and Publishing Software

Word processing and desktop publishing has replaced paper and pen as the predominate way people write and communicate. Though keyboarding is a skill many students struggle with, software programs such as Kidpix Deluxe 4 and Kid Pix se habla español! (Riverdeep) combine art, graphics, and word processing to provide opportunities for even very young children to express their emerging literacy abilities through electronic text. Labbo and Kuhn (1997) found that kindergartners used Kidpix to make the kinds of speech-to-text connections that young learners make when using more traditional writing materials.

Standard word processing programs such as Word (Microsoft) usually come preloaded on computers and include spell checkers, highlighters, clip art, drawing tools, and other components that allow students to easily write and illustrate their own stories. Most word processors also have features for accessibility for visually and hearing-impaired students. Stories can easily be modified, saved, printed, and placed in the classroom library for other students to read.

Kidspiration and Inspiration (Inspiration Software, Inc.) programs can be used in multiple contexts, but are particularly useful for brainstorming and organizing ideas for writing. Students build graphic organizers by combining pictures, text, and spoken words to represent thoughts and information.

## Hardware

Hardware comprises all of the physical parts of a computer or other digital device. Hardware used in schools includes desktop computers, digital cameras, digital camcorders, handheld devices, and digital audio players.

**Digital Cameras and Camcorders** Books, field trips, and classroom experiences provide great ideas for stories or to document learning. Digital cameras and camcorders provide a way to capture ideas and events that can be turned into student-made books and movies. With digital storytelling, students take their written stories and incorporate illustrations and/or photographs and add voice recordings to create a QuickTime movie that can be posted on the Internet. In addition to creating enthusiasm for writing, digital storytelling also provides authentic opportunities for students to learn to use digital photography and audio, image, and video software. Free down-



## engaging in Visual Literacy

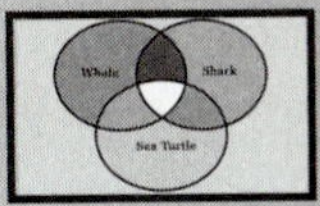

### Using Digital Cameras

Mrs. Kruel believes that students need skills and strategies for reading pictures just as they do for reading text. She wanted her fourth-graders to use images to create and convey meaning, so she designed a project in which her students would use digital cameras to document the most important events during the school day. Their work would then be posted on the class web page. The students were divided into groups, and they planned their project by creating storyboards of the events they wanted to capture. Because the school did not allow students' pictures to be posted on the school website, the students were challenged to take pictures of events without showing any fourth-graders. The students had to use their creativity to capture the day using only images. The project was successful in assisting the fourth-graders in understanding how to use images to convey meaning. See the final project "A Day in 4K" at www.mskreul.com/dayin4K/dayin4k.htm.

loadable software, such as Microsoft Photo Story 3 (www.microsoft.com), Picasa (picasa.google.com), and Movie Maker (www.microsoft.com), are easy to use and provide a way for students to organize, edit, narrate, and publish digital stories. For more information about digital storytelling, visit the digital story telling site (http://electronicportfolios.com/digistory). See the Engaging in Visual Literacy feature for an example of how to use digital cameras in your class.

IRA/NCTE 8

**Handheld Devices** Though desktop computers and printers have become staples in today's classrooms, handheld devices are a more recent arrival. **Handheld devices,** more commonly known as PDAs (Personal Data Assistants), are small computers that have many of the same capabilities as full-size computers but with the additional technology of cell phones, digital cameras, calculators, voice recorders, wireless Internet, and infrared transmission. Most of these devices contain traditional software programs such as word processors and spreadsheets but additional programs are available, most of which are free of charge, that provide flashcards, dictionaries, vocabulary, spelling, and math practice. Wireless, foldable keyboards are available for easy input. Handheld devices also serve as e-books. Children's books in print or audio can be downloaded and viewed or played in several languages. Handheld devices are also being used by teachers as a means of assessment. Students' written responses to a book or another assignment can be sent via infrared transmission to the teacher's handheld device. Software programs such as Wireless Generation (www.wirelessgeneration.com) allow teachers to take running records of students' reading with a handheld device. The Engaging in Assessment feature has more information on using handheld devices in the classroom.

**Digital Audio Players** A **digital audio player** (DAP), commonly referred to as an MP3 player, is a device that stores, organizes, and plays digital music files (and other

## engaging in Assessment

### Using Handheld Devices

Mrs. Hahn finished reading aloud *The Tale of Despereaux* written by Kate DiCamillo to the students in her fifth-grade class. The students really enjoyed the book and were anxious to discuss it. Before Mrs. Hahn engaged the students in talk, she asked them to respond to the prompts, "I liked . . ." or "I didn't like. . . ." The students pulled out their handheld devices and keyboards and quickly typed in their responses. When they finished, they sent their responses by infrared transmission to Mrs. Hahn's handheld device. While waiting for everyone to send their responses, Mrs. Hahn quickly scanned the different responses to get a sense of the students' thoughts about the book. A few of the responses indicated that some students might have been confused by certain events in the book. This prompted Mrs. Hahn to quickly review the events in the book to check for student understanding before the class discussion. In this way, Mrs. Hahn was assured that all students understood the major events in the story that might otherwise be confusing or might prevent some from participating in the discussion.

file formats as well). The Apple iPod is the most popular of these devices, but many other brands exist that are very affordable for classroom use. In addition to digital music, DAPs can be used to listen to audiobooks downloaded from online files or uploaded to the DAP from an audiobook on CD-ROM. DAPs can hold many hours of audio, depending on the capacity of the device, making it an easy storage device for many audiobooks rather than keeping track of several CDs for one audiobook.

DAPs can also be used to listen to podcasts, radio-like programs that can be downloaded from the Internet into the device. Thousands of podcasts are being published daily for both local and global audiences on a multitude of topics. An excellent place to find classroom podcasts is the Education Podcast Network (epnweb.org). Even a low-capacity digital audio player can store several hours of podcasts. Additionally, teachers and students can create their own podcasts to share classroom learning experiences with other classrooms around the world and the broader community. The use of podcasts encourages students to read, write, and conduct research. Read about the Room 208 Podcast (www.apple.com/education/profiles/wells) where third- and fourth-graders at Wells Elementary School in Wells, Maine, create and record podcasts.



## Selecting and Evaluating Software

The expense of software and hardware has decreased in cost over the years, but they are still considered major purchases for most schools with limited budgets. Careful consideration must be given to the selection of software to support the literacy curriculum. Software reviews are available, such as Children's Software (www.childrenssoftware.com/links.html), but these reviews are not always conducted by educators or people familiar with educational applications. Furthermore, these reviewers do not know your students. Software that has received the best reviews and has won numerous awards may not meet the needs of some students in your classroom. Therefore, teachers should conduct their own software reviews, with the knowledge of their students' needs in mind. The following questions can serve as a guide (Wepner, Valmont, and Thurlow, 2000, p. 91):

- Are the activities and tasks within the program compelling enough to hold students' interest?
- Are instructions to students clear, concise, and easy to follow without significant adult help?
- Are the graphics and sound of a high quality, are they integral part of the concepts and content taught, and are they appropriate for the age level intended?
- Does the content fit into or expand beyond what students are learning?
- Does the program stretch students' imagination and creativity beyond ordinary means?
- Does the program provide enough practice on important concepts, especially if you are looking for a program that builds skills?
- Does the program foster interaction and cooperative activities, especially if you are looking for these kinds of activities within your classroom?
- Is the text narrated so that students can read the book or passage independently, and is the text highlighted as it is read so that students can follow along?

- Will the program develop with the students over the course of the year and accommodate differing ability or age levels?
- Are record-keeping or assessment features built into the program, especially if this is an important issue providing accountability for your use of technology?
- Does the publisher provide a teacher's guide, with lessons, ways to introduce the program to your students, and supplementary handout materials to assist you?
- Is a printed copy of a book on screen available for students to use independently?

## Internet

Though computer software and hardware provide many advantages for students and teachers, it is through the Internet and other ICTs that the computer realizes its greatest potential. Leu and Coiro (2004, p. 160) state:

> Simply using technology in the classroom does not assure that students are acquiring the new literacies they require. Using technologies such as Accelerated Reader (Topping and Paul, 1999) or other software packages designed to support the acquisition of foundational literacies will not prepare students for the new literacies of the Internet and other ICTs. Using these instructional technologies does nothing to develop the essential skills, strategies, and dispositions that define the new literacies. This type of thinking has been one reason why the field has not moved faster at integrating new literacies into classroom instruction; using software programs to teach foundational literacies is the only vision many have for integrating literacy and technology in classrooms.

Almost 100 percent of public schools have access to the Internet (Parsad and Jones, 2005). The Internet is a powerful network tool that can bring the world into the classroom. The following section describes ways teachers and students can use the Internet for literacy learning:

**Online Books** The Internet allows teachers and librarians to literally bring a whole world of books into the classroom. Some of these books are simply traditional forms of books that have been put on the Internet. Others are interactive, in that students can have the book read to them, have words pronounced or defined for them, or engage in related activities. The Internet also opens up opportunities to find out more information about a book's setting, events, and author that make for a richer and more meaningful reading experience.

Thousands of free digitized versions of traditional print books are available on the Internet. A unique and invaluable collection is the International Children's Digital Library (www.icdlbooks.org). This global collection currently includes 2,412 books in 41 languages for children (ages three to thirteen). The browser interface can display in eleven languages. The ICDL website allows students to search for new books and to retrieve previously read books through categories students can easily understand, such as true or make-believe, book color, length, how a book makes them feel, or by spinning a globe. An advanced search interface is also available for older students and adults. The collection is focused on books that help students to understand the world around them and the global society in which they live. The books represent exemplary artistic, historical, and literary qualities. Books are presented in the way they are read in their country

**Figure 15.2** International Children's Digital Library Website

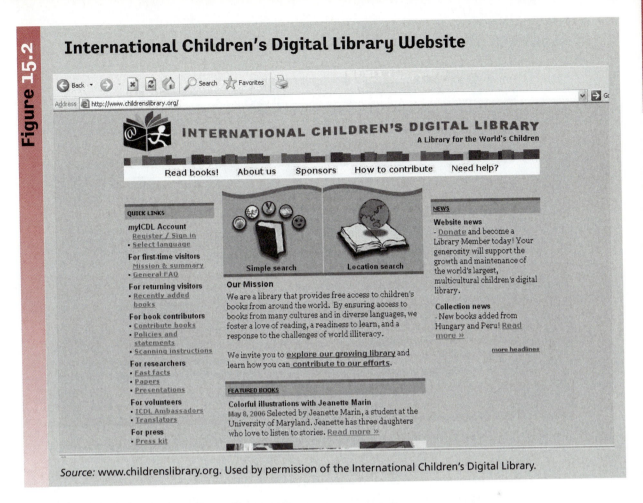

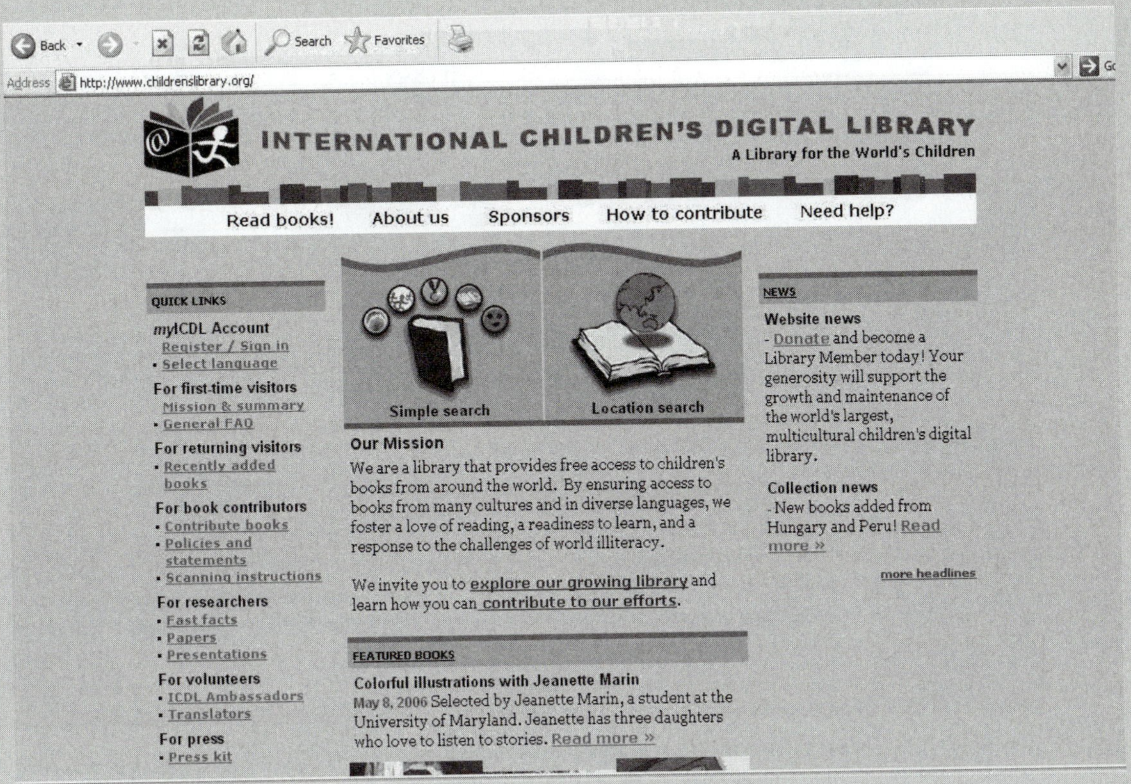


*Source:* www.childrenslibrary.org. Used by permission of the International Children's Digital Library.



(i.e., written from left to right). Many books are written in dual languages. This collection is especially beneficial for English Language Learners because books in their home language may be difficult to find in print in America. For instance, there are 377 books from Persia written in Farsi and 24 books from the Philippines written in Tagalog. These books are also interesting to monolingual students so they can see what other languages look like in print. Sometimes, the artwork can also be analyzed to help students conjecture about other cultures and cultural ways of representing ideas. See Figure 15.2 for an example of the ICDL interface.

Students enjoy hearing books read aloud by their parents, teachers, and librarians who serve as models for reading. The Screen Actors Guild Foundation (www.sagfoundation.org/index.shtml) has capitalized on this influence by hosting BookPALS Storyline Online (www.storylineonline.net) in which students can watch streaming videos of celebrities such as Elijah Wood, Amanda Bynes, and Jason Alexander reading and discussing children's picture books. Currently, twenty-one picture books appeal to students of all ages. Information about each book, author, and celebrity reader is provided along with related activities. See Figure 15.3 for the BookPALS Storyline Online home page.

**Online interactive storybooks** are much like CD-ROM storybooks. One outstanding site for interactive storybooks is the TumbleBook Library (www.tumblebooks.com), a collection of animated talking picture books offered through participating public

**Figure 15-3** **BookPALS Storyline Online Website**

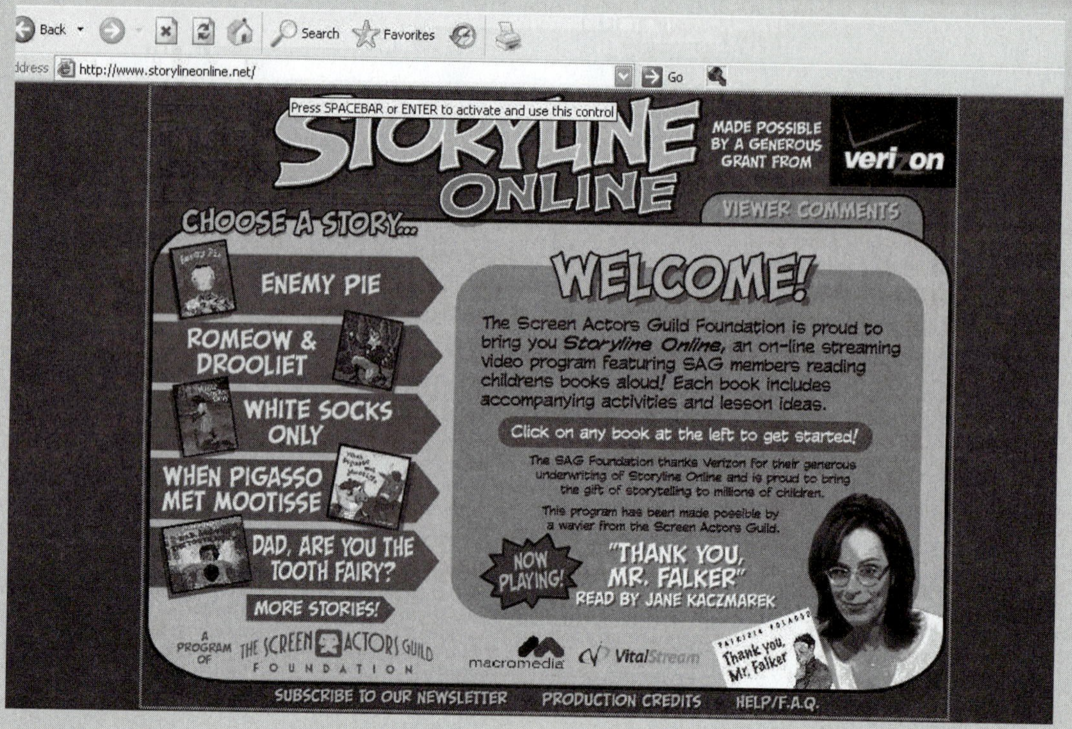


*Source:* Used by permission of the Screen Actors Guild Foundation.

libraries. The TumbleBook Library consists of over one hundred highly popular picture books for K-5 students. The audio and graphics can be turned off and students can read the books for themselves. Some books include a word helper that defines certain words in the story. See Figure 15.4 for a page from an online storybook called *The Diary of a Worm.*

**Virtual Author Visits, Websites/Weblogs** Though there is no substitute for the thrill of meeting an author in person, author visits can be very expensive and time consuming for schools to host. The Internet allows students and teachers to meet authors "virtually" that they cannot meet in person. There are several advantages to virtual visits: They are more affordable, they provide access to authors who are geographically distant or who prefer not to travel, and they permit a more extended, thoughtful discussion of the author's work. The best way to locate an author to participate in a virtual visit is to do a quick Internet search for the author's website or e-mail address or contact the book publisher directly. Virtual author visits can be conducted via e-mail, bulletin board, virtual chat, or live broadcast via webcam. The type of communication technology, the cost, and date/time frame will be a decision made between the author/publisher and the teacher/librarian.

Almost every author has a website or is part of the publisher's website. Author websites often offer a showcase of his or her works, schedule of appearances, upcoming interviews or speeches, and other news about the author. In addition, some authors include a web log (or *blog*) that serves as an online journal and updates the audience on their daily

**Figure 15.4** *The Diary of a Worm* **Website**

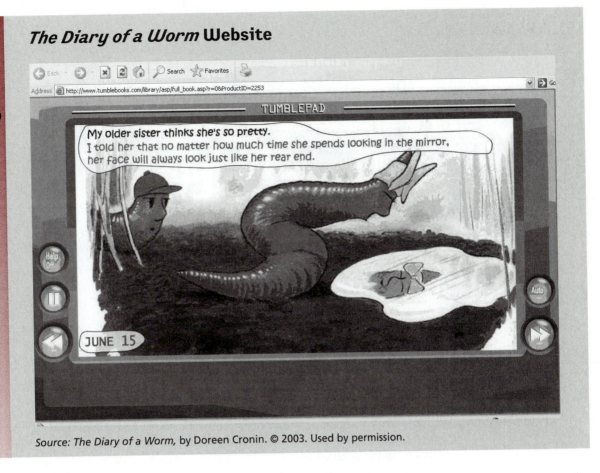

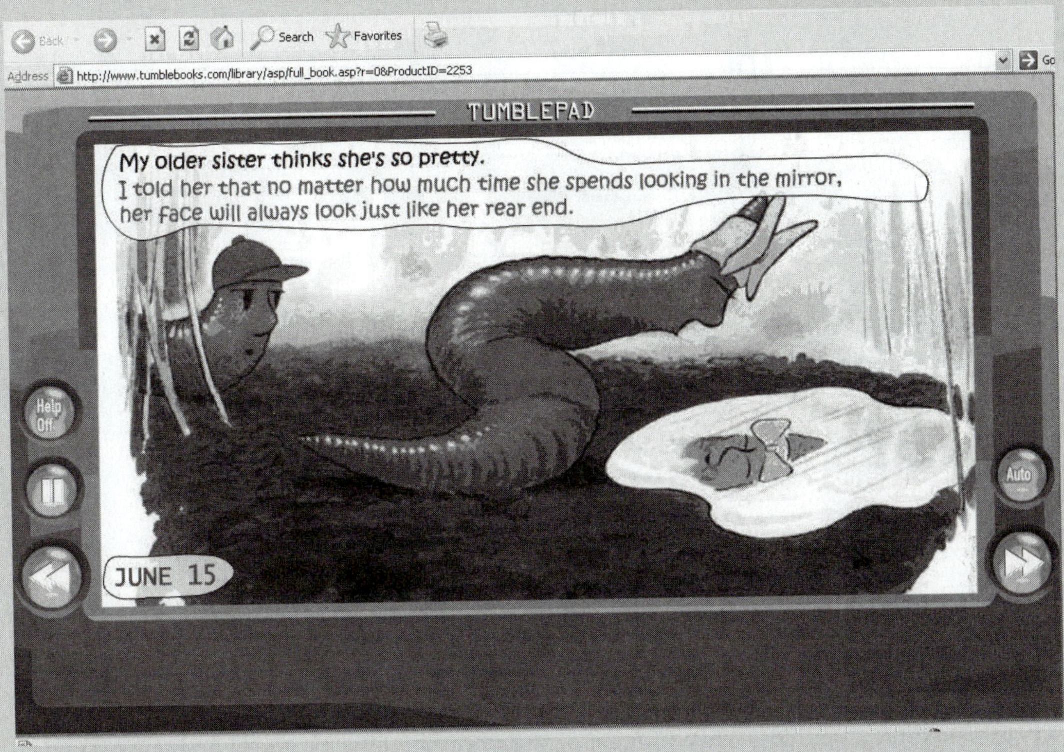


*Source: The Diary of a Worm,* by Doreen Cronin. © 2003. Used by permission.

lives, what they are currently writing, or their opinions on a variety of topics. Some author sites have activity resources, such as worksheets, that go along with their books.

**Online Communication and Book Discussions** The Internet has closed the gap between people around the world. Unlike the old days, when a letter could take several weeks to arrive at its destination, Internet communication is almost instantaneous. Electronic mail (e-mail), listservs, instant messaging (IM), chat rooms, discussion boards, wikis, and web logs (blogs) allow people to share ideas, opinions, and information with others around the world.

Internet communication can promote authentic interactions between students or a broader audience outside of the school. For example, students can communicate with astronauts, authors, historians, scientists, and other students about topics being studied in class or events happening in the world. See Figure 15.5 for an example of an online community (www.**epals**.com). Writing is more conversational and brief (even one word) when using Internet communications such as e-mail (Wollman-Bonilla, 2003) than traditional print. Because of the speed of the communication, e-mail can become similar to conversation which can also have an effect on the way e-mail is read. Wollman-Bonilla (2003) writes, "The notion that computers encourage superficial browsing rather than careful, extended attention to screen content suggests that writers might not attend to the details of e-mail messages as they would to printed (non-screen) texts where reading is thought to be deeper and composing more deliberate"

**Figure 15-5**

## ePals Website

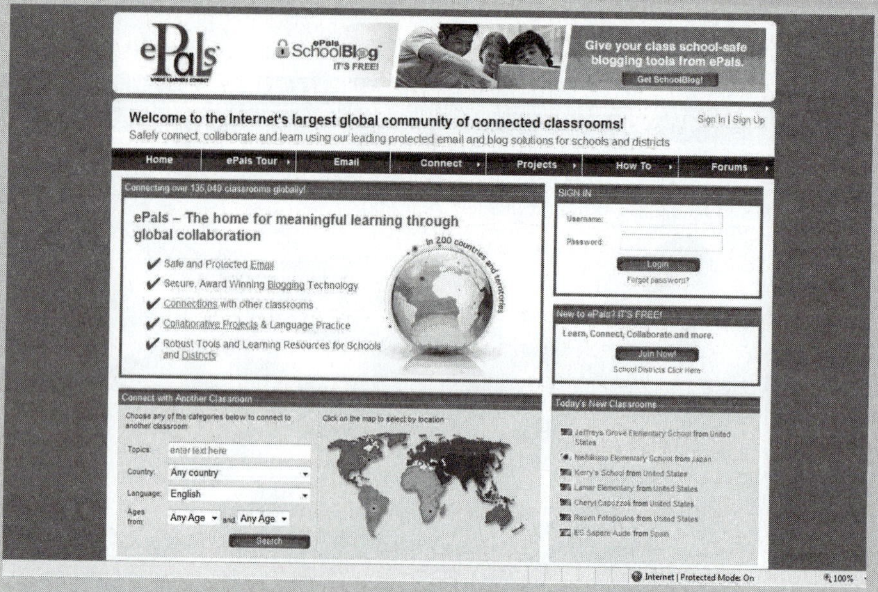


*Source:* Used by permission of ePals.

(p. 128). While Internet communication differs from printed text in terms of writing and reading, it is an important tool of communication—one with which students need exposure and explicit instruction. The Internet makes it easier for kids to talk with other kids locally, regionally, nationally, or internationally about books. Book discussions, sometimes called *book raps* or *book chats,* are online discussion groups about books that take place using e-mail, chat rooms, or discussion boards. Classes from different parts of the world can read and discuss books together. At the same time, students can learn about culture and diversity (Leu et al., 2004).

In order for online discussions to be meaningful conversations rather than superficial one-line responses, students must understand how to engage in meaningful face-to-face discussions about books. Online discussions should not replace in-class literature groups or book clubs but should be used as an important extension that allows students to connect with a broader audience with diverse perspectives, cultures, and experiences. When students understand how to participate in meaningful in-class discussions with other students and the teacher, it serves as a foundation for meaningful online discussions. Yet, online communication is different than face-to-face discussions and it is important for teachers to scaffold students' understanding of how to read and respond to online communication.

**Writing and Publishing on the Internet** The Internet provides a great way for students to share their work with others, including parents, grandparents, relatives, and other students around the world. Publishing student writing on the Internet is motivating, and it expands the audience of readers. There are many websites that post student stories, poems, and art for other students to read and respond to. Several sites also offer support for young writers. Scholastic's *Writing with Writers* site (teacher.scholastic.com/writewit) provides an online opportunity for prominent authors to serve as mentors by offering tips and writing advice, along with the author's biographical information, selected works, and recommended books. The authors are able to make explicit connections between the craft of writing and reading. This site also has students' stories posted at different age levels that students can read. One or two of the stories have feedback from the author. When students' writing is posted on the Internet, their work becomes a part of the large network of stories and information on the World Wide Web, and the students learn that they too can become published authors.

There are many ways to publish students' writing on the Internet. A school or class home page is a great place to publish students' writing, but many other locations exist as well. Other websites that offer support for student writing include:

- The Writers' Window (http://english.unitecnology.ac.nz/writers) allows students (ages five to eighteen) to publish their writing and to communicate with others through a discussion board about different aspects of the writing process.
- The Biography Maker (www.bham.wednet.edu/bio/biomaker.htm) takes students through a series of steps to help them write a biography: questioning, learning, synthesis, and storytelling.
- Poetry Express (www.poetryexpress.org) contains activities and advice regarding the making, sharing, revising, and editing of poems.

**WebQuests** A WebQuest facilitates the acquisition, integration, and extension of a vast amount of information through tasks specifically designed to engage the learner in analysis and demonstration of understanding. According to Bernie Dodge (San Diego State University) and Tom March (ozline.com), creators of the **WebQuest,** "A WebQuest is an inquiry-oriented activity in which most or all of the information used by learners is drawn from the Web. WebQuests are designed to use learners' time well, to focus on using information rather than looking for it, and to support learners' thinking at the levels of analysis, synthesis, and evaluation" (www.webquest.org/index.php).

The design of a WebQuest is critical to its effectiveness as an instructional resource. WebQuests consist of the following critical attributes:

- **Introduction.** The purpose of this section is to both prepare and hook the reader. The introduction draws the reader into the learning situation by relating to the reader's interests or goals and/or engagingly describing a compelling question or problem. The introduction builds on the reader's prior knowledge by explicitly mentioning important concepts or principles, and it effectively prepares the learner for the lesson by foreshadowing new concepts and principles.

- **Task.** The task focuses learners on what they are going to do—specifically, the culminating performance or product that drives all of the learning activities. The task requires synthesis of multiple sources of information, and/or taking a position, and/or going beyond the data given and making a generalization or product.

- **Process.** This section outlines how the learners will accomplish the task. Scaffolding includes clear steps, resources, and tools for organizing information. The process through which readers should proceed to complete the project is broken out into well-written, clearly described steps. There is variety in the activities performed and/or roles and perspectives to be taken on by the reader.

- **Resources.** All links to web resources are pertinent to the task, and they make excellent use of the web.

- **Evaluation.** This section describes the evaluation criteria needed to meet performance and content standards. Explicit directions tell how the readers will demonstrate their growth in knowledge. The "product" reflects this growth.



For example, Mrs. Henry in the Classroom Challenge decides that a WebQuest would be an excellent way to introduce her students to finding information on the Internet while learning about the battles of the Revolutionary War. She has her students compete in the Revolutionary War Battle Site Tour WebQuest at www.fcps.k12.va.us/LondonTowneES/Webquests/rw/rwtourwebquest/tourwebquest.htm. The introduction to the WebQuest states, "Your class is competing for a grant that will allow you to tour Revolutionary War battle sites. You will learn about the battles and the important people who were involved in the battles. You will also have the opportunity to learn about planning a trip." The task requires students to gather information about Revolutionary War battle sites in one of three regions of the country (New England, Mid-Atlantic, or South), to decide which sites to visit, and to create a plan for the trip. The students must convince the grant committee that their class should be awarded the grant to take the tour. The process involves students working in groups to decide which area of the country to tour and then to conduct research on the battle fields they choose to visit. Finally, the students are to create a plan with information about the battles and leaders of the battles and the budget for the trip. The resources include several links to timelines, battlefields, and the National Park Service. The WebQuest includes a rubric for the teacher to use to evaluate the project. By engaging in this WebQuest, the students in Mrs. Henry's class have participated in a motivating project that prevents the frustration of haphazardly searching on the Internet, by presenting the students with a few links recommended by an educator.

According to Bernie Dodge, "Putting a WebQuest together is not much different from creating any kind of lesson. It requires getting your learners oriented, giving them an interesting and doable task, giving them the resources they need and guidance to complete the task, telling them how they'll be evaluated, and then summarizing and extending the lesson." WebQuests can be either long-term or short-term, depending on the instructional goal. Short-term WebQuests can take from one to three sessions, and they involve the learner in knowledge acquisition and integration of new information. Long-term WebQuests can take anywhere from one week to a month, and they involve the learner in extending and refining information through analysis and demonstration.

## Internet Projects

IRA/NCTE 7

**Internet projects** are collaborative learning experiences conducted between two or more classrooms at different locations via the Internet. These projects can be initiated by individual teachers or coordinated through a website. Susan Silverman, formerly a second-grade teacher and now a technology consultant, created many collaborative literature extension activities around a book, genre, or topic. For an example of a teacher-initiated Internet project, visit Mrs. Silverman's Webfolio at http://kids-learn.org. The Internet project Journey North (www.learner.org/jnorth/index.html) engages students in a global study of wildlife migration and seasonal change. Students in kindergarten through twelfth grade share their own field observations with classmates across North America. They track the coming of spring through the migration patterns of monarch butterflies, bald eagles, robins, hummingbirds, whooping cranes, and other birds and mammals; the budding of plants; changing sunlight; and other natural events. Other websites that host Internet projects include:

- Global Schoolhouse (www.globalschoolnet.org/GSH/pr/index.cfm). Contains interactive projects designed so students worldwide can collaborate, communicate, and learn from each other. Teachers can sign up to participate in these projects.
- Project Centre (www.2learn.ca/projects/projectcentre/projintro.html). Teachers can sign up for telecollaborative projects that provide real-world contexts such as opportunities for students to interact with experts and other professionals.
- Oz Projects (www.ozprojects.edna.edu.au/sibling/home). Contains projects set around concept or theme. Students and teachers can search for project by grade range, date, and subject.
- iEarn (www.iearn.org). Over 150 projects designed by teachers to help foster critical thinking and research skills, cultural awareness, and community involvement.
- Flat Stanley: A Travel Buddy Project (eduscapes.com/tap/topic1h.htm). E-mail project based on the book *Flat Stanley* by Jeff Brown. Classrooms make their own Flat Stanleys and keep a journal that is sent to other schools. Not limited to e-mail; postal mail can also be used.

## Internet Inquiry

To find websites that support their research and interests, students must learn how to effectively use a web browser to conduct a search. This is essential, because a haphazard approach to finding information can lead to frustration (as seen in the Classroom Challenge at the beginning of the chapter). The skills and strategies for conducting a productive search are unique to the Internet. Henry (2006, p. 618) suggests the SEARCH strategy for teaching students how to search for information on the Internet:

1. **Set a purpose for searching.** The first and most crucial step is for students to have a goal in mind to focus their search task. Teachers can help students with this step by asking students to think about what information they are trying to locate.
2. **Employ effective search strategies.** Next, teachers can help students to activate prior knowledge about the topic of the search and use keywords as effective search strategies. Henry (2006) relates, "Providing students with a basic knowledge foundation of the topic to be explored causes searches to become more focused as the selection of appropriate keywords becomes easier" (p. 618).
3. **Analyze search-engine results.** Once the search results have been displayed, students must then be able to determine which results will provide the most relevant information to the search goal. When a web page has been selected, students should skim the page for the URL (Uniform Resource Locator, the address of the website), make inferences, and look for highlighted terms to determine whether or not the information is relevant.
4. **Read critically and synthesize information.** After a web page has been selected, critically evaluate the content for authenticity and relevancy. "Because anyone can publish anything on the Web, students need to learn how to determine the source of information and if the source is reliable or reputable" (p. 620). Teachers can provide students with guidelines for what to look for when reading a website:

identify the author or institution associated with the website, the purpose for the website, the intended audience, the appropriate copyright data, and whether the information meets the needs of their intended audience. An easy source to use for checking basic information is the textbook or encyclopedia in the classroom. Clearly erroneous information may be identified quickly this way.

5. **Cite your sources.** Documenting your sources used (even from the Internet) is a necessary part of any research. Landmarks Citation Machine (http://citationmachine.net) is a free, easy-to-use citation service that can assist students in the formatting of source citations. "Students simply select the type of resource they want to cite, fill in the corresponding form, and the citation is provided that can then be copied and pasted into their reference list" (p. 622).
6. **How successful was your search?** Finally, students should reflect on the search process to identify the strategies they employed that were successful or unsuccessful and how they would approach the search task differently in the future.

The information needed to fulfill the goal of the search more than likely will come from several websites. Students will then need to synthesize the information into one response. Determining authenticity and relevancy of information from multiple websites, integration of that information into existing prior knowledge, and then synthesizing that information into a coherent response are difficult tasks to say the least. Students will need a great deal of modeling and scaffolding by the teacher slowly releasing responsibility to them over time until they become independent. This kind of research can be helped by the school librarian-media specialist. He or she may be able to introduce students to the research process, serve as another guide as students collect information and frame their reports, and help you, the teacher, identify good websites to use.

Ithaki 4 KiDs (kids.ithaki.net) is a metasearch engine designed specifically to help young students find the best sites just for them by searching in real time several search engines for kids (e.g., DmozKids, Yahooligans, FactMonster, ArtKIDSRule, AolKIDS, AwesomeLibrary, and KidsClick). Ithaki Metasearch (www.ithaki.net) is for older students (ages ten to twelve) and searches worldwide search engines, such as Google, Yahoo, OpenDirectory, AskJeeves, Teoma, Hotbot, Wisenut, and Alltheweb). Ithaki does not add sponsored results.

There are also several online encyclopedias to assist students with research. Some include audio and video clips and links to other pertinent articles. A few online encyclopedias include:

- Encyclopedia Mythica (www.pantheon.org) is an encyclopedia of mythology, folklore, and religion from around the world. The content is separated into six geographical regions, with an information search feature.
- Encarta (http://encarta.msn.com) allows users to search articles and historical documents. It also contains literature guides and homework starts; some features may require membership.
- Encyclopedia.com (www.encyclopedia.com) allows users to search for articles by letter or keyword.
- DK/Google's e-encyclopedia (www.dke-encyc.com) allows users to search for information sorted by nine categories from space to arts and entertainment.

Because there is such a wide spectrum of online research tools available, determining authenticity and relevancy of information from multiple websites is an important part of online research projects.



## Safety and Censorship

The Internet is an open network in which anyone can post almost anything. Because Internet search engines find information based on keywords that might appear in a variety of contexts, the search results might include content inappropriate for students. To prevent this from happening, schools require filtering software, such as NetNanny (www.netnanny.com), that blocks access to inappropriate sites and keywords which are updated regularly. If a teacher would like access to a site that is blocked, it can be unblocked. Students can also use search engines that are designed for them, such as Ithaka4KiDs, discussed above. Teachers can also "bookmark" sites that are safe for students to access.

Though parents and teachers need to be cautious about students' Internet browsing, it is equally important to teach students how to protect themselves. Educators must discuss with students why some information is not appropriate for them and teach students how to evaluate websites for credibility and to never give out personal information on the Internet. Additional resources for teachers and families on child Internet safety include:

- The American Library Association's Online Safety Rules and Regulations web page (www.ala.org/ala/oif/foryoungpeople/youngpeopleparents/especiallyyoungpeople.htm) provides a list of websites on child Internet safety.
- The Net Smartz (www.netsmartz.org) website, sponsored by the National Center for Missing and Exploited Children and Boys and Girls Clubs of America, provides educational resources for children (ages five to seventeen), parents, and teachers on how to stay safer on the Internet.
- The SafeKids.com (http://safekids.com) website provides guidelines for parents and rules to ensure kids' online safety.

## Selecting and Evaluating Internet Sites

Just as not all websites are appropriate for students, not all websites are reader friendly or contain worthwhile information. When selecting websites for students, a number of considerations must be made to ensure that the site is a source of good information and is designed to support the emerging navigational skills of students, rather than becoming a frustrating experience (Schrock, 2008). The following questions will guide your selection:

- Does the page take a long time to load?
- Are there big pictures on the page?
- Is the author's name and e-mail address displayed on the page?
- Is there a picture on the page that you can use to choose links (such as a site map)?
- If you go to another page, is there a way to get back to the first page?
- Is there a date that tells you when the page was made?
- If there are photographs, do they look real?
- If there are sounds, do they sound read?
- Does the title of the page tell you what the site is about?
- Is there an introduction on the page telling you what is included?
- Are the facts shown on the page what you were looking for?
- Would you have gotten more information from an encyclopedia?
- Would the information have been better in the encyclopedia?
- Does the author of the page say anything with which you disagree?
- Does the page lead you to some other good information (links)?
- Does the page include information that you know is wrong?
- Do the pictures and photographs on the page help you to learn?

These questions should also be shared with students, so they can learn to judge the credibility and value of Internet sites.

## What Do We Know about Learning and Technology?

Educators must focus their attention not only on *how* students read, but also *why*. Guthrie and Anderson (1999) explain that "motivations and social interactions are equal to cognitions as foundations for reading" (p. 17). They believe that reading can be seen as engagement because "Engaged readers not only have acquired reading skills, but use them for their own purposes in many contexts" (p. 17); in fact, "an interested reader identifies with the conceptual context of a text so fully that absorbing its meaning is an effortless activity" (p. 19). Engaged readers are involved, interested, and constantly learning from their text.

## Motivation and Engagement

Teachers have observed the motivational effect of computers on students since computers were first introduced into classrooms. Reinking (2001) asserts, "Electronic texts that exploit multimedia inherently foster engagement because they naturally promote an active orientation to reading, are easier to read for more readers, fulfill a broad range of social and psychological needs, and more naturally make reading a creative, playful, and less serious activity" (p. 216). Computer technology also has a positive effect on ESL students' attitudes toward learning. LeLoup and Ponterio (2003) state, "Language learners report a positive attitude toward computer use overall when engaged in language learning tasks" (p. 1). See the Exploring Diversity feature for an example of using technology to bring together multiple cultures.

> **Video Homework Exercise**
>
> *Interview: Presentation*
>
> Go to the Homework and Exercises section of Chapter 15 of MyEducationLab and view the video, "Interview: Presentation," in which a teacher shares the final product characteristics of students' research projects and a student shares a brief demonstration. Complete the activities that follow, and save your work or transmit it to your professor as assigned.

### exploring diversity

### Technology Brings Cultures Together

Hans has just moved from Germany to the United States and entered Mr. Styles' second-grade classroom. He only speaks German and is not able to converse with other students or read books or other materials in the class. It will be a few days before the district is able to provide an ESL teacher to assist Hans. Mr. Styles uses the computer to engage Hans in reading and writing in his home language. First, Mr. Styles accesses the International Children's Digital Library (www.icdlbooks.org) and finds several books in German for Hans to read. He also finds an audio version of *The Tale of Peter Rabbit* in German on the Kids' Corner website (http://wiredforbooks.org/kids.htm). When necessary, Mr. Styles accesses an online dictionary for German-to-English translations (http://dictionary.reference.com/translate/text.html). Mr. Styles also worked with Hans' family on a project in which Hans used the Internet to create a collage of pictures and information about his previous hometown and extended family living in Germany. Hans also used a digital camera to take pictures of his family and favorite activities to share with the class.

The computer and other digital media allow Hans to have access to books and information in German. These tools also provide a motivational way for him to share his German background and family with his classmates. The visual information creates a bridge between Hans and the class that transcends words.

## Comprehension and the New Literacies

IRA/NCTE 3

The main aspect of digital texts that distinguishes them from traditional texts is their interactive nature. Digital texts are not linear. Hyperlinks embedded in websites allow the reader to go to completely different web pages or to a digital picture, video, or audio. The path of hyperlinks selected by the reader influences the direction and content of the text. In this way, the reader's purpose and choices determine the reading sequence (rather than the author). Because of the unique nature of digital text, we use different comprehension strategies than with traditional print texts (see Table 15.1). Thus, knowing when and why to click a particular hyperlink is a strategic process that influences comprehension. For example, have you ever been reading a website, clicked on a hyperlink for more information, started reading the new information, and continued to click on interesting links only to realize after a while that you have no idea how you came to be where you are now and no idea how to get back to the original website? This can be frustrating for adults and students alike. Negative experiences can develop into poor attitudes toward reading online just as with reading traditional print.

### Table 15.1

### Examples of Skills, Strategies, and Dispositions Required by the New Literacies of the Internet and Other ICTs

| Central Functions During Internet Use | Some of the New Literacy Skills, Strategies, and Dispositions That Are Required |
|---|---|
| **Identify** important questions | • Possessing a "problem definition disposition," recognizing that Internet resources are often helpful in order to better understand a problem. As you gather background information about the general nature of the issues involved, the Internet helps you ask the right question.<br>• Possessing an "ethics of Internet use disposition," recognizing the important ethical responsibilities in using a tool as powerful as the Internet and how this tool needs to be used to identify problems that will make our world a better place for all of us.<br>• Knowing when the Internet is likely to be useful and when it is not for exploring a particular problem. |
| **Navigate** information networks to locate relevant information | • Having a "multiple search strategy disposition," considering multiple search strategy possibilities and quickly evaluating the potential of each one for a given purpose.<br>• Having the disposition to maintain focus on a task and not be distracted by interesting, but irrelevant, information.<br>• Being able to select search strategies that best accomplish a particular task.<br>• When appropriate, selecting the appropriate search engine to use in a search.<br>• Using a search engine effectively to locate relevant information.<br>• Reading and comprehending the results that a search engine produces. |

*(Continued)*

## Table 15.1 *(Continued)*

| Central Functions During Internet Use | Some of the New Literacy Skills, Strategies, and Dispositions That Are Required |
|---|---|
| | • Navigating rapidly through webpages to locate the most appropriate information.<br>• Correctly inferring the contents behind a hyperlink.<br>• Searching through bulletin board or discussion list archives to locate relevant information.<br>• Searching through personal email messages and folders for relevant information.<br>• Using a listserv, email, Instant Messaging, or other communication tools to request and obtain information from knowledgeable others.<br>• Additional searching skills, depending upon the technology. |
| **Critically Evaluate** the usefulness of information that is found | • Having a "healthy skeptic disposition," always evaluating each piece of information that you encounter, thinking critically about information found on the Internet.<br>• Distinguishing relevant from irrelevant information that one encounters during a search.<br>• Using clues at a site to infer who created this information, what "stance" the author takes, and how this stance "shapes" the information that is presented.<br>• Checking multiple sources of information that differ in important ways to evaluate "truthfulness." |
| **Synthesize** information to answer the question or solve the problem | • Understanding the significance of URL endings in terms of what purposes might be served by information at a site: ".com," ".org," ".edu," and others.<br>• Having a "non-linear disposition," seeking out multiple types and sources of information and continually thinking across texts and other media about their meaning.<br>• Bookmarking and organizing bookmarks to save and organize information sources for later retrieval. |
| **Communicate** the answer to others | • Being able to rapidly coordinate and synthesize multiple sources of information from multiple media sources.<br>• Organizing informational elements using a digital mapping tool such as Inspiration.<br>• Having a "communication disposition," knowing that communication with a large number of people can have an important impact if done successfully, efficiently, and ethically.<br>• Using email to communicate the answer or solution to the problem.<br>• Knowing how and when to use Instant Messaging most effectively to communicate information.<br>• Using a weblog to communicate information effectively.<br>• Creating a webpage to communicate information effectively. |

*(Continued)*

## Table 15.1 (Continued)

| Central Functions During Internet Use | Some of the New Literacy Skills, Strategies, and Dispositions That Are Required |
|---|---|
| | • Using a word processor and associated functions effectively.<br>• Using video conferencing technologies, such as iSight and others, to communicate with others. |

*Source: Teaching with the Internet K-12: New Literacies for New Times,* 4th ed., by Leu, Leu, and Coiro. Used by permission.



**BUILDING TEACHING SKILLS: Video Exercise**

*Presentation 1*

Go to the Building Teaching Skills section of Chapter 15 of MyEducationLab and view the video, "Presentation 1," which features a student sharing her presentation on a research report about the Statue of Liberty. Complete the activities that follow, and save your work or transmit it to your professor as assigned.

# How Can We Use Technology in Language Arts Instruction?

Students today are digital natives. Ninety percent of students between the ages of five and seventeen use computers (U.S. Department of Education, 2004). Four in ten kids use a technology device to read and are often high-frequency readers (Yankelovich, 2006). Very young students come to school either having experienced their own or their parents' or siblings' use of e-mail, cell phones, iPods, and digital cameras to send pictures and music or the use of the Internet to conduct online banking, shopping, or travel. Though students come to school with experiences using digital media, they do not necessarily know how to fully access and engage with them. Digital texts and ICTs are quickly becoming the predominant way people read and communicate at work and home, and this phenomenon will only become more pervasive. Teachers can use these tools to extend students' understanding, motivation, and engagement with literacy in authentic ways that also extend opportunities to acquire the skills and strategies needed to live and work in the rapidly changing technological world.

## Scaffolding Students' Understanding of Technology

Students often navigate the Web and use online resources without being taught to comprehend the process of information selection or evaluate the quality of the content presented and think metacognitively about their search strategies. According to Kymes (2005), "This is similar to teaching students to decode print text without teaching them cognitive strategies for comprehension or metacognitive strategies to internally control learning and processing" (p. 493).

The think-aloud is an effective strategy used with print-based reading to assess students' use of comprehension strategies. Thinking aloud while reading aloud makes the invisible processes of reading visible. Teachers can use think-alouds as an instructional method. "Think-alouds allow all students to hear how others sleuth out and make sense of all these text clues so that they can recognize and adopt these strategies as their own" (Wilhelm, 2001, p. 19). After observing the teacher model the think-aloud process, students can use think-alouds to vocalize what and why they are using particular strategies, thus helping students become aware of their own strategy use.

Kymes's (2005, pp. 494–496) research on print-based think-alouds and online comprehension found that many strategies used by good readers are also important to comprehension of online information. These strategies include:

- Awareness of purpose
- Skimming, scanning, and reading selectively
- Activating prior knowledge and maintaining the dialectic
- Discovering new meanings of words
- Rereading and note-taking for retention of key information
- Interpreting or paraphrasing text and "conversing" with the author
- Evaluating text structure and quality
- Reviewing information

Kymes (2005) contends that teachers can use think-alouds as an instructional tool to model appropriate comprehension strategies when using multimedia and online ICTs. A projection device can be used to display a website on a classroom wall or screen so all students can observe the teacher navigate the website while hearing her think-aloud about strategy use. For example, the teacher might read a passage on a website in which she models how to figure out an unknown word. She might say, "I don't know this word, but because it is red, I know it's a link. If I click on the word, it might provide the definition or take me to another site that gives more context. But, I want to be careful not to click too many links that lead me away from this site."

Teachers should encourage students to engage in this same kind of self-dialogue to become aware of their own comprehension strategies when navigating online environments. Kymes (2005) states, "For students to develop higher levels of understanding, explicit or direct instruction in metacognitive strategies that regulate self-awareness, self-control, and self-monitoring are necessary. Only with specific instruction will students be able to use the technologies, such as online information sources, effectively and productively" (p. 498).

## Setting Up the Environment

Though it is common for schools to have a computer lab with enough computers to accommodate an entire class of students, most classrooms also have one or more computers. Sometimes, teachers are hesitant to allow students to use computers independently for a variety of reasons: potential misuse of software programs, accessing inappropriate websites, talking and other off-task behavior, or the constant need for assistance with software programs or an assignment. Time away from the teacher should be just as beneficial as time with the teacher, so it is justifiable that teachers are concerned about the educational value of students' computer time. Yet, teachers can do much to lay a foundation for success in the computer area.

First and most important, teachers must have a thorough working knowledge of the computer software or websites in which students will be engaged. This coupled with knowledge of students' needs will ensure an appropriate match so that the student is working at an instructional level rather than too easy or too hard, which can lead to boredom or frustration. Second, teachers should model for students exactly what is expected, behaviorally and instructionally, when students use the computer. Directions can be posted so students will be reminded of these expectations. Make sure to include a plan for what to do if a student has hardware or software problems and doesn't know what to do. Finally, a schedule can be posted so students are aware of when and how long they have to work on the computer.

## Internet Workshop

IRA/NCTE 8

**Internet workshop** is an instructional framework developed by Don Leu (2002). Much like reading/writing workshop, it is designed to assist students with understanding the new literacies of the present and future. At the core of new literacies is learning how to learn. "It is not just that we want students to know how to read and write; we want them to know how to continuously learn new skills and strategies required by the new technologies of literacy that will regularly emerge" (p. 467). Internet workshop generally includes the following procedures:

1. Locate a site on the Internet with content related to a classroom unit of instruction and set a bookmark for the location. This ensures that the site is appropriate for the age and readability of the students, and it limits random surfing.
2. Design an activity, inviting students to use the site as they accomplish content, critical literacy, or strategic knowledge goals in your curriculum (as students progress, you may also invite them to develop independent inquiry projects). This step introduces students to the site and develops important background knowledge and navigation strategies for effective use of the Internet. The activity should be open-ended so students have some inquiry options about the information they will bring back to share at the end of the workshop.
3. Complete the research project. Assigning students to a schedule will assure they have enough time during the week to complete the activity.
4. Have students share their work, questions, and new insights at the end of the week during a workshop session. You may also use this time to prepare students for the next workshop experience that may extend opportunities to explore questions raised or emerging interests from the previous workshop activity.

This framework can be used to explore many topics through simulations, WebQuests, and other inquiry/Internet projects. For an example of an Internet Workshop that simulates the U.S. Senate hearings on the *Titanic* disaster, see Ms. Fields' Internet Workshop on the *Titanic* (Figure 15.6) at www.sp.uconn.edu/~djleu/titanic.html. Internet Workshops can also be designed around children's literature and author studies. Cyberguides (www.sdcoe.k12.ca.us/score/cyberguide.html), developed around the language arts standards of California, provide Internet activities around major works of children's literature.

In addition to content, students learn crucial literacy skills and strategies, including how to conduct an effective search on the Internet; how to determine if information on the Internet is valid, reliable, and current; how to use the Internet to extend learning beyond traditional forms of information; and how the Internet and other ICTs allow communication with others around the world to broaden our perspectives and understanding.

**Figure 15.6** Ms. Fields' Internet Workshop on the Titanic

In this activity you will do the following:

- · Conduct research on the Internet and discover information about people who were on the Titanic.
- · Read and take notes about people on the Titanic.
- Try and learn the complete story about these people.

Back + O - X 2 6 Search Favorites 6

- When you are ready, you will be called as a witness to the U. S. Senate Hearings on the Titanic Disaster. You will take the part of the person(s) you have studied and tell your story about what happened.
- · You will be asked to respond to questions as if you were this person.

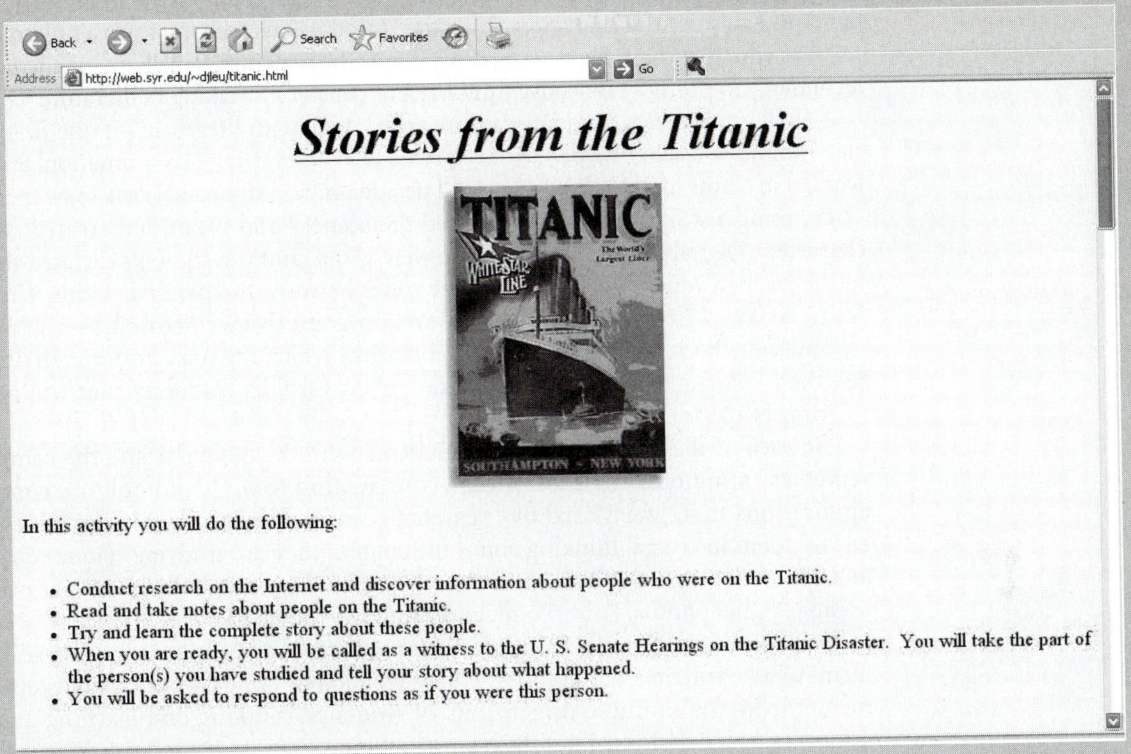


Used by permission.

## How Can We Assess Students' Reading and Writing with Technology?

In today's high-stakes testing environment, often teachers feel pressure to raise test scores. As a result, low-level skill and drill computer programs are employed to the exclusion of activities that require higher-level critical thinking. The use of technology to promote basic literacy skills is evident in both high- and low-income schools, but is particularly devastating to students in low-income schools. The best use of technology in support of learning is for knowledge generation and inquiry. Technology applications can be used in unique and powerful ways to assess students' learning in which teachers and students focus on knowledge acquisition rather than regurgitation.

In his book *I Have Computers in My Classroom—Now What?*, Bob Johnstone (2006) writes about several ways he and his colleagues use technology to capture students' learning in a way that other more traditional assessments cannot. For instance, open-minded portraits is "an activity to help students think more deeply about the characters in a book and reflect on events in the book from the characters' points of view" (p. 63), thus, leading students to deeper comprehension. Using PowerPoint, students select several defining moments when two or three of the main characters change. Then, the student creates a menu with hyperlinks to pages representing each of these defining moments. Each page includes the supporting text from the book and the student's drawings of the characters. Over the "mind" of each character is a link to a page that has what the characters are thinking about the situation. This is an excellent use of technology to promote reflective thinking and perspective-taking in literature.

At all grade levels, students can use technology with literature. In one first-grade classroom, the teacher helped children retell fairy tales using clay animation. Students worked in teams to reread the story and decide on the important parts to be included. Then, using a storyboard, they designed the scenery and props and created the clay characters. Digital photos of each scene were taken, and the students dictated the text to the teacher, which would become the slides between the pictures. Using Windows Movie Maker, a free downloadable software program (www.microsoft.com), the photos and slides became short claymation movies of which the students were very proud. See the Exploring Children's Literature feature for web resources that will help in selecting books for your students.

In each of these applications, the students were the designers and the computers served as "mindtools" or a knowledge construction tool. "Mindtools are computer applications that, when used by learners to represent what they know, necessarily engage them in crucial thinking about the content they are studying" (Jonassen, Carr, and Yuch, 1998, p. 24). Each application of technology just highlighted—word processing, digital photos, PowerPoint, and Windows Movie Maker—allowed the teacher to assess students' "crucial thinking about content" in a way that more traditional forms of assessment could not. In this way, technology applications can assist teachers in capturing the multiple dimensions of students' thinking and learning and can inform critical decisions about future instruction.

## exploring Children's Literature

### Web Resources for Selecting Children's Literature

**www.africaaccessreview.org/about.cfm**
Africa Access Review

**www.carolhurst.com/titles/allreviewed.html**
Carol Hurst's Children's Literature Site

**childrensbookreviews.pbwiki.com**
Children's Book Reviews

**www.midwestbookreview.com/cbw/index.htm**
Children's Bookwatch Newsletter

**www.ucalgary.ca/~dkbrown/index.html**
Children's Literature Web Guide

**www.dawcl.com**
Database of Award-Winning Children's Literature

**www.theedgeoftheforest.com**
*The Edge of the Forest*: A Children's Literature Monthly online journal

**www.mcpl.lib.mo.us/readers/series/juv**
Database of Juvenile Series and Sequels

**www.kid-lit.com/search.htm**
Kid-Lit.com

**www.nytimes.com**
*New York Times* Children's Book Reviews

**www.noflyingnotights.com/sidekicks/index.html**
Side Kicks: Graphic Novel Reviews

# How Can We Support Diversity and Differentiated Instruction in the Classroom?

IRA/NCTE 6

Cummins, Brown, and Sayers (2007) believe technology-supported instruction and projects can increase academic engagement among students of diverse backgrounds based on the extent to which two significant factors are present: (1) students are encouraged to explore and appreciate aspects of their own cultural and linguistic heritage, and (2) students come to see themselves as intelligent and capable human beings in the process of carrying out these projects (p. 216). Labbo (2005) states, "It is clear that when students gather and share cultural information for a cross-cultural Internet project, students engage in reading that is inherently meaningful, insightful, and motivating. The Internet opens up the world to students and helps them develop a respect for diversity" (p. 174).

The following are two examples of teacher-created Internet projects that engage students in sharing relevant and meaningful cultural information:

- Project FRESA (eden.clmer.csulb.edu/netshare/cti ) is a collaborative project designed by two teachers in the Ocean View School District in Oxnard, California (see Figure 15.7). Together, their classes created a multimedia, cross-curricular anthology about the relationship between the strawberry crops that surround and sustain the local community, the environment, and the economy to their lives. In the process, many questions were raised about the impact of the strawberry farming on the physical health of the workers. The project also helped the students make their lives more visible and linked them in ways not possible before.
- The Cinderella around the World project (www.northcanton.sparcc.org/~ptk1nc/cinderella) is a global project that brings together classes from around the world to read multicultural versions of *Cinderella*. After reading the story, students engage in language arts, social studies, math, or science activities showcased online (see Figure 15.8).

**Lesson Plan Homework Exercise**

*Literacy and Computers*

Go to the Homework and Exercises section of Chapter 15 of MyEducationLab and read the lesson, "Literacy and Computers," about a struggling writer who is motivated to write by incorporating technology-based clip art. Complete the activities that follow, and save your work or transmit it to your professor as assigned.

Online resources such as Intercultural E-mail Classroom Connections (www.iecc.org) and Global SchoolNet (www.globalschoolnet.org/index.html) are free services to help teachers link with partners in other cultures and countries for e-mail classroom pen pals and other project exchanges. Teachers can involve students in creating personal technology-supported projects such as digital storytelling and biographies that provide authentic opportunities for students to bring their home culture into the classroom and share with other students around the world.

Technology resources for English language learners include:

- The Ultralingua Online Dictionary (www.ultralingua.com/onlinedictionary) provides a word look-up in multiple languages and also turns any website into a dictionary. Just type in the web address of any website, and it becomes dictionary enabled. The site also provides a grammar reference.
- The ESL Podcast website (eslpod.com) is a free online service that provides stories in English at a slower speed and uses everyday phrases and expressions.

**Figure 15.7**

## Project FRESA Website

Back Search Favorites

### Journals

I am related to the strawberries because my whole family has worked in the strawberry fields. Every day, my mom used to get up at 4:00 a.m., make her lunch, and go to work. When she got home I would be already asleep. My two aunts also worked in the strawberry fields. When they would get home they were very tired. It was really hard for them because they would have to stand up all day.
-Eliana

Yo aprendí de que el veneno puede dañar al ser humano, matar a las plantas y también a los pájaros.
-Yuri



The uses of English expressions are explained after the story is presented. All podcasts have an 8- to 10-page learning guide, with complete transcripts and more vocabulary, explanations, and cultural information.

- The International Children's Digital Library (www.icdlbooks.org) provides online access to print books and audiobooks in many languages. The Reading Is Fundamental site (www.rif.org/readingplanet) and Story Place (www.storyplace.org) have stories read aloud in Spanish and English. Audiobooks for Free (www.audiobooksforfree.com) hosts hundreds of audiobooks in several genres and languages available to download to MP3 players free of charge. A filter is available to allow the visitor to search for audiobooks appropriate for students. Audiobooks are in abridged or unabridged formats.

## Assistive Technology

IRA/NCTE 4

Computers and other technologies allow students to work in multimodal ways, providing the opportunity to differentiate instruction. Supportive technology can be especially helpful in assisting students with learning disabilities and mental, physical, and emotional challenges.

**Figure 15.8**

## Cinderella around the World Website

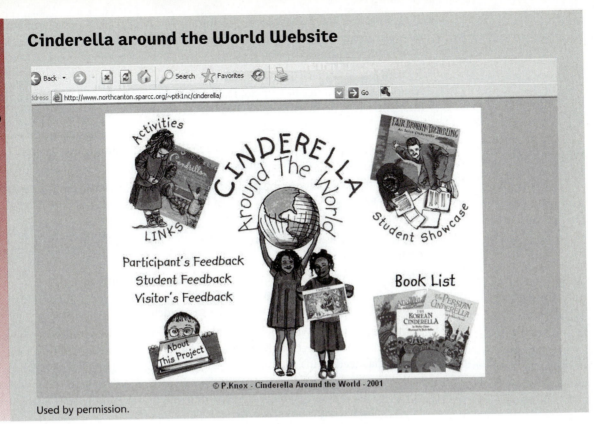

Used by permission.

- Accessibility options: Microsoft (www.microsoft.com/enable) and Apple (www.apple.com/education/accessibility) have many accessibility options available as part of the software or browser functions. For visual impairments, the contrast, scroll bar, icon size, and the width and speed of the cursor can be adjusted; also a magnifier that enlarges a portion of the screen where the cursor is placed and a voice recognition and text-to-speech screen reader can be turned on. For hearing impairments, SoundSentry provides a visual alert when the computer makes a sound, and ShowSounds displays captions for the speech and sound elements of various programs. Both can simply be switched on.
- Specialized adaptive technology: The adjustments to web browsers and software just mentioned may not meet the needs of all students with special needs to work around their areas of challenge. Alternative keyboards, such as IntelliKeys (www.intellitools.com), can be customized in appearance and functions with special printed overlays. Input devices, such as Kurzweil 3000 (www.kurzweiledu.com/kurz3000.aspx) allows any printed material to be scanned in and then read aloud (or it will read aloud a student's typed text). Also, high-powered screen magnifiers such as ZoomText (www.aisquared.com) provide magnified displays of text in high definition for easy viewing.
- Talking books: Talking storybooks on CD or online provide decoding, vocabulary, pronunciation, and fluency opportunities to students who struggle with reading. The National Center for Accessible Media (ncam.wgbh.org/ebooks/comparison.html) provides a matrix that identifies the capabilities and technological aspects of e-books and digital talking books software and hardware that make print accessible to readers with learning difficulties or vision impairments.

- Skills software: The Texas Assistive Technology Networks offer a review of current software programs that may assist struggling readers (www.texasat.net/default.aspx?name=trainmod.reading).
- Text-to-speech readers: Text-to-speech readers, such as ReadPlease (www.readplease.com), a free download, read any text including websites, e-mails, and files. The voice speed, word color, and background color can also be adjusted.
- Online translators: The American Sign Language browser (commtechlab.msu.edu/sites/aslWeb/browser.htm) and Online Braille Translator (pbskids.org/arthur/print/Braille) provide online translations of any text.
- Internet site accessibility: WebXACT (www.webxact.com) is a free online service that lets users test single pages of web content for quality, accessibility, and privacy issues.
- E-Buddies (www.ebuddies.org): This site is dedicated to enhancing the lives of people with intellectual disabilities by providing opportunities for one-to-one friendships.
- Internet inquiry: Visit the Center for Applied Special Technology (www.cast.org/teachingeverystudent/toolkits) for an online toolkit and model lesson on Internet inquiry opportunities for students with special needs.
- Internet projects and WebQuests provide unique opportunities for students with and without special needs to build understanding and friendships with students with special needs. Kids' Quests (www.cdc.gov/ncbddd/kids/kidhome.htm) are six WebQuests designed for students in fourth, fifth, and sixth grades intended to get kids to think about people with disabilities and some of the issues related to daily activities, health, and accessibility.
- Reading Matrix, sponsored by the National Center for Technology Innovation (www.nationaltechcenter.org/matrix): This matrix matches technology tools with supporting literature on promising practices for the instruction of reading for students with disabilities.

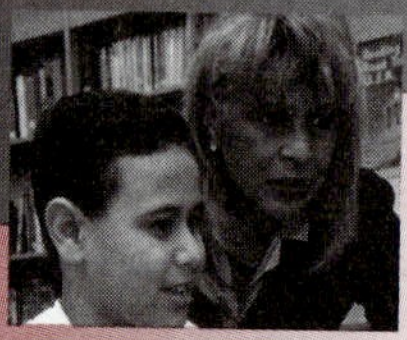

## What Professional Development Resources Can Help Us Learn about Technology?

The emphasis at the beginning of this chapter was on the changing nature of literacy and how new technologies continue to emerge, which requires educators to think about the changing definition of literacy. According to the International Reading Association's (IRA) Position Statement *Integrating Literacy and Technology in the Curriculum* (2001) at www.reading.org/resources/issues/positions_technology.html: "To become fully literate in today's world, students must become proficient in the new literacies of ICT. Therefore, literacy educators have a responsibility to effectively integrate these technologies into the literacy curriculum in order to prepare students for the literacy future they deserve" (p. 2). The position statement recommends that teachers:

- Take full advantage of professional development opportunities in technologies such as the Internet.
- Systematically integrate Internet applications and other ICTs in thoughtful ways into the literacy curriculum, especially in developing the critical literacies essential to effective information use.
- Explore the instructional strategies and resources developed by other teachers on the Internet.
- Regularly read professional publications such as books, print journals, and online journals to stay current on the research on and practical ideas for using technology to improve students' literacy learning.
- Join professional electronic mailing lists to exchange insights about effective instructional strategies (p. 3).

The Internet and other ICTs can be powerful resources for professional development for teachers of literacy. Increasingly, the Internet is being used as a way to deliver professional development to teachers in the form of online courses; listservs and discussion boards; live chats with experts in education; and websites with articles, materials, and lesson plans.

- The ReadWriteThink site (www.readwritethink.org) is sponsored by the International Reading Association (IRA) and the National Council of Teachers of English (NCTE) and offers teachers a wealth of lesson plans that connect literacy to technology.
- The IRA's technology resources website (www.reading.org/resources/issues/focus_technology.html) lists resources on the use of technology in literacy. The NCTE has a web page on online reading and writing (www.ncte.org/collections/weblit).
- Listservs, mailing lists, and discussion groups are available for educators to join if you have an e-mail account. A message sent to the mailing list address is distributed to all member subscribers. Mailing lists are used for discussions between people with similar interests. A list of discussion forums is provided through the IRA website (www.reading.org/resources/community/discussions.html). A list of all listservs can be found at www.tile.net/lists.
- Reading Rockets (www.readingrockets.org) and Reading Is Fundamental (www.rif.org) are two excellent websites that provide information for educators about literacy. There are many other excellent literacy sites on the Internet.
- Podcasts (www.podcastforteachers.org) and Blogs for Teachers (educational.blogs.com) are websites that list podcasts and blogs specifically for educators.
- Websites created by other teachers and students offer a great way to find out how other teachers are integrating literacy and technology. The IRA hosts a site that highlights the websites of the Miss Rumphius winners—educators who develop and share exceptional Internet resources for literacy and learning (www.reading.org/resources/community/links_rumphius_links.html).

revisit the

## classroomchallenge

How did Mrs. Henry help her students conduct successful Internet searches? First, she showed them how to use a search engine designed specifically for younger students. Then, she modeled the steps of the SEARCH strategy using one of the battles from the Revolutionary War as an example. After modeling the strategy several times, Mrs. Henry divided the students into groups and guided them through the process of using the SEARCH strategy.

How did Mrs. Henry help students navigate the text once they found a site? Once students were successful with finding a site, it was important that they know how to navigate it to find information. Mrs. Henry decided to conduct a think-aloud of her own thoughts as she navigated a website. The think-aloud allowed students to see how Mrs. Henry made decisions about when to click on a link, icon, or photo to find more information, when to skim information, and when to slow down and read carefully.

What other technology resources can students use to find information on their Revolutionary War battle? As discussed earlier, Mrs. Henry used a WebQuest on Revolutionary War battles. Students could also participate in Internet projects, take virtual field trips, and use online encyclopedias. Digital cameras and camcorders could be used to document field trips to Revolutionary War sites, and students could write reflections of their visits and post them on the class web page.

## chapterreview

### Why Is Technology Important for Reading and Writing?

Digital technologies are motivating and engaging for students. The Internet and other ICTs provide students with access to information that enhances their educational opportunities. Students of today will enter an information-based job market of tomorrow. Therefore, it is essential that they develop the literacy skills necessary to acquire and use information from computers and other ICTs.

### What Do We Know about Technology?

Computer hardware and software can effectively supplement and enhance the literacy curriculum. Software such as drill-and-practice, tutorials, and gamelike programs, can provide independent practice of literacy skills. Simulation, multimedia, and writing and publishing software can promote critical and creative thinking. Hardware such as digital cameras, camcorders, handheld devices, and audio players can provide students with opportunities to create or capture their ideas and share them with others. The selection of software and hardware should be based on the needs of the students in the classroom. The Internet brings the world into the classroom. Teachers and students have access to books, audiobooks, and authors, and students can publish their writing and talk to other students around the world. Curricular connections can be enhanced through Internet projects, WebQuests, and Internet inquiry. Teachers must ensure student safety when accessing the Internet and teach students to be cautious about Internet browsing. Teachers and students must also carefully select and evaluate websites.

### What Do We Know about Learning and Technology?

Computers and other technology can be motivational for students. When students are motivated to read, they are more likely to become engaged readers. Yet, becoming engaged in reading depends on the students' ability to comprehend digital texts. Because of the unique nature of digital texts, students need to develop and use different comprehension strategies than they would with traditional texts.

### How Can We Use Technology in Language Arts Instruction?

Teachers can do much to scaffold students' understanding of how to read and comprehend digital texts. Teachers can model their own thinking as they navigate web pages by thinking aloud and teaching students to engage in the think-aloud process themselves. Teachers can also set up the classroom computer area to promote success by becoming knowledgeable of the software or Internet activity the students will be doing, by providing clear and consistent directions for what is expected behaviorally and instructionally in the computer area, and by posting a schedule for student work times in the computer area. Internet workshop is a framework for assisting students with learning the new literacies of the digital age.

### How Can We Assess Students' Reading and Writing with Technology?

Technology applications allow teachers to capture students' learning in new ways. Students become the designers, and computers serve as the knowledge construction tool. Teachers can use creative applications of technology to assess students' thinking about content, context, and collaboration in ways that traditional forms of assessment can not.

### How Can We Support Diversity and Differentiated Instruction in the Classroom?

Technology can support academic engagement among students of diverse backgrounds. Internet projects, e-pals, and other technology-supported activities open up the world to students and engage them in learning and sharing relevant and meaningful cultural information. Assistive technology resources provide opportunities to differentiate instruction and support learning for ESL learners and learners with special needs.

### What Professional Development Resources Can Help Us Learn about Technology?

Increasingly, the Internet is being used as a way to deliver professional development. Today's teachers can access online courses, correspond through listservs and discussion boards, chat with education experts, and even find online lesson plans. With the continuous availability of the Internet for anyone with an e-mail account and Internet access, as well as the constant flow of new and relevant content becoming available by the minute, literacy educators have an unprecedented set of powerful ICTs to help them engage with professional development.

PEARSON myeducationlab™
Where the Classroom Comes to Life

Now go to www.myeducationlab.com to: take a Pretest to assess your initial comprehension of the chapter content, study chapter content with your individualized Study Plan; take a Posttest to assess your understanding of chapter content, practice your teaching skills with Building Teaching Skills exercises, and build a deeper, more applied understanding of chapter content with Homework and Exercises.

# References




Acheson, K., & Gall, M. (1997). *Techniques in the clinical supervision of teachers.* New York: Longman.

Adams, M. (1990). *Beginning to read: Thinking and learning about print.* Cambridge, MA: MIT Press.

Adams, M. (2001). Alphabetical anxiety and explicit, systematic phonics instruction: Cognitive science perspectives. In S. Neuman & D. Dickinson (eds.), *Handbook of early literacy research.* New York: Guilford Press, 66–80.

Adams, M., Foorman, B., Lundberg, I., & Beeler, T. (1998). *Phonemic awareness in young children: A classroom curriculum.* Baltimore: Paul H. Brookes Publishing.

Albers, P. (2006). Imagining the possibilities of multimodal curriculum design. *English Education, 38*(2), 75–101.

Allen, J. (1999). *Words, words, words: Teaching vocabulary in grades 4–12.* Portland, ME: Stenhouse.

Allen, R. (2003). Expanding writing's role in learning: Teacher training holds the key to change. *Curriculum Update.* Association for Supervision and Curriculum Development.

Allen, V. (1991). Teaching bilingual and ESL children. In J. Flood, J. Jensen, D. Lapp, and J. Squire (eds.), *Handbook of research on teaching the English language arts.* New York: Macmillan, 356–364.

Allington, R. (2006). *What really matters for struggling readers* (2nd ed.). New York: Longman.

Allington, R. L. & Johnston, P. H. (2002). *Reading to learn: Lessons from exemplary fourth-grade classrooms.* New York: Guilford Press.

Almasi, J. F. (1995). The nature of fourth graders' sociocognitive conflicts in peer-led and teacher-led discussions of literature. *Reading Research Quarterly, 30,* 314–351.

Alvermann, D. (1991). The discussion web: A graphic aid for learning across the curriculum. *The Reading Teacher, 45*(2), 92–99.

Anderson, R., Hiebert, E., Scott, J., & Wilkinson, I. (1984). *Becoming a nation of readers.* Champaign–Urbana, IL: Center for the Study of Reading.

Anderson, R. C. & Nagy, W. (1992). The vocabulary conundrum. *American Educator, 16*(4), 14–18, 44–47.

Anderson, R. C. & Pearson, P. D. (1984). A schema theoretic view of basic processes in reading comprehension. In P. D. Pearson, R. Bar, M. L. Kamil, and P. Mosenthal (eds.), *Handbook of reading research* (Vol. I). White Plains, NY: Longman, 255–291.

Anderson, R. C., Wilson, P. T., & Fielding, L. G. (1988). Growth in reading and how children spend their time outside school. *Reading Research Quarterly, 23,* 285–303.

Applebee, A. (1994). Toward a thoughtful curriculum: Fostering discipline-based conversation. *English Journal, 83*(3), 45–52.

Armbruster, B. & Osborn, J. (2003). *Put reading first.* Jessup, MD: National Institute for Literacy.

Arnold, K. (1998). *Meow!* New York: Holiday House.

Aronson, E., Blaney, N., Sikes, J., Stephan, G., & Snapp, P. (1978). *The jigsaw classroom.* Beverly Hills, CA: Sage.

Atwell, N. (1998). *In the middle: New understandings about writing, reading, and learning* (2nd ed.). Portsmouth, NH: Heinemann.

Au, K. (1998). Social constructivism and the school literacy learning of students of diverse backgrounds. *Journal of Literacy Research, 30*(2), 297–319.

Au, K. (2002). Elementary programs: Guiding change in a time of standards. In S. B. Wepner, D. S. Strickland, and J. T. Feeley (eds.), *The administration and supervision of reading programs* (3rd ed.). New York: Teachers College Press, 42–58.

August, D. & Shanahan, T. (2006). *Handbook of research on the teaching of language learners.* Mahwah, NJ: Lawrence Erlbaum.

Babbitt, N. (1975). *Tuck everlasting.* New York: Square Fish.

Bacmeister, R. (1969). "Galoshes" from *Voices in the night.* New York: Dutton Children's Books.

Bajaj, V. (2004). *How many kisses do you want tonight?* New York: Little, Brown and Co.

Baker, L., Dreher, M. J., & Guthrie, J. T. (2000). Why teachers should promote reading engagement. In L. Baker, M. J. Dreher, and J. T. Guthrie (eds.), *Engaging young readers.* New York: Guilford Press, 1–16.

Baker, S., Gersten, R., & Graham, S. (2003). Teaching expressive writing to students with learning disabilities. *Journal of Learning Disabilities, 36*(2), 109–123.

Bang, B. (1978). *The old woman and the rice thief.* New York: Greenwillow Books.

Barr, Rebecca. (1986). Studying Classroom Reading Instruction. *Reading Research Quarterly 21*(3), 231–236.

Barrera, R., Liguori, O., & Salas, L. (1993). Ideas a literature can grow on: Key insights for enriching and expanding children's literature about the Mexican-American experience. In V. J. Harris (ed.), *Teaching multicultural literature in grades K–8.* Norwood, MA: Christopher-Gordon, 203–241.

Mildred L. Batchelder Award: www.ala.org/ala/alsc/awardsscholarships/literaryawds/batchelderaward/batchelderaward.htm

Bear, D., Invernizzi, M., Templeton, S., & Johnston, F. (2004). *Words their way* (3rd ed.). Upper Saddle River, NJ: Pearson Education.

Beck, I., McKeown, M. G., & Kucen, L. (2002). *Bring words to life: Robust vocabulary instruction.* New York: Guilford Press.

Beers, C. & Beers, J. (1991). Understanding children's spelling. In D. Booth (ed.), *Spelling links.* Portsmouth, NH: Heinemann.

Beers, C. & Beers, J. (1991). Children's Knowledge of Inflected Morphology in Spelling. In S. Templeton and D. Bear (eds.) *Development of orthographic knowledge: Foundations of literacy.* Hillsdale, NJ: Lawrence Erlbaum.

Beers, C. & Beers, J. (1992). Children's spelling of English inflectional morphology. In S. Templeton and D. Bear (eds.), *Development of orthographic knowledge and the foundations of literacy.* Hillsdale, NJ: Lawrence Erlbaum, 231–252.

Beers, J. (1995). Spelling development: Stages and strategies. In *Spelling research and information: An overview of current research and practices.* Glenview, IL: Scott Foresman.

Beers, J. (2005). *Developmental spelling assessment.* Unpublished test.

Beers, J. & Henderson, E. (1977). A study of developing orthographic concepts among first graders. *Research in the Teaching of English, 11*(2), 133–148.

Pura Belpré Medal: www.ala.org/ala/alsc/awardsscholarships/literaryawds/belpremedal/belprmedal.htm

Benedict, H. (1979). Early lexical development: Comprehension and production. *Journal of Child Language, 6,* 183–200.

Bereiter, C. & Scardamalia, M. (1987). *The psychology of written composition.* Hillsdale, NJ: Lawrence Erlbaum.

Berko, J. (1958). The child's learning of English morphology. *Word, 14,* 140–177.

Biemiller, A. (2004). Teaching vocabulary in the primary grades: Vocabulary instruction needed. In J. F. Baumann and E. J. Kame'enui (eds.), *Vocabulary instruction: Research into practice.* New York: Guilford Press, 28–40.

Blachowicz, C., Fisher, P., Ogle, D., & Watts-Taffe, S. (2006). Vocabulary: Questions from the classroom. *Reading Research Quarterly, 41*(4), 524–539.

Blachowicz, C. & Fisher, P. (2006). *Teaching vocabulary in all classrooms* (3rd ed.). Upper Saddle River, NJ: Pearson-Prentice Hall.

Blachowicz, C. & Obrochta, C. (2005). Vocabulary visits: Developing content vocabulary in the primary grades. *The Reading Teacher, 59,* 262–269.

Blachowicz, C. & Ogle, D. (2008). *Reading comprehension: Strategies for independent learners* (2nd ed.). New York: Guilford Press.

Black, A. & Stave, A. M. (2007). *A comprehensive guide to readers theater: Enhancing fluency and comprehension in the middle school and beyond.* Newark, DE: International Reading Association.

Blok, H., Oostdam, R., Otter, M., & Overmaat, M. (2002). Computer-assisted instruction in support of beginning reading instruction: A review. *Review of Educational Research, 72,* 101–130.

Bloom, L. (1970). *Language development: Form and function of emerging grammars.* Cambridge, MA: MIT Press.

Bloom, P. (2000). *How children learn the meaning of words.* Cambridge, MA: MIT Press.

Bode, B. (1989). Dialogue journal writing. *The Reading Teacher.* Newark, DE: International Reading Association, *42,* 568–571.

Bodrova, E. & Leong, D. (1996). *Tools of the mind: The Vygotskian approach to early childhood education.* Englewood Cliffs, NJ: Merrill.

Bohn, C., Roehrig, A., & Pressley, M. (2004). The first days of school in the classrooms of two more effective and four less effective primary-grades teachers. *The Elementary School Journal, 104*(4), 269–287.

Boyle, O. & Peregoy, S. (1998). Literacy scaffolds: Strategies for first- and second-language readers and writers. In M. Opitz (Ed.), *Literacy instruction for culturally and linguistically diverse students.* Newark, DE: International Reading Association.

Britton, J. (1970). *Language and learning.* London: Penguin.

Britton, J., Burgess, T., Martin, N., McLeod, A., & Rosen, H. (1975). *The development of writing abilities.* London: Macmillan Education.

Bromley, K. (2003). Building a sound writing program. In L. Morrow, L. Gambrell, and M. Pressley (eds.), *Best practices in literary instruction.* New York: Guilford Press, 143–165.

Brown, M. (1991). *Goodnight moon* (C. Hurd, Illus.). New York: Harper.

Brown, R. (1973). *A first language: The early stages.* Cambridge, MA: Harvard University Press.

Bruner, J. (1986). *Actual minds, possible worlds.* Cambridge, MA: Harvard University Press.

Brunwin, B. (2004). *Crafting the language of poetry: Seven process approaches for developing poetic expression.* North Humberside, UK: Working with Your Children Publications.

Buss, K. & Karnowski, L. (2002). *Reading and writing nonfiction genres.* Newark, DE: International Reading Association.

Byrne, B. & Fielding-Barnsley, R. (1995). Evaluation of a program to teach phonemic awareness to young children. *Journal of Educational Psychology, 87*(3), Sept. 1995, 488–503.

Cai, M. (2002). *Multicultural literature for children and young adults: Critical issues.* Westport, CT: Greenwood Press.

Calkins, L. (1994). *The art of teaching writing.* Portsmouth, NH: Heinemann.

Calkins, L. (2001). *The art of teaching reading.* Portsmouth, NH: Heinemann.

Canado, M. (2005). English and Spanish spelling: Are they really different? *The Reading Teacher, 58,* 522–530.

Carey, A. (1978). The child as word learner. In M. Halle, J. Bresnan, and G. Miller (eds.), *Linguistic theory and psychological reality.* Cambridge, MA: MIT Press, 264–293.

Carle, E. (1984). *The very hungry caterpillar.* New York: Philomel.

Carlson, N. (1990). *I like me!* New York: Puffin.

Carson, A. (October 20, 2005). *The New York review of books.* New York: NYREV, Inc., *52*(16).

Chatton, B. (2004). Critiquing the critics: Adult values, children's responses, postmodern picture books, and Arlene Sardine. *Journal of Children's Literature, 30*(1), 31–37.

Chicago Public Schools Office of Literacy (2004). *The Chicago reading initiative.* Chicago, IL: Chicago Public Schools.

Chomsky, C. (1969). *The acquisition of syntax in children from 5–10.* Cambridge, MA: MIT Press.

Chomsky, N. (1965). *Aspects of a theory of syntax*. Cambridge, MA: MIT Press.
Chomsky, N. (1975). *Reflections on language*. New York: Pantheon.
Chomsky, N. (1986). *Knowledge of language*. New York: Praeger.
Chomsky, N. (1995). *A minimalist program*. Cambridge, MA: MIT Press.
Christensen, F. (1967). *Notes towards a new rhetoric: Six essays for teachers*. New York: Harper & Row.
Chukovsky, K. (1963). *From two to five*. Berkeley: University of California Press.
Clark, E. V. (1974). Some aspects of the conceptual basis for first language acquisition. In R. Schiefelbusch and L. Lloyd (eds.), *Language perspectives—Acquisition, retardation, and intervention*. Baltimore: University Park Press.
Clay, M. (1975). *What did I write?* Portsmouth, NH: Heinemann.
Clay, M. (2002). *An observation survey of early literacy achievement*. (2nd ed.). Portsmouth, NH: Heinemann.
Coiro, J. (2003). Reading comprehension on the Internet: Expanding our understanding of reading comprehension to encompass new literacies. *The Reading Teacher, 56*, 458–464.
Cole, A. (2003). *Knee to knee, eye to eye: Circling in on comprehension*. Portsmouth, NH: Heinemann.
Cole, J. (2003). What motivates students to read? Four literacy personalities. *The Reading Teacher, 56*(4), 326–336.
Conway, P. & Clark, C. (2003). The journey inward and outward: A reexamination of Fuller's concerns-based model of teacher development. *Teacher and Teacher Education, 19*(5), 465–482.
Cooke, G. (2002). *Keys to success for urban school principals*. Skylight Training and Publishing. Thousand Oaks, CA: Corwin Press.
Cooper, C. & Odell, L. (eds.). (1977). Evaluating writing. Urbana, IL: National Council of Teachers of English.
Cooper, J. (2003). *Helping children construct meaning* (5th ed.). Boston: Allyn & Bacon.
Cooper, J. & Kiger, N. (2005). *Literacy assessment: Helping teachers plan instruction* (2nd ed.). Boston: Houghton Mifflin.
Cooper, T. C. (1981). Sentence combining: An experiment in teaching writing. *Modern Language Journal, 65*, 158–165.
Corson, D. (1984). The case for oral language in schooling. *The Elementary School Journal, 84*, 458–467.
Crais, E. (1992). Fast mapping: A new look at word learning. In R. Chapman (ed.), *Processes in language acquisition and disorders*. St. Louis: Mosby Year Book.
Cramer, R. (1998). *The spelling connection*. New York: Guilford Press.
Cramer, R. (2004). *The language arts: A balanced approach to teaching reading, writing, listening, talking, and thinking*. Boston: Allyn & Bacon.
Cramer, R. & Cipielewski, J. (1995). A study of spelling errors in 18,599 written compositions of children in grades 1–8. In *Spelling research and information: An overview of current research and practices*. Glenview, IL: Scott Foresman.
Culham, R. (2003). *6 + 1 traits of writing: The complete guide*. Portland, OR: Northwest Regional Educational Laboratory.
Cummins, J., Brown, K., & Sayers, D. (2007). *Literacy, technology, and diversity: Teaching for success in changing times*. New York: Allyn & Bacon.
Cummins, J. & Corson, D. (1997). *Bilingual education*, Vol. 5, *International Encyclopedia of Language and Education*. Dordrecht, The Netherlands: Kluwer Academic Publishers.
Cunningham, A. E. (2005). Vocabulary growth through independent reading and reading aloud to children. In E. Heibert and M. Kamil (eds.), *Teaching and learning vocabulary: Bringing research to practice*. Mahwah, NJ: Lawrence Erlbaum.
Cunningham, A. E. & Stanovich, K. E. (1998). What reading does for the mind. *American Educator, 2*, 8–17.
Cunningham, P. (1992). Making words: Enhancing the invented spelling-decoding connection. *The Reading Teacher, 46*, 106–115.
Cunningham, P., Hall, D., & Defee, M. (1998). Non-ability grouped, multi-level instruction: Eight years later. *The Reading Teacher, 51*(8), 652–664.
Dahl, K. & Freppon, P. (1995). A comparison of inner-city children's interpretations of reading and writing instruction in the early grades in skills-based and whole language classrooms. *Reading Research Quarterly, 30*(1), 50–74.
Daiker, D. A., Kerek, A., & Morenberg, M. (eds.). (1985). *Sentence combining: A rhetorical perspective*. Carbondale and Edwardsville, IL: Southern Illinois University Press.
Daniels, H. (2002). *Literature circles: Voice and choice in book clubs and reading groups*. Portland, ME: Stenhouse.
Dandy, E. (1991). *Black communications: Breaking down the barriers*. Chicago: African American Images.
Dansereau, D. (1986). *Dyadic and cooperative learning and performance strategies*. Paper presented at annual meeting of American Educational Research Association. San Francisco.
Deshler, D. D. & Schumaker, J. B. (2006). *High school students with disabilities: Strategies for accessing the curriculum*. New York: Corwin Press.
Dewey, J. (2001). *The school and society & the child and curriculum*. Mineola, NY: Dover Publications.
Diedrich, P. B. (1974). *Measuring growth in English*. Urbana, IL: National Council of Teachers of English.
Dobson, L. (1989). Connections in learning to read and write. In J. Mason (ed.), *Reading and writing connections*. Boston: Allyn & Bacon.
Dreher, M. & Singer, H. (1980). Story grammar unnecessary for intermediate grades. *The Reading Teacher, 34*, 261–268.
Duke, N. (2000). 3.6 minutes per day: The scarcity of informational texts in first grade. *Reading Research Quarterly, 35*(2), 202–224.
Dymock, S. (1999). Learning about text structure. In G. B. Thompson & T. Nicholson (eds.). *Learning to read: Beyond phonics and whole language*. New York: Teacher's College Press, 174–192.

Dyson, A. H. (1982). The emergence of visible language: Interrelationships between drawing and early writing. *Visible Language, 16*, 360–381.

Dyson, A. (1989). *Multiple worlds of child writers: Friends learning to write.* New York: Teachers College Press.

Dyson, A. (1993). *Social worlds of children learning to write.* New York: Teachers College Press.

Dyson, A. & Freedman, S. (1991). Writing. In J. Flood, J. Jensen, D. Lapp, and J. Squire (eds.), *Handbook of research on teaching the English language arts.* New York: Macmillan, 754–774.

Echevarria, J., Vogt, M. E., & Short, D. J. (2007). *Making content comprehension for English learners: The SIOP model* (3rd (eds.). Boston: Allyn & Bacon.

Educational Testing Service (2003). *Early literacy assessment systems: Essential elements.* Princeton, NJ: Educational Testing Service.

Eeds, M. & Wells, D. (1989). Grand conversations: An exploration of meaning construction in literature study groups. *Research in the Teaching of English, 23*, 4–29.

Ehri, L. (1991). Development of the ability to read words. In R. Barr, M. Kamil, P. Mosenthal, and P. D. Pearson (eds.). *Handbook of Reading Research.* New York: Longman, 1991.

Elbow, P. (1973). *Writing without teachers.* New York: Oxford University Press.

Elbow, P. (1983). *Writing with power: Techniques for mastering the writing process.* New York: Oxford University Press.

Ellery, V. (2005). *Techniques for developing competency in phonemic awareness, fluency, vocabulary, and comprehension.* Newark, DE: International Reading Association.

Emig, J. (1971). *The composing process of twelfth graders.* Urbana, IL: National Council of Teachers of English.

Ericson, L. & Juliebo, M. F. (1998). *The Phonological Awareness Handbook for Kindergarten and Primary Teachers.* Newark, DE: International Reading Association.

Fielding, L. & Pearson, P. (1994). Reading comprehension: What works. *Educational Leadership, 51*(5), 62–68.

Fink, R. (2006). *When Jane and John couldn't read—And how they learned.* Newark, DE: International Reading Association, 71, 145.

Fischer, P. (1993). *The sounds and spelling patterns of English.* Farmington, ME: Oxton House Publishing.

Fitzgerald, J. & Spiegel, D. L. (1983). Enhancing children's reading comprehension through instruction in narrative structure. *Journal of Reading Behavior, 15*, 1–17.

Fitzgerald, J. & Teasley, A. (1986). Effects of instruction in narrative structure on children's writing. *Journal of Educational Psychology, 78*, 424–432.

Fletcher, R. & Portalupi, J. (2001). *Writing workshop: The essential guide.* Portsmouth, NH: Heinemann.

Fogelberg, E., Skalinder, C., Staz, P., Hiller, B., Bernstein, L., & Vitantonio, S. (2008). *Integrating literacy and math: Strategies for K–6 teachers.* New York: Guilford Press.

Fountas, I. & Pinnell, G. (1996). *Guided reading: good first teaching for all children.* Portsmouth, NH: Heinemann.

Fountas, I. & Pinnell, G. S. (2005). *Leveled books, K–8: Matching texts to readers for effective teaching.* Portsmouth, NH: Heinemann.

Fountas, I. & Pinnell, G. S. (2005). *The Fountas and Pinnell leveled book list, K–8, 2006–08 Edition.* Portsmouth, NH: Heinemann.

Fountas, I. & Pinnell, G. (2006). *Teaching for comprehension and fluency: Thinking, talking, and writing about reading, K–8.* Portsmouth, NH: Heinemann.

Fresch, M. (1995). Self-selection of early literacy learners. *The Reading Teacher, 49*(3), 220–227.

Fulwiler, T. (1987). *The journal book.* Portsmouth, NH: Heinemann.

Gagne, R. & Smith, E. (1962). A study of the effects of verbalization on problem solving. *Journal of Experimental Psychology, 63*, 12–18.

Galda, L. (1984). The relations between reading and writing in young children. In R. Beach and L. Birdwell (eds.), *New directions in composition research.* New York: Guilford Press, 191–203.

Gambrell, L. (1996). What research reveals about discussion. In L. Gambrell and J. Almasi (eds.), *Lively discussions! Fostering engaged reading.* Newark, DE: International Reading Association.

Gambrell, L. & Bales, R. (1986). Mental imagery and the comprehension-monitoring performance of fourth- and fifth-grade poor readers. *Reading Research Quarterly, 21*(4) (Autumn, 1986), 454–464.

Ganske, K. (2000). *Word journeys: Assessment-guided phonics, spelling, and vocabulary instruction.* New York: Guilford Press.

Gardner, H. (1993). *Multiple intelligences: The theory in practice.* New York: Basic Books.

Gaskins, I., Ehri, L., Cress, C., O'Hara, C., & Donnelly, K. (1997). Procedures for word learning: Making discoveries about words. *The Reading Teacher, 50*(4), 312–327.

Gaswami, U. (2001). Early phonological development and the acquisition of literacy. In S. Neuman and D. Dickinson (eds.), *Handbook of early literacy research.* New York: Guilford Press, 111–125.

Genesee, F., Lindholm-Leary, K., Saunders, W., & Christian, D. (2005). English language learners in U.S. schools: An overview of research findings. *Journal of Education for Students Placed at Risk, 10*(4), 363–385.

Gentry, J. (1987). *Spel is a four-letter word.* Portsmouth, NH: Heinemann.

Gilbert, S. (2001). A conversation with Elliot Aronson: No one left to hate: Averting Columbines. *New York Times.*

Gillet, J., Temple, C., & Crawford, A. (2004). *Understanding reading problems* (7th ed.). Boston: Allyn & Bacon.

Glasgow, J. N. (1996). It's my turn! Motivating young readers. *Learning and Leading with Technology, 24*(3), 20–23.

Goodlad, J. (1984). *A place called school.* New York: McGraw Hill.

Goodman, K. & Goodman, Y. (1982). Learning about psycholinguistic processes by analyzing oral reading. In F. Gollasch (ed.), *Language and literacy: The selected writings of Kenneth S. Goodman.* Boston: Routledge & Kegan Paul.

Graves, D. (1983). *Writing: Teachers and children at work.* Exeter, NH: Heinemann.

Graves, D. (1990). *Discover your own literacy.* Portsmouth, NH: Heinemann.

Graves, D. (1994). *A fresh look at writing.* Portsmouth, NH: Heinemann.

Graves, D. & Hansen, J. (1983). The author's chair. *Language Arts, 60,* 176–182.

Graves, M. F. (2006). *The vocabulary book: Learning and instruction.* New York: Teachers College Press.

Gray, R., Saski, J., McEntire, M., & Larsen, S. (1980). Is proficiency in oral language a predictor of academic success? *Elementary School Journal, 80,* 260–268.

Griffiths, P. (1986). Early vocabulary. In P. Fletcher and M. Garman (eds.), *Language acquisition* (2nd ed). New York: Cambridge University Press.

Guarino, D. (1989). *Is your mama a llama?* New York: Scholastic.

Gunning, T. (1998). *Assessing and correcting reading and writing difficulties.* Boston: Allyn & Bacon.

Guthrie, J. T. (2003). Concept oriented reading instruction. In C. E. Snow and A. P. Sweet (eds.), *Rethinking reading comprehension.* New York: Guilford Press.

Guthrie, J. T. & Anderson, E. (1999). Engagement in reading: Processes of motivated strategic, knowledgeable, social readers. In J. T. Guthrie and D. E. Alvermann (eds.), *Engaged reading.* New York: Teachers College Press.

Guthrie, J. T., Wigfield, A., & Perencevich, K. C. (eds.). (2004). *Motivating reading comprehension: Concept-oriented reading instruction.* Mahwah, NJ: Lawrence Erlbaum.

Hall, M. (1981). *Teaching reading as a language experience.* Columbus, OH: Merrill.

Halliday, M. A. K. (1973). *Explorations in the functions of language.* London: Edward Arnold.

Halliday, M. A. K. (1982). Relevant models of language. In B. Waide (ed.), *Language perspectives: Papers from the Educational Review.* London: Heinemann.

Hanna, P., Hanna, J., Hodges, R., & Rudorf, E. (1966). *Phoneme-grapheme correspondences as cues to spelling improvement.* Washington, DC: U.S. Government Printing Office.

Harste, J. C., Short, K. G., & Burke, C. I. (1988). *Creating classrooms for authors: The reading writing connections.* Portsmouth, NH: Heinemann.

Harste, J. C., Woodward, V. A., & Burke, C. I. (1984). *Language stories and literacy lessons.* Portsmouth, NH: Heinemann.

Hart, B. & Risley, T. R. (1995). *Meaningful differences in the everyday experiences of young American children.* Baltimore: Brookes.

Harvey, S. & Goudvis, A. (2000). *Strategies that work: Teaching comprehension to enhance understanding.* Portland, ME: Stenhouse.

Hawkins, C. & Hawkins, J. (1987). New York: Putnam.

Heatherington, M. (1980). *How language works.* Cambridge, MA: Winthrop Publishers.

Hegarty, M., Carpenter, P., & Just, M. A. (1991). Diagrams in the comprehension of scientific texts. In R. Barr, M. Kamil, P. Mosenthal, and P. D. Pearson (eds.), *Handbook of reading research* (Vol. II.). New York: Longman, 641–668.

Heimlich, J. E. & Pittelman, S. D. (1986). *Semantic mapping: Classroom applications.* Newark, DE: International Reading Association.

Heller, R. (2000). *Fastastic! wow! and unreal!* New York: Putnam Juvenile.

Henderson, E. (1990). *Teaching spelling* (2nd ed.). Boston: Houghton Mifflin.

Henry, L. (2006). SEARCHing for an answer: The critical role of new literacies while reading on the Internet. *The Reading Teacher, 59*(7), 614–627.

Hidi, S. & Harackiewicz, J. (2000). Motivating the academically unmotivated: A critical issue for the 21st century. *Review of Educational Research, 70*(2), 151–179.

Hillocks, G., Jr. (1986). *Research on written composition: New directions for teaching.* Urbana, IL: National Council of Teachers of English.

Hockett, Charles F. (1958). *A course in modern linguistics.* New York: Macmillan.

Hoffman, J. (1979). The intra-act procedure for critical reading. *Journal of Reading, 22*(7), 605–608.

Hoffman, J. V. (1992). Critical reading/thinking across the curriculum: Using I-Charts to support learning. *Language Arts, 69,* 121–127.

Holdaway, D. (1979). *The foundations of literacy.* Sydney: Ashton Scholastic.

Hudgins, B. & Edelman, S. (1986). Teaching critical thinking skills to fourth and fifth graders through teacher-led small group discussions. *Journal of Educational Research, 79,* 333–342.

Hughey, J. & Slack, C. (2001). *Teaching children to write.* Upper Saddle Ridge, NJ: Prentice Hall.

Hunt, K. (1965). *Grammatical structures written at three grade levels.* Urbana, IL: National Council of Teachers of English.

Hunt, K. (1977). Early blooming and later blooming syntactic structures. In C. Cooper and L. Odell (eds.), *Evaluating writing.* Urbana, IL: National Council of Teachers of English.

Individuals with Disabilities Education Act (2004). U.S. Department of Education.

International Reading Association (1996). *Standards for English Language Arts.* Newark, DE: International Reading Association.

International Reading Association (2001). *Integrating literacy and technology in the curriculum: A position statement.* Retrieved September 1, 2006 from www.reading.org/resources/issues/positons_technology.html.

International Reading Association and National Council of Teachers of English (1996). *Standards for the English language arts.* Newark, DE: International Reading Association.

Irvin, J. I. (1990). *Reading and the middle school student.* Boston, MA: Allyn & Bacon.

Jacobs, J. & Tunnell, M. (2004). *Children's literature, briefly* (3rd ed.). Upper Saddle River, NJ: Pearson.

Janeczko, P. (1990). *The place my words are looking for.* New York: Bradbury Press.

Jiminez, R. Jiménez, R. T. (2003). Literacy and Latino students in the United States: Some considerations, questions, and new directions. *Reading Research Quarterly, 38*(1), 122–128.

Johns, J. (2001). *Basic reading inventory* (8th ed.). Dubuque, IA: Kendall/Hunt.

Johnson, D. (2009). *The joy of children's literature.* Boston: Houghton Mifflin.

Johnston, P. (1987). Teachers as evaluation experts. *The Reading Teacher, 40,* 744–748.

Johnstone, B. (2006). *I have computers in my classroom—Now what?* Portsmouth, NH: Heinemann.

Jonassen, D., Carr, C., & Yuch, H. (1998). Computers as mindtools for engaging learners in critical thinking. *TechTrends, 43*(2), 24–32.

Jones, J. (2003). *Early literacy assessment systems: Essential elements.* Princeton, NJ: Educational Testing Service.

Jones, S. & Myhill, D. (2004). Seeing things differently: Teachers' construction of underachievement. *Gender and Education, 16,* 4.

Jordan, J. (1988). Nobody mean more to me than you and the future life of Willie Jordan. *Harvard Educational Review, 58,* 363–374.

Juel, C. (1988). Learning to read and write: A longitudinal study of 54 children from first through fourth grades. *Journal of Educational Psychology, 80,* 437–447.

Juel, C. (1991). Beginning reading. In R. Barr, M. Kamil, P. Mosenthal, and P. D. Pearson, eds. *Handbook of Reading Research.* New York: Longman, 759–788.

Karchmer, R., Mallette, M., Kara-Soteriou, J., & Leu, J. D., Jr. (eds.). (2005). *Innovative approaches to literacy education: Using the Internet to support new literacies.* Newark, DE: International Reading Association.

Ketch, A. (2005). Conversation: The comprehension connection. *The Reading Teacher, 59*(1), 8–13.

Killgallon, D. (1998). *Sentence composing for middle schools.* Portsmouth, NH: Heinemann. Coretta Scott King Award: www.ala.org/ala/ emiert/corettascottkingbookawards/ corettascott.cfm

Koch, K. (2000). *Wishes, lies, and dreams: Teaching children to write poetry.* New York: Harper.

Kong, A. & Fitch, E. (2003). Using book clubs to engage culturally and linguistically diverse learners in reading, writing, and talking about books. *The Reading Teacher, 56*(4), 352–363.

Krashen, S. D. (1991). *Bilingual education: A focus on current research.* Washington, DC: National Clearinghouse for Bilingual Education.

Krashen, S. D. (1992). Principles and practice in second language acquisition. Oxford, NY: Pergamon.

Krashen, S. (2004). *The power of reading: Insights from research* (2nd ed.). Portsmouth, NH: Heinemann/Libraries Unlimited.

Krashen, S. D. & Terrell, T. D. (1983). *The natural approach: Language acquisition in the classroom.* New York: Pergamon/Alemany.

Kroll, B. (1981). Developmental relationships between speaking and writing. In B. Kroll and R. Vann (eds.), *Exploring speaking-writing relationships: Connections and contrasts.* Urbana, IL: National Council of Teachers of English, 32–54.

Kroll, B. (1985). Cognitive egocentrism and the problem of audience awareness in written discourse. *Research in the Teaching of English, 12,* 269–281.

Kucan, L. & Beck, I. (2003). Inviting students to talk about expository texts: A comparison of two discourse environments and their effects on comprehension. *Reading Research and Instruction, 42,* 1–29.

Kymes, A. (2005). Teaching online comprehension strategies using think-alouds. *Journal of Adolescent and Adult Literacy, 48*(8), 492–500.

Labbo, L. (2005). Fundamental qualities of effective Internet literacy instruction: An exploration of worthwhile classroom practices. In R. Karchmer, M. Mallette, J. Kara-Soteriou, and D. Leu (eds.), *Innovative approaches to literacy education: Using the Internet to support new literacies.* Newark, DE: International Reading Association, 165–179.

Labbo, L. D. & Kuhn, M. R. (1997). *Computers and emergent literacy: Expanding upon reading.* Paper presented at the annual meeting of the College Reading Association, Boston (November).

LaFaye, A. (2001). *Dad, in spirit.* New York: Simon & Schuster Children's Publishing.

Laminack, L. & Wadsworth, R. (2006). *Learning under the influence of language and literature: Making the most of read-alouds across the day.* Portsmouth, NH: Heinemann.

Laminack, L. & Wood, K. (1996). *Spelling in use.* Urbana, IL: National Council of Teachers of English.

Langer, J. (2002). *Effective literacy instruction: Building successful reading and writing programs.* Urbana, IL: National Council of Teachers of English.

Langer, J. & Applebee, A. (1987). *How writing shapes thinking: A study of teaching and learning.* NCTE Research report No. 22. Urbana, IL: National Council of Teachers of English.

LeClair, T. (1993). The language must not sweat: A conversation with Toni Morrison. In H. Gates, Jr. and K. Appiah (eds.), *Toni Morrison: Critical perspectives past and present.* New York: Amistad Press.

Lederer, R. (1998). *Crazy English: The ultimate joy ride through our language.* Pocket Books.

Lee, C. (1991). Big picture talkers/words walking without masters: The instructional implications of ethnic voices for an expanded literacy. *Journal of Negro Education, 60,* 291–304.

Leedy, L. (1994). *Message in the mailbox: How to write a letter.* New York: Holiday House.

LeLoup, J. & Ponterio, R. (2003). Second language acquisition and technology: A review of the research. *CAL Digest*. Washington, DC: Center for Applied Linguistics.

Lenneberg, E. H. (1981). Developmental milestones in motor and language development. In V. Clark, P. Escholz, and A. Rosa (eds.), *Language: Introductory readings*. New York: St. Martin's Press.

Lenz, K. (2008). The Unit Organizer. Sent through personal communication on February 15, 2008.

Leu, D. (2002). Internet workshop: Making time for literacy. *The Reading Teacher, 55*(5), 466–472.

Leu, D. & Coiro, J. (2004). *Teaching with the Internet: New literacies for new times* (4th ed.). Norwood, MA: Christopher Gordon.

Leu, D., Grace, T., & Bevans, J. (2000). Hidden treasures: Discovering new experiences with story on the Internet. *The Dragon Lode, 19*(1), 1–5.

Leu, D., Kinzer, C., Coiro, J., & Cammack, D. (2004). Toward a theory of new literacies emerging from the Internet and other information and communication technologies. In R. B. Ruddell and N. Unrau (eds.), *Theoretical models and processes of reading* (5th ed.). Newark, DE: International Reading Association, 1570–1613.

Lewis, M. & Wray, J. (1995). *Developing children's non-fiction writing*. Leamington Spa, UK: Scholastic.

Lindfors, J. (1991). *Children's language and learning*. Boston: Allyn & Bacon.

Lipson, M. Y. & Wixson, K. K. (1991). Perspectives on reading disability research. In R. Barr, M. Kamil, P. Mosenthal, and P. D. Pearson (eds.). *Handbook of Reading Research*. New York: Longman, 1991, pp. 539–570.

Lobel, A. (1970). *Frog and toad are friends*. New York: Harper & Row.

Long, T. W. & Gove, M. K. (2003). How engagement strategies and literature circles promote critical response in a fourth-grade urban classroom. *The Reading Teacher, 57*, 350–360.

Louie, B. (2006). Guiding principles for teaching multicultural literature. *The Reading Teacher, 59*(5), 438–448.

Lubliner, S. & Smetana, L. (2005). The effects of comprehensive vocabulary instruction on Title I students' metacognitive word-learning skills and reading comprehension. *Journal of Literacy Research, 37*(2), 163–200.

Macon, J., Bewell, D., & Voight, M. (1991). *Responses to literature—Grades K–8*. Newark, DE: International Reading Association.

Maizel, J. & Petty, K. (1996). *The amazing pop-up grammar book*. New York: Dutton Juvenile.

Margulies, N. (1991). *Mapping inner space: Learning and teaching mind mapping*. Tucson, AZ: Zephyr Press.

Markson, L. & Bloom, P. (1997). Evidence against a dedicated system for word learning in children. *Nature, 385*, 813–815.

Martin, B., Jr. (1995). *Brown, brown bear, what do you see?* New York: Holt, Rinehart, and Winston.

Marzano, R. (2005). *Building background knowledge: Academic vocabulary*. Alexandria, VA: Association for Supervision and Curriculum Development.

Mason, J., Peterman, C., Powell, B., & Kerr, M. (1989). Reading and writing attempts by kindergartners after book reading by teachers. In J. Mason (ed.), *Reading and writing connections*. Boston: Allyn & Bacon.

Mayher, J., Lester, N., & Pradl, G. (1983). *Learning to write/writing to learn*. New York: Boynton/Cook.

McGee, L. (1992). An exploration of meaning construction in first graders' grand conversations. In C. Kinzer and D. Leu (eds.), *Literacy research, theory, and practice: Views from many perspectives*. Chicago: National Reading Conference.

McGinley, W. & Denner, P. R. (1987). Story impressions: A prereading/writing activity. *Journal of Reading, 31*, 248–253.

McGowan, M. (2005). My Internet projects and other online resources for the literacy classroom. In R. Karchmer et al. (eds.), *Innovative approaches to literacy education: Using the Internet to support new literacies*. Newark, DE: International Reading Association.

McKee, J. & Ogle, D. (2005). *Integrating instruction: Literacy and science*. New York: Guilford Press.

McKenna, M. & Kear, D. (1990). Measuring attitude toward reading: A new tool for teachers. *The Reading Teacher, 43*(8), 626–639.

McLaughlin, M. & Allen, M. (2002). *Guided comprehension: A teaching model for grades 3–8*. Newark, DE: International Reading Association.

McMahon, S. I. & Raphael, T. E. (eds.). (1997). *The book club connection: Literary learning and classroom talk*. New York: Teachers College Press.

McTighe, J. & Fyman, F. T., Jr. (1988). Cueing thinking in the classroom. *Educational Leadership, 45*(7), 18–24.

Mehan, H. (1979). *Learning lessons*. Cambridge, MA: Harvard University Press.

Mehler, J. & Christophe, A. (1995). Maturation and learning of language in the first year of life. In M. S. Gazzaniga (ed.), *The cognitive neurosciences*. Cambridge, MA: MIT Press, 943–954.

Miller, C. (1994). Genre as social action. In A. Freedman and P. Medway (eds.), *Genre and the New Rhetoric*. London: Taylor & Francis, 23–42.

Morris, D. & Slavin, R. (2003). *Every child reading*. Boston: Allyn & Bacon.

Morrow, L. & Brittain, R. (2003). The nature of storybook reading in elementary school: Current practices. In A. van Kleeck, S. Stahl, and E. Bauer (eds.), *On reading books to children: Parents and teachers*. Mahwah, NJ: Lawrence Erlbaum, 140–158.

Morrow, L. & Smith, J. (1990). The effects of group size on interactive storybook reading. *Reading Research Quarterly, 25*, 213–231.

Moss, B. & Newton, E. (2002). An examination of the informational text genre in basal readers. *Reading Psychology*, 23, 1–13.

Murray, D. (1985). *A writer teaches writing*. Boston: Houghton Mifflin.

Murray, D. (2004). *A writer teaches writing* (2nd ed.). Boston: Heinle.

Myhill, D. (2006). Teaching and learning in whole class discourse. *Research Papers in Education, 21*(1), 19–41.

Nagy, W. (1988). *Teaching vocabulary to improve reading comprehension.* Newark, DE: International Reading Association.

Nagy, W. (1988). *Teaching vocabulary to improve reading comprehension*. Champaign, IL: National Council of Teachers of English.

Nagy, W. E., Anderson, R. C., & Herman, P.A. (1987). Learning word meanings from context during normal reading. *American Educational Research Journal, 24*, 237–270.

Nagy, W. & Herman, P. A. (1987). Breadth and depth of vocabulary knowledge: Implications for acquisition and instruction. In M. G. McKeown and M. E. Curtis (eds.), *The nature of vocabulary acquisition.* Hillsdale, NJ: Lawrence Erlbaum, 19–35.

National Assessment of Educational Progress (2004). *The condition of education 2004.* Annual Reports Program.

National Assessment Governing Board (2009). *Reading framework for the 2009 national assessment of educational progress* (pre-publication edition). Washington, DC: American Institutes for Research.

National Communication Association. *NCA K-12 standards of communication* (pdf). Retrieved June 20, 2007, from www.natcom.org/nca/Template2.asp?bid=269.

National Council of Teachers of English (1985). *On grammar exercises to teach speaking and writing. A resolution adopted by the NCTE Board of Directors.* Urbana, IL: National Council of Teachers of English.

National Council of Teachers of English and the International Reading Association (1996). *Standards for the English language arts.* Urbana, IL/Newark, DE: National Council of Teachers of English/International Reading Association.

National Reading Panel (2000). Teaching children to read: An evidence-based assessment of the scientific research literature on reading and its implications for reading instruction. (Reports of the Subgroups; NIH Publication No. 00–4754). Washington, DC: National Institute of Child Health and Human Development, National Institutes of Health.

National Writing Project & Nagin, C. (2003). *Because writing matters: Improving student writing in our schools.* San Francisco: Jossey-Bass.

NCES (2003). *Digest of education statistics 2003.* Available: http://nces.ed.gov/programs/digest/

Neeld, E. C. & Kiefer, K. E. (1990). *Writing.* Glenview: Scott Foresman.

Nelson, K. (1973). Structure and strategy in learning to talk. *Monographs of the Society for Research in Child Development,* 38.

Nelson, K. (1974). Concept, word, and sentence: Interrelations in acquisition and development. *Psychological Review, 81*, 267–285.

Neuman, S. B. & Dickinson, D. K. (eds.). (2001). *Handbook of early literacy research.* New York: Guilford Press.

Newman, M., Ogle, D., & Costas, S. (2005). *Adventure of the American mind: NLU visual literacy project.* Presentation for Federation of Independent Illinois Colleges and Universities (April).

Newman, M., Spirou, C., & Danzer, G. (2007). *Chicago stories 1830s–World War I: Visual images for classroom instruction.* Chicago: National-Louis University.

Nieto, S. (1996). *Affirming diversity* (2nd ed.). New York: Longman.

Noden, H. (1999). *Image grammar: Using grammatical structures to teaching writing.* Portsmouth, NH: Boynton/Cook.

Noguchi, R. (1991). *Grammar and the teaching of writing: Limits and possibilities.* Urbana, IL: National of Teachers of English.

O'Connor, K. (2002). *How to grade for learning: Linking grades to standards* (2nd ed.). Glenview, IL: Pearson Professional Development.

Ogle, D. (1986). K-W-L: A teaching model that develops active reading of expository text. *Reading Teacher, 40,* 564–570.

Ogle, D. (2006). *Partner reading for ELL and struggling readers.* Presentation at Area Chicago Public Schools, Office of Literacy Professional Development Day. (March).

Ogle, D. (2008). *Coming together as readers.* Thousand Oaks, CA: Corwin Press.

Ogle, D. & Blachowicz, C. (2001). Beyond literature circles: Helping students comprehend informational texts. In C. C. Block and M. Pressley (eds.), *Comprehension instruction: Research-based practices.* New York: Guilford Press.

Ogle, D. & Blachowicz, C. (2008). *Reading comprehension: Strategies for independent learners* (2nd ed.). New York: Guilford Press.

Ogle, D., Klemp, R., & McBride, W. (2007). *Building literacy in social studies.* Alexandria, VA: Association for Supervision and Curriculum Development.

Ogle, D. & McMahon, S. (2003). *Curriculum integration to promote literate thinking: Dilemmas and possibilities.* In J. Flood, J. R. Squires, and J. M. Jensen (eds.), *Handbook of research on the teaching the English language arts* (2nd ed.). Mahwah, NJ: Lawrence Erlbaum, 1035–1051.

Ollman, H. (1993). Choosing literature wisely: Students speak out. *Journal of Reading, 36*(8), 648–653.

Olness, R. (2005). *Using literature to enhance writing instruction.* Newark, DE: International Reading Association.

Olsen, W. (1959). *Child development.* Boston: D. C. Heath.

O'Neil, M. (1966). "Sounds of water" from *What is that sound!* New York: Atheneum, 1966.

Organization for Economic Cooperation and Development. (2003). *The PISA 2003 assessment framework: Mathematics, reading, science and problem solving knowledge and skills.* Paris: Author.

Owens, R. (2005). *Language development* (5th ed.). Boston: Allyn & Bacon.

Owens, R. (2005). *Language development: An introduction* (6th ed.). Boston: Pearson.

Palinscar, A. (1987). Reciprocal teaching: Can student discussions boost comprehension? *Instructor,* 56–60.

Palinscar, A. & Brown, A. (1984). Reciprocal teaching of comprehension-fostering and comprehension-monitoring activities. *Cognition and Instruction, 12,* 117–175.

Paratore, J. & McCormick, R. (1998). *Peer talk in the classroom: Learning from research.* Newark, DE: International Reading Association.

Paris, S. G. & Ayers, L. R. (1994). *Becoming reflective students and teachers with portfolios and authentic assessment.* Washington, DC: American Psychological Association.

Parsad, B. & Jones, J. (2005). *Internet access in U.S. public schools and classrooms 1994–2005.* Washington, DC: National Center for Educational Statistics. Retrieved August 24, 2006 from http://nces.ed.gov/ pubsearch/ pubsinfo.asp?pubid=2005015.

Patterson, K. (1977). *Bridge to Terabithia.* New York: Scholastic.

Paynter, D. E., Bodrova, E., & Doty, J. K. (2005). *For the love of words: Vocabulary instruction that works.* San Francisco: Jossey-Bass.

Pearson, B. M. (2003). Taylor, B. M., & Pearson, P. D. (eds.) (2002). *Teaching reading: Effective schools, accomplished teachers.* Mahwah NJ: Lawrence Erlbaum.

Pearson, P. D. & Gallagher, M. C. (1983). The instruction of reading comprehension. *Contemporary Educational Psychology, 8*(3), 317–344.

Pegler-Gordon, A. (2006). "Seeing Images in History," *Perspectives, 44,* 28–31

Pennsylvania State Department of Instruction (2000). *Local community project.* Harrisburg, PA: Pennsylvania State Department of Instruction.

Peregoy, S. & Boyle, O. (2008). *Reading, writing, and learning in ESL: A resource book for teaching K–12 learners* (5th ed.). Boston: Allyn & Bacon.

Perl, S. (1979). The composing process of unskilled college writers. *Research in the Teaching of English, 13,* 317–336.

Peters, R. S. (1967). *The concept of education.* London: Routledge & Kegan Paul.

Piaget, J. (1954). *The construction of reality in the child.* New York: Basic Books.

Piaget, J. (1969). *The psychology of intelligence.* Paterson, NJ: Littlefield, Adams.

Piazza, C. (2003). *Journeys: The teaching of writing in elementary schools.* Upper Saddle River, NJ: Pearson.

Pierce, S. (October 2006). Personal conversation.

Pinker, S. (1994). *The language instinct: How the mind creates language.* New York: Prentice Hall.

Pinnell, G. (1989). Reading recovery: Helping at-risk children learn to read. *The Elementary School Journal, 90,* 161–183.

Pinnell, G. S. & Jagger, A. M. (1991). Oral language: Speaking and listening in the classroom. In J. Flood, J. Jensen, D. Lapp, and J. Squire (eds.), *Handbook of research on teaching the English language arts.* New York: Macmillan, 691–720.

PIRLS (Progress in International Reading Literacy Study) (2006). Retrieved from http.isa.bc.edu/PDF/ Chapt 1. pdf, P.3

Prelutsky, J. (1977). *It's Halloween.* New York: Greenwillow.

Pressley, M. (1976). Mental imagery helps eight-year-olds remember what they read. *Journal of Educational Psychology, 68,* 355–359.

Pressley, M. (2005). *Reading instruction that works: The case for balanced teaching* (3rd ed.). New York: Guilford Press.

Pressley, M. (2006.) *Reading instruction that works: The case for balanced teaching* (3rd Ed.) New York: Guilford Press.

Pressley, M., Allington, R. L., Wharton-McDonald, R., Block, C. C., and Morrow, L. M. (2001). *Learning to read: Lessons from exemplary first-grade classrooms:* New York: Guilford Press.

Pressley, M., Levin, J., & Delaney, H. D. (1983). The mnemonic keyword method. *Review of Educational Research, 52,* 6–91.

Pressley, M., Wharton-McDonald, R., Mistretta, J., & Echevarria, M. (1998). The nature of literacy instruction in ten grade 4/5 classrooms in upstate New York. *Scientific Studies of Reading, 2,* 159–194.

Quiroz, B., Greenfield, P. M., & Altchech, M. (1999). Bridging cultures with a parent-teacher conference. *Educational Leadership 56*(7), pp. 68–70.

RAND Reading Study Group (2002). *Reading for understanding: Toward an R & D program in reading comprehension.* Santa Monica, CA: RAND.

Raphael, T. & McMahon, S. I. (1994). Book club: An alternative framework for reading instruction. *The Reading Teacher, 48,* 102–116.

Raphael, T. E., Pardo, L. S., & Highfield, K. (2002). *Book club: A literature-based curriculum.* Lawrence, MA: Small Planet.

Read, C. (1971). Preschool children's knowledge of English phonology. *Harvard Educational Review, 41,* 1–34.

Read, C. (1975). *Children's categorization of speech sounds in English.* Urbana, IL: National Council of Teachers of English.

Reinking, D. (2001). Multimedia and engaged reading in a digital world. In L. Verhoeven and K. Snow (eds.), *Literacy and motivation: Reading engagement in individuals and groups.* Mahwah, NJ: Lawrence Erlbaum, 195–221.

Reutzel, R. & Fawson, P. (2002). *Your classroom library: New ways to give it more teaching power.* New York: Scholastic.

Reznitskaya, A., Anderson, R. C., McNurlen, B., Nguyen-Jahiel, K., Archodidou, A., & Kim, S. (2001). Influence of oral discussion on written argument. *Discourse Processes, 32,* 155–175.

Richards, K. (2006). Being the teacher: Identity and classroom conversation. *Applied Linguistics, 27*(1), 51–77.

Richardson, B. (2003). *Sally dog little.* Toronto, ON: Annick Press.

Richardson, J. & Morgan, R. (2003). *Reading to learn in the content areas.* Belmont, CA: Wadsworth/Thomson Learning.

Richgels, D. (2001). Invented spelling, phonemic awareness, and reading and writing instruction. In S. Neuman and D. Dickinson (eds.), *Handbook of early literacy.* New York: Guilford Press, 142–158.

Rogers, T. (2000). *Journal of Literacy Research.*

Rogoff, B. (1990). *Apprenticeship in thinking: Cognitive development in social contexts.* New York: Oxford University Press.

Rosenblatt, L. (1978). *The reader, the text, the poem: The transactional theory of the literary work*. Carbondale, IL: Southern Illinois University Press.

Routman, R. (2003). *Reading essentials: The specifics you need to teach reading well*. Portsmouth, NH: Heinemann.

Routman, R. (2005). *Writing essentials: Raising expectations and results while simplifying teaching*. Portsmouth, NH: Heinemann.

Rylant, C. (1985). *The relatives came*. New York: Bradbury Press.

Sadoski, M. & Paivio, A. (2001). *The dual coding theory of reading*. Mahwah, NJ: Lawrence Erlbaum.

Samuels, S. (1994). Toward a theory of automatic information processing in reading, revisited. In R. B. Ruddell, M. R. Ruddell, and H. Singer (eds.), *Theoretical models and processes of reading* (4th ed.). Newark, DE: International Reading Association, 816–837.

Samuels, S. J. (1988). *Characteristics of exemplary reading programs*. In S. J. Samuels & P. D. Pearson (eds.). *Changing school reading programs: Principles and case studies*. Newark, DE: International Reading Association, 3–9.

Scarborough, H. (2001). Connecting early language and literacy to later reading (dis)abilities: Evidence, theory, and practice. In S. Neuman & D. Dickinson (eds.). *Handbook of early literacy research*. New York: Guilford Press, 97–110.

Scholastic. 2005. Retrieved from: http://www.scholastic.com/administrator/

Schlager, N. (1978). Predicting children's choices in literature: A developmental approach. *Children's Literature in Education, 9*(3), 136–142.

Schrock, K. *Kathy Schrock's Guide for Educators,* Critical evaluation information at: http://school.discoveryeducation.com/schrockguide/eval.html (2008).

Schwartz, R. M. & Raphael, T. E. (1985). Concept of definition: A key to improving students' vocabulary. *The Reading Teacher, 39*, 198–205.

Schwarz, N. (2005). North American dialects. *National Geographic*.

Scott, J. A., Jamieson-Noel, D., & Asselin, M. (2003). Vocabulary instruction throughout the day in twenty-three Canadian upper-elementary classrooms. *The Elementary School Journal, 103*, 269–286.

Shanahan, T. (2001). Chicago reading framework project. University of Illinois at Chicago.

Short, K., Harste, J., & Burke, C. (1996). *Creating classrooms for authors and inquirers* (2nd ed.). Portsmouth, NH: Heinemann.

Shuy, R., & Staton, J. (1982). Assessing oral language ability in children. In L. Feagans & D. Farran (eds.). *The language of children reared in poverty: Implications for evaluation and intervention*. New York: Academic Press, 181–195.

Sibberson, F. & Szymusiak, K. (2003). *Still learning to read: Teaching students in grades 3–6*. Portland, ME: Stenhouse.

Silvaroli, N. (2000). *Classroom reading inventory* (6th ed.). Dubuque, IA: Wm. C. Brown Publishers.

Skinner, B. F. (1957). *Verbal behavior*. New York: Appleton-Century-Crofts.

Slobin, D. (1978). Cognitive prerequisites for the development of grammar. In L. Bloom and M. Lahey (eds.), *Readings in language development*. New York: Wiley.

Slobodkina, E. (1940). *Caps for sale*. New York: Harper & Row.

Smith, M. C. (2000). The real-word reading practices of adults. *Journal of Literacy Research, 32*(1), 25–52.

Smith, P. H., Jiménez, R. T., & Martínez-León, N. (2005). Other countries' literacies. What U.S. educators can learn from Mexican schools. In P. Shannon and J. Edmonson (eds.), *Reading Education Policy*. Newark, DE: International Reading Association, 325–340. (Reprint of article in *The Reading Teacher, 56*(8), 2–11.)

Snow, C. E. (2002). *Reading for understanding: Toward a R & D program in reading comprehension*. Santa Monica, CA: RAND.

Snow, C. E., Burns, M. S., & Griffin, P. (eds.). (1998). *Preventing reading difficulties in young children*. Committee on the Prevention of Reading Difficulties in Young Children. Commission on Behavior and Social Sciences and Education. National Research Council Washington, DC: National Academy Press.

Sommers, N. (1980). Revision strategies of student writers and experienced adult writers. *College Composition and Communication, 31*, 378–388.

Soto, G. (1990). *A fire in my hands*. New York: Scholastic.

Spears-Bunton, L. (1990). Welcome to my house: African American and European American students' responses to Virginia Hamilton's *House of Dies Drear. Journal of Negro Education, 59*, 566–576.

Staab, C. (1992). *Oral language for today's classroom*. Don Mills, ON: Pippin.

Stahl, S. (2001). Teaching phonics and phonological awareness. In S. Neuman and D. Dickinson (eds.), *Handbook of early literacy*. New York: Guilford Press, 333–347.

*Standards for the English language arts*. Urbana, IL: International Reading Association and National Council of Teachers of English. Retrieved on February 19, 2008 from www.ncte.org/about/over/standards/110846.htm.

Stanovich, K. (1980). Toward an interactive-compensatory model of individual differences in the development of reading fluency. *Reading Research Quarterly, 16*, 32–71.

Stanovich, K. E. & Siegel, L. S. (1994). Phenotypic performance profile of children with reading disabilities: A regression-based test of the phonological-core variable-difference model. *Journal of Educational Psychology, 86*, 24–53.

Staton, J. (1987). The power of responding to dialogue journals. In T. Fulwiler (ed.), *The journal book*. Portsmouth, NH: Boynton/Cook, 1987.

Staton, J., Shuy, R. W., Kreeft, J., & Reed, L. (1982). *Dialogue journal writing as a communicative event*. National Institute of Education. NIE-G-80–0122. Washington, DC: Center for Applied Linguistics.

Stauffer, R. (1969). *Developing reading maturity as a cognitive process.* New York: Harper & Row.
Stauffer, R. (1976). *Action research in L.E.A. instructional procedures.* Newark, DE: University of Delaware.
Stauffer, R. (1980). *The language-experience approach to the teaching of reading.* New York: HarperCollins.
Steffensen, M. & deJong, (1999). Steffensen, M.S., Joag-Dev, C. & Anderson, R.C. (1979). A Cross-Cultural Perspective On Reading Comprehension. *Reading Research Quarterly, 15,* 10–29.
Steffensen, M. S., Joag-Dev, C., & Anderson, R. C. (1979). A cross-cultural perspective on reading comprehension. *Reading Research Quarterly, 15*(1), 11–29.
Strickland, D. S. (1998). What's basic in beginning reading? Finding common ground. *Educational Leadership, 55*(6).
Strickland, D. (1998). Principles of instruction. In M. F. Opitz (ed.), *Literacy instruction for culturally and linguistically diverse students.* Newark, DE: International Reading Association, 50–53.
Strickland, D. & Morrow, L. (1989). Oral language development: Children as storytellers. *The Reading Teacher, 43*(4), 260–261.
Strong, W. (1996). *Writer's toolbox: A sentence-combining workshop.* New York: McGraw Hill.
Sullivan, J. E. & Sharp, J. (2000). Using technology for writing development. In S. Wepner, W. Valmont, and R. Thurlow (eds.), *Linking literacy and technology: A guide for K–8 classrooms.* Newark, DE: International Reading Association.
Tatum, B. D. (1997). *"Why are all the black kids sitting together in the cafeteria?" and other conversations about race.* New York: Basic Books.
Taylor, B. & Pearson, P. (2002). *Teaching reading: Effective schools, accomplished teachers.* Mahwah, NJ: Lawrence Erlbaum.
Taylor, B. M. & Pearson, P. D. (2004). Research on learning to read—at school, at home, and in the community. *Elementary School Journal, 105*(2), 168–181.
Teale, W. & Sulzby, E. (eds.). (1986). *Emergent literacy: Writing and reading.* Norwood, NJ: Ablex.
Temple, C., Martinez, M., Yokota, J., & Naylor, A. (2002). *Children's books in children's hands: An introduction to their literature* (2nd ed.). Boston: Allyn & Bacon.
Templeton, S. (1992). Theory, nature, and pedagogy of higher-order orthographic development in older children. In S. Templeton and D. Bear (eds.), *Development of orthographic knowledge and the foundations of literacy.* Hillsdale, NJ: Lawrence Erlbaum, 253–278.
Terrell, T. D. (1981). The natural approach in bilingual education. In California State Department of Education, Office of Bilingual Bicultural Education, *Schooling and language minority students: A theoretical framework.* Los Angeles: California State University, Evaluation, Dissemination and Assessment Center, 115–146.
Thomas, W. P. & Collier, V. P. (2002). *A national study of school effectiveness for language minority students' long-term academic achievement final report: Project 1.1.* Santa Cruz, CA: Center for Research on Education, Diversity and Excellence.
Tiedt, I. (2002). *Tiger lilies, toadstools, and thunderbolts: Engaging K–8 students with poetry.* Newark, DE: International Reading Association.
Tomlinson, C. A. (2000). Differentiation of instruction in the elementary grades. *ERIC Digest.* Champaign, IL: ERIC Clearinghouse on Elementary and Early Childhood Education.
Tompkins, G. (2005). *Language arts: Patterns of practice* (6th ed.). Boston: Allyn & Bacon.
Topping, K. J. & Paul, T. D. (1999). Computer-assisted assessment of practice at reading: A large scale survey using accelerated reader data. *Reading & Writing Quarterly, 15*(3), 213–231.
Tough, J. (1981). *Talk for teaching and learning.* London: Ward Lock Educational.
Tough, J. (1982). Children's use of language. In B. Waide (ed.), *Language perspectives: Papers from the educational review.* London: Heinemann Press.
Trumbull, E., Rothstein-Fisch, C., Greenfield, P. M., & Quiroz, B. (2001). *Bridging cultures between home and school: A guide for teachers.* Mahwah, NJ: Lawrence Erlbaum.
U.S. Department of Education, National Center for Education Statistics (2004). *Young children's access to computers in the home and at school in 1999 and 2000.* Washington, DC: U.S. Department of Education.
Valencia, S., Hiebert, E., & Afflerbach, P. (eds.). (1994). *Authentic reading assessment: Practices and possibilities.* Newark, DE: International Reading Association.
van Kleeck, A. & Stahl, S. (2003). Preface. In A. van Kleeck, S. Stahl, and E. Bauer (eds.), *On reading books to children: Parents and teachers.* Mahwah, NJ: Lawrence Erlbaum.
Vogt, M. E. (1996). Creating a response-centered curriculum with literature discussion groups. In L. Gambrell. and J. Almasi (eds.), *Lively discussions! Fostering engaged reading.* Newark, DE: International Reading Association.
Vogt, M. E. (1996). *Resources for Teachers: Standards for the English Language Arts.* Newark, DE: International Reading Association.
Vygotsky, L. (1978). *Mind in society: The development of higher psychological processes.* In M. Cole, V. John-Steiner, S. Scribner, and E. Souberman (eds.). Cambridge MA: Harvard University Press.
Vygotsky, L. S. (1962). *Thought and language.* In E. Hanfmann and G. Vakar (eds. and trans.). Cambridge, MA: MIT Press.
Wagstaff, J. (1994). *Phonics that work! New strategies for the reading/writing classroom.* New York: Scholastic.
Way, B. (1967). *Development through drama.* London: Longman Group.
Weaver, C. (1996). *Teaching grammar in context: Why and how.* Portsmouth, NH: Heinemann-Boynton/Cook.
Wepner, S., Valmont, W., & Thurlow, R. (2000). *Linking literacy and technology.* Newark, DE: International Reading Association, 91.

Wham, M., Barnhart, J., & Cook, G. (1996). Enhancing multicultural awareness through the storybook reading experience. *Journal of Research and Development in Education, 30,* 1–9.

*Where we stand on learning to read and write* (1998). Washington, DC: National Association for the Education of Young Children. Retrieved on February 19, 2008 from www.naeyc.org/about/positions/pdf/WWSSLearningToReadAndWriteEnglish.pdf

Whitehurst, G. J., Falcon, F., Lonigan, C. J., Fischel, J. E., et al. (1988). Accelerating language development through picture book reading. *Developmental Psychology, 24,* 552–559.

Wickstron, S. K. (1988). *The wheels on the bus.* New York: Crown.

WIDA (2004). *Framework for large-scale assessment.* Madison, WI: Department of Public Instruction, State of Wisconsin.

Wilhelm, J. (2001). *Improving comprehension with think-aloud strategies.* New York: Scholastic.

Williams, J. (1989). *Preparing to teach writing.* Belmont, CA: Wadsworth.

Wollman-Bonilla, J. E. (2003). E-mail as genre: A beginning writer learns the conventions. *Language Arts, 81,* 126–134.

Woods, M. & Moe, A. (2003). *Analytic reading inventory* (7th ed.). Upper Saddle River, NJ: Pearson Education.

Worthy, J. (1996). Removing barriers to voluntary reading for reluctant readers: The role of school and classroom libraries. *Language Arts, 73*(7), 483–492.

Worthy, J., Moorman, M., & Turner, M. (1999). What Johnny likes to read is hard to find in school. *Reading Research Quarterly, 34*(1), 12–27.

Wu, X. (2007). Visual literacy for second language learners. In Mark Newman, Costas Spirou, and Gerald Danzer (eds.), *Chicago stories 1830s–World War I: Visual images for classroom instruction.* Chicago: National-Louis University.

www.natcom.org. Guidelines for Developing Oral Communication Curricula in Kindergarten through Twelfth Grade (pdf file), 8.

Wylie, R. & Durrell, D. (1970). Teaching vowels through phonograms. *Elementary English, 47,* 787–791.

Yankelovich. (2006). *Kids and family reading report.* Available: www.scholastic.com/ readingreport Your Dictionary Website: www.yourdictionary.com, a comprehensive online resource for your dictionary needs; accessed in 2006.

Zevenbergen, A. A. & Whitehurst, G. J. (2003). Dialogic reading: A shared picture book reading intervention for preschoolers. In A. van Kleeck, S. S. Stahl, and E. B. Bauer (eds.), *On reading books to children: Parents and teachers.* Mahwah, NJ: Lawrence Erlbaum, 177–200.

Zutell, J. & Rasinski, T. V. (1991). Training teachers to attend to their students' oral reading fluency. *Theory into Practice, 30,* 211–217.

# Index



## A



## B

## C

# D

# E



# F



# G

# H



# I

## J



## K



## L

## M

## N



## O

## P



## Q



## R

# S

# T

## U



## V



## W

## Y



## Z

*This page constitutes a continuation of the copyright page.*



## Text Acknowledgments:



## Photo Credits: